MATHEMATICS
Structure and Method
COURSE I

MARY P. DOLCIANI

ROBERT H. SORGENFREY

JOHN A. GRAHAM

EDITORIAL ADVISORS:

RICHARD G. BROWN

ROBERT B. KANE

HOUGHTON MIFFLIN COMPANY • Boston
Atlanta   Dallas   Geneva, Ill.   Palo Alto   Princeton   Toronto

AUTHORS

Mary P. Dolciani   Formerly Professor of Mathematical Sciences, Hunter College of the City University of New York

Robert H. Sorgenfrey   Professor of Mathematics, University of California, Los Angeles

John A. Graham   Mathematics Teacher, Buckingham Browne and Nichols School, Cambridge, Massachusetts

Editorial Advisers

Richard G. Brown   Mathematics Teacher, Phillips Exeter Academy, Exeter, New Hampshire

Robert B. Kane   Dean of the School of Education and Professor of Mathematics Education, Purdue University, Lafayette, Indiana

Teacher Consultants

Carolyn Connolly   Mathematics Teacher, Pierce School, Brookline, Massachusetts

Rebecca K. Cook   Department Chairman and Mathematics Teacher, Gifted and Talented Grades 7 and 8, Wiley Junior High School, Winston-Salem, North Carolina

James C. Price   Mathematics Teacher, Coleman Junior High School, Wichita, Kansas

Jane F. Schielack   Lecturer, Mathematics Department, Texas A & M University, College Station, Texas

Acknowledgment

The authors wish to thank Robert H. Cornell, Mathematics Teacher, Milton Academy, Milton, Massachusetts, for his valuable contribution to this edition.

Printed in U.S.A.

ISBN: 0-395-48098-1

DEFGHIJ-VH-99876543

Contents

1 OPERATIONS WITH WHOLE NUMBERS

xlii

2 USING VARIABLES

30

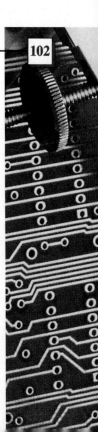

5

NUMBER THEORY

6

FRACTIONS: DEFINITIONS AND RELATIONSHIPS

v

7 OPERATIONS WITH FRACTIONS

8 SOLVING EQUATIONS

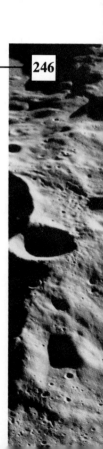

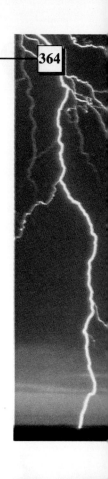

Mathematics as Problem Solving

PROBLEM SOLVING LESSONS

NONROUTINE PROBLEM SOLVING

PROBLEM SOLVING REMINDERS

Mathematics as Communication

COMMUNICATION LESSONS

COMMUNICATION IN MATHEMATICS

Mathematics as Reasoning

EXPLORATION LESSONS

Mathematical Connections

Technology

Review and Testing

Reading Mathematics

This page shows the metric measures and symbols that are used in this book. Use this page as a reference when you read the book.

Symbols

·	times	2	ㄥ	is a right angle	114
. . .	and so on	5	$\triangle ABC$	triangle ABC	118
$<$	is less than	39	π	pi	128
$>$	is greater than	39	4!	4 factorial	152
$\overleftrightarrow{PQ}$	line PQ	104	131 R1	131 with remainder 1	154
$\overrightarrow{BA}$	ray BA	104	$\sqrt{}$	square root	157
$\overline{PQ}$	segment PQ	104	GCF	greatest common factor	163
$\parallel$	is parallel to	105	LCM	least common multiple	166
AB	length of $\overline{AB}$	109	$0.6\overline{81}$	81 repeats without end	196
$\approx$	is approximately equal to	109	LCD	least common	211
$\cong$	is congruent to	109		denominator	
$\angle A$	angle A	113	1:5	1 to 5	226
$m\angle A$	measure of angle A	113	$^-4$	negative 4	366
60°	60 degrees	113	$|n|$	absolute value of n	366
$\perp$	is perpendicular to	113	$P(A)$	probability of event A	427

Metric Measures

Prefixes

Prefix	kilo	centi	milli
Factor	1000	0.01	0.001
Symbol	k	c	m

Base Units

Length: **meter** (m)
Mass: **kilogram** (kg)
Capacity: **liter** (L)

Temperature: **Degree Celsius** (°C)

Length	1 mm = 0.001 m	1 cm = 0.01 m	1 km = 1000 m
	1 m = 1000 mm	1 m = 100 cm	1 cm = 10 mm
Mass	1 kg = 1000 g	1 mg = 0.001 g	1 g = 0.001 kg
Capacity	1 mL = 0.001 L	1 L = 1000 mL	1 L = 1000 cm^3
Time	60 s = 1 min	60 min = 1 h	3600 s = 1 h

Examples of compound units   kilometers per hour: km/h
square centimeters: cm^2 cubic meters: m^3

Diagnostic Test of Whole Number Skills

This test reviews the skills of addition, subtraction, multiplication, and division necessary to begin Chapter 1. More practice of these skills can be found on pages 444–445.

Addition

Add.

1. 142 + 237	**2.** 374 + 213	**3.** 602 + 257	**4.** 549 + 386	**5.** 759 + 684

6. 103 19 + 42	**7.** 1007 285 + 59	**8.** 642 58 73 + 256 830	**9.** 17 2041 490 + 683	**10.** 246 9 1064 842 + 83

11. 32 + 56　　　　　**12.** 17 + 20 + 32　　　　　**13.** 693 + 105

14. 65 + 29　　　　　**15.** 34 + 17 + 25　　　　　**16.** 671 + 248

17. 246 + 9 + 3011 + 495　　　　**18.** 2306 + 19 + 429 + 1443

19. 18 + 593 + 641 + 1111　　　　**20.** 495 + 301 + 4 + 5803 + 78

Subtraction

Subtract.

1. 864 − 231	**2.** 9748 − 2635	**3.** 4693 − 2758	**4.** 838 − 619	**5.** 711 − 493

6. 4931 − 4498	**7.** 609 − 423	**8.** 801 − 543	**9.** 5021 − 2479	**10.** 3004 − 2567

11. 768 − 654　　　　　**12.** 925 − 713　　　　　**13.** 853 − 432

14. 762 − 149　　　　　**15.** 3147 − 1028　　　　**16.** 2651 − 1278

17. 2670 − 357　　　　**18.** 3980 − 2734　　　　**19.** 4803 − 567

20. 7216 − 4567　　　　**21.** 5323 − 789　　　　**22.** 6255 − 4367

Multiplication

Multiply.

1.	63	2.	42	3.	24	4.	131	5.	214
	× 21		× 34		× 56		× 25		× 37

6.	246	7.	310	8.	407	9.	213	10.	381
	× 30		× 29		× 132		× 312		× 206

11. 46×21
12. 51×73
13. 92×34
14. 732×24
15. 260×35
16. 947×62
17. 237×826
18. 367×503
19. 7011×281
20. 2407×390
21. 4023×570
22. 9108×6027

Division

Divide.

1. $7\overline{)91}$
2. $4\overline{)64}$
3. $8\overline{)296}$
4. $6\overline{)288}$

5. $12\overline{)972}$
6. $29\overline{)522}$
7. $23\overline{)782}$
8. $33\overline{)1782}$

9. $42\overline{)2436}$
10. $74\overline{)3478}$
11. $607\overline{)6677}$
12. $198\overline{)4554}$

Divide. Be sure to state the remainder.

13. $56 \div 3$
14. $49 \div 8$
15. $107 \div 6$
16. $425 \div 7$
17. $319 \div 15$
18. $628 \div 20$
19. $943 \div 48$
20. $856 \div 82$
21. $1143 \div 56$
22. $4053 \div 62$
23. $9963 \div 542$
24. $5327 \div 482$

A **magic square** consists of rows and columns of numbers arranged so that the sums of any row, column, or diagonal are equal. This sum is called the magic number.

17	24	1	8	15
23	5	7	14	16
4	6	13	20	22
10	12	19	21	3
11	18	25	2	9

1. What is the magic number for the magic square shown?

We want to make the square at the right below into a magic square using the numbers 6 through 14:

$$\{6, 7, 8, 9, 10, 11, 12, 13, 14\}.$$

Each number can be used only once.

2. How will finding the sum of all nine numbers help determine the magic number for this magic square?

3. Tim got the sum of the nine numbers by multiplying 10×9. Why does this work?

Since every row, column, and main diagonal contains three numbers, we will refer to them as **triplets.**

4. In how many different triplets must the number in the middle box be used?

5. In how many triplets must a number in one of the corner boxes be used?

6. In how many triplets must a number in one of the shaded boxes be used?

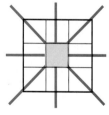

There are two pairs of numbers that can be used in a triplet with a 6 to make a sum of 30: $6 + M + N = 30$

7. What must be the sum of M and N?

8. Why *can't* we use $6 + 12 + 12 = 30$?

9. What are the only two possible pairs of values for *M* and *N?*

10. Since six can be used in only two different triplets, what are the four boxes in which it could be placed?

11. Suppose we put 6 in the first column. Why must the number in the middle box be 10, 11, 13, or 14?

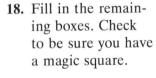

These are all the different triplets
with a sum of 30 using 10.

10 + 8 + 12   **10** + 7 + 13
10 + 9 + 11   **10** + 6 + 14

Write all the possible triplets with a sum of 30:

12. using 11   **13.** using 12   **14.** using 13

15. Why must 10 be the number in the middle box?

16. With 10 in the middle box, what number must go in the shaded box?

17. What numbers must go in these boxes? Why?

18. Fill in the remaining boxes. Check to be sure you have a magic square.

Suppose you are to make a magic square using the numbers 4 through 12:

$$\{4, 5, 6, 7, 8, 9, 10, 11, \text{and } 12\}$$

19. What is the sum of all the boxes in this square?

20. What will be the magic number? What number will go in the middle box? Complete the square.

21. What would be the number in the middle square of a 5 by 5 magic square containing the numbers 30 through 54?

Equations

In elementary school, the only way to work the following problem was to keep guessing and checking until you got the number. In algebra, you write an equation to fit the problem, then solve the equation. Being able to write an equation that represents a problem is an important mathematical skill.

I am thinking of a number. If I triple the number and add 7 the result is 55. What is the number?

1. Suppose the problem had been, "I triple the number 5 and add 7." Write a numerical expression for this statement.

2. What would you write for, "I triple the number 8 and add 7?

To write the variable expression for, "I triple a number *n* and add 7," treat *n* as though it were a number. Write $3 \times n + 7$ as $3n + 7$. To solve the original problem, "If I triple a number and add 7 the result is 55," you can write the equation

$$3n + 7 = 55.$$

To write an equation to fit a problem, use a variable as you would use any number.

The result when 4 is subtracted from 5 times a number is 21.

3. Suppose the problem had been, "The result when 4 is subtracted from 5 times 2." Write a numerical expression for this word sentence.

4. Suppose the problem had been, "The result when 4 is subtracted from 5 times 6." Write a numerical expression for this word sentence.

5. Write a math expression for, "The result when 4 is subtracted from 5 times a number."

6. Write an equation that fits the original problem.

Write an equation for each word sentence. Use n to represent the unknown number.

7. A number decreased by 3 is 12.

8. When a certain number is doubled the result is 36.

9. Nine less than 5 times a number is 61.

10. Five more than $\frac{1}{3}$ of a number is 17.

Write an equation for each word sentence. Use n to represent the unknown number.

11. When 60 is divided by a number and 6 is then subtracted, the result is 24.

12. Three times some number divided by 4 is 36.

Write an equation for each problem. Use m to represent the original amount of money.

13. Matt spent $8 and has $20 left.

14. Anne found $6 and now has $36.

15. Mom tripled her savings and now has $78.

16. Al shared his money with three people. Each got $13.

17. After sharing his money with his 2 brothers, Lou spent $6 and had $24 left.

Write a variable expression for each problem.

EXAMPLE

The length of a rectangle is 3 inches longer than twice its width. Let w = the width of the rectangle.

Solution

Think: If the width were 5 in., the length would be 3 inches + 2 × 5. Since the width is w, the length is $3 + 2w$.

18. Sarah is paid $300 per week plus $50 for every car she sells. Let c = the number of cars sold.

19. Joan got a $100 discount for buying several guitars at the $350 price. Let g = the number of guitars bought.

20. Carlos decided to keep $100 of his bonus for himself and share the rest with his three sisters. Let b = the amount of his bonus.

21. The circumference of a circle is 3.14 times as long as its diameter. Let d = the diameter.

Write a word problem to fit each equation.

22. $2n + 8 = 20$

23. $3k - 7 = 50$

24. $(n - 4) \div 3 = 34$

25. $m \div 5 = 25$

26. $3h - 5 = 22$

27. $75 - 3n = 0$

Ten to the third power (10^3) means $10 \times 10 \times 10$.
Ten to the second power (10^2) means 10×10.
If you multiply 10^3 and 10^2, the result is 10^5.

$$10^3 \times 10^2 = (10 \times 10 \times 10) \times (10 \times 10) = 10 \times 10 \times 10 \times 10 \times 10 = 10^5$$

Find each answer. Write the answers with exponents.

1. $10^2 \times 10^1$ **2.** $10^3 \times 10^3$

3. $10^4 \times 10^4$ **4.** $10^8 \times 10^4$

5. Look for a pattern in your answers to the exercises above. Write a rule for multiplying numbers with exponents that have the same base.

If you divide 10^3 by 10^1, the result is 10^2.

$$10^3 \div 10^1 = \frac{10^3}{10^1} = \frac{10 \times 10 \times 10}{10} = \frac{\overset{1}{\cancel{10}} \times 10 \times 10}{\underset{1}{\cancel{10}}} = \frac{10 \times 10}{1} = \frac{10^2}{1} = 10^2$$

Find each answer. Write the answers with exponents.

6. $10^4 \div 10^3$ **7.** $10^4 \div 10^2$ **8.** $10^8 \div 10^3$

9. Write a rule for dividing numbers with exponents that have the same base.

Rules

1. To multiply numbers with exponents that have the same base, add the exponents.

$$n^a \times n^b = n^{a+b}$$

2. To divide numbers with exponents that have the same base, subtract the exponent of the divisor from that of the dividend.

$$n^a \div n^b = n^{a-b}$$

Using the rules, find each answer. Write the answers with exponents.

10. a. $10^5 \times 10^3$ **b.** $10^5 \div 10^3$

11. a. $10^{20} \times 10^5$ **b.** $10^{20} \div 10^5$

Using the rules, find each answer. Write the answers with exponents.

12. a. $10^7 \times 10^2$ **b.** $10^7 \div 10^2$

13. a. $23^9 \times 23^4$ **b.** $23^9 \div 23^4$

When we apply the rule to $10^2 \div 10^2$ we get 10^0. Any number with a zero exponent has a specific value. Examine the following list of powers of 10.

Fifth power:	$10^5 = 10 \times 10 \times 10 \times 10 \times 10$	$= 100,000$
Fourth power:	$10^4 = 10 \times 10 \times 10 \times 10$	$= 10,000$
Third power:	$10^3 = 10 \times 10 \times 10$	$= 1,000$
Second power:	$10^2 = 10 \times 10$	$= 100$
First power:	$10^1 =$ (exponent usually not written) $= 10$	
Zero power:	$10^0 = $?	$= ?$

14. From the pattern for the powers of ten above, what should be the value of 10^0?

15. Explain how you determined the value of 10^0.

16. Write $10^2 \div 10^2$ without exponents. When you divide, what is the result?

17. Since $10^0 = 1$, what will happen if you multiply a number by 10^0? Why?

Use the rule for multiplying numbers with exponents to find the following products. Write your answers without exponents.

18. $10^3 \times 10^0$ **19.** $10^0 \times 10,000$ **20.** $10^5 \times 10^0$

21. $6^5 \times 6^0$ **22.** $8^0 \times 8^3$ **23.** $9^0 \times 9^0$

24. Write an explanation of how you would show a friend that $8^0 = 1$. Include examples you would use in your explanation.

This factor tree has been used to find the prime factorization of 60.

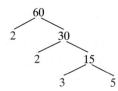

$$60 = 2 \times 2 \times 3 \times 5$$
$$= 2^2 \times 3 \times 5$$

1. Why should you *never* use 1 on a factor tree?

Complete each factor tree shown below. Then use exponents to write each prime factorization.

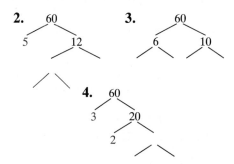

2. 60 / 5, 12

3. 60 / 6, 10

4. 60 / 3, 20, 2

5. Make at least one other factor tree for 60 that is different from those above.

The exercises above illustrate the Fundamental Theorem of Arithmetic.

Fundamental Theorem of Arithmetic

Every composite number greater than 1 can be written as a product of prime factors in exactly one way, except for the order of the factors.

The one and only prime factorization of **24** is **2 × 2 × 2 × 3** or **2^3 × 3**. This means that no matter how you make the factor tree for 24, the factors will always be 2, 2, 2, and 3.

Write true or false for each statement about M and N in the factor tree.

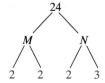

6. Neither *M* nor *N* is equal to 1.

7. *M* and *N* are both prime numbers.

8. Three is a factor of *N*.

9. *M* is equal to 4.

10. Explain why the following is true: The prime factorization of 24 can be written as 3×2^3.

$36 = 2 \times 2 \times 3 \times 3$ or $2^2 \times 3^2$
18 *is* a factor of 36 because $18 = 2 \times 3^2$, and all of its factors are in the prime factorization of 36.

$60 = 2 \times 2 \times 3 \times 5$ or $2^2 \times 3 \times 5$
18 is *not* a factor of 60 because $18 = 2 \times 3^2$, and the prime factorization of 60 has only one 3.

In Exercises 11–14, refer to the prime factorizations for 36 and 60 on the previous page.

11. Why is 10 a factor of 60?

12. Why *isn't* 10 a factor of 36?

13. Why is 12 a factor of both 36 and 60?

14. Why *isn't* 2 the smallest factor of both 36 and 60? What number is?

SAM is a big number:

$$SAM = 2^2 \times 3^5 \times 7^8 \times 13^{47} \times 23^{12}$$

The only numbers (other than 1) that are factors of SAM are numbers that are in SAM's prime factorization. Since $98 = 2 \times 7^2$ and all of these factors are in SAM's prime factorization, 98 is a factor of SAM.

In Exercises 15–17, refer to the factorization of SAM given above.

15. Why *isn't* 60 a factor?

16. Why *isn't* 24 a factor?

17. Why is 36 a factor?

The **Greatest Common Factor (GCF)** is the greatest whole number that is a factor of two or more given whole numbers.

$$36 = 2 \times 2 \times 3 \times 3 \text{ or } 2^2 \times 3^2$$

$$120 = 2 \times 2 \times 2 \times 3 \times 5$$
$$\text{or } 2^3 \times 3 \times 5$$

The greatest common factor (GCF) of 36 and 120 is the greatest whole number that is a factor of both 36 and 120. The GCF of 36 and 120 is $2 \times 2 \times 3$ or $2^2 \times 3 = 12$.

In Exercises 18–21, refer to the prime factorizations for 36 and 120.

18. Why *can't* you use a 5 in the GCF?

19. Why can you use only 2's and 3's?

20. Why can you use only two 2's?

21. Why can you use only one 3?

| $400 = 2^4 \times 5^2$ | $280 = 2^3 \times 5 \times 7$ |

---

22. Why can you use one 5 in the GCF of 400 and 280?

23. Why *can't* you use a 7?

24. Why can you use only three 2's?

25. What is the GCF of 400 and 280?

Write the prime factorization of each number. Then find the GCF of each pair.

26. 28 and 70   27. 84 and 75

28. 60 and 105

$$SAM = 2^2 \times 3^5 \times 7^8 \times 13^{47} \times 23^{12}$$

Since $84 = 2^2 \times 3 \times 7$, all of the prime factors of 84 are contained in SAM's prime factorization. Thus, 84 is a factor of SAM and SAM is a **multiple** of 84.

SAM is *not* a multiple of 20 because $20 = 2^2 \times 5$ and SAM's factorization does not contain a 5. Because we know SAM's prime factorization does not contain a 5, we may conclude that SAM is not a multiple of *any* number whose prime factorization contains a 5.

1. Is SAM a multiple of 8? Explain your answer.

2. Is SAM a multiple of 84? Explain your answer.

3. Write a rule for determining whether SAM is a multiple of a number n.

4. Find a number greater than 100 but less than 200 of which SAM is a multiple.

5. Find a number between 100 and 200 of which SAM is *not* a multiple.

6. What is the smallest whole number of which SAM is a multiple?

7. What is the smallest whole number of which SAM is *not* a multiple?

8. Explain why every number is a multiple of itself.

The **Least Common Multiple (LCM)** of two numbers is the smallest nonzero number that is a multiple of both numbers.

Find the LCM of each pair of numbers.

9. 3 and 5   **10.** 6 and 4

11. 8 and 4   **12.** 6 and 12

Find the LCM of 56 and 60 given that $56 = 2^3 \times 7$ and $60 = 2^2 \times 3 \times 5$.

13. To be a multiple of 60, the LCM of 56 and 60 must contain the entire factorization of 60. Why?

14. To be a multiple of 56, the LCM of 56 and 60 must also contain the entire factorization of 56. Why must the LCM of 56 and 60 contain 2^3 rather than 2^2?

15. Why must the LCM contain a 7?

16. What is the LCM of 56 and 60?

17. Why can't you remove the 5 from the LCM?

18. Why can't you add an 11 to the LCM?

Find the LCM of 24 and 36.

19. Write the prime factorization of

20. Add the factors needed to make it a multiple of 24.

21. Why was only one 2 added?

22. Why can't you remove a 3?

Find the LCM of 120 and 24.

23. Write the prime factorization of 120.

24. Must any factors be added to make it a multiple of 24? Why?

25. What is the LCM of 120 and 24?

Find the LCM of each pair of numbers.

26. $36 = 2^2 \times 3^2$
$120 = 2^3 \times 3 \times 5$

27. $100 = 2^2 \times 5^2$
$120 = 2^3 \times 3 \times 5$

28. $196 = 2^2 \times 7^2$
$42 = 2 \times 3 \times 7$

29. $30 = 2 \times 3 \times 5$
$120 = 2^3 \times 3 \times 5$

30. $400 = 2^4 \times 5^2$
$120 = 2^3 \times 3 \times 5$

31. $1960 = 2^3 \times 5 \times 7^2$
$560 = 2^4 \times 5 \times 7$

32. In the following examples the LCM and GCF have been found. Factors used in the LCM are shown in boldface type. Find the pattern.

$$200 = \mathbf{2^3} \times \mathbf{5^2}$$
$$120 = 2^3 \times \mathbf{3} \times 5$$
$$LCM = \mathbf{2^3} \times \mathbf{3} \times \mathbf{5^2}$$
$$GCF = 2^3 \times 5$$

$$1960 = 2^3 \times 5 \times \mathbf{7^2}$$
$$400 = \mathbf{2^4} \times \mathbf{5^2}$$
$$LCM = \mathbf{2^4} \times \mathbf{5^2} \times \mathbf{7^2}$$
$$GCF = 2^3 \times 5$$

$$560 = \mathbf{2^4} \times 5 \times \mathbf{7}$$
$$400 = 2^4 \times \mathbf{5^2}$$
$$LCM = \mathbf{2^4} \times \mathbf{5^2} \times \mathbf{7}$$
$$GCF = 2^4 \times 5$$

$$630 = 2 \times \mathbf{3^2} \times 5 \times \mathbf{7}$$
$$120 = \mathbf{2^3} \times 3 \times 5$$
$$LCM = \mathbf{2^3} \times \mathbf{3^2} \times 5 \times \mathbf{7}$$
$$GCF = 2 \times 3 \times 5$$

Fractions that represent the same number are called **equivalent fractions.** There are two important properties for working with equivalent fractions.

Property 1

For any whole numbers a, b, and c, with $b \neq 0$ and $c \neq 0$:

$$\frac{a}{b} = \frac{a \times c}{b \times c}$$

When you apply Property 1, it appears as if the *value* of the fraction should increase. Let's explore why the value does not increase but stays the same.

A paper with $\frac{2}{3}$ shaded is folded into two parts as shown by the dotted line.

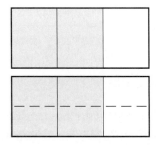

1. On the folded paper, the shaded part now represents what fraction?

2. How do the values of $\frac{2}{3}$ and $\frac{4}{6}$ compare?

3. How does the number of *shaded* parts compare before and after folding?

4. How does the *total* number of parts compare before and after folding?

5. Looking at the folded paper, Jake said, "How can $\frac{2}{3} = \frac{4}{6}$ when there are twice as many parts?" How would you answer Jake's question?

Applying Property 1 in Exercises 1–5:

$$\begin{array}{r} \text{shaded} \rightarrow \\ \text{total} \rightarrow \end{array} \frac{2}{3} = \frac{2 \times 2}{3 \times 2} = \frac{4}{6}$$

A paper with $\frac{1}{2}$ shaded is folded into four parts.

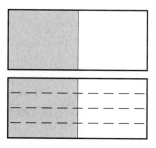

6. How do the values of $\frac{1}{2}$ and $\frac{4}{8}$ compare?

7. How does the number of *shaded* parts compare before and after folding?

8. How does the *total* number of parts compare before and after folding?

Applying Property 1 in
Exercises 6–8:

$$\begin{array}{c}\text{shaded} \rightarrow \\ \text{total} \rightarrow\end{array}\ \frac{1}{2} = \frac{1 \times 4}{2 \times 4} = \frac{4}{8}$$

Complete each statement to find a second fraction with the same value as the first fraction.

9. $\dfrac{3}{5} = \dfrac{\times}{\times} = \dfrac{}{25}$

10. $\dfrac{6}{7} = \dfrac{\times}{\times} = \dfrac{}{14}$

11. $\dfrac{5}{8} = \dfrac{\times}{\times} = \dfrac{}{56}$

Property 2

For any whole numbers a, b, and c, with $b \neq 0$ and $c \neq 0$:

$$\frac{a}{b} = \frac{a \div c}{b \div c}$$

When you apply Property 2, it appears as if the value of the fraction should decrease. However, the value stays the same.

Consider the swimming lane ropes as making parts.

12. What fraction of the swimming pool is deep water?

13. What fraction is deep water if the lane ropes are removed?

Both $\frac{6}{12}$ and $\frac{1}{2}$ tell us that part of the pool is deep water:

$$\frac{6}{12} = \frac{6 \div 6}{12 \div 6} = \frac{1}{2}$$

Using or removing the rope doesn't change the fraction of the pool that is deep water.

The dotted lines represent folds in the paper. Write the fraction for the shaded portion using the folds. Then write the fraction you would get without the folds.

14.
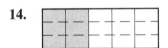

15.
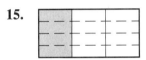

16.
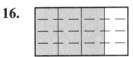

Complete each statement to find a second fraction with the same value as the first fraction.

17. $\dfrac{24}{32} = \dfrac{\div}{\div} = \dfrac{3}{4}$

18. $\dfrac{12}{75} = \dfrac{\div}{\div} = \dfrac{4}{25}$

19. $\dfrac{36}{42} = \dfrac{\div}{\div} = \dfrac{}{7}$

Division of Fractions

A pattern for an apron calls for $\frac{3}{4}$ yd of material for an apron. How many aprons can be made from a piece of material 3 yd long? You can use three fraction bars to represent the 3 yd of material as shown below.

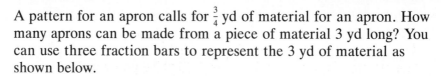

1. What does one bar represent?

A fraction bar showing $\frac{3}{4}$ has been placed next to the 3 fraction bars.

2. What does the $\frac{3}{4}$-bar represent?

3. Use the $\frac{3}{4}$-bars. How many aprons can be made from the 3 yd of material?

One way of finding the number of $\frac{3}{4}$-yd aprons in 3 yd is to divide $3 \div \frac{3}{4} = 4$.

$$3 \div \frac{3}{4} = 4$$

Use a piece of paper to represent 1 yd of material. Divide the paper into four equal parts.

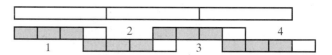

Cut off enough of the paper bar to represent one copy of the pattern.

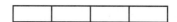

One apron and part of another can be made from 1 yd.

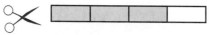

← Part of a copy

4. What fraction of another can be made from the remaining part? Use the cut-out parts to decide.

E13

Altogether, you can make $1\frac{1}{3}$ aprons from one yard of material.

5. If you can make $1\frac{1}{3}$ aprons from 1 yard of material, how many aprons can you make from 3 yd? Use paper to find your answer.

To find the number of aprons from 3 yd we can multiply:
$3 \times 1\frac{1}{3} = 3 \times \frac{4}{3} = 4$

$$3 \times \frac{4}{3} = 4$$

Use fraction bars to solve each problem.

6. A dog collar can be made from a $\frac{2}{3}$-yd piece of leather. How many collars can be made from a 4-yd piece of leather?

7. A recipe calls for $\frac{5}{8}$ cup of milk. How many batches of the recipe can be made with 2 cups of milk?

Since $3 \div \frac{3}{4} = 4$ and $3 \times \frac{4}{3} = 4$, then $3 \div \frac{3}{4} = 3 \times \frac{4}{3}$. This demonstrates the rule for dividing fractions.

Rule

If a, b, c, and d are whole numbers with $b \neq 0$, $c \neq 0$, and $d \neq 0$, then $\quad \frac{a}{b} \div \frac{c}{d} = \frac{a}{b} \times \frac{d}{c}$

Using the rule, $\frac{1}{4} \div \frac{5}{4} = \frac{1}{4} \times \frac{4}{5} = \frac{1}{5}$.

Use the rule to divide.

8. $2 \div \frac{2}{3}$

9. $9 \div \frac{9}{13}$

10. $5 \div \frac{5}{8}$

11. $\frac{1}{2} \div \frac{2}{3}$

12. $\frac{3}{4} \div \frac{7}{8}$

13. $\frac{4}{5} \div \frac{3}{10}$

The bars in Figure A show that 50% of 20 = 10.

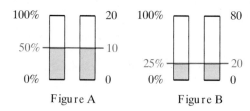

Figure A   Figure B

The bars in Figure B show that 25% of 80 = 20.

Use bars to represent each statement.

1. 50% of 200 = 100

2. 25% of 20 = 5

3. 75% of 60 = 45

Janelle made 40% of her shots in the first four games. If Janelle took 80 shots, how many did she make?

Use one bar to represent the percent and another to represent the shots.

a) You know she made 40% of her shots. Label the percent bar.

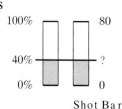

Percent Bar

b) The total number of shots taken is 80. You are to find the part she made. Label the shot bar.

Shot Bar

Rick made 30% of his shots in the last four games. If Rick made 21 shots, how many shots did he take?

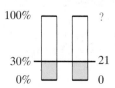

This time you know the number of shots made and are asked to find the total number of shots taken. Since 21 is the part of the shots he made and you are trying to find the total number he took, label the shot bar as shown.

Joe made 24 of the 60 shots he took. What percent of his shots did he make?

Label the entire shot bar. It is part of the percent bar that is missing.

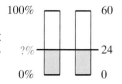

In Exercises 4–7, write the number that should replace each letter. If the letter is an unknown quantity, write a question mark.

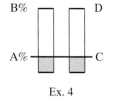

Ex. 4   Ex. 5

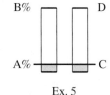

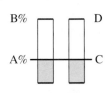

Ex. 6   Ex. 7

4. Of the 60 students in the band, 25% own their instruments. How many own their instruments?

5. About 12% of the students at Garcia High play in the band. How many students are in the band if the school enrollment is 500?

6. Jan got 80% of the test questions right. If she got 44 questions right, how many questions were on the test?

7. Of 80 students questioned, 28 preferred rap music to rock. What percent preferred rap?

Bars can also be used to write a proportion to solve a problem.

Letisha made 80 baskets during the season. If this was 40% of the shots she took, how many shots did she take?

$$\frac{40}{100} = \frac{80}{n}$$

$40n = 8000$

$n = 200$

Letisha took 200 shots.

The team made 51 of the 68 free throws shot during the tournament. What percent of their free throws did they make?

$$\frac{n}{100} = \frac{51}{68}$$

$68n = 5100$

$n = 75$

The team made 75% of their free throws.

In Exercises 8–11, write a proportion and solve.

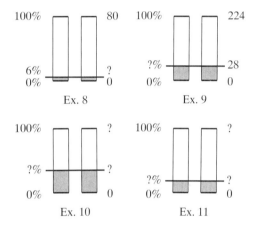

Ex. 8   Ex. 9

Ex. 10   Ex. 11

8. Quan buys an $80 jacket. If the sales tax is 6%, how much tax must he pay?

9. In a survey of 224 people, 28 answered *yes* to one question. This is what percent of the total?

10. Only 30% of the registered voters voted in the city election. If 4200 people voted, how many registered voters are there?

11. Marge gets a bonus of 5% of her sales. What amount of sales will earn her a $500 bonus?

Sometimes percents greater than 100 make sense and sometimes they don't.

> A car normally costing $10,000 is on sale with a discount of 150%. This is *not reasonable*. This means the price is reduced 100% ($10,000) plus another 50% ($5000). You would receive a discount greater than the cost of the car.

> The price of a car costing $10,000 last year is now 125% of what it was last year. This means the price is 25% ($2500) more than it was last year. This is *reasonable*.

Determine if the following statements are reasonable. If a statement is not reasonable explain why.

1. 130% of the coins in a jar are pennies.

2. The population of Rockville Centre is 110% of what it was last year.

3. In the basketball game, Rochelle made 125% of her shots.

4. Write two situations with percents greater than 100 that are reasonable and two situations that are not.

5. Explain why 187% of 60 must be greater than 60.

The bars show 125% of 40 is 50.   *The bars show 175% of 80 is 140.*

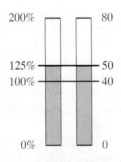

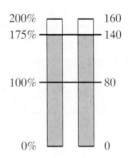

100% of 40 = 40   100% of 80 = 80
 25% of 40 = 10   75% of 80 = 60
so 125% of 40 = 50   so 175% of 80 = 140

Use bars to represent each statement.

6. 160% of 100 = 160   **7.** 125% of 20 = 25   **8.** 140% of 60 = 84

Proportions can be used to solve problems with percents greater than 100.

125% of 60 is ?   175% of ? is 42   ? % of 20 is 30

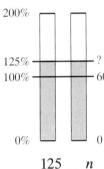   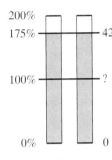   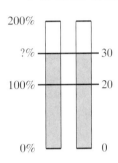

$$\frac{125}{100} = \frac{n}{60}$$ $$\frac{175}{100} = \frac{42}{n}$$ $$\frac{n}{100} = \frac{30}{20}$$

9. Explain how the bars help you write the proportion for each problem above.

10. Solve the proportions. In each case, explain why your answer is reasonable.

Use bars to represent each problem. Write a proportion and solve.

11. ? % of 36 is 48   **12.** 110% of ? is 44   **13.** 130% of 85 is ?

14. This year, enrollment at Bohan High is 130% of what it was last year. If 1560 students are enrolled this year, what was the enrollment last year?

15. A company sells goods at 150% of their purchase price. If the company purchased an item for $12.50, at what price would it be sold?

16. A baseball trading card that originally cost Greg $5 is now worth $9. What percent of the original price is the new price?

Without using integers, equations like $n + 5 = 0$ do not have a solution. Suppose we were to invent a solution to this equation called a **5-eliminator.**

1. Why is a 5-eliminator a good name for this number?

Write the solution to each equation as an eliminator.

2. $n + 8 = 0$

3. $12 + n = 0$

4. $n + 175 = 0$

5. $230 + n = 0$

To have an easier way to read and write eliminator numbers, we will use a number followed by the letter E. For example,

$$5 \text{ eliminator} = 5\text{-E}$$
$$\text{and}$$
$$20 \text{ eliminator} = 20\text{-E.}$$

Write the solution to each equation using eliminator notation if necessary.

6. $n + 4 = 0$

7. $22 + n = 0$

8. $6 + 6\text{-E} = n$

9. $9\text{-E} + n = 0$

10. $n + 85 = 0$

11. $105 + n = 0$

12. $34\text{-E} + 34 = n$

13. $n + 15\text{-E} = 0$

Every time an eliminator bumps into its corresponding number an explosion occurs and the number and the eliminator cancel each other out. Picture 8-eliminators floating around looking for eights to eliminate.

14. What would happen if an 8-eliminator, not paying attention to where it was going, accidentally bumped into a 10?

15. What part of the 10 can the 8-eliminator actually eliminate?

16. What part of the 10 would be left?

Find each sum.

17. $6 + 2\text{-E}$

18. $12 + 3\text{-E}$

19. $9\text{-E} + 15$

20. $35\text{-E} + 50$

21. Write a rule for adding an eliminator and a number when there is more number than eliminator.

Suppose our careless 8-eliminator, again not paying attention to where it was going, accidentally bumped into a 3.

22. Can the 8-eliminator eliminate a 3?

23. How much of its eliminating power will the 8-eliminator have left after eliminating the 3?

Find each sum.

24. 6 + 10-E

25. 2 + 3-E

26. 20-E + 15

27. 135-E + 20

28. Write a rule for adding an eliminator and a number when the eliminator has more power than is needed to eliminate the number.

Find each sum.

29. 10 + 10-E

30. 2 + 8-E

31. 20-E + 5

32. 5-E + 20

33. 14 + 7-E

34. 20-E + 20

35. 45 + 17-E

36. 100 + 75-E

37. Write a rule covering *all possible* situations involving adding a number and an eliminator.

Suppose a 3-eliminator and a 2-eliminator decided to join forces.

38. What could they accomplish together?

39. Explain how they could go about eliminating a 5.

Find each sum.

40. 6-E + 10-E

41. 7-E + 3-E

42. 20-E + 15-E

43. 35-E + 20-E

44. Write a rule for adding two eliminators.

Find each sum.

45. 5 + 10-E

46. 2-E + 8-E

47. 20-E + 15

48. 5-E + 20-E

49. 14 + 7E

50. 20-E + 20-E

51. 45 + 27-E

You can solve equations using inverse operations. For example,

$$n - 4 = 6 \rightarrow n = 4 + 6 = 10.$$

Subtraction *undoes* addition.   Addition *undoes* subtraction.

$$
\begin{aligned}
n + 34 &= 83 \\
n + 34 - 34 &= 83 - 34 \\
n &= 49
\end{aligned}
\qquad
\begin{aligned}
n - 57 &= 130 \\
n - 57 + 57 &= 130 + 57 \\
n &= 187
\end{aligned}
$$

Sometimes the rule for subtracting integers gives answers that are right but which are not immediately obvious.

Consider the problem ⁻3 − ⁻8.

1. What do you get if you change the sign of the second number and add?

2. Does 5 seem like a reasonable answer to you? If not, why not?

The problem ⁻3 − ⁻8 asks the question, "What must I add to ⁻8 to get ⁻3"? The numbers ⁻3 and ⁻8 have been circled on the number line.

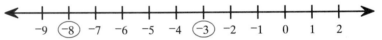

3. Why *can't* the number we add to ⁻8 to get ⁻3 be a negative number?

4. What *positive* number must the answer be?

The number line shows that you must take 5 jumps forward to get from ⁻8 to ⁻3.

The numbers ⁻3 and 2 have been circled on the number line below.

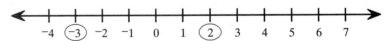

5. What question is asked by the problem ⁻3 − 2?

6. Must the answer be negative or positive? Why?

Since you must make 5 jumps backward, you must add ⁻5 to 2 in order to get ⁻3.

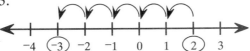

The numbers 3 and ⁻4 have been circled on the number line below.

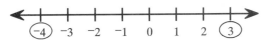

7. What question is asked by the problem 3 − ⁻4?

8. Must the answer be negative or positive? Why?

Since you must make 7 jumps forward, you must add 7 to ⁻4 in order to get 3.

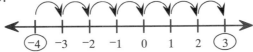

9. How would the number line representation for ⁻4 − 3 be *like* that for 3 − ⁻4?

10. Why would the answer to ⁻4 − 3 be *negative 7*? Use the number line to explain.

Write and solve the two subtraction problems that can be worked using each number line.

11.

12.

Draw a number line showing the answer.

13. 5 − ⁻2   14. ⁻5 − ⁻3   15. ⁻3 − 4 .   16. ⁻3 − ⁻6

The **median** of a set of numbers, like the median of a highway, is the point that separates the numbers into two equal parts. It is the number that falls in the middle when data are listed from least to greatest. If the number of data is even, the median is the mean, or *average,* of the two middle items.

Find the median for each set of test and quiz scores.

1. 78, 79, 84, 86, 88, 94, 96

2. 34, 45, 56, 58, 59, 60

3. 32, 34, 45, 48, 56, 58

4. 3, 5, 6, 6, 7, 8, 10, 6

Sometimes knowing only the median of a set of numbers can be misleading.

5. Lydia has the following math scores: 84, 86, **86,** 94, 98
Mark has the following math scores: 20, 46, **86,** 87, 88
Is Lydia doing better than Mark? Explain.

6. Median salaries for two companies are $35,000 and $40,000. What additional information would be helpful to have before deciding which company you would like to work for?

Because they show more information, **box-and-whisker plots,** can help avoid misunderstandings caused by looking at just the median.

To make a box-and-whisker plot you need to separate the data into four equal parts and identify the highest and lowest scores.

Test Scores for 17 Students

56,	86,	74,	90,	80,
85,	96,	94,	86,	84,
76,	92,	87,	70,	68,
79,	100			

Start by arranging the scores in order from lowest to highest. Then find the median.

the median
56 68 70 74 76 79 80 84 **85** 86 86 87 90 92 94 96 100

Use what you know about finding a median to find the following.

7. The median of the data below 85

8. The median of the data above 85

56 68 70 74 **75** 76 79 80 84 **85** 86 86 87 90 **91** 92 94 96 **100**

56 is the least score and 100 is the greatest. The numbers 75, 85, and 91 are called *quartiles* because they separate the scores into four parts. These numbers are shown with dots below the number line.

Draw a **box** with edges passing through the first and third quartiles (75 and 91). Draw a line through the box to show the median (85). Now add the **whiskers** to the plot by connecting the box to the lowest and highest scores.

Test Scores for 17 Students

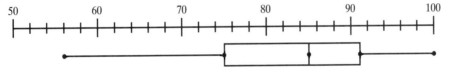

Make box-and-whisker plots for each set of data.

9. Minutes spent exercising each day: 23, 25, 28, 28, 29, 39, 43, 46, 47, 54, 55, 60, 63

10. Cost of a dress: 45, 87, 67, 98, 81, 66, 89, 76, 86, 94, 96, 67, 95

The box-and-whisker plot shows test scores for two classes.

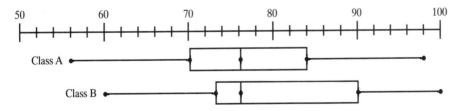

11. How do the medians compare?

12. How many of the 20 people in Class B scored 90 or above?

13. How many of the 40 people in Class A scored below 84?

14. Which class did better on the test? Explain.

1 Operations with Whole Numbers

APPLYING MATHEMATICS
BUSINESS

The Financial District of New York City is located in Manhattan. It is here that every major bank in the world has its main office or a branch office. It is also the location of the world's largest investment companies. New York City is the home of The New York Stock Exchange and The American Stock Exchange. In this small section of the city, many of the world's major economic and financial transactions take place. In recent years the rapid expansion of the use of data, numbers, and money has pushed mathematics and business into the computer age. Likewise, the development and use of computers has been responsible for the creation of many new businesses. In this chapter you will learn about basic properties of operations with whole numbers.

CAREER CONNECTION

ACCOUNTANT

Accountants may be self-employed or may work for industry or government. They compute profits and losses, classify assets and liabilities, and prepare income tax returns for businesses and private clients. Most companies appoint an accountant to be the comptroller or financial officer for the company. An accountant has a bachelors degree in accounting. Certified Public Accountants are required to pass a comprehensive examination and are licensed by the state.

Photo: Computer graphics provide rapid data displays, so business decision makers can view trends.

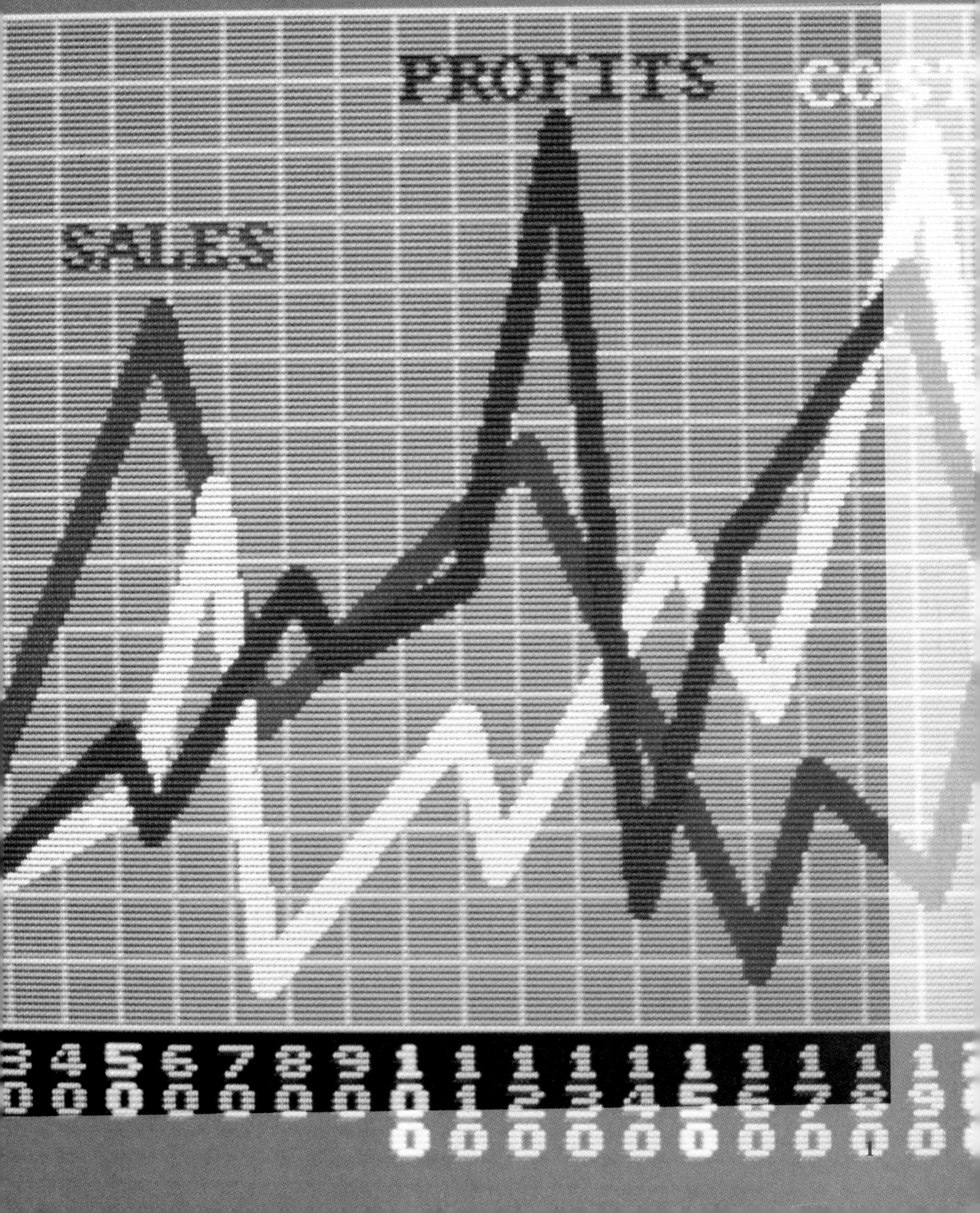
PROFITS
SALES

1-1 Mathematical Expressions

A checkout clerk in a supermarket takes three minutes to pass an average customer's groceries over a code reader. The following table shows how long it will take the clerk to wait on a given number of customers.

Number of Customers	Minutes Required
1	$3 \times 1 = 3$
2	$3 \times 2 = 6$
3	$3 \times 3 = 9$
4	$3 \times 4 = 12$
5	$3 \times 5 = 15$

Each of the expressions for minutes fits the pattern

$$3 \times n$$

when n stands for 1, 2, 3, 4, or 5. We call n a *variable*.

A **variable** is a symbol used to represent one or more numbers. The numbers are called the **values** of the variable.

An expression, such as $3 \times n$, that involves a variable is called a **variable expression.** Expressions, such as 3×2, that name a certain number are called **numerical expressions.**

When we write a product that involves a variable, we usually omit the multiplication symbol. Thus,

$$3 \times n \text{ is written as } 3n$$

and $2 \times a \times b$ is written as $2ab$.

In numerical expressions for products a multiplication symbol must be used to avoid confusion. We sometimes use a raised dot for the multiplication symbol. For example,

$$9 \times 7 \text{ may be written as } 9 \cdot 7.$$

The number named by a numerical expression is called the **value** of the expression. Since the expressions $4 + 5$ and 9 name the same number, they have the same value. To show that these expressions have the same value, we use the equals sign, $=$. We write $4 + 5 = 9$ and say "four plus five equals (or is equal to) nine." Of course, 9 is the simplest name for the number nine. When we write 9 for the expression $4 + 5$, we say that we have **simplified** the expression $4 + 5$.

When a mathematical sentence uses an equals sign, it is called an *equation*. An **equation** tells us that two expressions name the same number. The expression to the left of the equals sign is called the **left side** of the equation and the expression to the right of the equals sign is called the **right side.**

When a number is **substituted** for a variable in a variable expression and the indicated operation is carried out, we say that the variable expression has been **evaluated.** For example, if n has the value 6 in the variable expression $3 \times n$, then

$$3 \times n \text{ has the value } 3 \times 6, \text{ or } 18.$$

EXAMPLE 1   Simplify.

      a. $81 + 62$ **b.** 13×8 **c.** $148 \div 4$ **d.** $209 - 46$

Solution   **a.** $81 + 62 = 143$

      b. $13 \times 8 = 104$

      c. $148 \div 4 = 37$

      d. $209 - 46 = 163$

EXAMPLE 2   Evaluate each expression if $m = 3$ and $n = 18$.

      a. mn **b.** $n - m$ **c.** $m + n$ **d.** $n \div m$

Solution   **a.** $mn = 3 \times 18 = 54$

      b. $n - m = 18 - 3 = 15$

      c. $m + n = 3 + 18 = 21$

      d. $n \div m = 18 \div 3 = 6$

Class Exercises

Simplify.

    1. $183 + 59$ **2.** $261 - 194$ **3.** 23×15 **4.** $459 \div 3$

Evaluate each expression if $a = 7$ and $b = 2$.

    5. $5a$ **6.** $24 - a$ **7.** $b + 17$ **8.** $84 \div b$

    9. $98 \div a$ **10.** $4ab$ **11.** $a + b + 13$ **12.** $a - b$

Written Exercises

Simplify.

A 1. $163 + 348$ 2. 21×18 3. $283 - 198$ 4. $510 \div 3$

5. $27 \cdot 34$ 6. $421 - 256$ 7. $432 \div 6$ 8. $397 + 248$

Evaluate each expression when the variable has the values listed.

9. $4x$; 1, 2, 3, 4   10. $6a$; 2, 4, 6, 8   11. $23 + z$; 5, 7, 11, 13

12. $123 - c$; 89, 47, 68   13. $84 \div y$; 4, 12, 42   14. $b \div 3$; 27, 81, 108

Evaluate each expression if $a = 12$ and $b = 15$.

15. $8b$ 16. $7a$ 17. $91 - a$ 18. $b + 79$

19. $444 \div a$ 20. $4ab$ 21. $420 \div b$ 22. $101 - b$

Evaluate each expression if $x = 8$, $y = 18$, and $z = 20$.

B 23. $x + y + 41$ 24. $z - x + 38$ 25. $108 - y + x$ 26. $93 + y - z$

27. $5xy$ 28. $13yz$ 29. $xy \div 12$ 30. $yz \div 15$

31. $x + y + z$ 32. xyz 33. $9xyz$ 34. $yz \div x$

C 35. $3x + 4y$ 36. $2z \div x$ 37. $5y - 4z$ 38. $4y \div 3x$

39. $3xy + 5z$ 40. $yz - 21x$ 41. $10xy + 7xz$ 42. $5xy \div 2z$

Review Exercises

Perform the indicated operation.

1. $\begin{array}{r} 1328 \\ + \ 4017 \\ \hline \end{array}$ 2. $\begin{array}{r} 98 \\ 107 \\ + \ 58 \\ \hline \end{array}$ 3. $\begin{array}{r} 349 \\ \times \ 29 \\ \hline \end{array}$ 4. $\begin{array}{r} 507 \\ \times \ 62 \\ \hline \end{array}$

5. $9 + 45 + 706$ 6. $413 + 1028$ 7. 504×18 8. 965×37

 NONROUTINE PROBLEM SOLVING: *Working Backward*

Four bacteria are placed in a jar, and the number of bacteria doubles every day. The jar is full at the end of 28 days. How long did it take the bacteria to fill half the jar?

1-2 Properties of Addition and Multiplication

The set of numbers

$$1, 2, 3, 4, 5, \ldots$$

is called the **counting numbers.** The three dots, read "and so on," show that the set continues without end. If 0 is included in the set, we obtain the set of **whole numbers:**

$$0, 1, 2, 3, 4, \ldots$$

The order in which two whole numbers are added or multiplied does not change their sum or their product. For example,

$$3 + 4 = 7 \qquad \text{and} \qquad 4 + 3 = 7$$

and

$$3 \times 4 = 12 \qquad \text{and} \qquad 4 \times 3 = 12.$$

These examples illustrate the *commutative property of addition* and the *commutative property of multiplication.*

Commutative Properties

For any whole numbers a and b, $a + b = b + a$.

For any whole numbers a and b, $a \times b = b \times a$.

Suppose we wish to add three or more numbers. We first have to add two of the numbers, then add the third number to their sum. The order in which we add the numbers has no effect on the sum. We can use parentheses to show which numbers are added first. For example,

$$(6 + 5) + 7 = 11 + 7 = 18$$

and

$$6 + (5 + 7) = 6 + 12 = 18$$

illustrate that

$$(6 + 5) + 7 = 6 + (5 + 7).$$

Operations indicated within parentheses in any expression are done before the others. Consider the following products.

$$(9 \times 2) \times 5 = 18 \times 5 = 90$$

$$9 \times (2 \times 5) = 9 \times 10 = 90$$

These examples illustrate that the order in which we multiply whole numbers has no effect on the product. Thus,

$$(9 \times 2) \times 5 = 9 \times (2 \times 5).$$

Operations with Whole Numbers **5**

The properties of addition and multiplication shown on the previous page are called the *associative property of addition* and the *associative property of multiplication*.

Associative Properties

For any whole numbers a, b, and c,

$$(a + b) + c = a + (b + c).$$

For any whole numbers a, b, and c,

$$(a \times b) \times c = a \times (b \times c).$$

The commutative and associative properties are helpful in simplifying expressions.

EXAMPLE 1 Simplify, using the commutative and associative properties.

a. $13 + 8 + 7$ **b.** $5 \times 7 \times 2$

Solution

a. $13 + 8 + 7 = 13 + (8 + 7)$
$= 13 + (7 + 8)$
$= (13 + 7) + 8$
$= 20 + 8$
$= 28$

b. $5 \times 7 \times 2 = 5 \times (7 \times 2)$
$= 5 \times (2 \times 7)$
$= (5 \times 2) \times 7$
$= 10 \times 7$
$= 70$

The numbers 0 and 1 have special properties. You know that

$$6 + 0 = 6 \quad \text{and} \quad 0 + 6 = 6.$$

Since the sum of any whole number and 0 is the same whole number, 0 is called the **identity element for addition.**

Addition Property of Zero

For any whole number a,

$$a + 0 = a \quad \text{and} \quad 0 + a = a.$$

You know that

$$6 \times 1 = 6 \quad \text{and} \quad 1 \times 6 = 6.$$

As the preceding equations suggest, 1 is the **identity element for multiplication** since the product of any whole number and 1 is the same whole number.

> ## *Multiplication Property of One*
>
> For any whole number a,
>
> $$a \times 1 = a \quad \text{and} \quad 1 \times a = a.$$

The equations

$$6 \times 0 = 0 \quad \text{and} \quad 0 \times 6 = 0$$

illustrate an important property of 0, namely that the product of any whole number and 0 is 0.

> ## *Multiplication Property of Zero*
>
> For any whole number a,
>
> $$a \times 0 = 0 \quad \text{and} \quad 0 \times a = 0.$$

COMMUNICATION IN MATHEMATICS: *Study Helps*

When reading your mathematics textbook, pay particular attention to words in heavy type and to material in boxes. The words in heavy type are mathematical terms that are being defined. The boxes contain important formulas, rules, or properties.

EXAMPLE 2 Simplify, using the properties.

a. $8 \times 0 \times 11$ **b.** $4 \times 6 \times 1$

Solution **a.** $8 \times 0 \times 11 = (8 \times 0) \times 11$
$= 0 \times 11$
$= 0$

b. $4 \times 6 \times 1 = 4 \times (6 \times 1)$
$= 4 \times 6$
$= 24$

Class Exercises

Simplify, using the properties.

1. $18 + 17 + 2$

2. $21 + 14 + 19$

3. $33 + 27 + 9$

4. $4 \times 9 \times 5$

5. $13 \times 5 \times 2$

6. $14 \times 0 \times 9$

7. $19 + 0 + 24$

8. $37 + 24 + 13$

9. $44 + 18 + 2$

10. $34 \times 20 \times 5$

11. $42 \times 11 \times 1$

12. $25 \times 17 \times 4$

Written Exercises

Simplify, using the properties.

A

1. $16 + 29 + 34$

2. $14 + 0 + 41$

3. $27 + 19 + 23$

4. $18 \times 1 \times 9$

5. $14 \times 13 \times 5$

6. $11 \times 24 \times 0$

7. $13 + 37 + 19$

8. $24 + 16 + 1$

9. $31 + 42 + 29$

10. $15 \times 17 \times 12$

11. $13 \times 1 \times 27$

12. $16 \times 0 \times 5$

13. $26 + 32 + 34$

14. $81 + 29 + 34$

15. $62 + 38 + 43$

16. $28 \times 13 \times 25$

17. $19 \times 0 \times 10$

18. $31 \times 14 \times 25$

B

19. $81 + 37 + 49 + 23$

20. $108 + 74 + 96 + 42$

21. $25 \times 2 \times 14 \times 2$

22. $14 \times 15 \times 2 \times 10$

23. $164 + 47 + 53 + 36$

24. $192 + 28 + 81 + 149$

25. $20 \times 12 \times 5 \times 10$

26. $8 \times 25 \times 14 \times 5$

27. $263 + 428 + 32 + 147$

28. $181 + 256 + 319 + 234$

29. $5 \times 18 \times 10 \times 20$

30. $32 \times 9 \times 5 \times 15$

31. $24 \times 6 \times 5 \times 15$

32. $46 \times 8 \times 0 \times 40$

Review Exercises

Perform the indicated operation.

1. $\begin{array}{r} 5000 \\ -783 \\ \hline \end{array}$

2. $\begin{array}{r} 3840 \\ -79 \\ \hline \end{array}$

3. $72\overline{)360}$

4. $16\overline{)8048}$

5. $721 - 39$

6. $1008 - 762$

7. $553 \div 79$

8. $8000 \div 16$

1-3 Inverse Operations

The operation of subtraction is related to the operation of addition. The following table shows some addition facts and the related subtraction facts.

Addition Facts	Related Subtraction Facts
$9 + 6 = 15$	$15 - 6 = 9$
$6 + 9 = 15$	$15 - 9 = 6$

Notice in the above table that the subtraction of 6 undoes the addition of 6 and that the subtraction of 9 undoes the addition of 9. We call addition of a given number and subtraction of the same number **inverse operations.**

A similar statement may be made for division in relation to multiplication; that is, multiplication by a given number and division by the same number are inverse operations.

Multiplication Facts	Related Division Facts
$6 \times 3 = 18$	$18 \div 3 = 6$
$3 \times 6 = 18$	$18 \div 6 = 3$

EXAMPLE 1 a. State the related subtraction facts for $14 + 7 = 21$ and $7 + 14 = 21$.

b. State the related division facts for $8 \times 6 = 48$ and $6 \times 8 = 48$.

Solution a. $21 - 7 = 14$ and $21 - 14 = 7$

b. $48 \div 6 = 8$ and $48 \div 8 = 6$

We can use the relationship between inverse operations to simplify some numerical and variable expressions.

EXAMPLE 2 Simplify, using inverse operations.

a. $17 - 8 + 8$ b. $9 + x - x$

Solution a. Subtracting 8 and adding 8 are inverse operations.
$17 - 8 + 8 = 17$

b. Adding x and subtracting x are inverse operations.
$9 + x - x = 9$

EXAMPLE 3   Simplify, using inverse operations.

       a. $108 \div 6 \times 6$ **b.** $3n \div 3$

Solution   **a.** Dividing by 6 and multiplying by 6 are inverse operations.
        $108 \div 6 \times 6 = 108$

        b. Multiplying by 3 and dividing by 3 are inverse operations.
        $3n \div 3 = n$

    The addition and multiplication properties of 0 and 1 lead us to the subtraction and division properties of 0 and 1. For example, the addition facts

$$9 + 0 = 9 \quad \text{and} \quad 0 + 9 = 9$$

give us the related subtraction facts

$$9 - 0 = 9 \quad \text{and} \quad 9 - 9 = 0,$$

which illustrate the following property.

Subtraction Property of Zero

For any whole number a,

$$a - 0 = a \quad \text{and} \quad a - a = 0.$$

    Similarly, the multiplication facts

$$7 \times 1 = 7 \quad \text{and} \quad 1 \times 7 = 7$$

give us the related division facts

$$7 \div 1 = 7 \quad \text{and} \quad 7 \div 7 = 1,$$

which illustrate the following property.

Division Property of One

For any whole number a, except 0,

$$a \div 1 = a \quad \text{and} \quad a \div a = 1.$$

    Also, the multiplication fact $0 \times 5 = 0$ gives us the related division fact $0 \div 5 = 0$, which suggests the following property.

Division Property of Zero

For any whole number a, except 0,

$$0 \div a = 0.$$

Notice in the division property of 0 that the divisor, a, represents any whole number, *except for 0*. If 0 were allowed as a divisor, the multiplication fact $5 \times 0 = 0$ might suggest the related division "fact" $0 \div 0 = 5$. Also, the fact $2 \times 0 = 0$ might suggest the "fact" $0 \div 0 = 2$. Since the two facts suggest different quotients for $0 \div 0$, there is no way to pick a specific number to be the quotient. Therefore, we *never divide 0 by 0*.

Can we divide 5 by 0? If there were a whole number n such that $5 \div 0 = n$, then $0 \times n = 5$. But $0 \times n = 0$. Hence, we cannot divide 5 by 0. In fact, we *never divide any number by 0*.

Class Exercises

Give two related subtraction facts.

1. $13 + 9 = 22$ **2.** $41 + 18 = 59$ **3.** $37 + 48 = 85$ **4.** $39 + 51 = 90$

Give two related division facts.

5. $13 \times 8 = 104$ **6.** $9 \times 17 = 153$ **7.** $12 \times 21 = 252$ **8.** $14 \times 22 = 308$

Simplify, using inverse operations.

9. $31 - 8 + 8$ **10.** $x + 3 - 3$ **11.** $84 \div 4 \times 4$ **12.** $a \times 19 \div 19$

13. $45 + 17 - 45$ **14.** $7 \times 24 \div 7$ **15.** $16 + z - 16$ **16.** $6y \div 6$

Written Exercises

Write two related facts for each of the following.

A

1. $32 + 26 = 58$ **2.** $16 \times 8 = 128$ **3.** $103 - 41 = 62$

4. $182 \div 14 = 13$ **5.** $21 \times 13 = 273$ **6.** $87 + 59 = 146$

7. $217 - 149 = 68$ **8.** $352 \div 16 = 22$ **9.** $305 - 249 = 56$

10. $23 \times 31 = 713$ **11.** $361 + 288 = 649$ **12.** $792 \div 33 = 24$

Simplify.

13. $38 - 0$

14. $15 \div 1$

15. $0 \div 12$

16. $19 \div 19$

17. $0 + 24$

18. 38×1

Simplify, using inverse operations.

19. $48 \div 6 \times 6$

20. $81 - 24 + 24$

21. $32 \times 5 \div 5$

22. $46 - 17 + 17$

23. $y \div 12 \times 12$

24. $z \times 9 \div 9$

B **25.** $16 + x - x$

26. $a \div 84 \times 84$

27. $39b \div 39$

28. $24 + 39 - 24$

29. $24 \times 36 \div 24$

30. $87 + 119 - 87$

31. $43 \times 29 \div 43$

32. $42 + x - 42$

33. $14z \div 14$

34. $26a \div 26$

35. $58 + c - 58$

36. $y + 38 - y$

37. $16 \times t \div 16$

38. $34 \times p \div 34$

39. $b + 41 - b$

For any whole numbers x, y, and z, except 0, simplify using inverse operations.

C **40.** $y + z - z$

41. $x \div y \times y$

42. $xz \div z$

43. $x + y - x$

44. $x - x + z$

45. $xy \div x$

Review Exercises

Perform the indicated operation.

1.
$$\begin{array}{r} 29 \\ 2156 \\ +\ 937 \end{array}$$

2.
$$\begin{array}{r} 5004 \\ -\ 797 \end{array}$$

3.
$$\begin{array}{r} 58 \\ \times\ 19 \end{array}$$

4.
$$\begin{array}{r} 712 \\ \times\ 309 \end{array}$$

5. $312 + 76 + 102$

6. $700 - 394$

7. 103×87

8. 567×908

■■■■ **CALCULATOR INVESTIGATION:** *Patterns*

Use your calculator to solve this problem: One day you tell a secret to a friend. The next day your friend tells your secret to two other friends. On the third day, each of the friends who was told your secret the day before tells it to two other friends. If this pattern continues from day to day, how many people will be told your secret on the fourteenth day?

1-4 The Distributive Property

The fee at State Park is $4 for each person and $2 for a bicycle. Therefore, the total fee in dollars for the 12 members of the Bicycle Club is

$$12 \times (4 + 2) = 12 \times 6 = 72.$$

The total fee is also the sum of the fees for the people and the fees for the bikes, that is,

$$12 \times 4 + 12 \times 2 = 48 + 24 = 72.$$

No matter which way the fee is computed, it is the same. Therefore,

$$12 \times (4 + 2) = (12 \times 4) + (12 \times 2).$$

This example, where the 12 has been distributed as a multiplier of each addend of the expression $4 + 2$, illustrates the following property.

> ## Distributive Property of Multiplication with Respect to Addition
>
> For any whole numbers a, b, and c,
>
> $$a \times (b + c) = (a \times b) + (a \times c)$$
>
> and $\quad (b + c) \times a = (b \times a) + (c \times a).$

Remember that the parentheses indicate which operation to do first.

EXAMPLE 1   Simplify, using the distributive property.

        a. 13×15 **b.** $(11 \times 4) + (11 \times 6)$.

Solution   **a.** $13 \times 15 = (13 \times 10) + (13 \times 5) = 130 + 65 = 195$

        b. $(11 \times 4) + (11 \times 6) = 11 \times (4 + 6) = 11 \times 10 = 110$

Example 2 illustrates the fact that multiplication is distributive with respect to subtraction, just as it is with respect to addition.

EXAMPLE 2   Show that $7 \times (11 - 3) = (7 \times 11) - (7 \times 3)$.

Solution $7 \times (11 - 3) = 7 \times 8 = 56$

        $(7 \times 11) - (7 \times 3) = 77 - 21 = 56$

        Therefore, $7 \times (11 - 3) = (7 \times 11) - (7 \times 3)$.

Distributive Property of Multiplication with Respect to Subtraction

For any whole numbers a, b, and c,

$$a \times (b - c) = (a \times b) - (a \times c)$$

and $\quad (b - c) \times a = (b \times a) - (c \times a).$

Since multiplication is distributive with respect to both addition and subtraction, we refer to both properties as the *distributive property*.

Class Exercises

Complete.

1. $4(3 + 8) = 4 \times 3 + 4 \times \underline{}$

2. $6(5 + 9) = 6 \times 5 + \underline{} \times 9$

3. $9(7 - 4) = 9 \times \underline{} - 9 \times 4$

4. $\underline{}(11 - 3) = 5 \times 11 - 5 \times 3$

5. $12(\underline{} + 7) = 12 \times 15 + 12 \times 7$

6. $8(9 + 14) = \underline{} \times 9 + \underline{} \times 14$

7. $11(17 - 12) = 11 \times \underline{} - 11 \times \underline{}$

8. $7(\underline{} + \underline{}) = 7 \times 12 + 7 \times 15$

Written Exercises

Simplify, using the distributive property.

A

1. $(8 \times 6) + (2 \times 6)$
2. $(7 \times 9) + (13 \times 9)$
3. $(8 \times 9) + (8 \times 1)$

4. $(117 \times 4) - (17 \times 4)$
5. $(41 \times 8) - (11 \times 8)$
6. $(84 \times 9) - (34 \times 9)$

7. $(24 \times 6) + (6 \times 6)$
8. $(43 \times 9) + (17 \times 9)$
9. $(73 \times 8) + (27 \times 8)$

10. $(89 \times 5) - (19 \times 5)$
11. $(93 \times 7) - (23 \times 7)$
12. $(54 \times 11) - (24 \times 11)$

13. $7(24 + 19)$
14. $4(17 + 42)$
15. $8(54 - 13)$
16. $5(62 - 38)$

17. $12(49 + 18)$
18. $15(61 + 24)$
19. $11(88 - 42)$
20. $18(76 - 59)$

B

21. 28×15
22. 23×11
23. 36×20
24. 9×57

25. 25×38
26. 51×27
27. 101×34
28. 74×49

29. 19×72
30. 99×43
31. 35×18
32. 29×54

33. 90×37
34. 210×23
35. 190×27
36. 110×43

In parts (a)–(c) of Exercises 37 and 38, simplify each side of the equation to tell whether the given statement is true or false. If the given sentence involves quotients that are not whole numbers, so state.

C **37. a.** $(12 \div 4) + (16 \div 4) = (12 + 16) \div 4$

    b. $(4 + 8) \div 3 = (4 \div 3) + (8 \div 3)$

    c. $120 \div (3 + 5) = (120 \div 3) + (120 \div 5)$

    d. In view of your answers to parts (a)–(c), what guess would you make about division being distributive with respect to addition?

38. a. $(24 \div 6) - (18 \div 6) = (24 - 18) \div 6$

    b. $(35 - 2) \div 11 = (35 \div 11) - (2 \div 11)$

    c. $84 \div (7 - 4) = (84 \div 7) - (84 \div 4)$

    d. In view of your answers to parts (a)–(c), what guess would you make about division being distributive with respect to subtraction?

Self-Test A

Evaluate each expression if $a = 9$ and $b = 24$.

1. $7b$	**2.** $8a$	**3.** $42 - a$	**4.** $b + 130$	**[1-1]**
5. $a - 5$	**6.** $3ab$	**7.** $108 \div a$	**8.** $6b \div 8$	

Simplify, using the properties.

9. $31 + 0 + 19$	**10.** $84 + 7 + 16$	**11.** $72 + 57 + 43$	**[1-2]**
12. $15 \times 0 \times 10$	**13.** $40 \times 17 \times 25$	**14.** $120 \times 1 \times 70$	

Simplify, using inverse operations.

15. $32 + a - a$	**16.** $56b \div 56$	**17.** $c + 62 - c$	**[1-3]**
18. $12 \times e \div 12$	**19.** $349 + d - 349$	**20.** $94 \times f \div 94$	

Simplify, using the distributive property.

21. $(87 \times 9) - (27 \times 9)$	**22.** $17(30 + 6)$	**23.** $24(90 - 8)$	**[1-4]**
24. 102×56	**25.** 110×78	**26.** 98×205	

Self-Test answers and Extra Practice are at the back of the book.

1-5 Order of Operations

Symbols, such as parentheses and brackets, [ ], that show which operations are to be performed first are called **grouping symbols.** When one pair of grouping symbols is enclosed in another, we always perform the operation enclosed in the inner pair of symbols first.

EXAMPLE 1 Simplify.

$$\textbf{a. } (14 + 77) \div 7 \qquad \textbf{b. } [3 + (4 \times 5)] \times 10$$

Solution

a. $(14 + 77) \div 7$
$91 \div 7$
13

b. $[3 + (4 \times 5)] \times 10$
$[3 + 20] \times 10$
23×10
230

Some expressions, such as

$$8 + 3 - 9 \times 2 \div 3,$$

are written without grouping symbols. In order to simplify these expressions we use the following rule.

Rule

When there are no grouping symbols:

1. Do all multiplications and divisions in order from left to right.
2. Then do all additions and subtractions in order from left to right.

EXAMPLE 2 Simplify.

$$\textbf{a. } 72 - 24 \div 3 \qquad \textbf{b. } 8 + 3 - 9 \times 2 \div 3$$

Solution

a. $72 - 24 \div 3$
$72 - 8$
64

b. $8 + 3 - 9 \times 2 \div 3$
$8 + 3 - 18 \div 3$
$8 + 3 - 6$
$11 - 6$
5

Class Exercises

State which operation is to be performed first.

1. $12(18 + 36)$
2. $(100 - 16) \div 7$
3. $4[(6 + 17)2]$
4. $[(54 - 12) + 26] \div 25$
5. $15 + 12 \times 3$
6. $87 - 16 \times 4$
7. $31 + 88 \div 11$
8. $96 \div 2 + 10$
9. $96 \div (2 + 10)$
10. $55 - 30 \div 5$
11. $(55 - 30) \div 5$
12. $84 \div (2 + 5)$

Written Exercises

Simplify.

A
1. $7 + (9 \times 2)$
2. $(5 \times 7) + 4$
3. $(19 - 3) \div 4$
4. $(12 + 9)3$
5. $7 + (15 - 3)$
6. $18 + (42 \div 6)$
7. $48 - (5 \times 4)$
8. $12(11 - 5)$
9. $72 \div (8 - 2)$
10. $3 \times 9 + 18$
11. $64 \div 16 + 16$
12. $37 + 13 \times 2$
13. $20 + 6 \times 8$
14. $(37 + 13)4$
15. $102 \div 3 - 1$
16. $86 - 40 \div 2$
17. $(18 - 5)(23 - 9)$
18. $(32 + 24) \div (30 - 22)$
19. $(12 \times 9) - (8 \times 11)$
20. $(11 \times 7) + (90 \div 6)$
21. $(135 \div 3) - (17 \times 2)$
22. $(148 \div 4) + (16 \times 5)$

B
23. $[48 - (4 \times 3)] \div 3$
24. $38 - [25 \div (43 - 18)]$
25. $[18 + (15 - 3)] + 14$
26. $[42 + (24 \div 6)] \div 2$
27. $53 + [64 - (10 \times 3)]$
28. $49 \div [81 - (37 \times 2)]$
29. $34 + 16 \times 2 - 29$
30. $126 - 9 \div 3 \times 28$
31. $181 - 24 \times 3 \div 8$
32. $8 + 6 \times 12 \div 4 + 6$
33. $19 + 84 \div 4 \times 8 - 11$
34. $97 - 75 \div 5 \times 3 + 68$

Evaluate if $t = 12$, $w = 10$, $x = 9$, $y = 4$, and $z = 3$.

C
35. $tx - wz$
36. $x(y + w)$
37. $3z \div (y - z)$
38. $tw \div z + xy$
39. $ty + wx \div z$
40. $xy \div t + wz$

Review Exercises

Perform the indicated operation.

1. $195 + 206 + 17$
2. $5004 - 729$
3. 607×74
4. $1280 \div 16$
5. $918 + 87 + 105$
6. $9018 - 119$
7. 727×102
8. $6539 \div 13$

1-6 A Problem Solving Model

Problem solving in both mathematics and real-life situations requires advance planning and careful thought. This can be accomplished by asking questions in regard to the problem. For example, we must know what is asked for in the problem. Also, we must know what facts are given and whether there are too few or too many. It is also a good idea to consider whether or not a diagram or sketch will be of help.

These considerations are part of the following overall plan for solving word problems. We will refer to this as the **five-step plan.**

Plan for Solving Word Problems

1. Read the problem carefully. Make sure that you understand what it says. You may need to read it more than once.

2. Use questions like these in planning the solution:

What is asked for?
What facts are given?
Are enough facts given? If not, what else is needed?
Are unnecessary facts given? If so, what are they?
Will a sketch or diagram help?

3. Determine which operation or operations can be used to solve the problem.

4. Carry out the operations carefully.

5. Check your results with the facts given in the problem. Give the answer.

EXAMPLE   The Golden Gate Bridge, completed in 1937, has a span of 4200 ft. The Brooklyn Bridge, completed in 1883, has a span of 1595 ft. How much longer is the span of the Golden Gate Bridge than the span of the Brooklyn Bridge?

Answer the following questions about the problem.

a. What number or numbers does the problem ask for?

b. Are enough facts given? If not, what else is needed?

c. Are unneeded facts given? If so, what are they?

d. What operation or operations would you use to find the answer?

Solution　**a.** The problem asks for the difference in the lengths of the spans of the two bridges.

b. The lengths of the two spans are given. Therefore, enough facts are given to do the problem.

c. The years of completion are given but are not needed.

d. You subtract to find the answer.

COMMUNICATION IN MATHEMATICS:　*Study Skills*

It is important to read the directions for the exercises or problems. The directions will tell you exactly what to do. For instance, the directions for the worked-out example in this lesson do not ask you to solve the problem, only to answer some questions about it.

Class Exercises

The following problems have unnecessary facts. Tell what facts are not needed to solve the problem.

1. Jean is 12 years old. She sold 42 newspapers on Monday and 37 on Tuesday. How many papers did she sell in the two days?

2. Phil rented a sailboat at a cost of $6 per hour. If he rented the boat at 1:00 P.M. and returned the boat 4 hours later, how much did the rental cost?

The following problems do not have enough facts. Tell what facts are needed to solve the problem.

3. Elrod jogs 3 km a day for exercise. How many hours did he spend jogging in June?

4. Melody bought 3 cans of tennis balls. She paid for the cans with a $20 bill. What was her change?

Tell what operation can be used to solve the problem.

5. Yvonne Chu drives 7 km to and from work each day. How many kilometers does she drive to and from work each week if she works 5 days a week?

6. The Hancock Center in Chicago is 1127 ft tall. The Hancock Tower in Boston is 790 ft tall. How much taller is the Hancock Center than the Hancock Tower?

Written Exercises

For each problem, answer the following questions.

a. What number or numbers does the problem ask for?
b. Are enough facts given? If not, what else is needed?
c. Are unnecessary facts given? If so, what are they?
d. What operation or operations would you use to find the answer?

A 1. Sam has 12 model planes. He bought several more. How many model planes did he have then?

2. Helene's father is 3 times as old as Helene. If Helene is 9 years old, how old is her father?

3. A store advertised softball bats at $7 each. How much will 5 bats cost?

4. While on vacation, the Wesman family drove 200 miles a day. How far did they drive during their vacation?

5. Bill's car, a 1982 model, gets 27 miles per gallon. Maria's car, a 1984 model, gets 34 miles per gallon. How many more miles per gallon does Maria's car get than Bill's car?

6. A truck can carry 4 cords of wood. How many trips must the truck make to deliver 36 cords?

B 7. Jolene bought the following items: a tennis racket for $39, a can of tennis balls for $5, a bicycle tire tube for $8, tennis shoes for $29, and a bicycle pump for $11. How much did Jolene spend on tennis equipment?

8. To get to her job, Louise drives 12 miles to the train station. After a 25 min train ride, Louise walks 8 min to her office. How long does it take Louise to get to work?

9. There were 43 small bags of nuts in the kitchen cabinet. During the week, Tim ate 9 bags, Jane ate 11 bags, and Dana ate 5 bags. If 14 more bags were served at a party, how many bags were left?

Review Exercises

Perform the indicated operations.

1. $5208 + 7962$
2. $1034 - 940$
3. 1208×17
4. $384 \div 48$
5. $12 + 9 + 6 + 57$
6. $5000 - 112$
7. 366×109
8. $1288 \div 161$

1-7 Problem Solving Applications

In the previous lesson we used the five-step plan to check the facts of a word problem and to see which operation was needed to solve the problem. We shall now use the plan to solve word problems.

EXAMPLE 1 During the four quarters of a basketball game, the Hoopsters scored 16 points, 21 points, 19 points, and 17 points. How many points did the Hoopsters score during the game?

Solution
- The problem asks for the total number of points scored.

- The given facts are as follows.

  First quarter: 16 points
  Second quarter: 21 points
  Third quarter: 19 points
  Fourth quarter: 17 points

- Since we know the points scored in the four quarters, we have enough facts.

- To find the total number of points, we *add* the scores.

$$16 + 21 + 19 + 17 = 73$$

Therefore, the Hoopsters scored 73 points during the game.

Some word problems involve more than one operation. Using a plan to solve this type of problem is very important since we not only have to decide which operations to use, but in what order to use them.

EXAMPLE 2 Simon had $165 in his checking account. He wrote checks for $32, $19, and $47. How much did Simon have left in his account?

Solution
- The problem asks for the amount of money Simon had left in his checking account.

- The given facts are as follows.

  Original amount: $165
  Checks written: $32, $19, $47

- We have enough facts since we know the original amount and all the amounts of the checks.

- To find the amount left in the account, we first *add* the amounts of the checks.

$$32 + 19 + 47 = 98$$

We then *subtract* this amount from $165.

$$165 - 98 = 67$$

Simon had $67 left in his checking account.

Class Exercises

State which operations you would use to solve the problems and in what order you would use them.

1. Sue bought 6 pencils at 20¢ each, 3 pens at 59¢ each, and 4 notebooks at 89¢ each. How much did Sue spend?

2. Four friends each had a bag of marbles. One bag had 41 marbles in it, the second bag had 34 marbles, the third bag had 49 marbles, and the fourth bag had 28 marbles. If the friends decided to share the marbles equally, how many marbles would each get?

3. Juanita had $75 in her checking account. She made a $95 deposit, wrote a check for $30, and then wrote another check for $47. She also made a $50 deposit and wrote a third check for $68. How much money does Juanita have in her account now?

4. The Explorers' Club was going on a camping trip. The club members filled four 15 L cans of water, six 18 L cans, and two 20 L cans. How many liters of water did they take on the trip?

Problems

Solve, using the five-step plan.

A   1. Marvin bought one shirt for $20, a second shirt for $18, and a pair of jeans for $27. How much did Marvin spend?

2. The admission charge to the museum for a group of 18 adults is $72. How much is this for each adult?

3. The Puerto Rico Trench in the Atlantic Ocean is 9460 m deep. The Marianas Trench in the Pacific is 11,776 m deep. How much deeper is the Marianas Trench than the Puerto Rico Trench?

4. The library had 1843 books. After 7 cases of new books arrived, the library had 1955 books. How many new books had arrived?

5. At the college bookstore, Martina bought a calculus textbook for $17, a chemistry textbook for $19, some notebooks for $13, and some pens for $9. Later she bought a history textbook for $21 and some posters for $11. How much did Martina spend on textbooks?

B   6. Marcia's Restaurant received a shipment of 12 cases of dinner plates and 15 cases of salad plates. Each case of dinner plates had 24 plates in it and each case of salad plates had 36 plates in it. How many plates did the restaurant receive?

7. Lou's bank statement showed the following: deposit $80, deposit $37, withdrawal $96, deposit $51, withdrawal $40. How much more money did Lou deposit in the bank than he withdrew?

8. The daily rental is $48 for a sailboat, $24 for a rowboat, and $36 for a canoe. The rental receipts for Sunday showed $912 for sailboats, $312 for rowboats, and $828 for canoes. How many boats were rented?

9. The school athletic department purchased the following: 8 footballs at $37 each, 12 soccer balls at $29 each, 16 football helmets at $44 each, and 38 sets of soccer shin pads at $9 a set. The school also purchased 2 football goal posts at $299 each and 2 soccer goals at $198 each. How much was spent on soccer equipment?

Self-Test B

Simplify.

1. $(8 + 2)(38 - 3)$ 2. $(37 + 3) \div (5 \times 8)$ 3. $25 \times 4 + 16 \div 4$ [1-5]

For each problem, answer the following questions.

a. What number or numbers does the problem ask for?
b. Are enough facts given? If not, what else is needed?
c. What operation or operations would you use to find the answer?

4. How many 35¢ bus tokens can Marcie buy with 3 quarters?   [1-6]

5. While on vacation, Sean collected 7 rocks to add to his rock collection. How many rocks were in Sean's collection after vacation?

Solve, using the five-step plan.

6. The Green Sox hit 13 more home runs this year than last year. Last year they hit 2 home runs fewer than the year before. How many home runs did the Green Sox hit this year if two years ago they hit 39 home runs?   [1-7]

Self-Test answers and Extra Practice are at the back of the book.

Computer Applications

Computers have become an important tool in many professions. Banks, airlines, and insurance companies are some of the businesses that depend on computers to process large amounts of information quickly and accurately. Using computers scientists can analyze large quantities of data, teachers can calculate multiple test scores, and people like engineers can develop models that require millions of computations. Many schools use computers for teaching, recordkeeping, and testing purposes. In the home, computers are now a source of learning and entertainment.

The list of computer applications is constantly growing, as people develop and find new uses for the computer's special abilities. Just to name a few, these include the improved ability to:

> store, sort, and retrieve information
> generate multi-color displays
> better simulate musical notes and speech tones
> reduce response time to user input

Below, and on the following page, are some of the many applications that have been developed. Computers are used to:

> control air traffic
> help doctors make diagnoses
> guide spacecraft to other planets
> forecast weather
> read product codes and determine prices at the supermarket
> run robots used in assembly-line manufacturing
> set type for books and newspapers
> play chess, adventure games, and games of skill
> schedule students' class assignments
> keep inventories and process orders

edit and print letters and reports
generate musical notes and rhythms
draw pictures for engineers, designers, and film animators
teach typing and other technical skills

Through these applications, and others like them, computers have changed the way people work and learn. But computers are still just a tool. It is people who have the imagination to see new uses for computers and who write the programs that make them possible.

Research Activities: Writing in Mathematics

1. Imagine how a computer can help in your school, for example, in the cafeteria, in English class, in athletics, or in the principal's office. Think of some useful applications and write a brief description of (a) how a computer can help and (b) how teachers and students can benefit from the use of a computer. The list of applications above and on the preceding page may give you some ideas.

2. Write an article about your school's computer facilities. Find answers to the following questions.
   a. How many computers does your school have for both administrative use and teaching purposes?
   b. What types of computers are they?
   c. Do they have disk drives and printers?
   d. Where are they located?
   e. Who is in charge of them?
   f. Who has access to the computers?
   g. Are the computers connected to other computer facilities?
   h. How much does it cost the school to maintain the computers?

Career Connection

Visit a person who uses a computer at work and write a brief report on how the computer helps this person do his or her job. Some careers that now often involve computers are travel agent, librarian, police officer, bank teller, teacher, and newspaper reporter.

Chapter Review

Evaluate each expression if $a = 8$, $b = 13$, and $c = 7$.

1. bc **2.** $169 \div b$ **3.** $2a + b - 3c$ **4.** $(a + b)c$ [1–1]

Match.

5. $18 \times 1 \times 7$ **6.** $89 \times 0 \times 18$ **A.** 69   **E.** 71   [1–2]

7. $42 + 19 + 8$ **8.** $32 + 0 + 8$ **B.** 40   **F.** 0

9. $72 + 83 - 83$ **10.** $m + 16 - m$ **C.** 84   **G.** 16   [1–3]

11. $84 \div 12 \times 12$ **12.** $8 \times 71 \div 8$ **D.** 126   **H.** 72

Write the letter of the correct answer.

13. $(7 \times 4) + (3 \times 4)$ **14.** $27(20 - 6)$ [1–4]
  a. 40   **b.** 55   **c.** 124   **a.** 378   **b.** 702   **c.** 546

15. 92×18 **16.** $(86 \times 12) - (56 \times 12)$
  a. 1840   **b.** 928   **c.** 1656   **a.** 30   **b.** 360   **c.** 1704

17. $90 \div 3 + 2$ **18.** $36 + 14 \times 3$ [1–5]
  a. 18   **b.** 60   **c.** 32   **a.** 150   **b.** 53   **c.** 78

19. $(31 + 4)(12 - 2)$ **20.** $[5 + (2 \times 7)]10$
  a. 350   **b.** 418   **c.** 71   **a.** 490   **b.** 190   **c.** 140

Which fact is not needed to solve the problem? Write the letter of the correct answer.

21. Monique worked for 8 hours to earn $24. She has $21 in bills and   [1–6]
the balance in coins. What is the value of the coins?
  a. 8 hours   **b.** $24   **c.** $21 in bills

22. Joshua delivered 154 newspapers last week and earned $6 in tips.
The week before, he delivered 133 papers and earned $4 in tips.
What was the average of the tips Joshua earned for the two weeks?
  a. 154 newspapers   **b.** $6 in tips   **c.** $4 in tips

Write the letter of the correct answer.

23. A troop of 18 Girl Scouts and their 2 leaders spent a total of $60 for   [1–7]
bus fare and admission to the zoo. Tickets to the zoo cost $40 in all.
How much did they spend on bus fare?
  a. Less than $20   **b.** $20   **c.** More than $20

Chapter Test

Evaluate each expression when the variable has the values listed.

1. $5x$; 0, 10, 20
2. $95 - y$; 17, 31, 40
3. $120 \div z$; 8, 15, 24   [1-1]
4. $a + 17$; 1, 11, 51
5. $b - 7$; 100, 10, 7
6. $13c$; 1, 12, 37

Simplify, using the properties.

7. $13 + 0 + 57$
8. $26 + 18 + 4$
9. $6 \times 8 \times 5$ [1-2]
10. 18×0
11. $32 \times 1 \times 10$
12. $120 \times 5 \times 40$

Simplify, using inverse operations.

13. $937 + 17 - 17$
14. $168 \times 17 \div 168$
15. $98a \div 98$ [1-3]
16. $39 + b - 39$
17. $28c \div 28$
18. $19 + d - d$

Simplify, using the distributive property.

19. $(32 \times 7) + (8 \times 7)$
20. $18(90 - 3)$
21. $25(60 + 4)$ [1-4]
22. 48×15
23. 73×94
24. 81×79

Simplify.

25. $21 + 21 \div 21$
26. $8(13 + 7)$
27. $(49 + 6) \div 5$ [1-5]
28. $(164 - 4) \div (56 + 24)$
29. $[32 \div (8 - 6)]3$
30. $19 - [(13 - 7)3]$

For each problem, answer the following questions. a. What number or numbers does the problem ask for? b. Are enough facts given? If not, what else is needed? c. Are unnecessary facts given? If so, what are they? d. What operation or operations would you use to find the answer?

31. A telephone directory of 328 pages lists telephone numbers in 4 columns on each page. If there are 460 numbers on each page, how many numbers are in the directory?   [1-6]

32. The population of Claxton is 1232 more than that of Truro. What is the population of Truro?

Solve, using the five-step plan.

33. The 16 members of the Science Club want to raise money for a field trip to the Science Museum. If admission is $3 per person and the bus fare is $2 per person each way, how much money do they need to raise?   [1-7]

Cumulative Review

Exercises

Perform the indicated operations.

1. 907
    + 68

2. 160
    − 47

3. 316
    − 109

4. 20
    304
    + 17

5. 58
    × 19

6. 402
    × 37

7. 18$\overline{)540}$

8. 123$\overline{)7011}$

9. $130 + 294 + 14$

10. $1401 - 720$

11. $12 \times 19 \times 57$

12. $27,716 \div 52$

13. 37×194

14. $18 + 105 + 90$

15. $19 - 6 \times 2$

16. $104 \times 90 - 78$

17. $78 + 10 \div 5$

18. $3(18 - 5)$

19. $21 - (14 + 2)$

20. $(12 + 9) \div 7$

21. $8 + 2(15 - 7) \div 4$

22. $291 - (36 - 8)7$

23. $240 \div [21 - (3 + 8)]$

Evaluate each expression if $u = 21$, $t = 15$, and $w = 3$.

24. $u + 12$

25. $31 - t$

26. $10w$

27. $189 \div u$

28. $t + w$

29. $u - t$

30. $t \div w$

31. uw

32. $u + t - 7$

33. $37 - u - t$

34. $12ut$

35. utw

Simplify, using the properties.

36. $36 + 0 + 14$

37. $340 \div 1 \times 10$

38. $(9 \times 14) + (9 \times 6)$

39. $a \times 0 \times 6$

40. 16×198

41. $4 \times 19 \times 25$

42. $3(140 - 7)$

43. $18 + b - b$

44. $(86 \times 3) + (4 \times 3)$

45. $0 \times 95 \times 108$

46. $47 \times 0 \times 124$

47. $27 + 0 + 73$

48. $850 \div 1$

49. $20 \times 31 \times 5$

50. $8 \times 35 \times 25$

51. $5 \times 1 \times c$

52. $1 \times 25 \times 8$

53. $x + 72 - x$

54. $15 \times 19 \times 4$

55. $8(300 - 4)$

56. $3 \times z \div 3$

57. $15(500 + 20)$

58. $38 + 12 + 62$

59. $19 \times 7 \div 19$

Problems

Solve, using the five-step plan.

1. Johanna bought 2 skirts at $18 each and 3 blouses at $15 each. How much did she spend?

2. Martin earned $25. He spent $5 at the movies and $3 for lunch. How much did Martin have left?

3. Maxine and Laura have saved $68 to buy a 4-person tent that costs $120. If Maxine saves $13 more and Laura saves $17 more, how much money do they still need to save to buy the tent?

4. Paul won a $100 gift certificate at Altwell's Department Store. He wants to buy a jogging suit for $42, a calculator for $18, a pair of jeans for $35, and a belt for $12. Will the gift certificate pay for all of these items or will Paul have to pay more money?

5. Susan and Jake can buy a used snow blower for $180. How many driveways must they clear at $15 apiece to pay for the equipment?

6. Jeff is 15 years old and earns $3 an hour. He worked 2 h on Monday, 4 h on Wednesday, and 7 h on Saturday. How much did he earn for working on those three days?

7. Kerry and her sister paid $7 apiece for admission to the circus and $1 apiece each way for bus fare. Together they paid $5 for a program and souvenirs, and $3 in all for snacks. How much did they spend in all?

8. At Baxter High School there are 403 freshmen, 416 sophomores, 397 juniors, and 389 seniors. If 314 students are involved in a school sport, how many are not involved in a school sport?

9. The 4 seventh-grade homerooms sold 87, 75, 83, and 98 advance tickets to the class play. The rest of the 400 tickets available were sold at the door. If the tickets cost $2 in advance and $3 at the door, how much money was made in selling the tickets?

2 Using Variables

APPLYING MATHEMATICS
BALLOONING

A balloon race is a test of a balloonist's skill in piloting the craft. Sun, wind speed, wind direction, and atmospheric conditions are some of the variables a balloonist has to evaluate. The combined weight of the balloon and its supplies must also be taken into consideration. This weight must be less than the corresponding volume of the air it displaces, if the balloon is to rise. The amount of lift is controlled by the amount of heated air inside the balloon. To maintain a certain altitude, the air inside the balloon occasionally needs reheating. Sometimes a cooling vent is opened so the balloon can make a quick descent. In this chapter you will learn about mathematical variables and how they are used to solve inequalities and equations.

CAREER CONNECTION

MECHANICAL ENGINEER

Mechanical engineers are concerned with the production and use of mechanical power. They are employed in transportation, power generation, and manufacturing. Mechanical engineers design, build, and test engines that produce power from steam, fossil fuels, and nuclear energy. Special fields of mechanical engineering include: aeronautical, automotive, environmental, and industrial engineering. All require a college degree.

Photo: Balloon enthusiasts float over Snowmass, Colorado.

31

2-1 Writing Mathematical Expressions

In mathematics we often need to translate a word phrase into a mathematical expression. In order to do this, we must be able to determine the mathematical operation or operations associated with the word phrase. The following table lists some of the word phrases that we associate with each of the four basic operations.

+	−	×	÷
add	subtract	multiply	divide
sum	difference	product	quotient
plus	minus	times	
total	remainder		
more than	less than		
increased by	decreased by		

Thus we can use the same mathematical expression to translate many different word phrases. For example, the three phrases:

Five less than a number n

The number n decreased by five

The difference when five is subtracted from a number n

can each be translated into the variable expression

$$n - 5.$$

EXAMPLE 1 Write a variable expression for each word phrase.

a. The quotient of a number y divided by ten

b. Seven increased by a number x

c. Twelve more than three times a number m

Solution

a. In this expression, the word *quotient* and the phrase *divided by* indicate the operation of division. $y \div 10$

b. In this expression, the phrase *increased by* indicates the operation of addition. $7 + x$

c. In this expression, the phrase *more than* and the word *times* indicate that two operations, addition and multiplication, are involved. $12 + 3 \times m$, or $12 + 3m$

Not all word phrases translate *directly* into mathematical expressions. Sometimes we first need to interpret a situation, and we may need to call to mind a familiar fact.

EXAMPLE 2 Write a variable expression for each word phrase.

     a. The number of hours in w workdays, if each workday consists of 8 h (hours)

     b. The total value in cents of q quarters and d dimes

Solution   **a.** One workday consists of 8×1 h, or 8 h.
         Two workdays consist of 8×2 h, or 16 h.
         Therefore, w workdays consist of $8 \times w$ h, or $8w$ h.

     b. The value of one quarter is 25 cents.
         The value of q quarters is $25 \times q$ cents, or $25q$ cents.

         The value of one dime is 10 cents.
         The value of d dimes is $10 \times d$ cents, or $10d$ cents.

         In this expression, the word *total* indicates the operation of addition. The total value in cents is $25q + 10d$.

Often relationships between numbers are expressed with words that we use in everyday speech. For example, **consecutive** whole numbers are whole numbers that increase by 1, such as the numbers 4, 5, 6, and 7. For any given whole number, the **preceding** whole number is the whole number that is 1 less and the **next** whole number is the whole number that is 1 greater.

EXAMPLE 3   **a.** Write a variable expression for each of the next three consecutive whole numbers following a whole number t.

     b. If $p + 7$ represents a whole number, write variable expressions for the preceding whole number and for the next whole number.

Solution   **a.** $t + 1$, $t + 2$, $t + 3$

     b. The *preceding* whole number is $p + 7 - 1$, or $p + 6$.
         The *next* whole number is $p + 7 + 1$, or $p + 8$.

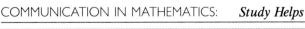

COMMUNICATION IN MATHEMATICS: *Study Helps*

Notice that variables are printed in *italic* type. This helps to distinguish variables from letters that are abbreviations. For instance, in part (a) of Example 2, the italic letter w is a variable that represents the number of workdays, while h is an abbreviation that represents the word "hours."

Class Exercises

Write a variable expression for each word phrase.

1. Six more than a number t

2. Eight decreased by a number m

3. The product of 4 and a number x

4. Six less than a number x

5. The sum of ten and a number t

6. Twice a number p

7. Nine divided by a number m

8. Two more than twice a number r

9. The value in cents of k dimes

10. The whole number preceding a whole number n

Written Exercises

Write a variable expression for each word phrase.

A

1. Ten more than a number b

2. The product of seven and a number y

3. Seven increased by a number m

4. Twelve minus a number v

5. Three times a number x

6. A number c plus eight

7. A number u multiplied by eleven

8. Three less than a number p

9. The total of five and a number m

10. A number n divided by nine

11. A number k less 78

12. A number n added to a number c

13. The remainder when five is subtracted from six times a number a

14. The product of two and a number p added to seven

15. The quotient when a number z is divided by fourteen

16. The difference when ten is subtracted from a number q

17. Mary's age 2 years from now if she is m years old now

18. Martin's age now if he will be y years old 10 years from now

19. The value in cents of n nickels

20. The value in cents of d dimes and p pennies

21. The value in cents of w dollars

22. The value in dollars of y cents

23. The next whole number following a whole number w

24. The whole number preceding a whole number $2x$

B 25. The number of hours in d days

26. The number of eggs in p dozen

27. The number of millimeters in y centimeters

28. The number of centimeters in g meters

29. The number of feet in k yards

30. The number of inches in r feet

31. The number of feet in t inches

32. The number of gallons in w quarts

33. Jill's age x years from now if she is t years old now

34. The amount in dollars that Malcolm earns if he works h hours at a dollars per hour

35. The greatest of three consecutive whole numbers, the smallest of which is m

36. The smallest of four consecutive whole numbers, the greatest of which is r

C 37. Joan receives d dollars for mowing a lawn, but she has to pay g dollars per gallon for the gasoline to run the mower. If the job requires x gallons of gasoline to complete, write a variable expression for the amount of money Joan earns after deducting the cost of the gasoline.

38. The school band is planning a car wash to raise money and will charge c dollars to wash each car. If the total cost for the soap and water is d dollars and w cars are washed, write a variable expression for the amount of money the band will earn after deducting the cost of the soap and water.

Review Exercises

Simplify.

1. $17(14 + 21)$

2. $(48 - 19)13$

3. $(21 - 9)(15 + 6)$

4. $(154 - 14) \div (39 - 25)$

5. $56 + 24 \div 8 - 29$

6. $31 \times 8 \div 4 + 89$

7. $88 - 44 \div 11 \times 9$

8. $155 \times 3 \div 15 + 108$

2-2 Writing Equations

In the previous lesson we translated word phrases into variable expressions. Now we will translate word sentences into equations. Recall that an equation states that two expressions name the same number. We can translate *is equal to*, *equals*, or *is* by using the equals sign.

EXAMPLE 1 Write an equation for each word sentence.

        a. Eight increased by a number x is equal to thirty-seven.

        b. Ten is two less than a number t.

        c. Twice a number w equals the sum of the number and four.

Solution **a.** Write the word phrase "eight increased by a number x" as the variable expression $8 + x$. Use the symbol $=$ to translate "is equal to." $8 + x = 37$

        b. Write "two less than a number t" as $t - 2$. Use the symbol $=$ to translate "is." $10 = t - 2$

        c. Write "twice a number w" and "the sum of the number and four" as $2w$ and $w + 4$, respectively. Use the symbol $=$ to translate "equals." $2w = w + 4$

Note that part (c) of Example 1 shows that both sides of an equation may be variable expressions.

Sometimes we need to write an equation for a word sentence that involves measurements. In such cases, it is important that each side of the equation represents a number related to the same *unit* of measurement.

EXAMPLE 2 Write an equation for the word sentence:
      The value of n dimes is $27.50.

Solution We know that the value of n dimes is $10n$ *cents*, while $27.50 is written in terms of *dollars*. In order to have the same unit on both sides of the equation, we write $27.50 as 2750 cents. $10n = 2750$

COMMUNICATION IN MATHEMATICS: *Study Skills*

As you work on the exercises, you may find it helpful to reread the examples in the lesson. They will give you a model to follow or an idea to get you started toward a solution.

Class Exercises

Write an equation for each word sentence.

1. Twelve more than a number x is seventeen.

2. Thirty-two less than a number m is eighteen.

3. A number t is eight more than fifty-one.

4. Six added to twice a number g is seventy-two.

5. Three times a number x is thirty-three.

6. By working eight hours for k dollars an hour, Kim earns a total of $50.00.

7. Twelve goldfish are worth d dollars each and have a total worth of fifteen dollars.

8. Mark has q quarters worth a total of $12.50.

Written Exercises

Write an equation for each word sentence. Use n as the variable.

A 1. Four times a number is eight.

2. Three less than a number is twelve.

3. Nine divided by a number is one.

4. Twelve times a number is four hundred thirty-two.

5. Fourteen less than a number is forty-one.

6. Fourteen more than a number is forty-one.

7. A number divided by nine is three hundred thirty-three.

8. Nine more than a number is six times the number.

9. Twenty-eight minus a number is twice the number.

10. A number increased by three is two more than twice the number.

11. A number times four is six less than twice the number.

12. Twenty-five divided by a number equals the number.

13. Ten less than a number is forty-three.

14. Eighty-six minus a number is equal to twice the number plus four.

Write an equation for each word sentence.

B **15.** Martha is x years old now and will be twenty-three years old in eight years.

16. A bird flies x km and then continues 1100 km farther, covering a total distance of 2700 km.

17. Sean has n nickels worth a total of $27.55.

18. David has p pennies and q quarters worth a total of $27.55.

19. Ten cars worth k dollars each have a total worth of $127,000.

20. The Ski Club has n members who have each paid $3.00 which totals $63.00.

21. The sum of a whole number n and the next three consecutive whole numbers is 106.

22. Lee buys p pencils for c cents each and spends a total of t cents.

23. The sum of the numbers a, b, and c is twice the number a. $(a+b+c) \times 2 = a$

24. The number x is y more than the number y times x. $y \times x$

25. The number r increased by t is t less than twice the number r.

26. Two more than six times a number m is ten less than m.

27. Six times a number s increased by two is ten less than s.

C **28.** Jo has p pennies, n nickels, and d dimes worth a total of r dollars.

29. George grows t tomato plants worth a cents each and p pepper plants worth b cents each for a total value of k dollars.

Review Exercises

Evaluate the expression if $x = 48$, $y = 92$, and $z = 125$.

1. $x + 342$

2. $y - 41$

3. $273 - z$

4. $146 + y$

5. $231 + y + x$

6. $z + 98 + x$

7. $z - 87 + 93$

8. $y + z - 201$

9. $y - 83 + x + z$

2-3 Writing Inequalities

The following are two **inequalities** that state the relationship between the numbers 2 and 7.

$$2 < 7 \qquad\qquad 7 > 2$$

2 *is less than* 7 \qquad 7 *is greater than* 2

The symbols $<$ and $>$ are called *inequality symbols.* We often use these symbols when we compare two numbers. To avoid confusing the two symbols with each other, it may help to think of them as arrowheads whose small ends point toward the smaller numbers.

The inequalities $2 < 7$ and $7 > 2$ describe the *order* of the numbers 2 and 7. One way that we can picture the order of numbers is by using a **number line.** On a number line, we assign consecutive whole numbers to points that are equally spaced along the line. We place the numbers in increasing order from left to right.

The point of the number line that is paired with a number is called the **graph** of that number. For example, pictured below are the graphs of the numbers 2, 5, and 7.

Using this number line, we see not only that $2 < 7$ and $7 > 2$, but also that 5 *is between* 2 and 7. We can use inequalities to write this relationship in the following ways.

$$2 < 5 \text{ and } 5 < 7 \qquad 7 > 5 \text{ and } 5 > 2$$
$$2 < 5 < 7 \qquad\qquad 7 > 5 > 2$$

EXAMPLE 1 Replace __?__ with $<$ or $>$.

  a. 14 __?__ 2   **b.** 1 __?__ 11   **c.** 8 __?__ 3 __?__ 0

Solution **a.** $14 > 2$ **b.** $1 < 11$ **c.** $8 > 3 > 0$

EXAMPLE 2 Write an inequality for each word sentence.

  a. Two is less than ten.

  b. A number $2 + x$ is greater than a number t.

  c. A number n is between 6 and 12.

Solution **a.** $2 < 10$ **b.** $2 + x > t$

  c. $6 < n < 12$, or $12 > n > 6$

Class Exercises

Imagine that the numbers given in Exercises 1–6 have been graphed on a number line. Replace the first __?__ with "left" or "right." Replace the second __?__ with < or >.

1. The graph of 9 is to the __?__ of the graph of 2.   9 __?__ 2

2. The graph of 4 is to the __?__ of the graph of 7.   4 __?__ 7

3. The graph of 3 is to the __?__ of the graph of 8.   3 __?__ 8

4. The graph of 10 is to the __?__ of the graph of 0.   10 __?__ 0

5. The graph of 0 is to the __?__ of the graph of 5.   0 __?__ 5

6. The graph of 6 is to the __?__ of the graph of 1.   6 __?__ 1

True or false? m represents a whole number.

7. $6 < 10$

8. $0 > 1$

9. $1 < 1$

10. $m < m + 1$

11. $m > m + 1$

12. $m < m$

13. $8 < 10 < 9$

14. $8 < 9 > 10$

15. $m < m + 1 < m + 2$

Written Exercises

Replace __?__ with < or >. The variables represent whole numbers.

A

1. 22 __?__ 11

2. 16 __?__ 15

3. 0 __?__ 12

4. 18 __?__ 0

5. 152 __?__ 251

6. 256 __?__ 562

7. 6 __?__ 10 __?__ 12

8. 8 __?__ 88 __?__ 888

9. 149 __?__ 139 __?__ 129

10. m __?__ $m + 7$

11. $a + 1$ __?__ a

12. $p + 2$ __?__ $p + 1$

13. $a + 9$ __?__ $a + 2$

14. m __?__ $m + 3$ __?__ $m + 5$

15. $t + 7$ __?__ $t + 2$ __?__ t

Write an inequality for each word sentence.

16. Twelve is less than twenty-two.

17. Six is greater than zero.

18. Nineteen is greater than nine.

19. Twenty-two is less than thirty-three.

20. On a number line eight is between zero and ten.

21. On a number line twenty-five is between fifty-two and five.

Pictured below is a portion of a number line showing the graph of a whole number *m*. Copy this number line and graph each of the following numbers.

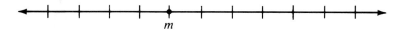

B **22.** $m + 1$ **23.** $m - 2$ **24.** $m + 2 - 3$ **25.** $m - 2 + 3$

Write an inequality for each word sentence.

26. Six is greater than a number *t*.

27. Twenty-seven is less than a number $3m$.

28. A number *p* is greater than a number *q*.

29. A number *a* is less than a number *b*.

30. The value in cents of *d* dimes is less than the value in cents of *n* nickels.

31. The value in cents of *m* pennies is greater than the value in cents of *y* quarters.

32. On a number line a number $2n$ is between 6 and 8.

33. On a number line a number $r + 1$ is between 10 and 4.

34. On a number line a number *a* is between a number *x* and a number *y*, where $x < y$.

35. On a number line a number $4x$ is between a number *m* and a number *n*, where $m > n$.

C **36.** On a number line 6 is between 2 and 10, and 20 is between 10 and 50.

37. On a number line a number *x* is between 0 and 10, and a number *y* is between 10 and 14.

38. On a number line 5 is between a number *a* and a number *b*, where $a < b$, and 8 is also between *a* and *b*.

39. On a number line a number *m* is between the numbers $m + 1$ and $m - 1$, and a number $m + 2$ is between the numbers $m + 1$ and $m + 3$.

40. On a number line a number *a* is between the numbers *t* and $t + a$, where $0 < a$, and a number *b* is between the numbers $t + a$ and $t + b$, where $a < b$.

Self-Test A

Write a variable expression for each word phrase.

1. Nine less than a number *h*   [2-1]

2. Seven times a number *a*

3. A number *x* increased by fifteen

4. Six more than the product of two and a number *z*.

Write an equation for each word sentence.

5. A number *y* divided by five is equal to thirty-one.   [2-2]

6. Seventeen more than a number *t* is sixty.

7. Fourteen times a number *a* equals ninety-eight.

Replace __?__ with < or >.

8. 6 __?__ 15   **9.** 146 __?__ 461   **10.** 41 __?__ 63 __?__ 87   [2-3]

Write an inequality for each word sentence.

11. Thirty is less than forty-eight.

12. Seventeen is between eleven and twenty-two.

13. Fifteen is greater than six.

14. A number *y* is between two and thirteen.

Self-Test answers and Extra Practice are at the back of the book.

 NONROUTINE PROBLEM SOLVING: *Finding a Pattern*

Each of the following represents an addition or multiplication exercise. Within each exercise, each letter represents a different digit. Determine which digit each letter represents.

1.	2.	3.	4.
$\begin{array}{r} A \\ A \\ +\,A \\ \hline HA \end{array}$	$\begin{array}{r} SEND \\ +\,MORE \\ \hline MONEY \end{array}$	$\begin{array}{r} ZX \\ \times\ W \\ \hline ZZZ \end{array}$	$\begin{array}{r} KL \\ \times\ JL \\ \hline JKL \\ KL \\ \hline PQL \end{array}$

2-4 Solving Equations and Inequalities

As we have seen, equations and inequalities are mathematical sentences. These sentences may be either true or false. For example, $6 + 9 = 15$ and $8 > 5$ are true sentences, while $7 + 2 = 10$ and $9 < 5$ are false sentences.

We have also seen that an equation or inequality may contain a variable. Any value of the variable that makes the equation or inequality a true sentence is called a **solution.** We **solve** an equation or inequality when we find *all* its solutions.

Sometimes an equation or inequality can be solved by using our knowledge of basic facts.

EXAMPLE 1 Solve, using basic facts.

  a. $12 - x = 4$ **b.** $y + 9 > 14$

Solution **a.** We know the fact $12 - 8 = 4$.
Thus, the solution is 8.

  b. We know the fact $5 + 9 = 14$.
The number 5 is not itself a solution, but any number *greater than* 5 is a solution.

Another method of solving equations and inequalities is to use inverse operations. To understand this method, recall that addition and subtraction are inverse operations, as shown by the following related facts.

$$8 + 9 = 17$$
$$8 = 17 - 9$$

This relationship between addition and subtraction also holds when we work with an equation that contains a variable. Thus, if we start with the equation

$$z + 9 = 17,$$

we can then write the related equation

$$z = 17 - 9.$$

Therefore, $17 - 9$, or 8, must be the *solution* of the given equation, $z + 9 = 17$.

EXAMPLE 2   Solve, using inverse operations.

   a. $r - 46 = 79$ **b.** $m + 2 > 14$

Solution   **a.** $r = 79 + 46$ **b.** $m > 14 - 2$
                  $r = 125$ $m > 12$

To check each solution, substitute the value of the variable in the original equation or inequality.

   a. $r - 46 = 79$ **b.** $m + 2 > 14$
          $125 - 46 = 79$ ✓ $12 + 2 = 14$
                                Any number *greater than* 12
                                is a solution. ✓

COMMUNICATION IN MATHEMATICS: ***Study Skills***

After you read a lesson and before you begin the exercises, stop to think about the main points of the lesson. A main point may be, for example, a mathematical idea, a definition, or a method for solving an exercise.

Class Exercises

Write the basic fact that can be used in solving the given equation or inequality.

   1. $c + 7 = 16$ **2.** $x + 5 = 12$ **3.** $13 - p = 8$

   4. $11 - t = 3$ **5.** $2 + m = 2$ **6.** $8 - h = 0$

   7. $y + 9 > 18$ **8.** $8 + x < 12$ **9.** $x - 8 < 6$

   10. $7 + g > 11$ **11.** $k - 8 > 9$ **12.** $r - 3 < 7$

Write the related addition or subtraction equation that can be used in solving the given equations.

   13. $a + 19 = 78$ **14.** $56 + d = 92$ **15.** $s - 75 = 83$

   16. $n - 18 = 44$ **17.** $14 + q = 123$ **18.** $z - 137 = 19$

Write the related inequality that can be used in solving the given inequality.

   19. $t + 4 > 17$ **20.** $9 + x < 22$ **21.** $v - 16 < 45$

   22. $b - 31 > 29$ **23.** $j + 24 > 111$ **24.** $w - 41 < 138$

Written Exercises

Solve, using basic facts.

A 1. $x + 6 = 12$ 2. $r + 7 = 13$ 3. $t - 5 = 9$

4. $12 - c = 3$ 5. $8 + x = 16$ 6. $5 + x = 14$

7. $12 - x = 12$ 8. $14 - x = 0$ 9. $k + 0 = 10$

10. $b + 7 > 8$ 11. $w + 8 < 15$ 12. $m - 4 < 7$

13. $a - 9 > 2$ 14. $4 + q < 13$ 15. $z - 4 > 9$

16. $s + 0 < 5$ 17. $y + 9 > 9$ 18. $h - 7 > 7$

Solve, using inverse operations.

19. $x + 17 = 101$ 20. $v + 24 = 70$ 21. $n - 39 = 47$

22. $t - 20 = 35$ 23. $26 + g = 73$ 24. $17 + y = 94$

25. $b + 12 > 57$ 26. $h - 14 > 78$ 27. $x - 53 < 19$

28. $d + 61 < 100$ 29. $28 + t > 42$ 30. $m - 25 < 16$

B 31. $18 + a = 118$ 32. $k + 73 = 273$ 33. $p - 34 = 100$

34. $b - 3 = 150$ 35. $t + 100 = 1100$ 36. $t - 100 = 2100$

37. $647 + x = 2647$ 38. $y - 582 = 3000$ 39. $z - 1452 = 0$

40. $x - 158 = 271$ 41. $1234 + x = 4321$ 42. $x + 272 = 727$

43. $x - 987 = 645$ 44. $n - 327 = 492$ 45. $n - 248 = 603$

46. $n + 1412 = 3061$ 47. $2037 + n = 4911$ 48. $y - 4691 = 1909$

49. $y + 1659 = 6470$ 50. $1743 + z = 2651$ 51. $z - 1893 = 5729$

C 52. $x + 0 = 0$ 53. $x - 0 = 0$ 54. $x + 0 = x$

Review Exercises

Evaluate the expression if $a = 4$, $b = 9$, and $c = 12$.

1. $17a$ 2. $243 \div b$ 3. $12c$

4. $108 \div a$ 5. $bc \div 3$ 6. $18ab$

7. $1008 \div ac$ 8. $abc \div 16$ 9. $12b \div 9c$

2-5 Solving Other Equations and Inequalities

Just as we can solve some equations and inequalities by using our knowledge of addition and subtraction facts, we can solve other equations and inequalities by using multiplication and division facts.

EXAMPLE 1 Solve, using basic facts.

  a. $t \div 7 = 8$ **b.** $3k > 18$

Solution   **a.** We know the fact $56 \div 7 = 8$.
     Thus, the solution is 56.

   b. We know the fact $3 \times 6 = 18$.
     The number 6 is not itself a solution, but any number *greater than* 6 is a solution.

We can also use inverse operations in solving equations and inequalities involving multiplication and division. Recall the relationship between multiplication and division, as shown by the following related facts.

$$9 \times 6 = 54$$

$$6 = 54 \div 9$$

Thus, if we start with the equation

$$9a = 54,$$

we can then write the related equation

$$a = 54 \div 9.$$

Therefore, $54 \div 9$, or 6, is the solution of the given equation, $9a = 54$.

EXAMPLE 2 Solve, using inverse operations.

  a. $q \div 4 = 16$ **b.** $3w < 42$

Solution   **a.** $q = 16 \times 4$ **b.** $w < 42 \div 3$
     $q = 64$ $w < 14$

     Check: $q \div 4 = 16$ Check: $3w < 42$
        $64 \div 4 = 16$ ✓ $3 \times 14 = 42$
                         Any number *less than*
                         14 is a solution. ✓

Some equations involve two operations. The following example illustrates how to solve such an equation using inverse operations.

EXAMPLE 3 Solve, using inverse operations.

$$4x + 172 = 248$$

Solution First write the related subtraction equation that will give the value of $4x$.

$$4x = 248 - 172$$
$$4x = 76$$

Now write the related division equation that will give the value of x.

$$x = 76 \div 4$$
$$x = 19$$

Check the solution.

$$4x + 172 = 248$$
$$4 \times 19 + 172 = 248$$
$$76 + 172 = 248 \ \sqrt{}$$

The solution is 19.

Class Exercises

Write the basic fact that can be used in solving the given equation or inequality.

1. $5t = 35$ 2. $6y = 48$ 3. $9m = 81$

4. $r \div 9 = 2$ 5. $42 \div m = 6$ 6. $u \div 9 = 1$

7. $2a > 14$ 8. $7x < 28$ 9. $3y > 27$

10. $z \div 6 < 5$ 11. $s \div 4 > 8$ 12. $b \div 9 < 4$

Write the related equation or inequality that can be used in solving the given equation or inequality.

13. $6c = 96$ 14. $4q = 72$ 15. $9a = 144$

16. $r \div 3 = 18$ 17. $w \div 18 = 8$ 18. $n \div 2 = 84$

19. $8h < 96$ 20. $3d > 87$ 21. $12p < 132$

22. $y \div 5 > 50$ 23. $m \div 6 < 78$ 24. $t \div 10 > 30$

Written Exercises

Solve, using basic facts.

A **1.** $4x = 28$ **2.** $8y = 56$ **3.** $5t = 45$

4. $m \div 7 = 7$ **5.** $p \div 3 = 9$ **6.** $9 \div w = 3$

7. $8a > 8$ **8.** $6n > 54$ **9.** $7q < 63$

10. $r \div 8 < 5$ **11.** $z \div 6 > 5$ **12.** $d \div 9 < 8$

Solve, using inverse operations.

13. $5b = 95$ **14.** $8h = 112$ **15.** $12u = 156$

16. $k \div 4 = 23$ **17.** $s \div 17 = 6$ **18.** $j \div 12 = 12$

19. $6m > 84$ **20.** $9x < 198$ **21.** $11t < 154$

22. $z \div 5 > 18$ **23.** $g \div 13 < 9$ **24.** $w \div 24 > 12$

25. $10p = 1000$ **26.** $7t = 7777$ **27.** $1234c = 1234$

28. $x \div 50 = 500$ **29.** $j \div 1111 = 9$ **30.** $n \div 9876 = 1$

B **31.** $2c + 6 = 12$ **32.** $5r + 20 = 40$ **33.** $3y - 12 = 9$

34. $4z - 16 = 20$ **35.** $6x + 11 = 83$ **36.** $4p + 86 = 154$

37. $3a - 10 = 53$ **38.** $5h - 53 = 12$ **39.** $2n + 51 = 89$

40. $7t + 62 = 153$ **41.** $5x - 12 = 78$ **42.** $6x + 17 = 83$

C **43.** Find two solutions of $t \times t = t$. **44.** Find a solution of $m \div m = m$.

Solve.

45. $x \div 1 = 1$ **46.** $1 \div x = 1$ **47.** $x \div 1 = x$

Review Exercises

Write a variable expression for each word phrase.

1. Thirteen more than a number x **2.** Fifty-one decreased by a number y

3. Twenty times a number n **4.** Ninety-four divided by a number q

5. The product of a number d and eighteen increased by fifty-four

6. Four less than the quotient when a number c is divided by seven

2-6 Problem Solving: Using Mathematical Expressions

Often we can represent a word problem by a relationship between mathematical expressions. If we can state this relationship as an equation, we can solve the word problem by solving the equation.

EXAMPLE 1   Seventeen less than a number is fifty-six. Find the number.

Solution   • The problem asks for a certain number. Let n = the number.

• In this word problem, the phrase *less than* indicates subtraction. Write an equation for the word problem.
$$n - 17 = 56$$

• Solve the equation, using the related addition equation.
$$n = 56 + 17$$
$$n = 73$$

• Check: Is seventeen less than 73 equal to fifty-six?
$$73 - 17 = 56 \ \checkmark$$

The number is 73.

EXAMPLE 2   The Explorers' Club needs a total of $125 for new supplies. They already have $57. How many cars must they wash at $2 per car in order to raise the money they need?

Solution   • The problem asks for the number of cars they must wash. Let c = the number of cars.

• If they wash c cars, they raise $2 \times c$ dollars, or $2c$ dollars.

• In this word problem, the word *total* indicates addition. Write an equation for the word problem.
$$57 + 2c = 125$$

• Solve the equation, using inverse operations.
$$2c = 125 - 57$$
$$2c = 68$$
$$c = 68 \div 2$$
$$c = 34$$

• Check: Will they raise enough money if they wash 34 cars?
$$57 + 2 \times 34 = 125$$
$$57 + 68 = 125 \ \checkmark$$

They need to wash 34 cars.

Class Exercises

Write an equation for each problem. Do not solve.

1. The product of a number and twenty-one is one thousand eight.

2. Forty-six increased by a number is equal to ninety-three.

3. The quotient when a number is divided by four is eighty-four.

4. Twenty-nine less than a number equals two hundred twelve.

5. Six times a number decreased by forty-five equals fifty-one.

6. Nineteen more than twice a number is four hundred sixty-one.

Problems

Write an equation for each problem, then find the number.

A 1. Twelve times a number is two hundred fifty-two.

2. Thirty-six divided by a number is equal to nine.

3. Forty-five less than a number is one hundred.

4. Fifteen decreased by a number is six.

5. Two more than six times a number is eighty-six.

6. Twice a number minus nine is ninety-five.

7. If one is subtracted from five times a number, the difference is one hundred fourteen.

8. A number is multiplied by thirteen, and seven is added to the product. The result is two hundred fifteen.

9. The product of a number and seven increased by twenty-three is equal to one hundred seven.

10. The remainder when fifteen is subtracted from four times a number is eighty-one.

Write an equation for each problem, then solve.

B **11.** Sylvie scored 221 points in all during basketball season. If she averaged 13 points per game, how many games did she play?

12. Sharon has $27, and she will earn $2 per hour at work this weekend. How many hours will she have to work to have a total of $61?

13. David has $15.75 in nickels and pennies. If he has 770 pennies, how many nickels does he have?

14. Admission to the art museum is $3 per person. When the museum opened this morning, there was $150 on hand in the ticket booth. At closing time, there was $1254. How many people paid admission today?

15. Carol spent a total of $20.55 on stamps. She bought 35 thirteen-cent stamps, and the rest were twenty-cent stamps. How many twenty-cent stamps did she buy?

C **16.** Fifteen-year-old Estaban is three years older than twice the age of his brother Julio. Their sister, Maria, is two years younger than twice Julio's age. How old are Julio and Maria?

Self-Test B

Solve.

1. $x - 7 = 6$ **2.** $h + 6 < 14$ [2-4]

3. $r + 10 = 35$ **4.** $y - 15 > 29$

5. $3a = 24$ **6.** $n \div 6 < 8$ [2-5]

7. $t \div 5 = 10$ **8.** $4c > 52$

9. $5a + 27 = 62$ **10.** $2d - 19 = 51$

11. A number divided by four is twenty-one. Find the number.   [2-6]

12. Sally has a collection of nickels and quarters. If the collection is worth $18.45 and forty coins are quarters, how many are nickels?

Self-Test answers and Extra Practice are at the back of the book.

Introduction to BASIC

The work of a computer is determined by a set of instructions called a *program,* which is written in a special *programming language.* A number of these languages exist today. One of the most commonly used languages is called **BASIC.**

A BASIC program is composed of a list of *numbered lines.* These lines are often listed in intervals of 10 to allow lines to be inserted later, if necessary. Each line number is followed by a *statement* that indicates what the computer is to do. One of the uses of a **PRINT** statement tells the computer to evaluate the expression listed on that line. A program usually finishes with an **END** statement telling the computer that the program is over.

In BASIC, mathematical operations are represented by the following symbols:

+	for addition	*	for multiplication
−	for subtraction	/	for division

The use of these operations and parentheses follows the order of operation rules stated in Chapter 1.

EXAMPLE   Write a two-line program to find the value of

$$(4 + 5) \times 10 + (9 - 3) \div 2.$$

Solution
```
10   PRINT (4 + 5) * 10 + (9 − 3)/2
20   END
```

To get the computer to *execute* the program, type the command **RUN** (a command has no line number), and press the **RETURN,** or **ENTER,** key. The computer then finds the solution based on the PRINT statement in line 10 and displays the result, or **output,** 93.

A computer handles variables in the same manner as we do. For example, the computer can evaluate the expression $x + 7$ when we give it the value of x by using an **INPUT** statement. When the computer comes to this statement, it displays a question mark and waits for the value of x to be typed in. After a value has been typed in and the RETURN key pressed, the computer proceeds with the program.

A program to evaluate the expression $x + 7$ is shown below at the left. The display to its right shows what happens when we execute it.

```
10   INPUT X                      RUN
20   PRINT X + 7                  ? 16  ←── you type in
30   END                          23
```

To make the program above clearer, we can display an expression telling the viewer what to type in after the question mark, and another expression describing the result. We enclose these expressions between quotation marks after the PRINT command.

A modified program to evaluate $x + 7$ is shown below at the left. The display to its right shows what happens when we execute it.

```
5    PRINT  "WHAT IS YOUR VALUE OF X";   RUN
10   INPUT X                             WHAT IS YOUR VALUE OF X? 16
20   PRINT "X + 7 = "; X + 7             X + 7 = 23
30   END
```

In BASIC, the *semicolon* instructs the computer to bring expressions closer together. In the program above, the semicolon in line 5 tells the computer to print the question mark, from the INPUT statement, at the end of our first message. The semicolon in line 20 informs the computer that there is more than one expression on the same line.

By using the PRINT and INPUT statements and the semicolon, we can write a program that will solve any equation in the form $x + a = b$.

```
10   PRINT "TO SOLVE X + A = B."     RUN
20   PRINT "VALUE OF A";             TO SOLVE X + A = B.
30   INPUT A                         VALUE OF A? 29
40   PRINT "VALUE OF B";             VALUE OF B? 51
50   INPUT B                         THE VALUE OF X IS: 22
60   PRINT "THE VALUE OF X IS: ";B - A
70   END
```

1. Use the program above to solve the following equations.
   a. $x + 94 = 352$ b. $67 + x = 149$ c. $x + 587 = 1065$

2. Write a program to solve any equation in the form:
   a. $x - a = b$ b. $ax = b$ c. $x \div a = b$

Chapter Review

True or false?

[2–1]

1. $16 - n$ represents "a number n decreased by sixteen."

2. "The total of nine and a number y" is represented by $9 + y$.

3. "The product of seven and a number q" is represented by $7q$.

4. $3x = 45$ represents "the sum of three and a number x is forty-five." [2–2]

5. $2p - 10 = 50$ represents "twice a number p, minus ten, is equal to fifty."

6. $8 < 14$ represents "eight is less than fourteen." [2–3]

7. $6 > m$ represents "six is less than a number m."

8. "On a number line, a number y is between two and ten" is represented by $2 < y < 10$.

Solve. Write the letter of the correct answer.

9. $x + 53 = 131$ [2–4]

    a. 184   **b.** 88   **c.** 78   **d.** 661

10. $y - 39 = 146$

    a. 175   **b.** 185   **c.** 107   **d.** 117

11. $a - 4 < 2$

    a. all numbers less than 6   **b.** all numbers greater than 6

    c. all numbers less than 2   **d.** all numbers greater than 2

12. $6t = 84$ [2–5]

    a. 90   **b.** 78   **c.** 504   **d.** 14

13. $x \div 7 = 21$

    a. 147   **b.** 3   **c.** 28   **d.** 14

14. $3z + 12 = 42$

    a. 2   **b.** 10   **c.** 30   **d.** 14

15. Katherine's bank contains nickels and dimes. The coins have a total value of $19.85. If 137 of the coins are dimes, how many nickels are there in the bank? [2–6]

    a. 137   **b.** $13.70   **c.** 123   **d.** $6.15

Chapter Test

Write a variable expression for each word phrase.

1. The total of sixteen and a number n [2-1]

2. A number c divided by nine

3. Forty-two decreased by a number x

4. The product of twelve and a number a

Write an equation for each word sentence.

5. The sum of five and a number p is ninety.   [2-2]

6. Eleven multiplied by a number x is one hundred thirty-two.

7. Sixty-four divided by a number u is equal to sixteen.

8. Twice a number y minus eight equals seventy-four.

Replace __?__ with < or >.

9. 121 __?__ 112   **10.** 423 __?__ 234   **11.** 113 __?__ 131 __?__ 311   [2-3]

Write an inequality for each word sentence.

12. Sixty-eight is less than eighty.

13. Nineteen is between fourteen and thirty.

14. Zero is less than a number y.

15. A number z is greater than a number r.

Solve.

16. $x + 57 = 149$ **17.** $y - 45 = 74$ [2-4]

18. $z - 11 < 16$ **19.** $a + 9 > 20$

20. $4t = 144$ **21.** $x \div 5 = 615$ [2-5]

22. $6c < 42$ **23.** $s \div 7 > 8$

24. $5y - 1 = 19$ **25.** $4m + 59 = 159$

26. Ten more than twice a number is sixty-six. Find the number.   [2-6]

27. Eunice and Martin spent a total of $23.75 on decorations for the school dance. They bought fifteen rolls of streamers costing 75¢ a roll. The remainder of the money was spent on ornaments costing 50¢ each. How many ornaments did Eunice and Martin buy?

Cumulative Review (Chapters 1–2)
Exercises

Perform the indicated operation.

1. $\begin{array}{r} 746 \\ + 598 \\ \hline \end{array}$

2. $\begin{array}{r} 2059 \\ + 1384 \\ \hline \end{array}$

3. $\begin{array}{r} 3698 \\ + 965 \\ \hline \end{array}$

4. $\begin{array}{r} 781 \\ - 279 \\ \hline \end{array}$

5. $\begin{array}{r} 3036 \\ - 1758 \\ \hline \end{array}$

6. $\begin{array}{r} 1608 \\ - 594 \\ \hline \end{array}$

7. $\begin{array}{r} 46 \\ \times 18 \\ \hline \end{array}$

8. $\begin{array}{r} 341 \\ \times 24 \\ \hline \end{array}$

9. $\begin{array}{r} 498 \\ \times 35 \\ \hline \end{array}$

10. $17\overline{)646}$

11. $23\overline{)1173}$

12. $28\overline{)1568}$

13. $1865 + 247$

14. $2498 + 4651$

15. $849 + 4972$

16. $2041 - 1472$

17. $1894 - 389$

18. $3201 - 1875$

19. 134×23

20. 427×39

21. 586×42

22. $888 \div 24$

23. $1728 \div 32$

24. $2968 \div 53$

Simplify.

25. $13(18 + 41)$

26. $29(41 + 19)$

27. $34(26 + 37)$

28. $(28 + 11)(9 + 14)$

29. $(41 - 19)(13 + 12)$

30. $(37 - 11)(29 - 7)$

31. $29 - 8 \times 2 + 67$

32. $15 + 84 \div 7 + 75 - 3$

33. $12 \times 18 \div 3 + 74$

34. $168 - 100 \div 20 \times 14$

35. $(31 + 49) \div 8 \times 15$

36. $(74 - 20)3 - 52$

37. $36 \div (114 - 105)58$

38. $48 \div 8 \times 67 - 151$

39. $18 \times 15 \div 5 \times 0 \times 16$

40. $79 - 150 \div 15 \times 0 \div 3$

Solve.

41. $p + 9 = 18$

42. $8z = 32$

43. $19 + b = 71$

44. $m - 27 = 79$

45. $d - 14 > 76$

46. $t + 35 < 101$

47. $8x = 896$

48. $s \div 12 = 60$

49. $10k < 700$

50. $n \div 2 > 70$

51. $4r + 9 = 33$

52. $11y - 31 = 123$

Problems

Solve.

1. The librarian at Creston High ordered the following books: 39 novels, 17 books of poetry, 12 biographies, 41 science books, 32 history books, and an encyclopedia composed of 24 separate volumes. How many books in all did the librarian order?

2. The land areas of North Dakota and South Dakota are 70,837 and 77,615 square miles, respectively. How much larger is South Dakota than North Dakota?

3. If the federal tax on each gallon of gasoline sold is 9¢ while the state tax is 8¢, what is the total amount of federal and state tax on 15 gallons of gasoline?

4. Sue had 210 ft of string on the ball of string she used to fly a kite. After 164 ft were unwound, how many feet remained on the ball?

5. A parking garage charges the following rates:

   > 75¢ for the first half-hour,
   > 50¢ for the next half-hour,
   > 50¢ for each additional hour.

   How much does this garage charge to park a car for six hours?

6. A survey showed that there were 15,392 houses in a certain town on January 1. If 1341 more houses were built during the year, how many houses were there in the town at the end of that year?

7. The enrollment in the Science Club was 39. After 15 more students joined, the club advisor decided to split the club into 3 groups of equal size. How many students were in each group?

8. In a furniture factory it takes 20 min to assemble a table and 30 min to assemble a chair. How long does it take to assemble 15 dinette sets, each made up of 1 table and 4 chairs?

9. A printing machine controlled by a computer can print 80 lines a minute. How many lines can this machine print in two hours?

3 The Decimal System

APPLYING MATHEMATICS
MONETARY SYSTEM

The United States monetary system is a decimal system in which the basic unit is the dollar. The dollar contains one hundred cents, and so the cent is one hundredth of the dollar. Thus the value of any coin in the system can be identified as a decimal part of the dollar. For example, since a dime represents ten cents, its value can be identified as ten hundredths, or one tenth, of the dollar. We add, subtract, multiply, or divide amounts of money using the rules of our decimal system of numeration. During and after the American Revolution, there was no single monetary system in the United States. Thirteen states as well as Congress issued money, and people also used foreign coins. When Congress decided to establish a United States mint to coin money for the entire country, Thomas Jefferson suggested that a decimal system be adopted.

CAREER CONNECTION

COIN DEALER

Many people collect coins either as a hobby, as an investment, or as a means of studying art and history. A coin dealer is a person who runs a business through which these collectors can buy and sell coins and can obtain coin-collecting supplies. There are also dealers who specialize in the purchase and sale of other collectible items, such as antiques, books, and old photographs.

Photo: Pennies are the smallest unit of currency in the U.S.

3-1 Exponents and Powers of Ten

When two or more numbers are multiplied together, each of the numbers is called a **factor** of the product. For example, in the multiplication

$$3 \times 5 = 15,$$

3 and 5 are the factors of 15.

A product in which each factor is the same is called a **power** of that factor. For example, since

$$2 \times 2 \times 2 \times 2 = 16,$$

16 is called the *fourth power* of 2. We can write this as

$$2^4 = 16.$$

The small numeral 4 is called an **exponent** and represents the number of times 2 is a factor of 16. The number 2 is called the **base.**

EXAMPLE 1   Evaluate 4^3.

Solution $4^3 = 4 \times 4 \times 4 = 16 \times 4 = 64$

The second and third powers of a number have special names. The second power is called the **square** of the number and the third power is called the **cube.**

EXAMPLE 2   Read, then evaluate.

        a. 12^2 **b.** 9^3

Solution   **a.** 12^2 is read "twelve squared."
            $12^2 = 12 \times 12 = 144$

        b. 9^3 is read "nine cubed."
            $9^3 = 9 \times 9 \times 9 = 81 \times 9 = 729$

Powers of 10 are important in our number system. Here is a list of the first five powers of 10.

First power: 10^1 (exponent usually not written) $= 10$
Second power: $10^2 = 10 \times 10$ $= 100$
Third power: $10^3 = 10 \times 10 \times 10$ $= 1000$
Fourth power: $10^4 = 10 \times 10 \times 10 \times 10$ $= 10,000$
Fifth power: $10^5 = 10 \times 10 \times 10 \times 10 \times 10$ $= 100,000$

If you study the list on the previous page carefully, you can see that the following general rules apply.

> **Rules**
>
> 1. The exponent in a power of 10 is the same as the number of zeros when the number is written out.
> 2. The number of zeros in the product of powers of 10 is the sum of the numbers of zeros in the factors.

EXAMPLE 3 Multiply 100×1000.

Solution Since there are 2 zeros in 100 and 3 zeros in 1000, the product will have $2 + 3$, or 5, zeros.

$$100 \times 1000 = 100,000$$

Class Exercises

Name the exponent and the base.

1. 8^3 **2.** 9^7 **3.** 3^5 **4.** 6^4

Tell the number of zeros in the number or product.

5. 10^4 **6.** 10^8 **7.** 1000×1000 **8.** $100 \times 1,000,000$

Read the following, then evaluate each.

9. 7^2 **10.** 9^2 **11.** 3^3 **12.** 5^3

Written Exercises

Use exponents to write each of the following expressions.

A **1.** $5 \times 5 \times 5 \times 5 \times 5 \times 5$ **2.** $12 \times 12 \times 12 \times 12$

3. $8 \times 8 \times 8 \times 8 \times 8 \times 8 \times 8 \times 8 \times 8$ **4.** $20 \times 20 \times 20 \times 20 \times 20$

Multiply.

5. 1000×1000 **6.** $10 \times 10,000$ **7.** 100×100 **8.** $100 \times 100,000$

9. $1000 \times 1,000,000$ **10.** $10 \times 100,000$ **11.** $1000 \times 10,000$ **12.** $10 \times 1,000,000$

Evaluate.

13. 4^2 14. 11^3 15. 16^2 16. 15^2

17. 20^2 18. 5^4 19. 15^3 20. 2^5

21. 80^2 22. 40^3 23. 2^8 24. 12^3

25. 6^4 26. 5^5 27. 16^3 28. 3^5

Multiply.

EXAMPLE $3^4 \times 2^3$

Solution $3^4 \times 2^3 = (3 \times 3 \times 3 \times 3) \times (2 \times 2 \times 2)$
$$= 81 \times 8 = 648$$

B 29. $2^4 \times 5^2$ 30. $1^3 \times 16^2$ 31. $70^2 \times 7^3$ 32. $3^4 \times 10^5$

33. $0^4 \times 15^8$ 34. $15^2 \times 10^3$ 35. $31^2 \times 1^5$ 36. $20^5 \times 3^2$

37. $2^8 \times 1^5$ 38. $5^3 \times 3^4$ 39. $12^3 \times 2^2$ 40. $200^3 \times 3^2$

41. $2^3 \times 3^2 \times 10^3$ 42. $8^2 \times 5^3 \times 1^4$ 43. $119^2 \times 2^5 \times 0^8$ 44. $50^4 \times 2 \times 1^5$

Evaluate if $a = 3$ and $b = 5$.

C 45. a^3 46. b^3 47. $a^5 - b^2$ 48. $a^3 + b^2$

49. $50 - b^2$ 50. $20a^2$ 51. $(ab)^2$ 52. a^2b^3

Review Exercises

Evaluate.

1. $5(1000)$ 2. $6(100,000)$ 3. $3(100)$

4. $400 + 20 + 8$ 5. $3000 + 40 + 7$ 6. $50,000 + 600 + 7$

7. $2(100) + 3(10) + 6$ 8. $9(1000) + 5(10) + 1$ 9. $8(10,000) + 5(100) + 2$

NONROUTINE PROBLEM SOLVING: *Trial and Error*

Write 100 using four 5's and any operation symbols you need.

Write 100 using the numbers 1 through 9 and any operation symbols you need.

Write 100 using four 9's and any operation symbols you need.

3-2 The Decimal System

Our system of writing numbers uses the ten digits

$$0, 1, 2, 3, 4, 5, 6, 7, 8, 9.$$

Whole numbers greater than 9 can be represented as sums. For example, the number 386 can be represented as follows.

$$386 = 300 + 80 + 6 = 3(100) + 8(10) + 6(1)$$

─── ones' place (the place value is 1)
─── tens' place (the place value is 10)
─── hundreds' place (the place value is 100)

Notice that each place value is ten times the value of the place to its right. The number 10 is called the **base** of this system of writing numbers. The system itself is called the **decimal system** from the Latin word *decem,* meaning ten.

The first twelve place names are shown in the following chart.

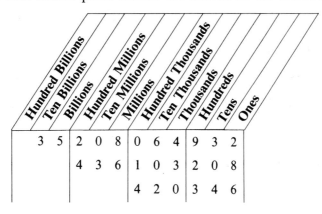

Hundred Billions	Ten Billions	Billions	Hundred Millions	Ten Millions	Millions	Hundred Thousands	Ten Thousands	Thousands	Hundreds	Tens	Ones
3	5	2	0	8	0	6	4	9	3	2	
		4	3	6	1	0	3	2	0	8	
				4	2	0	3	4	6		

To make numbers with more than four digits easier to read, commas are generally used to separate the digits into groups of three starting from the right. For example, the first number represented in the chart above is written

$$35,208,064,932.$$

In words, the number 420,346 is written as "four hundred twenty thousand, three hundred forty-six."

The **expanded notation** for 420,346 is given by:

$$4(100,000) + 2(10,000) + 0(1000) + 3(100) + 4(10) + 6(1)$$

Using exponents the expanded notation may be given as:

$$4(10^5) + 2(10^4) + 0(10^3) + 3(10^2) + 4(10) + 6(1)$$

EXAMPLE Write 279,043 (a) in words and (b) in expanded notation with exponents.

Solution   **a.** two hundred seventy-nine thousand, forty-three

b. $279{,}043 = 2(100{,}000) + 7(10{,}000) + 9(1000) + 0(100) + 4(10) + 3(1)$
$= 2(10^5) + 7(10^4) + 9(10^3) + 0(10^2) + 4(10) + 3(1)$

Class Exercises

Express in words.

1. 11,028
2. 92,047
3. 308,471
4. 14,982

5. 25,620
6. 1,098,470
7. 475,049,390
8. 14,907,059,111

State the place value of the underlined digit in each number.

9. 4̲2
10. 9̲37
11. 3̲049
12. 6̲20,190

13. 78̲4,903
14. 8,7̲21,047
15. 5,237,6̲49
16. 25̲,693,298

Written Exercises

Write in words.

A   **1.** 1962
2. 20,374
3. 57,419
4. 516,082

5. 1,037,908
6. 720,005,000
7. 1,416,980,016
8. 6,909,116,011

Write the number.

9. three thousand four
10. eighteen million, five hundred

11. one hundred thirteen thousand
12. six thousand seventy-two

13. three billion, fourteen million, seven hundred two

14. fourteen billion, sixty-two million, nine thousand eighty

Write the number in expanded notation with exponents.

15. 329
16. 5208
17. 10,472
18. 4058

19. 369
20. 905
21. 723
22. 4601

23. 96,209
24. 417,096
25. 804,725
26. 1,037,472

27. 5902
28. 38,047
29. 905,720
30. 32,905

31. 107,047	**32.** 5,098,472	**33.** 104,317,510

B **34.** 470,562,037   **35.** 14,049,596,111   **36.** 15,116,281,982

    37. 19,410,002,500   **38.** 414,300,511,261   **39.** 71,214,511

    40. 281,471,912   **41.** 18,412,931   **42.** 938,444,281

Write a variable expression to represent the two-digit number described.

EXAMPLE   The tens' digit is t; the ones' digit is 2.

Solution $10t + 2$

43. The tens' digit is t; the ones' digit is 7.

44. The tens' digit is 5; the ones' digit is x.

45. The tens' digit is 3; the ones' digit is u.

46. The tens' digit is t; the ones' digit is u.

47. The tens' digit is t; the ones' digit is $5t$.

48. The tens' digit is t; the ones' digit is an odd number less than 3.

49. The tens' digit is t; the ones' digit is 4 times the tens' digit.

50. The tens' digit is t; the ones' digit is 1 more than the tens' digit.

Write a variable expression to represent the number specified.

C **51.** A three-digit number; the hundreds' digit is h; the tens' digit is t; the ones' digit is 0.

    52. A four-digit number; the thousands' digit is x; the hundreds' digit is y; the tens' digit is z; the ones' digit is u.

    53. A three-digit number; the ones' digit is u; the tens' digit is t; the hundreds' digit equals 2 times the tens' digit.

Review Exercises

Graph the numbers on a number line.

  1. 6, 8, 10   **2.** 0, 3, 5   **3.** 4, 7, 9   **4.** 9, 11, 15   **5.** 7, 12, 14

  6. counting numbers less than 5   **7.** odd numbers between 2 and 6

  8. even numbers between 5 and 11   **9.** whole numbers less than 7

3-3 Decimals

Computation with fractions has presented difficulties in science and engineering throughout history. In 1585 Simon Stevin, a Belgian engineer, thought of a simple way to write the fractions $\frac{1}{10}$, $\frac{1}{100}$, $\frac{1}{1000}$, and so on. He first wrote the fractions using exponents in the denominators.

$$\frac{1}{10} = \frac{1}{10^1}, \quad \frac{1}{100} = \frac{1}{10^2}, \quad \frac{1}{1000} = \frac{1}{10^3}, \ldots$$

Stevin then replaced each fraction with strings of digits preceded by a dot called a **decimal point,** in such a way that the number of digits to the right of the decimal point in the string is equal to the exponent of 10 in the denominator of the given fraction.

$$\frac{1}{10} = 0.1, \quad \frac{1}{10^2} = 0.01, \quad \frac{1}{10^3} = 0.001, \ldots$$

These strings of digits are called **decimals.**

EXAMPLE 1 Write each fraction as a decimal.

  a. $\dfrac{1}{100,000}$ **b.** $\dfrac{1}{1,000,000}$

Solution   **a.** $\dfrac{1}{100,000} = \dfrac{1}{10^5} = 0.00001$

   b. $\dfrac{1}{1,000,000} = \dfrac{1}{10^6} = 0.000001$

As with whole numbers, decimals use *place values*. These places are located to the *right* of the decimal point. Each place value is ten times the place value to its right.

The values of the first six places to the right of the decimal point are shown in the chart at the right. (Compare this chart with the one for whole numbers in the previous lesson.)

Ones	Decimal point	Tenths	Hundredths	Thousandths	Ten-thousandths	Hundred-thousandths	Millionths
1	.	5	6	1	7	0	3
0	.	4	3	0	9	4	2
2	.	3	6	4	0	1	7

Decimals may be written in words and in expanded notation.

EXAMPLE 2 Write 0.6394 (a) in words and (b) in expanded notation.

Solution **a.** six thousand three hundred ninety-four ten-thousandths

b. $0.6394 = 0 + 0.6 + 0.03 + 0.009 + 0.0004$
$= 0(1) + 6(0.1) + 3(0.01) + 9(0.001) + 4(0.0001)$

Notice that we read the entire number to the right of the decimal point as if it represented a whole number, and then we give the place value of the digit farthest to the right.

EXAMPLE 3 Show that $0.400 = 0.4$.

Solution $0.400 = 0(1) + 4(0.1) + 0(0.01) + 0(0.001)$
$= 0 + 4(0.1) + 0 + 0$
$= 0.4$

Thus, as Example 3 suggests,

$0.4 = 0.40 = 0.400$, and so on.

In general, annexing zeros to the right of a decimal in this way does not change the number represented.

Decimals and whole numbers may be combined to give decimals for numbers greater than 1. For example,

14.35 is read "fourteen and thirty-five hundredths."

Notice that the decimal point is read "and."

Decimals may be represented on a number line as shown in the following figures.

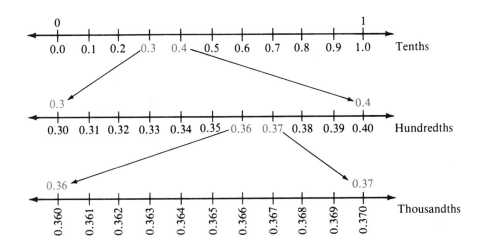

Class Exercises

Express in words.

1. 0.4   2. 0.08   3. 0.009   4. 0.0007

5. 0.41   6. 0.18   7. 0.029   8. 0.0097

9. 0.000002   10. 0.000125   11. 0.6025   12. 0.005098

13. 1.5   14. 3.06   15. 5.008   16. 16.0009

Written Exercises

a. Write in words.
b. Write in expanded notation.

A

1. 0.04   2. 0.3   3. 0.007   4. 0.0002

5. 0.12   6. 0.312   7. 0.0078   8. 0.000961

9. 1.3   10. 6.23   11. 17.008   12. 304.0162

Write the decimal.

13. five tenths   14. six hundredths

15. seventeen thousandths   16. forty-two thousandths

17. six and nine tenths   18. four and eleven hundredths

19. one hundred sixty-one millionths   20. fifty one hundred-thousandths

21. nine and seventy-six millionths   22. two and seven ten-thousandths

Write as a decimal.

23. $\frac{1}{100}$ 24. $\frac{1}{10}$ 25. $\frac{1}{10,000}$ 26. $\frac{1}{1,000,000}$

27. $\frac{1}{10^1}$ 28. $\frac{1}{10^4}$ 29. $\frac{1}{10^2}$ 30. $\frac{1}{10^3}$

B

31. $3(0.1)$ 32. $5(0.01)$ 33. $7(0.001)$ 34. $9(0.00001)$

35. $6\left(\frac{1}{10}\right)$ 36. $8\left(\frac{1}{10^3}\right)$ 37. $4\left(\frac{1}{10^2}\right)$ 38. $5\left(\frac{1}{10^5}\right)$

Write the decimal.

39. sixty-eight and ninety-nine ten-thousandths

40. one hundred eleven and twelve millionths

41. forty and four hundred thirty-one ten-thousandths

42. nineteen and eighty-four hundred-thousandths

43. four hundred sixty-two and seventy-one hundred-thousandths

44. sixteen and one thousand ninety-eight millionths

Copy the number line. Draw the graph of each decimal on the number line.

EXAMPLE 0.762

Solution

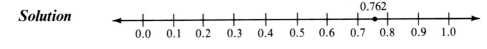

C **45.** 0.68   **46.** 0.34   **47.** 0.912   **48.** 0.175

49. 0.142   **50.** 0.52   **51.** 0.992   **52.** 0.009

Review Exercises

Write the numbers in order from least to greatest.

1. 324; 423; 234   **2.** 46; 194; 23   **3.** 154; 15,400; 451

4. 905; 590; 950   **5.** 60; 600; 6   **6.** 99; 100; 1001

7. 920; 219; 912   **8.** 116; 601; 610   **9.** 138; 803; 80,300

 CALCULATOR INVESTIGATION: *Writing Messages*

Use your calculator to solve this problem: A group of hikers from Idaho walked 69.3417 m north, 84.7953 m west, 461.283 m south, 9781.68 m east, 24,710.9 m south, and then stopped to rest.

1. How many meters did they hike in all?

2. In what city did they stop to rest? (*Hint:* Turn your calculator upside-down.)

    You can make up your own calculator messages by matching the letters with the numbers as shown at the right and then reversing the numbers. You can translate your messages by simply turning your calculator upside-down. For example, your pet GOOSE would now be your pet "35009." Instead of wishing your friends a good morning, you may say, "0.19786 − 0.12052."

B	⟶	8
E	⟶	3
G	⟶	9
H	⟶	4
I	⟶	1
L	⟶	7
O	⟶	0
S	⟶	5

3-4 Comparing Decimals

We have used number lines to show comparisons of whole numbers. Number lines can also be used to show comparisons of decimals. As with whole numbers, a larger number is graphed to the right of a smaller number.

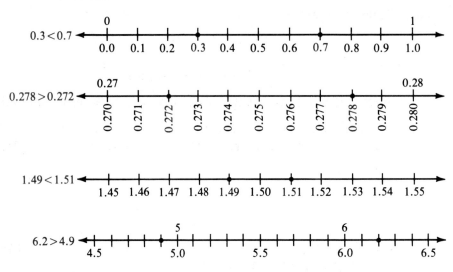

In order to compare decimals, we compare the digits in the place farthest to the left where the decimals have different digits.

EXAMPLE 1 Compare the following.

         a. 0.64 and 0.68   **b.** 2.58 and 2.62

Solution   **a.** 0.64   0.68   **b.** 2.58   2.62

                        └─compare─┘   └─compare─┘

              Since $4 < 8$, $0.64 < 0.68$.   Since $5 < 6$, $2.58 < 2.62$.

EXAMPLE 2 Compare 0.83 and 0.833.

Solution   To make the comparison easier, first express 0.83 to the same number of decimal places as 0.833.

$$0.83 = 0.830$$

Then, compare.   0.830   0.833

                             └─compare─┘

Since $0 < 3$, $0.830 < 0.833$.

EXAMPLE 3   Write in order from least to greatest.

$$4.164, \ 4.16, \ 4.163, \ 4.1$$

Solution   First, express each number to the same number of decimal places.

$$4.16 = 4.16\,0 \quad 4.1 = 4.1\,00$$

Then, compare.

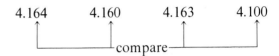

Since $0 < 6$, we can see that 4.1 is less than 4.164, 4.163, and 4.16.

We must still determine the order of 4.164, 4.163, and 4.16. We again write these numbers to the same number of decimal places and compare.

4.164   4.160   4.163

compare

Since $0 < 3$ and $0 < 4$, 4.16 is less than 4.164 and 4.163. Since $3 < 4$, $4.163 < 4.164$.

The order of the numbers from least to greatest is

4.1, 4.16, 4.163, and 4.164.

Class Exercises

For each pair of numbers, state the greater number if one is greater than the other. If the two numbers are equal, so state.

1. 7.50; 7.05   2. 0.11; 0.02   3. 5.6813; 0.0095

4. 3.80; 3.84   5. 0.0129; 0.0117   6. 0.308; 0.0301

7. 0.415; 0.578   8. 0.283; 0.291   9. 29.2; 29.20

10. 0.697; 0.6960   11. 0.50; 0.5000   12. 1.825; 1.8027

Name the decimal represented by A, B, and C on the number line.

13.

    A B C
    2.9   3.0

14.

    C A B
    1.7   1.8

15.

            A C B
    0.21   0.22

16.

        C B A
    7.48   7.49

Written Exercises

Replace the __?__ with <, >, or = to make a true sentence.

A **1.** 0.741 __?__ 0.734   **2.** 1.2 __?__ 1.20   **3.** 0.357 __?__ 0.289

   4. 0.139 __?__ 0.132   **5.** 3.86 __?__ 3.87   **6.** 0.819 __?__ 0.892

   7. 0.37 __?__ 0.370   **8.** 1.2407 __?__ 1.2047   **9.** 0.8862 __?__ 0.8826

In racing competitions, the shortest time wins. Which is the winning time?

10. Men's 500 m speed skating
   a. 39.54 s   **b.** 39.17 s   **c.** 39.25 s

11. Women's downhill skiing
   a. 46.16 s   **b.** 47.50 s   **c.** 46.68 s

In diving and skating competitions, the highest score wins. Which is the winning score?

12. Men's platform diving
   a. 548.61   **b.** 607.51   **c.** 576.99

13. Women's figure skating
   a. 188.16   **b.** 190.24   **c.** 193.80

Write the numbers in order from least to greatest.

14. 8.23, 8.32, 8.30   **15.** 3.12, 3.21, 3.19   **16.** 4.09, 4.90, 4.39

17. 6.08, 6, 6.80   **18.** 1.001, 1.010, 1.0010   **19.** 532.78, 532.9, 532.882

Write two values of x for which the inequality is true.

B **20.** $4.5 < x < 4.6$ **21.** $1.82 < x < 1.83$ **22.** $3.012 < x < 3.013$

   23. $15 < x < 15.001$ **24.** $0.19 < x < 0.2$ **25.** $0.121 < x < 0.1215$

Review Exercises

Write the value of the digit that is in the place specified.

   1. 516,706; hundreds   **2.** 47,921; ones   **3.** 918,037,700; ten millions

   4. 0.875; hundredths   **5.** 9.82; tenths   **6.** 0.01234; ten-thousandths

   7. 98.47; tenths   **8.** 142.579; hundreds   **9.** 41.795; ones

3-5 Rounding

Many times people use *rounded* numbers. For example, if a new phonograph record is priced at $7.98, we might say that it costs almost $8. Or, if there were 421 people at the school play, we could say that about 400 people attended the play.

Rounding may be pictured on a number line.

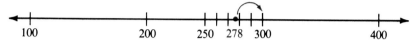

We see that 278 is closer to 300 than it is to 200. We say that

278 has been **rounded** to 300,
to the nearest hundred.

A method for rounding whole numbers can be stated as follows.

> **1.** Find the place to which you wish to round, and mark it with a caret (∧). Look at the digit to the right.
>
> **2.** If the digit to the right is 5 or greater, add 1 to the marked digit. If the digit to the right is less than 5, leave the marked digit unchanged.
>
> **3.** Replace each digit to the right of the marked place with 0.

EXAMPLE 1   Round 32,567 to (a) the nearest ten thousand, (b) the nearest thousand, (c) the nearest hundred, and (d) the nearest ten.

Solution   a. 32,567: Since 2 is less than 5, we leave the 3 unchanged and
              ∧   replace 2, 5, 6, and 7 with zeros.
           30,000

b. 32,567: Since the digit to the right of 2 is 5, we add 1 to 2 to get
    ∧   3 and replace 5, 6, and 7 with zeros.
 33,000

c. 32,567: Since 6 is greater than 5, we add 1 to 5 and replace 6 and
      ∧   7 with zeros.
 32,600

d. 32,567: Since 7 is greater than 5, we add 1 to 6 and replace 7 with
        ∧   a zero.
 32,570

A similar method of rounding can be used for decimals. The difference between the two methods is that when rounding decimals, we do not have to replace the dropped digits with zeros. This method is illustrated in Example 2.

EXAMPLE 2   Round 4.8637 to (a) the nearest thousandth, (b) the nearest hundredth, (c) the nearest tenth, and (d) the nearest unit.

Solution
   a. 4.8637: Since 7 is greater than 5, we add 1 to 3 to get 4 and then
   $\quad\quad\quad\wedge\quad$ drop the 7.
   4.864

   b. 4.8637: Since 3 is less than 5, we leave the 6 unchanged and drop
   $\quad\quad\quad\wedge\quad$ 3 and 7.
   4.86

   c. 4.8637: Since 6 is greater than 5, we add 1 to 8 and drop 6, 3,
   $\quad\quad\wedge\quad$ and 7.
   4.9

   d. 4.8637: Since 8 is greater than 5, we add 1 to 4 and drop 8, 6, 3,
   $\quad\quad\wedge\quad$ and 7.
   5

COMMUNICATION IN MATHEMATICS: *Reading for Meaning*

Mathematics should be read carefully. For instance, consider what might happen if you misread hundred as hundredth in a direction line.

Class Exercises

a. Round the number to the nearest ten.
b. Round the number to the nearest hundred.

1. 156	**2.** 325	**3.** 769	**4.** 905	**5.** 614
6. 2082	**7.** 16,407	**8.** 200,973	**9.** 21,448	**10.** 11,998
11. 4132	**12.** 31,399	**13.** 468,778	**14.** 325,491	**15.** 84,348

a. Round the number to the nearest tenth.
b. Round the number to the nearest hundredth.

16. 0.862	**17.** 2.915	**18.** 0.619	**19.** 0.898	**20.** 1.657
21. 3.009	**22.** 0.976	**23.** 1.071	**24.** 6.509	**25.** 1.099
26. 7.218	**27.** 9.112	**28.** 1.915	**29.** 0.421	**30.** 3.845

Written Exercises

Round 613,572,947 to the given place.

A **1.** tens   **2.** millions   **3.** ten thousands   **4.** hundred millions

5. hundreds   **6.** thousands   **7.** ten millions   **8.** hundred thousands

9–16. Repeat Exercises 1–8 for 196,037,908.

Round 216.098256 to the given place.

17. tenths   **18.** hundredths   **19.** tens   **20.** hundred-thousandths

21. ones   **22.** hundreds   **23.** thousandths   **24.** ten-thousandths

25–32. Repeat Exercises 17–24 for 509.690285.

a. What is the least whole number that satisfies the condition?
b. What is the greatest whole number that satisfies the condition?

EXAMPLE   A whole number, rounded to the nearest ten, is 520.

Solution   Rounding the whole numbers 515, 516, 517, . . . , 523, 524 to the nearest ten gives 520.

Thus, the least whole number is 515.
The greatest whole number is 524.

B **33.** A whole number, rounded to the nearest ten, is 650.

34. A whole number, rounded to the nearest hundred, is 1200.

35. A whole number, rounded to the nearest thousand, is 8000.

36. A whole number, rounded to the nearest ten, is 1280.

37. A whole number, rounded to the nearest hundred, is 2,534,700.

38. A whole number, rounded to the nearest hundred, is 38,700.

C **39.** A whole number, rounded to the nearest hundred thousand, is 7,560,300,000.

a. What is the least possible amount of money that satisfies the condition?
b. What is the greatest possible amount?

40. A sum of money, rounded to the nearest dollar, is $58.

41. A sum of money, rounded to the nearest ten dollars, is $5980.

42. A sum of money, rounded to the nearest ten dollars, is $3140.

43. A sum of money, rounded to the nearest ten dollars, is $8520.

Self-Test A

Evaluate.

1. 15^2 **2.** 4^4 **3.** $10^5 \times 9^1$ **4.** $2^3 \times 5^2$ [3–1]

Write the number in expanded notation with exponents.

5. 617   **6.** 5038   **7.** 12,402   **8.** 256,030   [3–2]

Write the number in expanded notation.

9. 0.06   **10.** 1.3   **11.** 2.007   **12.** 0.0142   [3–3]

Write as a decimal.

13. $9(0.01)$ **14.** $5\left(\dfrac{1}{10^2}\right)$ **15.** $3\left(\dfrac{1}{10^5}\right)$ **16.** $2(0.0001)$

Write the numbers in order from least to greatest.

17. 1.32, 1.23, 1.30   **18.** 9, 9.08, 9.8   [3–4]

Round 372.0685 to the given place.

19. hundreds   **20.** ones   **21.** tenths   **22.** thousandths   [3–5]

Self-Test answers and Extra Practice are at the back of the book.

▮▮▮ CALCULATOR INVESTIGATION: *Order of Operations*

Some calculators follow the order of operations given in Chapter 1. Other calculators do not.

To see if your calculator follows the order of operations, enter

$$7 + 3 \times 5.$$

If the calculator displays 22, then it followed the order of operations. If it shows 50, then the calculator added 7 and 3 before multiplying by 5. To correct this, you should multiply 3 and 5 first and then add 7.

Use a calculator to simplify each expression.

1. $93 - 5 \times 7$ **2.** $41 + 14 \times 8$ **3.** $64 - 32 \div 4$

4. $156 + 210 \div 15$ **5.** $11 \times 7 - 4 \times 9$ **6.** $87 \div 3 + 88 \div 4$

7. $315 - 540 \div 18$ **8.** $490 \div 70 - 7$ **9.** $127 + 13 \times 16$

3-6 Adding and Subtracting Decimals

Decimals can be added or subtracted using the same rules as whole numbers. The rule below lists the steps used to add or subtract decimals.

Rules

1. Write the given numbers one above the other with the decimal points in line.

2. Annex zeros to get the same number of decimal places and then add or subtract as if the numbers were whole numbers.

3. Place a decimal point in the number for the sum or difference in position under the decimal points in the given numbers.

The example below shows how we use steps 1–3 to add decimals with different decimal places.

EXAMPLE 1   Add 6.47 + 340.8 + 73.523.

Solution

Step 1	Step 2	Step 3
6.47	6.470	6.470
340.8	340.800	340.800
+ 73.523	+ 73.523	+ 73.523
	420 793	420.793

Therefore 6.47 + 340.8 + 73.523 = 420.793.

The example below shows how we use steps 1–3 to subtract decimals with different decimal places.

EXAMPLE 2   Subtract 13.94 − 7.693.

Solution

Step 1	Step 2	Step 3
13.94	13.940	13.940
− 7.693	− 7.693	− 7.693
	6 247	6.247

Therefore 13.94 − 7.693 = 6.247.

EXAMPLE 3   Leonora had $317.58. She made purchases of $19.95, $27.49, and $89.98. How much did she have left?

Solution   Add the amounts of the purchases Leonora made.

$$
\begin{array}{r}
19.95 \\
27.49 \\
+\ 89.98 \\
\hline
137.42
\end{array}
$$

Subtract this total from the amount of money Leonora had.

$$
\begin{array}{r}
317.58 \\
-\ 137.42 \\
\hline
180.16
\end{array}
$$

Leonora had $180.16 left.

PROBLEM SOLVING REMINDER

Planning how to do a problem before starting it can often save some work. For instance, Example 3 could be solved by subtracting each purchase separately, a procedure that would require 3 subtraction operations. The method used in the example requires only 2 operations, one addition and one subtraction.

The use of rounded numbers to get an approximate answer is called **estimation.** We use estimates to check actual answers. To find an estimated sum or difference, first round to the highest place value of the smallest number, then compute.

EXAMPLE 4   Add 8.574 + 81.03 + 59.432. Estimate to check the answer.

Solution   First, find the sum.

$$
\begin{array}{r}
8.574 \\
81.030 \\
+\ 59.432 \\
\hline
149.036
\end{array}
$$

To check your answer, round all addends to the nearest unit.

$$8.574 \longrightarrow 9 \quad 81.030 \longrightarrow 81 \quad 59.432 \longrightarrow 59$$

Find the sum of the rounded addends.

$$9 + 81 + 59 = 149$$

The actual answer is in close agreement with the estimate. The actual answer is probably correct.

Class Exercises

a. **Estimate the answer.**
b. **Add or subtract.**

1. $\begin{array}{r} 13.1 \\ +\ 43.6 \\ \hline \end{array}$	**2.** $\begin{array}{r} 43.2 \\ +\ 22.5 \\ \hline \end{array}$	**3.** $\begin{array}{r} 36.75 \\ +\ 52.14 \\ \hline \end{array}$	**4.** $\begin{array}{r} 6.175 \\ +\ 0.142 \\ \hline \end{array}$
5. $\begin{array}{r} 16.72 \\ -\ 0.29 \\ \hline \end{array}$	**6.** $\begin{array}{r} 5.84 \\ -\ 0.37 \\ \hline \end{array}$	**7.** $\begin{array}{r} 7.35 \\ -\ 2.21 \\ \hline \end{array}$	**8.** $\begin{array}{r} 9.73 \\ -\ 3.41 \\ \hline \end{array}$

9. $121.56 + 40.131$ **10.** $79.92 + 16.213$

11. $561.92 - 41.81$ **12.** $108.16 - 18.03$

Written Exercises

Add or subtract. Estimate to check the answer.

A

1. $\begin{array}{r} 9.86 \\ +\ 1.12 \\ \hline \end{array}$	**2.** $\begin{array}{r} 15.7 \\ +\ 74.2 \\ \hline \end{array}$	**3.** $\begin{array}{r} 3.78 \\ +\ 0.21 \\ \hline \end{array}$	**4.** $\begin{array}{r} 0.056 \\ +\ 1.903 \\ \hline \end{array}$
5. $\begin{array}{r} 5.86 \\ -\ 1.51 \\ \hline \end{array}$	**6.** $\begin{array}{r} 0.132 \\ -\ 0.021 \\ \hline \end{array}$	**7.** $\begin{array}{r} 9.87 \\ -\ 3.52 \\ \hline \end{array}$	**8.** $\begin{array}{r} 15.75 \\ -\ 9.64 \\ \hline \end{array}$
9. $\begin{array}{r} 258.1 \\ +\ 32.139 \\ \hline \end{array}$	**10.** $\begin{array}{r} 76.061 \\ -\ 3.211 \\ \hline \end{array}$	**11.** $\begin{array}{r} 189.31 \\ -\ 22.872 \\ \hline \end{array}$	**12.** $\begin{array}{r} 12.3 \\ -\ 0.847 \\ \hline \end{array}$
13. $\begin{array}{r} 15.3009 \\ -\ 4.34 \\ \hline \end{array}$	**14.** $\begin{array}{r} 0.986 \\ +\ 0.21954 \\ \hline \end{array}$	**15.** $\begin{array}{r} 5.219 \\ -\ 1.0265 \\ \hline \end{array}$	**16.** $\begin{array}{r} 54.31 \\ -\ 47.4337 \\ \hline \end{array}$
17. $\begin{array}{r} 2100.2 \\ 74.09186 \\ 5.8032 \\ +\ 32.39 \\ \hline \end{array}$	**18.** $\begin{array}{r} 312.31 \\ 1269.174 \\ 501.01824 \\ +\ 0.0113 \\ \hline \end{array}$	**19.** $\begin{array}{r} 0.191 \\ 25.0197 \\ 3.00184 \\ 52.9 \\ +\ 82.763 \\ \hline \end{array}$	**20.** $\begin{array}{r} 13.219 \\ 3.41 \\ 6.4176 \\ 0.9 \\ +\ 20.618 \\ \hline \end{array}$

21. $9.1 - 5.628$ **22.** $13.6 + 112.903$

23. $0.1125 + 1.0297$ **24.** $8 - 3.095$

25. $5 - 1.302$ **26.** $0.48 + 2.9015$

27. $16.3 - 9.8602$ **28.** $2.15 - 0.9998$

29. $5.8 + 7.29 + 1.56$ **30.** $32.7 + 18.5 + 6.29 + 1.602$

Add or subtract. Estimate to check the answer.

B **31.** (3.24 + 16.139) − (1.14 + 8.176)   **32.** (75.004 − 1.32) + (41.13 − 2.891)

33. (0.918 + 23.705) − (2 − 1.556)   **34.** (49.603 − 14.09) + (31.4 + 15.801)

35. 0.0345 + 0.0216 − 0.0076   **36.** 2.312 − 1.0672 + 2.8

37. 14.321 + 0.389 + 22.14 − 0.5   **38.** 0.819 + 0.9 + 3.9

39. (12.14 + 0.587 + 6.138) − (2.007 + 9.991)

40. (43.149 + 6.312 + 5.145) − (15.762 − 2.659)

41. (16.008 + 21.43) − (23.4 − 4.018) + (43 − 2.119)

42. (4.314 + 13.896) − (20.9 − 19.004) + (2 − 0.1415)

43. 4.519 + 9.132 − 0.2 + 1.745 + 30

44. 99.86 − 13.08 − 45.17 + 0.33 + 1.2687

45. 0.56 − 0.22 − 0.02 + 14.46 + 8.84

46. 110 − 34.76 + 15.439 − 67.82 + 101.3

47. 1340 − 893.45 + 308.56 − 204.789 − 550

Problems

Solve, using the five-step plan.

A **1.** The four members of the swimming relay team swam 100 m each in the following times: 1 min 20.4 s, 1 min 10.3 s, 1 min 30.5 s, and 1 min 25.8 s. What was the total time for the 400 m relay?

2. At 7:00 A.M. the temperature was 86.7°F. By 3:00 P.M. the temperature had risen 5.3°. Four hours later it had dropped 10.5° below the reading at 3:00 P.M. What was the temperature at 7:00 P.M.?

3. In a 100 gram (g) serving of bran flakes with raisins, there are 8.3 g of protein, 8 g of vitamins and minerals, 3 g of fiber, 1.4 g of fat, and the remaining part is carbohydrates. How many grams of carbohydrates are there in the 100 g serving?

4. Paolo earns $209.92 each week. The following deductions are subtracted from his pay: federal income tax, $18.95; state income tax, $7.50; FICA (Social Security), $13.23; medical insurance, $10.12; union dues, $8.40. How much money does Paolo take home each week?

5. Janice had $285.35 at the beginning of the month. During the month she made purchases of $17.89, $26.90, $116.35, and $15.82. She also earned an additional $58.16. How much money did Janice have at the end of the month?

B **6.** During the past month Consuelo used her credit card to make four purchases costing $57.75, $36.95, $16.85, and $8.98. She exchanged the $16.85 item for one costing $18.25. What is the total of the new charges on her account for the month?

7. The Cronin family's monthly budget allows $50 per month for telephone charges. Their basic monthly service costs $18.75. Last month they made long-distance calls costing $2.85, $6.32, $.42, $.90, $1.63, $12.97, and $7.86. By how much did they exceed their budget for the month?

8. At the beginning of each day of a five-day trip, Carl recorded the odometer reading on his car and the purpose of that day's trip. When he returned home at the end of the fifth day, the odometer on his car read 81,262.3 miles. How many miles did Carl drive for business purposes during the 5 days?

Day	Odometer Reading	Purpose
1	79,802.7	Business
2	80,170.1	Business
3	80,340.9	Pleasure
4	80,562.3	Business
5	80,795.1	Business

Review Exercises

Multiply or divide.

1. 39×1000 **2.** $421 \times 10,000$ **3.** 9×10^3 **4.** 81×10^4

5. $420 \div 10$ **6.** $98,000 \div 100$ **7.** $7000 \div 10^3$ **8.** $82,000,000 \div 10^4$

3-7 Multiplying or Dividing by a Power of Ten

We have learned that in a decimal or a whole number each place value is ten times the place value to its right.

$$10 \times 1 = 10 \qquad 10 \times 10 = 100 \qquad 10 \times 100 = 1000$$
$$10 \times 0.1 = 1 \qquad 10 \times 0.01 = 0.1 \qquad 10 \times 0.001 = 0.01$$

Notice that multiplying by 10 has resulted in the decimal point being moved one place to the right and in zeros being inserted or dropped.

EXAMPLE 1 Multiply.

    a. 10×762 **b.** 10×4.931

Solution Multiplying by 10 moves the decimal point one place to the right.

    a. $10 \times 762 = 7620 = 7620$

    b. $10 \times 4.931 = 49.31 = 49.31$

At the beginning of this chapter we learned about powers of ten. For example, the fourth power of ten is

$$10^4 = 10 \times 10 \times 10 \times 10 = 10{,}000.$$

We can see that multiplying by a power of 10 is the same as multiplying by 10 repeatedly. For example, if we multiply 2.63874 by 10^4 we have

$$2.63874 \times 10^4 = 2.63874 = 26{,}387.4.$$

Notice that we have moved the decimal point *four* places to the right.

Rule

To multiply a number by the *n*th power of ten, move the decimal point *n* places to the right.

EXAMPLE 2 Multiply 0.0047 by the following.

    a. 100   **b.** 1000

Solution **a.** $0.0047 \times 100 = 0.0047 \times 10^2$
           Move the decimal point 2 places to the right.

$$0.0047 \longrightarrow 0.47$$

b. $0.0047 \times 1000 = 0.0047 \times 10^3$

Move the decimal point 3 places to the right.

$$0.0047 \longrightarrow 4.7$$

Powers of 10 provide a convenient way to write very large numbers. Numbers that are expressed as products of a number greater than or equal to 1, but less than 10, and a power of 10 are said to be written in **scientific notation.**

To write a number in scientific notation we move the decimal point to the *left* until the resulting number is between 1 and 10. We then multiply this number by the power of 10 whose exponent is equal to the number of places we moved the decimal point.

EXAMPLE 3   Write 4,592,000,000 in scientific notation.

Solution   First move the decimal point to the left to get a number between 1 and 10.

$$4592000000 \longrightarrow 4.592$$

Since the decimal point was moved 9 places we multiply 4.592 by 10^9 to express the number in scientific notation.

$$4.592 \times 10^9$$

When we move a decimal point to the left, we are actually dividing by a power of 10. Recall that multiplication and division are inverse operations. Therefore, from

$$2.386 \times 10^3 = 2386$$

we know that $2386 \div 10^3 = 2.386.$

Notice that in dividing by a power of 10 we move the decimal point to the left the same number of places as the exponent. Sometimes, we may have to annex zeros. For example,

$$3.1 \div 10^4 = 00031 = 0.00031$$

Rule

To divide a number by the nth power of ten, move the decimal point n places to the left, annexing zeros as necessary.

EXAMPLE 4   Divide 1784 by the following.

   a. 100   **b.** 100,000

Solution   **a.** $1784 \div 100 = 1784 \div 10^2$
             Move the decimal point 2 places to the left.

$$17\underset{\smile}{84} \longrightarrow 17.84$$

          b. $1784 \div 100,000 = 1784 \div 10^5$
             Move the decimal point 5 places to the left.

$$\underset{\smile}{01784} \longrightarrow 0.01784$$

Class Exercises

Multiply each number by (a) 10, (b) 100, and (c) 1000.

1. 51	**2.** 247	**3.** 41.9	**4.** 83.4
5. 906	**6.** 2.836	**7.** 0.5581	**8.** 6.00904

Divide each number by (a) 10, (b) 100, and (c) 1000.

9. 253	**10.** 17,300	**11.** 68	**12.** 14.7
13. 9.8	**14.** 50.35	**15.** 958.6	**16.** 0.04

Complete.

17. $6300 = 6.3 \times \underline{\quad ? \quad}$ **18.** $98,000,000 = 9.8 \times \underline{\quad ? \quad}$

19. $4750 = \underline{\quad ? \quad} \times 10^3$ **20.** $3,560,000 = \underline{\quad ? \quad} \times 10^6$

21. $\underline{\quad ? \quad} = 3.2 \times 10^5$ **22.** $\underline{\quad ? \quad} = 7.04 \times 10^8$

Written Exercises

Multiply each number by (a) 1000, (b) 10,000, and (c) 1,000,000.

A

1. 52	**2.** 123	**3.** 5.7	**4.** 610
5. 12.7	**6.** 56.79	**7.** 5.069	**8.** 0.0017
9. 0.08901	**10.** 0.3695	**11.** 16.475	**12.** 0.2108

Divide each number by (a) 100, (b) 10,000, and (c) 100,000.

13. 24,000	**14.** 516	**15.** 75.7	**16.** 1300

| **17.** 4.8 | **18.** 90.3 | **19.** 2.8 | **20.** 0.14 |
| **21.** 160,000 | **22.** 3,400,000 | **23.** 514,000 | **24.** 1628 |

Write in scientific notation.

25. 558,000	**26.** 11,230	**27.** 3800
28. 38,000,000	**29.** 81,507,000	**30.** 426,000,000
31. 527,000,000,000	**32.** 107,900,000,000	**33.** 3,269,000,000
34. 3,570,000	**35.** 127,376,000,000	**36.** 14,390,000,000

Write the given number in scientific notation.

B **37.** In a recent year about 1,593,600,000 books were sold in the United States.

38. There are about 70,797,133 acres in the national park system.

39. Approximately 29,715,000 people fish in fresh water lakes annually.

40. There are more than 154,400,000 registered automobiles, trucks, and buses in the United States.

41. The canoe industry manufactures about 101,000 canoes every year.

42. More than 189,200,000,000 m^3 of water flow over Niagara Falls each year.

43. The annual retail gross from canoe sales is about $40,200,000.

44. The estimated temperature of the sun's core is 25 million degrees Fahrenheit.

Review Exercises

Multiply.

| **1.** 17×98 | **2.** 560×9 | **3.** 84×198 | **4.** 140×500 |
| **5.** 147×208 | **6.** 109×508 | **7.** 871×306 | **8.** 1705×980 |

3-8 Multiplying Decimals

Decimals are multiplied in the same manner as whole numbers. To place the decimal point in the correct position in the product, we use the following rule.

Rule

Place the decimal point in the product so that the number of places to the right of the decimal point in the product is the sum of the number of places to the right of the decimal point in the factors.

EXAMPLE 1 Multiply 14.92×7.2.

Solution
$$
\begin{array}{r}
14.92 \\
\times\ 7.2 \\
\hline
2\ 984 \\
104\ 44 \\
\hline
107.424
\end{array}
$$

2 places
1 place

3 places

In order to avoid misplacing the decimal point, a computation using round numbers can be very helpful.

EXAMPLE 2 Estimate the product. Then multiply 11.32×8.73.

Solution Round 11.32 to 11 and 8.73 to 9.
$$11 \times 9 = 99$$
Thus, 11.32×8.73 should be close to 99.

$$
\begin{array}{r}
11.32 \\
\times\ 8.73 \\
\hline
3396 \\
7\ 924 \\
90\ 56 \\
\hline
98.8236
\end{array}
$$

2 places
2 places

4 places

EXAMPLE 3 A jet flew at 820.3 km/h for 3.2 h. How far did the jet travel?

Solution Use the formula distance = rate $\times$ time.
$$d = 820.3 \text{ km/h} \times 3.2 \text{ h}$$
Round 820.3 to 820 and 3.2 to 3.
$$820 \times 3 = 2460$$

Thus, 820.3×3.2 should be close to 2460.

$$
\begin{array}{rl}
820.3 & \text{1 place} \\
\times\ 3.2 & \text{1 place} \\
\hline
164\ 06 & \\
2460\ 9 & \\
\hline
2624.96 & \text{2 places}
\end{array}
$$

The jet flew 2624.96 km.

Class Exercises

Multiply.

1. 6×0.1 **2.** 2×0.3 **3.** 8×0.01 **4.** 30×0.02

5. 3×1.5 **6.** 4×0.12 **7.** 40×0.25 **8.** 50×0.12

State a whole number estimate for the product.

9. 0.02×0.08 **10.** 72.3×2.01 **11.** 5.19×1.26 **12.** 207.3×0.04

The correct digits are given for the product. State the product with the decimal point correctly inserted.

13. 6.8×0.94; 6392   **14.** 0.37×6.2; 2294   **15.** 8.4×9.6; 8064

16. 13.2×0.05; 660   **17.** 641.8×0.25; 160450   **18.** 103.2×1.248; 1287936

Written Exercises

a. Estimate the product.
b. Multiply.

A   **1.** 1.7   **2.** 9.3   **3.** 15.8   **4.** 1.39
       $\times\ 8$ $\times\ 5$ $\times\ 12$ $\times\ 15$

5. 4.17   **6.** 21.8   **7.** 5.08   **8.** 3.98
       $\times\ 3.2$ $\times\ 3.9$ $\times\ 0.19$ $\times\ 0.32$

9. 92.14×2.4 **10.** 5.71×0.03 **11.** 19.8×0.006

12. 2.581×3.9 **13.** $0.12 \times 80,000$ **14.** 0.14×0.14

15. 0.003×0.0156 **16.** 1.89×12.61 **17.** $6.005 \times 15,000$

18. 0.0125×0.008 **19.** 0.0042×0.018 **20.** 0.116×0.219

Simplify.

B **21.** $(19.81 \times 7.1) + (19.81 \times 2.9)$ **22.** $50(0.25 \times 0.125)$

23. $(0.04 + 0.2 + 0.001)30$ **24.** $80 \times 36.74 \times 0.125$

25. $(3.68 \times 0.064) - (2.05 \times 0.064) - (1.63 \times 0.064)$

Compute the cost of the electricity used (kW·h) at the specified rate.

C **26.** 164 kW·h at the following rate:
Minimum charge for first 20 kW·h: $2.25
Next 50 kW·h at 6.913¢ per kW·h
Next 100 kW·h at 5.821¢ per kW·h

Problems

Solve, using the five-step plan.

A **1.** How thick is a ream of 500 sheets of paper if each sheet is 0.0025 in. thick?

2. A 12-in. steel cable weighs 0.428 lb. How much does 12.8 ft weigh?

3. A nautical mile is equivalent to 6080.27 ft. If a ship is 3.8 nautical miles from a lighthouse, what is the distance in feet?

B **4.** Carla Russo's wages are increased from $3.80 per hour to $4.25 per hour. If she works 36 hours each week, how much more money will she earn in one year?

5. Max earns $4.35 per hour if he works 40 hours or less in one week. When he works more than 40 hours in one week, his hourly rate for the number of hours over 40 is 1.5 times his regular rate. How much will he be paid for working 53 hours in one week?

Review Exercises

Divide.

1. $78\overline{)702}$ **2.** $49\overline{)833}$ **3.** $102\overline{)4896}$ **4.** $15\overline{)8940}$

5. $456 \div 8$ **6.** $3424 \div 32$ **7.** $2040 \div 24$ **8.** $12,880 \div 16$

3-9 Dividing Decimals

To divide a decimal by a counting number we proceed as if we were dividing two counting numbers.

EXAMPLE 1   Divide 25.2 by 6.

Solution

$$
\begin{array}{r}
4.2 \\
6\overline{)25.2} \\
24 \\
\hline
1\,2 \\
1\,2 \\
\hline
0
\end{array}
$$

Check:
$$
\begin{array}{r}
4.2 \\
\times\,6 \\
\hline
25.2
\end{array}
$$

Notice the placement of the decimal point in the quotient.

Rule

In using the division process to divide a decimal by a counting number, place the decimal point in the quotient directly over the decimal point in the dividend.

When a division does not terminate, or does not come out evenly, we may wish to find an approximate quotient to a specified number of decimal places. This can be accomplished by annexing zeros to the end of the dividend, which does not change the value of the decimal. We then divide to one place beyond the specified number of places. The quotient is then rounded to the specified number of decimal places.

EXAMPLE 2   Divide 2.745 by 8 to the nearest thousandth.

Solution   First annex a zero to the end of the dividend. Then divide.

$$
\begin{array}{r}
0.3431 \\
8\overline{)2.7450} \\
2\,4 \\
\hline
34 \\
32 \\
\hline
25 \\
24 \\
\hline
10 \\
8 \\
\hline
2
\end{array}
$$

Rounding 0.3431 to the nearest thousandth gives 0.343.

To divide one decimal by another, recall that multiplication is the inverse of division. Therefore, from

$$5 \times 0.7 = 3.5$$

we can conclude that $3.5 \div 0.7 = 5$.

When we multiply both the dividend and divisor above by 10, you can see that the quotient remains the same. That is,

$$35 \div 7 = 5$$

This gives the following rule for dividing by a decimal.

Rules

1. Multiply the dividend and divisor by a power of ten that makes the divisor a counting number.

2. Divide the new dividend by the new divisor.

3. Check by multiplying the quotient and divisor.

EXAMPLE 3 Divide 3.154 by 1.25 to the nearest hundredth.

Solution First, multiply the dividend and divisor by 100.

Annex two zeros to the end of the dividend.

Then divide.

```
            2.523
      _____
1.25)3.15400
      2 50
      ____
       654
       625
       ___
       290
       250
       ___
       400
       375
       ___
        25
```

Rounding 2.523 to the nearest hundredth gives 2.52.

Check: multiply the rounded quotient by the divisor

```
       2.52
     × 1.25
     _____
      1260
       504
     2 52
     _____
     3.1500
```

Since 3.15 and 3.154 are equal in the hundredths' place, the rounded answer 2.52 is probably correct.

EXAMPLE 4 Tickets to the school play cost $5.25 each. The total receipts were
$651. How many tickets were sold?

Solution Divide $651 by $5.25.

$$
\begin{array}{r}
124 \\
5.25\overline{)65100.} \\
\underline{525} \\
1260 \\
\underline{1050} \\
2100 \\
\underline{2100} \\
0
\end{array}
$$

A total of 124 tickets were sold.

Class Exercises

Divide.

1. $4.8 \div 4$

2. $2.5 \div 5$

3. $0.18 \div 3$

4. $0.045 \div 9$

5. $32 \div 0.1$

6. $163 \div 0.1$

7. $72 \div 0.01$

8. $96 \div 0.001$

9. $5.6 \div 0.8$

10. $14.4 \div 1.2$

11. $1.69 \div 0.13$

12. $3.15 \div 0.05$

State the least power of ten which makes the divisor a counting number.

13. $0.6\overline{)16}$

14. $0.3\overline{)9.8}$

15. $1.25\overline{)80.5}$

16. $9.45\overline{)5}$

**The correct digits are given for the quotient. State the quotient with the
decimal point correctly inserted.**

17. $0.8\overline{)32.0}$ quotient 40

18. $1.4\overline{)1.050}$ quotient 75

19. $0.03\overline{)0.36}$ quotient 12

20. $0.57\overline{)0.171}$ quotient 3

Written Exercises

Divide and check. If necessary, round to the nearest tenth.

A

1. $6\overline{)453}$

2. $4\overline{)126}$

3. $17\overline{)11.9}$

4. $28\overline{)30.2}$

5. $1.2\overline{)18.74}$

6. $3.7\overline{)17.7}$

7. $0.18\overline{)76.2}$

8. $1.95\overline{)3.06}$

Divide and check. If necessary, round to the nearest hundredth.

9. $0.276 \div 7$

10. $52.12 \div 4$

11. $812 \div 0.8$

12. $783.9 \div 9$

13. $38.6 \div 1.4$

14. $6.3 \div 0.06$

15. $19.8 \div 0.32$

16. $5 \div 0.015$

Divide and check. If necessary, round to the nearest hundredth.

17. $0.812 \div 1.7$ 18. $3.26 \div 0.013$ 19. $42 \div 1.96$ 20. $0.21 \div 1.4$

21. $10.18 \div 130$ 22. $47.6 \div 7.2$ 23. $197 \div 0.09$ 24. $12.86 \div 0.08$

25. $39.6 \div 0.126$ 26. $4.72 \div 1.24$ 27. $0.4 \div 0.024$ 28. $1.26 \div 0.0081$

Simplify.

B 29. $(942.6 - 37.5) \div 1.5$ 30. $296.06 \div (18.7 + 3.9)$

31. $25.08 \div (16.3 - 9.7)$ 32. $(47.1 - 16.9) \div (21.9 - 6.8)$

Problems

Solve, using the five-step plan.

A 1. Paula earns $250 a week. If she works 35 h each week, what is her hourly rate of pay?

2. At an average rate of 55 km/h, how long will it take to drive 225 km, to the nearest tenth of an hour?

B 3. A job is advertised at a yearly salary of $16,800. If there are 245 working days a year and 7 h in a working day, what is the hourly rate to the nearest cent?

4. Gene bought a typewriter for $175.50. After 4.5 years, he sold it for $37.75. To the nearest cent, how much per year did it cost Gene to use the typewriter?

C 5. A monthly pass for a commuter train costs $84. A book of tickets for 12 rides costs $30.25. A single ticket costs $2.75. Johanna rides the train an average of 44 times per month.
   a. To the nearest cent, how much does Johanna save per ride by buying a monthly pass instead of buying single tickets?
   b. To the nearest cent, how much does Johanna save per ride by buying the monthly pass instead of buying books of 12 tickets?

Review Exercises

Estimate the answer. Then compute the answer.

1. $1027 + 5679$ 2. $14,000 - 1492$ 3. 778×19 4. 612×108

5. $980 \div 35$ 6. $4032 \div 63$ 7. $(212 - 132) \div 5$ 8. $(98 - 13)47$

3-10 Problem Solving: Using Estimation

In the previous lessons we used estimation to check our solutions. When we do not need exact answers, we can use estimates to approximate an answer.

EXAMPLE 1   A serving of carrots costs 39.7¢. About how much will it cost to serve 58 people?

Solution   To find an estimate, round 39.7¢ to 40¢, or $.40, and 58 to 60.

$$0.40 \times 60 = 24.00$$

It will cost about $24.00 to serve 58 people.

EXAMPLE 2   A twin room at the Pine Hills Inn costs $79.50 a night. Jean and Shari shared a room for 5 nights. About how much did each one spend for lodging?

Solution   Round $79.50 to $80, then multiply.

$$80 \times 5 = 400$$

Divide the product by 2.

$$400 \div 2 = 200$$

They each spend about $200 for lodging.

EXAMPLE 3   Omar wants to buy a sweater for $18.95, a belt for $5.95, a pair of socks for $3.75, and a bottle of lotion for $5.60. He has $40. Does he have enough money to make the purchases?

Solution   Find an estimated sum of the purchases. First round $18.95 to $19, $5.95 to $6, $3.75 to $4, and $5.60 to $6. Then add.

$$19 + 6 + 4 + 6 = 35$$

He has enough money to make the purchases.

Class Exercises

Estimate the answer.

1. If John works 12.8 h and his hourly rate of pay is $4.35, about how much will he earn?

Estimate the answer.

2. Shelves cost $17.84 each and brackets cost $6.95 each. About how much will 5 shelves and 10 brackets cost?

3. Ming worked 22 h and earned $84.70. About how much was his hourly rate of pay?

4. A package of ground beef costs $4.44. If it is divided into 5 portions, about how much will each portion cost?

5. Sarah is buying books that cost $4.90, $9.45, and $2.25 and magazines that cost $.75 and $1.50. About how much change will she receive from a $50-bill?

Problems

Solve, using the five-step plan. Estimate to check the solution.

A 1. Flannel sheets for a twin bed cost $22.95 each. A package of 2 matching pillow cases costs $9.95. How much will 2 sheets and 2 pillow cases cost?

2. Jamie bicycled 245 mi in 2.5 days. How many miles did Jamie bicycle per day?

3. An airplane flew 1750 km in 4.5 h. To the nearest tenth, what was its speed in kilometers per hour?

Estimate the answer. Then solve, using the five-step plan.

4. How many silk flowers at $1.25 each can you buy with $25.00?

B 5. Susan can buy a single place setting of stainless steel flatware for $12.45. She can buy a boxed set of 8 place settings in the same pattern for $96. How much will she save per place setting if she buys the set of 8?

6. A carton of artificial bricks costs $12.95 and a gallon of adhesive costs $15.99. Sheila and Paul need 6 cartons of bricks and 3 gallons of adhesive for a wall in their den. They saved $300 to decorate the den.
   a. How much will the brick and adhesive cost them?
   b. Do they have enough money for the project?
   c. After they finish the den, they want to buy a rug. How much money will they have left to use?

7. A GTX-6 sports car gets 36 mi per gallon without air conditioning. With air conditioning it gets 3.5 fewer miles per gallon. How many gallons of gas are needed to drive 312 mi with the air conditioning?

8. Leo drove 1256.8 mi last month on 40 gal of gas. How many miles to the gallon did his car get?

9. What is the value of 18 quarters, 32 dimes, 15 nickels, and 56 pennies?

10. A long distance phone call costs $1.95 for the first 3 min and $.30 for each additional minute. How much will an 8-minute phone call cost?

Self-Test B

Add or subtract.

1. 13.8 + 0.79   2. 128.02 − 39.118   3. 4.2 + 7.9 − 1.8   [3-6]

Write in scientific notation.

4. 5,640,000   5. 17,490,000,000   [3-7]

Multiply and divide each number by (a) 100 and (b) 1000.

6. 45,783   7. 2.635   8. 0.5166

Multiply or divide.

9. 38.2 × 0.015   10. 1.04 × 3.5   [3-8]

11. 84 ÷ 0.12   12. 0.24 ÷ 1.5   [3-9]

Estimate the answer. Then solve, using the five-step plan.

13. Claire bought 3 bags of flower seeds at $.75 each and 2 bags at $1.20. Rose bushes cost $4.95 each or 3 for $12.60. If she plans to spend no more than $20 in all, how many rose bushes can she buy?   [3-10]

Self-Test answers and Extra Practice are at the back of the book.

Checking Accounts

Many people have checking accounts so that they can pay bills with checks instead of cash. Checks are safer to carry around and to send through the mail. A checking account also gives you a written record of the money you spend.

The amount of money in a bank account is called the **balance.** Money that you put into an account is a **deposit.**

A **check** instructs your bank to take money from your account and give it to someone else. For example, suppose Naomi Ferber buys shoes for $32.95 at the Sport Store. She would write the check as shown below.

Naomi Ferber	No. _125_
	Nov. 8 19 ___ 51-3/100
PAY TO THE ORDER OF _The Sport Store_	$32 95/100
Thirty-two and 95/100 ——— DOLLARS	
City Bank	_Naomi Ferber_
MEMO _Shoes_	
0⌐00 0059⌐547 002 8	

City Bank will take $32.95 out of Naomi's account and give it to the Sport Store. Then the bank will cancel the check and return it to Naomi, so she will know that it has been paid.

You use a **check register** to keep a record of the checks you write and the balance in your account. When you write a check you subtract the amount from the balance. When you make a deposit you add the amount to the balance.

$$\begin{matrix} \text{PRESENT} \\ \text{BALANCE} \end{matrix} = \begin{matrix} \text{PREVIOUS} \\ \text{BALANCE} \end{matrix} + \begin{matrix} \text{DEPOSITS} \\ \text{RECORDED} \end{matrix} - \begin{matrix} \text{CHECKS} \\ \text{PAID} \end{matrix}$$

CHECK NO.	DATE	CHECK ISSUED TO	AMOUNT OF CHECK		✔	DATE OF DEP.	AMOUNT OF DEPOSIT		BALANCE	
			BALANCE BROUGHT FORWARD→						632	41
417	3/28	Quick Cleaners	37	49					594	92
418	4/2	Auto Repair, Inc.	143	72					451	20
419	4/6	Appliance Center	349	95					101	25
						4/11	250	00	351	25

Melissa 86 – 90

Your bank may charge you a service fee every month. You subtract this fee from your balance. If the bank pays you money called **interest,** you add it to your balance.

Solve.

1. Manuel Perez's previous balance was $342.53. He wrote checks for $119.46 and $78.95, and made a deposit of $147.50. What is his new balance?

2. Susan Toshiri had a previous balance of $213.47 in her checking account. She wrote checks for $18.49, $62.57, and $41.89. After depositing $150, Susan wrote another check for $110.98. How much does Susan have in her account now?

3. Elgin Smith's previous balance was $113.96. He wrote checks for $14.95, $24.88, $17.50, and $31.49, and made deposits of $47.50 and $25. The bank also charged him a service fee of $2.50. What is his new balance?

4. Claudia Jackson had a previous balance of $259.66. She wrote checks for $34.73 and $121.11, and made a deposit of $235.00. She received $1.18 in interest. What is her new balance?

5. Sue Liang had a previous balance of $520.91. She wrote a check for $138.14 and deposited $416.00. She received interest of $1.56 and was charged a $2.00 service fee. What is her new balance?

6. Hans Kerr had a previous balance of $526.13. On January 5, he wrote a check for $70.47. Five days later he deposited $253.50 and withdrew $45.30. On January 20, he wrote a check for $112.80 and withdrew $50.00 cash. How much money did he have in his account on January 21?

Research Activity: Writing in Mathematics

Get information on checking accounts offered by local banks. Compare their service fees, interest rates, and minimum balances. Report on the advantages and disadvantages of each account.

Chapter Review

Write the letter of the equivalent item.

1. 21^3

2. 5^4

3. 2^8

4. $2(1000) + 5(100) + 6(1)$

5. $9(10^4) + 2(10^2) + 6(1)$

6. $2(10^3) + 5(10) + 6$

7. $2(0.1) + 5(0.01) + 6(0.001)$

8. $2 + 5(0.01) + 6(0.001)$

9. $6 + 2(0.1) + 5(0.001)$

A. 256

B. 90,206

C. 2506

D. 625

E. 6.205

F. 2.056

G. 9261

H. 0.256

I. 2056

[3-2]

[3-3]

True or false?

10. $7.084 > 7.84$

11. $13.81 > 13.818$

12. The number 6.0957, rounded to the nearest tenth, is 6.1.

[3-4]

]3-5]

Complete.

13. $15.6 + 2.385 = \underline{}$

14. $8.042 - 1.956 = \underline{}$

[3-6]

15. $11.2 + 1.98 - 3.05 = \underline{}$

16. $5.8 - (3.2 + 1.02) = \underline{}$

17. $7.3 \times 10^5 = \underline{}$

18. $540,000 \div 10^4 = \underline{}$

[3-7]

19. $984,000 = 9.84 \times \underline{}$

20. $2,800,000 = \underline{} \times 10^6$

21. $42 \times 16.5 = \underline{}$

22. $0.86 \times 9.5 = \underline{}$

[3-8]

23. $4.9 \div 28 = \underline{}$

24. $0.96 \div 1.2 = \underline{}$

[3-9]

25. $(5.6 - 1.4) \div 0.6 = \underline{}$

26. $21.51 \div (1.18 + 3.6) = \underline{}$

Write the letter of the correct answer.

27. The toll charged for driving a vehicle over a bridge depends on the kind of vehicle. One day, the following tolls were collected:

[3-10]

    53 Class 1 vehicles @ $.75   13 Class 3 vehicles @ $5.00
    14 Class 2 vehicles @ $1.25   7 Class 4 vehicles @ $18.75

How much money was collected that day?
a. $2240.25   **b.** $25.75   **c.** $253.50   **d.** $39.75

Chapter Test

Evaluate.

1. 13^2
2. 10^8
3. 20^3
4. 2^5
[3-1]

Write the number in expanded notation with exponents.

5. 29
6. 507
7. 17,042
8. 109,804
[3-2]

Write the decimal.

9. three and eight thousandths 10. two and fifty-three hundredths
[3-3]

Write the numbers in order from least to greatest.

11. 4.17, 4.71, 4.10
12. 8.80, 8.18, 8.81
[3-4]

Round 408.5671 to the given place.

13. tens
14. ones
15. hundredths
16. thousandths
[3-5]

Estimate the answer. Then compute the answer.

17. $0.813 + 1.28$
18. $2.18 - 1.019$
[3-6]

19. $47.2 + 18.8 - 9.28$
20. $4.98 - (3.12 + 1.08)$

21. 5.17×10^3
22. $49.6 \div 10^2$

Write in scientific notation.

23. 629,000
24. 4,591,000
25. 7,419,000,000
[3-7]

Estimate the answer. Then compute the answer.

26. 28×0.045
27. 13.9×3.2
28. 0.018×0.15
[3-8]

29. $103.2 \div 12$
30. $21.08 \div 31$
31. $0.152 \div 0.04$
[3-9]

32. $(19.8 - 8.9) \div 5.45$
33. $1.4 + 2.2 \div 1.2$
34. $42 \div (0.06 + 0.5)$

Estimate the answer. Then solve, using the five-step plan.

35. How much will 3.8 lb of seafood cost at $6.19 a pound?
[3-10]

36. A round-trip bus ticket to Center City will cost Mark $7.60. If he drives, he estimates his costs will be $4.85 for gas and $1.50 per hour to park. If he plans to be in the city for 3.5 h, will it cost less to drive or to take the bus? How much less?

Cumulative Review (Chapters 1–3)

Exercises

Evaluate the expression if $a = 6$ and $b = 10$.

1. $a + b$ **2.** $b - a + 4$ **3.** b^2 **4.** $16b$

5. ab **6.** $5a$ **7.** $12 - b + a$ **8.** $10(b - a)$

Simplify.

9. $21 - 8 \times 2$ **10.** $32 + 8 \div 4$ **11.** $3 \times 9 + 8 \div 2$

12. $6(13 - 5)$ **13.** $(18 + 2) \div 2$ **14.** $(48 \div 6) - (12 - 9)$

15. $112 - (8 \times 5 - 40)$ **16.** $48 \times 13 \div 48$ **17.** $324 + 16 - 324$

18. $(8 \times 31) + (8 \times 9)$ **19.** $(16 \times 5) - (16 \times 3)$ **20.** $(864 \div 16 + 5) - 32$

21. $16.5 \times 0.84 - 8.5$ **22.** $38.7 - (16.05 + 1.1)$ **23.** $105 + (8.4 \div 12)$

24. $(68.2 + 6.8) \div 15$ **25.** $460 \div (9.2 - 8.8)$ **26.** $4.32 \div (600 \div 0.6)$

27. $6.4(13.2 - 8.7)$ **28.** $116 \div (1.6 \times 0.05)$ **29.** $(6.2 + 1.2 \times 3) \div 0.4$

Solve.

30. $42 + x - 42 = 138$ **31.** $14y \div 14 = 203$

32. $h + 81 - 81 < 52$ **33.** $174k \div 174 > 18$

34. $217 + m = 308$ **35.** $p - 17 = 93$

36. $9c = 189$ **37.** $d \div 3 = 14$

38. $16r > 96$ **39.** $u \div 6 < 108$

Write a variable expression for each word phrase.

40. Sixteen more than a number n

41. A number x decreased by seventeen

42. The product of a number v and thirty-two

Write an equation for each word sentence. Use n for the variable.

43. A number increased by fourteen is sixty-eight.

44. Five times a number is one hundred sixty-five.

45. Seventeen less a number is eleven.

46. The sum of a number and thirty is two hundred three.

Problems

PROBLEM SOLVING REMINDERS

Here are some reminders that may help you solve some of the problems on this page.
- Estimate to check your answers.
- Is more than one operation needed?
- Consider whether drawing a sketch will help.

Solve.

1. The buyer at Bears' Department Store ordered 56 solar-powered calculators, 89 battery-powered calculators, and 47 electric calculators. How many new calculators were ordered?

2. Pauline read 56 pages of a 316-page novel yesterday, and 139 pages today. How many more pages must she read to finish the book?

3. A 115-lb barbell set includes four 10-lb cast iron plates, four 5-lb plates, and six 2.5-lb plates. What is the combined weight of the remaining parts of the set?

4. A library has 412 books in circulation and 59 of those are overdue. How many are not overdue?

5. Total receipts for a bus tour were $756. If the 42-passenger bus was filled, how much did each passenger pay for the tour?

6. One morning a cashier counted 17 customers who paid for purchases with credit cards and 24 who paid with checks. The rest paid with cash. If there were 82 customers in all, how many paid for purchases with cash?

7. Paper plates for a birthday party are sold in packages of 15. If you want to allow 2 plates per person, and 24 persons are invited, how many packages must you buy?

8. The Clarksons bought a personal computer for $629. They also bought a disk drive for $379 and software modules for $67.95, $42.95, and $34.95. If they received a $50 rebate on the total cost, what was their final cost?

9. Economy Car Rental charges a basic fee of $29 per day for a compact car. The first 25 mi are free; $.24 per mile is charged for additional miles. Dietz Rent-a-Car charges $56 per day for the same car with unlimited mileage. If you need to rent a car for one day and plan to drive 100 miles, which rental service will charge you less? How much less?

4 Geometric Figures

APPLYING MATHEMATICS
INDUSTRIAL DESIGN

Almost everything in our home, school, or work environment is the result of industrial designing. The design of a product evolves from the concept stage to the actual manufacture of the item. In every phase of design the fundamental concepts of geometry and measurement are evident. First, a designer interviews the client to find out what is needed. From the interviews preliminary sketches are made and submitted for approval. When the client agrees with the sketches, concept drawings are made which are developed into three-dimensional drawings. Finally, mechanical drawings are completed. They detail specifically the dimensions of the product and the precise size of each of the materials used. In this chapter you will learn the fundamental concepts of plane geometry, its language, and its notation.

CAREER CONNECTION

DRAFTER

A drafter draws the detailed plans for the construction of architectural structures and machines. The drafter very often works with an architect or an engineer during all stages of design and construction. Skill in drawing, an understanding of mathematical and mechanical concepts, and knowledge of the use of computer graphics are required. Courses in mechanical drawing are offered in high schools, technical schools, and colleges.

Photo: Computer drafting software may replace traditional drafting tools like the compass.

4-1 Points, Lines, Planes

All of the figures that we study in geometry are made up of **points.** We usually picture a single point by making a dot and labeling it with a capital letter.

$$P \qquad\qquad Q$$
$$\bullet \qquad\qquad \bullet$$
Point P \qquad Point Q

Among the most important geometric figures that we study are straight lines, or simply **lines.** You probably know this important fact about lines:

> Two points determine exactly one line.

This means that through two points P and Q we can draw one line, and only one line, which we denote by $\overleftrightarrow{PQ}$ (or $\overleftrightarrow{QP}$).

Line PQ: $\overleftrightarrow{PQ}$, or $\overleftrightarrow{QP}$

Notice the use of arrowheads to show that a line extends without end in either direction.

Three points may or may not lie on the same line. Three or more points that do lie on the same line are called **collinear.** Points not on the same line are called **noncollinear.**

If we take a point P on a line and all the points on the line that lie on one side of P, we have a **ray** with **endpoint** P. We name a ray by naming first its endpoint and then any other point on it.

Ray PQ: $\overrightarrow{PQ}$ \qquad\qquad Ray BA: $\overrightarrow{BA}$

It is important to remember that the endpoint is always named first. $\overrightarrow{AB}$ is *not* the same ray as $\overrightarrow{BA}$.

If we take two points P and Q on a line and all the points that lie between P and Q, we have a **segment** denoted by $\overline{PQ}$ (or $\overline{QP}$). The points P and Q are called the **endpoints** of $\overline{PQ}$.

Segment PQ: $\overline{PQ}$, or $\overline{QP}$

EXAMPLE 1   Name (a) one line, (b) two rays, (c) three segments, (d) three collinear points, and (e) three noncollinear points in the given diagram. (Various answers are possible.)

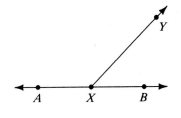

Solution   a. $\overleftrightarrow{AB}$ b. $\overrightarrow{XY}$, $\overrightarrow{AB}$ c. $\overline{AX}$, $\overline{XB}$, $\overline{XY}$ d. A, X, B e. A, Y, B

Just as two points determine a line, three noncollinear points in space determine a flat surface called a **plane.** We can name a plane by naming any three noncollinear points on it. Because a plane extends without limit in all directions of the surface, we can show only part of it, as in the figure below.

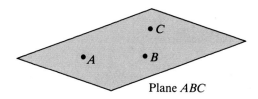

Plane *ABC*

Lines in the same plane that do not intersect are called **parallel lines.** Two segments or rays are parallel if they are parts of parallel lines. "$\overleftrightarrow{AB}$ is parallel to $\overleftrightarrow{CD}$" may be written as $\overleftrightarrow{AB} \parallel \overleftrightarrow{CD}$.

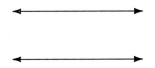

Intersecting lines intersect in a point.

Parallel lines do not intersect.

Planes that do not intersect are called **parallel planes.**

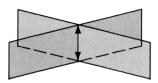

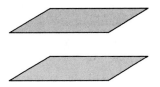

Intersecting planes intersect in a line.

Parallel planes do not intersect.

EXAMPLE 2 Use the box to name (a) two parallel lines, (b) two parallel planes, (c) two intersecting lines, (d) two intersecting planes, and (e) two nonparallel lines that do not intersect. (Various answers are possible.)

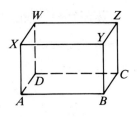

Solution

a. $\overleftrightarrow{AX}$ and $\overleftrightarrow{BY}$ b. plane ABC and plane XYZ

c. $\overleftrightarrow{AB}$ and $\overleftrightarrow{AX}$ d. plane ABC and plane ABY

e. $\overleftrightarrow{AD}$ and $\overleftrightarrow{BY}$

Two nonparallel lines that do not intersect, such as $\overleftrightarrow{AD}$ and $\overleftrightarrow{BY}$ in Example 2, are called **skew lines.**

Class Exercises

Tell how many endpoints each figure has.

1. a segment   **2.** a line   **3.** a plane   **4.** a ray

Exercises 5–9 refer to the diagram at the right in which $\overleftrightarrow{AB}$ and $\overleftrightarrow{CD}$ are parallel lines.

5. Name three collinear points.

6. Name two parallel rays.

7. Name two parallel segments.

8. Name two segments that are not parallel.

9. Name two rays that are not parallel.

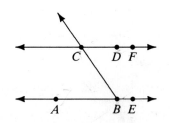

Exercises 10–14 refer to the box at the right. Classify each pair of planes as parallel or intersecting. If the planes are intersecting, name the line of intersection.

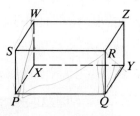

10. planes QRY and WSP **11.** planes PQR and PSW

12. planes SPW and XYQ **13.** planes PQR and WXY

14. In the box are $\overleftrightarrow{WX}$ and $\overleftrightarrow{RS}$ parallel, intersecting, or skew?

Written Exercises

In Exercises 1–4, give another name for the indicated figure.

A 1. $\overleftrightarrow{XY}$

2. $\overleftrightarrow{BC}$

3. $\overrightarrow{PR}$

4. $\overrightarrow{VU}$

5. Name one line and three rays in the diagram below.

6. Name three rays and three segments in the diagram below.

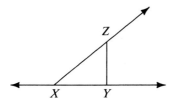

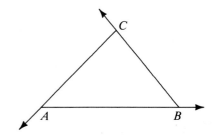

Exercises 7–20 refer to the diagram at the right. $\overleftrightarrow{PQ}$ and $\overleftrightarrow{ST}$ are parallel. (There may be several correct answers to each exercise.)

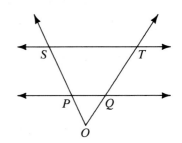

7. Name three collinear points.

8. Name three noncollinear points.

9. Name three segments that intersect at P.

10. Name two parallel rays.

11. Name two parallel segments.

12. Name two nonparallel segments that do not intersect.

13. Name two nonparallel rays that do not intersect.

14. Name two segments that intersect in exactly one point.

15. Name two rays that intersect in exactly one point.

16. Name a ray that is contained in $\overrightarrow{OT}$.

17. Name a ray that contains $\overline{SP}$.

18. Name the segment that is in $\overrightarrow{PQ}$ and $\overrightarrow{QP}$.

19. Name four segments that contain O.

20. Name two rays that intersect in more than one point.

Exercises 21–24 refer to the box at the right. (There may be several correct answers to each exercise.)

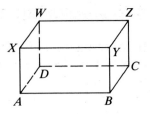

21. Name two intersecting lines and their point of intersection.

22. Name two intersecting planes and their line of intersection.

23. Name two parallel lines and the plane that contains them both.

24. Name two skew lines.

In Exercises 25–32, tell whether the statement is true or false.

B 25. Two lines cannot intersect in more than one point.

26. Two rays cannot intersect in more than one point.

27. Two segments cannot intersect in more than one point.

28. If two rays are parallel, they do not intersect.

29. If two rays do not intersect, they are parallel.

30. If two points of a segment are contained in a line, then the whole segment is contained in the line.

31. If two points of a ray are contained in a line, then the whole ray is contained in the line.

32. If two points of a segment are contained in a ray, then the whole segment is contained in the ray.

C 33. Draw $\overleftrightarrow{AB}$ and a point P not on $\overleftrightarrow{AB}$. Now draw a line through P parallel to $\overleftrightarrow{AB}$. How many such lines can be drawn?

34. Draw four points A, B, C, and D so that $\overline{AB}$ is parallel to $\overline{CD}$ and $\overline{AD}$ is parallel to $\overline{BC}$. Do you think that $\overline{AC}$ and $\overline{BD}$ must intersect?

35. We know that two points determine a line. Explain what we mean by saying that two nonparallel lines in a plane determine a point.

Review Exercises

Round to the nearest tenth.

1. 2.87 **2.** 6.32 **3.** 4.56 **4.** 7.08

5. 2.98 **6.** 11.753 **7.** 9.347 **8.** 6.482

4-2 Measuring Segments

In Washington, D.C., Jill estimated the length of a jet to be about 165 feet. When the plane landed in Paris, Jacques guessed the jet's length to be about 50 meters. Although the numbers 165 and 50 are quite different, the two estimates are about the same. This is so because of the difference in the units of measurement used.

The metric system of measurement uses the **meter (m)** as its basic unit of length. For smaller measurements we divide the meter into 100 equal parts called **centimeters (cm).**

We can measure a length to the nearest centimeter by using a ruler marked off in centimeters, as illustrated below.

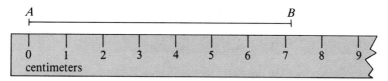

We see that the length of $\overline{AB}$ is closer to 7 cm than to 8 cm. The length of $\overline{AB}$ is written AB. The symbol $\approx$ means *is approximately equal to.* Therefore, $AB \approx 7$ cm.

The drawing at the right shows that the length of $\overline{XY}$ is about 3 cm.

$$XY \approx 3 \text{ cm}$$

Measurements made with small units are more precise than those made with larger units. We can measure lengths more precisely by using a ruler on which each centimeter has been divided into ten equal parts called **millimeters (mm).** We see that to the nearest millimeter the length of $\overline{AB}$ is 73 mm.

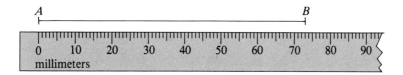

The drawing at the right shows that the length of $\overline{XY}$ is 28 mm and the lengths of $\overline{XM}$ and $\overline{MY}$ are 14 mm each. A point, such as M, that divides a segment into two other segments of equal length is called the **midpoint** of the segment. Thus, M is the midpoint of $\overline{XY}$. Segments of equal length are called **congruent segments.** The symbol $\cong$ means *is congruent to.* Since $XM = MY$, $\overline{XM} \cong \overline{MY}$.

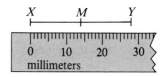

Usually centimeters and millimeters are marked on the same ruler, as shown below.

centimeters (with millimeters)

To measure longer lengths, such as distances between cities, we use **kilometers (km).** A kilometer is 1000 meters.

$$1 \text{ m} = 100 \text{ cm} = 1000 \text{ mm} \qquad 1 \text{ cm} = 10 \text{ mm}$$

1 cm = 0.01 m   (*centi* means *hundredths*)

1 mm = 0.001 m   (*milli* means *thousandths*)

1 km = 1000 m   (*kilo* means *thousand*)

Never mix metric units of length. For example, do not write 3 m 18 cm; write 3.18 m or 318 cm instead.

Class Exercises

Copy and complete these tables.

	1.	2.	3.	4.
Number of meters	4	?	?	?
Number of centimeters	?	60	52	?
Number of millimeters	?	?	?	36

	5.	6.	7.	8.
Number of meters	3500	?	475	?
Number of kilometers	?	4.2	?	0.034

9. Estimate the length and width of your desk top to the nearest centimeter.

10. Estimate the length and width of this book to the nearest centimeter.

11. Estimate the height of the classroom door to the nearest centimeter.

12. Estimate your height to the nearest centimeter.

13. Estimate the thickness of your pencil to the nearest millimeter.

14. Estimate the distance from your home to school in meters and in kilometers.

In Exercises 15 and 16, *M* is the midpoint of $\overline{AB}$. Draw a sketch to help you complete these sentences.

15. If $AB = 18$ cm, then $AM =$ _?_ cm and $MB =$ _?_ cm.

16. If $AM = 4$ mm, then $MB =$ _?_ mm and $AB =$ _?_ mm.

In Exercises 17 and 18, *P* is a point of $\overline{XY}$. Draw a sketch to help you complete these sentences.

17. If $XP = YP$, then $\overline{XP}$ is _?_ to $\overline{YP}$.

18. If $\overline{XP} \cong \overline{YP}$, then *P* is the _?_ of $\overline{XY}$.

Written Exercises

Measure each segment (a) to the nearest centimeter and (b) to the nearest millimeter. **(If you do not have a metric ruler, mark each segment on the edge of a piece of paper and use the ruler pictured earlier.)**

A **1.** $\overline{AE}$

2. $\overline{VZ}$

3. $\overline{MQ}$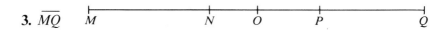

4. $\overline{GJ}$

5. $\overline{PT}$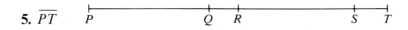

6. $\overline{NX}$

7. In Exercises 1–6, which pairs of the segments $\overline{AE}$, $\overline{VZ}$, $\overline{MQ}$, $\overline{GJ}$, $\overline{PT}$, and $\overline{NX}$ are approximately equal in length?

8. In Exercises 1–6, name the midpoints of $\overline{AE}$, $\overline{VZ}$, $\overline{MQ}$, $\overline{GJ}$, $\overline{PT}$, and $\overline{NX}$ given that the midpoint is named in each diagram.

Copy and complete these tables.

	9.	10.	11.	12.	13.	14.
Number of meters	4.5	1.63	?	?	?	?
Number of centimeters	?	?	250	82.6	?	?
Number of millimeters	?	?	?	?	60,000	368

	15.	16.	17.	18.	19.	20.
Number of meters	2000	20	625	?	?	?
Number of kilometers	?	?	?	3	4.5	0.25

Small units are often used to avoid decimals. However, it is sometimes easier to think about lengths given in meters. Change the following dimensions to meters.

B **21.** 374 cm by 520 cm   **22.** 425 cm by 650 cm

23. 4675 mm by 7050 mm   **24.** 5925 mm by 8275 mm

Rewrite each measurement using a unit that will avoid decimals.

25. 2.7 cm   **26.** 4.32 km   **27.** 0.65 m   **28.** 10.6 cm

For Exercises 29–32 use the following diagram and information.

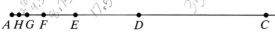

$A\ H\ G\ F\quad E\qquad\qquad D\qquad\qquad\qquad C\qquad\qquad\qquad\qquad\qquad\qquad\qquad B$

C is the midpoint of $\overline{AB}$; D is the midpoint of $\overline{AC}$;
E is the midpoint of $\overline{AD}$; F is the midpoint of $\overline{AE}$;
G is the midpoint of $\overline{AF}$; H is the midpoint of $\overline{AG}$.

C **29.** If $AB = 140$ mm, $AH = \underline{\ ?\ }$ mm.   **30.** If $BC = 70$ mm, $AF = \underline{\ ?\ }$ mm.

31. If $AG = 4.375$ mm, $AD = \underline{\ ?\ }$ mm.   **32.** If $FE = 8.75$ mm, $DC = \underline{\ ?\ }$ mm.

Review Exercises

Solve.

1. $x + 90 = 180$ **2.** $x + 20 = 90$ **3.** $x + 35 = 75$

4. $100 - x = 45$ **5.** $180 - x = 40$ **6.** $90 - x = 30$

7. $75 + x = 180$ **8.** $180 - x = 115$ **9.** $25 + x = 90$

4-3 Angles and Angle Measure

An **angle** is a figure formed by two rays with the same endpoint. The common endpoint is called the **vertex,** and the rays are called the **sides.**

We may name an angle by giving its vertex letter if this is the only angle with that vertex, or by listing letters for points on the two sides with the vertex letter in the middle. We use the symbol $\angle$ for *angle*. The diagram at the right shows several ways of naming an angle.

Angle *A*, angle *BAC*, or angle *CAB*
$\angle A$, $\angle BAC$,   or $\angle CAB$

To measure segments we used a ruler marked off in unit lengths. To measure angles, we use a **protractor** that is marked off in units of angle measure, called **degrees.** To use a protractor, place its center point at the vertex of the angle to be measured and one of its zero points on a side. In the drawing at the left below we use the outer scale and read the measure of $\angle E$ to be 60 degrees (60°). We write m $\angle E = 60°$.

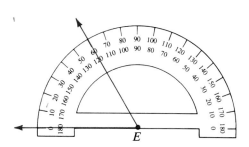 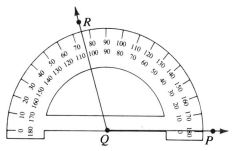

In the drawing on the right above the inner scale shows that m $\angle PQR = 105°$.

We often label angles with their measures, as shown in the figures. Since $\angle A$ and $\angle B$ have equal measures we can write m $\angle A =$ m $\angle B$. We say that $\angle A$ and $\angle B$ are **congruent angles** and we write $\angle A \cong \angle B$.

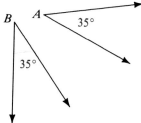

If two lines intersect so that the angles they form are all congruent, the lines are **perpendicular.** We use the symbol $\perp$ to mean *is perpendicular to.* In the figure $\overline{WY} \perp \overline{XZ}$.

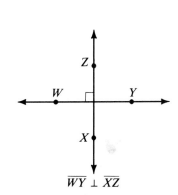

$\overline{WY} \perp \overline{XZ}$

Angles formed by perpendicular lines each have measure 90°. A 90° angle is called a **right angle.** A small square is often used to indicate a right angle in a diagram.

An **acute angle** is an angle with measure less than 90°. An **obtuse angle** has measure between 90° and 180°.

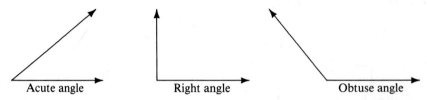

Acute angle   Right angle   Obtuse angle

Two angles are **complementary** if the sum of their measures is 90°. Two angles are **supplementary** if the sum of their measures is 180°.

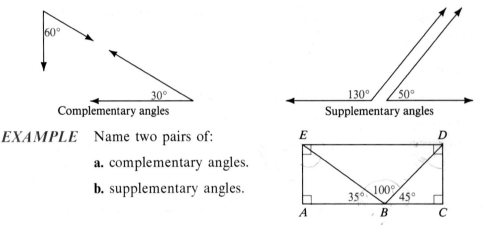

Complementary angles   Supplementary angles

EXAMPLE   Name two pairs of:

    a. complementary angles.

    b. supplementary angles.

Solution   **a.** Since $\angle AEB$ and $\angle BED$ form a right angle, they are complementary. Similarly, $\angle CDB$ and $\angle BDE$ are complementary.

    b. Since the sum of m$\angle ABE$ and m$\angle EBC$ is 180°, they are supplementary. Similarly, $\angle ABD$ and $\angle DBC$ are supplementary.

Although the sides of angles are rays, we often show the sides as segments, as in the figure for the example.

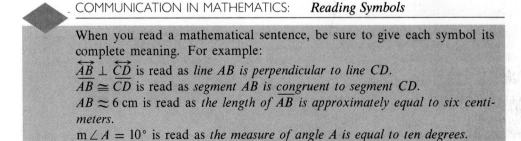

COMMUNICATION IN MATHEMATICS: *Reading Symbols*

When you read a mathematical sentence, be sure to give each symbol its complete meaning. For example:

$\overleftrightarrow{AB} \perp \overleftrightarrow{CD}$ is read as *line AB is perpendicular to line CD.*

$\overline{AB} \cong \overline{CD}$ is read as *segment AB is congruent to segment CD.*

$AB \approx 6$ cm is read as *the length of $\overline{AB}$ is approximately equal to six centimeters.*

m$\angle A = 10°$ is read as *the measure of angle A is equal to ten degrees.*

Class Exercises

1. If an angle is named ∠ *EFG*, its vertex is __?__.

2. If an angle is named ∠ *GEF*, its vertex is __?__.

Give three names for each angle.

3.
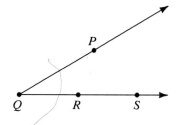

4.
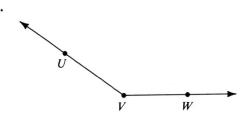

5. Use a protractor to find the measures of the angles in Exercises 3 and 4.

Exercises 6–9 refer to the diagram at the right.

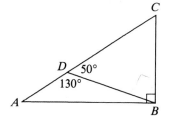

6. Name five acute angles and one obtuse angle.

7. Name a pair of perpendicular segments.

8. Name a pair of complementary angles.

9. Name a pair of supplementary angles.

State the measures of the complement and supplement of each angle.

10. m∠*F* = 70°   11. m∠*G* = 15°   12. m∠*H* = 45°   13. m∠*J* = 60°

Written Exercises

Use a protractor to draw an angle having the given measure.

A   1. 75°   2. 20°   3. 120°   4. 155°

Use a protractor to measure the given angle. State whether the angle is acute or obtuse.

5.
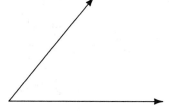

6.
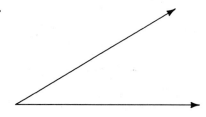

Measure the given angle. Is the angle acute or obtuse?

7.

8.

Copy and complete the table.

	9.	10.	11.	12.	13.	14.
$\angle X$	43°	9°	135°	?	?	?
Complement of $\angle X$	?	?	✕	12°	71°	?
Supplement of $\angle X$	?	?	?	?	?	150°

Use a protractor to draw an angle congruent to the angle in each given exercise.

15. Exercise 5   **16.** Exercise 6   **17.** Exercise 7   **18.** Exercise 8

Exercises 19–22 refer to the diagram at the right.

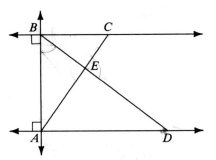

19. Name two pairs of perpendicular lines.

20. Name two pairs of complementary angles.

21. Name two pairs of supplementary angles.

22. What is the sum of the measures of the four angles having vertex E?

Angles that share a common vertex and a common side, but with no common points in their interiors, are called *adjacent angles*.

B **23.** Draw two adjacent complementary angles, one of which has measure 65°.

24. Draw two adjacent supplementary angles, one of which has measure 105°.

25. Draw two congruent adjacent supplementary angles. What is the measure of each?

26. Draw two congruent adjacent complementary angles. What is the measure of each?

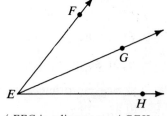

$\angle FEG$ is adjacent to $\angle GEH$
$\angle FEG$ is *not* adjacent to $\angle FEH$

True or false?

27. The supplement of an obtuse angle is acute.

28. The complement of an acute angle is obtuse.

C **29.** Measure the angles labeled 1, 2, 3, and 4. What general fact do your results suggest about angles formed by intersecting lines?

30. Measure the angles labeled 1, 2, 3, and 4. What general facts do your results suggest about two parallel lines intersected by a third line?

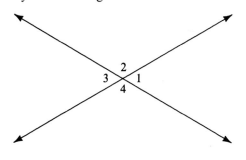

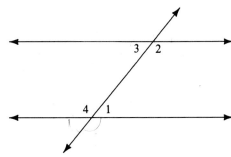

Self-Test A

Draw a sketch to illustrate each of the following.

 1. $\overline{CD}$ **2.** $\overleftrightarrow{AX}$ **3.** $\overrightarrow{RS}$ [4-1]

Exercises 4–7 refer to the diagram below.

 4. two parallel lines

 5. two parallel planes

 6. two intersecting lines

 7. two intersecting planes

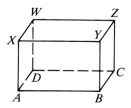

Complete each statement.

 8. 4000 m = _?_ km   **9.** 87 cm = _?_ m   [4-2]

10. 785 mm = _?_ m   **11.** 109 mm = _?_ cm

12. If M is the midpoint of $\overline{AB}$, then $AM =$ _?_ and $\overline{AM} \cong$ _?_ .

13. A right angle has measure _?_ .   [4-3]

14. Two angles with the same measures are _?_ .

15. ⊥ is the symbol for _?_ .

16. A 37° angle is a(n) _?_ angle.

17. The complement of a 42° angle has measure _?_ °.

18. The supplement of a 107° angle has measure _?_ °.

Self-Test answers and Extra Practice are at the back of the book.

4-4 Triangles

A **triangle** is the figure formed when three points not on a line are joined by segments. The drawing at the right shows triangle *ABC*, written △*ABC*, having the segments $\overline{AB}$, $\overline{BC}$, and $\overline{CA}$ as its **sides.** Each of the points *A*, *B*, and *C* is called a **vertex** (plural: *vertices*) of △*ABC*. Each of the angles ∠*A*, ∠*B*, and ∠*C* is called an **angle** of △*ABC*.

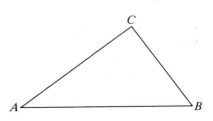

Suppose *A*, *B*, and *C* in the triangle above represent three points on a map. Do you think it is farther to travel from *A* to *B* and then to *C* or to travel directly from *A* to *C*? Measure to check. This illustrates the first fact about triangles stated below.

> In any triangle:
>
> **1.** The sum of the lengths of any two sides is greater than the length of the third side.
>
> **2.** The sum of the measures of the angles is 180°.

You can verify the second fact by tearing off the corners of any paper triangle and fitting them together as shown at the right.

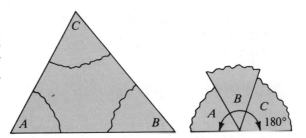

EXAMPLE 1   One angle of a triangle measures 40° and the other two angles have equal measures. Find the measures of the congruent angles.

Solution   The sum of the measures of the angles of a triangle is 180°. The sum of the measures of the congruent angles must be 180° − 40°, or 140°. Therefore each of the two congruent angles has measure 70°.

◆ PROBLEM SOLVING REMINDER
_____

Some problems do not give enough information. Sometimes you must *supply previously learned facts.* In the example above, you need to supply the additional information about the sum of the measures of the angles of a triangle.

There are several ways to name triangles. One way is by angles.

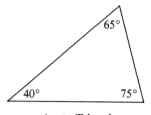

Acute Triangle
Three acute angles

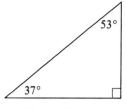

Right Triangle
One right angle

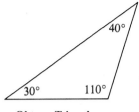

Obtuse Triangle
One obtuse angle

Triangles can also be classified by their sides.

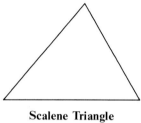

Scalene Triangle
No two sides
congruent

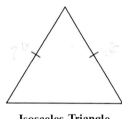

Isosceles Triangle
At least two sides
congruent

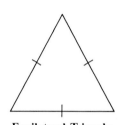

Equilateral Triangle
All three sides
congruent

As you might expect, the longest side of a tri-angle is opposite the largest angle, and the shortest side is opposite the smallest angle. Two angles are congruent if and only if the sides opposite them are congruent.

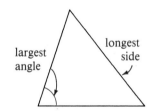

EXAMPLE 2   Classify each triangle by sides and by angles.

a.

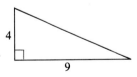

b.

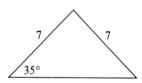

Solution

a. No two sides are congruent; the triangle is scalene.
There is one right angle; the triangle is a right triangle.
Scalene right triangle

b. Two sides are congruent; the triangle is isosceles.
The angles opposite the congruent sides are congruent; thus, the third angle has a measure of 110°; the triangle is obtuse.
Isosceles obtuse triangle

Class Exercises

How do you know, without measuring, that these triangles are labeled incorrectly?

1.
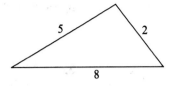

2.
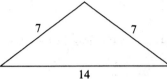

3.
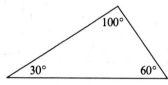

4.
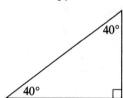

Exercises 5 and 6 refer to the triangles below.

a.

b.

c.
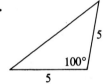

d.

5. Classify each triangle by sides.

6. Classify each triangle by angles.

7. Explain how you know that a triangle with two congruent angles is isosceles.

8. Explain how you know that a triangle with three congruent angles is equilateral.

Exercises 9–13 refer to the diagram at the right.

9. What segment is a common side of △ADC and △BCD?

10. What segment is a common side of △ABC and △BCD?

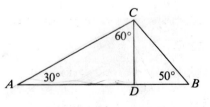

11. What angle is common to △ABC and △CAD?

12. Name two right triangles.

13. Name an obtuse triangle.

Written Exercises

The measures of two angles of a triangle are given. Find the measure of the third angle.

A **1.** 40°, 60°   **2.** 15°, 105°   **3.** 35°, 55°   **4.** 160°, 10°

Classify each triangle by its sides.

5. 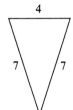   **6.** 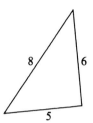   **7.** 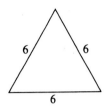   **8.**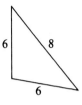

Classify each triangle by its sides and by its angles.

9. 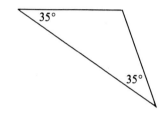   **10.**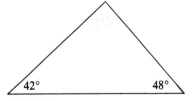

11. 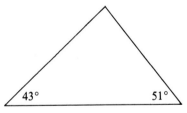   **12.**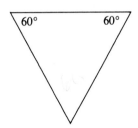

Exercises 13–16 refer to the diagram at the right.

13. Name three right triangles.

14. Name an isosceles triangle.

15. Name an acute scalene triangle.

16. Name an obtuse triangle.

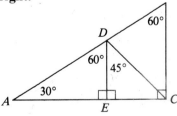

17. Use a ruler and a protractor to draw (a) a scalene acute triangle and (b) an isosceles obtuse triangle.

18. Use a ruler and a protractor to draw (a) a scalene obtuse triangle and (b) an isosceles acute triangle.

B **19.** What measures do the angles of an equilateral triangle have?

20. One of the congruent angles of an isosceles triangle has measure 40°. What measures do the other angles have?

21. One of the acute angles of a right triangle measures 75°. What measure does the other acute angle have?

22. What measures do the angles of an isosceles right triangle have?

23. An isosceles triangle has a 96° angle. What are the measures of its other angles?

24. An isosceles triangle has a 60° angle. What are the measures of its other angles?

25. One acute angle of a right triangle is 45°. What relationship, if any, is there between the two shorter sides?

26. Why is it not possible to have an equilateral right triangle?

C **27.** In $\triangle ABC$, $AB = 8$ and $BC = 5$. Then (a) $AC < \underline{\ ?\ }$, and (b) $AC > \underline{\ ?\ }$.

28. In $\triangle PQR$, $PR = 10$ and $RQ = 7$. Then (a) $PQ < \underline{\ ?\ }$, and (b) $PQ > \underline{\ ?\ }$.

29. Explain why in any triangle the difference of the lengths of any two sides cannot be greater than the length of the third side.

30. Draw a triangle. Draw rays that divide each of its angles into two congruent angles. Do this for several triangles of different shapes. What seems always to be true of the three rays?

31. Draw a triangle. Then draw segments joining each vertex to the midpoint of the opposite side. (These segments are called **medians** of the triangle.) Do this for several triangles of different shapes. What seems always to be truc?

Review Exercises

Add.

1. $3.75 + 4.92 + 6.41$
2. $7.83 + 6.91 + 5.29$
3. $8.36 + 4.95 + 2.21$
4. $5.3 + 6.21 + 7.3$
5. $8.02 + 5.1 + 7.21$
6. $3.07 + 4 + 5.93$
7. $11.27 + 6.513 + 4.09$
8. $10.03 + 5.7 + 4.93$
9. $12.004 + 4.9 + 7.864$

4-5 Polygons

A **polygon** is a closed figure formed by joining segments (**sides** of the polygon) at their endpoints (**vertices** of the polygon). We name polygons according to the number of sides they have.

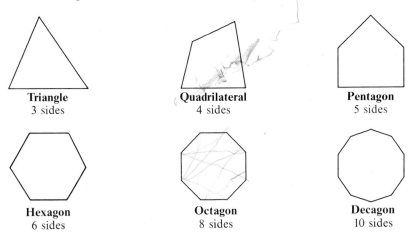

| Triangle | Quadrilateral | Pentagon |
| 3 sides | 4 sides | 5 sides |

| Hexagon | Octagon | Decagon |
| 6 sides | 8 sides | 10 sides |

A polygon is **regular** if all its sides are congruent and all its angles are congruent. As drawn above, the hexagon, the octagon, and the decagon are regular while the triangle, the quadrilateral, and the pentagon are not.

To name a polygon, we name its consecutive vertices in order. The quadrilateral shown at the right may be named quadrilateral $PQRS$.

A **diagonal** of a polygon is a segment joining two nonconsecutive vertices. Thus, $\overline{PR}$ and $\overline{QS}$ are the diagonals of quadrilateral $PQRS$.

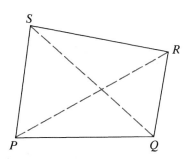

Certain quadrilaterals have special names.

A **parallelogram** has its opposite sides parallel and congruent.

A **trapezoid** has just one pair of parallel sides.

Certain parallelograms also have special names.

A **rhombus** has all its sides congruent.　　A **square** has congruent sides and congruent angles.　　A **rectangle** has all its angles congruent.

COMMUNICATION IN MATHEMATICS: *Vocabulary*

Many terms in mathematics have definitions with more than one condition. Be certain to read and learn the full definition. For example, a polygon is regular if (1) all its sides are congruent and (2) all its angles are congruent. Because the rhombus shown above does not meet condition 2, it is not a regular polygon. The square meets both conditions, so it is regular.

The **perimeter** of a figure is the distance around it. Thus, the perimeter of a polygon is the sum of the lengths of its sides.

EXAMPLE　Find the perimeter of each polygon.

a.
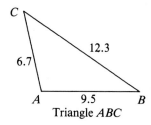
Triangle *ABC*

b.
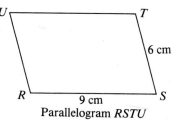
Parallelogram *RSTU*

Solution　**a.** Perimeter $= 9.5 + 12.3 + 6.7 = 28.5$

b. Because opposite sides of a parallelogram are congruent, the unlabeled sides have lengths 9 cm and 6 cm. Therefore:

$$\text{Perimeter} = (9 + 6 + 9 + 6)\text{ cm} = 30\text{ cm}$$

Class Exercises

Name each polygon according to the number of sides.

1.
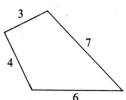

2.
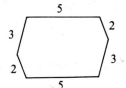

Name each polygon according to the number of sides.

3.

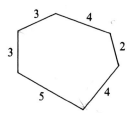

4.

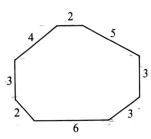

5–8. Find the perimeter of each polygon in Exercises 1–4.

9–12. State the number of diagonals that can be drawn from any one vertex of each figure in Exercises 1–4.

Give the most special name for each quadrilateral.

13.

Four congruent sides
Four congruent angles

14.

Four congruent angles

15.

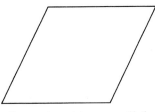

Opposite sides parallel
and congruent

16.

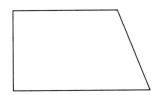

One pair of parallel sides

Written Exercises

Name the polygon having the given number of sides.

A **1.** 5   **2.** 4   **3.** 6   **4.** 10   **5.** 3   **6.** 8

7. What is another name for a regular quadrilateral?

8. What is another name for a regular triangle?

Find the perimeter of each pentagon.

9.

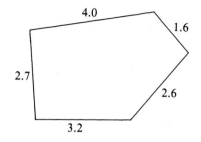

10.

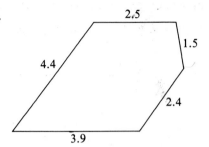

Find the perimeter of a regular polygon whose sides have the given length.

11. Hexagon, 52 cm

12. Pentagon, 43 mm

13. Triangle, 24.2 mm

14. Quadrilateral, 16.5 m

15. Decagon, 135.6 m

16. Octagon, 4.25 m

17. The sum of the measures of the angles of a pentagon is 540°. Find the measure of each angle of a regular pentagon.

18. The sum of the measures of the angles of a hexagon is 720°. Find the measure of each angle of a regular hexagon.

19. A STOP sign is a regular octagon 32 cm on a side. Express its perimeter in meters.

20. The Pentagon building in Washington, D.C., is in the form of a regular pentagon 276 m on a side. Express its perimeter in kilometers.

21. The perimeter of a regular pentagon is 60 m. How long is each side?

Exercises 22–24 refer to the hexagon at the right. The shorter sides are half as long as the longer sides.

22. Each shorter side is 3.2 cm long. What is the perimeter?

23. How many diagonals can be drawn from vertex A?

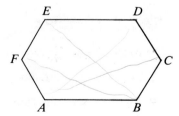

B 24. How many diagonals are there in all?

Use a protractor and a ruler for Exercises 25 and 26. The sum of the measures of the angles of a hexagon is 720°.

25. Draw a hexagon that is not regular, but has all its angles congruent.

26. Draw a hexagon that is not regular, but has all its sides congruent.

27. In the diagram below, $ABDE$ is a rhombus and $\angle DBC \cong \angle DCB$. Find the perimeter of trapezoid $ACDE$.

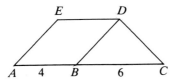

For Exercises 28 and 29 draw several polygons with different numbers of sides. Pick a vertex and draw all the diagonals from this vertex.

28. Count the number of triangles formed by the diagonals. How does the number of triangles compare to the number of sides of each polygon?

29. If the sum of the measures of the angles of the triangles formed equals the sum of the measures of the angles of the polygon, find the sum of the measures of the angles of the following.
   a. quadrilateral   **b.** decagon   **c.** trapezoid   **d.** octagon

C 30. Write a general formula for the sum of the measures of the angles of any polygon with n sides. (*Hint:* See Exercises 28 and 29.)

31. Every pentagon has the same number of diagonals. How many? (*Hint:* First decide how many diagonals can be drawn from one vertex.)

32. Every octagon has the same number of diagonals. How many? (See the hint for Exercise 31.)

Review Exercises

Evaluate if $a = 7$, $b = 3.2$, and $c = 5.45$.

   1. ab **2.** ac **3.** a^2 **4.** $15b$

   5. $2c$ **6.** $2bc$ **7.** $2ab$ **8.** abc

4-6 Circles

A **circle** is the set of all points in a plane at a given distance from a given point O called the **center.** The drawing at the right shows how to use a **compass** to draw a circle with center O.

A segment, such as $\overline{OP}$, joining the center to a point on the circle is called a **radius** (plural: *radii*) of the circle. All radii of a given circle have the same length, and this length is called **the radius** of the circle.

A segment, such as $\overline{XY}$, joining two points on a circle is called a **chord,** and a chord passing through the center is a **diameter** of the circle. The ends of a diameter divide the circle into two **semicircles.** The length of a diameter is called **the diameter** of the circle.

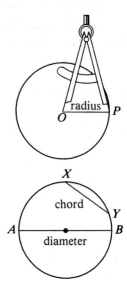

The perimeter of a circle is called the **circumference.** The quotient

$$\text{circumference} \div \text{diameter}$$

can be shown to be the same for all circles, regardless of their size. This quotient is denoted by the Greek letter π (pronounced "pie"). No decimal gives π exactly, but a fairly good approximation is 3.14.

If we denote the circumference by C and the diameter by d, we can write

$$C \div d = \pi.$$

This formula can be put into several useful forms.

Formulas

Let $C = $ circumference, $d = $ diameter, and $r = $ radius $(d = 2r)$. Then:

$$C = \pi d \qquad d = C \div \pi$$

$$C = 2\pi r \qquad r = C \div (2\pi)$$

EXAMPLE 1 The diameter of a circle is 6 cm. Find the circumference.

Solution We are given d and asked to find C. We use the formula $C = \pi d$.

$$C = \pi d$$
$$C \approx 3.14 \times 6 = 18.84$$
$$C \approx 18.8 \text{ cm, or } 188 \text{ mm}$$

When using the approximation $\pi \approx 3.14$, give your answer to only three digits (as in Example 1) because the approximation is good only to three digits. That is, we round to the place occupied by the third digit from the left.

EXAMPLE 2 The circumference of a circle is 20. Find the radius.

Solution   To find the radius, use the formula $r = C \div (2\pi)$.
$$r = C \div (2\pi)$$
$$r \approx 20 \div (2 \times 3.14) \approx 3.1847$$

Since the third digit from the left is in the hundredths' place, round to the nearest hundredth. Thus, $r \approx 3.18$.

A polygon is **inscribed** in a circle if all of its vertices are on the circle. The diagram at the right shows a triangle inscribed in a circle.

It can be shown that three points *not on a line* determine a circle. This means that there is one circle, and only one circle, that passes through the three given points.

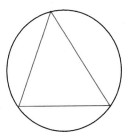

Class Exercises

Exercises 1–5 refer to the diagram below. *B* is the center of the circle. Name each of the following.

1. a diameter

2. three radii

3. five chords

4. two inscribed triangles

5. two isosceles triangles

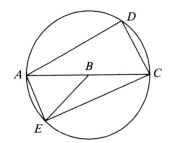

Exercises 6–8 refer to the diagram above.

6. If $BE = 8$, find AC.   **7.** If $AC = 10$, find AB.

8. If $BC = 20$, find the circumference of the circle.

Draw a circle and an inscribed polygon of the specified kind.

9. a pentagon   **10.** a hexagon   **11.** an octagon

Written Exercises

Use $\pi \approx 3.14$ and round to three digits.

Find the circumference of each circle with the given diameter or radius.

A   **1.** diameter = 8 cm   **2.** diameter = 20 km

      3. radius = 450 mm   **4.** radius = 16 cm

      5. diameter = 42.6 m   **6.** radius = 278 mm

Find the diameter of each circle.

      7. circumference = 283 m   **8.** circumference = 175 cm

      9. circumference = 450 km   **10.** circumference = 468 mm

    11. circumference = 625 m   **12.** circumference = 180 km

Find the radius of each circle.

   13. circumference = 10 mm   **14.** circumference = 20 m

   15. circumference = 23.5 km   **16.** circumference = 33.3 km

   17. circumference = 17.5 cm   **18.** circumference = 27.2 m

19. The equator of Earth is approximately a circle of radius 6378 km. What is the circumference of Earth at the equator? Use the approximation $\pi \approx 3.1416$ and give your answer to five digits.

20. A park near Cristi's home contains a circular pool with a fountain at the center. Cristi paced off the distance around the pool and found it to be 220 m. How far is the fountain from the edge of the pool?

21. The diameter of a circular lake is measured and found to be 15 km. What is the circumference of the lake?

22. It is 45 m from the center of a circular field to the inside edge of the track surrounding it. The distance from the center of the field to the outside edge is 55 m. Find the circumference of each edge.

B **23.** One circle has a radius of 15 m and a second has a radius of 30 m. How much larger is the circumference of the larger circle?

The curves in the diagrams below are parts of circles, and the angles are right angles. Find the perimeter of each figure.

24.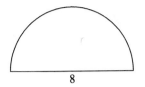
8

25.
10

26.
4
4

27.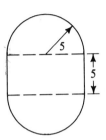
5
5

28.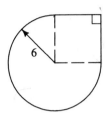
6

29.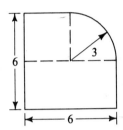
6
3
6

30. Find a formula that expresses the length, S, of a semicircle in terms of the radius, r.

31. Find a formula that expresses the length, S, of a semicircle in terms of the diameter, d.

In Exercises 32 and 33 use the fact that three points not on a line determine a circle.

32. Every triangle can be inscribed in some circle. Explain why this is so.

33. Explain how to draw a quadrilateral that cannot be inscribed in any circle.

C **34.** What is the radius of the semicircle that forms the curve of a 400 meter track if each straightaway is 116 m long?

35. Draw a circle and one of its diameters, $\overline{AB}$. Then draw and measure $\angle APB$, where P is a point on the circle. Repeat this for several positions of P. What does this experiment suggest?

Review Exercises

Simplify.

1. $6 + 4 \times 3$ **2.** $16 \div 2 + 2$ **3.** $3(4 + 5)$ **4.** $8(7 - 3)$

5. $64 \div (2 + 6)$ **6.** $(18 + 3)2$ **7.** $14 + 3 \times 2 - 6$ **8.** $52 - 18 \div 3 + 16$

Geometric Figures **131**

4-7 Congruent Figures

Two figures are **congruent** if they have the same size and shape. Triangles ABC and XYZ shown below are congruent.

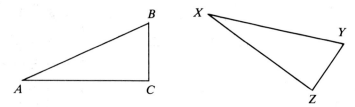

If we could lift $\triangle ABC$ and place it on $\triangle XYZ$, A would fall on X, B on Y, and C on Z. These matching vertices are called **corresponding vertices.** Angles at corresponding vertices are **corresponding angles,** and the sides joining corresponding vertices are **corresponding sides.**

> Corresponding angles of congruent figures are congruent.
>
> Corresponding sides of congruent figures are congruent.

When we name two congruent figures, we list corresponding vertices in the same order. Thus, when we see

$$\triangle ABC \cong \triangle XYZ \quad \text{or} \quad \triangle CAB \cong \triangle ZXY,$$

we know that:

$$\angle A \cong \angle X, \qquad \angle B \cong \angle Y, \qquad \angle C \cong \angle Z$$
$$\overline{AB} \cong \overline{XY}, \qquad \overline{BC} \cong \overline{YZ}, \qquad \overline{CA} \cong \overline{ZX}$$

EXAMPLE 1 pentagon $PQUVW \cong$ pentagon $LMHKT$

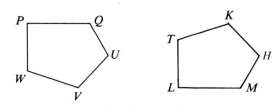

Complete these statements:

$$\angle W \cong \angle \underline{\ ?\ } \qquad \overline{QU} \cong \underline{\ ?\ } \qquad \angle H \cong \angle \underline{\ ?\ } \qquad \overline{TL} \cong \underline{\ ?\ }$$

Solution $\angle W \cong \angle T \qquad \overline{QU} \cong \overline{MH} \qquad \angle H \cong \angle U \qquad \overline{TL} \cong \overline{WP}$

If two figures are congruent, we can make them coincide (occupy the same place) by using one or more of these basic **rigid motions:**

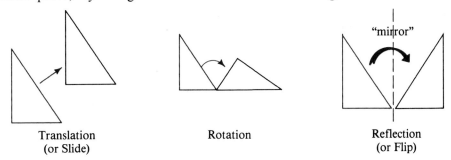

Translation
(or Slide)

Rotation

Reflection
(or Flip)

Consider the congruent trapezoids in panel (1) below. We can make $ABCD$ coincide with $PQRS$ by first reflecting $ABCD$ in the line $\overleftrightarrow{BC}$ as in panel (2), and then translating this reflection as shown in panel (3).

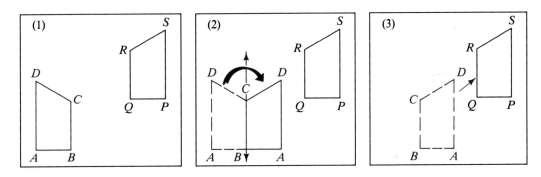

EXAMPLE 2 What type of rigid motion would make the red figure coincide with the black one?

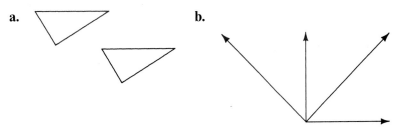

Solution

a. a translation: sliding the red triangle down and to the right would make it coincide with the black triangle

b. a rotation or a reflection: rotating the red angle around the vertex would make it coincide with the black angle; flipping the red angle over a line passing through the vertex would also make it coincide with the black angle

Geometric Figures **133**

Class Exercises

Each figure in Exercises 1–8 is congruent to one of the figures A – E. State which one.

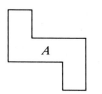

1.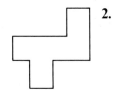
2.
3.
4.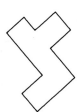

5.
6.
7.
8.

Complete the statements about each pair of congruent figures.

9.

a. △ MNO ≅ ___?___
b. ∠N ≅ _?_
c. $\overline{MO}$ ≅ _?_

10.

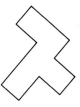

a. Quadrilateral HKLM ≅ ___?___
b. ∠B ≅ _?_
c. $\overline{HM}$ ≅ _?_

Name the kind of rigid motion that would make the red figure coincide with the black one.

11.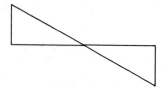

12.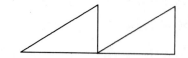

Written Exercises

Which statement is correct?

A **1.**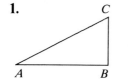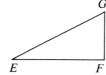

     a. $\triangle BCA \cong \triangle GEF$
     b. $\triangle ABC \cong \triangle EGF$
     c. $\triangle BCA \cong \triangle FGE$

2.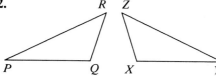

     a. $\triangle PQR \cong \triangle XYZ$
     b. $\triangle QRP \cong \triangle XZY$
     c. $\triangle PQR \cong \triangle XZY$

3.

     a. quad. $ABCD \cong$ quad. $WXYZ$
     b. quad. $CBAD \cong$ quad. $WXYZ$
     c. quad. $ABCD \cong$ quad. $XYZW$

4.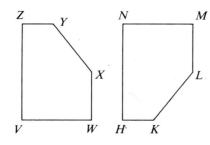

     a. pentagon $WXYZV \cong$ pentagon $MLKHN$
     b. pentagon $VWXYZ \cong$ pentagon $NMKLH$
     c. pentagon $XYZVW \cong$ pentagon $LMNHK$

Complete each statement about the figures in the given exercise.

5. Exercise 1.   **a.** $\triangle CBA \cong$ ___?___   **b.** $\angle C \cong$ _?_   **c.** $\overline{GE} \cong$ _?_

6. Exercise 2.   **a.** $\triangle ZYX \cong$ ___?___   **b.** $\angle X \cong$ _?_   **c.** $\overline{PQ} \cong$ _?_

7. Exercise 3.   **a.** quadrilateral $ADCB \cong$ ___?___   **b.** $\angle Z \cong$ _?_   **c.** $\overline{BC} \cong$ _?_

8. Exercise 4.   **a.** pentagon $XYZVW \cong$ ___?___   **b.** $\angle X \cong$ _?_   **c.** $\overline{VW} \cong$ _?_

What type of rigid motion would make the red figure coincide with the black one?

9.

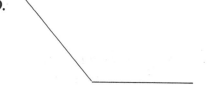

10.

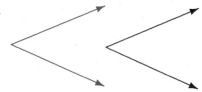

11.

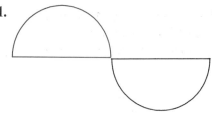

12.

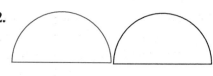

True or false?

B 13. Two segments are congruent if they have equal lengths.

14. Two angles are congruent if they have equal measures.

15. Two triangles are congruent if they have equal perimeters.

16. Two circles are congruent if they have equal circumferences.

17. Two squares are congruent if they have equal perimeters.

18. Two rectangles are congruent if they have equal perimeters.

19. If $\triangle GHK \cong \triangle RST$, which of the following are true?
    a. $\triangle RST \cong \triangle GHK$ **b.** $\triangle GHK \cong \triangle STR$ **c.** $\triangle HKG \cong \triangle STR$

20. If $DAMP \cong BING$, which of the following are true?
    a. $INGB \cong AMPD$ **b.** $PMAD \cong GNIB$ **c.** $ADPM \cong IBGN$

Complete each statement.

21. $\triangle XRL \cong \triangle NYS$
    a. $\angle X \cong$?   **b.** $\angle R \cong$?   **c.** $\overline{XL} \cong$?   **d.** $\overline{YS} \cong$?

22. $PQTV \cong HJKM$
    a. $\angle Q \cong$?   **b.** $\angle M \cong$?   **c.** $\overline{VP} \cong$?   **d.** $\overline{JK} \cong$?

23. $ABCD \cong EFGH$
    a. $\overline{BC} \cong$?   **b.** $\overline{AD} \cong$?   **c.** $\angle ABC \cong$?   **d.** $\overline{GH} \cong$?

24. $WXYZ \cong LMNP$
    a. $\overline{ZY} \cong$?   **b.** $\overline{XY} \cong$?   **c.** $\angle XYZ \cong$?   **d.** $\overline{PL} \cong$?

C 25. *ABCDEF* is a regular hexagon. If all the diagonals from *F* are drawn, name the following.
   a. all pairs of congruent triangles formed
   b. a pair of congruent quadrilaterals
   c. a pair of congruent pentagons

26. Let $\overline{AB}$ and $\overline{PQ}$ be corresponding sides of two congruent polygons. If one polygon is moved so that $\overline{AB}$ falls on $\overline{PQ}$, must the two polygons coincide?

27. Draw a large triangle. Measure the sides. Draw a second triangle using the same lengths for sides. Do the triangles appear to be congruent? Repeat the exercise for several more triangles. Give a general rule that appears to be true.

28. Draw a large triangle. Measure two sides and the angle that they form. Draw a second triangle using the same lengths and the same angle measure. Do the triangles appear to be congruent? Repeat the exercise for several more triangles. Give a general rule that appears to be true.

29. Draw a large triangle. Measure two angles and the side between them. Draw a second triangle using the same angle measures and the same length side. Do the triangles appear to be congruent? Repeat the exercise for several more triangles. Give a general rule that appears to be true.

Review Exercises

Solve.

1. $6x = 42$	**2.** $5x = 50$	**3.** $y \times 4 = 44$	**4.** $y \times 7 = 56$
5. $x \div 9 = 8$	**6.** $x \div 11 = 6$	**7.** $84 \div y = 21$	**8.** $65 \div y = 13$

▪▪▪ **CALCULATOR INVESTIGATION:** *Approximations for* π

Many ancient civilizations used approximations for π. Use a calculator to determine the following approximations for π as decimals. Which approximation is closest to the modern approximation of 3.14159265358?

1. Egyptian: $\frac{256}{81}$

2. Greek: $\frac{223}{71}$

3. Roman: $\frac{377}{120}$

4. Chinese: $\frac{355}{113}$

5. Hindu: $\frac{3927}{1250}$

6. Babylonian: $\frac{25}{8}$

4-8 Geometric Constructions

There is a difference between making a drawing and a **geometric construction.** For drawings, we may measure segments and angles; that is, we may use a ruler and a protractor to draw the figures. For geometric constructions, however, we may use only a compass and a straightedge. (We may use a ruler, but we must ignore the markings.)

Here are some important constructions. Construction I and Construction II involve dividing a segment or angle into two congruent parts. This process is called **bisecting** the segment or the angle.

Construction I: To bisect a segment $\overline{AB}$.

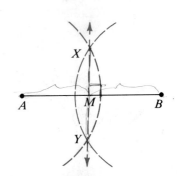

Use the compass to draw an arc (part of a circle) with center A and radius greater than $\frac{1}{2}AB$. Using the same radius but with center B, draw another arc. Call the points of intersection X and Y. $\overleftrightarrow{XY}$ is the **perpendicular bisector** of $\overline{AB}$ because it is perpendicular to $\overline{AB}$ and divides $\overline{AB}$ into two congruent segments.

Construction II: To bisect an angle BAC.

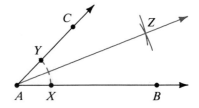

Draw an arc with center A. Let X and Y be the points where the arc intersects the sides of the angle. Draw arcs of equal radii with centers X and Y. Call the point of intersection Z. $\overrightarrow{AZ}$ is the **angle bisector** of $\angle BAC$, and $\angle CAZ \cong \angle ZAB$.

Construction III: To construct an angle congruent to a given angle Y.

Draw $\overrightarrow{MN}$. Draw an arc on $\angle Y$ with center Y. Let X and Z be the points where the arc intersects the sides of the angle. Draw an arc with center M and the same radius as arc XZ. Let S be the point where this arc intersects $\overrightarrow{MN}$. Call the other end of the arc R. With S as center draw an arc with radius equal to XZ. Let Q be the point where this arc intersects arc RS. Draw $\overrightarrow{MQ}$. $\angle NMQ \cong \angle Y$.

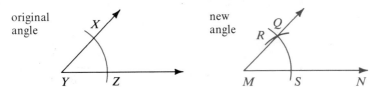

EXAMPLE 1   Construct a line that is perpendicular to $\overleftrightarrow{AB}$ and contains A.

Solution

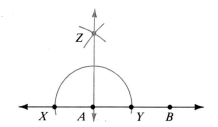

1. Place the compass at point A and draw an arc intersecting $\overleftrightarrow{AB}$ at two points. Call these two points X and Y, respectively. A is now the midpoint of $\overline{XY}$.

2. Place the compass at X and, as in Construction I, draw an arc with radius greater than $\overline{YA}$. Keeping the same radius, place the compass at Y and draw a second arc that intersects the first arc. Call the point of intersection of the two arcs Z.

3. Draw $\overleftrightarrow{AZ}$. Since $\overleftrightarrow{AZ}$ is the perpendicular bisector of $\overline{XY}$, and thus perpendicular to $\overleftrightarrow{AB}$, it is the required line.

EXAMPLE 2   Construct a 60° angle.

Solution

1. Draw a ray with endpoint A.

2. Draw an arc, with center A and any radius, intersecting the ray at B.

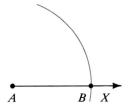

3. Draw an arc, with center B and the same radius as in step 2, intersecting the first arc at C.

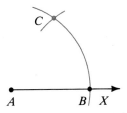

4. Draw $\overrightarrow{AC}$. Since $\triangle ABC$ is equilateral,   m $\angle BAC = 60°$.

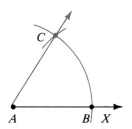

Written Exercises

In this exercise set use a compass and straightedge as your only construction tools.

A 1. Construct a 45° angle. (Method: Construct a right angle as in Example 1 and then bisect it.)

2. Construct a 30° angle. (Method: Construct a 60° angle as in Example 2 and then bisect it.)

3. Construct a 22.5° angle. (Use Exercise 1.)

4. Construct a 15° angle. (Use Exercise 2.)

5. Use a protractor to draw an angle with measure 75°. Construct an angle congruent to this angle.

6. Use a protractor to draw an angle with measure 130°. Construct an angle congruent to this angle.

7. Draw a large isosceles triangle. Using this triangle, construct the perpendicular bisector of the base. Through what point does the perpendicular bisector appear to pass?

8. Draw a large scalene triangle. Bisect its three angles. Are the angle bisectors **concurrent;** that is, do all three have a point in common?

9. Draw a large scalene triangle. Construct the perpendicular bisectors of its sides. Are these bisectors concurrent?

In Exercises 10 and 11, draw $\overleftrightarrow{ST}$ and a point P not on $\overleftrightarrow{ST}$.

B 10. Construct a line through P perpendicular to $\overleftrightarrow{ST}$. (Method: Draw an arc with center P to intersect $\overleftrightarrow{ST}$ in two points, A and B. Construct the perpendicular bisector of $\overline{AB}$.)

11. Construct a line through P parallel to $\overleftrightarrow{ST}$. (Method: 1. Construct $\overleftrightarrow{PQ}$ perpendicular to $\overleftrightarrow{ST}$ as in Exercise 10. 2. Construct $\overleftrightarrow{PR}$ perpendicular to $\overleftrightarrow{PQ}$ as in Example 1.)

12. Draw a large scalene triangle. A line through a vertex that is perpendicular to the opposite side is called an **altitude** of the triangle. Construct the three altitudes of the triangle (see Exercise 10). Are they concurrent?

13. Draw a large scalene triangle. A line through a vertex and the midpoint of the side opposite the vertex is called a **median** of the triangle. Construct the three medians (see Construction 1). Are they concurrent?

C 14. Draw three noncollinear points, A, B, and C. Construct the circle that passes through these points. (*Hint:* The perpendicular bisectors of $\overline{AB}$ and $\overline{BC}$ both pass through the center of the circle.)

15. Use a compass to construct a regular hexagon. (*Hint:* The length of each side of a regular hexagon inscribed in a circle equals the radius of the circle.)

Self-Test B

Complete each statement.

1. A triangle with three congruent sides is ___?___.   [4-4]

2. The sum of the measures of the angles of a triangle is __?__°.

3. An acute triangle has ___?___ acute angle(s).

4. A(n) ___?___ has eight sides.   [4-5]

5. A ___?___ has its opposite sides parallel and congruent.

6. A trapezoid has sides of 7 cm, 5 cm, 7 cm, and 14 cm. Find its perimeter.

7. The radius of a circle is 16 cm. Find its circumference. Use $\pi \approx 3.14$ and round to three digits.   [4-6]

True or false?

8. A diameter cuts a circle into two semicircles.

9. A radius is a chord.

10. Pentagon $ABCDE \cong$ Pentagon $FGHIJ$. Complete each statement.   [4-7]
    a. $\overline{AB} \cong$ __?__   **b.** $\angle E \cong \angle$ __?__   **c.** $\angle DEA \cong \angle$ __?__

11. Construct an isosceles right triangle.   [4-8]

12. Construct an equilateral triangle.

Self-Test answers and Extra Practice are at the back of the book.

■■■ **NONROUTINE PROBLEM SOLVING:** *Acting out the Problem*

You have your choice of your height in nickels that are stacked or in quarters that are laid side by side. Which would you choose?

More Programming in BASIC

In Chapter 2 we learned that to enter different values of a variable in BASIC we can use the INPUT statement.

To assign a value to a variable that will be repeated over and over again, we use the **LET** statement. For example, the statement

$$20 \quad \text{LET } K = 4037$$

assigns the value 4037 to the variable K. This statement tells the computer to store 4037 in its memory at location K. The value of a variable can be changed by assigning a new value. When we write

$$20 \quad \text{LET } K = 0.025$$

the original value, 4037, is replaced by the new value, 0.025.

The program below converts miles to kilometers by using the fact that 1 mi = 1.61 km.

```
10   PRINT "FROM MILES TO KILOMETERS"
20   PRINT "DISTANCE IN MILES";
30   INPUT X
40   LET A = 1.61
50   PRINT X;" MI = ";A*X;" KM"
60   END
```

Let us use the program to convert the approximate distance in miles from the planet Saturn to the Sun. That is, convert 887,000,000 mi to kilometers.

```
RUN
FROM MILES TO KILOMETERS
DISTANCE IN MILES? 887000000          do not use commas
887000000 MI = 1428070000 KM          to enter the distance
```

Use the program on the previous page to complete the table.

	Planet	Distance (in mi) from the Sun	Distance (in km) from the Sun
1.	Mercury	36,000,000	?
2.	Venus	67,000,000	?
3.	Earth	93,000,000	?

Instead of running the program three times, we can modify it to repeat lines 20 through 50 so that all three distances are converted in one RUN. To do this, we use the **FOR** and **NEXT** statements to create a *loop*. The loop starts with the FOR statement, and ends with the NEXT statement. These two statements tell the computer how many times to repeat a group of statements located between them. The program below is now modified to repeat the loop three times. The output for Exercises 1–3 is shown at the right.

```
10   PRINT "FROM MILES TO KILOMETERS"      RUN
15   FOR I = 1 TO 3                        FROM MILES TO KILOMETERS
20   PRINT "DISTANCE IN MILES";            DISTANCE IN MILES? 36000000
30   INPUT X                               36000000 MI = 57960000 KM
40   LET A = 1.61                          DISTANCE IN MILES? 67000000
50   PRINT X;" MI = ";A*X;" KM"            67000000 MI = 107870000 KM
55   NEXT I                                DISTANCE IN MILES? 93000000
60   END                                   93000000 MI = 149730000 KM
```

Depending on the computer you are using, the output displayed for the conversions above may be expressed in *scientific notation*. That is, a number such as 376770000 may be expressed as

$$3.7677E+08.$$

The code E+08 means "times 10 raised to the power of 8." Therefore

$$3.7677E+08 \text{ means } 3.7677 \times 10^8, \text{ or } 376770000.$$

Complete.

4. $37,492,000,000 = 3.7492E + \underline{\ ?\ }$

5. $5,491,000,000,000 = 5.491E + \underline{\ ?\ }$

6. $9.4678E+07 = \underline{\ ?\ }$

7. $3.2186E+10 = \underline{\ ?\ }$

8. Write a program to print out the multiples of 2 from one to ten.

9. Write a program to print out the distance traveled at a constant rate of 760 mi/h for 15, 27, 31, 40, and 55 hours. Use the formula $d = rt$.

Chapter Review

Complete.

1. Points on the same line are called ___?___.   [4-1]

2. A ___?___ has one endpoint.

3. Z divides $\overline{XY}$ into two congruent segments. Z is called the ___?___   [4-2]
   of $\overline{XY}$.

4. 927 mm = ___?___ cm = ___?___ m

True or false?

5. A right angle is obtuse.   [4-3]

6. In $\angle ABC$, A is the vertex.

7. The supplement of a 40° angle has measure 140°.

8. A triangle that has three sides of different lengths is called scalene.   [4-4]

9. In a triangle, the longest side is opposite the smallest angle.

10. All quadrilaterals are parallelograms.   [4-5]

Write the letter of the correct answer.

11. A hexagon is regular. One side has length 8 cm. What is the perimeter?
    a. 40 cm   **b.** 64 cm   **c.** 80 cm   **d.** 48 cm

12. Name the segment joining the center of a circle to a point on the   [4-6]
    circle.
    a. diameter   **b.** chord   **c.** radius   **d.** circumference

13. A circle has diameter 16 cm. Use $\pi \approx 3.14$ to find the circumference and round to three digits.
    a. 50.24 cm   **b.** 50.3 cm   **c.** 50.2 cm   **d.** 50 cm

14. Which is the symbol for congruence?   [4-7]
    a. $\cong$ **b.** $\perp$ **c.** $\angle$ **d.** $\triangle$

15. Construct a 120° angle.   [4-8]

16. Construct a right triangle.

Chapter Test

Exercises 1–3 refer to the diagram at the right.

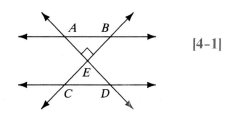

1. Name a pair of perpendicular lines.

2. Name two rays that are not parallel, but do not intersect.

3. Name three collinear points.

Complete.

4. 27 m = __?__ cm

5. 3.6 km = __?__ m

6. 5000 cm = __?__ km

7. 4 mm = __?__ m

8. Give the measures of the complement and the supplement of $\angle A$ if $m\angle A = 27°$.

9. If $\angle X \cong \angle Y$, then $m\angle X = $ __?__.

10. True or false? The sides of a right angle are perpendicular.

11. One angle of an isosceles triangle has measure 98°. Find the measures of the two congruent angles.

12. An obtuse triangle has how many obtuse angles?

13. True or false? A square is a rhombus.

14. A quadrilateral has sides of length 8 cm, 13 cm, 9 cm, and 16 cm. Find the perimeter.

15. A regular hexagon has perimeter 84 mm. Find the length of each side.

16. The diameter of a circle is 18 cm. Find the radius.

17. A circle has radius 50 mm. Find the circumference. Use $\pi \approx 3.14$.

18. True or false? Every triangle can be inscribed in a circle.

19. If quadrilateral $ABCD \cong$ quadrilateral $WXYZ$, then $\overline{AD} \cong$ __?__.

20. Draw a segment. Construct the perpendicular bisector. Then construct the bisector of one of the right angles.

[4-1]

[4-2]

[4-3]

[4-4]

[4-5]

[4-6]

[4-7]

[4-8]

Cumulative Review (Chapters 1–4)

Exercises

Perform the indicated operations.

1. 398
    + 471

2. 157
    × 92

3. 589
    − 237

4. 1179
    + 864

5. 378
    × 24

6. 956
    × 38

7. 2735
    − 1496

8. 3000
    − 1785

9.   271
     1098
    + 417

10. 2091
    × 26

11. 6045
    − 3488

12.   429
      3155
       71
    + 1096

13. $23\overline{)5658}$

14. $18\overline{)3006}$

15. $9112 \div 34$

16. $3264 \div 16$

17. $3.84 + 4.92 + 3.18$

18. 3.26×2.13

19. $7.94 - 5.82$

20. 4.931×2.48

21. $11.91 - 7.84$

22. $5.93 + 6.1 + 8.478$

23. $2.4\overline{)9.504}$

24. $35.6796 \div 5.83$

25. $2.09\overline{)7.1478}$

Simplify.

26. $61(89 + 118)$

27. $43(436 - 307)$

28. $214(842 + 351)$

29. $(219 + 12)(123 - 47)$

30. $(262 - 143)(125 + 317)$

31. $(837 \div 20) + (112 \times 217)$

32. $(113 \times 231) - (210 \div 14)$

33. $114 - 17 \times 3 + 8 \times 31$

34. $272 \div 8 + 11 \times 6 - 43$

35. $64 + 9 \times 5 - 59 + 86$

36. $444 \div 12 + 8 \times 11 - 49$

37. $17 \times 21 \div 7 + 84 - 16$

38. $448 \div 32 \times 2 + 87 \div 3$

Solve each equation.

39. $6x = 42$

40. $x + 50 = 97$

41. $x - 25 = 11$

42. $x \div 12 = 10$

43. $x - 35 = 40$

44. $8x = 88$

45. $45 + x = 100$

46. $64 \div x = 8$

47. $115 - x = 60$

48. $22 + x = 85$

49. $9x = 81$

50. $140 \div x = 20$

Problems

PROBLEM SOLVING REMINDERS

Here are some reminders that may help you solve some of the problems on this page.
- Determine which facts are necessary to solve the problem.
- Determine whether more than one operation is needed.
- Estimate to check your answers.

Solve.

1. Susan purchased the following items for the school dance: streamers, $2.89; tape, $4.59; bunting, $8.88; paper decorations, $14.75. How much did Susan spend?

2. Fred's Fish Farm started the week with 2078 fish. On Monday Fred sold 473 fish, on Tuesday he sold 509 fish, and on Wednesday 617 fish were sold. Fred bought 675 fish on Thursday and sold 349 on Friday. How many fish did Fred have at the end of the week?

3. Mr. Chou was putting a certain amount into his savings account each month. Last month he increased the amount by $38. If Mr. Chou deposited $162 into his savings account last month, how much was he putting in before the increase?

4. Yonora bought 7 gallons of paint at $16.95 a gallon, 3 brushes at $6.99 each, 4 rollers at $2.95 each, and a dropcloth for $7.88. How much did Yonora spend on painting supplies?

5. A side of a square is 13 m long. Find the perimeter.

6. If a number is multiplied by 3, the result is 51. Find the number.

7. The seventh grade sold greeting cards to raise money for a trip. There were 12 cards and 12 envelopes in each box. If the class sold 1524 cards with envelopes, how many boxes did they sell?

8. Elgin had $150 in his checking account. He wrote checks for $17.95, $23.98, $45.17, and $31.26. How much does Elgin have left in his account?

9. Becky bought a round pool that is 7 m in diameter. What is the circumference of the pool to the nearest meter?

10. Juanita is 7 years older than her brother Carlos, who is 3 years older than their sister Maria. If Carlos is 6 years old, how old are Juanita and Maria?

5 Number Theory

APPLYING MATHEMATICS
COMPUTER MEMORY

In combination with oxygen, the element
silicon is the chief ingredient of beach sand. Yet
silicon is also the base of these razor-thin wafers that
have been etched with hundreds of tiny electronic *chips*.
Chips like these rarely measure more than a quarter-inch on a
side, but each maybe able to perform millions of calculations per
second or to store hundreds of thousands of bits of data. If a chip is capable of
storing data, it is said to have a *memory*. The basic unit of measure for
memory is the K. The K represents 1024, or 2^{10}, bits of data, and the
storage capacity of a chip's memory is described in multiples
of K. Thus a memory that is identified as 64K can
store up to 64×1024, or 65,536, bits of data. In
this chapter you will learn about multiples,
factors, primes, divisibility, and
other topics in number theory.

CAREER CONNECTION

ELECTRICAL ENGINEER

Electronic chips are at the heart of modern
computers. Therefore, the rapid progress in the
development of chips has increased opportunities
in a wide variety of computer-related careers.
For example, electrical engineers develop the
hardware, or machinery, of computer systems.
Among the people who produce software, or the
instructions that make computers run, are
systems analysts and programmers.

Photo: A silicon computer chip is part of an integrated
circuit board.

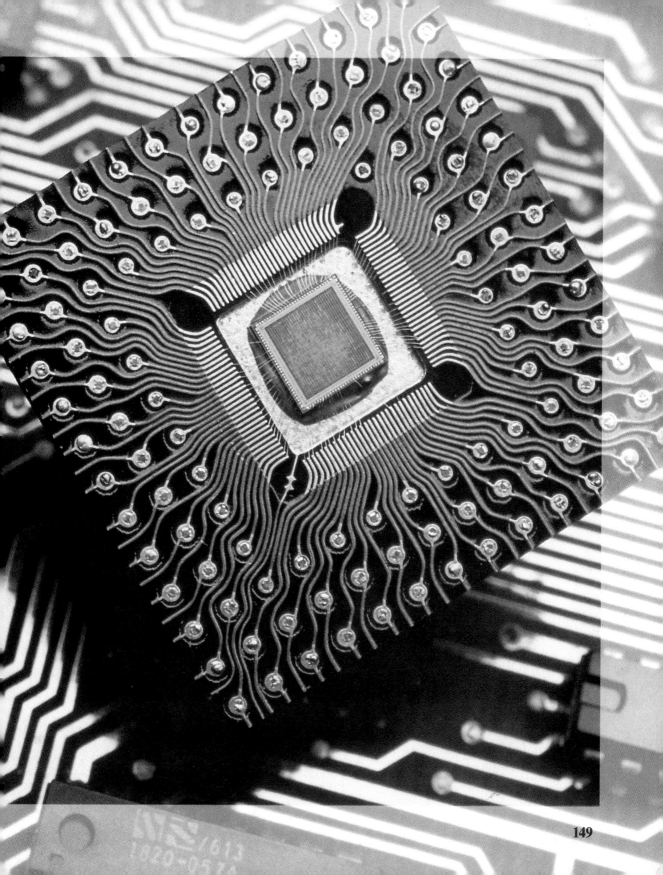

5-1 Finding Factors and Multiples

You know that 60 can be written as the product of 5 and 12. Whenever a number, such as 60, can be written as the product of two whole numbers, such as 5 and 12, these two numbers are called **whole number factors** of the first number. A number is said to be **divisible** by its whole number factors. Thus, 60 is divisible by the factors 5 and 12.

To find out if a smaller whole number is a factor of a larger whole number, we divide the larger number by the smaller. If the remainder is 0, then the smaller number is a factor of the larger number. If the remainder is *not* 0, then the smaller number is *not* a factor of the larger number.

EXAMPLE 1 State whether or not the smaller number is a factor of the larger.

        a. 6; 138   **b.** 8; 154

Solution **a.** Divide 138 by 6.

        $138 \div 6 = 23 \text{ R } 0$

        Since the remainder is 0, 6 is a factor of 138.

        b. Divide 154 by 8.

        $154 \div 8 = 19 \text{ R } 2$

        Since the remainder is not 0, 8 is not a factor of 154.

EXAMPLE 2 Find all the factors of 24.

Solution Try each whole number as a divisor, starting with 1.

$24 \div 1 = 24$ Thus, 1 and 24 are factors.
$24 \div 2 = 12$ Thus, 2 and 12 are factors.
$24 \div 3 = 8$ Thus, 3 and 8 are factors.
$24 \div 4 = 6$ Thus, 4 and 6 are factors.
$24 \div 5 = 4 \text{ R } 4$ Thus, 5 is not a factor.

Since $24 \div 6 = 4$, the factors begin to repeat, and we do not have to try any whole number greater than 5 as a divisor. Thus, the factors of 24 are 1, 2, 3, 4, 6, 8, 12, and 24.

A **multiple** of a whole number is the product of that number and any whole number. You can find the multiples of a given whole number by multiplying that number by 0, 1, 2, 3, 4, and so on. For example, the first four multiples of 7 are 0, 7, 14, and 21, since:

    $0 \cdot 7 = 0$ $1 \cdot 7 = 7$ $2 \cdot 7 = 14$ $3 \cdot 7 = 21$

In general, any number is a multiple of each of its factors. For example, 21 is a multiple of 7 and of 3.

Any multiple of 2 is called an **even number.** A whole number that is not an even number is called an **odd number.** Notice that since

$$0 = 0 \cdot 2,$$

0 is a multiple of 2 and is therefore an even number.

Class Exercises

State all the factors of each number.

1. 6   2. 10   3. 20   4. 18   5. 30

6. What number is a factor of every whole number?

State the first four multiples of each number.

7. 5   8. 4   9. 6   10. 9   11. 11

12. What number is a multiple of every whole number?

Written Exercises

A   **List all the factors of each number.**

1. 42   2. 45   3. 32   4. 40   5. 56

6. 31   7. 84   8. 51   9. 41   10. 112

List the first five multiples of each number.

11. 12   12. 15   13. 17   14. 21   15. 10

16. 19   17. 24   18. 31   19. 36   20. 50

21. What is the greatest odd factor of 18?

22. What is the smallest even factor of 52?

State whether or not the first number is a factor of the second. If it is a factor, find a second factor other than 1.

23. 7; 142   24. 9; 612   25. 17; 136   26. 14; 312

27. 18; 5094   28. 15; 7532   29. 23; 6279   30. 32; 1028

B **31.** List some whole numbers that are multiples of both 2 and 3. Are all the numbers you listed multiples of 6?

32. If a number is a multiple of both 3 and 5, it must be a multiple of what other number?

33. If a number is a multiple of each of two numbers, does it appear to be a multiple of the product of the two numbers? Test the following pairs of numbers to help you answer the question.

$$4 \text{ and } 5 \qquad 3 \text{ and } 10 \qquad 4 \text{ and } 6 \qquad 10 \text{ and } 15$$

Complete each statement with *odd* or *even*.

34. The product of two even numbers is ___?___ .

35. The product of an odd number and an even number is ___?___ .

36. The product of two odd numbers is ___?___ .

37. The sum of two odd numbers is ___?___ .

The expression $4 \cdot 3 \cdot 2 \cdot 1$, which equals 24, is called 4 factorial and is written 4! Similarly, $5! = 5 \cdot 4 \cdot 3 \cdot 2 \cdot 1 = 120$.
Find the value of each expression.

38. $7!$ **39.** $8!$ **40.** $\frac{6!}{5!}$ **41.** $\frac{17!}{16!}$ **42.** $\frac{21!}{19!}$

C **43.** List the factors of each of the whole numbers 1 through 16. Which numbers have an odd number of factors? Name another whole number greater than 16 that has an odd number of factors.

44. The numbers 14 and 35 are both multiples of 7. Their sum, 49, is also a multiple of 7. Test this relationship for some other whole numbers. What appears to be true if a and b are both multiples of a whole number c?

45. The number 33 is a multiple of 11, but the number 24 is not. Is the sum of 33 and 24 a multiple of 11? Test this relationship for some other whole numbers. What appears to be true if a is a multiple of a whole number c, but b is not?

Review Exercises

Divide. Round to the nearest hundredth.

1. $11\overline{)693}$ **2.** $7\overline{)574}$ **3.** $1246 \div 14$ **4.** $1836 \div 17$

5. $13\overline{)1293}$ **6.** $21\overline{)2785}$ **7.** $3487 \div 19$ **8.** $4017 \div 11$

5-2 Tests for Divisibility

Sometimes it may be possible to find the factors of a number by an inspection of the digits of the number. For example, let us

consider multiples of 2: 0, 2, 4, 6, 8, 10, . . .
consider multiples of 5: 0, 5, 10, 15, 20, . . .
consider multiples of 10: 0, 10, 20, 30, 40, . . .

From the patterns we see in the last digits of the sets of multiples above, we can devise the following tests for divisibility.

> Divisibility by 2: A whole number has 2 as a factor if its last digit has 2 as a factor.
>
> Divisibility by 5: A whole number has 5 as a factor if its last digit is 5 or 0.
>
> Divisibility by 10: A whole number has 10 as a factor if its last digit is 0.

Suppose we want to check whether a number, such as 712, is divisible by 4. Since any multiple of 100 is divisible by 4, we know that 700 is divisible by 4. To test 712, then, we simply look at the last two digits. Since 12 is a multiple of 4, the number 712 is also a multiple of 4 (712 ÷ 4 = 178). A similar inspection shows that 950 is not a multiple of 4, since the number represented by the last two digits, 50, is not a multiple of 4 (950 ÷ 4 gives 237 R 2). This suggests the following test for divisibility.

> Divisibility by 4: A whole number has 4 as a factor if its last two digits represent a multiple of 4.

EXAMPLE 1 Test each number for divisibility by 2, 4, 5, and 10.

        a. 35   **b.** 150

Solution **a.** 35: Since the last digit is 5 and is odd, 2 and 10 are not factors. Since 35 is not a multiple of 4, 4 is not a factor. Since the last digit is 5, 5 is a factor.

b. 150: Since 0 is the last digit, 2, 5, and 10 are factors. 4 is not a factor, since 50 is not a multiple of 4.

EXAMPLE 2   Test each number for divisibility by 2, 4, 5, and 10.

a. 7736   **b.** 920

Solution   **a.** 7736: 2 is a factor, since the last digit, 6, is even. 4 is a factor, since 36 is a multiple of 4. 5 and 10 are not factors, since the last digit is not 5 or 0.

b. 920: 2, 5, and 10 are all factors, since the last digit is 0. 4 is a factor, since the last two digits, 20, represent a multiple of 4.

Rules for recognizing numbers divisible by 3 or 9 are a bit more difficult to discover. The rules relate to the sum of the digits of the number. Study the following numbers.

	Divisible by 3	Divisible by 9	Sum of digits
393	yes $393 \div 3 = 131$	no $393 \div 9$ gives 43 R 6	15
394	no $394 \div 3$ gives 131 R 1	no $394 \div 9$ gives 43 R 7	16
395	no $395 \div 3$ gives 131 R 2	no $395 \div 9$ gives 43 R 8	17
396	yes $396 \div 3 = 132$	yes $396 \div 9 = 44$	18

Notice that when the sum of the digits of the number is divisible by 3 (15 or 18), the number (393 or 396) is divisible by 3. Notice also that when the sum of the digits is divisible by 9 (18), the number (396) is divisible by 9. This illustrates the following tests.

> Divisibility by 3: A whole number has 3 as a factor if the sum of the digits of the number is a multiple of 3.
>
> Divisibility by 9: A whole number has 9 as a factor if the sum of the digits of the number is a multiple of 9.

EXAMPLE 3   Test each number for divisibility by 3 and 9.

a. 714   **b.** 6291   **c.** 4813

Solution   **a.** $7 + 1 + 4 = 12$. Since 12 is a multiple of 3 but not a multiple of 9, 714 is divisible by 3, but not by 9.

b. $6 + 2 + 9 + 1 = 18$. Since 18 is a multiple of 3 and of 9, 6291 is divisible by 3 and by 9.

c. $4 + 8 + 1 + 3 = 16$. Since 16 is not a multiple of 3 or of 9, 4813 is not divisible by 3 or by 9.

Class Exercises

Test each number for divisibility by 2.

1. 130　　　　　**2.** 4681　　　　　**3.** 105　　　　　**4.** 3576

Test each number for divisibility by 4.

5. 8310　　　　　**6.** 712　　　　　**7.** 86,222　　　　　**8.** 5732

Test each number for divisibility by 5 and 10.

9. 8325　　　　　**10.** 7602　　　　　**11.** 870　　　　　**12.** 6395

Test each number for divisibility by 3 and 9.

13. 175　　　　　**14.** 288　　　　　**15.** 651　　　　　**16.** 8766

Written Exercises

State which of the numbers 2, 3, 4, 5, 9, and 10 are factors of the given number. Use the tests for divisibility.

A　**1.** 132　　　**2.** 150　　　**3.** 195　　　**4.** 4280　　　**5.** 567

　　　6. 8155　　　**7.** 43,260　　　**8.** 720　　　**9.** 1147　　　**10.** 78,921

　　　11. 62,584　　　**12.** 50,001　　　**13.** 36,432　　　**14.** 123,456　　　**15.** 102,030

For each number, determine whether (a) 2 is a factor, (b) 3 is a factor, and (c) 6 is a factor. What appears to be true in order for 6 to be a factor?

16. 1316　　　　　**17.** 2,817,000　　　　　**18.** 31,027,302

19. 1224　　　　　**20.** 2,147,640　　　　　**21.** 36,111,114

Supply the missing digit of the first number if it is known to have the other two numbers as factors.

22. 35?; 2, 3　　　　　**23.** 876?; 2, 5　　　　　**24.** 910?; 3, 5

B　**25.** 472?; 3, 4　　　　**26.** 61?2; 4, 9　　　　**27.** 47?2; 4, 9

A number has **11** as a factor if and only if the sum of its first, third, fifth, . . . digits equals the sum of its second, fourth, sixth, . . . digits, or if these two sums differ by a multiple of 11. Test each number for divisibility by 11.

EXAMPLE   **a.** 17,314   **b.** 806,124   **c.** 7923

Solution   **a.** $1 + 3 + 4 = 8$ Since the two sums are equal, we know that the
               $7 + 1 = 8$ number 17,314 has 11 as a factor.

           b. $8 + 6 + 2 = 16$ $16 - 5 = 11$. Since the two sums differ by 11,
               $0 + 1 + 4 = 5$ we know that 806,124 has 11 as a factor.

           c. $7 + 2 = 9$ $12 - 9 = 3$. Since the difference is not a multi-
               $9 + 3 = 12$ ple of 11, 7923 does not have 11 as a factor.

28. 46,893   **29.** 720,536   **30.** 862,301   **31.** 749,386

32. Any multiple of 1000 is divisible by 8. Use this fact to devise a test for divisibility by 8.

33. The total number of pages in a book must be a multiple of 32. If the book consists of 10 chapters, each 24 pages long, and 8 pages of introductory material, how many blank pages will be left?

C **34.** Devise a test for divisibility by 25.

35. A **perfect number** is one that is the sum of all of its factors except itself. The smallest perfect number is 6, since $6 = 1 + 2 + 3$. Find the next perfect number.

Review Exercises

Multiply or divide.

1. 17×17 **2.** 14×14 **3.** 23×23 **4.** 31×31

5. $729 \div 27$ **6.** $1444 \div 38$ **7.** $1681 \div 41$ **8.** $4489 \div 67$

5-3 Square Numbers and Square Roots

Certain counting numbers can be written as the product of two equal factors. For example,

$$1 = 1 \cdot 1 \qquad 4 = 2 \cdot 2 \qquad 9 = 3 \cdot 3$$
$$16 = 4 \cdot 4 \qquad 25 = 5 \cdot 5 \qquad 36 = 6 \cdot 6$$

Numbers such as 1, 4, 9, 16, 25, and 36 are called **square numbers** or **perfect squares**. The reason for this name is suggested by the diagrams at the right. As you have learned, these numbers can be written using the exponent 2.

$$1 = 1^2 \qquad 4 = 2^2 \qquad 9 = 3^2$$
$$16 = 4^2 \qquad 25 = 5^2 \qquad 36 = 6^2$$

$3^2 = 9$ $\qquad$ $4^2 = 16$

One of the two equal factors of a square number is called the **square root** of the number. To denote the square root of a number, we use a **radical sign**, $\sqrt{}$. For example, to denote the square root of 25, we write $\sqrt{25}$.

EXAMPLE Evaluate. **a.** $\sqrt{49}$ **b.** $\sqrt{100}$

Solution   **a.** $\sqrt{49} = 7$, since $7^2 = 49$.   **b.** $\sqrt{100} = 10$, since $10^2 = 100$.

Class Exercises

Evaluate the square of each number.

1. 3	**2.** 7	**3.** 9	**4.** 0	**5.** 1	**6.** 40

Evaluate the square root of each number.

7. 16	**8.** 25	**9.** 81	**10.** 1	**11.** 0	**12.** 400

Written Exercises

Evaluate each expression.

A

1. 8^2	**2.** 11^2	**3.** 13^2	**4.** 15^2	**5.** 21^2
6. $3^2 + 4^2$	**7.** $7^2 + 9^2$	**8.** $\sqrt{81}$	**9.** $\sqrt{121}$	**10.** $\sqrt{144}$
11. $\sqrt{400}$	**12.** $\sqrt{900}$	**13.** $\sqrt{1600}$	**14.** $\sqrt{9} + \sqrt{16}$	**15.** $\sqrt{9 + 16}$

16. a. Evaluate $\sqrt{36}$.
 b. Evaluate $\sqrt{9} \cdot \sqrt{4}$.
 c. Is it true that
$$\sqrt{36} = \sqrt{9} \cdot \sqrt{4}?$$

17. a. Evaluate $\sqrt{225}$.
 b. Evaluate $\sqrt{9} \cdot \sqrt{25}$.
 c. Is it true that
$$\sqrt{225} = \sqrt{9} \cdot \sqrt{25}?$$

18. a. Evaluate $\sqrt{100}$.
 b. Evaluate $\sqrt{36} + \sqrt{64}$.
 c. Is it true that
$$\sqrt{100} = \sqrt{36} + \sqrt{64}?$$

19. a. Evaluate $\sqrt{169}$.
 b. Evaluate $\sqrt{25} + \sqrt{144}$.
 c. Is it true that
$$\sqrt{169} = \sqrt{25} + \sqrt{144}?$$

Evaluate.

B **20.** $\sqrt{196}$ **21.** $\sqrt{324}$ **22.** $\sqrt{441}$ **23.** $\sqrt{625}$ **24.** $\sqrt{784}$

25. List the squares of the first eight whole numbers starting with 1. Find the difference between each square number and the preceding square number. Without calculating, give the difference between the eighth and ninth square numbers, and between the ninth and tenth square numbers.

26. Add the first two odd numbers and write down their sum. Do the same for the first three odd numbers, then the first four, and so on up to the first eight odd numbers. What kind of number is each sum? Explain how the diagram illustrates your answer.

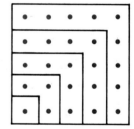

27. a. Find each of the following sums.

$$1$$
$$1 + 2$$
$$1 + 2 + 3$$
$$1 + 2 + 3 + 4, \text{ and so on up to}$$
$$1 + 2 + 3 + 4 + 5 + 6 + 7 + 8 + 9 + 10$$

 b. If you add any one of these sums to the one immediately following it in the list, what kind of number do you get?
 c. The number 1 and the sums in part (a) are called triangular numbers for the reason suggested by the diagram. Draw a diagram that illustrates the results of part (b).

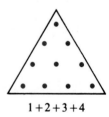

$1+2+3+4$

C **28.** The three numbers 3, 4, and 5 have the relationship
$$3^2 + 4^2 = 5^2. \qquad (9 + 16 = 25)$$

Find three other numbers that have this same relationship.

29. Take an odd perfect square, such as 9. Square the largest whole number that is less than half of it. (For 9 this would be 4.) If you add this square to the original number, what kind of number do you get? Try this with other odd perfect squares.

30. The number 130 can be written as a sum of two different perfect squares in two different ways:

$$11^2 + 3^2 = 121 + 9 = 130$$
$$7^2 + 9^2 = 49 + 81 = 130$$

Find the smallest whole number that can be written two ways as a sum of two different perfect squares.

Self-Test A

List all the factors of each number.

1. 60	**2.** 84	**3.** 100	**4.** 23	[5–1]

List the first five nonzero multiples of each number.

5. 13	**6.** 19	**7.** 24	**8.** 31

State which of the numbers 2, 3, 4, 5, 9, and 10 are factors of each number. Use the tests for divisibility.

9. 756	**10.** 630	**11.** 544	**12.** 7821	[5–2]
13. 9045	**14.** 11,340	**15.** 16,701	**16.** 319,447	

Evaluate each expression.

17. 14^2	**18.** $\sqrt{400}$	**19.** $\sqrt{256}$	**20.** 17^2	[5–3]
21. $\sqrt{361}$	**22.** 25^2	**23.** 36^2	**24.** $\sqrt{2500}$	

Self-Test answers and Extra Practice are at the back of the book.

▮ ▮ ▮ **NONROUTINE PROBLEM SOLVING:** *Number Sense*

Between the years of 1725 and 1875 the French won a battle on April 22. The French won another victory, 4382 days later, also on April 22. The sum of the digits of the years of the two battles is 40. If one battle took place in the 1700's and the other in the 1800's, in what years were the battles fought?

5-4 Prime Numbers and Composite Numbers

Consider the list of counting numbers and their factors given at the right. Notice that each of the numbers 2, 3, 5, 7, and 11 has *exactly* two factors: 1 and the number itself. A number with this property is called a **prime number.** A counting number that has more than two factors is called a **composite number.** In the list 4, 6, 8, 9, 10, and 12 are all composite numbers. Since 1 has exactly one factor, it is neither prime nor composite.

Number	Factors
1	1
2	1, 2
3	1, 3
4	1, 2, 4
5	1, 5
6	1, 2, 3, 6
7	1, 7
8	1, 2, 4, 8
9	1, 3, 9
10	1, 2, 5, 10
11	1, 11
12	1, 2, 3, 4, 6, 12

About 230 B.C. Eratosthenes, a Greek mathematician, suggested a way to find prime numbers in a list of all the counting numbers up to a certain number. Eratosthenes first crossed out all multiples of 2, except 2 itself. Next he crossed out all multiples of the next remaining number, 3, except 3 itself. He continued crossing out multiples of each successive remaining number except the number itself. The numbers remaining at the end of this process are the primes.

```
 1   2   3   4   5   6   7   8   9
10  11  12  13  14  15  16  17  18  19
20  21  22  23  24  25  26  27  28  29
30  31  32  33  34  35  36  37  . . .
```

The method just described is called the **Sieve of Eratosthenes,** because it picks out the prime numbers as a strainer, or sieve, picks out solid particles from a liquid.

Every counting number greater than 1 has at least one prime factor, which may be the number itself. You can factor a number into prime factors by using either of the following methods.

Inverted short division

```
2)42
3)21
   7
```

Factor tree

```
    42
   /  \
  2    21
      /  \
     3    7
```

Another factor tree for the number 42 is shown at the right. Notice that the prime factors of 42 are the same in either factor tree except for their order. Every whole number is similar to 42 in this respect. This fact is expressed in the following theorem.

$$42$$
$$3 \quad 14$$
$$7 \quad 2$$

Fundamental Theorem of Arithmetic

Every composite number greater than 1 can be written as a product of prime factors in exactly one way, except for the order of the factors.

When we write 42 as $2 \cdot 3 \cdot 7$, this product of prime factors is called the **prime factorization** of 42.

EXAMPLE   Give the prime factorization of 60.

Solution
Method 1

$2 \overline{)60}$
$2 \overline{)30}$
$3 \overline{)15}$
5

Method 2

$$60$$
$$2 \quad 30$$
$$2 \quad 15$$
$$3 \quad 5$$

Using either method, we find that the prime factorization of 60 is $2 \cdot 2 \cdot 3 \cdot 5$ or $2^2 \cdot 3 \cdot 5$.

Class Exercises

State whether each number is prime or composite.

1. 7 **2.** 9 **3.** 15 **4.** 23 **5.** 22 **6.** 19

Name the prime factors of each number.

7. 21 **8.** 10 **9.** 18 **10.** 26 **11.** 30 **12.** 70

Name the number whose prime factorization is given.

13. $3^2 \cdot 5$ **14.** $2^2 \cdot 3^2$ **15.** $2^3 \cdot 3$

16. $2 \cdot 7^2$ **17.** $3^2 \cdot 11$ **18.** $2^2 \cdot 5^2$

Written Exercises

State whether each number is prime or composite.

A   **1.** 39   **2.** 41   **3.** 51   **4.** 111   **5.** 124   **6.** 321

    7. 641   **8.** 753   **9.** 894   **10.** 1164   **11.** 2061   **12.** 3001

Give the prime factorization of each whole number.

    13. 12   **14.** 50   **15.** 24   **16.** 28   **17.** 39   **18.** 56

    19. 66   **20.** 51   **21.** 54   **22.** 63   **23.** 84   **24.** 90

    25. 196   **26.** 360   **27.** 308   **28.** 693   **29.** 114   **30.** 1150

B   **31.** Explain why 2 is the only even prime number.

    32. Write the prime factorizations of the square numbers 16, 36, 81, and 144 by using exponents. What do you think must be true of the exponents in the prime factorization of a square number?

    33. Explain why the sum of two prime numbers greater than 2 can never be a prime number.

    34. Explain how you know that each of the following numbers must be composite: 111; 111,111; 111,111,111; . . .

    35. List all the possible digits that can be the last digit of a prime number that is greater than 10.

C   **36.** Choose a six-digit number, such as 652,652, the last three digits of which are a repeat of the first three digits. Show that 7, 11, and 13 are all factors of the number you chose.

    37. Since 7, 11, and 13 are factors of any number of the type defined in Exercise 36, what is the largest composite number that is always a factor of such a number? What is the other factor?

    38. Give an example to show that the Fundamental Theorem of Arithmetic would be false if 1 were defined to be a prime number.

Review Exercises

Evaluate.

    1. 7^3 **2.** 3^5 **3.** 4^3 **4.** 2^6 **5.** 9^4

    6. 10^3 **7.** 10^5 **8.** $3^4 \cdot 2^3$ **9.** $5^3 \cdot 10^2$ **10.** $6^3 \cdot 4^4$

5-5 Greatest Common Factor

▲ See Pages E7–E8

If the factors of the numbers 30 and 42 are listed, the numbers 1, 2, 3, and 6 appear in both lists.

Factors of 30:   1, 2, 3, 5, 6, 10, 15, 30

Factors of 42:   1, 2, 3, 6, 7, 14, 21, 42

These numbers are called **common factors** of 30 and 42. The number 6 is the greatest of these and is therefore called the **greatest common factor** of the two numbers. We write

$$GCF(30, 42) = 6$$

to denote the greatest common factor of 30 and 42.

EXAMPLE 1   Find GCF(54, 72).

Solution   List the factors of each number.

Factors of 54: 1, 2, 3, 6, 9, 18, 27, 54

Factors of 72: 1, 2, 3, 4, 6, 8, 9, 12, 18, 24, 36, 72

The common factors are 1, 2, 3, 6, 9, and 18.
The greatest number in both lists is 18. Therefore,

$$GCF(54, 72) = 18.$$

Another way to find the GCF of two numbers is to use their prime factorizations. To find the GCF, multiply together the greatest power of each prime factor that occurs in *both* prime factorizations.

EXAMPLE 2   Find GCF(54, 72) using the prime factorization method.

Solution   First find the prime factorizations of 54 and 72.

$54 = 2 \cdot 3 \cdot 3 \cdot 3 = 2 \cdot 3^3$
$72 = 2 \cdot 2 \cdot 2 \cdot 3 \cdot 3 = 2^3 \cdot 3^2$

Find the greatest power of 2 that occurs in both prime factorizations.
The greatest power of 2 that occurs in both prime factorizations is 2.

Find the greatest power of 3 that occurs in both prime factorizations.
The greatest power of 3 that occurs in both prime factorizations is 3^2.

Therefore, $GCF(54, 72) = 2 \cdot 3^2 = 18.$

EXAMPLE 3   Find GCF(45, 60) using the prime factorization method.

Solution $45 = 3 \cdot 3 \cdot 5 = 3^2 \cdot 5$
$60 = 2 \cdot 2 \cdot 3 \cdot 5 = 2^2 \cdot 3 \cdot 5$

Since 2 is not a factor of 45, there is no greatest power of 2 that occurs in both prime factorizations.
The greatest power of 3 that occurs in both prime factorizations is 3.
The greatest power of 5 that occurs in both prime factorizations is 5.
Therefore, GCF(45, 60) = $3 \cdot 5 = 15$.

The number 1 is a common factor of any two whole numbers. If 1 is the GCF, then the two numbers are said to be **relatively prime.** As the next example shows, two numbers can be relatively prime even if one or both are composite.

EXAMPLE 4   Show that 15 and 16 are relatively prime.

Solution   List the factors of each number.

Factors of 15: 1, 3, 5, 15

Factors of 16: 1, 2, 4, 8, 16

Since GCF(15, 16) = 1, the two numbers are relatively prime.

Class Exercises

Give the GCF of each pair of numbers.

1. 4, 10   2. 15, 35   3. 6, 12   4. 9, 14   5. 18, 27

State whether the numbers in each pair are relatively prime.

6. 16, 20   7. 5, 15   8. 8, 9   9. 6, 35   10. 22, 26

Written Exercises

Find the GCF of each pair of numbers.

A   1. 16, 24   2. 18, 45   3. 24, 36   4. 26, 39

5. 15, 28   6. 44, 55   7. 28, 42   8. 75, 175

9. 60, 105   10. 54, 81   11. 56, 84   12. 63, 100

Use the prime factorization method to find each of the following.

13. GCF(360, 160)   **14.** GCF(625, 500)   **15.** GCF(196, 112)

16. GCF(264, 660)   **17.** GCF(350, 2450)   **18.** GCF(900, 1125)

B   **19.** GCF(20, 28, 40)   **20.** GCF(18, 36, 27)   **21.** GCF(30, 60, 80)

True or false?

22. Any two prime numbers are relatively prime.

23. If two numbers are relatively prime, one of them must be prime.

24. If one number is a factor of a second number, the GCF of the two numbers is the first number.

25. The GCF of any two even numbers is 2.

26. **a.** Find GCF(72, 270), using the prime factorization method. Then find $72 \div$ GCF(72, 270) and $270 \div$ GCF(72, 270).
     b. What is the GCF of your two answers?
     c. Repeat parts (a) and (b) with GCF(336, 600). What do you think is always true of the quotients when each of two numbers is divided by their GCF?

27. **a.** Find GCF(36, 90), GCF(90, 120), and GCF(36, 90, 120).
     b. Find GCF(60, 100), GCF(100, 150), and GCF(60, 100, 150).
     c. In each of parts (a) and (b) how is the third number you found related to the first two numbers?

C   **28.** Find two whole numbers whose product is 1500 and whose GCF is 10.

29. Find two whole numbers whose product is 540 and whose GCF is 6.

30. Explain why a number that is relatively prime to 21 and also to 110 must be relatively prime to 21×110.

31. Explain why 15 must be a factor of n if n denotes a whole number such that 15 is a factor of $8 \times n$.

Review Exercises

List the factors of each number.

1. 40   **2.** 84   **3.** 48   **4.** 54   **5.** 88

6. 120   **7.** 110   **8.** 96   **9.** 102   **10.** 125

5-6 Least Common Multiple

If the first few multiples of 8 and 12 are listed in order, certain numbers appear in both lists:

Multiples of 8:   0, 8, 16, 24, 32, 40, 48, 56, 64, 72, 80, . . .

Multiples of 12:   0, 12, 24, 36, 48, 60, 72, 84, . . .

The numbers 0, 24, 48, 72, . . . are called **common multiples** of 8 and 12. Excluding 0, the least of these multiples is 24 and is therefore called the **least common multiple.** We write the least common multiple of 8 and 12 as

$$\text{LCM}(8, 12) = 24.$$

To find the LCM of two whole numbers, we can write out lists of multiples of the two numbers as above. The LCM will be the first multiple, excluding 0, that occurs in both lists.

A second method is to write out the first few multiples of the larger of the two numbers and then test each multiple for divisibility by the smaller number. The first multiple of the larger number that is divisible by the smaller number is the LCM.

EXAMPLE 1   Find LCM(12, 15).

Solution   Write out the first few multiples of 15 (excluding 0).

$$15, 30, 45, 60, 75, 90$$

Test each for divisibility by 12.

$$\begin{array}{llll} \overset{1\ R\ 3}{12\overline{)15}} & \overset{2\ R\ 6}{12\overline{)30}} & \overset{3\ R\ 9}{12\overline{)45}} & \overset{5}{12\overline{)60}} \end{array}$$

Therefore, LCM(12, 15) = 60.

The LCM of two whole numbers can be found using their prime factorizations. For each prime factor of the two numbers, multiply together the greatest power of that factor that occurs in *either* prime factorization. The product will be the LCM.

EXAMPLE 2   Find LCM(54, 60).

Solution $54 = 2 \cdot 3 \cdot 3 \cdot 3 = 2 \cdot 3^3$
                     $60 = 2 \cdot 2 \cdot 3 \cdot 5 = 2^2 \cdot 3 \cdot 5$

The greatest power of 2 that occurs in either prime factorization is 2^2.

The greatest power of 3 that occurs in either prime factorization is 3^3.

The greatest power of 5 that occurs in either prime factorization is 5. Therefore, LCM(54, 60) $= 2^2 \cdot 3^3 \cdot 5 = 540$.

 COMMUNICATION IN MATHEMATICS: *Vocabulary*

To avoid being confused by the abbreviations GCF and LCM, recall what they stand for.

The GCF (greatest common factor) is a *factor*. The GCF of two numbers will be the smaller of the two or smaller than both.

The LCM (least common multiple) is a *multiple*. The LCM of two numbers will be the larger of the two or larger than both.

Class Exercises

State the first five nonzero multiples of each number. Then state the LCM of the pair.

1. 4, 6 **2.** 6, 9 **3.** 5, 10 **4.** 9, 12 **5.** 4, 5

Find the LCM of each pair of numbers by writing the first few multiples of the larger number and testing each for divisibility by the smaller number.

6. 15, 25 **7.** 8, 15 **8.** 12, 16 **9.** 10, 16 **10.** 15, 35

State the prime factorization of each number. Then state the prime factorization of the LCM.

11. 6, 8 **12.** 6, 14 **13.** 8, 12 **14.** 9, 15 **15.** 12, 21

Written Exercises

Find the LCM of each pair of numbers.

A **1.** 10, 12 **2.** 18, 27 **3.** 25, 45 **4.** 28, 98

 5. 24, 36 **6.** 28, 42 **7.** 45, 108 **8.** 66, 110

 9. 39, 130 **10.** 56, 196 **11.** 54, 180 **12.** 75, 175

Find the LCM of the three given numbers.

B **13.** 10, 15, 25 **14.** 18, 21, 36 **15.** 12, 16, 20 **16.** 18, 24, 28

17. If one whole number is a factor of a second whole number, what is the LCM of the two numbers?

18. If two whole numbers are relatively prime, what is their LCM?

19. a. Find LCM(6, 15) and LCM(15, 25). Then find LCM(6, 15, 25).
  b. Find LCM(12, 18), LCM(18, 30), and LCM(12, 18, 30).
  c. In each of parts (a) and (b), how is the third number you found related to the first two numbers?

20. a. Find LCM(12, 20) and GCF(12, 20). Find their product.
  b. Find LCM(30, 42) and GCF(30, 42). Find their product.
  c. What do you think is always true about the product of the GCF and the LCM of two numbers?

21. A granola bar producer puts a coupon for a free bar in every 80th bar and a coupon for two free bars in every 180th bar. How often does the producer put both coupons in a single bar?

22. If one car gets 18 miles per gallon and another gets 16 miles per gallon, what is the smallest whole number of gallons of gasoline each car will need to travel exactly the same distance as the other car?

23. If two kinds of bricks have heights 12 cm and 20 cm respectively, what is the least number of rows of each kind that will have equal heights?

C **24.** Find two whole numbers whose product is 90 and whose LCM is 30.

25. Find pairs of whole numbers whose LCM is 120 and whose GCF is 4. There is more than one solution.

26. The Plush Hotel received a shipment of glasses packed in full cartons of 40 glasses each. Another shipment of glasses packed 24 to a carton went to the Maison Restaurant. Glasses were also shipped to State University, but in this shipment cartons containing 25 glasses each were used. If the hotel, the restaurant and the university each received the same number of glasses and if none of them received more than a thousand glasses, how many glasses were in each shipment? How many cartons were in each shipment?

27. a. Show that GCF(24, 36) is a divisor of LCM(24, 36).
  b. Explain why the GCF of two counting numbers is always a divisor of the LCM of the numbers.

Self-Test B

Find out whether each number is prime or composite. If it is composite,
give its prime factorization.

1. 108	**2.** 79	**3.** 87	**4.** 109	[5-4]

Find the GCF of the numbers. If they are relatively prime, so state.

5. 30, 90	**6.** 98, 112	**7.** 45, 77	**8.** 75, 105	[5-5]

Find the LCM of each pair of numbers.

9. 28, 70	**10.** 21, 27	**11.** 39, 65	**12.** 45, 50	[5-6]

Self-Test answers and Extra Practice are at the back of the book.

 COMPUTER INVESTIGATION: *Factors*

The computer can be used to find all the pairs of factors of a number.
The program below will print all the pairs of factors of a given number.
If the number is a perfect square, there will be a pair of equal factors.

```
10   PRINT "TO FACTOR A NUMBER N:"
20   PRINT "N = ";
30   INPUT N
40   PRINT "PAIRS OF FACTORS ARE:"
50   FOR F = 1 TO N
60   LET Q = N / F
70   IF Q <  > INT (Q) THEN 90
80   PRINT F; TAB( 10);Q
90   NEXT F
100  END
```

RUN the program to print out the pairs of factors of the following.

1. 216	**2.** 256	**3.** 576	**4.** 672	**5.** 1680
6. 225	**7.** 625	**8.** 1450	**9.** 1840	**10.** 1059

You can see that we do not need to print all the pairs to find the
factors of the number. We can stop as soon as the quotient becomes less
than the factor being tested. Insert this line into the program.

$$65 \quad IF \; Q < F \; THEN \; 100$$

11-20. Repeat Exercises 1–10 with the shorter print-out. If a number is
a square number, state a square root of it.

A History of Numerals

The ancient **Egyptians** used an additive system for writing numerals. The values of the symbols were added, and the order in which they were written did not matter.

Numerals from 1 to 9 were written as shown at the right. Symbols for larger numbers are shown below.

All these symbols could be written from right to left or from left to right.

= 22,523

The **Babylonians** lived in Mesopotamia and wrote on clay tablets using wedge-shaped instruments. They usually wrote the numerals from 1 to 9 as shown at the right. Their symbol for 10 was ◁. They combined these symbols additively up to 59, ◁◁.

For numbers greater than 59, they used a place-value system with 60 as the base. Thus, 22,523 would be written in the following manner.

$$= 6(60^2) + 15(60) + 23 = 22,523$$

The Babylonians later used a symbol for zero to mark an "empty place." This is the first known use of such a symbol. The Babylonians' use of 60 as a base is reflected in our units of time, such as 60 s = 1 min and 60 min = 1 h.

The most well-known of the ancient numeral systems is that of the **Romans.** They used the symbols I, X, C, and M for 1, 10, 100, and 1000, respectively. The symbols V, L, and D stood for 5, 50, and 500, respectively. For numerals greater than 1000, a bar was placed over the symbols. The system was additive. Thus, 22,523 would be written as $\overline{XX}$MMDXXIII.

The **Mayas** flourished on the Yucatan peninsula of Mexico about 1300 years ago. They wrote numerals from 1 to 19 as follows, with a dot for 1 and a horizontal bar for 5. Once again, the symbols are additive.

On their stone calendars, the Mayas used a place-value system, arranged vertically. The place values are shown below.

$$22{,}523 = 3(20 \times 18 \times 20) + 2(18 \times 20) + 10(20) + 3 \longrightarrow$$

Notice that the third place value is 18×20, or 360, instead of 20×20, or 400. The Mayas also had a symbol for zero, $\bigcirc$.

The **Hindus** devised a place value system with base 10, using digits very much like those we use today. The **Arabs** adopted this system and spread its use to Asia, Africa, and Europe. The numerals we use today,

$$0,\ 1,\ 2,\ 3,\ 4,\ 5,\ 6,\ 7,\ 8,\ 9$$

are called **Hindu-Arabic numerals** because of their origin.

Write 1987:

1. with Egyptian numerals

2. with Babylonian numerals

3. with Roman numerals

4. with Mayan numerals

Write with decimal numerals:

5.   **6.**   **7.**

8.   **9.**   **10.**

Research Activity: Reading in Mathematics Read about numerals in an encyclopedia or a book about the history of mathematics.

Chapter Review

Complete.

1. 1, 2, 3, _?_, _?_, _?_, _?_, and _?_ are factors of 24. [5-1]

2. The first five multiples of 13 are _?_, _?_, _?_, _?_, and _?_.

3. The sum of an odd number and an even number is _?_.

4. The product of an odd number and an even number is _?_.

5. 40 is divisible by _?_, _?_, _?_, _?_, _?_, _?_, _?_, and _?_. [5-2]

6. All even numbers are divisible by 2 and _?_.

Write the letter of the correct answer.

7. Which of the following is not a factor of 156?
   a. 3   **b.** 4   **c.** 9   **d.** 2

8. Evaluate 17^2. [5-3]
   a. 189   **b.** 149   **c.** 249   **d.** 289

9. Evaluate $\sqrt{676}$.
   a. 24   **b.** 26   **c.** 23   **d.** 27

10. What is the next prime number after 47? [5-4]
    a. 49   **b.** 51   **c.** 53   **d.** 57

11. What is the prime factorization of 72?
    a. $1 \cdot 72$ **b.** $6^2 \cdot 2$ **c.** $2^3 \cdot 3^2$ **d.** $3^3 \cdot 2^2$

True or false?

12. 2 is the only even prime number.

13. Prime numbers have exactly two factors.

14. 121 is a prime number.

15. The only common factors of 6 and 12 are 2 and 3. [5-5]

16. GCF(56, 210) = 14

17. 135 and 531 are relatively prime.

18. The only common multiple of 7 and 11 is 77. [5-6]

19. 84 is a multiple of 3.

20. LCM(39, 65) = 2535

Chapter Test

List all the factors of each number.

1. 110   **2.** 126   **3.** 210   **4.** 435   [5-1]

List the first five multiples of each number.

5. 14   **6.** 18   **7.** 23   **8.** 26

State which of the numbers 2, 3, 4, 5, 9, and 10 are factors of each number. Use the tests for divisibility.

9. 822   **10.** 410   **11.** 315   **12.** 660   [5-2]

Evaluate each expression.

13. 18^2 **14.** $\sqrt{484}$ **15.** 27^2 **16.** $\sqrt{676}$ [5-3]

Find out whether each number is prime or composite. If it is composite, give its prime factorization.

17. 168   **18.** 96   **19.** 53   **20.** 111   [5-4]

Find the greatest common factor of each pair of numbers. If the numbers are relatively prime, so state.

21. 21, 55   **22.** 108, 168   **23.** 65, 104   **24.** 252, 264   [5-5]

Find the least common multiple of each pair of numbers.

25. 10, 18   **26.** 25, 30   **27.** 12, 108   **28.** 54, 102   [5-6]

Cumulative Review (Chapters 1–5)

Exercises

Perform the indicated operation.

1. $\begin{array}{r} 3641 \\ + 4783 \\ \hline \end{array}$

2. $\begin{array}{r} 7692 \\ - 3089 \\ \hline \end{array}$

3. $\begin{array}{r} 11{,}031 \\ - \quad 7{,}493 \\ \hline \end{array}$

4. $\begin{array}{r} 48 \\ 5632 \\ + \quad 493 \\ \hline \end{array}$

5. $\begin{array}{r} 7643 \\ 93 \\ + 3074 \\ \hline \end{array}$

6. $\begin{array}{r} 14{,}693 \\ 745 \\ + \qquad 9 \\ \hline \end{array}$

7. $\begin{array}{r} 4902 \\ - 4754 \\ \hline \end{array}$

8. $\begin{array}{r} 24{,}865 \\ + 69{,}738 \\ \hline \end{array}$

9. $\begin{array}{r} 42{,}007 \\ - 39{,}499 \\ \hline \end{array}$

10. $\begin{array}{r} 42.931 \\ + \quad 6.45 \\ \hline \end{array}$

11. $\begin{array}{r} 0.0061 \\ + 0.103 \\ \hline \end{array}$

12. $\begin{array}{r} 11.59 \\ + \quad 3.4291 \\ \hline \end{array}$

13. $\begin{array}{r} 1.0064 \\ - 0.4695 \\ \hline \end{array}$

14. $\begin{array}{r} 3.324 \\ - 3.195 \\ \hline \end{array}$

15. $\begin{array}{r} 14.097 \\ - \quad 6.359 \\ \hline \end{array}$

16. $\begin{array}{r} 364 \\ \times 37 \\ \hline \end{array}$

17. $\begin{array}{r} 1231 \\ \times 48 \\ \hline \end{array}$

18. $\begin{array}{r} 1093 \\ \times 104 \\ \hline \end{array}$

19. $23\overline{)19{,}688}$

20. $46\overline{)13{,}708}$

21. $34\overline{)22{,}848}$

22. $\begin{array}{r} 14.92 \\ \times 3.71 \\ \hline \end{array}$

23. $\begin{array}{r} 1.983 \\ \times 0.24 \\ \hline \end{array}$

24. $\begin{array}{r} 11.092 \\ \times 5.004 \\ \hline \end{array}$

25. $6\overline{)54.96}$

26. $12\overline{)0.05232}$

27. $0.43\overline{)11.051}$

Simplify.

28. $2.43(0.91 + 4.62)$

29. $1.87(5.63 - 2.94)$

30. $47 + 113 \times 16 \div 4$

31. $643 - 51 \times 3 + 87$

32. $369 \div 9 + 9 \times 241$

33. $87 \times 42 \div 7 + 431$

Solve.

34. $15x = 75$

35. $m + 91 = 408$

36. $22y = 242$

37. $c - 37 = 1089$

38. $v \div 12 = 15$

39. $910 \div z = 65$

Complete.

40. If X, Y, and Z are collinear and $XY = YZ$, then Y is the ___?___ of $\overline{XZ}$.

41. The sum of the measures of the angles of a triangle is ___?___°.

42. The sides of a triangle are 6.4 cm long, 8.7 cm long, and 15.9 cm long. The perimeter is ___?___ cm.

43. Two angles whose measures add to 90° are called ___?___.

44. All even numbers are divisible by ___?___ and ___?___.

45. 12 is the ___?___ of 24 and 36.

Problems

PROBLEM SOLVING REMINDERS

Here are some reminders that may help you solve some of the problems on this page.
• Supply additional information, if needed.
• Think of a simpler, related problem to help you plan.
• Estimate to check your answers.

Solve.

1. The school bus stop is a 12 min walk from Gordon's house. On Tuesday Gordon had to wait 7 min for the bus. If the ride to school is 21 min, how long did it take Gordon to get to school on Tuesday?

2. A school auditorium has 750 seats. During an assembly only 247 seventh-graders, 301 eighth-graders, and 33 teachers were present. How many empty seats were there?

3. Ella jogs 1235 m each day. How many meters did she jog in July?

4. A shipment of eggs is to be packed into cases. How many cases are needed if each holds 12 dozen eggs and there are 4032 eggs in all?

5. A certain number when decreased by 31 is 237. Find the number.

6. A number is tripled. The result is 402. Find the number.

7. A pentagon has sides with lengths of 7.2 cm, 8.31 cm, 6.47 cm, 7.9 cm, and 8.04 cm. Find the perimeter.

8. Salvatore bought 6 equally priced record albums. If the total cost was $47.76, how much was each record?

9. Five sides of a hexagon have lengths 4.2 cm, 8.73 cm, 6.9 cm, 7.22 cm, and 8.02 cm. If the perimeter is 41.92 cm, find the length of the sixth side.

10. How many empty 0.35 L jars can be filled from a tank with 41.3 L of water in it?

6 Fractions: Definitions and Relationships

APPLYING MATHEMATICS
CONSTRUCTION INDUSTRY

The construction industry employs millions of skilled workers to build bridges, highways, homes, factories, and skyscrapers. Vast amounts of materials such as steel, lumber, cement, glass, and brick are used. Many types of large trucks and equipment like bulldozers and cranes are used in the transport of these materials. Great amounts of money are spent. Mathematics is important at every phase of construction. Some examples are when plans are designed, materials are ordered measurements are taken, or when accounting tasks are performed. In this chapter you will develop your understanding of fractions, and learn how to convert them to decimals.

CAREER CONNECTION

CARPENTER

Carpenters cut, fit, and assemble wood in the construction of boats, buildings, and bridges — to mention a few of the more than one hundred specialties. Carpenters should have skill in the use of tools and be able to read blueprints. People who want to become carpenters often enter an apprenticeship program. Apprentices gain experience in layout, form building, inside and outside finishing, and care and use of tools.

Photo: Joists and rafters are arranged vertically to support the downward load of a roof.

6-1 Fractions

If an object is divided into 8 equal parts, each part is one eighth of the whole. We write this fraction as $\frac{1}{8}$.

$\frac{1}{8}$ means 1 divided by 8, or $1 \div 8$

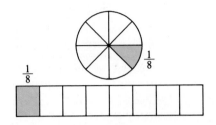

If an object is divided into 8 equal parts and three of these parts are being considered, the fraction that represents the parts under consideration is three eighths, or $\frac{3}{8}$.

$\frac{3}{8}$ means 3 divided by 8, or $3 \div 8$

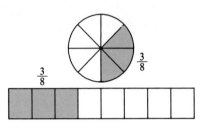

A fraction consists of two numbers. The **denominator** tells the number of equal parts into which the whole has been divided. The **numerator** tells how many of these parts are being considered. A fraction can have any nonzero whole number as denominator.

fraction bar ⟶ $\frac{7}{10}$ ⟵ numerator
⟵ denominator

As the diagrams illustrate:

$$\underbrace{\frac{1}{8} + \frac{1}{8} + \frac{1}{8} + \frac{1}{8} + \frac{1}{8} + \frac{1}{8} + \frac{1}{8} + \frac{1}{8}}_{\text{8 numbers added}} = \frac{8}{8} = 1, \quad \text{or} \quad 8 \times \frac{1}{8} = 1$$

$$\underbrace{\frac{1}{8} + \frac{1}{8} + \frac{1}{8}}_{\text{3 numbers added}} = \frac{3}{8}, \quad \text{or} \quad 3 \times \frac{1}{8} = \frac{3}{8}$$

Now think of a segment that is 3 units long. If this segment is divided into 8 congruent parts, each part is $3 \div 8$ or $\frac{3}{8}$ unit long. Thus, $\frac{3}{8}$ may also be thought of as $3 \div 8$.

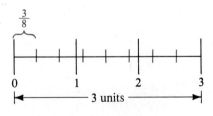

The diagram at the right illustrates how to multiply the fraction $\frac{2}{7}$ by the whole number 3.

$$\frac{2}{7} \times 3 = \frac{6}{7} \quad \text{or} \quad 3 \times \frac{2}{7} = \frac{6}{7}$$

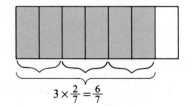

In general, we have the following properties of fractions.

Properties

For any whole numbers a, b, and c, with $b \neq 0$:

1. $\underbrace{\frac{1}{b} + \frac{1}{b} + \cdots + \frac{1}{b}}_{b \text{ numbers added}} = \frac{b}{b} = 1, \qquad b \times \frac{1}{b} = 1, \qquad \frac{1}{b} = 1 \div b$

2. $\underbrace{\frac{1}{b} + \frac{1}{b} + \cdots + \frac{1}{b}}_{a \text{ numbers added}} = \frac{a}{b}, \qquad a \times \frac{1}{b} = \frac{a}{b}, \qquad \frac{a}{b} = a \div b$

3. $\frac{a}{b} \times c = c \times \frac{a}{b} = \frac{a \times c}{b}$

EXAMPLE Complete.

a. $\frac{1}{3} + \frac{1}{3} + \frac{1}{3} = \underline{\quad ? \quad}$ **b.** $\frac{1}{5} + \frac{1}{5} = \underline{\quad ? \quad}$

c. $7 \div 12 = \underline{\quad ? \quad}$ **d.** $3 \times \frac{2}{11} = \underline{\quad ? \quad}$

Solution **a.** $\frac{1}{3} + \frac{1}{3} + \frac{1}{3} = 1$ **b.** $\frac{1}{5} + \frac{1}{5} = \frac{2}{5}$

c. $7 \div 12 = \frac{7}{12}$ **d.** $3 \times \frac{2}{11} = \frac{3 \times 2}{11} = \frac{6}{11}$

Class Exercises

What fraction of the whole figure does the shaded part represent?

1.   **2.**   **3.**   **4.**

5. If 4 students are absent from a class of 25, what fraction of the class is absent?

6. If a driver uses $\frac{1}{10}$ of a tank of gas every day, what fraction of a tank will she use in 3 days? in a week?

Complete.

7. $4 \times \frac{1}{4} = \underline{\quad ? \quad}$ **8.** $\frac{2}{9} = \underline{\quad ? \quad} \div \underline{\quad ? \quad}$ **9.** $2 \times \frac{1}{5} = \underline{\quad ? \quad}$ **10.** $4 \div 13 = \underline{\quad ? \quad}$

Written Exercises

What fraction of the whole figure does the shaded part represent?

A 1. 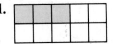   2. 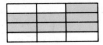   3.   4.

5.   6.   7.   8.

Complete.

9. $7 \times \frac{1}{7} = \underline{\ ?\ }$

10. $\frac{1}{5} + \frac{1}{5} + \frac{1}{5} = \underline{\ ?\ }$

11. $\frac{3}{4} = \underline{\ ?\ } \times \frac{1}{4}$

12. $5 \times \frac{1}{6} = \underline{\ ?\ }$

13. $5 \times \frac{2}{13} = \underline{\ ?\ }$

14. $\frac{3}{17} \times 4 = \underline{\ ?\ }$

15. $\underline{\ ?\ } \div \underline{\ ?\ } = \frac{3}{4}$

16. $\underline{\ ?\ } \div 5 = \frac{2}{?}$

17. $\underline{\ ?\ } \times \frac{1}{6} = 1$

18. $\underline{\ ?\ } \times \frac{1}{8} = \frac{7}{8}$

19. $\underline{\ ?\ } \times \frac{3}{25} = \frac{12}{25}$

20. $7 \times \frac{3}{22} = \underline{\ ?\ }$

21. $\frac{4}{27} \times 5 = \underline{\ ?\ }$

22. $\frac{7}{?} \times 2 = \frac{14}{15}$

23. $\underline{\ ?\ } \times \frac{5}{19} = \frac{15}{19}$

24. $\underline{\ ?\ } \times \frac{1}{9} = 1$

25. $14 \div \underline{\ ?\ } = \frac{?}{17}$

26. $\underline{\ ?\ } \div \underline{\ ?\ } = \frac{11}{21}$

A count of cars and trucks was taken at a parking lot on several different days. For each count, give the fraction of the total vehicles represented by (a) cars and (b) trucks.

EXAMPLE   8 cars, 7 trucks

Solution   Total vehicles $= 8 + 7 = 15$

a. Fraction represented by cars $= \frac{8}{15}$

b. Fraction represented by trucks $= \frac{7}{15}$

B 27. 9 cars, 11 trucks   28. 12 trucks, 15 cars

29. 15 trucks, 32 vehicles   30. 35 vehicles, 9 cars

In the school orchestra there are 26 strings, 10 woodwinds, 7 brasses, and 2 percussion instruments. What fraction of the orchestra is represented by each section?

31. Woodwind   32. String   33. Percussion   34. Brass

C 35. In a one-hour television program there were 13 minutes of commercials. What fraction of the total air time was taken up by (a) commercials and (b) programming?

36. In a two-hour track meet, 57 minutes were devoted to individual running events, and 34 minutes were devoted to relay races. What fraction of the total time was devoted to (a) individual running events, (b) relay races, and (c) other events?

Review Exercises

State whether the pairs of numbers are relatively prime.

1. 54, 17   **2.** 81, 27   **3.** 78, 13   **4.** 87, 6

5. 144, 24   **6.** 131, 18   **7.** 135, 48   **8.** 171, 19

 COMPUTER INVESTIGATION: *Finding the LCM*

The following program will find the LCM of two numbers.

```
10   PRINT "TO FIND LCM:"
20   PRINT "INPUT A, B";
30   INPUT A,B
40   FOR X = 1 TO B
50   LET A1 = A * X
60   LET Q = A1 / B
70   IF Q = INT (Q) THEN 90
80   NEXT X
90   PRINT "LCM(";A;",";B;") = ";A1
100  END
```

RUN the program to find the LCM of the following.

1. 12, 25   **2.** 5, 7   **3.** 18, 42   **4.** 72, 84

5. 34, 60   **6.** 45, 80   **7.** 110, 240   **8.** 235, 180

6-2 Equivalent Fractions

See Pages E11–E12 ▶

Fractions can be pictured on the number line. For example, $\frac{1}{2}$ is pictured as the midpoint of the segment from 0 to 1. Other fractions can be shown as follows.

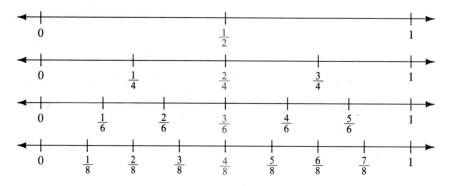

The number lines above show that the fractions

$$\frac{1}{2}, \frac{2}{4}, \frac{3}{6}, \text{ and } \frac{4}{8}$$

can all be pictured as the midpoint of the segment from 0 to 1. Thus, they denote the same number and are called **equivalent fractions.**

This suggests that if you multiply the numerator and denominator of a fraction, such as $\frac{1}{2}$, by the same nonzero whole number, the resulting fraction is equivalent to the original fraction. For example:

$$\frac{1}{2} = \frac{1 \times 3}{2 \times 3} = \frac{3}{6}$$

A similar process also works for division. If you divide the numerator and denominator of a fraction by the same nonzero whole number, the resulting fraction will be equivalent to the original fraction. For example:

$$\frac{4}{8} = \frac{4 \div 4}{8 \div 4} = \frac{1}{2}$$

In general, we have the following properties.

Properties

For any whole numbers a, b, and c, with $b \neq 0$ and $c \neq 0$:

$$\mathbf{1.} \; \frac{a}{b} = \frac{a \times c}{b \times c} \qquad \mathbf{2.} \; \frac{a}{b} = \frac{a \div c}{b \div c}$$

EXAMPLE 1 Find a fraction equivalent to $\frac{2}{3}$ with denominator 12.

Solution We want a number n such that

$$\frac{2}{3} = \frac{n}{12}.$$

Since $3 \times 4 = 12$, we multiply numerator and denominator by 4.

$$\frac{2}{3} = \frac{2 \times 4}{3 \times 4} = \frac{8}{12}$$

A fraction is in **lowest terms** if its numerator and denominator are relatively prime, that is, if their greatest common factor is 1.

$\frac{3}{4}$, $\frac{2}{7}$, and $\frac{3}{5}$ are in lowest terms.

$\frac{5}{10}$, $\frac{9}{12}$, and $\frac{6}{8}$ are *not* in lowest terms.

You can write a fraction in lowest terms by dividing the numerator and denominator by their GCF.

EXAMPLE 2 Write $\frac{12}{18}$ in lowest terms.

Solution Find the GCF of the numerator and denominator.

$$GCF(12, 18) = 6$$

$$\frac{12}{18} = \frac{12 \div 6}{18 \div 6} = \frac{2}{3}$$

Instead of finding the GCF in Example 2, we could have divided the numerator and denominator by common factors successively, until we got two relatively prime numbers. This method is illustrated at the right, where we divide first by 2 and then by 3.

$$\frac{\overset{6}{\cancel{12}}}{\underset{9}{\cancel{18}}} = \frac{\overset{2}{\cancel{6}}}{\underset{3}{\cancel{9}}} = \frac{2}{3}$$

EXAMPLE 3 Find two fractions with the same denominator that are equivalent to $\frac{7}{8}$ and to $\frac{5}{12}$.

Solution The common denominator of the two new fractions will have to be a multiple of both denominators, 8 and 12. The least common multiple is a convenient choice.

$$LCM(8, 12) = 24$$

$$\frac{7}{8} = \frac{7 \times 3}{8 \times 3} = \frac{21}{24}$$

$$\frac{5}{12} = \frac{5 \times 2}{12 \times 2} = \frac{10}{24}$$

The word *equivalent* comes from a Latin word meaning *equal in value.* Be sure you understand that two equivalent fractions, such as $\frac{7}{8}$ and $\frac{21}{24}$, are equal in value even though the numerals used to name the fractions are not the same.

Class Exercises

Multiply the numerator and denominator by the given whole number to get a fraction equivalent to the given fraction.

1. $\frac{2}{3}$; 2　　**2.** $\frac{3}{5}$; 4　　**3.** $\frac{4}{7}$; 3　　**4.** $\frac{3}{8}$; 5　　**5.** $\frac{3}{4}$; 7　　**6.** $\frac{5}{8}$; 2

Write in lowest terms.

7. $\frac{2}{6}$　　**8.** $\frac{10}{12}$　　**9.** $\frac{7}{14}$　　**10.** $\frac{15}{20}$　　**11.** $\frac{12}{15}$　　**12.** $\frac{8}{10}$

Name a whole number that could be the denominator of each of two fractions equivalent to the given fractions.

13. $\frac{2}{3}, \frac{1}{2}$　　　　**14.** $\frac{1}{3}, \frac{4}{5}$　　　　**15.** $\frac{1}{6}, \frac{3}{8}$　　　　**16.** $\frac{2}{9}, \frac{1}{12}$

Written Exercises

Complete the equivalent fraction.

A　**1.** $\frac{1}{4} = \frac{?}{20}$　　**2.** $\frac{1}{5} = \frac{?}{15}$　　**3.** $\frac{2}{3} = \frac{?}{30}$　　**4.** $\frac{3}{5} = \frac{?}{10}$

　　5. $\frac{6}{7} = \frac{24}{?}$　　**6.** $\frac{8}{9} = \frac{32}{?}$　　**7.** $\frac{5}{7} = \frac{35}{?}$　　**8.** $\frac{2}{9} = \frac{36}{?}$

　　9. $\frac{3}{11} = \frac{66}{?}$　　**10.** $\frac{5}{12} = \frac{?}{72}$　　**11.** $\frac{9}{14} = \frac{45}{?}$　　**12.** $\frac{6}{17} = \frac{?}{51}$

Write in lowest terms.

13. $\frac{8}{14}$　　**14.** $\frac{9}{15}$　　**15.** $\frac{20}{35}$　　**16.** $\frac{32}{48}$　　**17.** $\frac{30}{75}$　　**18.** $\frac{54}{72}$

Find the value of *n*.

19. $\frac{3}{5} = \frac{n}{15}$　　**20.** $\frac{20}{45} = \frac{n}{9}$　　**21.** $\frac{28}{56} = \frac{4}{n}$　　**22.** $\frac{3}{4} = \frac{24}{n}$

Find fractions with the same denominator that are equivalent to the given fractions. Use the LCM of the given denominators.

B　**23.** $\frac{3}{4}, \frac{2}{5}$　　　**24.** $\frac{5}{7}, \frac{2}{3}$　　　**25.** $\frac{5}{6}, \frac{2}{9}$　　　**26.** $\frac{3}{4}, \frac{1}{6}$

27. $\frac{7}{8}, \frac{5}{6}$ **28.** $\frac{15}{21}, \frac{8}{9}$ **29.** $\frac{5}{22}, \frac{3}{4}$ **30.** $\frac{9}{16}, \frac{7}{24}$

31. $\frac{3}{4}, \frac{5}{6}, \frac{7}{18}$ **32.** $\frac{2}{5}, \frac{7}{10}, \frac{4}{15}$ **33.** $\frac{4}{5}, \frac{3}{8}, \frac{1}{6}$ **34.** $\frac{3}{14}, \frac{1}{6}, \frac{5}{9}$

35. There are 9 juniors and 15 seniors on the varsity lacrosse team. What fraction of the team is seniors? Give your answer in lowest terms.

36. The results of a school election are shown at the right. Represent each fraction of the total vote in lowest terms.

        Mary   160
        Bob   240
        John   80

     a. Mary's vote   **b.** John's vote   **c.** Those not voting for Mary

C   **37. a.** Take two equivalent fractions, such as $\frac{6}{9}$ and $\frac{8}{12}$, and multiply the numerator of the first by the denominator of the second. Also multiply the numerator of the second by the denominator of the first. What do you notice about the two products?

     b. Repeat part (a) for several other pairs of equivalent fractions. If two fractions $\frac{a}{b}$ and $\frac{c}{d}$ are equivalent, state a relationship between the four numbers a, b, c, and d that does not involve fractions.

Find the value of n for which each statement is true.

38. $\frac{3}{n} = \frac{n}{12}$ **39.** $\frac{2}{n} = \frac{n}{8}$ **40.** $\frac{3}{n} = \frac{n}{27}$ **41.** $\frac{4}{n} = \frac{n}{25}$

42. $\frac{n}{16} = \frac{4}{n}$ **43.** $\frac{n}{9} = \frac{25}{n}$ **44.** $\frac{n}{48} = \frac{3}{n}$ **45.** $\frac{n}{10} = \frac{40}{n}$

Review Exercises

Simplify.

   1. $17 + 4 \times 5$ **2.** $18 + 42 \div 3$ **3.** $110 \div 5 + 5$

   4. $96 \div (4 + 8)$ **5.** $54 + 126 \div 3$ **6.** $14 \times 9 \div 6$

   7. $(81 + 18) \div 9$ **8.** $(130 + 15) \div 5$ **9.** $7(41 + 19)$

NONROUTINE PROBLEM SOLVING: *Thinking Skills*

A brick is placed on a balance scale. It balances exactly with a $\frac{3}{4}$ lb weight and $\frac{3}{4}$ of a brick. What is the weight of the brick?

6-3 Fractions and Mixed Numbers

You know that $\frac{1}{2} + \frac{1}{2} + \frac{1}{2} = \frac{3}{2}$. The fraction $\frac{3}{2}$ is shown on the number line.

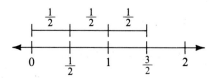

A fraction, such as $\frac{3}{2}$, whose numerator is greater than or equal to its denominator, is called an **improper fraction.** Every improper fraction is greater than or equal to 1. A **proper fraction** is a fraction whose numerator is less than its denominator. Thus, a proper fraction is always between 0 and 1.

Proper fractions	**Improper fractions**
$\dfrac{1}{4}, \dfrac{2}{3}, \dfrac{5}{9}, \dfrac{10}{12}, \dfrac{17}{18}$	$\dfrac{5}{2}, \dfrac{8}{3}, \dfrac{12}{5}, \dfrac{18}{15}, \dfrac{17}{4}$

You can express any improper fraction as the sum of a whole number and a proper fraction. For example, the number line shows that

$$\frac{3}{2} = 1 + \frac{1}{2}, \quad \text{or} \quad 1\frac{1}{2}.$$

A number, such as $1\frac{1}{2}$, that is expressed as the sum of a whole number and a fraction is called a **mixed number.** If the fractional part of a mixed number is a proper fraction in lowest terms, the mixed number is said to be in **simple form.**

To change an improper fraction to a mixed number in simple form, we divide the numerator by the denominator and express the remainder as a fraction.

EXAMPLE 1 Change $\frac{14}{3}$ to a mixed number in simple form.

Solution $\frac{14}{3} = 14 \div 3$. Here 4 R 2 is written as $4\frac{2}{3}$.

              Therefore $\frac{14}{3} = 4\frac{2}{3}$.

EXAMPLE 2 Change $\frac{30}{4}$ to a mixed number in simple form.

Solution   Method 1: $\frac{30}{4} = 30 \div 4 = 7\frac{2}{4} = 7\frac{1}{2}$

              Method 2: $\dfrac{\overset{15}{\cancel{30}}}{\underset{2}{\cancel{4}}} = \frac{15}{2} = 15 \div 2 = 7\frac{1}{2}$

To change a mixed number to an improper fraction, rewrite the whole number part as a fraction with the same denominator as the fractional part.

EXAMPLE 3   Change $1\frac{3}{8}$ to an improper fraction.

Solution $1\frac{3}{8} = 1 + \frac{3}{8} = \frac{8}{8} + \frac{3}{8} = \frac{11}{8}$

EXAMPLE 4   Change $2\frac{5}{6}$ to an improper fraction.

Solution $2\frac{5}{6} = 2 + \frac{5}{6} = \left(2 \times \frac{6}{6}\right) + \frac{5}{6} = \frac{12}{6} + \frac{5}{6} = \frac{17}{6}$

Example 4 suggests the following shortcut for changing a mixed number to an improper fraction.

$$2\frac{5}{6} = 2 \;\overset{+}{\underset{\times}{\curvearrowright}}\; \frac{5}{6} = \frac{(6 \times 2) + 5}{6} = \frac{12 + 5}{6} = \frac{17}{6}$$

EXAMPLE 5   An assembly period has 50 min available for speeches by 4 candidates for class president. If two minutes are allowed for each introduction and if the remaining time is divided equally, how long may each candidate speak?

Solution   A diagram showing the time periods involved will be helpful.

$$\overbrace{\text{50 min}}$$

| 2 | ? | 2 | ? | 2 | ? | 2 | ? |

From the diagram, we see that there are 50 − 8, or 42, minutes for the speeches. If each candidate is to have an equal amount of time to speak, we have

$$42 \div 4 = 10\frac{1}{2}.$$

Thus, each candidate has $10\frac{1}{2}$ minutes.

PROBLEM SOLVING REMINDER

Remember that *drawing diagrams* can be helpful in solving problems even if the problems are not geometric. In Example 5, looking at the diagram makes it easier to see that there are 50 − 8, or 42, minutes for speeches.

Class Exercises

Change to a whole number or a mixed number in simple form.

1. $\frac{5}{3}$ 2. $\frac{7}{4}$ 3. $\frac{17}{11}$ 4. $\frac{6}{3}$ 5. $\frac{9}{2}$ 6. $\frac{13}{4}$

Change to an improper fraction.

7. $1\frac{1}{3}$ 8. $1\frac{2}{5}$ 9. $2\frac{1}{2}$ 10. $3\frac{1}{4}$ 11. $1\frac{1}{12}$ 12. $5\frac{1}{2}$

Written Exercises

Change to a whole number or a mixed number in simple form.

A 1. $\frac{15}{4}$ 2. $\frac{22}{5}$ 3. $\frac{56}{9}$ 4. $\frac{51}{8}$ 5. $\frac{70}{7}$ 6. $\frac{53}{12}$

7. $\frac{26}{4}$ 8. $\frac{21}{9}$ 9. $\frac{45}{5}$ 10. $\frac{148}{6}$ 11. $\frac{175}{15}$ 12. $\frac{235}{30}$

Change to an improper fraction.

13. $6\frac{2}{3}$ 14. $6\frac{3}{5}$ 15. $7\frac{3}{8}$ 16. $9\frac{3}{11}$ 17. $12\frac{5}{6}$ 18. $16\frac{1}{5}$

19. $14\frac{5}{9}$ 20. $23\frac{2}{7}$ 21. $103\frac{1}{4}$ 22. $215\frac{5}{6}$ 23. $75\frac{7}{12}$ 24. $83\frac{1}{16}$

Express each quotient as a mixed number in simple form.

B 25. $3\overline{)785}$ 26. $5\overline{)852}$ 27. $13\overline{)4198}$ 28. $16\overline{)3751}$

29. $25\overline{)6785}$ 30. $32\overline{)8464}$ 31. $145\overline{)37025}$ 32. $231\overline{)98001}$

Complete.

C 33. $32\overline{)16?}^{\,5\frac{3}{32}}$ 34. $25\overline{)677?}^{\,271\frac{2}{25}}$ 35. $26\overline{)3??}^{\,12\frac{1}{26}}$ 36. $19\overline{)3??}^{\,20\frac{17}{19}}$

Problems

Express each answer as a proper fraction in lowest terms or a mixed number in simple form.

A 1. Sally and Bill prepared 40 sandwiches for a picnic with 14 friends. If the sandwiches were divided equally among 16 people, how many sandwiches would each person receive?

2. An assignment of 82 pages of a novel was given out on Monday to be read by Friday. If the students read equal amounts on Monday, Tuesday, Wednesday, and Thursday evenings, how many pages should be read each evening?

3. If 8 identical items together weigh 30 pounds, how much does each one weigh?

4. A class has 48 minutes available to hear reports from 15 students. If the time is to be divided equally, how long may each student have?

5. A fence is to be put along a side of a lot measuring 114 feet. Nineteen fence posts are to be used, one at each end and 17 equally spaced between the ends. What is the distance between centers of two consecutive fence posts?

B **6.** A play consists of 3 acts of equal length with 2 twenty-minute intermissions between acts. If the whole production takes 3 hours, how long is each act in minutes?

7. A one-hour TV program consists of four segments of equal length. There are 3 one-minute commercials between each segment. There is also a 2-minute introduction and a 2-minute closing. How long is each segment?

8. A table top is in the shape of a square 45 inches on a side. A chessboard is inlaid so that a border of 3 inches exists on all four sides. How wide is each of the eight rows of squares of the chessboard?

9. Five columns of lettering are to be laid out on a sign 35 inches wide. There will be a 1-inch space between pairs of adjacent columns and a 2-inch border at each side of the sign. How wide will each column be?

10. A circular dartboard has 12 regions of equal area where points can be scored. The total area of its outer border is 5 in². If the total area of the board is 144 in², what is the area of each point-scoring region?

11. In a 40-minute debate there were four speeches, each lasting 5 minutes, and two 3-minute rebuttals. If there were two breaks of equal duration between the speeches and rebuttals, how long was each break?

12. A highway is 78 feet wide. It has a breakdown lane on each side that is 12 feet wide. There is also a median divider that is 3 feet wide. How wide will each travel lane of the highway be if the road is divided into 4 travel lanes? 6 travel lanes?

C 13. A paper square has an area of 100 in². Into how many pieces of equal area must the square be cut if the area of each piece is to be between 8 in² and 9 in²? What is the area of each piece?

14. How many equal pieces that weigh between 12 and 13 ounces can be made from a 110-ounce block if the whole block is used? How much will each piece weigh?

Self-Test A

Complete.

1. $\frac{1}{7} + \frac{1}{7} + \frac{1}{7} + \frac{1}{7} = \underline{\ ?\ }$

2. $\frac{2}{15} \times \underline{\ ?\ } = \frac{14}{15}$ $\qquad$ [6-1]

3. $\underline{\ ?\ } \div \underline{\ ?\ } = \frac{9}{17}$

4. $\underline{\ ?\ } \times \frac{1}{8} = 1$

5. $\frac{1}{3} = \frac{?}{15}$

6. $\frac{3}{4} = \frac{75}{?}$

7. $\frac{4}{9} = \frac{36}{?}$ $\qquad$ [6-2]

Write in lowest terms.

8. $\frac{36}{40}$

9. $\frac{28}{60}$

10. $\frac{72}{108}$

Change to a mixed number in simple form.

11. $\frac{17}{9}$

12. $\frac{38}{12}$

13. $\frac{145}{18}$ $\qquad$ [6-3]

Change to an improper fraction.

14. $2\frac{4}{9}$

15. $14\frac{7}{8}$

16. $42\frac{7}{11}$

Self-Test answers and Extra Practice are at the back of the book.

 NONROUTINE PROBLEM SOLVING: *Using Deduction*

Give a fraction to represent the area of each lettered portion of the square.

6-4 Comparing Fractions

When two fractions have equal denominators, it is easy to tell which of the fractions is greater. We simply compare their numerators. For example,

$$\frac{3}{11} < \frac{5}{11}, \text{ since } 3 < 5.$$

If the fractions have different denominators, we can find a **common denominator.** That is, we find a whole number that can serve as the denominator of two fractions that are equivalent to the given ones. We then compare the numerators of these fractions.

EXAMPLE 1 Which is greater, $\frac{2}{3}$ or $\frac{4}{5}$?

Solution 15 is a multiple of both 3 and 5.
Therefore, we can use 15 as a common denominator.

$$\frac{2}{3} = \frac{2 \times 5}{3 \times 5} = \frac{10}{15} \qquad \frac{4}{5} = \frac{4 \times 3}{5 \times 3} = \frac{12}{15}$$

$$10 < 12$$

Therefore, we conclude that $\frac{2}{3} < \frac{4}{5}$.

A common denominator that is convenient to use in comparing fractions is the LCM of the denominators of the given fractions.

EXAMPLE 2 Which is greater, $\frac{5}{6}$ or $\frac{7}{9}$?

Solution LCM(6, 9) = 18
Therefore, we can use 18 as a common denominator.

$$\frac{5}{6} = \frac{5 \times 3}{6 \times 3} = \frac{15}{18} \qquad \frac{7}{9} = \frac{7 \times 2}{9 \times 2} = \frac{14}{18}$$

$$15 > 14$$

Therefore, we conclude that $\frac{5}{6} > \frac{7}{9}$.

EXAMPLE 3 Name a fraction between $\frac{1}{6}$ and $\frac{3}{8}$.

Solution First find fractions equivalent to the two given fractions and having a common denominator.

LCM(6, 8) = 24

$$\frac{1}{6} = \frac{1 \times 4}{6 \times 4} = \frac{4}{24} \qquad \frac{3}{8} = \frac{3 \times 3}{8 \times 3} = \frac{9}{24}$$

Now find a fraction between $\frac{4}{24}$ and $\frac{9}{24}$.

Thus $\frac{5}{24}, \frac{6}{24}, \frac{7}{24},$ and $\frac{8}{24}$ are fractions between $\frac{1}{6}$ and $\frac{3}{8}$.

Class Exercises

State the LCM of the denominators of each pair of fractions.

1. $\frac{2}{5}, \frac{1}{4}$ **2.** $\frac{2}{9}, \frac{5}{12}$ **3.** $\frac{5}{6}, \frac{7}{8}$ **4.** $\frac{7}{25}, \frac{3}{10}$

5–8. For each pair of fractions in Exercises 1–4, name a pair of fractions equivalent to the given fractions and having a common denominator.

9–12. State which fraction in each of Exercises 1–4 is greater.

Written Exercises

Which fraction is greater?

A   **1.** $\frac{3}{8}, \frac{1}{3}$ **2.** $\frac{7}{12}, \frac{4}{5}$ **3.** $\frac{5}{6}, \frac{7}{10}$ **4.** $\frac{17}{20}, \frac{13}{15}$

    5. $\frac{8}{25}, \frac{3}{10}$ **6.** $\frac{7}{18}, \frac{5}{12}$ **7.** $\frac{11}{16}, \frac{17}{24}$ **8.** $\frac{13}{28}, \frac{15}{21}$

    9. $\frac{14}{33}, \frac{9}{22}$ **10.** $\frac{21}{45}, \frac{29}{60}$ **11.** $\frac{7}{36}, \frac{3}{16}$ **12.** $\frac{7}{56}, \frac{5}{42}$

Name a fraction between the two given fractions.

13. $\frac{7}{12}, \frac{8}{15}$ **14.** $\frac{18}{25}, \frac{3}{4}$ **15.** $\frac{3}{14}, \frac{2}{21}$ **16.** $\frac{11}{35}, \frac{5}{14}$

B   **17.** $\frac{3}{7}, \frac{4}{7}$ (Hint: Use the denominator 14.)

    18. $\frac{7}{15}, \frac{8}{15}$ (Hint: Use the denominator 30.)

19. $\frac{5}{9}, \frac{7}{12}$ **20.** $\frac{7}{15}, \frac{12}{25}$ **21.** $\frac{1}{2}, \frac{7}{16}$ **22.** $\frac{5}{12}, \frac{3}{8}$

Which fraction is greatest?

23. $\frac{3}{8}, \frac{5}{12}, \frac{4}{9}$ **24.** $\frac{5}{21}, \frac{3}{14}, \frac{1}{6}$ **25.** $\frac{2}{3}, \frac{5}{7}, \frac{17}{21}$ **26.** $\frac{5}{13}, \frac{2}{5}, \frac{7}{15}$

If $n > 0$, complete using $<$, $>$, or $=$.

27. If $a < b$, then $\frac{a}{n}$ ___?___ $\frac{b}{n}$.   **28.** If $a < b$, then $\frac{n}{a}$ ___?___ $\frac{n}{b}$.

C 29. $\frac{n+1}{n}$ ___?___ 1 **30.** $\frac{n}{n+1}$ ___?___ 1

31. a. If $\frac{a}{b}$ and $\frac{c}{d}$ are two fractions, write two other fractions equivalent to these and having a common denominator. Use the letters a, b, c, and d in your answer.

   b. If $ad > bc$, which fraction is greater, $\frac{a}{b}$ or $\frac{c}{d}$?

Problems

A 1. Sandy made 7 baskets out of 18 shots in a basketball game, while Joan made 9 baskets out of 20 shots. Who made a greater fraction of her shots?

2. The Bears won 11 out of 16 games. The Eagles won 17 out of 24 games. Which team won a greater fraction of its games?

3. In a quality control test of 40-watt light bulbs, 4 out of 75 bulbs were found to be defective. In a test of 60-watt bulbs, 7 out of 120 bulbs were defective. Which type had a greater fraction of defective bulbs?

4. There were 10 sunny days out of 28 in February and 12 sunny days out of 30 in November. Which month had the higher fraction of sunny days?

B 5. In archery at summer camp Chris hit the target with 7 out of 12 shots. If Brett has 15 shots, how many must hit the target in order for him to have a higher fraction of successful shots?

Fractions: Definitions and Relationships **193**

6. The following table shows numbers of sedans and station wagons sold by three car dealers in March. What fraction of each dealer's sales were sedan sales? For which dealer was this fraction the greatest?

Dealer	Sedans	Station wagons
Autorama	15	12
Rolling Motors	18	14
Car City	16	12

C **7.** In a tennis match Melissa got 24 out of 30 first serves in. Jennifer got 22 first serves in. If Jennifer got a greater fraction of her first serves in than Melissa, what is the greatest total number of first serves Jennifer could have had?

Review Exercises

Divide. Give the remainder as a decimal rounded to the nearest hundredth, if necessary.

1. $117 \div 25$ **2.** $254 \div 40$ **3.** $183 \div 9$ **4.** $452 \div 16$

5. $363 \div 18$ **6.** $654 \div 15$ **7.** $582 \div 14$ **8.** $695 \div 17$

CALCULATOR INVESTIGATION: *Comparing Fractions*

Use a calculator to compare the following pairs of fractions.

1. $\frac{5}{8}, \frac{9}{14}$ **2.** $\frac{23}{18}, \frac{31}{24}$ **3.** $\frac{17}{25}, \frac{10}{17}$

4. $\frac{110}{17}, \frac{97}{13}$ **5.** $\frac{53}{62}, \frac{71}{81}$ **6.** $\frac{123}{235}, \frac{63}{119}$

NONROUTINE PROBLEM SOLVING: *Finding a Pattern*

Fill in the blanks.

1. 6, 10, 15, 21, __?__, 36, 45

2. 103, __?__, 305, 406, 507

3. 5, 3, 4, 2, __?__, 1, 2

4. 132, 243, 354, 465, __?__

5. 17, 16, 18, __?__, 19, 14, 20, 13

6-5 Changing a Fraction to a Decimal

There are two methods that can be used to change a fraction to a decimal. In one method we try to find an equivalent fraction whose denominator is a power of 10, although this may not always be possible. For example, to change $\frac{13}{25}$ to a decimal we can write

$$\frac{13}{25} = \frac{13 \times 4}{25 \times 4} = \frac{52}{100} = 0.52.$$

In the second method of changing a fraction to a decimal we divide the numerator by the denominator. For example, to change $\frac{3}{8}$ to a decimal, we proceed as shown below.

$$
\begin{array}{r}
0.375 \\
8\overline{)3.000} \\
\underline{2\,4} \\
60 \\
\underline{56} \\
40 \\
\underline{40} \\
0
\end{array}
\qquad
\frac{3}{8} = 3 \div 8 = 0.375
$$

When the remainder is 0, as in the division above, the decimal is referred to as a **terminating decimal.** By examining the denominator of a fraction in *lowest terms,* we can determine whether the fraction can be expressed as a terminating decimal. If the denominator has no prime factors other than 2 or 5, the decimal representation will terminate. This is so since the fraction can be written as an equivalent fraction whose denominator is a power of ten.

EXAMPLE 1   Determine whether each fraction can be expressed as a terminating decimal.

   a. $\frac{7}{40}$ **b.** $\frac{5}{12}$ **c.** $\frac{9}{12}$

Solution   **a.** $40 = 2^3 \times 5$. Since the only prime factors of the denominator are 2 and 5, the fraction can be expressed as a terminating decimal.

b. $12 = 2^2 \times 3$. Since 3 is a prime factor of the denominator, the fraction cannot be expressed as a terminating decimal.

c. $\frac{9}{12} = \frac{3}{4}$ and $4 = 2^2$. Since 4 has no prime factors other than 2, the fraction can be expressed as a terminating decimal.

The next example illustrates what happens when the denominator of a fraction has prime factors other than 2 or 5.

EXAMPLE 2 Change $\frac{15}{22}$ to a decimal.

Solution Since 22 has the prime factor 11, the remainder 0 will not be reached. Notice the pattern of repeating remainders 18 and 4. They produce the repeating block of digits, 81, in the quotient. We write

$$\frac{15}{22} = 0.6818181\ldots, \quad \text{or} \quad 0.68\overline{1}$$

where the bar means that the block 81 repeats without ending. The numbers 0.6, 0.68, 0.681, 0.6818, 0.68181, and so on, are closer and closer approximations to $\frac{15}{22}$.

```
        0.68181
22)15.00000
   13 2
    1 80
    1 76
      40
      22
     180
     176
      40
      22
      18
```

A decimal, such as $0.68\overline{1}$, in which a block of digits continues to repeat indefinitely is called a **repeating decimal.** In Example 2 the digits 81 continue to repeat because the remainders 18 and 4 continue to recur.

In fact, if you divide any whole number by any other whole number, the only possible remainders are the whole numbers less than the divisor. For example, if you divide a whole number by 7, the possible remainders are 0, 1, 2, 3, 4, 5, and 6. If the quotient does not terminate, some remainder will eventually reappear in the division, and then the same block of digits will reappear in the quotient. Therefore, we have the following property.

Property

Every fraction can be expressed as either a terminating decimal or a repeating decimal.

Class Exercises

State whether the decimal expansion of each fraction is a terminating decimal or a repeating decimal.

1. $\frac{3}{5}$ 2. $\frac{5}{12}$ 3. $\frac{21}{24}$ 4. $\frac{9}{40}$ 5. $\frac{13}{70}$ 6. $\frac{17}{32}$

State the decimal with two of the repeating blocks.

7. $0.\overline{712}$

8. $2.09\overline{37}$

9. $4.0\overline{1}$

10. $6.2\overline{136}$

Written Exercises

Change each fraction to a decimal.

A 1. $\frac{5}{8}$ 2. $\frac{7}{20}$ 3. $\frac{19}{25}$ 4. $\frac{13}{40}$ 5. $\frac{11}{16}$ 6. $\frac{113}{400}$

7. $\frac{5}{6}$ 8. $\frac{7}{12}$ 9. $\frac{8}{11}$ 10. $\frac{9}{22}$ 11. $\frac{16}{15}$ 12. $\frac{85}{99}$

13. $\frac{9}{8}$ 14. $\frac{19}{11}$ 15. $\frac{25}{12}$ 16. $\frac{21}{16}$ 17. $\frac{46}{25}$ 18. $\frac{29}{27}$

19. $\frac{5}{18}$ 20. $\frac{3}{16}$ 21. $\frac{18}{11}$ 22. $\frac{40}{33}$ 23. $\frac{15}{37}$ 24. $\frac{150}{99}$

Arrange the numbers in each list in order from least to greatest.

B 25. $0.45,\ 0.\overline{45},\ 0.4\overline{5},\ 0.\overline{4}$

26. $0.\overline{713},\ 0.7\overline{1},\ 0.713,\ 0.7\overline{13}$

27. $0.562,\ 0.5\overline{6},\ \frac{9}{16},\ 0.\overline{562}$

28. $0.8\overline{16},\ 0.\overline{8},\ 0.8\overline{1},\ \frac{49}{60}$

29. $0.\overline{626},\ \frac{2}{3},\ 0.67,\ \frac{62}{99}$

30. $\frac{25}{22},\ 1.\overline{13},\ \frac{103}{90},\ 1.\overline{136}$

Express as a terminating or repeating decimal.

31. $\frac{1.38}{3.3}$ 32. $\frac{16.4}{11.1}$ 33. $\frac{10}{1.6}$ 34. $\frac{94.255}{1.75}$

35. $\frac{0.0594}{0.027}$ 36. $\frac{9}{0.074}$ 37. $\frac{0.0377}{0.12}$ 38. $\frac{90}{0.64}$

C 39. Give a rule for the number of digits in the terminating decimal expansion of a proper fraction based on the prime factorizations of the denominators shown in the following table.

Denominator	Prime Factorization	Digits in Decimal Expansion
4	2^2	2
8	2^3	3
50	2×5^2	2
80	$2^4 \times 5$	4
200	$2^3 \times 5^2$	3
250	2×5^3	3
500	$2^2 \times 5^3$	3

Fractions: Definitions and Relationships **197**

a. **Find the prime factors of each denominator.**

b. **Use the rule determined in Exercise 39 to find the number of digits in the decimal expansion of each fraction.**

40. $\dfrac{5}{64}$ **41.** $\dfrac{7}{125}$ **42.** $\dfrac{3}{160}$ **43.** $\dfrac{4}{32}$ **44.** $\dfrac{9}{40}$ **45.** $\dfrac{11}{625}$

Review Exercises

Multiply.

1. 5.493×10^2 **2.** 8.451×10^1 **3.** 6.9832×10^3

4. 0.0092×10^3 **5.** 1.008×10^2 **6.** 4.92×10^4

7. 8.34962×10^3 **8.** 0.00006×10^2 **9.** 1.920008×10^5

CALCULATOR INVESTIGATION: *Patterns*

Use a calculator for these exercises. Copy and complete each of the following.

1. $(1 \times 9) + 1 = 9 + 1 \quad = 10$

2. $(12 \times 9) + 2 = 108 + 2 = 110$

3. $(123 \times 9) + 3 \quad = \underline{?}$

4. $(1234 \times 9) + 4 \quad = \underline{?}$

5. $(12345 \times 9) + 5 \quad = \underline{?}$

6. $(123456 \times 9) + 6 \quad = \underline{?}\ \star$

7. $(1234567 \times 9) + 7 \quad = \underline{?}$

8. $(12345678 \times 9) + 8 \quad = \underline{?}$

9. $(123456789 \times 9) + 9 \quad = \underline{?}$

10. $3 \times 37037 = 111111$

11. $6 \times 37037 = \underline{?}$

12. $9 \times 37037 = \underline{?}$

13. $12 \times 37037 = \underline{?}$

14. $15 \times 37037 = \underline{?}$

15. $18 \times 37037 = \underline{?}$

16. $21 \times 37037 = \underline{?}$

17. $24 \times 37037 = \underline{?}$

18. $27 \times 37037 = \underline{?}$

19. $30 \times 37037 = \underline{?}\ \star$

20. Compare the results marked $\star$.

21. Verify that $1001 = 7 \times 11 \times 13$.

22. Complete the factoring:

$1111110 = 30 \times 37037$

$= \underline{?} \times \underline{?} \times \underline{?} \times \underline{?} \times \underline{?} \times \underline{?} \times \underline{?}$

6-6 Changing a Decimal to a Fraction

As we have seen, every fraction is equal to either a terminating decimal or a repeating decimal. It is also true that every terminating or repeating decimal is equal to a fraction.

   To change a terminating decimal to a fraction in lowest terms, we write the decimal as a fraction whose denominator is a power of 10. We then write this fraction in lowest terms.

EXAMPLE 1 Change 0.385 to a fraction in lowest terms.

Solution $0.385 = \frac{385}{1000} = \frac{77}{200}$

EXAMPLE 2 Change 3.64 to a mixed number in simple form.

Solution $3.64 = 3 + \frac{64}{100} = 3 + \frac{16}{25} = 3\frac{16}{25}$

   The next two examples demonstrate a method of changing a repeating decimal to a fraction.

EXAMPLE 3 Change $0.\overline{243}$ to a fraction in lowest terms.

Solution Let $n = 0.\overline{243} = 0.243243\ldots$.
Then $1000n = 243.243243\ldots$.
We can subtract n from $1000n$ to get $999n$.

$$\begin{array}{r} 1000n = 243.243243\ldots \\ \underline{n = 0.243243\ldots} \\ 999n = 243.000000\ldots \end{array}$$

$999n = 243$

$n = 243 \div 999 = \frac{243}{999} = \frac{27}{111} = \frac{9}{37}$

EXAMPLE 4 Change $0.3\overline{18}$ to a fraction in lowest terms.

Solution Let $n = 0.3\overline{18} = 0.3181818\ldots$.
Then $100n = 31.818181\ldots$.
We can subtract n from $100n$ to get $99n$.

$$\begin{array}{r} 100n = 31.818181\ldots \\ \underline{n = 0.318181\ldots} \\ 99n = 31.500000\ldots \end{array}$$

$99n = 31.5$

$n = 31.5 \div 99 = \frac{31.5}{99} = \frac{31.5 \times 10}{99 \times 10} = \frac{315}{990} = \frac{63}{198} = \frac{7}{22}$

Notice that in Example 3 and Example 4, we multiplied the given repeating decimal by 10 to the power that is the number of digits in the repeating block.

COMMUNICATION IN MATHEMATICS: *Reading for Meaning*

Mathematics should be read slowly and carefully to avoid errors. For example, if read too quickly, $0.3\overline{18}$ could be read as 0.318, $0.\overline{318}$, or $0.31\overline{8}$, all of which represent different numbers.

Class Exercises

Change each decimal to a fraction.

1. 0.7   2. 0.61   3. 0.289   4. 0.03   5. 4.9   6. 2.057

State what power of 10 you would multiply each repeating decimal by in order to change it to a fraction.

7. $0.3\overline{06}$ 8. $0.5\overline{3}$ 9. $0.4\overline{82}$ 10. $0.13\overline{6}$

State which of the two decimals is greater.

11. $0.\overline{3}$, 0.3   12. $0.2\overline{5}$, 0.25   13. $0.1\overline{62}$, $0.\overline{62}$ 14. $0.3\overline{5}$, $0.\overline{35}$

Written Exercises

Change each decimal to either a proper fraction in lowest terms or a mixed number in simple form.

A 1. 0.32   2. 0.65   3. 0.375   4. 0.088

5. 5.26   6. 1.45   7. 9.075   8. 6.112

9. 0.1725   10. 0.124   11. $0.\overline{7}$ 12. $0.6\overline{3}$

13. $0.1\overline{44}$ 14. $0.\overline{216}$ 15. $0.0\overline{27}$ 16. $0.3\overline{15}$

B 17. $0.4\overline{189}$ 18. $0.\overline{2970}$ 19. $0.60\overline{975}$ 20. $0.37\overline{128}$

21. Change $0.3\overline{9}$ to a fraction in lowest terms. Do you know another decimal representation of this fraction?

22. Change $1.24\overline{9}$ to a mixed number in simple form. Give another decimal representation of this number.

a. Add the decimals. Change the sum of the decimals to a fraction.
b. Change each decimal to a fraction. Add the fractions.
c. Compare the answers to parts (a) and (b).

23. 0.5, $0.\overline{3}$ **24.** $0.\overline{7}$, 0.4

C **25.** $0.1\overline{6}$, 0.4 **26.** $0.\overline{3}$, $0.\overline{54}$

  27. $0.41\overline{6}$, $0.\overline{2}$ **28.** $0.\overline{27}$, $0.\overline{6}$

  29. $0.\overline{51}$, $0.\overline{6}$ **30.** $0.0\overline{8}$, $0.5\overline{83}$

  31. $0.\overline{36}$, $0.\overline{243}$ **32.** $0.\overline{5}$, $0.\overline{3}$

Self-Test B

Which fraction is greater?

1. $\frac{3}{8}$, $\frac{7}{20}$ **2.** $\frac{5}{9}$, $\frac{4}{7}$ **3.** $\frac{2}{7}$, $\frac{83}{290}$ **[6-4]**

Name a fraction between the two given fractions.

4. $\frac{1}{2}$, $\frac{7}{8}$ **5.** $\frac{9}{11}$, $\frac{9}{10}$ **6.** $\frac{5}{7}$, $\frac{6}{7}$

Change each fraction to a decimal.

7. $\frac{9}{40}$ **8.** $\frac{111}{200}$ **9.** $\frac{11}{16}$ **10.** $\frac{26}{33}$ **[6-5]**

Change each decimal to a fraction in lowest terms.

11. 0.84 **12.** 0.542 **13.** $0.3\overline{17}$ **14.** $0.2\overline{85}$ **[6-6]**

Self-Test answers and Extra Practice are at the back of the book.

 CALCULATOR INVESTIGATION: *Repeating Decimals*

Solve.

1. a. Use a calculator to express $\frac{1}{22}$ and $\frac{8}{55}$ as repeating decimals.

   b. Do both decimals have the same repeating block?
   c. Find the difference between the decimals in part (a).

2. a. Use a calculator to express $\frac{3}{22}$ as a repeating decimal.

   b. Predict the equivalent of $\frac{13}{55}$ in decimal form. (*Hint:* See Ex. 1)

   c. Use a calculator to express $\frac{13}{55}$ as a repeating decimal.

People in Mathematics

Archimedes (287–212 B.C.)

Archimedes is considered to be one of the great mathematicians of all time. He was a native of the Greek city of Syracuse, although he did spend some time at the University of Alexandria in Egypt.

Archimedes is the subject of many stories and legends. The most famous story about Archimedes is that of King Hieron's crown. The crown was supposedly all gold, but the king suspected that it contained silver and he asked Archimedes to determine whether it was pure gold. Archimedes hit upon the solution, while bathing, by discovering the first law of hydrostatics. The story relates that he jumped from the bath and ran through the streets shouting "Eureka."

Archimedes discovered many important mathematical facts. He found formulas for the volumes and surface areas of many geometric solids. He invented a method for approximating π and studied spirals, one of which bears his name. His work, as shown by a paper not found until 1906, even contained the beginning of calculus, a branch of mathematics not developed until the seventeenth century.

Sonya Kovaleski (1850–1891)

Sonya Kovaleski was one of the great mathematicians of the nineteenth century. Her work includes papers on such diverse topics as partial differential equations (a theorem is named in her honor), Abelian integrals, and the rings of Saturn. Her other work included research in the topics of analysis and physics. In 1888 her research paper entitled *On the Rotation of a Solid Body about a Fixed Point* was awarded the Prix Bordin of the French Academy of Sciences. It was considered so outstanding that the prize of 3000 francs was doubled.

Kovaleski's rise to prominence was far from easy. In order to leave Russia to study at a foreign university, she had to arrange a marriage, at age eighteen, to Vladimir Kovaleski. In 1868 they went to Heidelberg where she studied with Kirchhoff and Helmholtz, two famous physicists. In 1871 she went to Berlin to study with Karl Weierstrass. Since women were not admitted to university lectures, all her studying was done privately. Finally, in 1874, the University of Gottingen awarded her a doctorate *in absentia*. However, she was unable to find an academic position for ten years despite strong letters of recommendation from Weierstrass. Finally, in 1884, she was appointed as a lecturer at the University of Stockholm where she was made a full professor five years later.

Emmy Noether (1882–1935)

Emmy Noether is considered one of the brilliant mathematicians of the twentieth century. Her most important work was done in the field of advanced algebra, a branch of mathematics that deals with structures called "groups" and "rings." An important theorem in advanced algebra is called the Noether-Lasker Decomposition Theorem. Noether is also known for work she did on Einstein's theory of relativity.

Although her father was a mathematician, Noether faced many of the same obstacles as Sonya Kovaleski. She sat in on courses at the University of Erlangen (shown in the photograph) and the University of Gottingen from 1900 to 1903, but was not allowed to officially enroll until 1904 when Erlangen changed its policy toward women. She received her doctorate in 1907.

In 1915 Noether was invited to Gottingen by David Hilbert. There, she worked with Hilbert and Felix Klein, two prominent mathematicians, although she was not appointed to the faculty until 1922. She left Gottingen in 1933 and took a professorship at Bryn Mawr College in Pennsylvania.

Research Activities: History of Mathematics

1. Look up the statement of the law of physics known as Archimedes' principle. Using a measuring cup, devise a simple experiment to verify this law.

2. Archimedes discovered a way to calculate the number π very accurately. Look up the history of π in an encyclopedia. Find what values ancient civilizations thought it had.

3. Two other people considered important in the history of mathematics are Hypatia and Maria Agnesi. Find out about the lives and work of these mathematicians.

Chapter Review

Complete.

1. $\frac{1}{5} + \frac{1}{5} + \frac{1}{5} + \frac{1}{5} + \frac{1}{5} = $ ___?___   2. $\frac{5}{19} \times 3 = $ ___?___   [6-1]

3. $7 \div 9 = $ ___?___   4. ___?___ $\times \frac{3}{22} = \frac{15}{22}$

5. $\frac{2}{3}$ and $\frac{?}{12}$ are equivalent fractions.   [6-2]

6. $\frac{20}{35}$ in lowest terms is ___?___.

7. $\frac{30}{9}$ as a mixed number in simple form is ___?___.   [6-3]

8. $7\frac{5}{8}$ as an improper fraction is ___?___.

True or false?

9. An improper fraction is always between 0 and 1.

10. $\frac{7}{8}$ is between $\frac{10}{12}$ and $\frac{11}{12}$.   [6-4]

11. $\frac{11}{13}$ is greater than $\frac{15}{17}$.

12. Every fraction can be expressed as a terminating decimal or a repeating decimal.   [6-5]

13. The decimal representation of $\frac{7}{20}$ does not terminate.

Write the letter of the correct answer.

14. Change $\frac{16}{25}$ to a decimal.

    a. 0.64   **b.** $\frac{64}{100}$ **c.** $0.6\overline{4}$ **d.** $0.\overline{64}$

15. Change $\frac{19}{22}$ to a decimal.

    a. $0.\overline{863}$ **b.** $0.86\overline{3}$ **c.** $0.8\overline{63}$ **d.** 0.863

16. Change 0.544 to a fraction in lowest terms.   [6-6]

    a. $\frac{544}{1000}$ **b.** $\frac{272}{500}$ **c.** $\frac{136}{250}$ **d.** $\frac{68}{125}$

17. Change $0.\overline{25}$ to a fraction in lowest terms.

    a. $\frac{1}{4}$ **b.** $\frac{25}{99}$ **c.** $\frac{25}{100}$ **d.** $\frac{25}{990}$

Chapter Test

Complete.

1. $\frac{1}{9} + \frac{1}{9} + \frac{1}{9} + \frac{1}{9} = \underline{\ ?\ }$ 2. $3 \times \frac{1}{3} = \underline{\ ?\ }$ [6-1]

3. $\underline{\ ?\ } \times \frac{3}{13} = \frac{9}{13}$ 4. $11 \div \underline{\ ?\ } = \frac{11}{23}$

5. $\frac{1}{8} = \frac{?}{32}$ 6. $\frac{2}{3} = \frac{14}{?}$ 7. $\frac{3}{11} = \frac{18}{?}$ [6-2]

Write in lowest terms.

8. $\frac{15}{20}$ 9. $\frac{84}{100}$ 10. $\frac{96}{108}$

Change to a mixed number in simple form.

11. $\frac{11}{4}$ 12. $\frac{51}{9}$ 13. $\frac{125}{10}$ [6-3]

Change to an improper fraction.

14. $8\frac{3}{4}$ 15. $13\frac{5}{9}$ 16. $24\frac{6}{7}$

Which fraction is greater?

17. $\frac{13}{27}, \frac{15}{29}$ 18. $\frac{11}{17}, \frac{3}{4}$ 19. $\frac{17}{19}, \frac{8}{9}$ [6-4]

20. Name a fraction between $\frac{8}{15}$ and $\frac{7}{12}$.

Change each fraction to a decimal.

21. $\frac{7}{16}$ 22. $\frac{5}{33}$ 23. $\frac{17}{60}$ [6-5]

Change each decimal to a fraction in lowest terms.

24. 0.618 25. $0.7\overline{1}$ 26. $0.2\overline{384}$ [6-6]

Cumulative Review (Chapters 1–6)

Exercises

Add or subtract.

1. $\begin{array}{r} 17,842 \\ +\ 11,693 \\ \hline \end{array}$

2. $\begin{array}{r} 18,749 \\ -\ 12,972 \\ \hline \end{array}$

3. $\begin{array}{r} 13.9024 \\ -\ 4.3075 \\ \hline \end{array}$

4. $\begin{array}{r} 4.9372 \\ +\ 0.0985 \\ \hline \end{array}$

5. $\begin{array}{r} 6.0904 \\ -\ 3.6498 \\ \hline \end{array}$

6. $\begin{array}{r} 11.64 \\ +\ 5.6932 \\ \hline \end{array}$

7. $4931 + 11,846 + 19$

8. $429 + 15,692 + 1126$

9. $5.921 + 7.402 + 3.9$

10. $0.9101 + 11.2 - 0.003$

11. $23 - 16.9003 + 0.42$

12. $1.0961 - 0.3 + 113.25$

Multiply or divide.

13. $\begin{array}{r} 368 \\ \times\ 34 \\ \hline \end{array}$

14. $\begin{array}{r} 743 \\ \times\ 87 \\ \hline \end{array}$

15. $\begin{array}{r} 6.932 \\ \times\ 5.9 \\ \hline \end{array}$

16. 569×47

17. 8.61×4.79

18. 12.513×7.24

19. $63\overline{)17,325}$

20. $29\overline{)33,292}$

21. $2.56\overline{)20.7872}$

22. $88,752 \div 86$

23. $2.7594 \div 0.54$

24. $0.003488 \div 1.09$

Solve.

25. $8x = 640$

26. $225 \div x = 15$

27. $137 + x = 604$

28. $x - 203 = 467$

29. $x \div 3 = 214$

30. $12x = 960$

True or false?

31. The diameter is the distance around a circle.

32. An octagon is a polygon with eight sides.

33. An acute angle measures more than $90°$.

34. $0.068\overline{18}$ is a terminating decimal.

Find the LCM of each pair.

35. 6, 14

36. 10, 16

37. 15, 35

38. 28, 70

Find the GCF of each pair.

39. 15, 90

40. 98, 112

41. 56, 210

42. 252, 264

Problems

1. Lucinda had to run some errands last Saturday. She drove to a store 5.60 km from her home. She then drove 3.20 km to the next stop, 7.64 km to her third stop, and 6.95 km to her last stop. If she drove 5.30 km home, how many kilometers did she travel in all?

2. The Baseball Shoppe received a shipment of 275 items. The shipment included 48 gloves, 56 bats, and 84 caps. If the remaining items were baseballs, how many baseballs were in the shipment?

3. The radius of a circle is 7.58 cm. Find the circumference to the nearest tenth. Use $\pi \approx 3.14$ and round to three digits.

4. When a certain number is tripled, the result is 528. Find the number.

5. When a certain number is increased by 79, the result is 452. Find the number.

6. A pentagon has a perimeter of 111.8 cm. If four of its sides have lengths 17.4 cm, 21.6 cm, 18.7 cm, and 25.2 cm, find the length of the fifth side.

7. Alvin gets $5.25 per hour at his after-school job. He worked 2 h on Monday, 3 h on Tuesday, 2.5 h on Wednesday, 1.5 h on Thursday, and 3.5 h on Friday. How much did Alvin earn?

8. One base angle of an isosceles triangle is 39°. Find the measure of the other two angles.

9. A contractor used a truck that would carry 3 tons to move 20 tons of sand. If the truck was fully loaded each trip except the last one, how many trips did the truck make to move all the sand? How heavy was the last load?

10. Sally wishes to cut as many pieces of rope of equal length as she can from three strands that are 35 ft., 49 ft., and 56 ft. long. If the pieces are to be as long as possible and Sally does not wish to waste any rope, how long should she cut each piece?

7 Operations with Fractions

APPLYING MATHEMATICS
SCALE MODELS

An architect can use a model to show what a proposed building will look like and its relationship to its setting. Such models are particularly useful in presenting new designs to members of design review boards and citizens committees. Some models even simulate lighting, sound, or motion, like the forward and reverse motions of an automobile. Although a model building is smaller than the actual building, some models are much larger than the actual objects. For example, models of human cells are often used in the study of biology. In this chapter you will study fractions, ratios, and proportions. You will also study scales, such as those used in models and scale drawing.

CAREER CONNECTION

CITY PLANNER

City or urban planners coordinate programs to accommodate the growth and rapidly changing needs of metropolitan areas. They analyze and suggest solutions to the social, economic, and environmental problems that may arise. A diverse academic background is one of the requirements of this profession, as well as sensitivity to community needs.

Photo: A scale model presents the complex interactions of a series of connected structures.

7-1 Addition and Subtraction of Fractions

The diagram at the right illustrates that

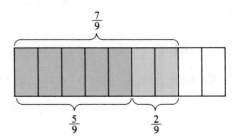

$$\frac{5}{9} + \frac{2}{9} = \frac{7}{9}$$

and

$$\frac{7}{9} - \frac{2}{9} = \frac{5}{9}.$$

This example suggests the following rules for adding and subtracting fractions with the same denominator.

Rules

For any whole numbers a, b, and c, with $c \neq 0$:

$$\frac{a}{c} + \frac{b}{c} = \frac{a + b}{c}$$

$$\frac{a}{c} - \frac{b}{c} = \frac{a - b}{c}$$

The properties of addition and subtraction of whole numbers also apply to fractions. To understand why the rules stated above work, we use the distributive property.

$$\frac{a}{c} + \frac{b}{c} = \left(a \times \frac{1}{c}\right) + \left(b \times \frac{1}{c}\right) = (a + b) \times \frac{1}{c} = \frac{a + b}{c}$$

$$\frac{a}{c} - \frac{b}{c} = \left(a \times \frac{1}{c}\right) - \left(b \times \frac{1}{c}\right) = (a - b) \times \frac{1}{c} = \frac{a - b}{c}$$

EXAMPLE 1 Add or subtract. Simplify.

  a. $\dfrac{8}{11} + \dfrac{7}{11}$ **b.** $\dfrac{13}{12} - \dfrac{5}{12}$

Solution **a.** $\dfrac{8}{11} + \dfrac{7}{11} = \dfrac{8 + 7}{11} = \dfrac{15}{11}$, or $1\dfrac{4}{11}$

  b. $\dfrac{13}{12} - \dfrac{5}{12} = \dfrac{13 - 5}{12} = \dfrac{8}{12} = \dfrac{2}{3}$

In order to add two fractions with different denominators, we first find two fractions, with a common denominator, equivalent to the given fractions. We then add these two fractions.

The most convenient denominator to use as a common denominator is the least common denominator, or LCD, of the two fractions. That is, the least common multiple of the two denominators.

$$\text{LCD}\left(\tfrac{a}{b}, \tfrac{c}{d}\right) = \text{LCM}(b, d) \text{ with } b \neq 0, d \neq 0$$

For example, $\text{LCD}\left(\tfrac{3}{4}, \tfrac{5}{6}\right) = \text{LCM}(4, 6) = 12$.

EXAMPLE 2 Add or subtract. Simplify.

  a. $\dfrac{7}{15} + \dfrac{8}{9}$ **b.** $\dfrac{5}{6} - \dfrac{11}{24}$

Solution **a.** First find the LCD.

$$\text{LCD}\left(\tfrac{7}{15}, \tfrac{8}{9}\right) = \text{LCM}(15, 9) = 45$$

Then find equivalent fractions with an LCD of 45, and add.

$$\frac{7}{15} + \frac{8}{9} = \frac{7 \times 3}{15 \times 3} + \frac{8 \times 5}{9 \times 5}$$

$$= \frac{21}{45} + \frac{40}{45} = \frac{61}{45}, \text{ or } 1\frac{16}{45}$$

b. $\text{LCD}\left(\tfrac{5}{6}, \tfrac{11}{24}\right) = \text{LCM}(6, 24) = 24$

$$\frac{5}{6} - \frac{11}{24} = \frac{5 \times 4}{6 \times 4} - \frac{11}{24}$$

$$= \frac{20}{24} - \frac{11}{24}$$

$$= \frac{9}{24} = \frac{3}{8}$$

Class Exercises

Add or subtract. Simplify.

1. $\dfrac{3}{7} + \dfrac{2}{7}$ **2.** $\dfrac{11}{13} - \dfrac{7}{13}$ **3.** $\dfrac{8}{9} + \dfrac{5}{9}$ **4.** $\dfrac{5}{6} - \dfrac{1}{6}$

In Exercises 5–12, first name the LCD and then add or subtract.

5. $\dfrac{1}{3} + \dfrac{1}{2}$ **6.** $\dfrac{3}{8} + \dfrac{1}{4}$ **7.** $\dfrac{1}{4} + \dfrac{1}{6}$ **8.** $\dfrac{2}{9} + \dfrac{1}{2}$

9. $\dfrac{7}{8} - \dfrac{1}{2}$ **10.** $\dfrac{4}{5} - \dfrac{1}{3}$ **11.** $\dfrac{5}{6} - \dfrac{2}{9}$ **12.** $1 - \dfrac{2}{7}$

Written Exercises

Add or subtract. Simplify.

A 1. $\frac{7}{13} + \frac{12}{13}$ 2. $\frac{22}{9} - \frac{10}{9}$ 3. $\frac{17}{5} - \frac{2}{5}$ 4. $\frac{7}{8} + \frac{9}{8}$

5. $\frac{13}{11} - \frac{9}{11}$ 6. $\frac{54}{99} - \frac{17}{99}$ 7. $\frac{18}{41} + \frac{17}{41}$ 8. $\frac{15}{64} + \frac{51}{64}$

9. $\frac{5}{6} + \frac{7}{12}$ 10. $\frac{17}{18} - \frac{5}{6}$ 11. $\frac{8}{9} - \frac{5}{12}$ 12. $\frac{7}{8} + \frac{5}{6}$

13. $\frac{37}{15} - \frac{13}{10}$ 14. $\frac{13}{14} + \frac{5}{6}$ 15. $\frac{18}{25} + \frac{7}{10}$ 16. $\frac{13}{14} - \frac{3}{4}$

17. $\frac{7}{22} + \frac{5}{6}$ 18. $\frac{13}{15} - \frac{4}{9}$ 19. $\frac{7}{10} + \frac{9}{8}$ 20. $\frac{5}{6} - \frac{9}{14}$

B 21. $\frac{2}{3} + \frac{3}{5} + \frac{5}{6}$ 22. $\frac{7}{12} + \frac{4}{9} + \frac{3}{4}$ 23. $\left(\frac{13}{15} + \frac{1}{4}\right) - \frac{2}{3}$

24. $\left(\frac{7}{12} + \frac{1}{8}\right) - \frac{5}{24}$ 25. $\frac{3}{4} - \left(\frac{5}{28} + \frac{2}{7}\right)$ 26. $\frac{17}{10} - \left(\frac{3}{5} + \frac{5}{6}\right)$

27. $\frac{14}{15} - \left(\frac{8}{5} - \frac{7}{6}\right)$ 28. $\frac{47}{72} - \left(\frac{7}{8} - \frac{5}{12}\right)$ 29. $\frac{3}{10} + \frac{3}{100} + \frac{3}{1000}$

30. $\frac{7}{100} + \frac{5}{1000} + \frac{1}{10,000}$ 31. $\frac{9}{10} - \left(\frac{5}{100} + \frac{63}{1000}\right)$ 32. $\left(\frac{1}{10} + \frac{41}{100}\right) - \frac{57}{1000}$

33. If a whole number d is a multiple of a whole number b, with $b \neq 0$ and $d \neq 0$, then $\text{LCD}\left(\frac{a}{b}, \frac{c}{d}\right) = \underline{\quad?\quad}$.

34. If two whole numbers b and d are relatively prime, with $b \neq 0$ and $d \neq 0$, then $\text{LCD}\left(\frac{a}{b}, \frac{c}{d}\right) = \underline{\quad?\quad}$.

Solve each equation.

EXAMPLE   a. $n + \frac{1}{2} = \frac{5}{6}$ b. $x - \frac{1}{2} = \frac{5}{6} - \frac{4}{9}$

Solution   a. $n + \frac{1}{2} = \frac{5}{6}$ b. $x - \frac{1}{2} = \frac{5}{6} - \frac{4}{9}$

$n = \frac{5}{6} - \frac{1}{2}$ $x - \frac{1}{2} = \frac{15}{18} - \frac{8}{18}$

$n = \frac{5}{6} - \frac{3}{6}$ $x - \frac{1}{2} = \frac{7}{18}$

$n = \frac{2}{6} = \frac{1}{3}$ $x = \frac{7}{18} + \frac{1}{2} = \frac{7}{18} + \frac{9}{18} = \frac{16}{18} = \frac{8}{9}$

C 35. $n + \frac{5}{12} = \frac{3}{4}$ 36. $c - \frac{5}{6} = \frac{13}{15}$ 37. $x + \frac{5}{18} = \frac{11}{12} - \frac{1}{4}$

38. $m + \frac{5}{6} = \frac{1}{2} + \frac{4}{9}$ 39. $y - \frac{3}{8} = \frac{5}{24} + \frac{1}{4}$ 40. $a - \frac{3}{4} = \frac{5}{12} - \frac{7}{18}$

Problems

Solve.

A **1.** The combined thickness of the pages of a book is $\frac{11}{16}$ in. The thickness of each cover is $\frac{1}{8}$ in. What is the total thickness of the book?

2. Luann started a trip with the gas tank of her car $\frac{3}{4}$ full. At the end of the trip the tank was $\frac{1}{6}$ full. What fraction of the tank of gasoline did she use on the trip?

3. Lee and Tracy were the only two candidates for class president. Lee received $\frac{7}{15}$ of the votes. What fraction of the votes did Tracy get?

4. A certain kind of steel is $\frac{23}{25}$ iron. What fraction is other elements?

5. It took Elroy $\frac{5}{12}$ h to wash his mother's car and $\frac{1}{5}$ h to wash his father's car. How much time did Elroy spend washing the cars?

6. The Chen family's house occupies $\frac{7}{20}$ of the area of their lot. The garage occupies $\frac{1}{15}$ of the area. What is the fraction of the total area occupied by the two structures?

B **7.** One fourth of Jesse's monthly income is used for rent, $\frac{3}{14}$ for food, and $\frac{2}{7}$ for clothes. What fraction of Jesse's income remains after he pays for rent, food, and clothing?

8. Fred bought a bag of nuts. He gave $\frac{1}{4}$ of it to one brother, $\frac{1}{6}$ to another, $\frac{1}{5}$ to his sister, and kept the rest. How much did he keep?

C **9.** Sally had 3 ft of board. She made two shelves, each $\frac{3}{4}$ ft long, and a third shelf that was $\frac{5}{6}$ ft long. Does she have enough board left to make another shelf $\frac{3}{4}$ ft long? Give a reason for your answer.

10. Jim bought three half-pound packages of whole-wheat flour. He used $\frac{3}{4}$ of a pound of the flour for one recipe and $\frac{2}{3}$ of a pound for another recipe. Does he have enough flour left for a third recipe that needs $\frac{1}{6}$ of a pound of flour?

Review Exercises

Change the following improper fractions to mixed numbers.

1. $\frac{37}{8}$ **2.** $\frac{43}{6}$ **3.** $\frac{28}{5}$ **4.** $\frac{51}{4}$ **5.** $\frac{72}{7}$ **6.** $\frac{59}{3}$

7-2 Addition and Subtraction of Mixed Numbers

To add or subtract mixed numbers, we can first change the mixed numbers to improper fractions and then use the methods of the previous lesson. For example,

$$1\tfrac{4}{9} + 3\tfrac{1}{9} = \tfrac{13}{9} + \tfrac{28}{9} = \tfrac{41}{9} = 4\tfrac{5}{9}.$$

A second method is illustrated in Example 1. In this method, we work separately with the fractional and whole-number parts of the given mixed numbers. Sometimes, as in part (b), we must change the form of a mixed number before we can subtract the fractional parts.

EXAMPLE 1 Add or subtract. Simplify.

    a. $3\tfrac{4}{9} + 1\tfrac{7}{9}$ **b.** $9\tfrac{3}{7} - 4\tfrac{5}{7}$

Solution

a.
$$3\tfrac{4}{9}$$
$$+\;1\tfrac{7}{9}$$
$$\overline{4\tfrac{11}{9}} = 4 + 1\tfrac{2}{9}$$
$$= 5\tfrac{2}{9}$$

b. $9\tfrac{3}{7} = \left(8 + \tfrac{7}{7}\right) + \tfrac{3}{7} = 8\tfrac{10}{7}$

$$9\tfrac{3}{7} = 8\tfrac{10}{7}$$
$$-\;4\tfrac{5}{7} = -\;4\tfrac{5}{7}$$
$$\overline{4\tfrac{5}{7}}$$

If the fractional parts of the given mixed numbers have different denominators, we find equivalent mixed numbers whose fractional parts have the same denominator, usually the LCD. Then we use the method of Example 1.

EXAMPLE 2 Add or subtract. Simplify.

    a. $5\tfrac{3}{10} + 7\tfrac{7}{15}$ **b.** $9\tfrac{5}{9} - 4\tfrac{13}{15}$

Solution   **a.** $\text{LCD}\left(\tfrac{3}{10}, \tfrac{7}{15}\right) = 30$ **b.** $\text{LCD}\left(\tfrac{5}{9}, \tfrac{13}{15}\right) = 45$

$$5\tfrac{3}{10} = 5\tfrac{9}{30}$$
$$+\;7\tfrac{7}{15} = +\;7\tfrac{14}{30}$$
$$\overline{12\tfrac{23}{30}}$$

$$9\tfrac{5}{9} = 9\tfrac{25}{45} = 8\tfrac{70}{45}$$
$$-\;4\tfrac{13}{15} = -\;4\tfrac{39}{45} = -\;4\tfrac{39}{45}$$
$$\overline{\phantom{-4\tfrac{39}{45}=}4\tfrac{31}{45}}$$

Class Exercises

Add and simplify.

1. $3\frac{3}{5} + 1\frac{4}{5}$ **2.** $2\frac{3}{4} + 5\frac{1}{4}$ **3.** $7\frac{3}{8} + 4\frac{7}{8}$ **4.** $6\frac{5}{9} + \frac{7}{9}$

a. Rewrite the first number so that you can subtract.
b. Subtract and simplify.

5. $3\frac{1}{5} - 2\frac{4}{5}$ **6.** $7 - 4\frac{3}{4}$ **7.** $5\frac{3}{8} - 1\frac{7}{8}$ **8.** $4\frac{1}{6} - \frac{5}{6}$

a. Name the LCD of the fractional parts of the two mixed numbers.
b. Add or subtract. Simplify.

9. $9\frac{1}{4} + 2\frac{3}{8}$ **10.** $3\frac{5}{6} - 1\frac{1}{2}$ **11.** $5\frac{1}{3} + 7\frac{3}{4}$ **12.** $6\frac{4}{5} - 4\frac{2}{3}$

13. $7\frac{1}{2} + 1\frac{9}{14}$ **14.** $5\frac{3}{5} - 4\frac{1}{10}$ **15.** $2\frac{5}{6} + 1\frac{1}{4}$ **16.** $8\frac{3}{4} - 5\frac{1}{3}$

Written Exercises

Add or subtract. Simplify.

A

1. $7\frac{5}{9} + 4\frac{7}{9}$ **2.** $5\frac{1}{8} + 6\frac{7}{8}$ **3.** $9\frac{3}{7} - 2\frac{5}{7}$ **4.** $8\frac{3}{10} - 6\frac{7}{10}$

5. $6\frac{8}{13} + 7\frac{7}{13}$ **6.** $9\frac{7}{12} + 5\frac{11}{12}$ **7.** $17\frac{3}{8} - 9\frac{7}{8}$ **8.** $16\frac{4}{13} - 15\frac{8}{13}$

9. $10\frac{1}{4} - 4\frac{3}{8}$ **10.** $3\frac{5}{12} - 1\frac{2}{3}$ **11.** $2\frac{5}{9} + \frac{5}{6}$ **12.** $9\frac{1}{4} + 7\frac{5}{6}$

13. $8\frac{2}{5} - 3\frac{2}{3}$ **14.** $7\frac{5}{14} - 2\frac{17}{28}$ **15.** $5\frac{9}{10} + 10\frac{1}{4}$ **16.** $6\frac{5}{6} + 4\frac{7}{9}$

17. $9\frac{7}{12} + 8\frac{13}{15}$ **18.** $5\frac{17}{20} + 4\frac{11}{15}$ **19.** $8\frac{3}{10} - 4\frac{3}{4}$ **20.** $7\frac{2}{9} - 3\frac{8}{15}$

B **21.** $3\frac{1}{2} + 4\frac{1}{3} + 5\frac{1}{4}$ **22.** $5\frac{1}{6} + 7\frac{2}{5} + 3\frac{1}{3}$ **23.** $6\frac{3}{8} + 3\frac{5}{16} + 1\frac{3}{4}$

24. $\left(3\frac{1}{3} + 5\frac{3}{4}\right) - 2\frac{5}{6}$ **25.** $\left(7\frac{1}{6} - 3\frac{2}{5}\right) + 8\frac{9}{10}$ **26.** $6\frac{1}{12} - \left(1\frac{5}{8} + 2\frac{1}{3}\right)$

27. $9\frac{3}{14} - \left(4\frac{3}{4} + 2\frac{5}{7}\right)$ **28.** $\left(4\frac{1}{3} + 8\frac{2}{5}\right) - \left(3\frac{1}{2} + 6\frac{2}{3}\right)$ **29.** $\left(8\frac{3}{4} - 2\frac{2}{3}\right) + \left(5\frac{5}{6} - 3\frac{1}{2}\right)$

Solve.

C **30.** $n + 3\frac{1}{2} = 5\frac{3}{4}$ **31.** $n - 1\frac{2}{3} = 7\frac{1}{6}$ **32.** $a - 3\frac{7}{15} = 2\frac{5}{6}$

33. $x + 2\frac{11}{14} = 5\frac{13}{21}$ **34.** $y + 3\frac{13}{33} = 7\frac{5}{22}$ **35.** $c - 4\frac{9}{14} = 6\frac{7}{10}$

Problems

Solve.

A 1. Mel bought $3\frac{1}{4}$ lb of peaches and $2\frac{5}{8}$ lb of seedless grapes. How many pounds of fruit did he buy altogether?

2. Alice's tennis racket has a grip that measures $3\frac{7}{8}$ in. The grip of Duncan's racket measures $4\frac{1}{2}$ in. How much larger is the grip on Duncan's racket?

3. On a baseball diamond the pitcher's mound is $60\frac{1}{2}$ ft from home plate. If second base is $127\frac{1}{4}$ ft from home plate, how far is the pitcher's mound from second base?

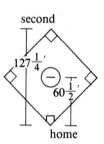

4. The flying time from New York to Los Angeles is $5\frac{2}{3}$ h. The return flight takes $4\frac{3}{4}$ h. How much longer does it take to go from New York to Los Angeles than from Los Angeles to New York?

5. Two pieces were cut from a sheet of tin $4\frac{5}{8}$ ft long. One piece was $2\frac{1}{2}$ ft long; the other was $1\frac{1}{3}$ ft long. How much of the sheet was left?

B 6. A certain stock started the day at a price of $57\frac{1}{8}$, rose $3\frac{1}{4}$ points, and then fell $5\frac{1}{2}$ points by closing time. What was the closing price of the stock?

7. A two-by-four actually measures $1\frac{5}{8}$ in. by $3\frac{1}{2}$ in. What is the total distance around a two-by-four?

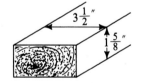

8. A book page that is $7\frac{1}{10}$ in. wide contains a picture that is $4\frac{5}{6}$ in. wide. How wide is each side margin if the two margins are of equal width?

C 9. Herb drives home from work on two straight roads. One road is $6\frac{1}{3}$ mi long and the other road is $4\frac{3}{4}$ mi long. The roads are at right angles to each other. If a direct road were built between Herb's office and his home, it would be $7\frac{11}{12}$ mi long. How many miles would this road save Herb each trip?

Review Exercises

Find the GCF of each pair of numbers.

1. 30, 54   2. 20, 28   3. 25, 110   4. 72, 84

5. 112, 120   6. 80, 96   7. 135, 150   8. 315, 280

7-3 Multiplication of Fractions

The diagram at the right shows that $\frac{2}{3}$ of $\frac{4}{5}$ is $\frac{8}{15}$. That is,

$$\frac{2}{3} \times \frac{4}{5} = \frac{8}{15}.$$

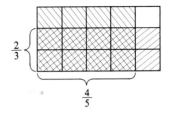

Notice that the numerator of the product, 8, is the product of the numerators, 2 and 4. The denominator of the product, 15, is the product of the denominators, 3 and 5.

Rule

If a, b, c, and d are whole numbers with $b \neq 0$ and $d \neq 0$, then

$$\frac{a}{b} \times \frac{c}{d} = \frac{a \times c}{b \times d}.$$

EXAMPLE 1   Multiply $\frac{6}{35} \times \frac{7}{3}$. Simplify.

Solution $\frac{6}{35} \times \frac{7}{3} = \frac{6 \times 7}{35 \times 3} = \frac{42}{105} = \frac{2}{5}$

In the solution to Example 1 you could have simplified $\frac{6}{35} \times \frac{7}{3}$ before multiplying, as follows.

$$\frac{6}{\underset{5}{\cancel{35}}} \times \frac{\overset{1}{\cancel{7}}}{3} = \frac{\overset{2}{\cancel{6}}}{5} \times \frac{1}{\underset{1}{\cancel{3}}} = \frac{2}{5} \times \frac{1}{1} = \frac{2 \times 1}{5 \times 1} = \frac{2}{5}$$

This suggests the following.

When multiplying two fractions, you can simplify the multiplication by dividing either of the numerators and either of the denominators by a common factor.

EXAMPLE 2   Multiply $\frac{25}{6} \times \frac{42}{5}$. Simplify.

Solution $\frac{25}{6} \times \frac{42}{5} = \frac{\overset{5}{\cancel{25}}}{\underset{1}{\cancel{6}}} \times \frac{\overset{7}{\cancel{42}}}{\underset{1}{\cancel{5}}} = \frac{5}{1} \times \frac{7}{1} = \frac{5 \times 7}{1 \times 1} = \frac{35}{1} = 35$

Class Exercises

Multiply. Simplify.

1. $3 \times \frac{2}{9}$ **2.** $4 \times \frac{1}{2}$ **3.** $\frac{2}{3} \times \frac{3}{5}$ **4.** $\frac{2}{3} \times \frac{4}{7}$

5. $\frac{4}{7} \times \frac{3}{5}$ **6.** $\frac{1}{4} \times \frac{8}{11}$ **7.** $\frac{5}{9} \times \frac{3}{4}$ **8.** $\frac{1}{5} \times \frac{10}{13}$

9. $\frac{5}{4} \times \frac{4}{5}$ **10.** $\frac{3}{8} \times \frac{8}{3}$ **11.** $\frac{5}{3} \times \frac{1}{10}$ **12.** $\frac{3}{10} \times \frac{5}{12}$

Written Exercises

Multiply. Simplify.

A **1.** $8 \times \frac{2}{3}$ **2.** $5 \times \frac{3}{8}$ **3.** $\frac{9}{5} \times 10$ **4.** $\frac{5}{4} \times 12$

5. $\frac{2}{3} \times \frac{5}{8}$ **6.** $\frac{4}{7} \times \frac{9}{4}$ **7.** $\frac{6}{35} \times \frac{7}{15}$ **8.** $\frac{3}{25} \times \frac{5}{16}$

9. $\frac{13}{16} \times \frac{32}{39}$ **10.** $\frac{14}{9} \times \frac{27}{28}$ **11.** $\frac{25}{44} \times \frac{33}{40}$ **12.** $\frac{26}{9} \times \frac{54}{13}$

13. $\frac{42}{55} \times \frac{30}{14}$ **14.** $\frac{45}{49} \times \frac{28}{63}$ **15.** $\frac{22}{81} \times \frac{36}{55}$ **16.** $\frac{56}{25} \times \frac{45}{77}$

B **17.** $\frac{5}{9} \times \frac{3}{10} \times \frac{2}{3}$ **18.** $\frac{8}{9} \times \frac{15}{32} \times \frac{9}{10}$ **19.** $\frac{4}{9} \times \frac{27}{25} \times \frac{5}{7}$

20. $\frac{16}{11} \times \frac{33}{20} \times \frac{5}{3}$ **21.** $\frac{7}{5} \times \frac{15}{28} \times \frac{4}{3}$ **22.** $\frac{2}{9} \times \frac{63}{65} \times \frac{15}{14}$

23. $\frac{26}{25} \times \frac{35}{39} \times \frac{45}{7}$ **24.** $\frac{57}{20} \times \frac{35}{38} \times \frac{22}{27}$ **25.** $\frac{60}{51} \times \frac{17}{24} \times \frac{4}{5}$

26. $\frac{130}{161} \times \frac{69}{40} \times \frac{4}{9}$ **27.** $\frac{9}{28} \times \frac{52}{35} \times \frac{98}{13}$ **28.** $\frac{54}{65} \times \frac{91}{330} \times \frac{50}{63}$

C **29. a.** $\left(\frac{6}{7} + \frac{3}{4}\right) \times \frac{7}{30}$ **30. a.** $\frac{15}{2} \times \left(\frac{7}{8} - \frac{5}{24}\right)$ **31. a.** $\left(\frac{3}{4} + \frac{5}{12}\right)\left(\frac{1}{7} + \frac{2}{3}\right)$

b. $\frac{6}{7} + \frac{3}{4} \times \frac{7}{30}$ **b.** $\frac{15}{2} \times \frac{7}{8} - \frac{5}{24}$ **b.** $\frac{3}{4} + \frac{5}{12} \times \frac{1}{7} + \frac{2}{3}$

Review Exercises

Solve.

1. $5x = 55$ **2.** $3x = 36$ **3.** $2x = 48$ **4.** $64 \div x = 8$

5. $x \div 12 = 5$ **6.** $40 \div x = 8$ **7.** $x \div 9 = 9$ **8.** $x \times 4 = 40$

7-4 Division of Fractions

Certain numbers, when multiplied together, have the product 1. For example,

$$5 \times \frac{1}{5} = 1 \quad \text{and} \quad \frac{3}{4} \times \frac{4}{3} = 1.$$

Two numbers whose product is 1 are called **reciprocals** of each other. Thus $\frac{3}{4}$ is the reciprocal of $\frac{4}{3}$, and $\frac{4}{3}$ is the reciprocal of $\frac{3}{4}$. Since the product of 0 and any number is always 0, the number 0 has no reciprocal. This suggests the following property.

> ## *Property*
>
> Every nonzero number has a unique (exactly one) reciprocal.

COMMUNICATION IN MATHEMATICS: *Study Skills*

It is important to know the meanings of all the words in a mathematical definition or property. If you are not sure about the mathematical meaning, check the glossary at the back of the book, or look up the meaning in a mathematics dictionary or reference book.

Recall that multiplication and division are inverse operations. Now study the following examples.

$$18 = 3 \times 6, \quad \text{so} \quad 18 \div 6 = 3. \quad \text{Also, } 18 \times \frac{1}{6} = 3.$$

$$7 = 28 \times \frac{1}{4}, \quad \text{so} \quad 7 \div \frac{1}{4} = 28. \quad \text{Also, } 7 \times 4 = 28.$$

$$20 = 24 \times \frac{5}{6}, \quad \text{so} \quad 20 \div \frac{5}{6} = 24. \quad \text{Also, } 20 \times \frac{6}{5} = 24.$$

These examples suggest that dividing a number by a fraction is the same as multiplying the number by the reciprocal of the fraction.

> ## *Rule*
>
> If a, b, c, and d are whole numbers with $b \neq 0$, $c \neq 0$, and $d \neq 0$, then
>
> $$\frac{a}{b} \div \frac{c}{d} = \frac{a}{b} \times \frac{d}{c}.$$

▲ See Pages E13–E14

EXAMPLE Divide. Simplify.

a. $\frac{4}{7} \div \frac{8}{3}$ b. $\frac{12}{5} \div 9$ c. $10 \div \frac{2}{5}$

Solution

a. $\frac{4}{7} \div \frac{8}{3} = \frac{4}{7} \times \frac{3}{8} = \frac{4}{7} \times \frac{3}{\overset{}{\underset{2}{8}}} = \frac{1 \times 3}{7 \times 2} = \frac{3}{14}$

b. $\frac{12}{5} \div 9 = \frac{12}{5} \times \frac{1}{9} = \frac{\overset{4}{12}}{5} \times \frac{1}{\underset{3}{9}} = \frac{4 \times 1}{5 \times 3} = \frac{4}{15}$

c. $10 \div \frac{2}{5} = 10 \times \frac{5}{2} = \frac{\overset{5}{10}}{1} \times \frac{5}{\underset{1}{2}} = \frac{5 \times 5}{1 \times 1} = 25$

Class Exercises

State the reciprocal of each number.

1. $\frac{5}{8}$ 2. $\frac{1}{6}$ 3. 9   4. $\frac{2}{9}$ 5. 10   6. $\frac{1}{5}$

a. Express the given division as a product.
b. Multiply and simplify.

7. $\frac{3}{5} \div 3$ 8. $7 \div \frac{14}{3}$ 9. $4 \div \frac{8}{5}$ 10. $\frac{3}{5} \div 12$

11. $\frac{5}{6} \div \frac{5}{3}$ 12. $\frac{1}{3} \div \frac{3}{5}$ 13. $\frac{1}{2} \div \frac{1}{7}$ 14. $\frac{7}{12} \div \frac{5}{4}$

Written Exercises

Divide. Simplify.

A 1. $\frac{8}{7} \div 12$ 2. $\frac{21}{11} \div 14$ 3. $18 \div \frac{6}{7}$ 4. $24 \div \frac{8}{9}$

5. $\frac{3}{8} \div \frac{9}{5}$ 6. $\frac{20}{9} \div \frac{16}{3}$ 7. $\frac{11}{8} \div \frac{33}{4}$ 8. $\frac{20}{21} \div \frac{15}{28}$

9. $\frac{5}{18} \div \frac{25}{12}$ 10. $\frac{26}{21} \div \frac{13}{9}$ 11. $\frac{15}{16} \div \frac{5}{24}$ 12. $\frac{32}{45} \div \frac{8}{35}$

13. $\frac{17}{30} \div \frac{34}{25}$ 14. $\frac{42}{55} \div \frac{36}{11}$ 15. $\frac{8}{13} \div \frac{18}{39}$ 16. $\frac{51}{56} \div \frac{17}{49}$

B 17. $\frac{12}{5} \div \left(\frac{3}{4} \div \frac{1}{8}\right)$ 18. $\frac{32}{5} \div \left(\frac{4}{5} \times \frac{6}{7}\right)$ 19. $\left(\frac{2}{5} + \frac{7}{30}\right) \div \frac{38}{105}$ 20. $\frac{55}{24} \div \left(\frac{7}{18} - \frac{1}{12}\right)$

21. $\left(\frac{13}{7} \times \frac{6}{5}\right) \div \left(\frac{4}{3} \div \frac{5}{9}\right)$

22. $\left(\frac{5}{12} \div \frac{25}{28}\right) \div \left(\frac{42}{65} \div \frac{30}{91}\right)$

23. $\left[\frac{5}{8}\left(\frac{7}{15} + \frac{1}{3}\right)\right] \div \left[\frac{56}{57}\left(\frac{3}{4} + \frac{1}{5}\right)\right]$

24. $\left[\frac{16}{33}\left(\frac{7}{8} - \frac{5}{12}\right)\right] \div \left[\frac{28}{27}\left(\frac{1}{2} + \frac{3}{14}\right)\right]$

Solve.

EXAMPLE   **a.** $\frac{9}{16} \times n = \frac{21}{20}$

b. $n \div \frac{18}{5} = \frac{10}{9}$

Solution   **a.** $\frac{9}{16} \times n = \frac{21}{20}$

$$n = \frac{21}{20} \times \frac{16}{9}$$

$$n = \frac{\overset{7}{\cancel{21}}}{\underset{5}{\cancel{20}}} \times \frac{\overset{4}{\cancel{16}}}{\underset{3}{\cancel{9}}}$$

$$n = \frac{7}{5} \times \frac{4}{3} = \frac{28}{15} = 1\frac{13}{15}$$

b. $n \div \frac{18}{5} = \frac{10}{9}$

$$n = \frac{10}{9} \times \frac{18}{5}$$

$$n = \frac{\overset{2}{\cancel{10}}}{\underset{1}{\cancel{9}}} \times \frac{\overset{2}{\cancel{18}}}{\underset{1}{\cancel{5}}}$$

$$n = \frac{2}{1} \times \frac{2}{1} = \frac{4}{1} = 4$$

C **25.** $\frac{5}{12} \times n = \frac{15}{8}$

26. $\frac{4}{7} \times n = \frac{16}{21}$

27. $n \div \frac{11}{6} = \frac{1}{2}$

28. $n \div \frac{18}{25} = \frac{10}{9}$

29. $\frac{5}{6} \times n = \frac{35}{3}$

30. $n \div \frac{20}{49} = \frac{7}{8}$

Review Exercises

Change each mixed number to an improper fraction.

1. $3\frac{5}{9}$ **2.** $7\frac{6}{11}$ **3.** $4\frac{3}{7}$ **4.** $5\frac{7}{12}$ **5.** $7\frac{12}{17}$

6. $11\frac{5}{8}$ **7.** $9\frac{7}{16}$ **8.** $3\frac{17}{19}$ **9.** $13\frac{5}{31}$ **10.** $12\frac{7}{27}$

██ ██ **CALCULATOR INVESTIGATION:** *Patterns*

Use a calculator to express these fractions as repeating decimals. Describe the number patterns that you find.

1. $\frac{1}{11}, \frac{2}{11}, \frac{3}{11}, \cdots, \frac{10}{11}$

2. $\frac{81}{99}, \frac{82}{99}, \frac{83}{99}, \cdots, \frac{90}{99}$

3. $\frac{1}{37}, \frac{2}{37}, \frac{3}{37}, \cdots, \frac{10}{37}$

4. $\frac{1}{55}, \frac{2}{55}, \frac{3}{55}, \cdots, \frac{10}{55}$

5. $\frac{1}{27}, \frac{2}{27}, \frac{3}{27}, \cdots, \frac{10}{27}$

6. $\frac{1}{165}, \frac{2}{165}, \frac{3}{165}, \cdots, \frac{10}{165}$

7-5 Multiplication and Division of Mixed Numbers

One method of finding the product of two mixed numbers is to first change the mixed numbers to improper fractions and then multiply. A second method makes use of the distributive property. This method is convenient for doing simple products mentally. Both methods are illustrated in the following example.

EXAMPLE 1   Multiply $6 \times 3\frac{1}{12}$. Simplify.

Solution   *Method 1*

$$6 \times 3\frac{1}{12} = \frac{6}{1} \times \frac{37}{12} = \frac{\overset{1}{\cancel{6}}}{1} \times \frac{37}{\underset{2}{\cancel{12}}} = \frac{37}{2} = 18\frac{1}{2}$$

Method 2

$$6 \times 3\frac{1}{12} = 6 \times \left(3 + \frac{1}{12}\right) = (6 \times 3) + \left(6 \times \frac{1}{12}\right)$$

$$= 18 + \frac{6}{12} = 18\frac{1}{2}$$

Estimates may be used to check our computation. We can estimate a product or a quotient by rounding each number to the nearest whole number.

EXAMPLE 2   Multiply $5\frac{3}{4} \times 4\frac{2}{3}$. Simplify.

Solution   Estimate: $6 \times 5 = 30$

$$5\frac{3}{4} \times 4\frac{2}{3} = \frac{23}{4} \times \frac{14}{3} = \frac{23}{\underset{2}{\cancel{4}}} \times \frac{\overset{7}{\cancel{14}}}{3} = \frac{161}{6} = 26\frac{5}{6}$$

To divide one mixed number by another, we change the mixed numbers to improper fractions and use the method of the previous lesson.

EXAMPLE 3   Divide $2\frac{2}{3} \div 10\frac{2}{3}$. Simplify.

Solution $2\frac{2}{3} \div 10\frac{2}{3} = \frac{8}{3} \div \frac{32}{3} = \frac{8}{3} \times \frac{3}{32} = \frac{\overset{1}{\cancel{8}}}{\underset{1}{\cancel{3}}} \times \frac{\overset{1}{\cancel{3}}}{\underset{4}{\cancel{32}}} = \frac{1}{1} \times \frac{1}{4} = \frac{1}{4}$

When problems involve computations with mixed numbers, it is a good idea to *estimate the answer* as in Example 2. This estimate can be used to check your answers.

Class Exercises

Multiply, using the distributive property. Simplify.

1. $8 \times 3\frac{1}{4}$
2. $18 \times 5\frac{1}{3}$
3. $20 \times 3\frac{3}{4}$
4. $6 \times 2\frac{1}{8}$

Estimate the product or quotient. Express each mixed number as an improper fraction. Multiply or divide. Simplify.

5. $1\frac{1}{3} \times 1\frac{1}{2}$
6. $4\frac{1}{5} \div 2\frac{1}{3}$
7. $1\frac{1}{4} \div 2\frac{1}{2}$

8. $18 \times 2\frac{5}{6}$
9. $2\frac{2}{3} \div 1\frac{1}{15}$
10. $1\frac{3}{4} \div 10\frac{1}{2}$

11. $6\frac{1}{4} \times 1\frac{3}{5}$
12. $2\frac{1}{7} \times 9\frac{1}{3}$
13. $3\frac{2}{3} \times \frac{3}{11}$

14. $2\frac{4}{7} \times 4\frac{2}{3}$
15. $\frac{11}{12} \div 1\frac{5}{6}$
16. $7\frac{1}{5} \div 7\frac{1}{5}$

Written Exercises

Multiply or divide. Simplify.

A

1. $3\frac{1}{2} \times \frac{4}{7}$
2. $2\frac{5}{8} \times \frac{3}{14}$
3. $3\frac{3}{5} \times 4\frac{1}{6}$

4. $4\frac{2}{3} \times 5\frac{1}{7}$
5. $2\frac{1}{10} \times 3\frac{4}{7}$
6. $5\frac{5}{12} \times 1\frac{2}{13}$

7. $5\frac{2}{5} \times 2\frac{4}{9}$
8. $6\frac{2}{9} \times 1\frac{7}{8}$
9. $3\frac{1}{8} \div 5$

10. $4\frac{4}{9} \div 8$
11. $1\frac{1}{8} \div 6\frac{3}{4}$
12. $2\frac{6}{7} \div 1\frac{1}{14}$

13. $8\frac{1}{6} \div 3\frac{8}{9}$
14. $1\frac{7}{15} \div 5\frac{1}{2}$
15. $6\frac{3}{10} \div 1\frac{2}{25}$

16. $4\frac{1}{30} \div 4\frac{2}{5}$
17. $9\frac{2}{7} \times 2\frac{2}{13}$
18. $13\frac{1}{3} \times 15\frac{3}{4}$

19. $7\frac{1}{5} \times 5\frac{5}{12}$
20. $10\frac{4}{5} \times 3\frac{1}{18}$
21. $4\frac{1}{12} \div 7\frac{7}{8}$

22. $4\frac{9}{10} \div 1\frac{3}{25}$
23. $2\frac{3}{11} \div 2\frac{1}{22}$
24. $42\frac{2}{3} \div 3\frac{5}{9}$

Solve.

EXAMPLE $n \times 2\frac{1}{3} = 6\frac{5}{12}$

Solution $n \times 2\frac{1}{3} = 6\frac{5}{12}$

$$n = 6\frac{5}{12} \div 2\frac{1}{3} = \frac{77}{12} \div \frac{7}{3}$$

$$n = \frac{\overset{11}{\cancel{77}}}{\underset{4}{\cancel{12}}} \times \frac{\overset{1}{\cancel{3}}}{\underset{1}{\cancel{7}}} = \frac{11}{4} \times \frac{1}{1} = \frac{11}{4} = 2\frac{3}{4}$$

B 25. $n \times 1\frac{1}{2} = 1\frac{7}{8}$

26. $m \times 5\frac{1}{5} = 1\frac{3}{10}$

27. $p \times 2\frac{1}{12} = 3\frac{1}{8}$

28. $y \div 5\frac{1}{4} = 5\frac{5}{6}$

29. $r \div 8\frac{3}{4} = 2\frac{13}{16}$

30. $n \times 7\frac{3}{7} = 2\frac{2}{13}$

C 31. $u \div 5\frac{1}{2} = 3\frac{2}{3} + 1\frac{2}{11}$

32. $s \div 4\frac{5}{6} = 6\frac{11}{20} - 2\frac{4}{5}$

33. $w \times 2\frac{4}{7} = 2\frac{5}{26} \times 1\frac{17}{35}$

34. $m \times 3\frac{3}{25} = 7\frac{1}{5} \times 4\frac{7}{8}$

Problems

Solve.

A 1. QED Company stock sells for $11\frac{1}{4}$ dollars per share. How many shares will Lisa be able to buy for $90?

2. A recipe for tomato sauce calls for $2\frac{2}{3}$ tablespoons of cooking oil. Brett wants to make $1\frac{1}{4}$ times the amount produced by the recipe. How many tablespoons of oil should he use?

3. The hour hand of a clock moves 30° every hour. Through how many degrees does it travel in $1\frac{3}{4}$ h?

4. A concrete-mixing truck can mix $4\frac{1}{2}$ tons of concrete at a time. How many truckloads are needed for the foundation of a building that will use 150 tons?

5. Each loaf of bread at Ellen's Bakery uses $9\frac{1}{2}$ oz of flour. How much flour is used to bake 3500 loaves of bread?

6. Roy wants to fill a 20 gal tank with water. If he uses a $2\frac{1}{2}$ gal container, how many times must it be filled?

7. The crankcase of a machine motor holds $5\frac{5}{8}$ quarts of oil. If the oil level has dropped to $\frac{3}{5}$ of its original amount, how many quarts of oil should be added to fill the crankcase?

8. The circulatory system of a human body contains about 5 L of blood, of which about $\frac{3}{5}$ is blood plasma and the rest is either red blood cells or white blood cells. What is the approximate volume of red or white blood cells in the circulatory system of a human body?

B 9. A recipe for whole-wheat rolls makes 40 rolls using $5\frac{1}{3}$ cups of flour. How many rolls can be made using 32 cups of flour?

10. Emory is mounting 3 shelves $12\frac{3}{4}$ in. apart on a wall. If each board is $\frac{3}{4}$ in. thick, what is the total vertical space occupied by the set of shelves?

11. A bag of fertilizer weighing $31\frac{1}{4}$ lb will cover 1000 ft². How much fertilizer will be needed to cover 1600 ft²?

12. Pam is building a deck at the back of her house. It will be made from 12 planks, each $7\frac{5}{8}$ in. wide. The total width of the deck will be 110 in. If there are equal spaces between adjacent planks, how wide must each space be?

Self-Test A

Add or subtract. Simplify.

1. $\frac{8}{17} + \frac{5}{17}$ 2. $\frac{3}{8} + \frac{7}{32}$ 3. $\frac{7}{9} - \frac{10}{27}$ [7-1]

4. $3\frac{5}{12} + 5\frac{1}{12}$ 5. $6\frac{3}{4} - 4\frac{7}{16}$ 6. $2\frac{5}{8} + 4\frac{7}{24}$ [7-2]

Multiply or divide. Simplify.

7. $45 \times \frac{5}{9}$ 8. $\frac{7}{12} \times \frac{3}{8}$ 9. $\frac{15}{28} \times \frac{7}{10}$ [7-3]

10. $\frac{3}{5} \div 15$ 11. $\frac{9}{25} \div \frac{4}{5}$ 12. $\frac{18}{55} \div \frac{3}{11}$ [7-4]

13. $5\frac{2}{3} \times \frac{5}{6}$ 14. $12\frac{3}{5} \div 2\frac{5}{8}$ 15. $4\frac{6}{7} \times 2\frac{6}{17}$ [7-5]

Self-Test answers and Extra Practice are at the back of the book.

7-6 Ratios

At Fair Oaks Junior High School there are 35 teachers and 525 students. We can compare the number of teachers to the number of students by writing a quotient.

$$\frac{\text{number of teachers}}{\text{number of students}} = \frac{35}{525}, \text{ or } \frac{1}{15}$$

The indicated quotient of one number divided by a second number is called the **ratio** of the first number to the second number. We can write the ratio above in the following ways.

$$\frac{1}{15} \qquad 1:15 \qquad 1 \text{ to } 15$$

All of these expressions are read *one to fifteen*. If the colon notation is used, the first number is divided by the second. A ratio is said to be in **lowest terms** if the two numbers are relatively prime. You do not change an improper fraction to a mixed number if the improper fraction represents a ratio.

EXAMPLE 1   There are 9 players on a baseball team. Four of these are infielders and 3 are outfielders. Find each ratio in lowest terms.

   a. infielders to outfielders

   b. outfielders to total players

Solution   **a.** $\dfrac{\text{infielders}}{\text{outfielders}} = \dfrac{4}{3}$ or   4:3   or   4 to 3

   b. $\dfrac{\text{outfielders}}{\text{total players}} = \dfrac{3}{9} = \dfrac{1}{3}$ or   1:3   or   1 to 3

   Some ratios compare measurements. In these cases, we must be sure that the measurements are expressed in the same unit.

EXAMPLE 2   It takes Herb 4 min to mix some paint. Herb can paint a room in 3 h. What is the ratio of the time it takes Herb to mix the paint to the time it takes Herb to paint the room?

Solution   Use minutes as a common unit for measuring time.

$$3 \text{ h} = 3 \times 60 \text{ min} = 180 \text{ min}$$

The ratio is $\dfrac{\text{min to mix}}{\text{min to paint}} = \dfrac{4}{180} = \dfrac{1}{45}$, or 1:45.

There is *not enough information* given in some problems. Then you must recall facts that are part of your general knowledge. In Example 2, you must recall that 1 h = 60 min.

Some ratios are of the form

40 miles per hour   or   5 for a dollar.

These ratios involve quantities of different kinds and are called **rates.**
Rates may be expressed as decimals or mixed numbers. Rates should be simplified to a *per unit* form.

EXAMPLE 3   Alice's car went 258 miles on 12 gallons of gas. Express the rate of fuel consumption in miles per gallon.

Solution   The rate of fuel consumption is

$$\frac{258}{12} = \frac{43}{2} = 21\frac{1}{2} \text{ miles per gallon.}$$

Some of the units in which rates are given are:

mi/gal (or mpg)	miles per gallon
mi/h (or mph)	miles per hour
km/L	kilometers per liter
km/h	kilometers per hour

Class Exercises

Express each ratio as a fraction in lowest terms.

1. 5 to 7   **2.** 11 to 6   **3.** 10:30   **4.** 12:24

5. 8 to 2   **6.** 32 to 4   **7.** 68:17   **8.** 45:18

Rewrite each ratio so that the numerator and denominator are expressed in the same unit of measure.

9. $\dfrac{2 \text{ dollars}}{50 \text{ cents}}$ **10.** $\dfrac{5 \text{ months}}{2 \text{ years}}$ **11.** $\dfrac{35 \text{ cm}}{1 \text{ m}}$ **12.** $\dfrac{12 \text{ min}}{2 \text{ h}}$

Express each rate in per unit form.

13. 120 km in 3 h   **14.** 70 mi on 5 gal of gas

15. $1000 in 4 months   **16.** 30 km on 3 L of gas

Written Exercises

For each diagram below, name each ratio as a fraction in lowest terms.
a. The number of shaded squares to the number of unshaded squares
b. The number of shaded squares to the total number of squares
c. The total number of squares to the number of unshaded squares

A **1.** 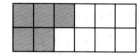   **2.**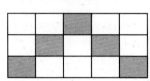

3. 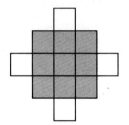   **4.**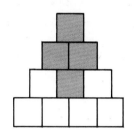

Express each ratio as a fraction in lowest terms.

5. 18 hours to 2 days   **6.** 25 cm to 3 m   **7.** 4 days : 2 weeks

8. 48 s : 5 min   **9.** 3 kg : 800 g   **10.** 6 lb : 24 oz

Express each rate in per unit form.

11. $\dfrac{60 \text{ km}}{24 \text{ L}}$ **12.** $\dfrac{126 \text{ km}}{4 \text{ h}}$ **13.** $\dfrac{248 \text{ mi}}{16 \text{ gal}}$ **14.** $\dfrac{36 \text{ g}}{48 \text{ cm}^3}$

15. $\dfrac{75 \text{ ft}}{30 \text{ s}}$ **16.** $\dfrac{125 \text{ lb}}{2 \text{ ft}^3}$ **17.** $\dfrac{26 \text{ mi}}{2.5 \text{ h}}$ **18.** $\dfrac{246 \text{ km}}{30 \text{ L}}$

Find each ratio as a fraction in lowest terms.

B **19. a.** The number of vowels to the number of consonants in the alphabet (consider *y* a consonant)
  b. The number of consonants to the total number of letters
  c. The total number of letters to the number of vowels

20. a. The number of weekdays to the number of weekend days (Saturdays and Sundays) in the month of February (not a leap year)
  b. The number of weekdays in the month of February (not a leap year) to the number of days in February
  c. The number of days to the number of Sundays in the month of February (not a leap year)

21. a. The number of diagonals drawn in the figure at the right to the total number of segments

b. The number of sides of the figure to the number of diagonals

c. The total number of segments to the number of sides

22. a. The number of prime numbers between 10 and 25 to the number of whole numbers between 10 and 25

b. The number of prime numbers between 10 and 25 to the number of composite numbers between 10 and 25

c. The number of whole numbers between 10 and 25 to the number of composite numbers between 10 and 25

In Exercises 23–26, $AB = 7\frac{1}{5}$, $CD = 10\frac{1}{2}$, $EF = 12$, and $GH = 6\frac{3}{4}$. Express each ratio in lowest terms.

C 23. $\dfrac{AB}{EF}$ 　　　　**24.** $\dfrac{EF}{GH}$ 　　　　**25.** $\dfrac{CD}{GH}$ 　　　　**26.** $\dfrac{GH}{AB}$

Problems

Solve.

A 1. What is the cost of grapes in dollars per kilogram if 4.5 kg of grapes cost $7.56?

2. The *index of refraction* of a transparent substance is the ratio of the speed of light in space to the speed of light in the substance. Using the table, find the index of refraction of
a. glass. 　　　**b.** water.

Substance	Speed of Light (in km/sec)
space	300,000
glass	200,000
water	225,000

3. The *mechanical advantage* of a simple machine is the ratio of the weight lifted by the machine to the force necessary to lift it. What is the mechanical advantage of a jack that lifts a 3200-pound car with a force of 120 pounds?

4. The C-string of a cello vibrates 654 times in 5 seconds. How many vibrations per second is this?

5. A four-cubic-foot volume of water at sea level weighs 250 lb. What is the density of water in pounds per cubic foot?

6. A share of stock that cost $88 earned $16 last year. What was the price-to-earnings ratio of this stock?

In Exercises 7 and 8, find the ratio in lowest terms.

B **7. a.** $\dfrac{AB}{DE}$

   b. $\dfrac{\text{Perimeter of } \triangle ABC}{\text{Perimeter of } \triangle DEF}$

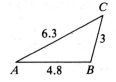

8. a. $PQ:TU$
   b. $QR:UV$
   c. $\dfrac{\text{Perimeter of } PQRS}{\text{Perimeter of } TUVW}$

 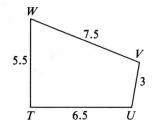

For Exercises 9–12, refer to the table to find the ratios in lowest terms.

9. The population of Centerville in 1980 to its population in 1970

10. The growth in the population of Easton to its 1980 population

Population (in thousands)		
Town	1970	1980
Centerville	36	44
Easton	16	28

11. The total population of both towns in 1970 to their total population in 1980

12. The total growth in the population of both towns to their total 1980 population

13. During a season, a baseball player hit safely in 135 times at bat; the player struck out or was fielded out in 340 times at bat. What is the player's ratio of hits to times at bat?

14. A fruit drink recipe requires fruit juice and milk in the ratio $3:5$. What fraction of the drink is milk? What fraction is juice?

Review Exercises

Solve.

1. $6x = 54$ **2.** $11x = 99$ **3.** $5x = 45$ **4.** $3x = 39$

5. $20x = 100$ **6.** $10x = 80$ **7.** $12x = 144$ **8.** $9x = 72$

7-7 Proportions

The seventh grade at Madison Junior High School has 160 students and 10 teachers. The seventh grade at Jefferson Junior High School has 144 students and 9 teachers. Let us compare the two teacher-student ratios.

$$\frac{10}{160} = \frac{1}{16} \qquad \frac{9}{144} = \frac{1}{16}$$

Thus, the two ratios are equal.

$$\frac{10}{160} = \frac{9}{144}$$

An equation that states that two ratios are equal is called a **proportion.** The proportion above may be read as

10 is to 160 as 9 is to 144.

The numbers 10, 160, 9, and 144 are called the **terms** of the proportion.

Sometimes one of the terms of a proportion is a variable. If, for example, 192 students will be in the seventh grade at Madison Junior High next year, how many teachers will be needed if the teacher-student ratio is to remain the same?

Let n be the number of teachers needed next year. Then, if the teacher-student ratio is to be the same, we must have

$$\frac{n}{192} = \frac{10}{160}.$$

To **solve** this proportion, we find the value of the variable that makes the equation true. This can be done by finding equivalent fractions with a common denominator. For example:

$$\frac{160 \times n}{160 \times 192} = \frac{10 \times 192}{160 \times 192}$$

Since the denominators are equal, the numerators also must be equal.

$$160 \times n = 10 \times 192$$

Notice that this result could also be obtained by **cross-multiplying** in the original proportion.

$$\frac{n}{192} \diagdown \frac{10}{160}$$

$$160 \times n = 10 \times 192$$
$$160n = 1920$$
$$n = 1920 \div 160 = 12$$

Therefore, the seventh grade will need 12 teachers next year.

The example on the previous page illustrates the following property of proportions.

Property

If $\frac{a}{b} = \frac{c}{d}$, with $b \neq 0$ and $d \neq 0$, then $ad = bc$.

EXAMPLE Solve $\frac{3}{8} = \frac{12}{n}$.

Solution

$$\frac{3}{8} = \frac{12}{n}$$
$$3 \times n = 8 \times 12$$
$$3n = 96$$
$$n = 96 \div 3 = 32$$

It is a simple matter to check your answer when solving a proportion. You merely substitute your answer for the variable and cross-multiply. For instance, in the example above:

$$\frac{3}{8} \overset{?}{=} \frac{12}{32}$$
$$3 \times 32 \overset{?}{=} 8 \times 12$$
$$96 = 96$$

Class Exercises

Cross-multiply and state an equation that does not involve fractions.

1. $\frac{n}{9} = \frac{2}{3}$ **2.** $\frac{3}{5} = \frac{n}{20}$ **3.** $\frac{2}{7} = \frac{6}{n}$ **4.** $\frac{3}{n} = \frac{6}{10}$

5. $\frac{12}{15} = \frac{n}{5}$ **6.** $\frac{2}{n} = \frac{3}{9}$ **7.** $\frac{n}{16} = \frac{3}{4}$ **8.** $\frac{8}{3} = \frac{24}{n}$

9. $\frac{13}{18} = \frac{5}{n}$ **10.** $\frac{n}{42} = \frac{14}{3}$ **11.** $\frac{17}{n} = \frac{102}{5}$ **12.** $\frac{37}{11} = \frac{51}{n}$

Written Exercises

Solve and check.

A **1.** $\frac{n}{3} = \frac{12}{9}$ **2.** $\frac{7}{2} = \frac{x}{10}$ **3.** $\frac{21}{r} = \frac{3}{8}$ **4.** $\frac{3}{75} = \frac{2}{m}$

5. $\frac{8}{5} = \frac{56}{u}$

6. $\frac{14}{n} = \frac{7}{9}$

7. $\frac{80}{c} = \frac{4}{3}$

8. $\frac{b}{24} = \frac{15}{9}$

9. $\frac{8}{7} = \frac{x}{63}$

10. $\frac{d}{20} = \frac{14}{8}$

11. $\frac{15}{11} = \frac{n}{33}$

12. $\frac{13}{11} = \frac{26}{m}$

13. $\frac{5}{r} = \frac{2}{3}$

14. $\frac{4}{3} = \frac{n}{7}$

15. $\frac{17}{20} = \frac{v}{10}$

16. $\frac{c}{2} = \frac{6}{18}$

B 17. $\frac{x}{5} = \frac{20}{x}$

18. $\frac{3}{m} = \frac{m}{27}$

19. $\frac{4}{n} = \frac{n}{36}$

20. $\frac{a}{16} = \frac{4}{a}$

21. $\frac{y}{25} = \frac{16}{y}$

22. $\frac{v}{50} = \frac{18}{v}$

23. $\frac{25}{x} = \frac{x}{9}$

24. $\frac{49}{n} = \frac{n}{4}$

25. If $\frac{x}{7} = \frac{3}{21}$, what is the ratio of x to 3?

26. If $\frac{27}{m} = \frac{9}{2}$, what is the ratio of m to 27?

27. If $\frac{3}{5} = \frac{12}{n}$, what is the ratio of n to 5?

C 28. Choose nonzero whole numbers a, b, c, d, x, and y such that $\frac{a}{b} = \frac{x}{y}$

and $\frac{c}{d} = \frac{x}{y}$. Use these numbers to check whether $\frac{a + c}{b + d} = \frac{x}{y}$.

29. Find nonzero whole numbers a, b, c, and d to show that if

$\frac{a + c}{b + d} = \frac{x}{y}$, it may not be true that $\frac{a}{b} = \frac{x}{y}$ and $\frac{c}{d} = \frac{x}{y}$.

Review Exercises

Multiply.

1. $2\frac{2}{3} \times 5$

2. $3\frac{5}{8} \times 6$

3. $5 \times 4\frac{5}{9}$

4. $7 \times 6\frac{3}{4}$

5. $3\frac{4}{9} \times 2\frac{1}{2}$

6. $4\frac{1}{3} \times 5\frac{1}{4}$

7. $6 \times 7\frac{1}{4}$

8. $5 \times 8\frac{3}{5}$

9. $9 \times 6\frac{7}{10}$

CALCULATOR INVESTIGATION: *Solving Proportions*

Calculators are useful in solving proportions involving decimals. Use a calculator to help solve the following proportions.

1. $\frac{x}{0.7} = \frac{5}{8}$

2. $\frac{n}{4} = \frac{0.8}{0.3}$

3. $\frac{6}{y} = \frac{0.5}{0.82}$

4. $\frac{12}{c} = \frac{0.37}{1.21}$

5. $\frac{x}{1.43} = \frac{3.61}{0.57}$

6. $\frac{a}{0.005} = \frac{2.972}{4.019}$

7-8 Problem Solving: Using Proportion

Proportions can be used to solve word problems. The following steps are helpful in solving problems using proportions.

1. Decide which quantity is to be found and represent it by a variable.
2. Determine whether the quantities involved can be compared using ratios (rates).
3. Equate the ratios in a proportion.
4. Solve the proportion.

EXAMPLE   Linda Chu bought 4 tires for her car at a cost of $264. How much would 5 tires cost at the same rate?

Solution   Let c = the cost of 5 tires. Set up a proportion.

$$\frac{4}{264} = \frac{5}{c} \quad \longleftarrow \quad \text{number of tires} \\ \longleftarrow \quad \text{cost}$$

Solve the proportion.

$$\frac{4}{264} = \frac{5}{c}$$
$$4c = 5 \times 264$$
$$4c = 1320$$
$$c = 330$$

Therefore, 5 tires would cost $330.

Notice that the proportion in the example could also be written as:

$$\frac{264}{4} = \frac{c}{5} \quad \longleftarrow \quad \text{cost} \\ \longleftarrow \quad \text{number of tires}$$

Class Exercises

State a proportion you could use to solve each problem.

1. If 4 bars of soap cost $1.50, how much would 8 bars cost?

2. If you can buy 4 containers of cottage cheese for $4.20, how many could you buy for $9.45?

3. If a satellite travels 19,500 km in 3 h, how far does it travel in 7 h?

4. If a car uses 5 gallons of gasoline to travel 160 miles, how many gallons would the car use in traveling 96 miles?

5. If 9 kg of fertilizer will feed 300 m² of grass, how much fertilizer would be required to feed 500 m²?

6. If 2 cans of paint will cover 900 ft², what area will 3 cans cover?

Problems

Solve.

A **1.** A train traveled 720 km in 9 h.
    a. How far would it travel in 11 h?
    b. How long would it take to go 1120 km?

2. Five pounds of apples cost $3.70.
    a. How many pounds could you buy for $5.92?
    b. How much would 9 pounds cost?

3. Eight oranges cost $1.50.
    a. How much would 20 oranges cost?
    b. How many oranges could you buy for $5.25?

4. Due to Earth's rotation, a point on the equator travels about 40,000 km every 24 h.
    a. How far does a point on the equator travel in 33 h?
    b. How long does it take a point on the equator to travel 95,000 km?

5. Seventy-five cubic centimeters of maple sap can be boiled down to make 2 cm³ of maple syrup.
    a. How much maple syrup would 200 cm³ of sap make?
    b. How much sap would be needed to make 9 cm³ of syrup?

6. A long-playing record revolves 100 times every 3 min.
    a. How many revolutions does it make in 2.25 min?
    b. How long does it take for 275 revolutions?

7. Three and a half pounds of peaches cost $1.68. How much would $2\frac{1}{2}$ lb of peaches cost?

8. A type of steel used for bicycle frames contains 5 g of manganese in every 400 g of steel. How much manganese would a 2200 g bicycle frame contain?

9. A printing press can print 350 sheets in 4 min. How long would it take to print 525 sheets?

10. A pharmacist mixes 5 g of a powder with 45 cm³ of water to make a prescription medicine. How much powder should she mix with 81 cm³ of water to make a larger amount of the same medicine?

162

B **11.** A baseball team has won 8 games and lost 6. If the team continues to have the same ratio of wins to losses, how many wins will the team have after playing 21 games?

12. The ratio of cars to trucks passing a certain intersection is found to be 7:2. If 63 vehicles (cars and trucks) pass the intersection, how many might be trucks?

C **13.** In the third century B.C., the Greek mathematician Eratosthenes calculated that an angle of $7\frac{1}{2}°$ at Earth's center cuts off an arc of about 1600 km on Earth's surface. From this information compute the circumference of Earth.

14. In the diagram $\overline{PQ}$ is perpendicular to $\overline{MN}$. It can be shown that $\frac{a}{x} = \frac{x}{b}$. If $a = 50$ and $b = 2$, find x.

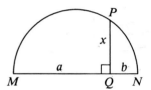

Review Exercises

Rewrite each ratio so that the numerator and denominator are expressed in the same unit of measure.

1. $\dfrac{2 \text{ m}}{15 \text{ cm}}$ **2.** $\dfrac{20 \text{ mm}}{7 \text{ cm}}$ **3.** $\dfrac{10 \text{ yd}}{5 \text{ ft}}$ **4.** $\dfrac{8 \text{ in.}}{3 \text{ ft}}$

5. $\dfrac{2 \text{ km}}{450 \text{ m}}$ **6.** $\dfrac{85 \text{ cm}}{4 \text{ m}}$ **7.** $\dfrac{1 \text{ yd}}{20 \text{ in.}}$ **8.** $\dfrac{310 \text{ m}}{3 \text{ km}}$

▮▮▮ CALCULATOR INVESTIGATION: *Reciprocals*

It is fairly simple to find the reciprocal of a fraction or a whole number. It is harder to find the reciprocal of a decimal. However, many calculators have a reciprocal key to carry out this procedure.

Use a calculator with a reciprocal key to find each reciprocal.

1. 0.67   **2.** 0.579   **3.** 0.2539   **4.** 1.564   **5.** 4.7851

7-9 Scale Drawing

In the drawing of the house the actual height of 9 m is represented by a length of 3 cm, and the actual length of 21 m is represented by a length of 7 cm. This means that 1 cm in the drawing represents 3 m in the actual building. Such a drawing in which all lengths are in the same ratio to actual lengths is called a **scale drawing**. The relationship of length in the drawing to actual length is called the **scale**. In the drawing of the house the scale is 1 cm:3 m.

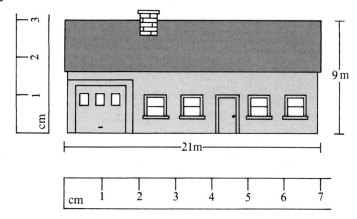

We can express the scale as a ratio, called the scale ratio, if a common unit of measure is used. Since 3 m equals 300 cm, the scale ratio above is $\frac{1}{300}$.

EXAMPLE Find the length and width of the room shown if the scale of the drawing is 1 cm:1.5 m.

Solution Measuring the drawing, we find that it has length 4 cm and width 3 cm.

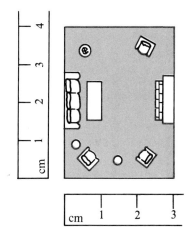

Method 1 Write a proportion for the length.

$$\frac{1}{1.5} = \frac{4}{l} \quad \leftarrow \text{ unit lengths in the drawing} \\ \leftarrow \text{ actual length}$$

$l = 1.5 \times 4 = 6$ The room is 6 m long.

Write a proportion for the width. $\frac{1}{1.5} = \frac{3}{w}$

$w = 1.5 \times 3 = 4.5$ The room is 4.5 m wide.

Method 2 Use the scale ratio: $\frac{1 \text{ cm}}{1.5 \text{ m}} = \frac{1 \text{ cm}}{150 \text{ cm}} = \frac{1}{150}$

The actual length is 150 times the length in the drawing.

$l = 150 \times 4 = 600 \text{ cm} = 6 \text{ m}$ $w = 150 \times 3 = 450 \text{ cm} = 4.5 \text{ m}$

Class Exercises

A drawing of a bureau is to be made with a scale of 1 cm to 10 cm. Find the dimension on the drawing if the actual dimension is given.

1. Height of bureau (70 cm)

2. Width of bureau (80 cm)

3. Height of legs (17.5 cm)

4. Width of top (75 cm)

5. Height of top drawer (10 cm)

6. Height of second drawer (12.5 cm)

7. Height of third drawer (15 cm)

8. Width of drawer (72.5 cm)

Written Exercises

An O-gauge model railroad has a scale of 1 in.:48 in. Find the actual length of each railroad car, given the scale dimension.

A **1.** Flat car: 23 in.

2. Freight car: 11 in.

3. Tank car: 12 in.

4. Caboose: 9 in.

5. Passenger car: 20 in.

6. Refrigerator car: 15 in.

Exercises 7–14, on the next page, refer to the map below.
a. Measure each distance in the map shown to the nearest 0.5 cm.
b. Compute the actual distance to the nearest 100 km.

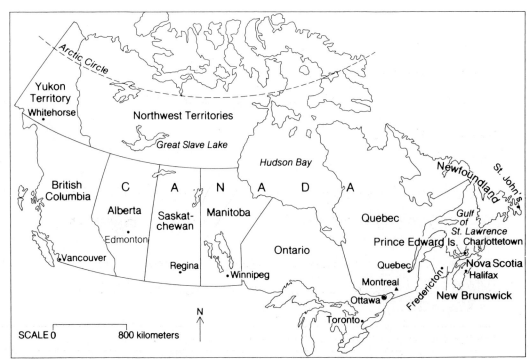

7. Vancouver to Edmonton

8. Toronto to Winnipeg

9. Whitehorse to Montreal

10. Ottawa to Charlottetown

11. Toronto to Halifax

12. Fredericton to St. John's

B 13. By how many kilometers would an airplane route from Winnipeg to Montreal be extended if the plane went by way of Toronto?

14. How much farther is it by air from Vancouver to Edmonton to Whitehorse than it is from Vancouver directly to Whitehorse?

If Earth had the diameter of a peppercorn (5 mm), the sun would have the diameter of a large beach ball (54.5 cm) and it would be about the length of two basketball courts (58.75 m) away. Assuming that the diameter of Earth is about 12,700 km, compute each measurement.

15. The actual diameter of the sun

16. The distance from Earth to the sun

17. The number of times larger in diameter the sun is than Earth

18. In the scale described above, the diameter of the planet Jupiter would be 55 mm. What is the actual diameter of Jupiter?

Self-Test B

Express each ratio as a fraction in lowest terms.

1. 12:8

2. 51 to 27

3. 18 to 99

[7-6]

Solve.

4. $\frac{x}{3} = \frac{8}{12}$

5. $\frac{12}{9} = \frac{n}{3}$

6. $\frac{180}{n} = \frac{4}{3}$

[7-7]

7. Find the price per gram of a metal that costs $154.10 for 230 g.

[7-8]

8. A company paid a dividend of $30 on 12 shares of stock. How much will it pay on 44 shares?

9. On a map, 3 in. represents 16 ft. What length represents $5\frac{1}{3}$ ft?

[7-9]

10. What is the scale in a drawing in which a vase 28 cm tall is drawn 1.75 cm high?

Self-Test answers and Extra Practice are at the back of the book.

The Computer and Series

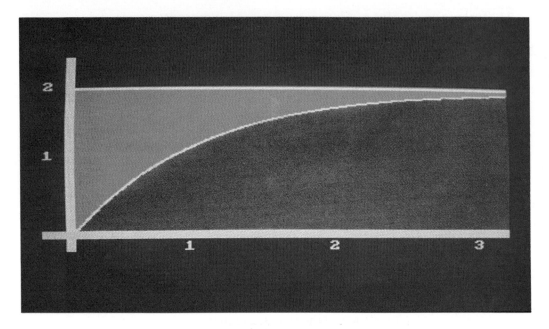

The following computer program will compute the sum of the first N terms of $1 + \frac{1}{2} + \frac{1}{4} + \frac{1}{8} + \cdots$.

```
10   LET M = 2
20   PRINT "NUMBER OF TERMS";
30   INPUT N
40   LET T = 1
50   LET S = 1
60   FOR K = 2 TO N
70   LET T = T/M
80   LET S = S + T
90   NEXT K
100  PRINT "SUM = ";S
110  END
```

  1. RUN the program for $N = 3$, $N = 4$, and $N = 5$.

  2. RUN the program for $N = 8$, $N = 10$, and $N = 12$. Using these results and the results of Exercise 1, tell what number these sums appear to be approaching.

   The number that you found in Exercise 2 is called the **sum** of the series $1 + \frac{1}{2} + \frac{1}{4} + \frac{1}{8} \cdots$. The indicated sum of a sequence of numbers is called a **series**. The more terms you add to $1 + \frac{1}{2} + \frac{1}{4} + \frac{1}{8} \cdots$, the closer the sum will be to this number.

3. Change line 10 of the program to LET M = 3 and find the sum of

$$1 + \frac{1}{3} + \frac{1}{9} + \frac{1}{27} + \cdots,$$

in which the denominator triples with each new term, for $N = 5$, $N = 7$, $N = 9$, and $N = 11$. What fraction do these sums appear to be approaching?

4. Change line 10 of the program to LET M = 4 and find the sum of

$$1 + \frac{1}{4} + \frac{1}{16} + \frac{1}{64} + \cdots$$

for several values of N. What fraction do these sums appear to be approaching as you increase the value of N?

For the remaining exercises, delete line 10 from the program.

Do all the series have sums? In order to answer this question, do the following exercise.

5. For $N = 3, 5, 7, 9, 20, 50,$ and 100, find the sum of

$$1 + \frac{1}{2} + \frac{1}{3} + \frac{1}{4} + \cdots$$

by changing the computer program as follows. Delete lines 40 and 70 and replace line 80 with 80 LET S = S+1/K. What appears to be happening?

Some series of fractions may have sums even when the series involve both addition and subtraction. This is shown by the following exercises.

6. For $N = 50, 51, 52, 53, 100, 101, 102,$ and 103, find the sum of

$$1 - \frac{1}{2} + \frac{1}{3} - \frac{1}{4} + \cdots$$

by changing the computer program as follows:

40 LET F = 1   70 LET F = −F   80 LET S = S+F/K

What appears to be happening?

7. Replace line 80 with 80 LET S = S+F/(2*K−1) and find sums of

$$1 - \frac{1}{3} + \frac{1}{5} - \frac{1}{7} + \cdots$$

for $N = 10, 100,$ and 500. Multiply the result by 4 and round to hundredths. What familiar number have you found?

Chapter Review

Write the letter of the correct answer.

1. $\frac{8}{11} + \frac{1}{11}$

    a. $\frac{8}{22}$ **b.** $\frac{9}{11}$ **c.** $\frac{8}{121}$ **d.** $\frac{9}{22}$

[7-1]

2. $\frac{17}{18} - \frac{3}{9}$

    a. $\frac{14}{9}$ **b.** $\frac{20}{27}$ **c.** $\frac{14}{18}$ **d.** $\frac{11}{18}$

3. $3\frac{5}{8} + 4\frac{1}{4}$

    a. $12\frac{7}{8}$ **b.** $7\frac{1}{8}$ **c.** $7\frac{7}{8}$ **d.** $8\frac{1}{8}$

[7-2]

4. $11\frac{1}{4} - 5\frac{3}{4}$

    a. $6\frac{1}{2}$ **b.** $6\frac{1}{4}$ **c.** $5\frac{1}{2}$ **d.** $5\frac{1}{4}$

5. $\frac{6}{13} \times \frac{5}{2}$

    a. $\frac{15}{13}$ **b.** $\frac{11}{26}$ **c.** $\frac{12}{65}$ **d.** $\frac{15}{26}$

[7-3]

6. $\frac{15}{7} \div \frac{2}{3}$

    a. $\frac{10}{7}$ **b.** $\frac{30}{21}$ **c.** $\frac{14}{45}$ **d.** $\frac{45}{14}$

[7-4]

7. $1\frac{1}{2} \times 1\frac{7}{9}$

    a. $1\frac{7}{18}$ **b.** $2\frac{2}{3}$ **c.** $2\frac{7}{18}$ **d.** $1\frac{2}{3}$

[7-5]

True or false?

8. 25 s to 2 h is in lowest terms.

9. $\frac{9}{3}$ may be written as $3:1$.

[7-6]

10. If $\frac{18}{21} = \frac{6}{n}$, then $n = 7$.

11. If $\frac{x}{45} = \frac{7}{9}$, then $x = 30$.

[7-7]

12. If a train travels 208 mi in 4 h, then it will travel 364 mi in 6 h.

[7-8]

13. If a pump empties a 420 L tank in 14 min, then it will empty a 540 L tank in 18 min.

14. On a scale drawing, 2 cm represents 5 m. The scale is 5 m : 2 cm.

[7-9]

Chapter Test

Add or subtract. Simplify.

1. $\frac{2}{15} + \frac{3}{15}$
2. $\frac{3}{8} + \frac{11}{12}$
3. $\frac{9}{4} - \frac{7}{10}$ [7-1]

4. $7\frac{4}{9} - 1\frac{2}{9}$
5. $5\frac{1}{6} + 7\frac{2}{5}$
6. $7\frac{5}{8} - 6\frac{5}{6}$ [7-2]

Multiply or divide. Simplify.

7. $8 \times \frac{2}{3}$
8. $\frac{4}{7} \times \frac{9}{5}$
9. $\frac{2}{3} \times \frac{15}{8}$ [7-3]

10. $\frac{14}{11} \div 2$
11. $\frac{7}{9} \div \frac{14}{15}$
12. $\frac{24}{17} \div \frac{36}{51}$ [7-4]

13. $3\frac{1}{4} \times 2\frac{1}{5}$
14. $12 \times 6\frac{2}{3}$
15. $5\frac{1}{4} \div 2\frac{1}{3}$ [7-5]

Express each ratio as a fraction in lowest terms.

16. 35 min:3 h
17. 2 m to 85 cm   [7-6]

Solve.

18. $\frac{n}{40} = \frac{3}{8}$
19. $\frac{24}{5} = \frac{x}{10}$
20. $\frac{5}{11} = \frac{20}{a}$ [7-7]

21. A car traveled 162 mi in 3 h. How many hours would it take to travel 351 mi?   [7-8]

22. On a map, 2 in. represents 300 mi. If two points are separated by 5 in. on the map, what is the actual distance between them?   [7-9]

Cumulative Review (Chapters 1–7)

Exercises

Perform the indicated operation.

1. $18{,}793 + 16{,}099$ **2.** $43{,}003 - 27{,}468$ **3.** $14.071 - 9.586$

4. $7.93 + 0.06 + 4.3 + 1.937$ **5.** $4.003 + 2.1 + 3 + 6.93$

6. 1036×41 **7.** $38\overline{)10{,}678}$ **8.** 3.091×0.37

9. 0.093×4.12 **10.** $0.24\overline{)0.78}$ **11.** $6.7774 \div 1.03$

Write in mathematical symbols.

12. Five more than a number n **13.** A number n is greater than fourteen.

14. Eight times a number n **15.** Twenty-seven is less than forty-one.

Solve.

16. $3x = 126$ **17.** $x - 47 = 117$ **18.** $x + 43 = 97$ **19.** $5x = 110$

20. $x \div 12 = 44$ **21.** $81 + x = 148$ **22.** $x \div 35 = 7$ **23.** $163 - x = 91$

Complete.

24. A(n) __?__ triangle has three congruent sides.

25. Any four-sided figure is called a(n) __?__ .

26. A line has __?__ endpoint(s).

27. The symbol $\perp$ means __?__ .

28. Two angles whose measures add to $180°$ are __?__ .

Find the LCM of each pair.

29. 4, 14   **30.** 6, 15   **31.** 10, 12   **32.** 24, 30

Find the GCF of each pair.

33. 42, 38   **34.** 34, 12   **35.** 70, 58   **36.** 84, 92

Change each improper fraction to a mixed number in simple form.

37. $\frac{42}{5}$ **38.** $\frac{17}{3}$ **39.** $\frac{61}{11}$ **40.** $\frac{231}{20}$ **41.** $\frac{437}{52}$

Change each mixed number to an improper fraction.

42. $4\frac{7}{8}$ **43.** $7\frac{4}{5}$ **44.** $11\frac{14}{15}$ **45.** $17\frac{9}{14}$ **46.** $26\frac{37}{50}$

Change each decimal to a fraction in lowest terms.

47. 0.86 **48.** 0.475 **49.** $0.\overline{72}$ **50.** $0.8\overline{25}$ **51.** $0.9\overline{3}$

Problems

Solve.

1. At the town art festival each artist was allowed to display 24 works. If there were 84 artists in all, and 40 displayed 24 works each, while the other 44 displayed 20 works each, how many works of art were displayed?

2. The film society was showing a three-reel movie. If the entire showing took 2 h and it took 5 min to change reels, how long was each reel?

3. The diameter of a phonograph record is 12 inches. Find the circumference to the nearest inch. Use $\pi \approx \frac{22}{7}$.

4. Susan bought a tennis racket for $44.95, three cans of tennis balls for $4.49 each, and two headbands for $6.99 each. How much did Susan spend?

5. Forty-seven less than a certain number is 268. Find the number.

6. Luis drives a total of $8\frac{1}{3}$ mi to work and back each day. If he drives $26\frac{4}{5}$ mi on the weekend and works 5 days a week, how far does Luis drive each week?

7. A regular hexagon has a perimeter of 43.590 cm. Find the length of each side.

8. Each booth at the school carnival has the same amount of space. If the row in which the booths are located is 132 feet long and there are 16 booths, how long is each booth?

9. Tickets for the new musical were sold as follows. There were 347 tickets sold in advance by mail, 431 tickets sold in advance by telephone, and 578 tickets sold in advance at the box office. There were also 294 tickets sold at the door. How many tickets were sold in advance?

10. A baseball stadium has 43,218 seats. There are 16,247 box seats and 21,469 reserved seats. The remaining seats are in the bleachers. How many bleacher seats are there?

8 Solving Equations

APPLYING MATHEMATICS
AERONAUTICS

NASA (National Aeronautics and Space Administration) is the U.S. government agency responsible for space exploration and experiments. Astronauts and other scientists conduct in-flight scientific experiments and observations. Much of the research takes months to analyze, but the results are of enormous importance in many fields. For example, some of the experiments concern the effect of weightlessness on the human body and on plants. The manufacture of some medicines may also be improved in a weightless environment. Radar equipment and infrared sensors are used to scan millions of square miles of Earth's surface, recording data on vegetation, mineral deposits, oceans, and clouds.

CAREER CONNECTION

SPACE SCIENTIST

Space scientists require a strong background in mathematics, physics, and related sciences. The work is demanding but exciting. The men and women who perform experiments in the Spacelab research station aboard the space shuttle are selected because of their specialized knowledge in various fields, for example, in biology, chemistry, or medicine.

Photo: A NASA image from the Apollo II spacecraft shows craters on the far side of the moon.

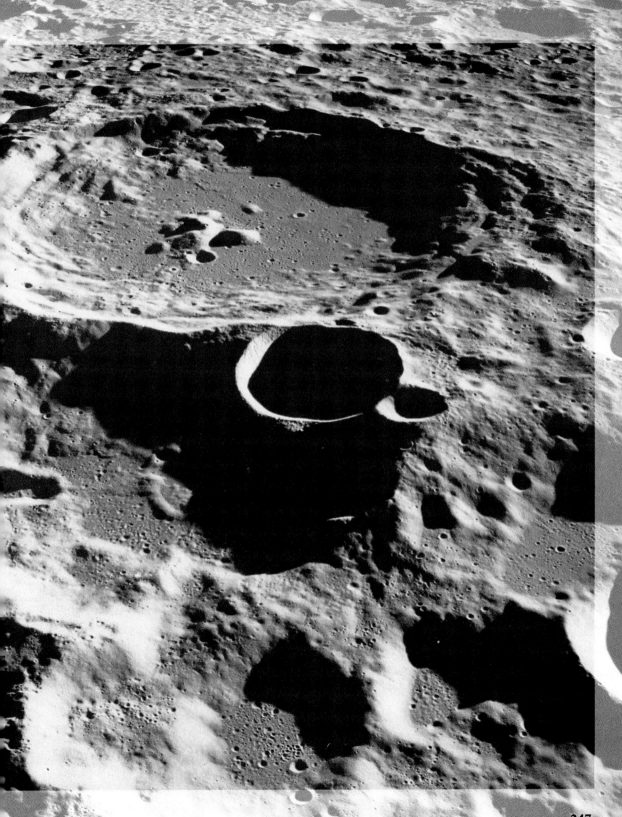

8-1 Equations and Variables

You know that a letter, such as n, that represents a number is called a *variable,* and an expression, such as $n + 3$, containing a variable is called a *variable expression.* In an equation involving a variable, such as

$$n + 3 = 7,$$

a value of the variable that makes the equation a true statement is said to **satisfy** the equation. This value is called a **solution** of the equation. An equation may have no solution, one solution, or more than one solution. The solution of $n + 3 = 7$ is 4 since $4 + 3 = 7$. The given set of numbers that a variable may represent is called the **replacement set.** We write the replacement set by enclosing the given numbers in braces, { }. For example, if the numbers in the replacement set are

$$1, 2, 3, 4,$$

we can write the set as $\{1, 2, 3, 4\}$.

Sometimes it may be practical to substitute each value of the replacement set for the variable to see which ones satisfy the equation.

EXAMPLE 1   Solve $2x + 5 = 17$, if the replacement set for x is $\{0, 2, 4, 6\}$.

Solution   Substitute each value in the replacement set for x in $2x + 5 = 17$.

$$2 \times 0 + 5 \neq 17$$
$$2 \times 2 + 5 \neq 17$$
$$2 \times 4 + 5 \neq 17$$
$$2 \times 6 + 5 = 17$$

The solution in $\{0, 2, 4, 6\}$ is 6.

EXAMPLE 2   Solve $8 - n = 2$, if the replacement set for n is $\{1, 2, 3\}$.

Solution   Substitute each value in the replacement set for n in $8 - n = 2$.

$$8 - 1 \neq 2$$
$$8 - 2 \neq 2$$
$$8 - 3 \neq 2$$

Since no value in the replacement set satisfies the equation, the equation has no solution *in the given replacement set.* (If the replacement set is the set of whole numbers, the solution is 6.)

EXAMPLE 3 Solve $x + 5 = 5 + x$, if the replacement set for x is $\{0, 2, 4\}$.

Solution   Substitute the values in the replacement set for x.

$$0 + 5 = 5 + 0; \; 5 = 5$$
$$2 + 5 = 5 + 2; \; 7 = 7$$
$$4 + 5 = 5 + 4; \; 9 = 9$$

Since all the values in the replacement set satisfy the equation, the solutions are 0, 2, and 4.

The equation in Example 3, $x + 5 = 5 + x$, would also be satisfied by all values if the replacement set were the set of all the numbers in our decimal system. Such an equation is called an **identity**.

Class Exercises

Evaluate each variable expression for each value in the replacement set $\{0, 1, 2, 3\}$.

1. $n + 4$ **2.** $7 - a$ **3.** $2n + 5$ **4.** $8 - 2c$

5. $\dfrac{d}{2}$ **6.** $\dfrac{1}{2} + z$ **7.** $5 - \dfrac{x}{2}$ **8.** $\dfrac{2n}{3}$

State whether or not each equation is satisfied by the given value of the variable.

9. $3n - 1 = 14; \; n = 5$ **10.** $2c + 7 = 13; \; c = 8$

11. $\dfrac{2}{3}b = 16; \; b = 9$ **12.** $\dfrac{n}{2} - 3 = 2; \; n = 10$

13. $9 - 2e = 3; \; e = 3$ **14.** $8 - \dfrac{x}{2} = 2; \; x = 5$

15. $\dfrac{2}{5}t + 5 = 11; \; t = 15$ **16.** $13 + \dfrac{b}{7} = 16; \; b = 21$

Written Exercises

Evaluate each expression for the given value of the variable.

A   **1.** $3x - 5; \; x = 12$ **2.** $\dfrac{2}{3}x + 1; \; x = 15$

     3. $\dfrac{3y + 2}{5}; \; y = 11$ **4.** $\dfrac{2y - 5}{3}; \; y = 13$

     5. $3(n + 2); \; n = 7$ **6.** $7(n - 3); \; n = 9$

Solving Equations **249**

Solve each equation using the given replacement set. If the equation has no solution in the replacement set, so state.

7. $17 + 2n = 25$; $\{0, 3, 4\}$

8. $14 - 3a = 8$; $\{0, 1, 2, 3\}$

9. $3n + 9 = 18$; $\{1, 2, 3, 4\}$

10. $7x - 19 = 9$; $\{0, 4, 8\}$

11. $5b + 3 = 3 + 5b$; $\{3, 6, 9, 10\}$

12. $2n - 7 = n + n - 7$; $\{0, 1, 2\}$

13. $4n + 11 = 55$; $\{1, 4, 11, 13\}$

14. $23 + 5x = 58$; $\{3, 5, 8\}$

15. $\frac{a}{3} = 5$; $\{9, 12, 15, 18\}$

16. $\frac{n}{2} + 5 = 7$; $\{1, 2, 3, 4\}$

17. $\frac{3e}{5} = 9$; $\{10, 15, 20, 25\}$

18. $\frac{5}{2}d = 15$; $\{8, 10, 12, 14\}$

19. $5 - \frac{z}{2} = 1$; $\{4, 6, 8, 10\}$

20. $\frac{n}{3} + 5 = 6$; $\{1, 3, 5, 7\}$

21. $20 - 3y = 2$; $\{4, 6, 8, 10\}$

22. $4 + 4n = 5$; $\{0, 1, 2, 3\}$

23. $\frac{1}{2}n + 3 = 7$; $\{0, 2, 4, 6\}$

24. $\frac{3}{4}y - 1 = 8$; $\{4, 8, 12, 16\}$

State whether or not each equation is satisfied by the given value of the variable.

B 25. $\frac{2}{3}(x + 8) = 14$; $x = 13$

26. $\frac{2}{5}(x - 1) = 6$; $x = 16$

27. $\frac{1}{2}(x + 3) - 2 = 5$; $x = 9$

28. $8 - \frac{1}{3}(x + 17) = 1$; $x = 4$

29. $2\left(9 - \frac{1}{4}x\right) = 10$; $x = 16$

30. $5\left(\frac{2}{3}x + 4\right) - 7 = 35$; $x = 15$

31. $\frac{1}{3}\left(12 + \frac{2}{5}x\right) = 6$; $x = 25$

32. $\frac{3}{4}(16x - 32) = 96$; $x = 9$

Solve each equation if the replacement set is the set of whole numbers. If the equation has no solution or is an identity, so state.

C 33. $3x + 2x = (3 + 2)x$

34. $x = x + 1$

35. $\frac{1}{2}x = x$

36. $\frac{x}{x} = 1$, $(x \neq 0)$

Review Exercises

Complete.

1. $x + 5 - \underline{\ ?\ } = x$

2. $y - 7 + \underline{\ ?\ } = y$

3. $4 + x - \underline{\ ?\ } = x$

4. $11 - y + \underline{\ ?\ } = 11$

5. $9 + a - a = \underline{\ ?\ }$

6. $13 - c + c = \underline{\ ?\ }$

7. $y - \underline{\ ?\ } + \underline{\ ?\ } = 17$

8. $\underline{\ ?\ } + 9 - \underline{\ ?\ } = x$

9. $\underline{\ ?\ } - \underline{\ ?\ } + a = 8$

8-2 Equations: Addition and Subtraction

If the replacement set for an equation is the set of whole numbers, it is not practical to use substitution to solve the equation. Instead, we **transform,** or change, the given equation into a simpler, **equivalent equation,** that is, one that has the same solution. When we transform the given equation, our goal is to arrive at an equivalent equation of the form

$$\text{variable} = \text{number.}$$

For example: $n = 5$

The number, 5, is then the solution of the original equation. The following transformations can be used to solve equations.

> Simplify numerical expressions and variable expressions.
>
> *Transformation by addition:* Add the same number to both sides.
>
> *Transformation by subtraction:* Subtract the same number from both sides.

EXAMPLE 1 Solve $x = 3 + 5$.

Solution Simplify the numerical expression $3 + 5$.

$$x = 3 + 5$$
$$x = 8$$

The solution is 8.

EXAMPLE 2 Solve $x - 2 = 8$.

Solution Our goal is to find an equivalent equation of the form

$$x = \text{a number.}$$

The left side of the given equation is $x - 2$. Recall that addition and subtraction are inverse operations. If we add 2 to both sides, the left side simplifies to x.

$$x - 2 = 8$$
$$x - 2 + 2 = 8 + 2$$
$$x = 10$$

The solution is 10.

EXAMPLE 3 Solve $x + 6 = 17$.

Solution Subtract 6 from both sides of the equation to get an equivalent equation of the form "$x =$ a number."

$$x + 6 = 17$$
$$x + 6 - 6 = 17 - 6$$
$$x = 11$$

The solution is 11.

In equations involving a number of steps, it is a good idea to check your answer. This can be done quite easily by substituting the answer in the *original* equation. The method of using a check is illustrated in Example 4.

EXAMPLE 4 Solve $5 + x + 4 = 17$.

Solution

$$5 + x + 4 = 17$$
$$9 + x = 17$$
$$9 + x - 9 = 17 - 9$$
$$x = 8$$

Check: $5 + x + 4 = 17$
$$5 + 8 + 4 \stackrel{?}{=} 17$$
$$13 + 4 = 17$$

The solution is 8.

The following example shows how to solve an equation, such as $34 - x = 27$, in which the variable is being subtracted.

EXAMPLE 5 Solve $34 - x = 27$.

Solution Add x to both sides.

$$34 - x = 27$$
$$34 - x + x = 27 + x$$
$$34 = 27 + x$$

Subtract 27 from both sides.

$$34 - 27 = 27 + x - 27$$
$$7 = x$$

The solution is 7.

◆ COMMUNICATION IN MATHEMATICS: *Study Skills*

Review the worked-out examples if you need help in solving any of the exercises. When reading or reviewing these examples, be certain to read carefully and to make sure that you understand what is happening in each step.

You may be able to solve some of the equations in the exercises without pencil and paper. Nevertheless, it is important to show all the steps in your work and to make sure you can tell which transformation you are using in each step.

Throughout the rest of this chapter, if no replacement set is given for an equation, you should assume that the replacement set is the set of all numbers in our decimal system.

Class Exercises

State which transformation was used to transform the first equation into the second.

1. $x - 3 = 5$
$x - 3 + 3 = 5 + 3$

2. $x = 8 + 7$
$x = 15$

3. $4 - 1 = 3 - x$
$3 = 3 - x$

4. $x - 5 = 9$
$x - 5 + 5 = 9 + 5$

5. $x + 4 = 6(2 + 3)$
$x + 4 = 30$

6. $9 - x = 3$
$9 - x + x = 3 + x$

Complete each equation. State which transformation has been used.

7. $x = 11 + 17$
$x = \underline{\ ?\ }$

8. $x - 11 = 12$
$x - 11 + 11 = 12 + \underline{\ ?\ }$

9. $x + 7 = 13$
$x + 7 - 7 = 13 \underline{\ ?\ } 7$

10. $15 - x = 6$
$15 - x + x = 6 \underline{\ ?\ } x$

11. $6 + x = 17$
$6 - 6 + x = 17 \underline{\ ?\ } 6$

12. $x - 15 = 8$
$x - 15 + 15 = 8 + \underline{\ ?\ }$

Written Exercises

Use transformations to solve each equation. Write down all the steps.

A

1. $x + 15 = 27$

2. $x - 8 = 21$

3. $x - 6 = 19$

4. $19 + x = 35$

5. $8 + 7 = x$

6. $3 + 16 = x$

7. $x = 38 - 15$

8. $x = 48 + 15$

9. $x + 7 = 3(6 + 2)$

10. $34 = 4(3 - 1) + x$

11. $23 = 30 - x$

12. $42 - x = 9$

Use transformations to solve each equation. Write down all the steps.

B **13.** $5(2 + 7) - x = 33$

14. $6(8 - 3) = 48 - x$

15. $9 + 12 = (3 \times 5) + x$

16. $3(72 \div 12) - x = 5$

17. $4(10 - 7) = x + 4$

18. $22 + x = 4(39 \div 3)$

19. $\frac{3}{5} + n = 2$

20. $n - \frac{3}{4} = 3$

21. $5 = 8\frac{2}{3} - a$

22. $4\frac{1}{5} - c = 2$

23. $n - 0.76 = 0.34$

24. $n + 0.519 = 0.597$

25. $0.894 - y = 0.641$

26. $0.321 + r = 0.58$

27. $x - 0.323 = 0.873$

28. $0.254 + t = 0.67$

29. $3\frac{1}{2} + 5\frac{1}{4} = n - 1$

30. $4\frac{1}{3} - 1\frac{5}{6} = b + 1$

31. $n + 3\frac{1}{6} + 4\frac{1}{4} = 10$

32. $n + 5\frac{7}{8} - 1\frac{1}{6} = 7$

33. $n + 0.813 - 0.529 = 0.642$

34. $a + 0.952 - 0.751 = 0.7$

C **35.** $8\left(4\frac{1}{10} - 3\frac{1}{4}\right) = y + 3$

36. $3\left(2\frac{1}{9} + 4\frac{5}{6}\right) = 25 - c$

37. $7(0.34 - 0.21) = b - 0.82$

38. $4(0.641 + 0.222) = n + 0.357$

Review Exercises

Complete.

1. $5x \div \underline{\quad?\quad} = x$

2. $y \times 8 \div 8 = \underline{\quad?\quad}$

3. $3z \div \underline{\quad?\quad} = z$

4. $\frac{x}{4} \times \underline{\quad?\quad} = x$

5. $\frac{x}{9} \times \underline{\quad?\quad} = x$

6. $\frac{z}{7} \times 7 = \underline{\quad?\quad}$

7. $15z \times \underline{\quad?\quad} = z$

8. $y \times \underline{\quad?\quad} \div 12 = y$

9. $\underline{\quad?\quad} \times 13 \div 13 = x$

█ █ █ **NONROUTINE PROBLEM SOLVING:** *Trial and Error*

The number of chirps that a cricket makes is given by the equation $n = 4t - 160$, where t is the temperature in degrees Fahrenheit and n is the number of chirps in one minute. At what temperature will the crickets stop chirping?

254 *Chapter 8*

8-3 Equations: Multiplication and Division

If an equation involves multiplication or division, the following transformations are used to solve the equation.

Transformation by multiplication: Multiply both sides of the equation by the same nonzero number.

Transformation by division: Divide both sides of the equation by the same nonzero number.

EXAMPLE 1 Solve $3n = 24$.

Solution Our goal is to find an equivalent equation of the form
$$n = \text{a number}.$$
Use the fact that multiplication and division are inverse operations and that $3n \div 3 = n$.
$$3n = 24$$
$$\frac{3n}{3} = \frac{24}{3}$$
$$n = 8$$
The solution is 8.

EXAMPLE 2 Solve $5x = 53$.

Solution Divide both sides by 5.
$$5x = 53$$
$$\frac{5x}{5} = \frac{53}{5}$$
$$x = 10\frac{3}{5}$$
The solution is $10\frac{3}{5}$.

EXAMPLE 3 Solve $\frac{n}{4} = 7$.

Solution Multiply both sides by 4.
$$\frac{n}{4} = 7$$
$$\frac{n}{4} \times 4 = 7 \times 4$$
$$n = 28$$
The solution is 28.

Class Exercises

a. State the transformation you would use to solve each equation.
b. Solve the equation.

1. $2n = 26$ **2.** $\frac{n}{2} = 5$ **3.** $\frac{n}{3} = 12$ **4.** $3n = 12$

5. $5n = 35$ **6.** $33 = 11n$ **7.** $7 = \frac{n}{4}$ **8.** $\frac{n}{5} = 20$

9. $4 + x = 7$ **10.** $4x = 24$ **11.** $28 = \frac{x}{7}$ **12.** $11 = x - 2$

Written Exercises

Use the transformations given in this chapter to solve each equation.
Show all steps. Check your solution.

A **1.** $5n = 75$ **2.** $87 = 3n$ **3.** $\frac{n}{3} = 6$ **4.** $3n = 15$

5. $7n = 42$ **6.** $\frac{n}{4} = 8$ **7.** $\frac{n}{6} = 9$ **8.** $\frac{n}{5} = 6$

9. $\frac{n}{4} = 21$ **10.** $10 = \frac{n}{6}$ **11.** $4 = \frac{n}{7}$ **12.** $5n = 55$

13. $9n = 45$ **14.** $\frac{n}{8} = 9$ **15.** $11n = 110$ **16.** $8n = 96$

17. $\frac{n}{13} = 7$ **18.** $\frac{n}{16} = 6$ **19.** $12n = 132$ **20.** $17n = 289$

B **21.** $6x = 45$ **22.** $18x = 12$ **23.** $\frac{x}{17} = 13$ **24.** $\frac{x}{15} = 11$

25. $\frac{x}{21} = 12$ **26.** $\frac{x}{27} = 23$ **27.** $24x = 20$ **28.** $12x = 76$

29. $9x = 80 + 7$ **30.** $64x = 100 - 48$ **31.** $\frac{x}{26} = 2(3 + 4)$

32. $42 + x = 179$ **33.** $x - 193 = 54$ **34.** $296 - x = 51$

C **35.** $7x = \frac{14}{19}$ **36.** $11x = \frac{13}{20}$ **37.** $\frac{x}{16} = \frac{21}{32}$ **38.** $\frac{x}{9} = \frac{13}{84}$

Review Exercises

Multiply or divide.

1. $\frac{5}{8} \times \frac{12}{35}$ **2.** $\frac{14}{30} \div \frac{2}{15}$ **3.** $\frac{17}{9} \times \frac{6}{85}$

4. $3\frac{2}{3} \times 5\frac{9}{11}$ **5.** $3\frac{5}{8} \div 1\frac{3}{16}$ **6.** 0.09×3.74

8-4 Equations: Decimals and Fractions

Sometimes the variable expression in an equation may involve a decimal. When this occurs, you can use the transformations that you have learned in the previous sections.

EXAMPLE 1 Solve the equation $0.42x = 1.05$.

Solution Divide both sides by 0.42.

$$0.42x = 1.05$$

$$\frac{0.42x}{0.42} = \frac{1.05}{0.42}$$

$$x = 2.5$$

The solution is 2.5.

EXAMPLE 2 Solve the equation $\frac{n}{0.15} = 92$.

Solution Multiply both sides by 0.15.

$$\frac{n}{0.15} = 92$$

$$0.15 \times \frac{n}{0.15} = 0.15 \times 92$$

$$n = 13.80$$

The solution is 13.80.

The variable expression in an equation may also involve a fraction. To see how to solve an equation such as $\frac{2}{3}x = 6$, think how you would solve an equation such as $2x = 6$. (You would divide both sides by 2, getting $x = 3$.) Thus, to solve $\frac{2}{3}x = 6$, you would divide both sides by $\frac{2}{3}$. This is the same as multiplying by the reciprocal of $\frac{2}{3}$, or $\frac{3}{2}$. We therefore solve equations involving fractions in the following way.

If an equation has the form

$$\frac{a}{b}x = c,$$

where both a and b are nonzero,

multiply both sides by $\frac{b}{a}$, the reciprocal of $\frac{a}{b}$.

EXAMPLE 3 Solve the equation $\frac{1}{3}y = 18$.

Solution Multiply both sides by 3, the reciprocal of $\frac{1}{3}$.

$$\frac{1}{3}y = 18$$

$$3 \times \frac{1}{3}y = 3 \times 18$$

$$y = 3 \times 18$$
$$y = 54$$

The solution is 54.

EXAMPLE 4 Solve the equation $\frac{6}{7}n = 8$. Check.

Solution Multiply both sides by $\frac{7}{6}$, the reciprocal of $\frac{6}{7}$.

$$\frac{6}{7}n = 8 \qquad\qquad \text{Check:} \qquad \frac{6}{7}n = 8$$

$$\frac{7}{6} \times \frac{6}{7}n = \frac{7}{6} \times 8 \qquad\qquad \frac{6}{7} \times \frac{28}{3} \stackrel{?}{=} 8$$

$$n = \frac{7}{6} \times \overset{4}{8} \qquad\qquad \frac{\overset{2}{6}}{\underset{1}{7}} \times \frac{\overset{4}{28}}{\underset{1}{3}} \stackrel{?}{=} 8$$
$$\phantom{n = \frac{7}{\underset{3}{6}} \times 8}$$

$$n = \frac{28}{3} \qquad\qquad \frac{2}{1} \times \frac{4}{1} = 8$$

The solution is $\frac{28}{3}$, or $9\frac{1}{3}$.

Class Exercises

a. State what number you would multiply or divide both sides of each equation by in order to solve it.
b. Solve the equation.

1. $\frac{3}{4}x = 15$ **2.** $0.2x = 6$ **3.** $\frac{x}{0.4} = 1.7$ **4.** $\frac{x}{1.3} = 2.4$

5. $\frac{1}{8}x = 7$ **6.** $\frac{17}{12}x = 34$ **7.** $\frac{8}{3}x = 24$ **8.** $\frac{1}{9}x = 14$

9. $\frac{x}{1.8} = 2.9$ **10.** $\frac{x}{2.3} = 5$ **11.** $0.35x = 10.5$ **12.** $0.55x = 2.20$

13. $0.28x = 2.24$ **14.** $0.67x = 6.03$ **15.** $\frac{x}{2.6} = 3.7$ **16.** $\frac{x}{5.9} = 14.2$

Written Exercises

Solve each equation.

A 1. $\frac{1}{8}x = 11$ 2. $\frac{1}{3}x = 13$ 3. $0.4x = 8$ 4. $0.6x = 24$

5. $\frac{x}{0.3} = 5$ 6. $\frac{x}{0.7} = 14$ 7. $\frac{2}{3}x = 16$ 8. $\frac{3}{4}x = 21$

9. $0.25x = 15$ 10. $0.44x = 22$ 11. $\frac{x}{1.5} = 13$ 12. $\frac{x}{2.2} = 22$

13. $\frac{3}{2}x = 27$ 14. $\frac{5}{9}x = 65$ 15. $\frac{12}{5}x = 48$ 16. $\frac{12}{7}x = 60$

17. $1.3x = 39$ 18. $3.2x = 128$ 19. $\frac{x}{4.5} = 11$ 20. $\frac{x}{6.2} = 17$

B 21. $\frac{4}{3}n = 18$ 22. $\frac{6}{5}n = 20$ 23. $\frac{8}{3}n = 28$ 24. $\frac{6}{7}n = 21$

25. $3.9 = 0.6n$ 26. $3.6 = 1.6n$ 27. $1.5n = 1.2$ 28. $1.25n = 3.5$

29. $2\frac{2}{5}n = \frac{4}{15}$ 30. $\frac{3}{11} = \frac{9}{5}n$ 31. $\frac{7}{9} = \frac{14}{15}n$ 32. $1\frac{5}{7}n = \frac{16}{35}$

33. $\frac{n}{2.45} = 3.1$ 34. $\frac{n}{6.31} = 2.12$ 35. $\frac{n}{5.37} = 0.004$ 36. $\frac{n}{0.09} = 2.79$

C 37. $\frac{2}{3}x = 3.8$ 38. $\frac{3}{4}x = 6.93$ 39. $\frac{3}{5}x = 9.36$

40. $\frac{x}{6.4} = \frac{5}{8}$ 41. $\frac{x}{2.7} = \frac{11}{9}$ 42. $\frac{x}{4.2} = \frac{17}{6}$

Review Exercises

Solve.

1. $x + 17 = 47$ 2. $55 + x = 75$ 3. $96 - x = 41$

4. $82 - x = 37$ 5. $x - 45 = 58$ 6. $5x = 95$

7. $3x = 51$ 8. $7x = 91$ 9. $4x = 76$

CALCULATOR INVESTIGATION: Solving Equations

Using a calculator can greatly simplify the computations involved in solving an equation with decimals. Use a calculator to solve the following equations.

1. $0.32x = 0.096$ 2. $3.02x = 1.84$ 3. $2.11x = 5.74$

4. $\frac{x}{0.79} = 1.08$ 5. $\frac{x}{1.91} = 1.77$ 6. $\frac{x}{4.002} = 0.107$

8-5 Combined Operations

In order to solve an equation of the form

$$ax + b = c \quad \text{or} \quad ax - b = c \quad \text{or} \quad b - ax = c,$$

where a, b, and c are given numbers and x is a variable, we must use more than one transformation.

EXAMPLE 1 Solve the equation $3n - 5 = 10 + 6$.

Solution Simplify the numerical expression.

$$3n - 5 = 10 + 6$$
$$3n - 5 = 16$$

Add 5 to both sides.

$$3n - 5 + 5 = 16 + 5$$
$$3n = 21$$

Divide both sides by 3.

$$\frac{3n}{3} = \frac{21}{3}$$
$$n = 7$$

The solution is 7.

Example 1 suggests the following general procedure for solving equations.

1. Simplify each side of the equation.

2. If there are still indicated additions or subtractions, use the inverse operations to undo them.

3. If there are indicated multiplications or divisions involving the variable, use the inverse operations to undo them.

It is important to remember that in using the procedure outlined above you must *always perform the same operation on both sides of the equation.* Also, you must use the steps in the procedure in the order indicated. That is, you first simplify each side of the equation, then undo additions and subtractions, and then undo multiplications and divisions.

EXAMPLE 2 Solve the equation $\frac{3}{2}n + 7 = 22$.

Solution Subtract 7 from both sides.

$$\frac{3}{2}n + 7 = 22$$

$$\frac{3}{2}n + 7 - 7 = 22 - 7$$

$$\frac{3}{2}n = 15$$

Multiply both sides by $\frac{2}{3}$, the reciprocal of $\frac{3}{2}$.

$$\frac{2}{3} \times \frac{3}{2}n = \frac{2}{3} \times 15$$

$$n = \frac{2}{3} \times \overset{5}{\cancel{15}}$$

$$\underset{1}{}$$

$$n = 10$$

The solution is 10.

EXAMPLE 3 Solve the equation $40 - \frac{5}{3}n = 15$.

Solution Add $\frac{5}{3}n$ to both sides.

$$40 - \frac{5}{3}n = 15$$

$$40 - \frac{5}{3}n + \frac{5}{3}n = 15 + \frac{5}{3}n$$

$$40 = 15 + \frac{5}{3}n$$

Subtract 15 from both sides.

$$40 - 15 = 15 + \frac{5}{3}n - 15$$

$$25 = \frac{5}{3}n$$

Multiply both sides by $\frac{3}{5}$.

$$\frac{3}{5} \times 25 = \frac{3}{5} \times \frac{5}{3}n$$

$$\frac{3}{\cancel{5}} \times \overset{5}{\cancel{25}} = n$$

$$\underset{1}{} \quad 15 = n$$

The solution is 15.

Class Exercises

State the two transformations you would use to find the solution of each equation. Be sure to specify which transformation you would use first.

1. $3n + 2 = 8$

2. $4n - 1 = 19$

3. $\frac{1}{2}n - 6 = 1$

4. $\frac{1}{3}n + 5 = 7$

5. $\frac{2}{3}n - 6 = 14$

6. $\frac{5}{2}n + 2 = 13$

7. $3n - 6 = 15$

8. $7n + 21 = 63$

9. $\frac{3}{4}n - 8 = 12$

10. $\frac{1}{2}n + 2 = 5$

11. $2\frac{1}{3}n - 2 = 8$

12. $1\frac{2}{3}n + 15 = 51$

Written Exercises

Solve each equation.

A

1. $2n - 5 = 17$

2. $3n + 8 = 23$

3. $5n + 6 = 41$

4. $4n - 15 = 9$

5. $6n + 11 = 77$

6. $8n - 13 = 51$

7. $50 - 3n = 20$

8. $42 - 5n = 7$

9. $29 - 6n = 11$

10. $79 - 8n = 15$

11. $\frac{1}{4}n + 5 = 25$

12. $\frac{1}{8}n - 11 = 21$

13. $\frac{1}{2}n + 3 = 18$

14. $\frac{1}{3}n - 7 = 11$

15. $\frac{1}{5}n - 2 = 9$

16. $\frac{1}{4}n + 3 = 8$

17. $\frac{2}{3}n + 12 = 28$

18. $\frac{3}{5}n - 11 = 7$

19. $6n - 7 = 19$

20. $10n + 4 = 39$

21. $\frac{6}{5}n - 7 = 20$

22. $\frac{15}{4}n + 7 = 32$

23. $2\frac{2}{5}n + 5 = 23$

24. $1\frac{1}{7}n - 9 = 27$

B

25. $\frac{3}{5}n + \frac{2}{3} = \frac{8}{3}$

26. $\frac{2}{3}n - \frac{5}{8} = \frac{7}{8}$

27. $\frac{3}{4}n - \frac{11}{15} = \frac{3}{5}$

28. $\frac{5}{6}n + \frac{1}{10} = \frac{29}{30}$

29. $\frac{7}{8}n - \frac{5}{6} = \frac{3}{4}$

30. $\frac{1}{3}n - \frac{11}{25} = \frac{7}{10}$

31. $\frac{2}{5}n + \frac{3}{7} = \frac{11}{5}$

32. $\frac{1}{6}n + \frac{1}{5} = \frac{7}{11}$

33. $1\frac{5}{8}n + \frac{13}{12} = \frac{51}{4}$

34. $2\frac{2}{3}n - \frac{4}{7} = \frac{8}{9}$

35. $\frac{11}{3}n - \frac{5}{9} = \frac{5}{6}$

36. $\frac{7}{2}n - \frac{11}{12} = \frac{5}{9}$

37. $1\frac{3}{8}n + \frac{1}{4} = \frac{7}{8}$

38. $\frac{3}{4}n - \frac{1}{12} = \frac{7}{3}$

39. $\frac{3}{7}n + \frac{4}{5} = \frac{6}{7}$

EXAMPLE   Solve $6x + 5x = 132$.

Solution   Use the distributive property.

$$6x + 5x = 132$$
$$(6 + 5)x = 132$$
$$11x = 132$$
$$x = 12$$

The solution is 12.

C **40.** $5n + 3n = 17 + 7$ **41.** $7n - 4n = 26 - 5$ **42.** $23 - 8 = 6n - n$

   43. $8n - 2n = 11 + 13$ **44.** $19 - 4 = 2n + n$ **45.** $6 + 24 = n + 4n$

   46. Solve $C = 2\pi r$ for r if $C = 220$ and $\pi \approx \frac{22}{7}$.

   47. Solve $P = 2l + 2w$ for w if $P = 64$ and $l = 5$.

   48. Solve $d = rt$ for r if $d = 308$ and $t = 3.5$.

Self-Test A

**Solve the following equations if the replacement set for x is
$\{0, 1, 2, 3, 4, 5\}$. If the equation has no solution, so state.**

   1. $5x - 2 = 13$ **2.** $\frac{x}{2} - 2 = 0$ [8-1]

   3. $x + 3 + x = 3 + 2x$ **4.** $\frac{1}{3}x + 4 = 6$

Use transformations to solve each equation.

   5. $x + 6 = 27 - 12$ **6.** $5(7 + 2) = x - 11$ [8-2]

   7. $7n = 91$ **8.** $\frac{n}{4} = 17$ [8-3]

   9. $\frac{1}{6}n = 25$ **10.** $\frac{13}{3}n = 11$ [8-4]

   11. $0.35x = 2.8$ **12.** $\frac{x}{0.03} = 58$

   13. $8n - 40 = 180$ **14.** $\frac{2}{3}n + 18 = 98$ [8-5]

Self-Test answers and Extra Practice are at the back of the book.

8-6 Word Sentences and Equations

An equation such as $32n = 80$ can be given meaning in the real world in many ways.

a. If a car goes 32 mi/h, how many hours (n) would it take to go 80 miles?

$$32 \text{ mi/h} \times n \text{ hours} = 80 \text{ mi}$$

b. If peaches cost 32¢ a pound, how many pounds (n) can you buy for 80¢?

$$32¢/\text{lb} \times n \text{ pounds} = 80¢$$

Notice that in both of the word problems above, one of the numbers is unknown and is represented by a variable.

Notice also that each problem asks a question. The related equation does not answer the question, but we can find the answer by solving the equation.

EXAMPLE 1 Write a word problem that can be represented by the equation $45 - n = 33$.

Solution Two possibilities are the following.

a. Lee had $45 in his wallet. After paying for dinner and a movie, he had $33 left. How much did he spend on dinner and the movie?

b. A shipment of baseball gloves to a sporting goods store contained 45 gloves. After a week, 33 gloves were still unsold. How many were sold that week?

EXAMPLE 2 Which of the following equations represents the problem?

a. $125 = 16x$ **b.** $125 = x + 16$ **c.** $125 = x - 16$

The seventh grade at Centerville Junior High has 125 students. This is 16 more than the number of seventh graders at Eastham Junior High. How many seventh graders (x) are there at Eastham?

Solution We want to find the number of seventh graders at Eastham Junior High. We are told that there are 16 more seventh graders at Centerville than there are at Eastham. Therefore, if we add 16 to the number of seventh graders (x) at Eastham, we get the number of seventh graders at Centerville, or $125 = x + 16$. **(b)**

Class Exercises

Write a problem that each equation could represent. Use the words in parentheses as the subject of the problem.

1. $x + 16 = 180$ (number of students in the eighth grade)

2. $0.59x = 2.36$ (buying groceries)

3. $48x = 630$ (traveling in a car)

4. $x - 25 = 175$ (number of cars in a parking lot)

5. $256 - x = 219$ (price reduction in a department store)

6. $10x = 26$ (running race)

7. $25x = 175$ (fuel economy in a car)

8. $139 + x = 165$ (price increase in a television store)

Written Exercises

Write a problem that each equation could represent. Use the words in parentheses for the subject of the problem.

A 1. $x + x + 7 = 37$ (perimeter of a triangle)

2. $2x + 24 = 38$ (perimeter of a rectangle)

3. $4x = 56$ (a square)

4. $78 + 23 + x = 180$ (a triangle)

Match each problem with one of the equations below.

a. $24x = 84$ b. $24 + x = 84$ c. $x - 24 = 84$ d. $84 - x = 24$ e. $84x = 24$

5. How many cans of soup (x) must be added to a supermarket inventory of 24 cans to increase the inventory to 84 cans?

6. Francine withdrew $24 from her bank account and found that $84 was left. How much money (x) was in the account before Francine made her withdrawal?

7. Cole's car gets 24 miles per gallon. How many gallons of gasoline (x) did he use on an 84-mile trip?

8. A share of stock traded at 84 points. Two years later it was traded at 24 points. How many points (x) did it lose in that time?

9. At 84 km/h how many hours (x) would a car take to go 24 km?

Write an equation for each word sentence.

10. Three more than a number n is fifteen.

11. Six less than a number n is seventeen.

12. The sum of a number n and twelve is forty.

13. The product of a number n and five is eighty.

B **14.** Five more than three times a number n is thirty.

15. The sum of a number n and twice the number is twenty-four.

16. The product of three and a number n is eight more than the number.

17. Three times a number n, minus one half the number, is the same as twice the sum of the number and one.

18. Fifteen more than a number n, divided by the number, is 5.

19. One half of a number n, plus one third of the number, is 4 less than the number.

20. Five times a number n divided by two is the same as one fourth of the number, plus forty-two.

C **21. a.** An airplane travels at an air speed (speed relative to the air) of 500 km/h. If the wind speed is w and the wind is blowing in the plane's direction of travel, write the plane's groundspeed (speed relative to the ground) as a variable expression involving w.
   b. If the plane in part (a) takes 3 h to make a flight of 1545 km, write an equation that would enable you to find the wind speed w.

22. What would your answers to parts (a) and (b) of Exercise 21 be if the wind were blowing against the plane's direction of travel and the plane took 3 h to make a flight of 1470 km?

Review Exercises

Write a mathematical expression for each word phrase.

1. Four less than a number

2. Five times a number

3. A number divided by seven

4. Ten more than a number

5. Forty minus a number

6. Twelve plus a number

7. A number times two

8. Ninety divided by a number

8-7 Translating Problems into Equations

In order to represent the conditions of a word problem by an equation, we first read the problem carefully.

Next, we decide what numbers are being asked for. We then choose a variable and use it with the given conditions of the problem to represent the number or numbers asked for. At this point a sketch may be helpful.

Now, we write an equation based on the given conditions of the problem. To do this, we write an expression involving the variable and set it equal to another variable expression or a number given in the problem that represents the same quantity.

The following example illustrates this procedure.

EXAMPLE   Write an equation for the following word problem.

The perimeter of an isosceles triangle is 40. What is the length of one of the two congruent sides if the length of the third side is 16?

Solution
- The problem asks for the length of one of the two congruent sides.

- Let l = length of one of the two congruent sides. (It often helps to use a letter for the variable that suggests the name of the quantity it represents.)

Draw a sketch and label it.

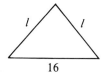

We are given 40 as the numerical value of the perimeter. From the sketch, we see that a variable expression for the perimeter is

$$l + l + 16 \quad \text{or} \quad 2l + 16.$$

- An equation that represents the conditions is

$$2l + 16 = 40.$$

PROBLEM SOLVING REMINDER

In problems involving geometric figures, *drawing a sketch* may help you to better visualize what is being asked for. A sketch may be helpful in other types of problems as well.

Class Exercises

a. Name the quantity you would represent by a variable.
b. State an equation that expresses the conditions of the word problem.

1. Jennifer bought 5 lb of apples for $3.45. What was the price per pound?

2. After Henry withdrew $350 from his account, he had $1150 left. How much money was in his account before this withdrawal?

3. A road that is 8.5 m wide is to be extended to 10.6 m wide. What is the width of the new paving?

4. In the seventh grade, 86 students made the honor roll. This is $\frac{2}{5}$ of the entire class. How many students are in the seventh grade?

5. A 25-story building is 105 m tall. What is the height of each story if they are all of equal height?

6. A 150 L tank in a chemical factory can be filled by a pipe in 60 s. At how many liters per second does the liquid enter the tank?

Problems

Choose a variable and write an equation for each problem.

A **1.** On one portion of a trip across the country, the Oates family covered 1170 miles in 9 days. How many miles per day is this?

2. Carey's car went 224 km on 28 L of gas. How many kilometers per liter is this?

3. The perimeter of a hexagon is 90 cm. What is the length of one side of the hexagon if all the sides are of equal length?

4. After $525 was spent on the class trip, there was $325 left in the class treasury. How much was in the treasury before the trip?

5. By the end of one month a hardware store had 116 socket wrench sets left out of a shipment of 144. How many sets were sold during the month?

6. After depositing his tax refund of $350, Manuel Ruiz had $1580 in his bank account. How much money was in the account before the deposit?

7. Two sides of a triangle have lengths 29 cm and 43 cm. What is the length of the third side if the perimeter is 100 cm?

8. The perimeter of a square is 60. What is the length of one side?

9. One of the two congruent sides of an isosceles triangle has length 26. What is the length of the third side if the perimeter is 65?

B 10. In a school election $\frac{4}{5}$ of the students voted. There were 180 ballots. How many students are in the school?

11. In a heat-loss survey it was found that $\frac{3}{10}$ of the total wall area of the Gables' house consists of windows. The combined area of the windows is 240 ft². What is the total wall area of the house?

12. A bookstore received a shipment of books. Twenty were sold and $\frac{2}{5}$ of those remaining were returned to the publisher. If 48 books were returned, how many books were in the original shipment?

C 13. A rectangle has length 24 cm and width 16 cm. By how much should the width be decreased in order to make the perimeter 74 cm?

Review Exercises

Write an equation for each word sentence.

1. Eight less than a number is forty-three.

2. Twelve times a number is one hundred eight.

3. Fourteen more than a number is seventy.

4. A number divided by nine is twenty-two.

5. A number minus seventeen is thirty-four.

6. Five times a number is sixty-five.

 **NONROUTINE PROBLEM SOLVING:** *Writing an Equation*

A thoroughbred is 80 m ahead of a quarter horse, and is running at the rate of 27 meters per second. The quarter horse is following at the rate of 31 meters per second. In how many seconds will the quarter horse overtake the thoroughbred?

8-8 A Problem Solving Model: Writing Equations

The following five-step method will be helpful in solving word problems using an equation.

Solving a Word Problem Using an Equation

Step 1 Read the problem carefully. Make sure that you understand what it says. You may need to read it more than once.

Step 2 Decide what numbers are asked for. Choose a variable and use it with the given conditions of the problem to represent the number(s) asked for.

Step 3 Write an equation based on the given conditions.

Step 4 Solve the equation and find the required numbers.

Step 5 Check your results with the words of the problem. Give the answer.

EXAMPLE 1   The congruent angles of an isosceles triangle each have a measure of 65°. Find the measure of the third angle of the triangle.

Solution

- The problem says
    one angle of the triangle has measure 65°
    a second angle also has measure 65°

- The problem asks for
    the measure of the third angle

    Let m = measure of the third angle.

    Draw a sketch and label it.

    The sum of the measures of the three angles is $65 + 65 + m$.

    The sum of the measures of the angles of a triangle is 180°.

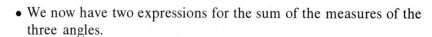

- We now have two expressions for the sum of the measures of the three angles.

    We set the two expressions equal to each other.

$$65 + 65 + m = 180$$

- Solve.
$$65 + 65 + m = 180$$
$$130 + m = 180$$
$$130 + m - 130 = 180 - 130$$
$$m = 50$$

- Check: The sum of the measures of the three angles of a triangle is 180°. $65 + 65 + 50 = 180$. The result checks.

The measure of the third angle is 50°.

EXAMPLE 2 An evergreen in Sam's yard is now 78 in. tall. If it grows 6 in. each year, how many years will it take to grow to a height of 105 in.?

Solution
- The problem says
    present tree height, 78 in.
    tree growth per year, 6 in.
    future tree height, 105 in.

- The problem asks for
    number of years for tree to grow to 105 in.

Let n = number of years for tree to grow to 105 in.

Since the tree grows 6 in. per year:
    height after 1 year, $78 + 6$
    height after 2 years, $78 + (6 \times 2)$
    height after 3 years, $78 + (6 \times 3)$
    height after n years, $78 + 6n$

- We now have two expressions for the height of the tree after n years. We set them equal to each other.
$$78 + 6n = 105$$

- Solve.
$$78 + 6n = 105$$
$$78 + 6n - 78 = 105 - 78$$
$$6n = 27$$
$$\frac{6n}{6} = \frac{27}{6}$$
$$n = 4\frac{1}{2}$$

- Check: If the tree grows 6 in. each year, in $4\frac{1}{2}$ years it will grow $4\frac{1}{2} \times 6$, or 27 in. The tree is now 78 in. tall. $78 + 27 = 105$. The result checks.

In $4\frac{1}{2}$ years the tree will grow to 105 in.

Problems

Solve each problem using the five-step method.

A 1. Two sides of a triangle have lengths 35 cm and 45 cm. What is the length of the third side if the perimeter of the triangle is 110 cm?

2. One angle of a triangle is 90° and the other two angles are congruent. Find the measure of one of these congruent angles.

3. The perimeter of a hexagon is 15. If all six sides are congruent, what is the length of one of these sides?

4. Three fourths of all the books in a school library are nonfiction. There are 360 nonfiction books. How many books are in the school library altogether?

5. The perimeter of a trapezoid is 68 cm. One side of the trapezoid has length 23 cm. What is the length of one of the other three sides if they are all equal in length?

6. A department store received five cartons of shirts. One week later 25 shirts had been sold and 95 shirts were left in stock. How many shirts came in each carton?

7. The four walls in Fran's room have equal areas. The combined area of the doors and windows of the room is 12 m². If the total wall area (including doors and windows) is 68 m², what is the area of one wall?

B 8. Three fifths of those attending a club picnic decided to play touch football. After one more person decided to play, there were 16 players. How many people attended the picnic?

9. Four fifths of the athletic club treasury was to be spent on an awards banquet. After $450 was paid for food, there was $150 left out of the funds designated for the banquet. How much money had been in the treasury originally?

10. After using $\frac{2}{3}$ of a bag of fertilizer on his garden, Kent gave 8 lb to a neighbor. If Kent had 42 lb left, how much had been in the full bag?

11. The length of each side of a pentagon is 28 cm. How much should each side be shortened in order to make the perimeter 115 cm?

12. Marcie biked to a point 5 km from her home. After a short rest, she then biked to a point 55 km from her home along the same road. If the second part of her trip took 4 hours, what was Marcie's speed, assuming her speed was constant? 12.5

C 13. When the gas gauge on her car was on the $\frac{3}{8}$ mark, Karen pumped 15 gallons of gas into the tank in order to fill it. How many gallons of gas does the tank in Karen's car hold?

Self-Test B

Match each problem with one of the following equations.

a. $x - 18 = 72$ **b.** $18x = 72$ **c.** $x + 18 = 72$ **d.** $72x = 18$

1. At 72 km/h how many hours would it take a car to travel 18 km? [8-6]

2. Seth bought 18 more model cars for his collection. If he now has 72 cars, how many did he have before?

3. After the first day, 18 people were eliminated from the tournament. If 72 people were still playing, how many people started the tournament?

Choose a variable and write an equation for each problem.

4. Luann's car gets 21 miles per gallon. How many gallons of gasoline will Luann use to drive 189 miles? [8-7]

5. John Silver made a withdrawal of $450 from his bank account. If there is $1845 left in the account, how much did he have in the bank before the withdrawal?

Solve each problem using the five-step method.

6. The Elgins wish to fence in a square field. If the perimeter of the field is 124 yards, how long will each side of the fence be? [8-8]

7. At a recent tennis tournament, $\frac{3}{4}$ of the new balls were used. If 309 balls were used, how many new balls were there at the start of the tournament?

Self-Test answers and Extra Practice are at the back of the book.

Balancing Equations in Chemistry

The basic chemical substances that make up the universe are called **elements.** Scientists often use standard symbols for the names of elements. Some of these symbols are given in the table below.

Element	Symbol	Element	Symbol	Element	Symbol
Hydrogen	H	Helium	He	Carbon	C
Nitrogen	N	Oxygen	O	Sodium	Na
Aluminum	Al	Sulfur	S	Potassium	K
Chlorine	Cl	Copper	Cu	Iron	Fe

The smallest particle of an element is called an **atom.** A pure substance made of atoms of two or more different elements is called a **compound.** In a compound the numbers of atoms of the elements always occur in a definite proportion. The formula for a compound shows this proportion. For example, the formula for water, H_2O, shows that in any sample of water there are twice as many hydrogen atoms as oxygen atoms.

In some elements and compounds, the atoms group together into **molecules.** The formula for a molecule is the same as the formula for the compound. The formula for oxygen is O_2 because a molecule of oxygen is made of two oxygen atoms. A molecule of water is made of two hydrogen atoms and one oxygen atom, so its formula is H_2O.

When compounds change chemically in a chemical reaction, we can describe this change by means of what chemists call an equation, although the equals sign is replaced by an arrow. An example of such a chemical equation is the following.

$$N_2 \quad + \quad 3\,H_2 \quad \longrightarrow \quad 2\,NH_3$$
$$\text{nitrogen} \qquad \text{hydrogen} \qquad \text{ammonia}$$

This equation indicates that a molecule of nitrogen (2 atoms) can combine with 3 molecules of hydrogen (2 atoms each) producing 2 molecules of ammonia.

Notice in the example that each side of the equation accounts for

$$2 \text{ atoms of nitrogen: } N_2 \ldots \quad \longrightarrow \quad 2\,N \ldots$$

and $\qquad$ 6 atoms of hydrogen: $\ldots 3\,H_2 \longrightarrow 2 \ldots H_3$

A chemical equation in which the same number of atoms of each element appears on both sides is said to be **balanced.** What number should replace the __?__ in order to balance the following equation?

$$S \quad + \quad 2\,H_2SO_4 \longrightarrow \underline{?}\,SO_2 \quad + \quad 2\,H_2O$$
$$\text{sulfur} \qquad \text{sulfuric} \qquad \text{sulfur} \qquad \text{water}$$
$$\text{acid} \qquad \text{dioxide}$$

To answer this question, let n represent the unknown number. Then by equating the number of oxygen atoms on each side, we have

$$2 \times 4 = (n \times 2) + (2 \times 1)$$
or $\qquad\qquad\qquad 8 = 2n + 2.$

Solving for n, we find that $n = 3$.

Replace each __?__ with a whole number to produce a balanced equation.

1. __?__ NO_2 $\quad + \quad$ H_2O $\quad \longrightarrow \quad$ $2\,HNO_3$ $\quad + \quad$ NO
   nitric oxide $\qquad\qquad$ water $\qquad\qquad$ nitric acid $\qquad\qquad$ nitrous acid

2. $4\,FeS_2$ $\quad + \quad$ __?__ O_2 $\quad \longrightarrow \quad$ $2\,Fe_2O_3$ $\quad + \quad$ $8\,SO_2$
   iron sulfide $\qquad\qquad$ oxygen $\qquad\qquad$ iron oxide $\qquad\qquad$ sulfur dioxide

3. $Al(OH)_3$ $\quad + \quad$ $3\,HCl$ $\quad \longrightarrow \quad$ $AlCl_3$ $\quad + \quad$ __?__ H_2O
   aluminum $\qquad\qquad$ hydrochloric $\qquad$ aluminum $\qquad\qquad$ water
   hydroxide $\qquad\qquad$ acid $\qquad\qquad$ chloride

4. C_2H_5OH $\quad + \quad$ __?__ O_2 $\quad \longrightarrow \quad$ $2\,CO_2$ $\quad + \quad$ $3\,H_2O$
   ethanol $\qquad\qquad$ oxygen $\qquad\qquad$ carbon dioxide $\qquad$ water

5. __?__ C_2H_6 $\quad + \quad$ __?__ O_2 $\quad \longrightarrow \quad$ $4\,CO_2$ $\quad + \quad$ $6\,H_2O$
   ethane $\qquad\qquad$ oxygen $\qquad\qquad$ carbon dioxide $\qquad$ water

Chapter Review

True or false?

1. If the replacement set is $\{2, 4, 6\}$, the solution to $\frac{7}{2}n - 21 = 0$ is 6.   [8-1]

2. $5x + 7 = 17$ has no solution if the replacement set is $\{1, 3, 5\}$.

3. An equivalent equation for $2x - 4 = 16$ is $2x = 12$.   [8-2]

Complete.

4. The solution to $5(11 - 3 + 12) = 2x$ is __?__.   [8-3]

5. To solve $4x = 82$, you would __?__ both sides by 4.

6. The solution to $\frac{n}{9} = 27$ is __?__.

Write the letter of the correct answer.

7. Solve $\frac{4}{3}x = 60$.

    a. 45   **b.** 80   **c.** $60\frac{3}{4}$

8. Solve $\frac{n}{0.15} = 15$.   [8-4]

    a. 1   **b.** 2.25   **c.** 22.5

9. Solve $\frac{3}{2}n - 5 = 70$.

    a. 40   **b.** $112\frac{1}{2}$ **c.** 50

10. Solve $\frac{n}{6} + 9 = 10.5$.   [8-5]

    a. 9   **b.** 120   **c.** 96

11. Which equation represents the problem?   [8-6]

Luis bought 3 records on sale. The original cost of the records had been $29.85, but Luis paid only $23.25 for all three. How much did Luis save on each record?

    a. $29.85 + 3x = 23.25$ **b.** $23.25 - 3x = 29.85$ **c.** $29.85 - 3x = 23.25$

12. Write an equation for the following problem.   [8-7]

A rectangle has a perimeter of 84 cm. Find the length if the width is 15 cm.

    a. $2l + 2w = 84$ **b.** $2l + 30 = 84$ **c.** $2l + 15 = 84$ **d.** $2l = 99$

13. Use the five-step method to solve the following problem.   [8-8]

Tanya and Sara went biking. When they returned, they found that they had gone 18 km in 0.75 h. What was their speed on the trip?

    a. 13.5 km/h   **b.** 32 km/h   **c.** 12 km/h   **d.** 24 km/h

Chapter Test

Solve each equation using the given replacement set. If the equation has no solution, so state.

1. $14 + 3n = 26$; $\{0, 2, 4, 6\}$ [8–1]

2. $\frac{2}{3}n - 7 = 7$; $\{21, 24, 27\}$

3. $3n - 5 = n - 5 + 2n$; $\{0, 1, 3\}$

4. $4n + 2 = 9$; $\{0, 2, 4, 6\}$

Use transformations to solve each equation.

5. $x - 18 = 11$ **6.** $3(7 - 2) + x = 19$ [8–2]

7. $9n = 1$ **8.** $\frac{n}{11} = 13$ **9.** $15n = 12$ [8–3]

10. $\frac{2}{3}x = 24$ **11.** $0.55x = 11$ **12.** $\frac{x}{1.2} = 8.6$ [8–4]

13. $4n - 16 = 32$ **14.** $\frac{3}{4}n + 18 = 51$ **15.** $30 - \frac{1}{2}n = 11$ [8–5]

Which equation represents the problem?

16. Toby Baylor wrote a check for $12 to pay a bill. Two days later he   [8–6]
deposited $20 in his checking account. If Toby had $88 in his account after these transactions, how much did he have originally?

     a. $20x - 12 = 88$ **b.** $x - 12 + 20 = 88$ **c.** $x - 88 = 12 + 20$

Write an equation for the following problem.

17. Annette Loo's car gets 23 miles per gallon. She is planning a trip to   [8–7]
San Diego. If Annette lives 345 miles from San Diego, how many gallons of gasoline will she use driving to San Diego?

Solve the following problem by the five-step method.

18. Bill and Roberta are shipping boxes to their new house. It costs $35   [8–8]
to ship each box and there is also a charge of $50 for the entire shipment. If the cost of shipping the boxes, including the $50 charge, comes to $610, how many boxes are being shipped?

Cumulative Review (Chapters 1–8)

Exercises

Perform the indicated operations.

1. $17,008 - 2599$

2. $16.091 + 0.02 + 4.3$

3. $13.0902 - 5.7648$

4. $\frac{7}{16} + \frac{5}{12}$

5. $2\frac{3}{8} + 4\frac{2}{3}$

6. $\frac{20}{21} - \frac{3}{4}$

7. $6\frac{5}{9} - 3\frac{7}{8}$

8. $\frac{41}{10} + \frac{21}{25}$

9. $\frac{37}{9} - \frac{13}{12}$

10. 3017×36

11. $26\overline{)17,082}$

12. $27,864 \div 43$

13. 7.04×3.8

14. 4.1×2.09

15. $9.26812 \div 2.63$

16. $\frac{4}{7} \times \frac{14}{25}$

17. $\frac{15}{34} \div \frac{5}{7}$

18. $4\frac{8}{9} \times 2\frac{13}{18}$

19. $6\frac{5}{12} \div 5\frac{1}{24}$

20. $\frac{16}{9} \times \frac{27}{4}$

21. $\frac{25}{8} \div \frac{35}{14}$

Write in mathematical symbols.

22. A number n is less than or equal to sixteen.

23. Ninety-three decreased by a number n.

24. Fifty-four is greater than a number n.

True or false?

25. A trapezoid is a quadrilateral.

26. A circumference is a chord.

27. A circle is a polygon.

28. A right angle has a measure of 90°.

Solve.

29. $8x = 104$

30. $x + 93 = 129$

31. $158 - x = 64$

32. $x \div 14 = 22$

33. $69 + x = 208$

34. $x - 113 = 41$

35. $3x = 648$

36. $564 \div x = 94$

37. $4x = 948$

Find the GCF of each pair.

38. 72, 84

39. 96, 80

40. 112, 120

41. 1620, 1776

Find the LCM of each pair.

42. 24, 36

43. 21, 27

44. 39, 65

45. 72, 84

Change each decimal to a fraction in lowest terms.

46. 0.635   **47.** 0.42   **48.** $0.8\overline{3}$ **49.** $1.9\overline{24}$ **50.** $1.6\overline{4}$

Problems

PROBLEM SOLVING REMINDERS

Here are some reminders that may help you solve some of the problems on this page.
- Determine which facts are necessary to solve the problem.
- Determine whether more than one operation is needed.
- Estimate to check your answers.

1. The recipe for mixed muffins calls for $2\frac{1}{3}$ cups of corn flour, $1\frac{7}{8}$ cups of bran flour, and $2\frac{1}{6}$ cups of wheat flour. How much flour is needed for the recipe?

2. The population of Elmwood was 26,547 in 1950, 31,068 in 1960, 30,327 in 1970, and 29,598 in 1980. What was the total increase in population between 1950 and 1980?

3. A square has a perimeter of 28.64 cm. Find the length of one side.

4. The school card sale had the following boxes of cards: greeting cards at $6.95 a box, get-well cards at $4.99 a box, and thank-you notes at $3.45 a box. If the school sold 53 boxes of greeting cards, 37 boxes of get-well cards, and 88 boxes of thank-you notes, how much money did the sale raise?

5. Cormo Corporation stock sells for $13\frac{5}{8}$ dollars a share. If Lorraine has $327, how many shares can she buy?

6. Tom Ying earns $491.75 a week. How much does he earn a day if he works 5 days each week?

7. A circle has a circumference of $16\frac{16}{21}$ in. Find the radius. Use $\pi \approx \frac{22}{7}$.

8. The scale on a map is 1 cm : 2.5 km. If Toynville and Readston are 13.45 cm apart on the map, what is the actual distance?

9. Marietta and Stan are working on a jigsaw puzzle. The puzzle contains 1032 pieces. If Marietta and Stan have 336 pieces left in all, how much of the puzzle have they done?

10. The scale on a drawing is 1 in. : $3\frac{3}{4}$ ft. What is the length of a line on the drawing if the actual length is $11\frac{5}{16}$ ft?

9 Percent

APPLYING MATHEMATICS
BANKING

The origin of modern banking can be traced to a system developed by the Babylonians more than four thousand years ago, for lending, borrowing, and holding money on deposit. Today banks perform a variety of services. They pay interest on deposits, and lend money to foreign countries, businesses, and individual clients. Some banks offer bill paying services, direct deposit of pension or social security checks, ATM machines, travelers checks, and insurance. Mathematics in banking involves not only the handling of money but the determining of percent and working with decimals. In this chapter you will learn to express percents as decimals and as fractions, and some useful applications using percents.

CAREER CONNECTION

BANK OFFICER

The title "Bank Officer" is a general title given to different banking professionals. For example, loan officers evaluate financial information and assist individuals, businesses, and corporations in obtaining loans. Bank managers are responsible for the daily operation of a bank's branch office. This includes the supervision of personnel. These administrative positions usually require a college degree in business, finance, or economics.

Photo: The mechanism of a bank vault door is designed to be impenetrable.

9-1 Percents and Fractions

During basketball season, Alice made 17 out of 25 free throws, while Nina made 7 out of 10. To see who did better, we compare the fractions representing each girl's successful free throws:

$$\frac{17}{25} \quad \text{and} \quad \frac{7}{10}$$

In comparing fractions it is often convenient to use the common denominator 100, even if 100 is not the LCD of the fractions.

$$\frac{17}{25} = \frac{17 \times 4}{25 \times 4} = \frac{68}{100} \qquad \frac{7}{10} = \frac{7 \times 10}{10 \times 10} = \frac{70}{100}$$

Since Alice makes 68 free throws per hundred and Nina makes 70 per hundred, Nina is the better free-throw shooter.

The ratio of a number to 100 is called a **percent.** We write percents by using the symbol %. For example,

$$\frac{17}{25} = \frac{68}{100} = 68\% \qquad \text{and} \qquad \frac{7}{10} = \frac{70}{100} = 70\%.$$

Rule

To express the fraction $\frac{a}{b}$ as a percent, solve the equation

$$\frac{n}{100} = \frac{a}{b}$$

for the variable n and write $n\%$.

EXAMPLE 1   Express $\frac{17}{40}$ as a percent.

Solution $\dfrac{n}{100} = \dfrac{17}{40}$

Multiply both sides by 100.

$$100 \times \frac{n}{100} = 100 \times \frac{17}{40}$$

$$n = \overset{5}{100} \times \frac{17}{\underset{2}{40}} = \frac{85}{2} = 42\frac{1}{2}$$

Therefore, $\frac{17}{40} = 42\frac{1}{2}\%$, or 42.5%.

EXAMPLE 2 Express $7\frac{1}{2}\%$ as a fraction in lowest terms.

Solution $7\frac{1}{2}\% = 7.5\% = \frac{7.5}{100} = \frac{7.5 \times 10}{100 \times 10} = \frac{75}{1000} = \frac{3}{40}$

Since a percent is the ratio of a number to 100, we can have percents that are greater than or equal to 100%. For example,

$$\frac{100}{100} = 100\% \qquad \text{and} \qquad \frac{165}{100} = 165\%.$$

EXAMPLE 3 Write 250% as a mixed number in simple form.

Solution $250\% = \frac{250}{100}$

$$= 2\frac{50}{100} = 2\frac{1}{2}$$

EXAMPLE 4 A certain town spends 42% of its budget on education. What percent is used for other purposes?

Solution The whole budget is represented by 100%. Therefore, the part used for other purposes is

$$100 - 42, \text{ or } 58\%.$$

Class Exercises

Express as a fraction in lowest terms or as a mixed number in simple form.

1. 17%	**2.** 90%	**3.** 50%	**4.** 25%
5. 20%	**6.** 100%	**7.** 4%	**8.** 150%
9. 300%	**10.** 30%	**11.** 35%	**12.** 210%

Express as a percent.

13. $\frac{1}{50}$ 14. $\frac{1}{10}$ 15. $\frac{7}{10}$ 16. 1

17. 2   18. $\frac{1}{20}$ 19. $3\frac{1}{2}$ 20. $\frac{9}{10}$

21. $\frac{3}{4}$ 22. $4\frac{1}{2}$ 23. $\frac{2}{25}$ 24. $\frac{3}{20}$

Written Exercises

Express as a fraction in lowest terms or as a mixed number in simple form.

A   1. 75%   2. 60%   3. 45%   4. 95%

5. 12%   6. 76%   7. 125%   8. 220%

9. $5\frac{3}{8}\%$ 10. $8\frac{4}{5}\%$ 11. $10\frac{3}{4}\%$ 12. $15\frac{1}{2}\%$

Express as a percent.

13. $\frac{4}{5}$ 14. $\frac{1}{4}$ 15. $\frac{3}{10}$ 16. $\frac{1}{25}$

17. $\frac{12}{25}$ 18. $\frac{17}{20}$ 19. $\frac{31}{50}$ 20. $1\frac{3}{4}$

21. $2\frac{1}{5}$ 22. $3\frac{11}{25}$ 23. $\frac{51}{50}$ 24. $\frac{31}{25}$

B   25. $\frac{7}{8}$ 26. $\frac{7}{40}$ 27. $\frac{1}{200}$ 28. $\frac{12}{125}$

29. $\frac{3}{400}$ 30. $\frac{9}{250}$ 31. $\frac{121}{40}$ 32. $\frac{25}{8}$

EXAMPLE   Express $33\frac{1}{3}\%$ as a fraction in lowest terms.

Solution $33\frac{1}{3}\% = \dfrac{33\frac{1}{3}}{100} = 33\frac{1}{3} \div 100$

$$= \frac{100}{3} \times \frac{1}{100} = \frac{1}{3}$$

Express each percent as a fraction in lowest terms.

C   33. $16\frac{2}{3}\%$ 34. $66\frac{2}{3}\%$ 35. $41\frac{2}{3}\%$ 36. $83\frac{1}{3}\%$

Problems

A 1. In a public opinion poll 62% of the questionnaires sent out were returned. What percent were not returned?

2. The efficiency of a machine is the percent of energy going into the machine that does useful work. A turbine in a hydroelectric plant is 92% efficient. What percent of the energy is wasted?

3. Of the 300 acres on Swanson's farm, 180 acres are used to grow wheat. What percent of the land is used to grow wheat?

4. Of the selling price of a pair of gloves, 42% pays the wholesale cost of the gloves, 33% pays store expenses, and the rest is profit. What percent is profit?

B 5. In a 500 kg bar, 475 kg is iron and the remainder is impurities. What percent of the bar is impurities?

6. A baseball team won 42 games out of its first 80. What percent of the games did the team win?

7. One year the Caterpillars lost 5 games out of 16. If the Caterpillars also tied 1 game, what percent of their games did they win?

C 8. The Bears won 40 games and lost 24, while the Bulls won 32 games and lost 18. Which team had the higher percent of wins?

9. At a company sales conference there were 4 executives, 28 salespeople, and 8 marketing consultants. What percent of the people were executives? Salespeople? Not marketing consultants?

Review Exercises

Change each fraction to a decimal.

1. $\frac{9}{20}$ 2. $\frac{19}{25}$ 3. $\frac{11}{40}$ 4. $\frac{17}{80}$ 5. $\frac{1}{25}$

6. $\frac{13}{30}$ 7. $\frac{8}{11}$ 8. $\frac{19}{22}$ 9. $\frac{43}{75}$ 10. $\frac{83}{90}$

9-2 Percents and Decimals

By looking at the following examples, you may be able to see a general relationship between decimals and percents.

$$57\% = \frac{57}{100} = 0.57 \qquad\qquad 0.79 = \frac{79}{100} = 79\%$$

$$113\% = \frac{113}{100} = 1\frac{13}{100} = 1.13 \qquad 0.06 = \frac{6}{100} = 6\%$$

These examples suggest the following rules.

Rules

1. To express a percent as a decimal, move the decimal point two places to the left and remove the percent sign.

$$57\% = 0.57 \qquad 113\% = 1.13$$

2. To express a decimal as a percent, move the decimal point two places to the right and add a percent sign.

$$0.79 = 79\% \qquad 0.06 = 6\%$$

EXAMPLE 1 Express each percent as a decimal.
  a. 83.5%   **b.** 450%   **c.** 0.25%

Solution   **a.** 83.5% = 0.835

  b. 450% = 4.50 = 4.5

  c. 0.25% = 0.0025

EXAMPLE 2 Express each decimal as a percent.
  a. 10.5   **b.** 0.0062   **c.** 0.574

Solution   **a.** 10.5 = 1050%

  b. 0.0062 = 00.62%

  c. 0.574 = 57.4%

In the previous lesson you learned one method of changing a fraction to a percent. The ease of changing a decimal to a percent suggests the following alternative method.

EXAMPLE 3 Express $\frac{7}{8}$ as a percent.

Solution Divide 7 by 8.

$$\begin{array}{r} 0.875 \\ 8\overline{)7.000} \\ \underline{6\,4} \\ 60 \\ \underline{56} \\ 40 \\ \underline{40} \\ 0 \end{array}$$

$\frac{7}{8} = 0.875 = 87.5\%$

EXAMPLE 4 Express $\frac{1}{3}$ as a percent to the nearest tenth of a percent.

Solution Divide 1 by 3 to the ten-thousandths'
place.

Round the quotient to the nearest
thousandth.

$0.3333 \approx 0.333$

Express the decimal as a percent.

$0.333 = 33.3\%$

$$\begin{array}{r} 0.3333 \\ 3\overline{)1.0000} \\ \underline{9} \\ 10 \\ \underline{9} \\ 10 \\ \underline{9} \\ 10 \\ \underline{9} \\ 1 \end{array}$$

To the nearest tenth of a percent, $\frac{1}{3} = 33.3\%$.

Class Exercises

Express each percent as a decimal.

1. 39%   2. 4%   3. 150%   4. 0.8%   5. 1080%   6. 1%

Express each decimal as a percent.

7. 0.56   8. 0.005   9. 0.07   10. 1.6   11. 5.3   12. 0.0001

Express each of the following first as a decimal and then as a percent.

13. $\frac{1}{2}$ 14. $\frac{1}{4}$ 15. $\frac{3}{5}$ 16. $2\frac{1}{2}$ 17. $\frac{1}{1000}$ 18. $\frac{23}{1000}$

Written Exercises

Express each percent as a decimal.

A
1. 93%
2. 46%
3. 114%
4. 175%

5. 260%
6. 1150%
7. 49.5%
8. 78.2%

9. 0.6%
10. 99.44%
11. 0.05%
12. 0.032%

Express each decimal as a percent.

13. 0.59
14. 0.87
15. 0.09
16. 0.075

17. 2.6
18. 10.6
19. 12.83
20. 5.01

21. 0.007
22. 0.033
23. 0.0867
24. 0.0026

Express each fraction as a decimal and then as a percent. Round to the nearest tenth of a percent if necessary.

B
25. $\frac{3}{8}$
26. $\frac{9}{125}$
27. $\frac{3}{500}$
28. $\frac{27}{40}$

29. $1\frac{5}{8}$
30. $2\frac{37}{40}$
31. $\frac{47}{80}$
32. $\frac{7}{11}$

33. $\frac{17}{24}$
34. $\frac{19}{12}$
35. $\frac{2}{7}$
36. $\frac{16}{9}$

Express each fraction as an exact percent.

EXAMPLE $\frac{1}{3}$

Solution Divide 1 by 3 to the hundredths' place: $1 \div 3 = 0.33 \text{ R } 1$, or $0.33\frac{1}{3}$

Express the quotient as a percent: $0.33\frac{1}{3} = 33\frac{1}{3}\%$

Thus as a percent $\frac{1}{3} = 33\frac{1}{3}\%$.

C
37. $\frac{1}{6}$
38. $\frac{2}{3}$
39. $\frac{8}{9}$
40. $\frac{1}{15}$
41. $\frac{5}{6}$

Review Exercises

Solve.

1. $x + 2.47 = 5.42$
2. $x - 3.43 = 1.91$
3. $x \div 3.72 = 4.15$

4. $2.48x = 8.1096$
5. $x \div 4.03 = 5.92$
6. $1.37x = 11.4806$

9-3 Computing with Percents

The statement 20% of 300 is 60 can be translated into the equations

$$\frac{20}{100} \times 300 = 60 \qquad \text{and} \qquad 0.20 \times 300 = 60.$$

Notice the following relationship between the words and the symbols.

A similar relationship occurs whenever a statement or a question involves a number that is a percent of another number.

EXAMPLE 1   What number is 8% of 75?

Solution   Let n represent the number asked for.

What number   is 8% of 75?

n $= 0.08 \times 75$

6 is 8% of 75.

EXAMPLE 2   What percent of 40 is 6?

Solution   Let $n\%$ represent the percent asked for. We can translate the question into an equation as follows.

What percent   of   40   is   6?

$n\%$ $\times$ 40 $=$ 6

$$n\% \times 40 = 6$$

$$n\% = \frac{6}{40}$$

$$\frac{n}{100} = \frac{3}{20}$$

$$n = \frac{3}{20} \times 100 = 15$$

15% of 40 is 6.

EXAMPLE 3   140 is 35% of what number?

Solution   Let n represent the number asked for.

$$\begin{array}{llll} 140 & \text{is} & 35\% & \text{of} \quad \text{what number?} \\ 140 & = 0.35 & \times & n \\ \end{array}$$

$$140 = 0.35n$$
$$140 \div 0.35 = 0.35n \div 0.35$$
$$140 \div 0.35 = n$$
$$400 = n$$

140 is 35% of 400.

Class Exercises

State an equation involving a variable that expresses the conditions of the question.

1. What number is 10% of 920?

2. What percent of 650 is 130?

3. 28 is 80% of what number?

4. 120 is what percent of 150?

5. 40% of 25 is what number?

6. What percent of 80 is 100?

7. 60 is 75% of what number?

8. What number is 125% of 160?

Written Exercises

Answer each question by writing an equation and solving it. Round your answer to the nearest tenth of a percent if necessary.

A   **1.** What percent of 225 is 90?

2. What number is 76% of 350?

3. 45% of 600 is what number?

4. What percent of 150 is 48?

5. 52 is 4% of what number?

6. 56 is 4% of what number?

7. What number is 36% of 15?

8. 96% of 85 is what number?

9. What percent of 36 is 30?

10. 48 is what percent of 72?

B   **11.** What is 110% of 95?

12. 0.5% of what number is 15?

13. 116% of 75 is what number?

14. What percent of 40 is 86?

15. What is 0.35% of 256?

16. 12 is 150% of what number?

17. What percent of 21 is 24?

18. What is 81% of 60?

19. 12.5% of what number is 28? **20.** What percent of 45 is 600?

C 21. 18 is $33\frac{1}{3}$% of what number? (*Hint:* Write the percent as a fraction in lowest terms.)

22. What is $41\frac{2}{3}$% of 300? **23.** 231 is $91\frac{2}{3}$% of what number?

Problems

Solve.

A 1. Lisa earns $250 a week and lives in a state that taxes income at 5%. How much does Lisa pay in state tax each week?

2. A baseball park has 40,000 seats of which 13,040 are box seats and 18,200 are reserved seats. What percent of the seats are box seats? reserved seats?

3. A basketball player made 62 out of 80 free-throw shots. What percent of the free throws did she make?

4. A sweater is 65% wool by weight. If the sweater weighs 12.4 ounces, how much wool is in the sweater?

B 5. In 1979 the United States produced 3112 million barrels of oil. This was 13.7% of the world oil output. What was the world oil output to the nearest million barrels?

6. Of the 427 people responding to a public opinion poll, 224 answered *Yes* to a certain question and 154 answered *No*. What percent of those responding were undecided? Give your answer to the nearest tenth of a percent.

Review Exercises

Perform the indicated operation.

1. $1.72 + 0.052 + 2.0072$ **2.** $3.492 + 4.11 + 3.07$ **3.** $1.901 + 2.51 + 3.023$

4. $9.813 - 2.591 - 1.074$ **5.** $8.537 - 0.01 - 1.432$ **6.** $2.039 - 0.008 - 1.071$

9-4 Percent of Increase or Decrease

A department store has a sale on audio equipment. An amplifier that originally sold for $260 is selling for $208. To find the **amount of change** in the price, we subtract the sale price from the original price.

$$\$260 - \$208 = \$52$$

To find the **percent of change** in the price we divide the amount of change by the original price and express the result as a percent.

$$\frac{52}{260} = 0.20 = 20\%$$

Formula

$$\text{percent of change} = \frac{\text{amount of change}}{\text{original amount}}$$

The denominator in the formula above is always the *original* amount, whether smaller or larger than the new amount.

EXAMPLE 1 Find the percent of increase from 20 to 24.

Solution amount of change $= 24 - 20 = 4$

$$\text{percent of change} = \frac{\text{amount of change}}{\text{original amount}} = \frac{4}{20} = 0.2 = 20\%$$

The formula above can be rewritten to find the amount of change when the original amount and the percent of change are known.

Formula

$$\text{amount of change} = \text{percent of change} \times \text{original amount}$$

EXAMPLE 2 Find the new number when 75 is decreased by 26%.

Solution First find the amount of change.

$$\text{amount of change} = \text{percent of change} \times \text{original amount}$$
$$= \qquad 26\% \qquad \times \qquad 75$$
$$= 0.26 \times 75 = 19.5$$

Since the original number is being decreased, we subtract to find the new number. $75 - 19.5 = 55.5$

EXAMPLE 3   The population of Eastown grew from 25,000 to 28,000 in 3 years. What was the percent of increase for this period?

Solution   The problem asks for the percent of increase.

amount of change $= 28,000 - 25,000 = 3000$

$$\text{percent of change} = \frac{\text{amount of change}}{\text{original amount}}$$

$$= \frac{3000}{25,000} = \frac{3}{25} = 0.12 = 12\%$$

The percent of increase was 12%.

PROBLEM SOLVING REMINDER

Sometimes *extra information* is given in a problem. The time period, 3 years, is not needed for the solution of the problem in Example 3.

Class Exercises

a. State the amount of change from the first number to the second.
b. State the percent of increase or decrease from the first number to the second.

1. 10 to 12	**2.** 4 to 3	**3.** 12 to 6	**4.** 6 to 12
5. 2 to 5	**6.** 5 to 7	**7.** 25 to 4	**8.** 1 to 4
9. 4 to 7	**10.** 100 to 55	**11.** 100 to 160	**12.** 125 to 100

Find the new number produced when the given number is increased or decreased by the given percent.

13. 120; 20% decrease	**14.** 30; 10% decrease
15. 48; 50% increase	**16.** 24; 25% increase

Written Exercises

Find the percent of increase or decrease from the first number to the second. Round to the nearest tenth of a percent if necessary.

A

1. 20 to 17	**2.** 25 to 12	**3.** 70 to 98	**4.** 16 to 10
5. 40 to 73	**6.** 63 to 79	**7.** 32 to 17	**8.** 8 to 19
9. 125 to 124	**10.** 160 to 380	**11.** 12 to 8.7	**12.** 240 to 245.5

Find the new number produced when the given number is increased or decreased by the given percent.

13. 165; 20% decrease

14. 76; 25% increase

15. 65; 12% decrease

16. 250; 63% decrease

17. 84; 145% increase

18. 260; 105% increase

19. 125; 0.4% decrease

20. 1950; 0.8% increase

Find the new number produced when the given number is changed by the first percent, and then the resulting number is changed by the second percent.

B **21.** 80; increase by 50%; decrease by 50%

22. 128; decrease by 25% increase by 25%

23. 150; increase by 40%; increase by 60%

24. 480; decrease by 35%; decrease by 65%

25. 350; increase by 76%; decrease by 45%

26. 136; decrease by 85%; increase by 175%

Find the original number if the given number is the result of increasing or decreasing the original number by the given percent.

C **27.** 80; original number increased by 25%

28. 63; original number increased by 75%

29. 78; original number decreased by 35%

30. 30; original number decreased by 85%

Problems

Solve. Round to the nearest tenth of a percent if necessary.

A **1.** The number of employees at a factory was increased by 5% from its original total of 1080 workers. What was the new number of employees?

2. The cost of a basket of groceries at the Shopfast Supermarket was $62.50 in April. In May the cost of the same groceries had risen by 0.8%. What was the cost in May?

3. The attendance at a baseball stadium went from 1,440,000 one year to 1,800,000 the next year. What was the percent of increase?

4. The number of registered motor vehicles in Smalltown dropped from 350 in 1978 to 329 in 1979. What percent of decrease is this?

5. The new Maple City Library budget will enable the library to increase its collection of books by 3.6%. If the library now has 7250 books, how many will it have after the increase?

B 6. The number of students at Center State University is 22,540. Ten years ago there were only 7000 students. What is the percent of increase?

7. The annual budget of Brictown was $9,000,000 last year. Currently, the budget is only $7,500,000. Find the percent of decrease.

Self-Test A

Express as a fraction in lowest terms or as a mixed number in simple form.

1. 27%   2. 83%   3. 164%   4. 290%   [9-1]

Express as a percent.

5. $\frac{1}{20}$ 6. $\frac{3}{8}$ 7. 4   8. $3\frac{1}{4}$

Express as a decimal.

9. 45%   10. 78%   11. 348%   12. 0.8%   [9-2]

Express as a percent.

13. 0.64   14. 0.81   15. 7.85   16. 0.068

17. What percent of 56 is 14?   18. 82 is what percent of 40?   [9-3]

19. What is 44% of 25?   20. 70% of what number is 84?

State the percent of increase or decrease from the first number to the second.

21. 50 to 47   22. 20 to 22   23. 70 to 91   24. 75 to 27   [9-4]

Self-Test answers and Extra Practice are at the back of the book.

9-5 Discount and Markup

A **discount** is a decrease in the price of an item. A **markup** is an increase in the price of an item. Both of these changes can be expressed as an amount of money or as a percent of the original price of the item. For example, a store may announce a discount of $3 off the original price of a $30 basketball, or a discount of 10%.

EXAMPLE 1   A warm-up suit that sold for $42.50 is on sale at a 12% discount. What is the sale price?

Solution   *Method 1* Use the formula:

amount of change = percent of change $\times$ original amount

=   12% $\times$ 42.50

Therefore, the discount is 0.12 $\times$ 42.50, or $5.10.

The amount of the discount is $5.10.
The sale price is 42.50 − 5.10, or $37.40.

Method 2 Since the discount is 12%, the sale price is 100% − 12%, or 88%, of the original price. The sale price is 0.88 $\times$ 42.50, or $37.40.

As shown in the solutions to Example 1, when you know the amount of discount you subtract to find the new price. When dealing with a markup, you add to find the new price.

EXAMPLE 2   The price of a new car model was marked up 6% over the previous year's model. If the previous year's model sold for $7800, what is the cost of the new car?

Solution   *Method 1* Use the formula:

amount of change = percent of change $\times$ original amount

=   6% $\times$ 7800

Therefore, the markup is 0.06 $\times$ 7800, or $468.

The amount of the markup is $468.
The new price is 7800 + 468, or $8268.

Method 2 Since the markup is 6%, the new price is 100% + 6%, or 106%, of the original price. The new price is 1.06 $\times$ 7800, or $8268.

A method similar to the second method of the previous examples can be used to solve problems like the one in the next example.

EXAMPLE 3   This year a pair of ice skates sells for $46 after a 15% markup over last year's price. What was last year's price?

Solution   This year's price is 100 + 15, or 115%, of last year's price. Let n represent last year's price.

$$46 = \frac{115}{100} \times n$$

$$46 = 1.15 \times n$$

$$\frac{46}{1.15} = n$$

$$40 = n$$

The price of the skates last year was $40.

Example 4 illustrates how to find the original price if you know the discounted price.

EXAMPLE 4   A department store advertised electric shavers at a sale price of $36. If this is a 20% discount, what was the original price?

Solution   The sale price is 100 − 20, or 80%, of the original price. Let n represent the original price.

$$36 = \frac{80}{100} \times n$$

$$36 = 0.8 \times n$$

$$36 \div 0.8 = n$$

$$45 = n$$

The original price was $45.

PROBLEM SOLVING REMINDER

Be sure that your *answers are reasonable*. In Example 3, last year's price should be less than this year's marked-up price. In Example 4, the original price should be greater than the sale price.

We can use the following formula to find the percent of discount or the percent of markup.

$$\text{percent of change} = \frac{\text{amount of change}}{\text{original amount}}$$

For example, if the original price of an item was $25 and the new price is $20, the amount of discount is $5 and the percent of discount is $5 \div 25 = 0.2$, or 20%.

Class Exercises

Copy and complete the following table.

	Old price	Percent of change	Amount of change	New price
1.	$12	25% discount	?	?
2.	$60	10% markup	?	?
3.	$50	?	?	$60
4.	$120	?	?	$240
5.	$200	?	$30 markup	?
6.	$250	?	$100 discount	?
7.	?	12% discount	$48 discount	?
8.	?	5% markup	$2.50 markup	?
9.	?	20% discount	?	$160
10.	?	150% markup	?	$50

Problems

Solve.

A 1. A basketball backboard set that sold for $79 is discounted 15%. What is the new price?

2. A parka that sold for $65 is marked up to $70.20. What is the percent of markup?

3. A stereo tape deck that sold for $235 was on sale for $202.10. What was the percent of discount?

4. At the end-of-summer sale, an air conditioner that sold for $310 was discounted 21%. What was the sale price?

5. Because of an increase of 8% in wholesale prices, a shoe store had to mark up its new stock by the same percent. What was the new price of a pair of shoes that had sold for $24.50?

6. A department store has a sale on gloves. The sale price is 18% less than the original price, resulting in a saving of $2.97. What was the original price of the gloves? What is the sale price?

7. A coat that originally cost $40 was marked up 50%. During a sale the coat was discounted 50%. What was the sale price?

8. A 7% sales tax added $3.15 to the selling price of a pair of ski boots. What was the selling price of the boots? What was the total price including the tax?

B 9. A tape recorder that cost $50 was discounted 20% for a sale. It was then returned to its original price. What percent of markup was the original price over the sale price?

10. At an end-of-season sale a power lawnmower was on sale for $168. A sign advertised that this was 20% off the original price. What was the original price?

11. At a paint sale a gallon can of latex was discounted 24%. If the sale price of a gallon is $9.50, what was the original price?

12. The cost of a record album was $10.53, including an 8% sales tax. What was the price of the album without the tax?

C 13. An item is discounted 20%. Then another 10% discount is given on the new price. What percent of the original price is the final price?

14. An item is marked up 20% and then discounted 15% based on the new price. What percent of the original price is the final price?

15. Which of the following situations will produce a lower final price on a given item?
   a. The item is marked up 30% and then discounted 30% of the new price.
   b. The item is discounted 30% and then marked up 30% of the new price.

Review Exercises

Complete.

1. circumference = $2\pi \times$ __?__

2. amount of change = __?__ $\times$ original amount

3. circumference = $\pi \times$ __?__

4. percent of change = $\dfrac{?}{\text{original amount}}$

9-6 Commission and Profit

In addition to a salary, many salespeople are paid a percent of the price of the products they sell. This payment is called a **commission.** Like a discount, a commission can be expressed as a percent or as an amount of money. The following formula applies to commissions.

> ## Formula
>
> amount of commission = percent of commission × total sales

EXAMPLE 1   Maria Bertram sold $42,000 worth of insurance in January. If her commission is 3% of the total sales, what was the amount of her commission in January?

Solution   amount of commission = percent × total sales
$$= 0.03 \times 42{,}000 = 1260$$

Her commission was $1260.

Profit is the difference between total income and total operating costs.

> ## Formula
>
> profit = total income − total costs

The **percent of profit** is the percent of total income that is profit.

> ## Formula
>
> $$\text{percent of profit} = \frac{\text{profit}}{\text{total income}}$$

EXAMPLE 2   In April, a shoe store had an income of $8600 and operating costs of $7310. What percent of the store's income was profit?

Solution   profit = total income − total costs = 8600 − 7310 = 1290
$$\text{percent of profit} = \frac{\text{profit}}{\text{total income}} = \frac{1290}{8600} = 0.15$$

The percent of profit was 15%.

Class Exercises

Copy and complete the following table.

	Total sales	Percent of commission	Amount of commission
1.	$3250	10%	?
2.	$680	20%	?
3.	$900	?	$225
4.	$2500	?	$125
5.	?	15%	$300
6.	?	10%	$14.50

a. State the amount of profit.
b. Give an equation that could be used to find the percent of profit.
c. Find the percent of profit.

7. Income $12,000; costs $9000

8. Income $10,000; costs $8700

9. Income $14,000; costs $12,600

10. Income $3000; costs $2850

11. Income $5000; costs $4950

12. Income $24,000; costs $16,800

13. Income $12,300; costs $9840

14. Income $105,360; costs $63,216

Problems

Solve.

A **1.** Esther Simpson receives a 15% commission on magazine subscriptions. One week her sales totaled $860. What was her commission for the week?

2. The Greenwood Lumber Company had an income of $7680 for one week in May. If the company's profit for this period was 15% of its income, what were its costs for the week?

3. Margaret DeRosa's day-care service makes a profit of $222 per week. What are her costs if this profit is 18.5% of her total income?

4. Harvey Williams sold new insurance policies worth $5120 in August. If he receives a 4.5% commission on new policies, how much did he earn in commissions in August?

B **5.** Sole Mates Shoes has expenses of $9592 per month. What must the store's total income be if it is to make a 12% profit?

6. The Top Drawer Furniture Company made a profit of $4360 in one month. What were its operating costs if this profit was 16% of its total income?

Nina Perez is a real estate agent who receives a commission of 6% of the selling price of each house she sells. The seller of the house pays Nina's commission out of the selling price and keeps the remainder. What should be the selling price of each house if the seller wants to keep the amount indicated below?

7. $61,000 **8.** $66,000 **9.** $55,000 **10.** $70,500

C **11.** Norman's Natural Foods has weekly expenses of $1075 and makes a profit of 14% of sales. If his weekly expenses increase to $1225 and he wants to make the same dollar profit as before, what percent of sales will this profit represent?

12. In May Sal's Bakery had operating costs of $6630 and made a profit of $1170. In June the operating costs are expected to be $6273. What must the bakery's income be if its profit is to remain the same percent of its income?

13. Each month Fran Parks receives a 6% commission on all her sales of barber supplies up to $15,000. She receives 8% commission on the portion of her sales that are above $15,000. Her commission for March was $1260. What were her sales?

14. Mildred Hofstadter receives a 5% commission on her sales of exercise equipment and a 6% commission on her sales of weight-training equipment. One month she sold $7900 worth of exercise equipment and made a total of $650 in commissions. How much were her sales of weight-training equipment that month?

Review Exercises

Evaluate if $w = 8$, $x = 0.25$, $y = 0.8$, and $z = 5$.

1. wxz **2.** xyz **3.** $wx + yz$ **4.** $wy - xz$

5. $(wyz) \div x$ **6.** $(wy) \div (xz)$ **7.** $0.2wx$ **8.** $1.3wyz$

9-7 Simple Interest

When you lease a car or an apartment, you pay the owner rent for the use of the car or the apartment. When you borrow money, you pay the lender **interest** for the use of the money. The amount of interest you pay is usually a percent of the amount borrowed figured on a yearly basis. This percent is called the **annual rate.** For example, if you borrow $150 at an annual rate of 12%, you pay:

$$\$150 \times 0.12 = \$18 \text{ interest for one year}$$
$$\$150 \times 0.12 \times 2 = \$36 \text{ interest for two years}$$
$$\$150 \times 0.12 \times 3 = \$54 \text{ interest for three years}$$

When interest is computed year by year in this manner we call it **simple interest.** The example above illustrates the following formula.

Formula

Let I = simple interest charged
P = amount borrowed, or **principal**
r = annual rate
t = time in years for which the amount is borrowed

Then, interest = principal × rate × time, or $I = Prt$.

EXAMPLE 1   How much simple interest do you pay if you borrow $640 for 3 years at an annual rate of 15%?

Solution   Use the formula: $I = Prt$
$$I = 640 \times 0.15 \times 3$$
$$= 288$$

The interest is $288.

EXAMPLE 2   Sarah Sachs borrowed $3650 for 4 years at an annual rate of 16%. How much money must she repay in all?

Solution   Use the formula: $I = Prt$
$$I = 3650 \times 0.16 \times 4$$
$$= 2336$$

The interest is $2336.
The total to be repaid is the principal plus the interest: 3650 + 2336, or $5986.

PROBLEM SOLVING REMINDER

When solving a problem, be certain to *answer the question asked.* In Example 2, you are asked to find the total amount to be repaid, not just the interest. To get the total amount to be repaid, you must add the interest to the amount borrowed.

EXAMPLE 3   Renny Soloman paid $375 simple interest on a loan of $1500 at 12.5%. What was the length of time for the loan?

Solution   Let t = time.

Use the formula: $I = Prt$
$$375 = 1500 \times 0.125 \times t$$
$$375 = 187.5t$$
$$\frac{375}{187.5} = t$$
$$t = 2$$

The loan was for 2 years.

EXAMPLE 4   George Landon paid $585 simple interest on a loan of $6500 for 6 months. What was the annual rate?

Solution   Let r = annual rate.

Use the formula: $I = Prt$
$$585 = 6500 \times r \times \frac{1}{2}$$
$$585 = 3250r$$
$$r = \frac{585}{3250} = 0.18$$

The annual rate was 18%.

In Example 4 notice that the time, 6 months, is expressed as $\frac{1}{2}$ year, since the rate of interest in the formula is the *annual or yearly rate.*

Class Exercises

Give the simple interest on each loan at the given annual rate for 1 year, 3 years, and 6 months.

1. $100 at 8%

2. $200 at 12%

3. $5000 at 10%

4. $400 at 5%

5. $1500 at 6%

6. $100 at 8.4%

Find the annual rate of interest for each loan.

7. principal: $1100, time: 2 years, simple interest: $220

8. principal: $1600, time: $1\frac{1}{2}$ years, simple interest: $120

Find the length of time for each loan.

9. principal: $1200, interest rate: 6%, simple interest: $144

10. principal: $500, interest rate: 8%, simple interest: $30

Find the total amount that must be repaid on each loan.

11. principal: $200, interest rate: 15%, time: 2 years

12. principal: $600, interest rate: 9%, time: 3 years

Written Exercises

Find the simple interest on each loan and the total amount to be repaid.

A
1. $1280 at 15% for 2 years
2. $4250 at 12% for 3 years

3. $2760 at 18% for 1 year, 6 months
4. $3500 at 16% for 9 months

5. $5640 at 7.5% for 4 years
6. $7250 at 12.8% for $2\frac{1}{2}$ years

7. $6380 at 14.5% for 6 years
8. $14,650 at 16.4% for $3\frac{1}{2}$ years

Find the annual rate of interest for each loan.

9. $4360 for 2 years, 6 months; simple interest: $1526

10. $1240 for 3 years, 6 months; simple interest: $651

11. $2600 for 4 years; total to be repaid: $3484

12. $5760 for 2 years, 9 months; total to be repaid: $8532

13. $6520 for 3 years, 3 months; simple interest: $3390.40

14. $3980 for $4\frac{1}{2}$ years; total to be repaid: $7024.70

Find the length of time for each loan.

15. $3775 at 12%; simple interest: $226.50

16. $7850 at 6.5%; simple interest: $510.25

Find the original amount (principal) of the given loan.

EXAMPLE   9% for 4 years; total to be repaid: $7140

Solution   Let P = the original amount of the loan.

$$\begin{aligned}
\text{amount to be repaid} &= P + Prt \\
&= P + P \times 0.09 \times 4 \\
&= P + 0.36P \\
&= P(1 + 0.36) \\
7140 &= 1.36P \\
P &= \tfrac{7140}{1.36} = 5250
\end{aligned}$$

The original amount of the loan was $5250.

B **17.** 8% for $4\frac{1}{2}$ years; total to be repaid: $6052

18. 13.5% for 5 years; total to be repaid: $3417

19. 16% for 2 years, 3 months; total to be repaid: $9139.20

20. 12.4% for 3 years, 6 months; total to be repaid: $2222.70

21. 9.6% for 4 years; total to be repaid: $2560.40

22. 10.8% for 2 years, 9 months; total to be repaid: $4734.05

Solve.

C **23.** If the simple interest on $250 for 1 year, 8 months is $30, how much is the interest on $425.50 for 3 years, 4 months?

24. If $150 earns $28.75 simple interest in 1 year and 8 months, what principal is required to earn $747.50 interest in 2 years, 6 months?

Problems

Solve.

A **1.** Lois Pocket owns bonds worth $10,500 that pay 11% annual interest. The interest is paid semiannually in two equal amounts. How much is each payment?

2. A car loan of $4650 at an annual rate of 16% for 2 years is to be repaid in 24 equal monthly payments, including principal and interest. How much is each of these payments?

3. Gilbert White wants to borrow $2250 for 3 years to remodel his garage. The annual rate is 18%. If the principal and interest are repaid in equal monthly installments, how much will each installment be?

4. Fernando Lopez can borrow $5640 at 12.5% for 4 years, or he can borrow the same amount for 3 years at 15%. Find the total amount to be repaid on each loan. Which amount is smaller?

B **5.** An education loan of $8400 for ten years is to be repaid in monthly installments of $122.50. What is the annual rate of this loan, computed as simple interest?

6. Will Darcy's three-year home improvement loan is to be repaid in monthly installments of $375.90 each. If the annual rate (as simple interest) is 14.4%, what is the principal of the loan?

C **7.** In how many years would the amount to be repaid on a loan at 12.5% simple interest be double the principal of the loan?

8. At what rate of simple interest would the amount to be repaid on a loan be triple the principal of the loan after 25 years?

Review Exercises

Multiply.

1. $\frac{1}{2} \times 0.75$

2. $\frac{1}{4} \times 0.3$

3. $\frac{1}{5} \times 0.25$

4. $\frac{3}{4} \times 0.61$

5. $\frac{4}{5} \times 1.87$

6. $\frac{3}{10} \times 2.03$

7. $\frac{2}{3} \times 1.25$

8. $\frac{7}{9} \times 2.375$

9. $\frac{5}{6} \times 2.875$

	CALCULATOR INVESTIGATION: *Percent Key*

Some calculators have a percent key. Use a calculator with a percent key to do the following exercises.

1. What is 8% of 200?

2. 35 is 20% of what number?

3. What percent of 75 is 36?

4. Express $\frac{17}{20}$ as a percent.

5. Express $\frac{13}{15}$ as a percent.

6. Express $\frac{7}{11}$ as a percent.

9-8 Compound Interest

If you deposited $100 in an account that paid 10% interest, you would have $10 interest after one year for a total of $110. You could then withdraw the $10 interest or leave it in the account. By withdrawing the interest, your principal would remain $100, and you would again receive simple interest. If, however, you left the $10 interest in the account, your principal would become $110, and you would accumulate **compound interest,** that is, interest on principal plus interest. The following chart illustrates these alternatives.

	Simple Interest		Compound Interest	
After	Interest	Principal	Interest	Principal
0 years	0	$100	0	$100
1 year	10% of $100 = $10	$100	10% of $100 = $10	$100 + $10 = $110
2 years	10% of $100 = $10	$100	10% of $110 = $11	$110 + $11 = $121
3 years	10% of $100 = $10	$100	10% of $121 = $12.10	$121 + $12.10 = $133.10
	Total interest: $30		Total interest: $33.10	

Notice that because the principal increases as interest is compounded, the total amount of interest paid on $100 after 3 years is greater than what is paid at the same rate of simple interest.

Interest is often compounded in one of the following manners.

> monthly: 12 times a year
> quarterly: 4 times a year
> semiannually: 2 times a year

EXAMPLE If $500 is deposited in an account paying 8% interest compounded quarterly, how much will the principal amount to after 1 year?

Solution Use the formula $I = Prt$.

After 1 quarter:
$I = 500 \times 0.08 \times \frac{1}{4} = \$10$ $P = 500 + 10 = \$510$

After 2 quarters:
$I = 510 \times 0.08 \times \frac{1}{4} = \$10.20$ $P = 510 + 10.20 = \$520.20$

After 3 quarters:
$I = 520.20 \times 0.08 \times \frac{1}{4} \approx \$10.40$ $P = 520.20 + 10.40 = \$530.60$

After 4 quarters:
$I = 530.60 \times 0.08 \times \frac{1}{4} \approx \$10.61$ $P = 530.60 + 10.61 = \$541.21$

After you read an interest problem, ask yourself the following questions:
What is asked for, simple interest or compound interest?
What is the time period? For example, is it 3 months or 3 years?
Is the answer to be the interest, the new principal, or the total amount to be repaid?

Class Exercises

$8000 is deposited in a bank that compounds interest annually at 5%. Find the following.

1. The interest paid at the end of the first year

2. The new principal at the beginning of the second year

3. The interest paid at the end of the second year

4. The new principal at the beginning of the third year

5. The interest paid at the end of the third year

$1000 is invested at 12%, compounded quarterly. Find the following.

6. The interest paid after 3 months

7. The new principal after 3 months

8. The interest paid after 6 months

9. The new principal after 6 months

Written Exercises

How much will each principal amount to if it is deposited for the given time at the given rate? (If you do not have a calculator, round to the nearest penny at each step.)

A **1.** $6400 for 2 years at 5%, compounded annually

2. $500 for 1 year at 8%, compounded semiannually

3. $1500 for 6 months at 8%, compounded quarterly

4. $8000 for 2 months at 6%, compounded monthly

5. $2500 for 18 months at 16%, compounded semiannually

6. $1280 for 9 months at 10%, compounded quarterly

7. $1800 for 1 year, 3 months at 14%, compounded quarterly

8. $3475 for $2\frac{1}{2}$ years at 6%, compounded semiannually

How much will each principal amount to if it is deposited for the given time at the given rate? (If you do not have a calculator, round to the nearest penny at each step.)

B 9. $3200 for 3 years at 7.5%, compounded annually

10. $3125 for 3 months at 9.6%, compounded monthly

11. $8000 for 2 years at 10%, compounded semiannually

12. $6250 for 1 year at 16%, compounded quarterly

13. What is the difference between the simple and compound (compounded semiannually) interest on $250 in 2 years at 14% per year?

14. What is the difference between the interest on $800 in 1 year at 8% per year compounded semiannually and compounded quarterly?

C 15. What principal will grow to $1367.10 after 1 year at 10% compounded semiannually?

16. How long would it take $2560 to grow to $2756.84 at 10% compounded quarterly?

Problems

Solve. (If you do not have a calculator, round to the nearest penny at each step.)

A 1. The River Bank and Trust Company pays 10%, compounded semiannually, on their 18-month certificates. How much would a certificate for $1600 be worth at maturity?

2. Mike Estrada invested $1250 at 9.6%, compounded monthly. How much was his investment worth at the end of 3 months?

B 3. Jennifer Thornton can invest $3200 at 12% simple interest or at 10% interest compounded quarterly. Which investment will earn more in 9 months?

4. Which is a better way to invest $6400 for $1\frac{1}{2}$ years: 16% simple interest or 15% compounded semiannually?

C 5. A money market fund pays 12.8% per year, compounded semiannually. For a deposit of $5000, this compound interest rate is equivalent to what simple interest rate for 1 year? Give your answer to the nearest tenth of a percent.

Self-Test B

Solve.

1. A $40 calculator is on sale for $34. What is the percent of discount? [9-5]

2. A hardware store pays $8 for a set of wrenches. If the store marks the set up 40%, what is the selling price of the wrenches?

3. Marcia Many earns 6% commission on her sales of real estate. If she sold a house for $95,000 last week, what was her commission? [9-6]

4. Computer Village had sales of $16,000 for December. The store's profits were $2880. What was the percent of profit?

5. Eldrige Jones owns bonds that pay 9% simple interest. If the bonds are worth $7000 and pay interest four times a year, how much is each payment? [9-7]

6. Sara Libby invested $3000 in a fund that pays 8% interest compounded quarterly. To the nearest penny, how much interest did she receive in all at the end of one year? [9-8]

Self-Test answers and Extra Practice are at the back of the book.

 COMPUTER INVESTIGATION: *Compound Interest*

The program at the right will find the new principal based on the initial principal *P*, the rate *R* as a decimal, compounded *N* times a year for *T* years.

Compute $200 at 5.5% for 3 years:

1. Compounded quarterly
2. Compounded monthly
3. Compounded daily (365 days)
4. Repeat Exercises 1–3 at 6%.

```
10   PRINT "COMPOUND INTEREST:"
20   PRINT "INPUT P, R(DECIMAL),";
30   PRINT "N, AND T";
40   INPUT P,R,N,T
50   LET M = N * T
60   FOR K = 1 TO M
70   LET P = P + P * R / N
75   NEXT K
80   LET P = INT(100 * P + .5)/100
90   PRINT "AMOUNT AFTER ";T;
100  PRINT " YEAR(S) = $";P
110  END
```

5. Fred Jones has $10,000 and the following choice of investments.
   a. A bank certificate paying 10.4% compounded daily for 5 years
   b. A municipal bond paying 11.8% compounded monthly for 4 years
   c. An investment fund paying 13.2% compounded quarterly for 3 years

   RUN the program for each investment. How much will Mr. Jones receive at the end of each investment?

Percents and Proportions

Proportions may be used to solve problems involving percent. To see how this can be done, let us consider the following example.

We know that 15 is 25% of 60. The number 15 is called the **percentage,** 25% is the **rate,** and 60 is called the **base.** Since a percent is an amount per hundred, 25% can be thought of as the ratio of 25 to 100, or $\frac{25}{100}$. Therefore,

$$\frac{15}{60} = \frac{25}{100}, \text{ or } \quad 15 \text{ is to } 60 \text{ as } 25 \text{ is to } 100.$$

Note that $\frac{15}{60}$ is the ratio of the percentage (p) to the base (b).

Percentage, base, and rate are related as shown in the following proportion:

$$\frac{p}{b} = \frac{n}{100},$$

where $\frac{n}{100}$ is the rate expressed as an amount per hundred.

EXAMPLE 1 What percent of 40 is 16?

Solution

16 is the percentage,
40 is the base, and

$\frac{n}{100}$ represents the rate.

16 is 40% of 40.

$$\frac{16}{40} = \frac{n}{100}$$

$$40n = 1600$$

$$n = \frac{1600}{40} = 40$$

EXAMPLE 2   If 4% of a certain ore is extractable as pure gold, how many grams of ore must be processed to obtain 2 g of pure gold?

Solution   The rate is 4% and the percentage is 2 g. Let b denote the number of grams of ore to be processed (the base).

$$\frac{2}{b} = \frac{4}{100}$$
$$200 = 4b$$
$$b = \frac{200}{4} = 50$$

50 g of ore must be processed to obtain 2 g of pure gold.

Find each percentage, base, or rate.

1. What percent of 90 is 18?

2. What is 5% of 120?

3. What percent of 40 is 6?

4. What is 4% of 75?

5. 12 is what percent of 32?

6. 18 is 20% of what number?

7. 42 is what percent of 48?

8. 9 is 15% of what number?

9. What is 10% of 240?

10. 42 is 40% of what number?

11. What is 70% of 480?

12. 533 is 82% of what number?

Solve.

13. Maria Sanchez gave 8% of her mathematics students a grade of A. If she had 125 students in her 4 classes, how many of these students received an A?

14. Approximately 60% of the weight in a human body is the weight of the water in the body. If a person weighs 160 pounds, about how many pounds of water are in that person's body?

15. How much zinc is in 28 kg of an alloy containing 5% zinc?

16. A survey found that one brand of light bulb lasted much longer than its guaranteed life of 240 hours. For instance, one light bulb lasted 420 hours. What percent of its guaranteed life did the light bulb last?

17. In studying a rock, a scientist found that 1.41 g of the 3.76 g rock was copper. What percent of the rock was copper?

18. 60% of the persons questioned in a public opinion poll approved of the job their city government was doing. If 90 persons approved, how many were questioned?

Chapter Review

Write the letter of the equivalent item.

1. 42%

2. $\frac{3}{5}$

3. $\frac{7}{8}$

4. 98%

5. 178%

6. 0.74

7. 38%

8. 15.8%

9. 3.66

10. 0.054

A. $\frac{49}{50}$

B. 366%

C. 0.74%

D. 60%

E. $\frac{21}{50}$

F. 74%

G. 54%

H. 87.5%

I. 3.66%

J. 0.158

K. $1\frac{39}{50}$

L. 0.38

M. $1\frac{34}{50}$

N. 5.4%

[9-1]

[9-2]

Complete each statement.

11. __?__ is 20% of 90.

12. 12 is __?__% of 64.

13. 336 is __?__% of 48.

14. 9 is 25% of __?__.

15. The percent of increase from 24 to 30 is __?__.

16. The percent of decrease from 50 to 37 is __?__.

17. The percent of increase from 76 to __?__ is 25%.

[9-3]

[9-4]

Write the letter of the correct answer.

18. A pair of shoes that regularly sells for $32 is on sale for $24. What is the percent of discount?

    a. $33\frac{1}{3}$%   **b.** 25%   **c.** 8%   **d.** 125%

[9-5]

19. The Vico Manufacturing Company makes a 12% profit. If the company sold $15,250 worth of goods in April, what was its profit?
    a. $13,420   **b.** $15,250   **c.** $1830   **d.** $18,300

[9-6]

20. John Anthony borrowed $1200 for $1\frac{1}{2}$ years at 13% simple interest. How much must he repay when the loan is due?
    a. $1434   **b.** $234   **c.** $1356   **d.** $156

[9-7]

21. Lorraine Eldar invested $6000 at 8% interest compounded semi-annually. How long will it take her investment to exceed $7000?

    a. 1 year   **b.** $1\frac{1}{2}$ years   **c.** 2 years   **d.** $2\frac{1}{2}$ years

[9-8]

Chapter Test

Express as a fraction in lowest terms or as a mixed number in simple form.

1. 48% **2.** 6% **3.** 215% **4.** 190% [9-1]

Express as a percent.

5. $\frac{11}{20}$ **6.** $\frac{5}{8}$ **7.** 3 **8.** $2\frac{1}{8}$

Express as a decimal.

9. 93% **10.** 42% **11.** 259% **12.** 0.86% [9-2]

Express as a percent.

13. 0.81 **14.** 0.07 **15.** 2.91 **16.** 1.01

17. What percent of 85 is 51? [9-3]

18. 27 is what percent of 60?

19. What is 30% of 80?

20. 20% of what number is 25?

Solve.

21. Sam Golden's salary increased $30 a week. If his salary was $400 a week before the raise, by what percent did his salary increase? [9-4]

22. A clock radio that sells for $30 is on sale at a 20% discount. What is the sale price? [9-5]

23. Edna's Autos sold $24,000 worth of cars last week. If Edna's costs were $16,800, how much profit did Edna make and what was the percent of profit? [9-6]

24. Joan Wu invested $5000 in an account that pays 13% simple interest. If the interest is paid 4 times a year, how much is each payment? [9-7]

25. Billtown Bank pays 8% interest compounded quarterly. To the nearest penny, how much will $2500 earn in one year? [9-8]

Cumulative Review (Chapters 1–9)

Exercises

Perform the indicated operations. Give answers in lowest terms.

1. $12 + 17 + 41$

2. $84 - 63 + 49$

3. $13 \times 9 \times 11$

4. $(96 \div 6)7$

5. $186 \div (60 \div 10)$

6. $42 \times 5 \div 7$

7. $0.39 + 0.87 + 0.09$

8. $5.94 - 1.92 - 3.41$

9. $6.81 - 4.93 + 0.07$

10. $0.82 \times 0.11 \times 0.5$

11. 3.14×6.5^2

12. $6.28 + 2.13 \times 4.1$

13. $5.88 \div 0.03$

14. $0.84 \div 1000$

15. $7.95 \div (0.1 \times 0.3)$

16. $\frac{3}{4} + \frac{5}{8} + \frac{7}{12}$

17. $3\frac{1}{2} - 1\frac{3}{5} + 2\frac{1}{8}$

18. $\frac{15}{9} + \frac{5}{6} - \frac{7}{15}$

19. $\frac{22}{7} \times 2\frac{1}{3} \times \frac{8}{9}$

20. $\frac{3}{16} + \frac{5}{8} \div \frac{5}{12}$

21. $\frac{11}{24} \div \frac{7}{12} \div 3\frac{3}{8}$

Evaluate the following for $a = 7$, $b = 3.14$, $c = \frac{22}{7}$, $d = 14$.

22. $ab + cd$

23. $2bd^2$

24. a^2bd

25. $2a(b + d)$

26. ca^2

27. bd^2a

Write as a percent.

28. 0.68

29. 0.01

30. 3.51

31. $\frac{3}{4}$

32. $4\frac{1}{2}$

33. $12\frac{3}{8}$

Find the perimeter or circumference. Use $\pi \approx 3.14$ and round to three digits.

34. square
side: 11 cm

35. circle
radius: 8 mm

36. rectangle
length: 5 m
width: 3 m

37. isosceles triangle
congruent sides: 7 m
base: 4 m

38. circle
diameter: 12 cm

39. regular hexagon
side: 15 mm

Solve.

40. $x + 17 = 41$

41. $y - 11 = 37$

42. $3r = 53$

43. $\frac{1}{2}t = 64$

44. $2x + 15 = 87$

45. $5z - 42 = 80$

46. $\frac{1}{n} = \frac{10}{15}$

47. $\frac{7}{12} = \frac{m}{60}$

48. $\frac{9}{21} = \frac{15}{b}$

Problems

1. In the downhill skiing event, three skiers raced through the course in these times: 1 min 45.73 s, 1 min 46.59 s, and 1 min 46.06 s. Which was the shortest time?

2. Describe one way to make change for an item costing $1.79, paid for with a five-dollar bill.

3. Estimate how long it will take a train to travel 137 miles at an average rate of 65 mph.

4. In a mechanical drawing, one angle of an isosceles triangle is labeled "120°." What is the measure of each of the other two angles of the triangle?

5. A length of gold braid $1\frac{1}{3}$ yd long was used to outline two congruent polygons in a craft project. How much braid will be needed to outline a third polygon that is congruent to the first two?

6. What is the least number greater than a million that is divisible by 3?

7. A fence is to be erected around a flower garden in the shape of an equilateral triangle. Find the total length of fencing needed if one side of the garden is 6 m long.

8. A pathway 8 m wide is to be built around a circular fountain. If the fountain is 12 m in diameter, find the inner and outer circumference of the path. Use $\pi = 3.14$ and round to three digits.

9. A water purification device can purify 15.5 L of water in one hour. How many liters can it purify in $3\frac{3}{4}$ hours?

10. The Bears scored twice as many points as the Cubs. If the Bears scored 42 points, how many points did the Cubs score?

11. The Onagas have a wall at the back of their property. They want to fence off a rectangular garden using 7 m of the existing wall for the back part of the fence. If they have 15 m of fencing, what will be the length of each of the shorter sides?

10 Areas and Volumes

APPLYING MATHEMATICS
BUILDING

The box-like shapes common in modern buildings are examples of space figures known in geometry as *right prisms*. The rectangular walls of such buildings rise vertically, at right angles to the ground level. The base of such a building may be an irregular polygon, whose shape is sometimes called a "footprint" by architects. As part of the design process, architects must calculate the volume contained by their buildings, and the total surface area that must be covered by sheathing materials. In this chapter you will study the geometry of space figures such as prisms, pyramids, and cylinders, and learn how to calculate their surface areas and volumes.

CAREER CONNECTION

ARCHITECT

Architects are responsible for the design and visual appearance of buildings. Good architectural designs are appealing, safe, and functional. Architects must combine technical skills with a strong sense of style. Course work in mathematics, engineering, and art provide the necessary background for this profession.

Photo: New York's World Financial Center features courses of rough and smooth granite sheathing.

319

10-1 Areas of Rectangles and Parallelograms

Earlier we measured lengths of segments and found perimeters of polygons. Now we will measure the part of the plane enclosed by a polygon. We call this measure the **area** of the polygon.

Just as we needed a unit length to measure segments, we now need a **unit area.** In the metric system a unit area often used is the **square centimeter (cm²).**

The rectangular regions shown in the diagrams have been divided into square centimeters to show the areas of the rectangles.

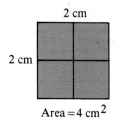

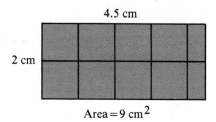

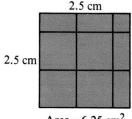

Notice that the area of each rectangle is the product of the lengths of two consecutive sides. These sides are called the **length** and the **width** of the rectangle. The length names the longer side and the width names the shorter side. We have the following formula for any rectangle.

Formula

Area of rectangle = length × width

$$A = lw$$

The length and width of a rectangle are called its **dimensions.**

In the case of a parallelogram, we may consider either pair of parallel sides to be the **bases.** (The word *base* is also used to denote the length of the base.) The **height** is the perpendicular distance between the bases.

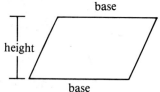

The colored region in the figure at the top of the next page can be moved to the right, as shown in the second figure, to form a rectangle having dimensions b and h. Thus, the area of the parallelogram is the same as the area of the rectangle, bh.

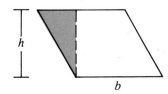 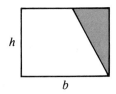

The area of any parallelogram can be found by using the following formula.

> ## Formula
>
> Area of parallelogram = base × height
>
> $$A = bh$$

EXAMPLE 1   Find the area of each parallelogram.

a.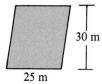

b.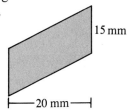

Solution

a. $A = bh$
   $= 25 \times 30 = 750$
   The area is 750 m².

b. $A = bh$
   $= 15 \times 20 = 300$
   The area is 300 mm².

EXAMPLE 2   A parallelogram has an area of 375 cm² and a height of 15 cm. Find the length of the base.

Solution

$A = bh$
$375 = b \times 15$
$\dfrac{375}{15} = b$
$25 = b$

The length of the base is 25 cm.

The unit areas used in the examples are **square meters (m²)**, **square millimeters (mm²)**, and **square centimeters (cm²)**. For very large regions, such as states or countries, we could use **square kilometers (km²)**.

Sometimes we may work with an unspecified unit of length. Then the unit of area is simply called a **square unit.** Thus, the area of the rectangle shown at the right is 250 square units.

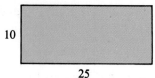

10

25

Class Exercises

Find the areas of the shaded regions.

1.  2. 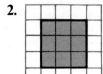 3.   4.

5. Find the perimeters of the regions in Exercises 1 and 2.

6. Find the area of a square with sides 4 cm long.

Complete.

7. $1 \text{ cm} = \underline{\ \ ?\ \ } \text{ mm}$

$1 \text{ cm}^2 = \underline{\ \ ?\ \ } \text{ mm}^2$

8. $1 \text{ m} = \underline{\ \ ?\ \ } \text{ cm}$

$1 \text{ m}^2 = \underline{\ \ ?\ \ } \text{ cm}^2$

9. $1 \text{ km} = \underline{\ \ ?\ \ } \text{ m}$

$1 \text{ km}^2 = \underline{\ \ ?\ \ } \text{ m}^2$

10. Explain why the blue parallelogram and the gray one have equal areas.

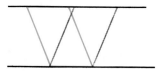

Written Exercises

Find the area and the perimeter of each rectangle or parallelogram.

A 1.

30 cm

35 cm

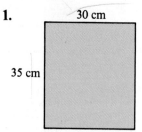

2.

11 m

4 m

5 m

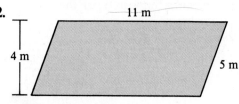

3.

65 km

41 km

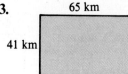

4.

5.6

1.3

1.2

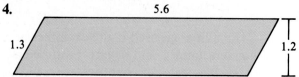

Find the area and the perimeter of a rectangle having the given dimensions.

5. 48 mm by 92 mm

6. 55 cm by 32 cm

7. 63.7 km by 39.1 km

8. 206.3 m by 33.15 m

Copy and complete the tables.

Rectangle	9.	10.	11.	12.	13.	14.
length	12.5	12	?	?	8.6	?
width	7.5	?	45	2.5	?	?
perimeter	?	?	?	17.0	18.0	4
Area	?	60	3600	?	?	1

Parallelogram	15.	16.	17.	18.	19.	20.
base	18.5	2.7	?	14.3	2.9	?
height	4.0	?	1.6	3.2	?	0.4
Area	?	8.1	0.8	?	11.6	3.6

Find the area of each region. (*Hint:* Subdivide each region into simpler ones, if necessary.)

B **21.**

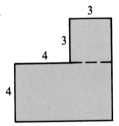

22.

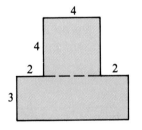

23.

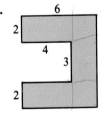

24.

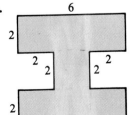

25.

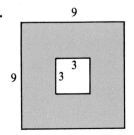

26.

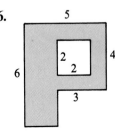

Problems

Solve.

A 1. How many square meters of wallpaper are needed to cover a wall 8 m long and 3 m high?

2. **a.** How many square yards of carpeting are needed to cover a floor that measures 8 yd by 5 yd?
   b. How much will the carpeting cost at $24 per square yard?

3. **a.** How many square feet of vinyl floor covering are needed to cover a floor measuring 60 ft by 12 ft?
   b. How much will the floor covering cost at $1.50 per square foot?

4. Jose wishes to line the open box shown at the right using five sheets of plastic. How many square centimeters will he need?

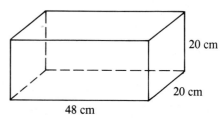

20 cm

20 cm

48 cm

B 5. Yoneko wishes to obtain 6 m² of plastic from a roll 40 cm wide. How many meters should she unroll?

6. A square pool 5 m on each side is surrounded by a brick walk 2 m wide. What is the area of the walk?

7. A construction site in the shape of a square is surrounded by a wooden wall 2 m high. If the length of one side of the wall is 45 m, find the area of the construction site.

8. A rectangular cow pasture has an area of 1925 m². If the length of one side of the pasture is 55 m, find the lengths of the other sides.

Review Exercises

Multiply.

1. $\frac{1}{2} \times 8 \times 7$

2. $\frac{1}{3} \times 11 \times 9$

3. $\frac{1}{2} \times 1.3 \times 1.6$

4. $\frac{1}{2}(8 + 9)11$

5. $\frac{1}{4}(20 + 12)5$

6. $\frac{1}{2}(0.11 + 0.17)0.6$

7. $\frac{1}{3}(0.26 + 0.52)0.3$

8. $\frac{1}{4}(1.76 + 2.69)1.94$

10-2 Areas of Triangles and Trapezoids

Any side of a triangle can be considered to be the **base.** The **height** is then the perpendicular distance from the opposite vertex to the base line.

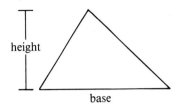

Let us find the area of a triangle having base b and height h. The triangle and a congruent copy of it can be put together to form a parallelogram as shown in the diagrams.

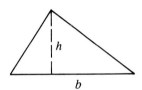
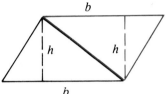

Since the area of the parallelogram is bh and the area of the triangle is half the parallelogram, we have the following formula.

Formula

Area of triangle $= \frac{1}{2} \times$ base $\times$ height

$$A = \frac{1}{2}bh$$

EXAMPLE 1   Find the area of each triangle.

a.

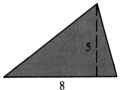

b.

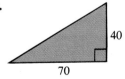

c.

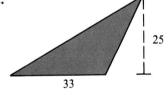

Solution

a. $A = \frac{1}{2}bh$

$\quad = \frac{1}{2} \times 8 \times 5 = 20$

$A = 20$ square units

b. $A = \frac{1}{2}bh$

$\quad = \frac{1}{2} \times 70 \times 40 = 1400$

$A = 1400$ square units

c. $A = \frac{1}{2}bh$

$\quad = \frac{1}{2} \times 33 \times 25 = 412.5$

$A = 412.5$ square units

Note in part (b) of Example 1 that the lengths of the sides of the *right angle* of the triangle were used as the base and the height. This can be done for any *right* triangle, even if the triangle is positioned so that it is "standing" on the side opposite the right angle.

The **height** of a trapezoid is the perpendicular distance between the parallel sides. These parallel sides are called the **bases** of the trapezoid. The method used to find the formula for the area of a triangle can be used to find the formula for the area of a trapezoid having bases b_1 and b_2 and

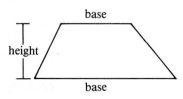

height h. The trapezoid and a congruent copy of it can be put together to form a parallelogram. The area of the parallelogram is $(b_1 + b_2)h$ and the area of the original trapezoid is half of the area of the parallelogram.

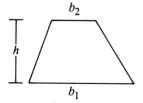 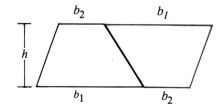

We, therefore, have the following formula.

Formula

Area of trapezoid $= \frac{1}{2} \times$ (sum of bases) $\times$ height

$$A = \frac{1}{2}(b_1 + b_2)h$$

EXAMPLE 2 Find the area of each trapezoid.

a.

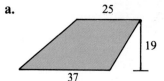

b.

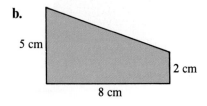

Solution

a. $A = \frac{1}{2}(b_1 + b_2)h$

$= \frac{1}{2} \times (37 + 25) \times 19 = 589$

$A = 589$ square units

b. $A = \frac{1}{2}(b_1 + b_2)h$

$= \frac{1}{2} \times (5 + 2) \times 8 = 28$

$A = 28$ m²

EXAMPLE 3 A trapezoid has an area of 200 cm² and bases of 15 cm and 25 cm. Find the height.

Solution

$$A = \frac{1}{2}(b_1 + b_2)h$$

$$200 = \frac{1}{2} \times (15 + 25) \times h$$

$$200 = \frac{1}{2} \times 40 \times h$$

$$200 = 20h$$
$$10 = h$$

The height is 10 cm.

Class Exercises

Find the area of each polygon.

1.

2.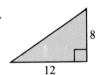

3.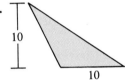

4.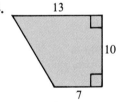

5.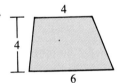

6.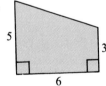

7.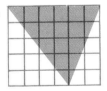

8.

9.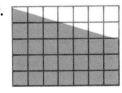

10.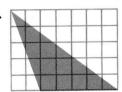

11.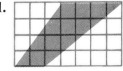

12.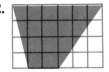

Written Exercises

Find the area of each polygon.

A 1.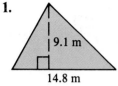
9.1 m
14.8 m

2.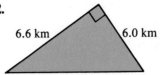
6.6 km   6.0 km

3.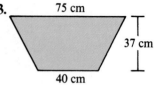
75 cm
37 cm
40 cm

4.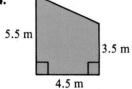
5.5 m
3.5 m
4.5 m

5.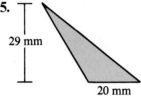
29 mm
20 mm

6.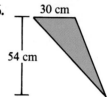
30 cm
54 cm

7. Triangle: base 122 km, height 30 km

8. Triangle: base 480 m, height 480 m

9. Trapezoid: bases 12.3 cm and 6.2 cm, height 4.8 cm

10. Trapezoid: bases 14.6 km and 22.4 km, height 14.0 km

Copy and complete the tables.

Triangle	11.	12.	13.	14.
base	6 cm	16 mm	?	?
height	?	?	2.4 m	1.4 m
Area	72 cm²	80 mm²	4.8 m²	0.42 m²

B

Trapezoid	15.	16.	17.	18.
base	0.7 mm	0.8 m	3	2
base	1.7 mm	1.2 m	?	?
height	?	?	2	3
Area	9.6 mm²	1.0 m²	18	18

19. In the figure at the right, $\overline{PQ}$ is parallel to $\overline{RT}$. Explain why triangles *PQR*, *PQS*, and *PQT* all have the same area.

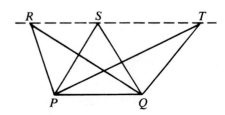

In Exercises 20 and 21 find the area of (a) the blue part and (b) the red part of the pennant.

20.

30 cm

|—20 cm—|——40 cm——|

21.

15 cm

15 cm

|——30 cm——|——30 cm——|

C **22.** One triangle has a base and a height that are twice as large as the base and the height of another triangle. What is the ratio of their areas?

23. One rectangle has a base and a height that are 3 times the base and the height of another rectangle. What is the ratio of their areas? their perimeters?

Review Exercises

Simplify.

1. 3×5^2

2. 1.2×9^2

3. 4×1.3^2

4. $3 \times 7^2 - 2 \times 4^2$

5. $4 \times 5^2 + 3 \times 8^2$

6. $11^2 \times 3 - 6^2 \times 4$

7. $5 \times 1.4^2 - 7 \times 1.1^2$

8. $2.5^2 \times 4 + 3.2^2 \times 7$

9. $17 \times 14^2 + 6 \times 16^2$

▮▮▮▮ **NONROUTINE PROBLEM SOLVING:** *Finding a Pattern*

The ancient Egyptians worked primarily with fractions with a numerator of 1. They expressed fractions such as $\frac{2}{5}$ as the sum of these fractions: $\frac{2}{5} = \frac{1}{3} + \frac{1}{15}$. These sums were listed in a table. Find the following sums selected from the Egyptian fraction table.

1. $\frac{1}{8} + \frac{1}{52} + \frac{1}{104}$

2. $\frac{1}{12} + \frac{1}{51} + \frac{1}{68}$

3. $\frac{1}{12} + \frac{1}{76} + \frac{1}{114}$

4. $\frac{1}{24} + \frac{1}{58} + \frac{1}{174} + \frac{1}{232}$

5. $\frac{1}{20} + \frac{1}{124} + \frac{1}{155}$

6. $\frac{1}{24} + \frac{1}{111} + \frac{1}{296}$

10-3 Areas of Circles

Recall that there are two formulas for the circumference, C, of a circle. If the diameter of the circle is denoted by d and the radius by r, then

$$C = \pi d \quad \text{and} \quad C = 2\pi r.$$

Two approximations for the number π are 3.14 and $\frac{22}{7}$.

The part of the plane enclosed by a circle is called the **area of the circle.** This area is given by the following formula.

Formula

Area of circle $= \pi \times (\text{radius})^2$

$$A = \pi r^2$$

EXAMPLE 1 Find the areas of the shaded regions. Use $\pi \approx 3.14$.

a.

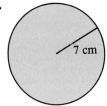
7 cm

b.

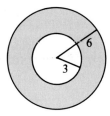
6
3

Solution

a. $A = \pi r^2$
$\quad \approx 3.14 \times 7^2$
$\quad \approx 3.14 \times 49 \approx 153.86$
$\quad A \approx 154 \text{ cm}^2$

b. $A = (\pi \times 6^2) - (\pi \times 3^2)$
$\quad = (\pi \times 36) - (\pi \times 9)$
$\quad = \pi(36 - 9) = \pi \times 27$
$\quad \approx 3.14 \times 27 \approx 84.78$
$\quad A \approx 84.8 \text{ square units}$

Recall that we give answers to only three digits when we use the approximation $\pi \approx 3.14$. Sometimes, to avoid approximations we give an answer in terms of π.

EXAMPLE 2 Find the area of the shaded region. Leave your answer in terms of π.

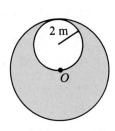
2 m
O

Solution Area of shaded region
$\quad = (\text{Area of large circle}) -$
$\quad\quad\quad\quad\quad\quad (\text{Area of small circle})$
We first find the area of the small circle.

$$A = \pi r^2 = \pi \times 2^2 = 4\pi$$

We then find the area of the large circle.

Since the radius of the large circle is the same as the diameter of the small circle, we know that the radius of the large circle is 4 m.

$$A = \pi r^2 = \pi \times 4^2 = 16\pi$$

Thus, area of shaded region is equal to $16\pi - 4\pi = 12\pi$

The area of the shaded region is 12π m².

To make the formula $A = \pi r^2$ seem reasonable to you, think of the circular region below cut like a pie.

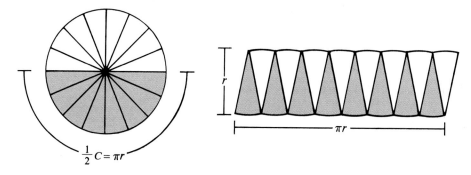

The pieces can be arranged to form a figure rather like a parallelogram with base πr and height r. This suggests that the area is given by

$$\pi r \times r = \pi r^2.$$

 COMMUNICATION IN MATHEMATICS: *Reading Diagrams*

To read and understand an explanation that is illustrated by a diagram, ask yourself questions about the diagram as you read. In the explanation above, for example, ask yourself, why is the figure "rather like" a parallelogram. How is it different? Why is the measure of the base πr?

Class Exercises

1. A circle has radius 10 cm. What is its area? Use $\pi \approx 3.14$.

2. A circle has diameter 14 units. What is its area? Use $\pi \approx \frac{22}{7}$.

3. A circle has diameter 6. What is its area? Give your answer in terms of π.

4. A circle has radius 5. What is its area? Give your answer in terms of π.

5. A circle has area 4π cm². What is its radius?

6. A circle has area 9π. What is its diameter?

7. Give a formula for the area of a semicircular region.

8. If a circle has a radius twice as large as another circle, the area of the first circle is __?__ times as great as the area of the second circle.

Written Exercises

Find the area of the circle. Use $\pi \approx 3.14$ and round to three digits.

A **1.** radius = 5 km

2. radius = 8 cm

3. diameter = 1.8

4. diameter = 0.6 m

Find the area of the circle described. Use $\pi \approx \frac{22}{7}$.

5. radius = 14 cm

6. diameter = 28 cm

7. diameter = $3\frac{1}{2}$

8. radius = $2\frac{1}{2}$

Find the area of the circle described. Leave your answer in terms of π.

9. diameter = 20 m

10. radius = 15 cm

11. circumference = 4π

12. circumference = π

Find the radius of a circle having the given area. Use $\pi \approx 3.14$.

13. $A = 78.5$ cm²

14. $A = 314$ m²

Find the diameter of a circle having the given area. Use $\pi \approx \frac{22}{7}$.

15. $A = 154$ km²

16. $A = 3\frac{1}{7}$ cm²

Find the circumference of a circle with the given area in terms of π.

B **17.** $A = 16\pi$

18. $A = 4\pi$

Find the area of the shaded region. Leave your answer in terms of π.

19.

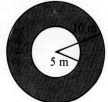

20.

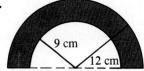

21.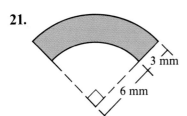

22.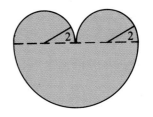

23.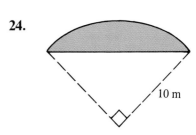

24.

C **25.** Find a formula giving the area of a circle in terms of the diameter.

26. Find a formula giving the area of a circle in terms of the circumference.

Problems

Solve. Draw a sketch illustrating the problem if necessary. Use $\pi \approx 3.14$ and round the area to three digits.

A **1.** A circular lawn 10 m in diameter is to be resodded at a cost of $14 per m². Find the total cost.

2. The Connaught Centre building in Hong Kong has 1748 circular plate glass windows, each 2.4 m in diameter. If glass costs $12 per m², what is the cost of the glass in a single window?

3. The circumference of a circular pond is 62.8 m. If its diameter is 20 m, find the area.

B **4.** A circular pond 20 m in diameter is surrounded by a gravel path 5 m wide. The path is to be replaced by a brick walk costing $30 per square meter. How much will the walk cost?

5. The inner and outer radii of the grooved part of a phonograph record are 7 cm and 14 cm. What is the area of the grooved part?

6. The bull's eye of a target is a circle 20 cm in diameter. It is surrounded by four rings, each 15 cm wide. Find the area of each ring.

7. A 12-inch quiche costs $7, and a 16-inch quiche costs $12. Which is the better buy, assuming that they are equally thick?

8. The inner and outer circumferences of a circular track are 314 m and 330 m. Find the area of the track. (*Hint:* Round the radius to the nearest tenth.)

Hint for Problems 9 and 10: Let the radius of the circle be 1 unit.

C 9. A circle is inscribed in a square. What fraction of the area of the square is taken up by the circle?

10. A square is inscribed in a circle. What fraction of the area of the circle is taken up by the square?

Review Exercises

Estimate to the nearest whole number.

1. $(3.9)^2$ 2. $(5.3)^2$ 3. $(2.72)^2$ 4. $(6.18)^2$

5. 2.7×6 6. 3.1×4.9 7. 3.14×5.3 8. 4.92×5.13

 NONROUTINE PROBLEM SOLVING: *Organizing Data*

Flanders, Fulton, and Farnsworth teach two subjects each in a small junior high school. The courses are mathematics, science, carpentry, music, social studies, and English.

1. The carpentry and music teachers are next-door neighbors.

2. The science teacher is older than the mathematics teacher.

3. The teachers ride together going to school and coming home. Farnsworth, the science teacher, and the music teacher each drive one week out of three.

4. Flanders is the youngest.

5. When they can find another player, the English teacher, the mathematics teacher, and Flanders spend their lunch period playing bridge.

What subjects does each teach?

10-4 Using Symmetry to Find Areas

We say that the figure at the right is **symmetric with respect to a line,** $\overleftrightarrow{AB}$, because if it were folded along $\overleftrightarrow{AB}$, the lower half would fall exactly on the upper half. $\overleftrightarrow{AB}$ is called a **line of symmetry.**

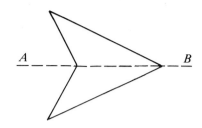

The diagrams below show that figures may have more than one line of symmetry.

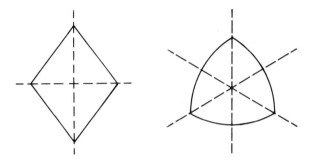

Symmetry can be helpful in finding areas.

EXAMPLE 1 Find the area of the symmetric figure.

Solution The symmetry of this figure is such that the four triangles are congruent. Therefore,

$$A = 4 \times \tfrac{1}{2}bh$$

$$= 4 \times \left(\tfrac{1}{2} \times 7 \times 6\right) = 84$$

Thus, the area is 84 square units.

Figures can also be **symmetric with respect to a point.** Although the figure at the right has no line of symmetry, it is symmetric with respect to point O. A figure is symmetric with respect to a point, O, if for every point P on the figure there corresponds an opposite point Q on the figure such that O is the midpoint of the segment $\overline{PQ}$. Every line through the point of symmetry divides the figure into two congruent figures.

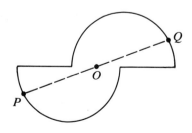

EXAMPLE 2   Find the area of the symmetric figure.

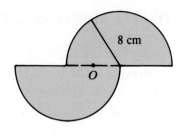

8 cm

Solution   The dashed line divides the region into two semicircles of radius 8 cm.

$$A = 2 \times \left(\frac{1}{2}\pi r^2\right)$$

$$= 2 \times \left(\frac{1}{2}\pi \times 8^2\right)$$

$$\approx 3.14 \times 64 = 200.96$$

The area is approximately 201 cm².

Class Exercises

Copy each figure and show on your drawing any lines or points of symmetry.

1.

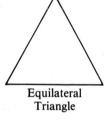

Equilateral Triangle

2.

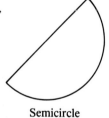

Semicircle

3.

Square

4.

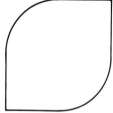

5.

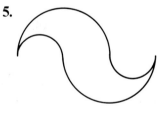

6.

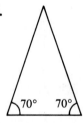

70°   70°

7.

8.

9.

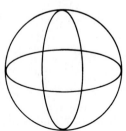

Written Exercises

Copy each figure and show on your drawing any lines or points of symmetry.

A **1.**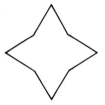

2.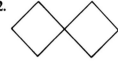

3.

4.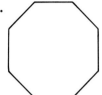

5.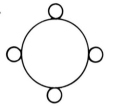

6.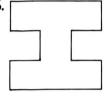

Find the areas of the following symmetric figures. Give your answers in terms of π, if necessary.

7.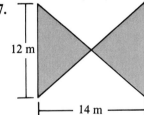

8.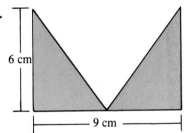

B **9.**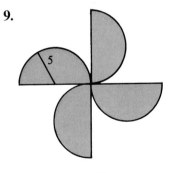

10.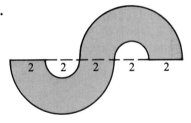

11.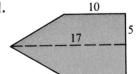

12.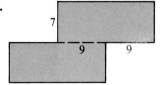

13.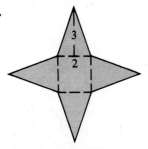

14.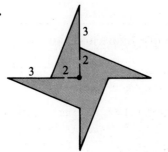

15.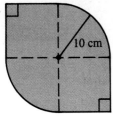

16.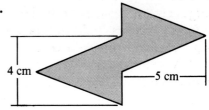

Self-Test A

Find the area. Round to three digits if necessary.

1. rectangle
   length: 21 cm
   width: 13 cm

2. parallelogram
   base: 7 m
   height: 12 m [10-1]

3. triangle
   base: 18 cm
   height: 8 cm

4. trapezoid
   bases: 11 m and 7 m
   height: 4 m [10-2]

5. circle: Use $\pi \approx 3.14$.
   radius: 15 mm

6. circle: Use $\pi \approx \frac{22}{7}$.
   diameter: 28 cm [10-3]

7. Copy the figure and show any lines or points of symmetry. [10-4]

8. Find the area of the symmetric figure.

Self-Test answers and Extra Practice are at the back of the book.

10-5 Polyhedrons

A **polyhedron** is a figure formed of polygonal parts of planes that enclose a region of space.

Among the simplest polyhedrons are **boxes.** The faces of a box are rectangular parts of planes. The faces intersect in segments, called **edges,** and the endpoints of the edges are the **vertices** of the box. Boxes have 6 faces, 12 edges, and 8 vertices. A box having square faces is called a **cube.**

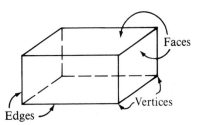

A box is an example of a *prism.* A **prism** is a polyhedron that has two congruent polygonal regions, called **bases,** that are parallel. The other faces are regions bounded by parallelograms. The bases may also be parallelograms.

Prisms are named according to their bases. Thus, a box is a rectangular prism. Some other examples of prisms are shown below.

A triangular prism

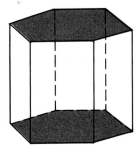

A hexagonal prism

The two polyhedrons below are **pyramids.** The shaded region of each is called the **base** of the pyramid. We name a pyramid by the shape of the polygonal base.

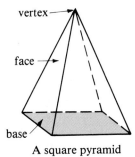

A square pyramid

A triangular pyramid, or tetrahedron

A **regular polyhedron** has all of its faces bounded by congruent, regular polygons. There are only five such polyhedrons: those having 4, 6, 8, 12, and 20 faces.

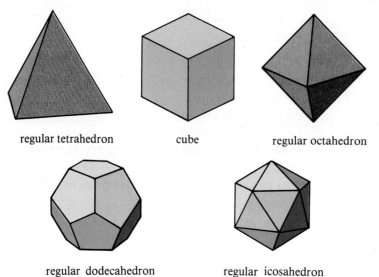

regular tetrahedron   cube   regular octahedron

regular dodecahedron   regular icosahedron

Let F denote the number of faces of a polyhedron, E the number of edges, and V the number of vertices. It is a surprising fact that the following formula is true for all polyhedrons.

$$F + V - E = 2$$

For example, in the case of a box, $F = 6$, $E = 12$, and $V = 8$.

$$F + V - E = 6 + 8 - 12 = 2$$

For a square pyramid, $F = 5$, $E = 8$, and $V = 5$.

$$F + V - E = 5 + 5 - 8 = 2$$

This formula is called *Euler's Formula*. It is named after the famous Swiss mathematician Leonhard Euler (1707–1783), who first proved it.

Class Exercises

Give the most specific name for each polyhedron.

1.

2.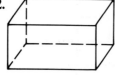

3.

4. 　　**5.** 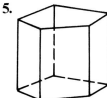　　**6.**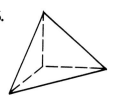

Written Exercises

Make a sketch of each polyhedron.

A　**1.** a pyramid with a trapezoidal base　　**2.** a prism with a trapezoidal base

　　3. a pentagonal prism　　　　　　　　**4.** a pentagonal pyramid

Check the formula $F + V - E = 2$ for each polyhedron.

5. 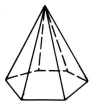　　　　　　　　　　**6.**

7. 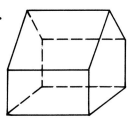　　　　　　　　　　**8.**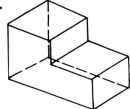

Copy and complete the following table for the regular polyhedrons. (*Hint:* Refer to the diagrams on the previous page to help you count the edges and vertices.)

	F	E	V	$F + V$	$E + 2$
9.	4	?	?	?	?
10.	6	?	?	?	?
11.	8	?	?	?	?
12.	12	?	?	?	?
13.	20	?	?	?	?

In each of Exercises 14–19, some information about a polyhedron is given. Answer the question asked. Use the formula $F + V - E = 2$ in the form $F + V = E + 2$.

EXAMPLE   15 edges, 10 vertices. How many faces?

Solution   Use $E = 15$ and $V = 10$ in the formula $F + V = E + 2$.

$F + 10 = 15 + 2$, or $F + 10 = 17$.

From this we see that $F = 7$.

B **14.** 10 edges, 6 vertices. How many faces?

15. 20 vertices, 30 edges. How many faces?

16. 8 faces, 6 vertices. How many edges?

17. 7 vertices, 7 faces. How many edges?

18. 12 edges, 6 faces. How many vertices?

19. 10 faces, 24 edges. How many vertices?

C **20. a.** Find a relationship between the number of vertices of any pyramid and the number of faces.

   b. Use the result of part (a) to find a relationship between the number of edges of any pyramid and the number of vertices.

Review Exercises

Evaluate each expression using the given values of the variables.

$m^2 n$ **1.** $m = 4$, $n = 1.1$ **2.** $m = 0.5$, $n = 4$

$\left(\frac{1}{2}xy\right)z$ **3.** $x = 22$, $y = 16$, $z = 5$ **4.** $x = 0.25$, $y = 0.40$, $z = 1.9$

$\frac{1}{2}(a + b)c$ **5.** $a = 3$, $b = 1.5$, $c = 2$ **6.** $a = 25$, $b = 16$, $c = 0.75$

CALCULATOR INVESTIGATION: *Square Roots*

If you know the area of a square, you can find the length of a side by taking the square root of the area. Find the length of the side of each square with the following area. Round to the nearest tenth.

   1. 1369   **2.** 841   **3.** 3844   **4.** 3249   **5.** 5184

   6. 9604   **7.** 13,924   **8.** 8412   **9.** 10,562   **10.** 14,256

10-6 Volumes of Prisms

A polyhedron together with the region inside it is called a **solid.** The measure of the space occupied by a solid is called the **volume** of the solid or the volume of the polyhedron.

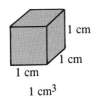

1 cm
1 cm
1 cm
1 cm³

To measure volumes, we need a **unit volume.** A common unit of volume in the metric system is the **cubic centimeter (cm³),** illustrated at the right.

To find the volume of the prism shown at the left below we can count the number of cubic centimeters it contains. We can fill the bottom of the prism with 4×2, or 8 cubes, as shown in the center below. (The figures are slightly reduced in scale.)

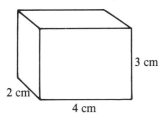
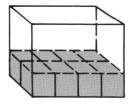
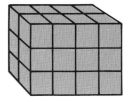

Three layers of cubes will fill the prism. Thus, 8×3, or 24 cubes will fill the prism. The volume is 24 cm³.

The prism above has a base with area 8 cm², and its height is 3 cm. Thus, the volume is the product of the base area and the height. The following formula holds for every prism.

Formula

Volume of prism = Base area $\times$ height

$$V = Bh$$

EXAMPLE Find the volume of the prism.

Solution The bases of the prism are the right triangles. Thus, the base area, B, is $\frac{1}{2} \times 4 \times 5$, or 10 m².

The height, h, is 8 m. Therefore,

$V = Bh = 10 \times 8$, or $V = 80$ m³.

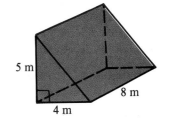

5 m
4 m
8 m

In the example, the unit of volume used was the **cubic meter (m³).** In other cases it might be the **cubic millimeter (mm³)** or some other cubic unit.

Class Exercises

In Exercises 1–6, find the volume of the prism shown or described.

1.

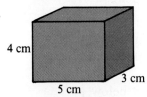

4 cm
3 cm
5 cm

2.

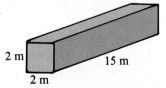

2 m
2 m
15 m

3.

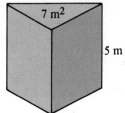

7 m²
5 m

4.

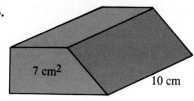

7 cm²
10 cm

5. A box 6 cm long, 2 cm wide, and 5 cm high

6. A box 10 cm long, 5 cm wide, and 5 cm high

Complete.

7. $1 \text{ km} = \underline{\ ?\ } \text{ m}$
$1 \text{ km}^3 = \underline{\ ?\ } \text{ m}^3$

8. $1 \text{ m} = \underline{\ ?\ } \text{ cm}$
$1 \text{ m}^3 = \underline{\ ?\ } \text{ cm}^3$

9. $1 \text{ cm} = \underline{\ ?\ } \text{ mm}$
$1 \text{ cm}^3 = \underline{\ ?\ } \text{ mm}^3$

Written Exercises

Find the volume of each prism.

A **1.**

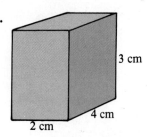

3 cm
4 cm
2 cm

2.

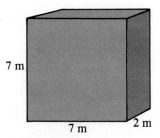

7 m
7 m
2 m

3.

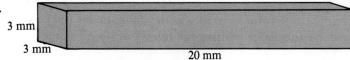

3 mm
3 mm
20 mm

4.

1 m
1 m
8 m

5.

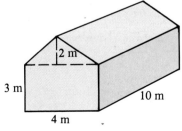

4 cm
8 cm
4.5 cm

6.

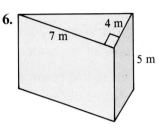

7 m
4 m
5 m

Find the volume of the rectangular prism having the given dimensions.

7. 1.1 cm on each edge

8. 2.1 m on each edge

9. 2 m by 1.5 m by 3 m

10. 5 cm by 12.5 cm by 3 cm

B **11.** One cube has edges twice as long as another cube. What is the ratio of their volumes?

12. The block shown at the right has been painted on all sides and then cut into unit cubes.
  a. How many of the cubes are painted on 3 faces?
  b. How many of the cubes are painted on only 2 faces?
  c. How many of the cubes are painted on only 1 face?
  d. How many of the cubes are unpainted?
  e. Does the sum of your answers to parts (a)–(d) equal the number of cubic units in the volume of the cube?

3 painted faces

2 painted faces

13. A prism has height 5 cm and volume 45 cm³. What is the area of its base?

14. The base of a prism is a 6 cm by 8 cm rectangle, and its volume is 240 cm³. What is its height?

Find the volume of each prism.

15.

2 m
3 m
4 m
10 m

16.

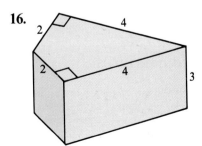

2
2
4
4
3

Problems

Solve.

A 1. A wooden door is 200 cm high, 90 cm wide, and 4 cm thick. Find the volume of the wood in cubic centimeters.

2. A tank at the fish hatchery is 7 m long, 4 m wide, and 2 m deep. Find the volume of the water in the tank when the tank is full.

3. The glass prism shown below is part of a camera's optical system. What is the volume of the glass?

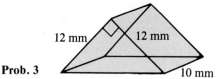

Prob. 3   12 mm   12 mm   10 mm

5 m   2 m   3 m

Prob. 4

4. The trapezoid above is the cross section of an aqueduct. What volume of water is in a ten-meter length of the aqueduct when it is running full?

B 5. The container shown below is empty. If 1200 cm³ of water is poured into it, how deep will the water be?

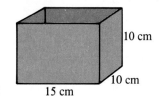

10 cm   10 cm

Prob. 5   15 cm

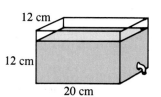

12 cm   12 cm

Prob. 6   20 cm

6. By how much will the depth of the water in the container above decrease if 720 cm³ are drawn off?

C 7. The outside dimensions of an open-topped toolbox are 100 cm by 30 cm by 30 cm. If the wood used to make the rectangular toolbox is 2 cm thick, find the inside volume of the box.

Review Exercises

Solve for x.

1. $24 = 6x$ 2. $0.8 = 2x$ 3. $19x = 9.5$ 4. $(1.1)^2x = 3.63$

5. $x^2 = 144$ 6. $176 = 11x^2$ 7. $\pi x = 28\pi$ 8. $2\pi x^2 = 50\pi$

10-7 Volumes of Cylinders

A **cylinder** is a space figure that has circular bases and one curved surface. The perpendicular distance between the bases is the **height,** h. If the base radius is r, then the base area, B, is πr^2. The volume is given by the following formula.

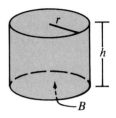

Formula

Volume of cylinder = Base area × height

$$V = Bh \qquad \text{or} \qquad V = \pi r^2 h$$

EXAMPLE 1 Find the volume of a cylinder having a base radius of 6 cm and a height of 8 cm. Use $\pi \approx 3.14$.

Solution *Method 1* Use two formulas: $B = \pi r^2$ and $V = Bh$.

$$B = \pi r^2 = \pi \times 6^2 \approx 3.14 \times 36 \approx 113$$
$$V = Bh \approx 113 \times 8 = 904$$

Method 2 Use one formula: $V = \pi r^2 h$.

$$V = \pi r^2 h \approx 3.14 \times 6^2 \times 8 \approx 904$$

The volume is approximately 904 cm³.

The volume of a cylinder or box is often called its capacity. For containers of liquids, capacity is usually measured in **liters (L)** or **milliliters (mL).**

$$1 \text{ L} = 1000 \text{ cm}^3 \qquad 1 \text{ mL} = 1 \text{ cm}^3$$

EXAMPLE 2 Find the capacity in liters of the water storage tank shown at the right.

Solution The base radius is $80 \div 2$, or 40 cm. The height is 90 cm.

$$V = \pi r^2 h = \pi \times 40^2 \times 90 \approx 3.14 \times 1600 \times 90 = 452{,}160$$
$$V \approx 452{,}160 \div 1000 \approx 452$$

The volume is approximately 452 L.

Certain terms in mathematics may have different meanings than they have in ordinary usage. For example, in everyday language *base* refers to the bottom of an object and *height* refers to how tall an object is. In mathematical usage these terms have special meanings. For instance, in the figure of Example 2, the height is 90 cm (even though it is measured horizontally) and the bases are the circular ends (even though they are on the sides).

Class Exercises

1. Name several common objects that are shaped like cylinders.

2. How many liters are there in one cubic meter?

Complete the statements for each cylinder.

3.

$$B = \pi \times \underline{\ ?\ }^2$$
$$V = \pi \times \underline{\ ?\ }^2 \times \underline{\ ?\ }$$

4.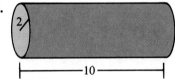

$$B = \pi \times \underline{\ ?\ }^2$$
$$V = \pi \times \underline{\ ?\ }^2 \times \underline{\ ?\ }$$

Find the volume of each cylinder.

5.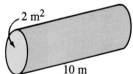

6.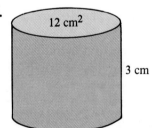

Written Exercises

Find the volume. Use $\pi \approx 3.14$ and round to three digits.

A **1.**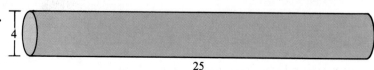

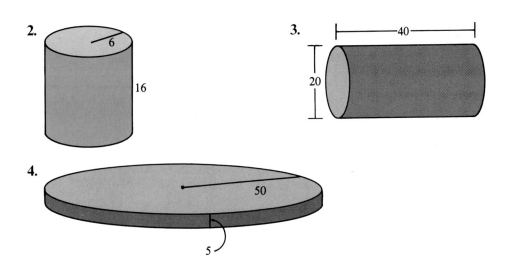

2. 6

16

3. 40

20

4. 50

5

Find the volume of each solid. Leave your answer in terms of π.

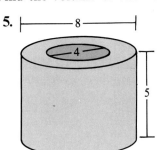

5. 8

4

5

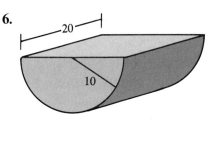

6. 20

10

Find the missing dimension of each cylinder.

7. $V = 36 \text{ cm}^3$, $B = 12 \text{ cm}^2$, $h = \underline{\ ?\ }$

8. $V = 0.8 \text{ mm}^3$, $B = 0.4 \text{ mm}^2$, $h = \underline{\ ?\ }$

9. $V = 24 \text{ m}^3$, $h = 6 \text{ m}$, $B = \underline{\ ?\ }$

10. $V = 15 \text{ m}^3$, $h = 30 \text{ m}$, $B = \underline{\ ?\ }$

11. $V = 100\pi$, $r = 5$, $h = \underline{\ ?\ }$

12. $V = 64\pi$, $r = 4$, $h = \underline{\ ?\ }$

B **13.** $V = 100\pi$, $h = 25$, $r = \underline{\ ?\ }$ **14.** $V = 15\pi$, $h = 15$, $r = \underline{\ ?\ }$

What happens to the volume of a cylinder if its dimensions are changed as indicated?

15. The height is doubled.   **16.** The base radius is doubled.

C **17.** The height is doubled and the base radius is doubled.

Problems

Solve. Use $\pi \approx 3.14$ and round to three digits.

A 1. A fuel tank in a booster rocket is a cylinder 8 m in diameter and 45 m high. Find its volume.

2. A natural gas storage tank is a cylinder 50 m in diameter and 15 m high. How many cubic meters of gas will it hold?

3. A fruit juice can is 14 cm in diameter and 15.6 cm high. Find its capacity in liters.

4. The figure at the right shows the cross section of a circular tunnel. The diameter of the tunnel is 12 m wide. How many cubic meters of dirt must be removed for each kilometer of tunnel?

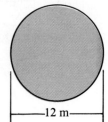

B 5. The tall jar of applesauce sells for $1.49, and the short jar sells for $2.69. Which is the better buy?

6. A coin 22 mm in diameter contains 76 mm³ of metal. How thick is the coin?

7. A cylindrical water bottle is 28 cm in diameter. How much is the water level lowered when 1 L is drawn off?

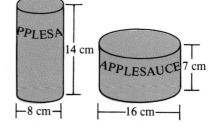

C 8. In order to design air-conditioning machinery for the auditorium shown at the right, an engineer needs to know its volume. How many cubic meters of air does the auditorium contain?

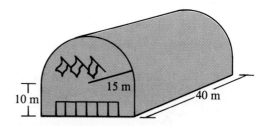

9. A 4 cm slice of watermelon is 24 cm in diameter and has a rind 2 cm thick. What percent of the slice is rind?

Review Exercises

Multiply or divide.

1. 3.2×5.7 2. 6.1×9.6 3. 4.28×3.6 4. 7.41×5.3

5. 0.6×3000 6. 2.5×700 7. $1.25 \div 1000$ 8. $0.87 \div 1000$

10-8 The Mass of an Object

The **mass** of an object is a measure of the amount of material it contains. The drawing illustrates the fact that one lead cube has greater mass than four aluminum cubes of the same size.

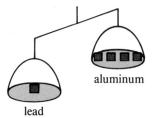

aluminum

lead

In the metric system, the mass of one cubic centimeter of water, under standard conditions, is one **gram (g).** Larger masses are measured in **kilograms (kg)** and **metric tons (t).**

$$1 \text{ kg} = 1000 \text{ g}$$
$$1 \text{ t} = 1000 \text{ kg}$$

The table at the right gives the mass of one cubic centimeter of several materials.

Material	Mass per cm³
aluminum	2.7 g
cork	0.2 g
gold	19.3 g
lead	11.4 g
oak	0.7 g
mercury	13.6 g
steel	7.8 g
water	1.0 g

EXAMPLE An oak plank has dimensions 2.5 cm by 16 cm by 2 m. Find its mass.

Solution An oak plank is a rectangular prism. The volume of the oak plank is

$$2.5 \times 16 \times 200 = 8000.$$

From the table, 1 cm³ of oak has mass 0.7 g. Since the volume of the plank is 8000 cm³, the mass is

$$0.7 \times 8000 = 5600.$$

The mass may also be written as 5600 g or 5.6 kg.

 PROBLEM SOLVING REMINDER

Sometimes *tables must be used* to find information necessary to solve a problem. In the example, the table must be used to find the mass of 1 cm³ of oak.

Class Exercises

Complete.

1. 1 kg = __?__ g

2. 1 t = __?__ kg

3. 1 t = __?__ g

4. 2500 g = __?__ kg

5. 0.8 t = __?__ kg

6. 2700 kg = __?__ t

Areas and Volumes **351**

In Exercises 7–10, use the table given in the lesson to find the mass.

7. 1000 cm³ of cork (g)

8. 1000 cm³ of gold (kg)

9. 2 L of water (kg)

10. 10 L of mercury (kg)

Written Exercises

Complete.

A **1.** $0.87 \text{ t} = \underline{\ ?\ } \text{ kg}$

2. $1.25 \text{ kg} = \underline{\ ?\ } \text{ g}$

3. $950 \text{ g} = \underline{\ ?\ } \text{ kg}$

4. $2500 \text{ kg} = \underline{\ ?\ } \text{ t}$

5. $20 \text{ kg} = \underline{\ ?\ } \text{ t}$

6. $33 \text{ g} = \underline{\ ?\ } \text{ kg}$

Use the table on the preceding page to find the mass of each of the following.

7. 300 cm³ of cork

8. 60 cm³ of lead

9. 5 L of water

10. 5 L of mercury

11. 1 m³ of gold

12. 1 m³ of aluminum

In Exercises 13–16, the solid pictured is made of the specified material. Find its mass. Use $\pi \approx 3.14$ and round to three digits.

B **13.**

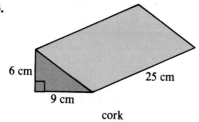

cork

14.

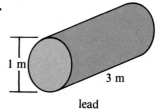

lead

15.

3.5 cm

2 mm

gold

16.

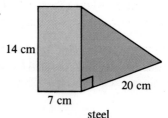

steel

An object placed in a liquid will float if its mass per cubic centimeter is less than the mass per cubic centimeter of the liquid. Use the materials listed in the table given in the lesson to answer each question.

C **17.** Which materials would float on water?

18. Which material would not float on mercury?

Problems

Solve.

A **1.** Find the mass of a gold block 10 cm by 20 cm by 40 cm.

2. A cork plank and an oak plank have the same dimensions. Find the ratio of their masses.

3. Each cubic meter of earth to be removed from the tunnel at the right has mass 2.5 t. What mass of earth must be removed if the tunnel is 5 km long?

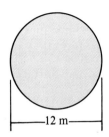
—12 m—

4. Find the mass in grams of the mercury in the jar below.

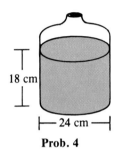

18 cm

—24 cm—

Prob. 4

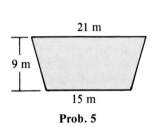

21 m

9 m

15 m

Prob. 5

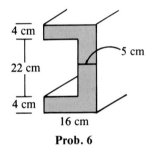

4 cm

22 cm

4 cm

5 cm

16 cm

Prob. 6

B **5.** A cross section of an aqueduct is shown above. How many metric tons of water are in one kilometer of the aqueduct when it is full?

6. A 10 m long steel channel bar has the cross section shown at the right above. Find its mass in metric tons to the nearest tenth.

A floating object displaces a volume of liquid equal to the volume of the object below the surface of the liquid.

C **7.** An oak cube with volume 100 cm³ is placed in water. If 70% of the cube is below the surface, find the mass of the displaced water.

8. A lead block with a volume of 45 cm³ is placed in a container of mercury. If 16% of the lead is above the surface of the mercury, find the mass of the displaced mercury to the nearest gram.

Review Exercises

Evaluate each expression using $a = 10$, $b = 0.5$, $c = 8$, and $d = 1.5$.

1. $2bc$

2. $ab + ac + ad$

3. $3a^2b$

4. $2ab + 2b^2$

5. $2\left(\frac{1}{2}cd\right)$

6. $\frac{1}{4}(ac + bd)$

7. $\frac{1}{3}cd + \frac{1}{5}ab$

8. $\frac{1}{6}(abcd)$

10-9 Surface Area

If one can of paint will cover 25 m², is one can enough to paint the outside of the box shown at the right? To answer this question we must calculate the **surface area** of the box, that is, the sum of the areas of its six faces.

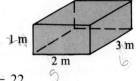

$$\text{Surface area} = 2(1 \times 2) + 2(2 \times 3) + 2(1 \times 3) = 22$$

Since the surface area is 22 m², one can of paint is enough to paint the box (with a little left over).

As we know, each prism or cylinder has two bases. The remainder of the prism or cylinder is called its **lateral surface.**

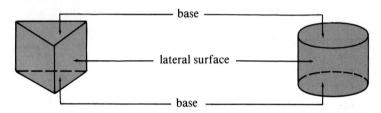

In this section we shall consider only **right prisms:** those in which all faces that are not bases are rectangles.

EXAMPLE 1 Find (a) the lateral area and (b) the total surface area of the right prism shown.

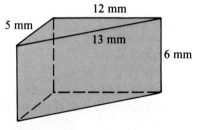

Solution
    a. The lateral surface consists of three rectangles.

$$\text{lateral surface area} = (6 \times 5) + (6 \times 12) + (6 \times 13)$$
$$= 180$$

    b. To obtain the total surface area, add the areas of the two triangular bases to the lateral surface area.

$$\text{total surface area} = 180 + 2\left(\frac{1}{2} \times 5 \times 12\right) = 180 + 60$$

$$= 240$$

Shown at the left at the top of the next page is a cylinder with base radius, r, and height, h. In the second drawing, the bases have been removed. The third drawing shows the circular bases and the lateral area, which has been unrolled into a rectangle. The length of this rectangle is equal to the circumference of a circular base, $2\pi r$.

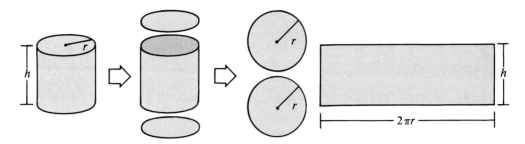

The drawings show us that we can calculate surface area for cylinders by using the following formula.

> ### Formula
>
> For any cylinder:
>
> lateral surface area $= 2\pi rh$
> total surface area $= 2\pi rh + 2\pi r^2$

EXAMPLE 2 For the cylinder shown at the right, find (a) the lateral surface area, (b) the total surface area, and (c) the volume. Use $\pi \approx 3.14$.

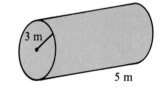

Solution

a. lateral surface area $= 2\pi rh \approx 2 \times 3.14 \times 3 \times 5 = 94.2$

b. total surface area $= 2\pi rh + 2\pi r^2 \approx 94.2 + 2 \times 3.14 \times 3^2$
≈ 151

c. volume $= \pi r^2 h \approx 3.14 \times 3^2 \times 5 \approx 141$

Class Exercises

1. Each face of a cube has area 10 cm². What is the total surface area?

2. Find the total surface area of a cube whose edge is 2 m long.

3. A box 2 m high has square bases 1 m on each edge. Find its total surface area.

4. The bases of a right prism 10 cm high are equilateral triangles 1 cm on each edge. Find the lateral surface area of the prism.

5. The lateral area of a right prism equals the perimeter of the ___?___ times the ___?___.

Written Exercises

Find the total surface area of each box having the given dimensions.

A **1.** 5 cm by 5 cm by 5 cm   **2.** 1.2 m by 1.2 m by 1.2 m

   3. 2 m by 5 m by 6 m   **4.** 10 mm by 15 mm by 20 mm

In Exercises 5–10, find the (a) lateral surface area, (b) total surface area, and (c) volume of the right prism or cylinder. Use $\pi \approx 3.14$ and round to three digits.

5.

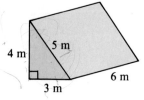

6.

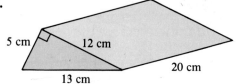

7.

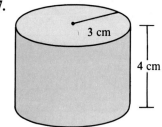

8.

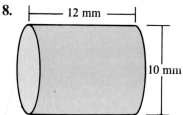

9.

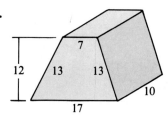

10.

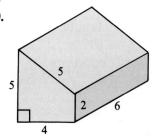

In Exercises 11–14, find the total surface area. Use $\pi \approx 3.14$ and round answer to three digits. (Do not forget the hidden parts.)

B **11.**

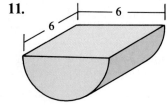

12.

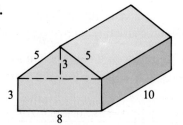

C 13.

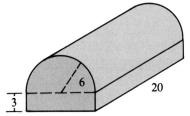

14.

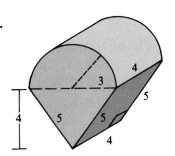

Self-Test B

Make a sketch of each polyhedron.

1. rectangular pyramid   **2.** hexagonal prism   [10-5]

Find the volume. Use $\pi \approx 3.14$ and round to three digits.

3.

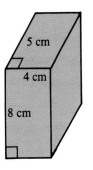

4.

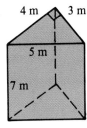

[10-6]

5.

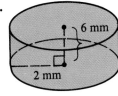

6.

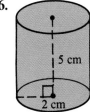

[10-7]

Use the table on page 351 to find the mass of the following.

7. 850 cm³ of steel   **8.** 345 cm³ of cork   [10-8]

9. Find the total surface area of the prism in Exercise 4.   [10-9]

10. Find the total surface area of the cylinder in Exercise 6. Use $\pi \approx 3.14$ and round to three digits.

Self-Test answers and Extra Practice are at the back of the book.

The Pythagorean Theorem

Look at the diagram at the right. Notice that the longest side, or **hypotenuse,** is 5 units long. The other two sides have lengths 3 units and 4 units long. If you square each length, you will find that

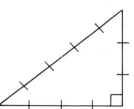

$$5^2 = 3^2 + 4^2 \qquad \text{or} \qquad 25 = 9 + 16.$$

Thus, *the square of the length of the hypotenuse equals the sum of the squares of the lengths of the other two sides.*

    It was over 2500 years ago that the Greek philosopher Pythagoras showed that every right triangle has the property stated above. Thus, for any right triangle with an hypotenuse of length c and sides of lengths a and b, we have $c^2 = a^2 + b^2$. This equation is called the **Pythagorean theorem.**

    To see why the equation $c^2 = a^2 + b^2$ is true, look at the diagrams below. In each diagram four copies of the triangle, shown in blue, have been placed in a square $(a + b)$ units on a side.

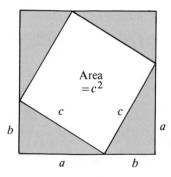

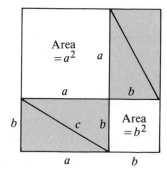

Can you explain why the area of the white region in the left-hand diagram must equal the area of the white regions in the right-hand diagram? From this fact you can see that $c^2 = a^2 + b^2$.

The Pythagorean theorem has many uses. For example, to find the length, a, of a pond, a surveyor marks a point P to form a right triangle as shown at the right. She then measures the lengths b and c and finds that $b = 24$ m and $c = 25$ m. She now uses the Pythagorean theorem.

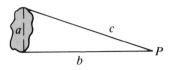

$$c^2 = a^2 + b^2$$
$$25^2 = a^2 + 24^2$$
$$625 = a^2 + 576$$
$$625 - 576 = a^2$$
$$49 = a^2$$
$$7 = a$$

Thus, the pond is 7 m long.

In Exercises 1–10, c is the length of the hypotenuse of a right triangle and a and b are the lengths of the other two sides. Find the missing length.

1. $a = 8$, $b = 6$, $c = $ _?_

2. $a = 7$, $b = 24$, $c = $ _?_

3. $a = 5$, $c = 13$, $b = $ _?_

4. $a = 60$, $c = 100$, $b = $ _?_

5. $b = 15$, $c = 17$, $a = $ _?_

6. $a = 21$, $c = 35$, $b = $ _?_

7. $a = 10$, $b = 24$, $c = $ _?_

8. $b = 60$, $c = 65$, $a = $ _?_

9. $b = 30$, $c = 34$, $a = $ _?_

10. $a = 14$, $b = 48$, $c = $ _?_

11. A television tower is to be braced by a cable reaching from a point 24 m up the tower to a point 18 m from its base. How long must the cable be?

12. How high up a building will a 13-foot ladder reach if its bottom end is 5 ft from the base of the building?

13. A rope is attached to the top of a flagpole. If the rope is 17 ft long and touches the ground 8 ft from the base of the pole, how high is the flagpole?

Research Activity: Reading about Mathematics

Find out more about the history of the Pythagorean theorem.

Chapter Review

Write the letter of the correct answer.

1. A rectangle has a length of 17 cm and a width of 5 cm. Find the area. [10–1]
   a. 44 cm²   **b.** 85 cm²   **c.** 42.5 cm²   **d.** 22 cm²

2. A parallelogram has a base of 16 m and a height of 4 m. Find the area.
   a. 32 m²   **b.** 40 m²   **c.** 20 m²   **d.** 64 m²

3. A triangle has a base of 14 m and a height of 10 m. Find the area. [10–2]
   a. 140 m²   **b.** 34 m²   **c.** 70 m²   **d.** 35 m²

4. A trapezoid has bases of 9 cm and 15 cm and a height of 6 cm. Find the area.
   a. 72 cm²   **b.** 144 cm²   **c.** 810 cm²   **d.** 189 cm²

5. A circle has a diameter of 18 cm. Find the area. Use $\pi \approx 3.14$. [10–3]
   a. 28.3 cm²   **b.** 1020 cm²   **c.** 56.5 cm²   **d.** 254 cm²

Complete.

6. Figures may be symmetric with respect to a __?__ or a __?__. [10–4]

7. A polyhedron with two parallel bases is a __?__ and a polyhedron with one base is a __?__. [10–5]

8. $F + V - E = $ __?__.

True or false?

9. The volume of a rectangular prism with dimensions 4 cm by 5 cm by 9 cm is 160 cm³. [10–6]

10. The volume of a triangular prism with a base area of 15 cm² and a height of 10 cm is 75 cm³.

11. The volume of a cylinder with a diameter of 10 m and a height of 20 m is 200 m³. [10–7]

12. If the mass of 1 cm³ of gold is 19.3 g, the mass of 1000 cm³ of gold is 19.3 kg. [10–8]

13. The lateral surface area of a cylinder is greater than the total surface area. [10–9]

14. The total surface area of a rectangular prism with dimensions 8 cm by 5 cm by 3 cm is 158 cm².

Chapter Test

Find the area. Use $\pi \approx 3.14$ and round to three digits.

1. rectangle
   length: 14 m
   width: 9 m

2. parallelogram
   base: 23 cm
   height: 11 cm

[10–1]

3. triangle
   base: 9 mm
   height: 16 mm

4. trapezoid
   bases: 8 m and 14 m
   height: 7 m

[10–2]

5. circle:
   radius: 17 mm

6. circle:
   diameter: 42 cm

[10–3]

7. Copy the figure at the right and show any lines
   or points of symmetry.

8. Find the area of the symmetric figure.

[10–4]

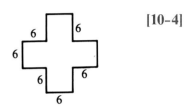

Make a sketch of each polyhedron.

9. tetrahedron

10. square prism

[10–5]

Find the volume. Use $\pi \approx 3.14$ and round to three digits.

11.

$h = 3$
$w = 2$
$l = 5$

12.

2 cm
$h = 5$ cm
2 cm
4 cm

[10–6]

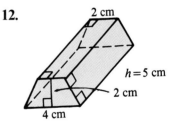

13.

12 cm
4 cm

14.

6
6

[10–7]

Use the table on page 351 to find the mass of the following.

15. 350 cm³ of lead

16. 3 L of mercury

[10–8]

17. Find the total surface area of the prism in Exercise 11.

[10–9]

18. Find the total surface area of the cylinder in Exercise 13.

Cumulative Review (Chapters 1–10)
Exercises

Perform the indicated operations.

1. $36 \times 14 \div 4$

2. $(88 + 79)7$

3. $(137 - 21) \div 4$

4. $0.39 \times 4.2 \times 5$

5. $15.2 \div 3.8 \times 1.06$

6. $25.5 \div 1.7 \div 0.05$

7. $(2.48 + 4.92)1.1$

8. $(7.021 - 1.021)0.21$

9. $(2.879 + 5.249) \div 2.54$

10. $\frac{1}{8} + \frac{3}{10} + \frac{13}{20}$

11. $\frac{49}{50} - \frac{2}{5} - \frac{1}{2}$

12. $6\frac{2}{3} - 2\frac{1}{4} + 1\frac{5}{8}$

13. $\frac{11}{7} \times \frac{42}{33} \times \frac{5}{2}$

14. $3\frac{1}{8} \times 2\frac{2}{3} \times 1\frac{1}{2}$

15. $\frac{27}{16} \times \frac{10}{39} \div \frac{3}{13}$

Evaluate the following for $x = 0.24$, $y = 15$, and $z = 3$.

16. $xy + yz$

17. xy^2

18. $4xyz$

19. z^2x

20. $2xyz + y^2z$

21. $2(x + y) + z^2$

Find the area. Use $\pi \approx 3.14$ and round to three digits.

22. square
    side: 14 cm

23. circle
    radius: 3.5 ft

24. rectangle
    length: 18 mm
    width: 11 mm

25. trapezoid
    bases: 30 m, 46 m
    height: 12 m

Solve.

26. $7x = 266$

27. $y - 106 = 29$

28. $4a - 59 = 33$

29. $3c + 71 = 173$

30. $r + 2.463 = 8.401$

31. $3.21x = 21.507$

32. $0.31z - 4.09 = 1.6512$

33. $2.4y + 3.79 = 19.534$

34. $\frac{2}{3}r - \frac{5}{12} = \frac{7}{8}$

35. $\frac{5}{9}c + \frac{3}{4} = \frac{81}{10}$

36. 42% of 125 is what number?

37. 2.5% of 32 is what number?

38. 48 is 6% of what number?

39. 39 is what percent of 52?

40. 3 is what percent of 120?

41. 17 is 20% of what number?

Problems

PROBLEM SOLVING REMINDERS

Here are some reminders that may help you solve some of the problems on this page.
- Consider whether drawing a sketch will help.
- Determine which facts are necessary to solve the problem.
- Determine whether more than one operation is needed.

1. A fence is to be built around a field that has the shape of an isosceles trapezoid. The shorter base of the trapezoid is 39 m. The longer base is 1.5 times as long as the shorter base. Each congruent side is 18.6 m long. Find the perimeter of the field.

2. Sally bought a tennis racquet for $42. She also bought 4 cans of tennis balls at $3.50 a can. If the sales tax is 7%, how much did Sally pay altogether?

3. A plane travels at a speed of 450 mph at a height of 36,000 ft. How long will it take the plane to make a flight of 2362.5 miles?

4. The population of Meridia was about 34,000 in 1970 and 28,000 in 1980. Find the percent of decrease to the nearest tenth.

5. Burt can lift 180 lb on the weight machine. Erny can lift only $\frac{4}{5}$ as much. How much weight can Erny lift?

6. A pentagon has a perimeter of 317 cm. One side has a length of 27 cm and a second has a length of 53 cm. If the other sides are congruent, find the length of each.

7. Elenore bought 12 pencils at $.18 each, 5 pads at $.79 each, a pen for $2.95, and 2 typewriter ribbons at $4.50 each. She paid for these items with a $20 bill. What was her change?

8. Sixteen more than 3 times a number is 139. Find the number.

9. A drawing has a scale of 2 cm: 1.25 m. Find the actual perimeter of a rectangle in the drawing with sides of 7 cm and 11 cm.

10. Darlene deposited $4500 in a special account that pays 8% interest compounded quarterly. How much interest will she receive after 1 year on that deposit?

11 Integers and Graphs

APPLYING MATHEMATICS
LIGHTNING

Lightning is a dramatic, electrical reaction that is usually associated with thunderclouds. It occurs as a result of a sudden, powerful exchange between the positive and negative centers within a cloud, between several clouds, or between a cloud, the air, and the ground. The long flash of light we see is part of the interaction. The positive and negative charges move through the atmosphere so rapidly that a tremendous amount of heat is generated, which warms up the surrounding air so quickly that a thunderous explosion results. In this chapter you will examine operations and equations with both positive and negative numbers as well as the graphs of such numbers in the coordinate plane.

CAREER CONNECTION

GEOLOGIST

Earthquakes are similar to lightning in that they are sudden, dramatic natural events. Geologists study earthquakes as part of their study of the earth. By studying the structure and history of the rocks beneath the earth's surface, geologists may be able to predict future earthquakes. Geologists can also specialize in locating oil and other raw materials.

Photo: A burst of lightning connects ground and clouds.

11-1 Negative Numbers

A weather thermometer indicates temperatures below 0° by *negative* numbers. During a rocket launch, time before ignition is regarded as negative. On a horizontal number line we use **negative numbers** for the coordinates of points to the left of 0.

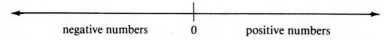

negative numbers   0   positive numbers

We denote the number called *negative four* by the symbol ⁻4. The graphs of ⁻4 and 4 are the same distance from 0, but in opposite directions. We call such a pair of numbers **opposites.** Thus,

⁻4 is the opposite of 4, and 4 is the opposite of ⁻4.

The opposite of 0 is 0.
The diagram below shows the graphs of several pairs of opposites.

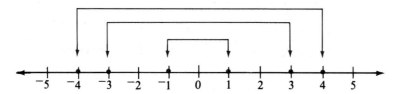

The distance from 0 to the graph of a number is called the **absolute value** of the number. Thus, 4 and ⁻4 have the same absolute value, namely 4. The symbol for the absolute value of a number, n, is $|n|$. We write $|4| = 4$ or $|⁻4| = 4$. The absolute value of 0 is 0.
The counting numbers

1, 2, 3, 4, 5, . . .

are the **positive integers,** while

⁻1, ⁻2, ⁻3, ⁻4, ⁻5, . . .

are the **negative integers.** The positive integers, the negative integers, and 0 make up the set of **integers.** The integer 0 is neither positive nor negative.
The farther we go to the *right* on the number line the *greater* the numbers become. Thus, we can compare two integers by looking at their positions on a number line.

EXAMPLE 1   Replace each __?__ with < or >.

         a. ⁻5 __?__ ⁻2   **b.** ⁻3 __?__ 2   **c.** 0 __?__ ⁻1

Solution

Use the number line shown on the previous page.

  a. ⁻5 is to the left of ⁻2.   ⁻5 < ⁻2
  b. ⁻3 is to the left of 2.   ⁻3 < 2
  c. 0 is to the right of ⁻1.   0 > ⁻1

We have been representing integers by their **graphs,** that is, by points on a number line. Another way to represent integers is with arrows, as illustrated below.

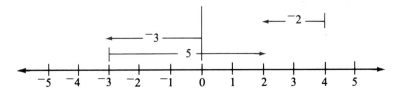

Notice that when an arrow represents a negative number, it points to the *left.*

EXAMPLE 2 Use an arrow diagram to represent each integer described.

  a. 3, starting at 0   **b.** 3, starting at ⁻1

  c. ⁻3, starting at 0   **d.** ⁻3, starting at 2

Solution   **a.**
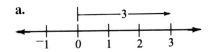

b.
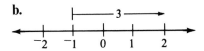

c.
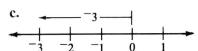

d.
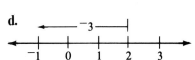

Class Exercises

Name the opposite of each integer.

  1. 7   **2.** 5   **3.** 3   **4.** ⁻9   **5.** ⁻11   **6.** ⁻3

Give the absolute value of each integer.

  7. 22   **8.** 31   **9.** 0   **10.** 14   **11.** ⁻91   **12.** ⁻82

Replace each __?__ with < or >.

  13. ⁻3 __?__ 1   **14.** ⁻6 __?__ ⁻8   **15.** 0 __?__ ⁻5   **16.** 5 __?__ ⁻2

Replace each __?__ with the integer that the arrow represents.

17.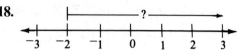

18.

Written Exercises

Graph the integers in each exercise on the same number line.

A   **1.** ⁻2, 0, 3   **2.** ⁻2, ⁻1, 0   **3.** ⁻4, ⁻3, ⁻2

    4. ⁻1, 0, 1   **5.** ⁻4, ⁻2, 0, 2   **6.** ⁻6, ⁻3, 0, 3

Graph the given integer and its opposite on the same number line.

    7. 5   **8.** ⁻2   **9.** ⁻3   **10.** 7   **11.** 1   **12.** ⁻8

13–18. Give the absolute value of each integer in Exercises 7–12.

Use an arrow diagram to represent each integer described.

    19. ⁻3, starting at 0   **20.** 5, starting at 0

    21. 3, starting at ⁻2   **22.** ⁻4, starting at 1

    23. ⁻5, starting at 5   **24.** 3, starting at ⁻3

In Exercises 25–39, (a) list the integers that can replace x to make a true statement and (b) graph the integers on a number line.

EXAMPLE   ⁻3 < x < 2

Solution   ⁻3 < x < 2 means that x is between ⁻3 and 2.

           a. ⁻2, ⁻1, 0, 1   **b.**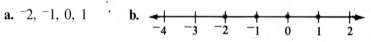

B   **25.** ⁻2 < x < 3   **26.** ⁻1 < x < 5   **27.** ⁻4 < x < 0

    28. ⁻3 < x < ⁻1   **29.** ⁻1 < x < 1   **30.** ⁻5 < x < 1

    31. ⁻5 < x < ⁻2   **32.** ⁻3 < x < 4   **33.** ⁻1 < x < 6

    34. ⁻6 < x < 0   **35.** 0 < x < 5   **36.** ⁻7 < x < ⁻1

    37. ⁻2 < x < 2   **38.** ⁻11 < x < ⁻7   **39.** ⁻8 < x < 2

Replace each __?__ by *positive* or *negative* to make a true statement.

C **40.** The opposite of a __?__ number is positive.

41. Zero is greater than every __?__ number.

42. If $x < 0$, then x is __?__.

43. Every __?__ integer is less than every __?__ integer.

Review Exercises

Find the sum using mental arithmetic. Use paper and pencil to check.

1. $9 + 42 + 51$ | **2.** $13 + 47 + 36$ | **3.** $119 + 17 + 81$

4. $17 + 48 + 21 + 83$ | **5.** $111 + 39 + 85 + 65$ | **6.** $31 + 67 + 126 + 83$

7. $31 + 74 + 49 + 61$ | **8.** $92 + 117 + 78 + 63$ | **9.** $153 + 254 + 97 + 195$

■ ■ ■ **COMPUTER INVESTIGATION:** *Patterns*

Simplify.

1. a. $(3 + 4)2$ **b.** $(3 \times 4) + 2$

2. a. $(5 + 6)3$ **b.** $(5 \times 6) + 3$

3. a. $(4 + 9)3$ **b.** $(4 \times 9) + 3$

4. a. $(7 + 8)4$ **b.** $(7 \times 8) + 4$

5. What pattern do you see in Exercises 1–4?

6. Find an example where this pattern does not work.

A computer can be used to find other examples. The following program in BASIC will check numbers from 1 to 15 and print out all groups of three numbers for which the pattern holds.

```
10   FOR A = 1 TO 15
20   FOR B = 1 TO 15
30   FOR C = 1 TO 15
40   IF A * B + C < > (A + B) * C THEN 60
50   PRINT A;",";B;",";C;";"    ";
60   NEXT C
70   NEXT B
80   NEXT A
90   END
```

11-2 Adding Integers

We can use arrows to add whole numbers as illustrated at the left below. We represent the numbers being added by solid arrows. We start at 0 and draw an arrow pointing to the right to represent the first number, 2. From the tip of this arrow we draw a second arrow to represent the other number to be added, 5. The dashed arrow represents the sum.

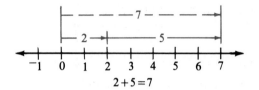

$$2+5=7$$

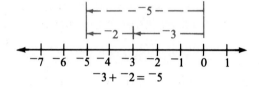

$$^-3 + ^-2 = ^-5$$

We can use arrows as well when the numbers being added are negative. The diagram at the right above illustrates the addition of two negative numbers. Note that we start at 0 and represent negative numbers by arrows pointing to the left.

Rules

The sum of two positive integers is a positive integer.

The sum of two negative integers is a negative integer.

When one number is positive and the other negative, the sum may be positive, negative, or zero. These possibilities are illustrated below and on the following page.

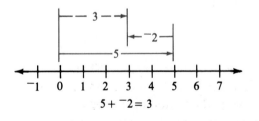

$$5 + ^-2 = 3$$

The positive number 5 has a greater absolute value than the negative number $^-2$. Therefore, the sum is positive.

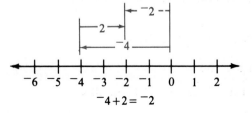

$$^-4 + 2 = ^-2$$

The negative number $^-4$ has a greater absolute value than the positive number 2. Therefore, the sum is negative.

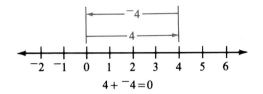

4 + ⁻4 = 0

The positive number 4 and the negative number ⁻4 have the same absolute value. Therefore, the sum is zero.

Rules

The sum of a positive integer and a negative integer is:
1. Positive if the positive number has the greater absolute value.
2. Negative if the negative number has the greater absolute value.
3. Zero if both numbers have the same absolute value.

When adding integers, you may wish to use an arrow diagram.

EXAMPLE 1 Use an arrow diagram to find each sum.

a. 7 + ⁻4   **b.** ⁻7 + 4

Solution

a.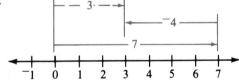

$$7 + {}^-4 = 3$$

b.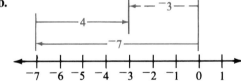

$${}^-7 + 4 = {}^-3$$

All the properties of whole numbers also hold for integers. When adding more than two integers, we may rearrange and group them in any way we wish by applying the associative and commutative properties. For example, we may group the numbers that give us sums of zero or tens.

$$^-4 + 27 + 4 + {}^-7 = ({}^-4 + 4) + (27 + {}^-7) = 0 + 20 = 20$$

Or we may group the positive numbers together.

$$^-4 + 27 + 4 + {}^-7 = (27 + 4) + ({}^-4 + {}^-7) = 31 + {}^-11 = 20$$

EXAMPLE 2 Jenny Chung started a checking account with $500. She later wrote a check for $150, made a deposit of $220, and wrote another check for $170. How much money was left in Jenny's account?

Solution Express the given data as a sum of integers.

$$500 + {}^-150 + 220 + {}^-170 = 400$$

The amount left in Jenny's account was $400.

COMMUNICATION IN MATHEMATICS: *Study Skills*

When you read mathematical rules, think of numerical examples to check your understanding.

Class Exercises

For each arrow diagram (a) state the integer that is represented by each arrow (starting with the bottom arrow), and (b) state the addition fact the diagram represents.

1.

2.

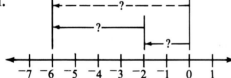

3.

4.
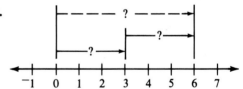

5.

6.
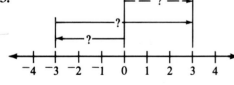

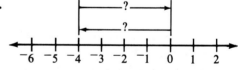

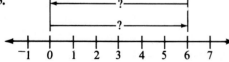

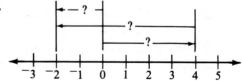

Find each sum. Use a number line if you need it.

7. $^-6 + 5$ **8.** $5 + {}^-6$ **9.** $4 + {}^-7$ **10.** $^-2 + {}^-5$

11. $^-7 + 7$ **12.** $^-4 + 6$ **13.** $9 + {}^-9$ **14.** $^-4 + {}^-8$

Written Exercises

Draw an arrow diagram to represent each sum.

A **1.** ⁻3 + ⁻2   **2.** 3 + ⁻3   **3.** ⁻6 + 6   **4.** ⁻4 + ⁻1

5. 6 + ⁻2   **6.** ⁻6 + 1   **7.** 3 + ⁻7   **8.** 7 + ⁻4

Find each sum.

9. 7 + ⁻10   **10.** ⁻9 + 6   **11.** ⁻8 + 13   **12.** 12 + ⁻3

13. ⁻10 + ⁻15   **14.** ⁻8 + 7   **15.** 20 + ⁻1   **16.** ⁻8 + ⁻7

17. a. ⁻2 + (3 + ⁻6)   **b.** (⁻2 + 3) + ⁻6

18. a. 6 + (⁻8 + 5)   **b.** (6 + ⁻8) + 5

19. a. (⁻4 + ⁻3) + 3   **b.** ⁻4 + (⁻3 + 3)

20. a. (⁻8 + 5) + ⁻5   **b.** ⁻8 + (5 + ⁻5)

B **21.** 9 + 18 + ⁻9 + ⁻17   **22.** 8 + ⁻10 + 11 + ⁻8

23. ⁻11 + 18 + ⁻10 + 11   **24.** ⁻14 + ⁻7 + 4 + 7

25. ⁻3 + ⁻2 + ⁻6 + 10   **26.** 9 + ⁻5 + 8 + ⁻7

True or false?

27. If the sum of two integers is positive, then at least one of the integers must be positive.

28. If the sum of two integers is negative, then at least one of the integers must be negative.

Exercises 29–34 refer to the addition table at the right. Notice that the sum 3 can be found in six ways in the table: 4 + ⁻1, 3 + 0, 2 + 1, 1 + 2, 0 + 3, and ⁻1 + 4. In how many ways can each of the following sums be found in the table?

29. 2   **30.** 6   **31.** ⁻3

32. ⁻2   **33.** ⁻1   **34.** 4

First number

0	1	2	3	4	4	5	6	7	8
⁻1	0	1	2	3	3	4	5	6	7
⁻2	⁻1	0	1	2	2	3	4	5	6
⁻3	⁻2	⁻1	0	1	1	2	3	4	5
⁻4	⁻3	⁻2	⁻1	0	0	1	2	3	4
⁻4	⁻3	⁻2	⁻1	+	0	1	2	3	4
⁻5	⁻4	⁻3	⁻2	⁻1	⁻1	0	1	2	3
⁻6	⁻5	⁻4	⁻3	⁻2	⁻2	⁻1	0	1	2
⁻7	⁻6	⁻5	⁻4	⁻3	⁻3	⁻2	⁻1	0	1
⁻8	⁻7	⁻6	⁻5	⁻4	⁻4	⁻3	⁻2	⁻1	0

Second number

Problems

Solve each problem by first expressing the given data as a sum of integers. Then, compute the sum of the integers and answer the question.

A
1. The elevation of Bad Water in Death Valley is 282 ft below sea level. If a helicopter starts from Bad Water and rises vertically for 1200 ft, how far above sea level is it?

2. An elevator starts at the 12th floor, goes down 7 floors and then up 15 floors. At what floor is it then?

3. Between noon and 1 P.M. the temperature rose 3°C from a reading of 25°C. Between 1 P.M. and 2 P.M. it fell 8°, and between 2 P.M. and 3 P.M. it fell 12°. What was the temperature at 3 P.M.?

4. A diving bell was lowered from a research ship to a depth of 1500 m. It was then raised 650 m and later lowered 1250 m to the ocean bottom. How deep is the ocean at the point where the diving bell was lowered?

5. Stock in the QED Corporation was issued at the end of 1981 at $100 per share. In the next three years it went up $21 per share, down $15, and up $3. What was the price of QED at the end of 1984?

B
6. Fred Wilson's bank permits an overdraft of up to $50 before it returns a check because of insufficient funds. Fred had $85 in his account. He deposited $45 more. Then he wrote checks for $15, $68, and $76. Did Fred have enough money in his account to cover these checks? If not, did his bank return any of these checks because of insufficient funds? Give reasons for your answers.

7. A ship set sail from Hawaii, whose latitude is 20°N. The ship sailed 15°S, then 8°N, then 59°S. What was the latitude of the ship at that point?

Review Exercises

Simplify.

1. the opposite of ⁻17

2. the opposite of 62

3. 9 + (the opposite of 9)

4. 12 + (the opposite of 7)

5. 18 + (the opposite of ⁻6)

6. ⁻75 + (the opposite of ⁻25)

7. ⁻47 + (the opposite of 31)

8. 66 + (the opposite of ⁻38)

11-3 Subtracting Integers

You know that $5 - 2 = 3$. You learned in the previous lesson that $5 + {}^-2 = 3$. We see that subtracting 2 gives the same result as adding the opposite of 2. In general, to subtract an integer, add its opposite.

> ## Rule
>
> For all integers a and b,
> $$a - b = a + (\text{opposite of } b).$$

EXAMPLE 1   Find each difference.

   a. $5 - {}^-2$ **b.** $2 - 5$ **c.** ${}^-2 - {}^-5$ **d.** ${}^-2 - 5$

Solution   Express as a sum according to the rules of the previous section.

   a. $5 - {}^-2 = 5 + (\text{opposite of } {}^-2) = 5 + 2 = 7$

   b. $2 - 5 = 2 + (\text{opposite of } 5) = 2 + {}^-5 = {}^-3$

   c. ${}^-2 - {}^-5 = {}^-2 + (\text{opposite of } {}^-5) = {}^-2 + 5 = 3$

   d. ${}^-2 - 5 = {}^-2 + (\text{opposite of } 5) = {}^-2 + {}^-5 = {}^-7$

EXAMPLE 2   A submarine is at a depth of 28 m. The submarine then dives 114 m. Find the new depth.

Solution   Express the given data as a difference of integers.

   $${}^-28 - 114 = {}^-28 + (\text{opposite of } 114) = {}^-28 + {}^-114 = {}^-142$$

   The new depth of the submarine is 142 m.

Class Exercises

Replace each _?_ to make a true statement.

1. $5 - {}^-7 = 5 + \underline{}$ **2.** ${}^-6 - 4 = {}^-6 + \underline{}$ **3.** ${}^-5 - {}^-8 = {}^-5 + \underline{}$

4. $4 - {}^-4 = 4 + \underline{}$ **5.** $1 - 5 = 1 + \underline{}$ **6.** ${}^-6 - {}^-7 = {}^-6 + \underline{}$

Find each difference.

7. $4 - 6$ **8.** ${}^-4 - {}^-7$ **9.** ${}^-3 - {}^-8$ **10.** $7 - 15$

11. $8 - {}^-2$ **12.** $5 - {}^-5$ **13.** ${}^-7 - 2$ **14.** ${}^-6 - {}^-6$

Written Exercises

Find each difference.

A
1. $6 - 10$
2. $^-4 - 5$
3. $^-8 - {}^-13$
4. $20 - 25$
5. $5 - {}^-10$
6. $12 - {}^-10$
7. $^-15 - 10$
8. $^-17 - {}^-8$
9. $0 - {}^-18$
10. $^-37 - 37$
11. $13 - 52$
12. $^-64 - {}^-32$
13. $39 - {}^-13$
14. $^-120 - 40$
15. $^-125 - {}^-75$
16. $462 - {}^-36$
17. $123 - {}^-321$
18. $1492 - 1776$

Simplify.

B
19. **a.** $(7 - {}^-18) - 20$ **b.** $7 - ({}^-18 - 20)$
20. **a.** $(^-14 - {}^-8) - 10$ **b.** $^-14 - ({}^-8 - 10)$
21. **a.** $(12 - {}^-4) - {}^-4$ **b.** $12 - ({}^-4 - {}^-4)$
22. **a.** $(^-8 - 10) - {}^-18$ **b.** $^-8 - (10 - {}^-18)$

True or false?

C
23. The sum of any two negative integers is negative.

24. The difference between any two negative integers is negative.

25. The sum of any two whole numbers is a whole number.

26. The sum of any two integers is an integer.

27. The difference between any two whole numbers is a whole number.

28. The difference between any two integers is an integer.

29. The opposite of b is a positive integer if b is a negative integer.

30. If ^-a represents the opposite of any integer a, then ^-a may stand for a positive integer, a negative integer, or zero.

Problems

Solve each problem by first expressing the given data as a difference of integers. Then, compute the difference and answer the question.

A
1. The temperature at noon was 5°C. At 5 P.M. it was $^-12$°C. How many degrees did the temperature fall?

2. The highest and lowest temperatures ever recorded on Earth are 57.8°C in Africa and ⁻88.3°C in Antarctica. How much higher is the highest temperature than the lowest?

3. From the highest point in California, Mount Whitney, elevation 14,494 ft, one can see the lowest point in the United States, Bad Water, elevation ⁻282 ft. How much higher is Mount Whitney than Bad Water?

4. The deepest lake on Earth is Baikal, in Siberia. Its surface is 1493 ft above sea level while its deepest part is 3822 ft below sea level. How deep is Lake Baikal?

5. The top of Mount Everest is 8708 m above sea level, while the bottom of the Marianas Trench is 11,776 m below sea level. How much higher is the top of Mount Everest than the bottom of the Marianas Trench?

6. These announcements were heard at a rocket launch: "Minus 45 seconds and counting," and "We have second-stage ignition at plus 110 seconds." How much time elapsed between the announcements?

B **7.** A plane flew from Sydney, Australia, latitude 34°S, to the North Pole at 90°N. (a) What was the plane's change in latitude? (b) One degree of latitude is equivalent to 111 km. How many kilometers did the plane fly?

8. Paul Garcia's first-of-the-month bank balance was $268.50. During the month, he withdrew $65.00 and $258.75, and made one deposit. How large was the deposit if his end-of-month balance was $526.25?

Review Exercises

Multiply.

1. 14 × 11 × 3   **2.** 26 × 13 × 7   **3.** 57 × 43 × 0   **4.** 81 × 92 × 5

5. 143 × 51 × 8   **6.** 246 × 74 × 10   **7.** 213 × 137 × 2   **8.** 302 × 255 × 1

11-4 Products with One Negative Factor

We can think of the product $3 \times {}^-2$ as a sum.

$$3 \times {}^-2 = {}^-2 + {}^-2 + {}^-2$$

The arrow diagram for this sum is shown below.

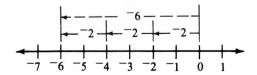

Thus we see that

$$3 \times {}^-2 = {}^-6.$$

All the multiplication properties for whole numbers hold for integers. Using the commutative property, $a \times b = b \times a$, we can write

$$3 \times {}^-2 = {}^-2 \times 3 = {}^-6.$$

We have the following rules.

Rules

The product of a positive integer and a negative integer is a negative integer.

The product of zero and any integer is zero.

EXAMPLE Find the product.

    a. ${}^-6 \times 3$ **b.** $5 \times {}^-4$ **c.** ${}^-7 \times 0$

Solution   **a.** ${}^-6 \times 3 = {}^-18$ **b.** $5 \times {}^-4 = {}^-20$ **c.** ${}^-7 \times 0 = 0$

Class Exercises

Find the product.

1. ${}^-6 \times 2$ **2.** ${}^-4 \times 2$ **3.** 0×7 **4.** $2 \times {}^-5$ **5.** $6 \times {}^-4$

6. $10 \times {}^-3$ **7.** ${}^-8 \times 0$ **8.** $12 \times {}^-1$ **9.** ${}^-1 \times 9$ **10.** ${}^-7 \times 5$

11. $({}^-1 \times 4)5$ **12.** $(2 \times {}^-3)2$ **13.** $({}^-4 \times 0)3$

14. ${}^-6(0 \times 3)$ **15.** $(4 + {}^-1){}^-2$ **16.** $({}^-2 + 3){}^-5$

Written Exercises

Find the product.

A **1.** $16 \times {}^-4$ **2.** ${}^-20 \times 0$ **3.** ${}^-6 \times 15$

4. $18 \times {}^-9$ **5.** ${}^-10 \times 66$ **6.** ${}^-14 \times 92$

7. $16 \times {}^-20$ **8.** $17 \times {}^-76$ **9.** ${}^-207 \times 41$

10. $862 \times {}^-57$ **11.** $327 \times {}^-49$ **12.** ${}^-16 \times 749$

13. $361 \times {}^-213$ **14.** ${}^-482 \times 505$ **15.** $3981 \times {}^-12$

16. $0 \times {}^-8476$ **17.** $(72 \times {}^-21)43$ **18.** $(25 \times 62){}^-17$

Simplify.

B **19. a.** $(4 \times {}^-5)3$ **b.** $4({}^-5 \times 3)$

20. a. $10({}^-2 \times 4)$ **b.** $(10 \times {}^-2)4$

21. a. $15({}^-3 \times 6)$ **b.** $(15 \times {}^-3)6$

22. a. $({}^-12 \times 3)5$ **b.** ${}^-12(3 \times 5)$

23. a. ${}^-8(14 - 5)$ **b.** $({}^-8 \times 14) - ({}^-8 \times 5)$

24. a. $(22 + {}^-22)7$ **b.** $(22 \times 7) + ({}^-22 \times 7)$

25. a. ${}^-12(32 - 32)$ **b.** $({}^-12 \times 32) - ({}^-12 \times 32)$

26. Which general property of integers do Exercises 19–22 illustrate?

27. Which general property of integers do Exercises 23–25 illustrate?

Simplify.

C **28.** $[10 + (2 \times {}^-3)]{}^-5$ **29.** ${}^-6[({}^-5 \times 2) + 15]$

30. ${}^-12[16 - ({}^-4 \times 5)]$ **31.** $[25 - (6 \times {}^-2)]{}^-3$

32. $[({}^-8 \times 5) - (6 \times {}^-9)]({}^-2 \times 3)$ **33.** $({}^-1 \times 6)[(4 \times {}^-2) - (6 \times {}^-2)]$

Review Exercises

Solve.

1. $x + 18 = 51$ **2.** $y - 27 = 11$ **3.** $y - 49 = 31$

4. $x + 47 = 93$ **5.** $x - 42 = 83$ **6.** $y + 39 = 117$

7. $2y - 28 = 54$ **8.** $5x + 38 = 153$ **9.** $3x + 42 = 285$

11-5 Products with Several Negative Factors

Study the following steps that use the distributive property.

$$(6 + {}^-1)({}^-1) = (6 \times {}^-1) + ({}^-1 \times {}^-1)$$
$$5 \times {}^-1 = {}^-6 + ({}^-1 \times {}^-1)$$
$${}^-5 = {}^-6 + ({}^-1 \times {}^-1)$$

Since ${}^-5 = {}^-6 + ({}^-1 \times {}^-1)$, and we know that

$${}^-5 = {}^-6 + 1,$$

we can conclude that

$${}^-1 \times {}^-1 = 1.$$

We can use the fact that ${}^-1 \times {}^-1 = 1$ to find the product of any two integers.

EXAMPLE 1 Find the product.

        a. ${}^-1 \times {}^-7$ **b.** ${}^-8 \times {}^-7$

Solution   **a.** ${}^-1 \times {}^-7 = {}^-1 \times ({}^-1 \times 7) = ({}^-1 \times {}^-1) \times 7 = 1 \times 7 = 7$

              b. ${}^-8 \times {}^-7 = ({}^-1 \times 8) \times ({}^-1 \times 7) = ({}^-1 \times {}^-1) \times (8 \times 7)$
                        $= 1 \times (8 \times 7) = 1 \times 56 = 56$

Notice that the products ${}^-1 \times {}^-7$ and ${}^-8 \times {}^-7$ are *positive*.

Rules

The product of ${}^-1$ and any integer equals the opposite of that integer.

The product of two negative integers is a positive integer.

We can now multiply any number of integers.

EXAMPLE 2 Find the product.

        a. ${}^-3 \times 4 \times {}^-2$ **b.** ${}^-5 \times 2 \times {}^-3 \times {}^-4$

Solution   **a.** ${}^-3 \times 4 \times {}^-2 = ({}^-3 \times 4) \times {}^-2 = {}^-12 \times {}^-2 = 24$

              b. ${}^-5 \times 2 \times {}^-3 \times {}^-4 = ({}^-5 \times 2) \times ({}^-3 \times {}^-4) = {}^-10 \times 12 = {}^-120$

These examples suggest the rules at the top of the next page.

Class Exercises

Find the product.

1. $^-2 \times {}^-5$ **2.** $^-6 \times {}^-3$ **3.** $^-8 \times {}^-1$ **4.** $^-5 \times {}^-5$

5. $5 \times {}^-5$ **6.** $^-6 \times 0$ **7.** $^-8 \times {}^-3$ **8.** $^-8 \times 3$

9. $^-2(8 + {}^-8)$ **10.** $^-2 \times {}^-3 \times {}^-4$ **11.** $8 \times {}^-2 \times {}^-1$

12. $^-6 \times 3 \times {}^-2$ **13.** $^-2 \times {}^-2 \times {}^-2$ **14.** $^-2 \times {}^-7 \times 0 \times 11$

Written Exercises

Find the product.

A **1.** $^-9 \times {}^-27$ **2.** $^-8 \times {}^-32$ **3.** $6 \times {}^-81$ **4.** $0 \times {}^-127$

5. $^-101 \times {}^-22$ **6.** $160 \times {}^-1$ **7.** $^-25 \times {}^-25$ **8.** $^-52 \times 45$

9. $^-30 \times 5 \times {}^-20$ **10.** $^-4 \times {}^-14 \times {}^-24$ **11.** $26 \times {}^-8 \times {}^-5$

12. $16 \times {}^-2 \times 30$ **13.** $2 \times {}^-3 \times 4 \times {}^-5$ **14.** $^-4 \times 4 \times 5 \times {}^-5$

15. $^-7 \times {}^-18 \times {}^-15 \times 4$ **16.** $13 \times {}^-11 \times 0 \times {}^-3$ **17.** $16 \times 4 \times {}^-5 \times 2$

18. $^-8 \times {}^-4 \times {}^-5 \times {}^-7$ **19.** $12 \times 0 \times {}^-11 \times {}^-2$ **20.** $^-6 \times {}^-3 \times 4 \times {}^-22$

Simplify.

B **21.** $^-8(7 + {}^-15)$ **22.** $(^-4 + {}^-5)^-6$

23. $(6 - 18)^-5$ **24.** $(14 - {}^-16)^-3$

25. $(3 \times {}^-6) + (^-4 \times {}^-7)$ **26.** $(^-6 \times {}^-3) + (4 \times {}^-5)$

27. $(^-4 \times {}^-7) - (3 \times {}^-6)$ **28.** $^-25 - (^-4 \times {}^-6 \times {}^-1)$

Simplify.

29. $[(^-3 \times {}^-8) + (4 \times {}^-6)](5 \times {}^-8)$

30. $(7 \times {}^-8)[(^-4 \times 6) - (^-3 \times 7)]$

31. $(^-2 \times 6)[(^-3 \times 8) + (^-5)^2]$

32. $[(^-6)^2 + (^-4 \times 9)](^-6 \times {}^-16)$

True or false?

C **33.** The square of every negative integer is positive.

34. Every integer and its opposite have equal squares.

35. The cube of every negative integer is positive.

36. Every integer and its opposite have equal cubes.

37. The greater of two integers has the greater square.

38. The greater of two integers has the greater cube.

Review Exercises

Find the value of n that makes the equation a true statement.

1. $654 = 6n$

2. $891 = 33n$

3. $1024 = 16n$

4. $512 = 64n$

5. $2166 = 6n$

6. $1344 = 7n$

7. $1892 = 4n$

8. $3123 = 9n$

9. $4008 = 3n$

▮▮▮ NONROUTINE PROBLEM SOLVING: *Number Sense*

Using each of the digits 1, 3, 5, 7, and 9 exactly once, create a three-digit integer and a two-digit integer. The integers may be either positive or negative.

1. What is the greatest possible sum of the two integers? the least possible sum?

2. What is the greatest possible difference between the two integers? the least possible difference?

3. What is the greatest possible product of the two integers? the least possible product?

11-6 Quotients of Integers

Associated with the product

$$2 \times 5 = 10$$

is the quotient

$$10 \div 5 = 2 \text{ or } \frac{10}{5} = 2.$$

Now study these examples.

$2 \times 5 = 10$	$10 \div 5 = 2,$	or $\frac{10}{5} = 2$
$2 \times {}^-5 = {}^-10$	${}^-10 \div {}^-5 = 2,$	or $\frac{{}^-10}{{}^-5} = 2$
${}^-2 \times 5 = {}^-10$	${}^-10 \div 5 = {}^-2,$	or $\frac{{}^-10}{5} = {}^-2$
${}^-2 \times {}^-5 = 10$	$10 \div {}^-5 = {}^-2,$	or $\frac{10}{{}^-5} = {}^-2$

The examples above suggest the following rules about division.

Rules

The quotient of two positive or two negative integers is positive.

The quotient of a positive integer and a negative integer is negative.

EXAMPLE Find the quotient. Check your result.

a. $\frac{15}{{}^-3}$ **b.** ${}^-24 \div 3$ **c.** $\frac{{}^-18}{{}^-3}$

Solution **a.** $\frac{15}{{}^-3} = {}^-5$ **b.** ${}^-24 \div 3 = {}^-8$ **c.** $\frac{{}^-18}{{}^-3} = 6$

Check: Check: Check:
${}^-3 \times {}^-5 = 15$ $3 \times {}^-8 = {}^-24$ ${}^-3 \times 6 = {}^-18$

Of course, the quotient of two integers need not be an integer. For example, there is no integer n such that $\frac{10}{{}^-4} = n$ because there is no integer n such that $n \times {}^-4 = 10$. Actually, the quotient $\frac{10}{{}^-4}$ equals ${}^-2.5$.

Also, remember that we *never* divide by 0.

Class Exercises

Find the quotient.

1. $\frac{4}{-2}$ **2.** $\frac{-9}{3}$ **3.** $\frac{-8}{-4}$ **4.** $\frac{-3}{-3}$

5. $\frac{6}{-1}$ **6.** $\frac{12}{-6}$ **7.** $\frac{-1}{1}$ **8.** $\frac{15}{-1}$

9. $\frac{-25}{-5}$ **10.** $1 \div {}^{-}1$ **11.** $\frac{16}{-2}$ **12.** $\frac{16}{-4}$

Written Exercises

Find the quotient. Check your result.

A   **1.** $\frac{98}{-7}$ **2.** $\frac{-56}{-14}$ **3.** $\frac{-52}{13}$ **4.** $\frac{105}{-35}$

5. $\frac{-187}{-17}$ **6.** ${}^{-}806 \div 13$ **7.** $270 \div {}^{-}18$ **8.** $\frac{378}{-18}$

9. $420 \div {}^{-}15$ **10.** ${}^{-}504 \div {}^{-}56$ **11.** ${}^{-}462 \div 21$ **12.** ${}^{-}551 \div {}^{-}29$

Find the value of n that makes each equation a true statement.

13. ${}^{-}2n = {}^{-}6$ **14.** $6n = {}^{-}12$ **15.** ${}^{-}3n = 9$

16. ${}^{-}12n = 96$ **17.** $13n = {}^{-}65$ **18.** ${}^{-}6n = {}^{-}72$

19. ${}^{-}7n = 91$ **20.** $12n = {}^{-}132$ **21.** ${}^{-}16n = {}^{-}144$

Simplify.

B   **22. a.** $48 \div ({}^{-}4 \div 2)$ **b.** $(48 \div {}^{-}4) \div 2$

23. a. $(72 \div 12) \div 3$ **b.** $72 \div (12 \div 3)$

24. $(3 \times {}^{-}16 \times 12) \div (36 \div {}^{-}6)$ **25.** $({}^{-}5 \times {}^{-}8 \times 24) \div (10 \times {}^{-}3)$

26. $\dfrac{6 \times 8 + {}^{-}3 \times 5}{7 \times 5 + {}^{-}3 \times 8}$ **27.** $\dfrac{{}^{-}5 \times 12 + {}^{-}4 \times 18}{5 \times 10 + {}^{-}4 \times 7}$

Let n be a positive integer and ${}^{-}n$ be its opposite. Replace the ___?___ by n, ${}^{-}n$, 1, or ${}^{-}1$ to make a true statement.

C   **28.** $n \div {}^{-}1 = $ ___?___   **29.** ${}^{-}n \div {}^{-}1 = $ ___?___

30. ${}^{-}n \div {}^{-}n = $ ___?___   **31.** ${}^{-}n \div n = $ ___?___

32. ${}^{-}n \times n = $ ___?___ $\times n^2$ **33.** ${}^{-}n \times {}^{-}n = $ ___?___ $\times n^2$

34. $n^2 \div {}^{-}n = $ ___?___   **35.** $n^2 \div n = $ ___?___

Self-Test A

Give the opposite and the absolute value of each integer.

1. 6   2. ⁻3   3. ⁻7   4. 0   5. 4   [11–1]

Replace each __?__ with < or >.

6. ⁻5 __?__ 2   7. 0 __?__ ⁻8   8. 3 __?__ ⁻1

Simplify.

9. $5 + {}^-9$ 10. ${}^-7 + {}^-6$ [11–2]

11. ${}^-2 + 8 + {}^-7 + 4$ 12. $35 + {}^-18 + {}^-40$

13. $78 - 104$ 14. ${}^-91 - {}^-15$ [11–3]

15. $(27 - {}^-18) - 43$ 16. ${}^-56 - ({}^-13 - {}^-28)$

17. $(5 \times {}^-3)7$ 18. ${}^-11(8 \times 14)$ [11–4]

19. ${}^-8 \times {}^-3 \times {}^-9$ 20. $(9 - 27)(32 - 51)$ [11–5]

21. $({}^-12 \times 8) - ({}^-31 \times 8)$ 22. ${}^-31 - ({}^-8 \times {}^-4) + 9$

23. $({}^-110 \div 5) \div {}^-11$ 24. $96 \div {}^-6 \div {}^-8$ [11–6]

Self-Test answers and Extra Practice are at the back of the book.

▌▌▌ CALCULATOR INVESTIGATION: +/− Key

Some calculators have a **+/−** key. This key can be used to add, subtract, multiply, or divide negative numbers on the calculator. Use a calculator to perform the following operations.

1. ${}^-8 + 7 + {}^-3 + {}^-5$ 2. $4 - {}^-6 - 9 - {}^-11$

3. ${}^-3 + 6 - {}^-8 - {}^-5$ 4. ${}^-11 \times 3 \times {}^-2 \times 4$

5. $3 \times {}^-5 \times {}^-14 \times {}^-7$ 6. ${}^-12 \div 2 \times 3 \div {}^-6$

▌▌▌ NONROUTINE PROBLEM SOLVING: *Trial and Error*

Using the first nine counting numbers, fill in the boxes so you get the same sum when you add vertically, horizontally, or diagonally. Can you do this with any nine consecutive counting numbers?

11-7 Solving Equations

Now that you have learned about negative integers, you can solve an equation such as $x + 7 = 2$.

$$x + 7 = 2$$

Subtract 7 from both sides.

$$x + 7 - 7 = 2 - 7$$
$$x = 2 + {}^-7$$
$$x = {}^-5$$

Notice that we are using the transformations discussed in Chapter 8.

COMMUNICATION IN MATHEMATICS: *Study Skill*

When you find a reference in the text to material you learned earlier, such as transformations on page 251 and page 255, reread that material to help you understand the new lesson.

EXAMPLE 1   Solve $\frac{1}{2}x + 3 = 0$.

Solution   Subtract 3 from both sides.

$$\frac{1}{2}x + 3 = 0$$

$$\frac{1}{2}x + 3 - 3 = 0 - 3$$

$$\frac{1}{2}x = 0 + {}^-3$$

$$\frac{1}{2}x = {}^-3$$

Multiply both sides by 2.

$$2 \times \frac{1}{2}x = 2 \times {}^-3$$

$$x = {}^-6$$

Check: $\frac{1}{2} \times {}^-6 + 3 \stackrel{?}{=} 0$

$${}^-3 + 3 \stackrel{?}{=} 0$$

$$0 = 0$$

EXAMPLE 2 Solve $^-3z - {}^-15 = 9$.

Solution Add $^-15$ to both sides.

$$^-3z - {}^-15 = 9$$
$$^-3z - {}^-15 + {}^-15 = 9 + {}^-15$$
$$^-3z = {}^-6$$

Divide both sides by $^-3$.

$$\frac{^-3}{^-3}z = \frac{^-6}{^-3}$$
$$z = 2$$

Check: $^-3 \times 2 - {}^-15 \overset{?}{=} 9$
$$^-6 - {}^-15 \overset{?}{=} 9$$
$$9 = 9$$

Class Exercises

Solve each equation.

1. $x + 5 = {}^-2$ **2.** $y - 5 = {}^-2$ **3.** $2x = {}^-6$ **4.** $\frac{w}{3} = {}^-2$

5. $x + 8 = 3$ **6.** $y - {}^-6 = 4$ **7.** $^-3x = {}^-9$ **8.** $\frac{w}{^-4} = 7$

9. $x + {}^-9 = {}^-12$ **10.** $y - {}^-7 = {}^-8$ **11.** $^-5x = 30$ **12.** $\frac{w}{^-8} = {}^-3$

Written Exercises

Solve each equation.

A **1.** $x + {}^-10 = 15$ **2.** $\frac{1}{4}z = {}^-6$ **3.** $^-5u = 125$

4. $x - {}^-8 = 22$ **5.** $12r = {}^-60$ **6.** $z + {}^-2 = {}^-18$

7. $t - 5 = {}^-4$ **8.** $\frac{1}{^-10}x = {}^-7$ **9.** $^-8y = 104$

10. $x + {}^-16 = {}^-14$ **11.** $15y = {}^-195$ **12.** $u + 10 = {}^-10$

13. $\frac{1}{^-9}r = 0$ **14.** $t - {}^-10 = 19$ **15.** $^-11z = 187$

16. $y + {}^-72 = 100$ **17.** $r - {}^-16 = {}^-34$ **18.** $\frac{1}{^-9}c = 33$

19. $\frac{4}{^-5}x = 120$ **20.** $m + {}^-37 = {}^-59$ **21.** $t + 84 = {}^-15$

22. $i + {}^-53 = 48$ **23.** $\frac{^-7}{10}c = {}^-147$ **24.** $n - 61 = 39$

Integers and Graphs **387**

Solve each equation.

B **25.** $2x + 5 = {}^-3$ **26.** $3u - 1 = {}^-7$ **27.** ${}^-5z + {}^-6 = 9$

28. ${}^-2t + 3 = {}^-7$ **29.** $4 - t = {}^-10$ **30.** ${}^-2 - x = {}^-7$

31. $10 = {}^-6 - 4n$ **32.** $6 = {}^-3 + 3k$ **33.** $\frac{1}{2}x + {}^-6 = 1$

34. $\frac{1}{3}y + 4 = {}^-3$ **35.** $\frac{2}{3}t + {}^-1 = 1$ **36.** $\frac{u}{5} + {}^-2 = 3$

37. $\frac{3}{2}z - 4 = {}^-1$ **38.** ${}^-1 + \frac{5}{3}n = 9$ **39.** $2 - \frac{1}{5}x = {}^-4$

40. ${}^-6 = \frac{1}{2}z + 4$ **41.** ${}^-13 = 1 - \frac{1}{2}y$ **42.** ${}^-3 - \frac{1}{7}t = {}^-11$

43. $2x + {}^-2 = {}^-6$ **44.** ${}^-3z + 18 = 9$ **45.** $13 + \frac{{}^-7}{9}m = 34$

46. ${}^-5 + \frac{1}{2}x = {}^-15$ **47.** ${}^-2 + x = {}^-2$ **48.** $\frac{9}{15}x - 43 = 74$

EXAMPLE   Solve $x = {}^-6 + 3x$.

Solution   Subtract $3x$ from both sides.

$$x = {}^-6 + 3x$$
$$x - 3x = {}^-6 + 3x - 3x$$
$$(1 - 3)x = {}^-6$$

Divide ${}^-2$ from both sides.

$$^-2x = {}^-6$$
$$x = 3$$

C **49.** ${}^-6 + z = 8 - z$ **50.** $3 - r = {}^-5 + r$

51. $\frac{1}{2}x - 2 = {}^-5 + x$ **52.** $1 + \frac{2}{3}t = 5 + t$

53. $\frac{2}{3}y + {}^-3 = 1 + y$ **54.** $\frac{3}{2}x = {}^-6 + 2x$

Review Exercises

Explain the meaning of each term.

1. perpendicular lines   2. square   3. rectangle

4. parallelogram   5. trapezoid   6. pentagon

7. hexagon   8. isosceles triangle   9. obtuse triangle

11-8 Graphs of Ordered Pairs

The location of a desk in a classroom can be described as "second row, third desk." If we write (2, 3) to represent this location, the order of the numbers is important, since (3, 2) would represent "third row, second desk." A pair of numbers whose order is important is called an **ordered pair.**

We graph a number as a point on a number line. We graph an ordered pair of numbers as a point on a plane marked with two perpendicular number lines, called **axes.** The first number of an ordered pair is associated with the horizontal number line, called the **x-axis,** and the second number with the vertical number line, called the **y-axis.** The axes meet in a point, called the **origin.**

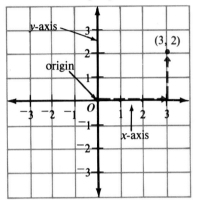

The diagram at the right shows the graph of the ordered pair (3, 2). To locate this point, start at the origin, go 3 units to the right, and then 2 units up. The numbers 3 and 2 are the **coordinates** of the graph of (3, 2). The plane itself is called a **coordinate plane.**

The following example shows how to graph ordered pairs having a negative or a zero coordinate.

EXAMPLE Graph the ordered pairs (⁻3, ⁻1), (⁻2, 0), (⁻1, 2), (0, 0), (1, 2), (2, 1), and (3, ⁻1).

Solution To graph (⁻3, ⁻1), start at the origin and go 3 units left and 1 unit down.

To graph (⁻2, 0), start at the origin and go 2 units left. Since the second number is 0, there is no up or down movement.

The other ordered pairs are graphed in a similar manner.

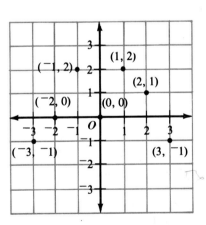

Notice in the example that (1, 2) and (2, 1) have different graphs. This is so because the order of the coordinates is important. The horizontal coordinate is always listed first.

Class Exercises

The graphs of twelve ordered pairs are given on the coordinate plane at the right. Give the letter associated with the graph of each ordered pair.

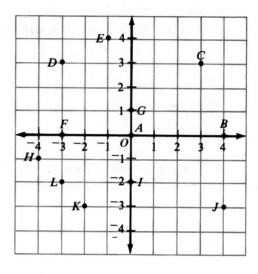

1. $(^-1, 4)$ 2. $(3, 3)$ 3. $(0, ^-2)$

4. $(4, ^-3)$ 5. $(0, 0)$ 6. $(^-3, 0)$

Give the ordered pair associated with each letter.

7. D 8. L 9. B

10. K 11. I 12. H

Written Exercises

For each exercise, graph the ordered pairs on the same coordinate plane.

A 1. $(3, 1), (0, 2), (^-2, 1)$ 2. $(1, 3), (^-4, 0), (2, ^-1)$

3. $(^-4, ^-1), (0, ^-3), (^-2, 4)$ 4. $(3, 3), (^-1, ^-1), (^-2, ^-2)$

5. $(4, ^-4), (0, 0), (^-2, 2)$ 6. $(^-4, 3), (^-1, ^-3), (1, ^-3)$

7. $(^-3, 2), (^-1, 3), (1, 4), (3, ^-2)$

8. $(^-3, 1), (^-2, ^-3), (2, 3), (3, ^-1)$

9. $(^-3, 3), (^-1, 0), (0, 2), (1, 0), (3, 3)$

10. $(^-3, 0), (^-2, 3), (0, 4), (2, 3), (3, 0)$

a. Graph the ordered pairs.
b. Join the points in the order A, B, C, D, A.
c. Identify the quadrilateral as a square, a rectangle, a parallelogram, or a trapezoid. Use the most specific name.

11. $A(4, 2), B(0, 2), C(^-2, ^-3), D(2, ^-3)$

12. $A(^-3, ^-1), B(2, ^-1), C(2, 3), D(^-3, 3)$

13. $A(1, ^-3), B(4, ^-3), C(4, 1), D(1, 1)$

14. $A(^-1, ^-1), B(4, ^-1), C(1, 3), D(^-1, 3)$

a. Graph the ordered pairs.
b. Join the points in the order given.
c. Identify the polygon as a quadrilateral, a pentagon, or a hexagon.

B 15. (3, 1), (0, 3), (⁻3, 1), (⁻2, ⁻2), (2, ⁻2), (3, 1)

16. (2, 0), (2, 2), (⁻2, 3), (⁻3, 0), (⁻1, 0), (2, 0)

17. (3, 1), (0, 3), (⁻3, 2), (⁻3, ⁻2), (1, ⁻2), (3, ⁻2), (3, 1)

18. (3, 0), (1, 3), (⁻1, 3), (⁻3, 0), (⁻2, ⁻3), (2, ⁻3), (3, 0)

a. Graph the ordered pairs and join the points to form a triangle.
b. Classify the triangle by angles and by sides.

C 19. (⁻2, ⁻1), (1, 1), (4, ⁻1)   20. (⁻3, 0), (0, 3), (1, 0)

21. (4, ⁻2), (⁻1, 3), (⁻1, ⁻2)   22. (2, 2), (⁻2, 2), (0, ⁻3)

23. (2, 2), (⁻3, 1), (3, ⁻1)   24. (1, ⁻1), (1, 2), (⁻4, 2)

Review Exercises

Find the value of y for the given value of x.

1. $y = x$; $x = 17$ 2. $y = 4x$; $x = 13$ 3. $y = x - 23$; $x = 41$

4. $3x + 9 = y$; $x = 14$ 5. $7x - 18 = y$; $x = 9$ 6. $y = 54 - 3x$; $x = 17$

7. $y = {}^-6x + 79$; $x = 13$ 8. $y = 9x + 19$; $x = 13$ 9. $y = {}^-12x + 103$; $x = 7$

 NONROUTINE PROBLEM SOLVING: *Drawing a Diagram*

Of 60 students, 25 play hockey, 47 swim, and 12 do both sports. How many students play hockey only? We can use a *Venn diagram*, shown at the right, to answer the question. We write the number of students who play both sports in the overlapping portion of the circles. We subtract this number from the total number of students in each sport.

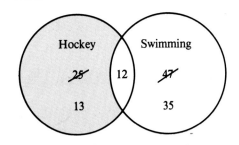

The shaded region shows the 13 students who play hockey only.

Draw a Venn diagram to help answer the question.
1. Of 127 students, 75 enjoy theater, 88 enjoy classical music, and 36 enjoy both theater and classical music. How many students enjoy theater but not classical music? How many students enjoy classical music but not theater?

Integers and Graphs **391**

11-9 Graphs of Equations

An equation in two variables such as

$$y = 2 - x$$

can produce many ordered pairs. If we give x the value 3, for example, a corresponding value of y is determined.

$$y = 2 - 3 = {}^-1$$

We describe this correspondence by the ordered pair $(3, {}^-1)$. The table below gives several other ordered pairs produced by $y = 2 - x$.

x	$2 - x = y$	Ordered pair (x, y)
${}^-1$	$2 - {}^-1 = 3$	$({}^-1, 3)$
0	$2 - 0 = 2$	$(0, 2)$
1	$2 - 1 = 1$	$(1, 1)$
2	$2 - 2 = 0$	$(2, 0)$
3	$2 - 3 = {}^-1$	$(3, {}^-1)$
4	$2 - 4 = {}^-2$	$(4, {}^-2)$

In the diagram at the left below we have graphed the ordered pairs computed in the table. Notice that the axes have been labeled with the names of the variables, x and y.

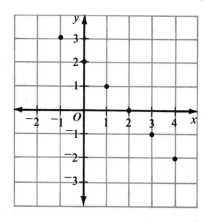
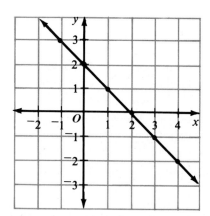

The diagram suggests that if we were able to graph *all* the ordered pairs produced by $y = 2 - x$ (including those with noninteger coordinates), we would obtain the line shown at the right above. This line is the **graph** of the equation $y = 2 - x$.

EXAMPLE Graph the equation $y = 2x - 3$. Use values of x from $^-1$ through 4.

Solution First make a table of ordered pairs and then graph the ordered pairs on a coordinate plane.

x	$2x - 3 = y$	Ordered pair
$^-1$	$2 \times ^-1 - 3 = ^-5$	$(^-1, ^-5)$
0	$2 \times 0 - 3 = ^-3$	$(0, ^-3)$
1	$2 \times 1 - 3 = ^-1$	$(1, ^-1)$
2	$2 \times 2 - 3 = 1$	$(2, 1)$
3	$2 \times 3 - 3 = 3$	$(3, 3)$
4	$2 \times 4 - 3 = 5$	$(4, 5)$

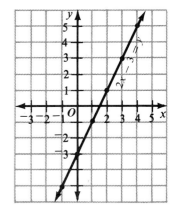

In the set of ordered pairs in the example, for each value of x there is exactly one value of y. A set of ordered pairs, such as this, in which no two ordered pairs have the same first component is called a **function**. A rule or correspondence that produces such ordered pairs defines a function. For example, we can say that $y = 2x - 3$ defines y as a function of x.

Class Exercises

Copy and complete each table.

1.

x	$x - 3 = y$	Ordered pair
$^-1$	$^-1 - 3 = ?$	$(^-1, ?)$
0	$0 - 3 = ?$	$(0, ?)$
1	$? - 3 = ?$	$(?, ?)$
2	$? - 3 = ?$	$(?, ?)$
3	$? - 3 = ?$	$(?, ?)$

2.

x	$2x + 1 = y$	Ordered pair
$^-2$	$2(^-2) + 1 = ?$	$(^-2, ?)$
$^-1$	$2(^-1) + 1 = ?$	$(^-1, ?)$
0	$2(?) + 1 = ?$	$(?, ?)$
1	$2(?) + 1 = ?$	$(?, ?)$
2	$2(?) + 1 = ?$	$(?, ?)$

Complete each ordered pair for the given equation.

$y = x + 4$ **3.** $(^-2, ?)$ **4.** $(^-1, ?)$ **5.** $(0, ?)$ **6.** $(1, ?)$ **7.** $(2, ?)$

$y = 3x$ **8.** $(^-2, ?)$ **9.** $(^-1, ?)$ **10.** $(0, ?)$ **11.** $(1, ?)$ **12.** $(2, ?)$

Integers and Graphs   **393**

Written Exercises

Copy and complete each table.

A **1.**

x	$x + {}^-1 = y$	Ordered pair
$^-3$	$^-3 + {}^-1 = ?$	?
$^-2$	$^-2 + {}^-1 = ?$	?
$^-1$	$^-1 + {}^-1 = ?$	?
0	$0 + {}^-1 = ?$	?
1	$1 + {}^-1 = ?$	?
2	$2 + {}^-1 = ?$	?
3	$3 + {}^-1 = ?$	?

2.

x	$2x + 3 = y$	Ordered pair
$^-3$	$2(^-3) + 3 = ?$	?
$^-2$	$2(^-2) + 3 = ?$	?
$^-1$	$2(^-1) + 3 = ?$	?
0	$2(0) + 3 = ?$	?
1	$2(1) + 3 = ?$	?
2	$2(2) + 3 = ?$	?
3	$2(3) + 3 = ?$	?

Graph the given equation. Use values of x from $^-2$ through 2.

3. $y = x$

4. $y = {}^-x$

5. $y = 1 - x$

6. $y = x + 1$

7. $y = 2x$

8. $y = 3 - x$

Graph the given equation. Use the following values of x: $^-6, ^-4, ^-2, 0, 2, 4, 6$.

9. $y = x - {}^-1$

10. $y = x + {}^-3$

11. $y = {}^-x + 2$

12. $y = {}^-x - {}^-5$

13. $y = x + {}^-2$

14. $y = x + {}^-6$

15. $y = {}^-x - 2$

16. $y = 7 - {}^-x$

17. $y = x + 4$

Graph the given equation. Use the following values of x: $^-3, ^-1, 0, 1, 3$.

B **18.** $y = 2x - 1$

19. $y = 2x + 1$

20. $y = 3x + 2$

21. $y = 3x - 2$

22. $y = {}^-2x + 2$

23. $y = {}^-2x - 2$

24. $y = 3x - {}^-2$

25. $y = 7 - {}^-2x$

26. $y = {}^-3 + {}^-2x$

Graph the given equation. Use the following values of x: $^-4, ^-3, ^-2, 0, 2$.

27. $y = {}^-3x - 1$

28. $y = 1 + {}^-2x$

29. $y = 4x + {}^-1$

30. $y = 2x - {}^-5$

31. $y = {}^-2 - {}^-2x$

32. $y = {}^-3x - {}^-3$

33. $y = 2(x + {}^-1)$

34. $y = 3({}^-x + {}^-4)$

35. $y = 4({}^-1 + x)$

36. $y = 3({}^-x - 1)$

37. $y = {}^-2({}^-3 + x)$

38. $y = 4({}^-x + {}^-1)$

Graph the given equation using values of x as specified. (These graphs are not lines. They are curves called parabolas.)

EXAMPLE $y = x^2 + 1$; x from $^-2$ through 2

Solution

x	$x^2 + 1 = y$	Ordered pairs
$^-2$	$(^-2)^2 + 1 = 5$	$(^-2, 5)$
$^-1$	$(^-1)^2 + 1 = 2$	$(^-1, 2)$
0	$(0)^2 + 1 = 1$	$(0, 1)$
1	$(1)^2 + 1 = 2$	$(1, 2)$
2	$(1)^2 + 1 = 5$	$(2, 5)$

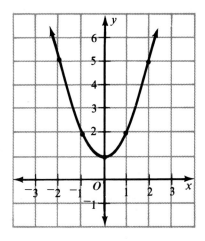

C **39.** $y = x^2$; x from $^-2$ through 2

40. $y = x^2 - 2$; x from $^-2$ through 2

41. $y = x^2 - 2x$; x from $^-1$ through 3

42. $y = 2 - x^2$; x from $^-2$ through 2

43. $y = 4 + x^2$; x: $^-3$, $^-1$, 0, 1, 3

44. $y = ^-3 + x^2$; x: $^-4$, $^-2$, 0, 2, 4

45. $y = x^2 - {}^-1$; x: $^-5$, $^-3$, 0, 3, 5

46. $y = x^2 + {}^-3$; x: $^-6$, $^-2$, 0, 2, 6

Self-Test B

Solve each equation.

1. $x + {}^-8 = 31$

2. $y + 14 = {}^-11$

3. $\frac{1}{{}^-4}t = 13$

[11-7]

4. $5n = {}^-105$

5. $x - 16 = {}^-9$

6. $y - {}^-6 = 18$

In each exercise, graph the ordered pairs on the same coordinate plane.

7. $(3, 1)$, $(^-4, 2)$, $(^-3, ^-2)$

8. $(0, ^-5)$, $(2, ^-1)$, $(4, 2)$

[11-8]

Graph the given equation. Use values of x from $^-2$ through 2.

9. $y = x + 3$

10. $y = ^-3x$

[11-9]

11. $y = 2x + 3$

12. $y = 3x - 1$

Self-Test answers and Extra Practice are at the back of the book.

Graphing Inequalities

You graphed inequalities such as $^-3 < x < 2$, where x is an integer, on page 368. Suppose we wish to graph $x < 2$ where x is an integer. The graph is shown on the left below. The heavy arrowhead indicates that the set continues to the left.

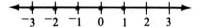 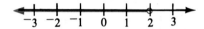

If we wish to graph *all* numbers less than 2, we put an open circle at 2, since 2 is not part of the set, and then put an arrow from this circle pointing to the left, as shown on the right above. If we wish 2 to be part of the set, we put a dot at 2. The inequality symbol in this case would be $\leq$, read "is less than or equal to." The symbol $\geq$ means "is greater than or equal to."

As was the case with equations, inequalities can involve two variables. Compare the table of values for the equation $y = 3 - x$ with the table for the inequality $y \leq 3 - x$.

$y = 3 - x$			$y \leq 3 - x$	
x	y		x	y
$^-1$	4		$^-1$	4, 3, 2, 1, …
0	3		0	3, 2, 1, 0, …
1	2		1	2, 1, 0, $^-1$, …
2	1		2	1, 0, $^-1$, $^-2$, …
3	0		3	0, $^-1$, $^-2$, $^-3$, …
4	$^-1$		4	$^-1$, $^-2$, $^-3$, $^-4$, …

Notice that in the case of the equation only one ordered pair has 2 as its first number, namely (2, 1). But in the case of the inequality, there are many such ordered pairs: (2, 1), (2, 0), (2, $^-1$), (2, $^-2$), and so on.

Any set of ordered pairs is called a **relation.** A relation is a function if no two ordered pairs have the same first number. Therefore, $y = 3 - x$ defines a function, while $y \leq 3 - x$ defines a relation that is not a function.

To draw the graphs of $y = 3 - x$ and $y \leq 3 - x$, we can use the tables of values shown above.

The line $y = 3 - x$ is called the **boundary line** of the graph of the inequality $y \leq 3 - x$.

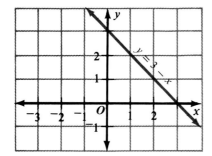
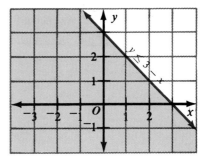

The following is a two-step method for graphing an inequality.

1. Draw the boundary line. Use a solid line if the boundary belongs to the graph ($\leq$ or $\geq$); use a dashed line if it does not ($<$ or $>$).

2. Shade either the part of the plane above the boundary line or the part below it. If the inequality reads $y >$ or $y \geq$, shade above the line. If it reads $y <$ or $y \leq$, shade below the line. As a check, choose a point in the shaded region and substitute its coordinates into the inequality. If the resulting inequality is true, then the shading is correct.

EXAMPLE Graph $y > 2x - 3$.

Solution

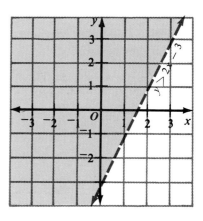

1. The boundary line has the equation $y = 2x - 3$. Make a table of values and draw the graph as a dashed line.

2. Because the inequality reads $y > 2x - 3$, shade the part of the plane above the boundary line. You can use $(0, 0)$ as a check. Since $0 > 2 \times 0 - 3$, the shading is correct.

Graph each inequality on a number line.

1. $x < 4$
2. $x > {}^-2$
3. $x \geq {}^-5$
4. $x \leq 0$

Graph each inequality on a coordinate plane.

5. $y < x$
6. $y \geq x$
7. $y \geq x - 1$
8. $y > 1 - x$
9. $y \leq 2x - 1$
10. $y < 2x + 2$
11. $y > 4 - x$
12. $y \leq x + 2$
13. $y > {}^-x + 2$
14. $y \leq 2 - x$
15. $y > {}^-3 + x$
16. $y \geq x - 6$

Integers and Graphs **397**

Chapter Review

Complete. Use < or > for Exercises 3 and 4.

1. The opposite of $^-4$ is __?__ .   [11-1]

2. The absolute value of 7 is __?__ .

3. $^-8$ __?__ 5   **4.** 0 __?__ $^-2$

Match.

5. $^-8 + 11$ **6.** $^-6 + ^-9$ **A.** $^-16$ **B.** $^-22$ [11-2]

7. $5 - 16$ **8.** $^-13 - ^-9$ **C.** $^-17$ **D.** $^-15$ [11-3]

9. $4 \times ^-4$ **10.** $^-8 \times 0$ **E.** $^-24$ **F.** $^-8$ [11-4]

11. $^-5 \times ^-11$ **12.** $^-3 \times ^-8 \times ^-1$ **G.** 3   **H.** 0   [11-5]

13. $84 \div ^-7$ **14.** $^-51 \div ^-3$ **I.** 17   **J.** $^-12$ [11-6]

                                                  K. $^-11$ **L.** $^-4$

                                                  M. 55   **N.** 21

Write the letter of the correct answer. Exercises 18–19 refer to the diagram below.

15. Solve $x - ^-9 = 11$.   [11-7]
   a. $^-20$ **b.** 20   **c.** 2   **d.** $^-2$

16. Solve $\frac{1}{^-6}y = 18$.
   a. $^-3$ **b.** $^-108$ **c.** 108   **d.** 3

17. Solve $^-4y = ^-36$.
   a. 9   **b.** $^-9$ **c.** 144   **d.** $^-144$

18. What are the coordinates of point A?   [11-8]
   a. $(^-1, 3)$ **b.** $(^-3, 1)$
   c. $(1, ^-3)$ **d.** $(3, ^-1)$

19. What are the coordinates of point B?
   a. $(^-5, ^-1)$ **b.** $(5, 1)$
   c. $(1, 5)$ **d.** $(^-1, ^-5)$

20. Which ordered pairs would you use to   [11-9]
   graph $y = 2x - 4$?
   a. (3, 10), (6, 16)   **b.** (3, 2), (6, 8)
   c. (6, 10), (12, 16)   **d.** (6, 2), (12, 8)

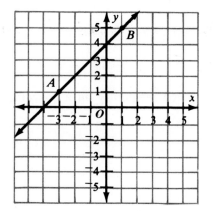

Chapter Test

Name the opposite and give the absolute value of each integer.

1. $^-11$ 2. 2   3. $^-6$ 4. $^-2$ 5. 0   [11-1]

Replace each __?__ with < or >.

6. $^-10$ __?__ $^-3$ 7. 0 __?__ $^-6$ 8. 5 __?__ $^-7$

Simplify.

9. $^-7 + 12$ 10. $18 + ^-13$ [11-2]

11. $^-9 + 3 + ^-15$ 12. $7 + 15 + ^-33$

13. $16 - ^-8$ 14. $2 - 13$ [11-3]

15. $^-12 - (47 - ^-76)$ 16. $^-36 - ^-25 - 43$

17. $^-7 \times 8$ 18. $9 \times ^-24$ [11-4]

19. $5(^-12 \times 30)$ 20. $^-9 \times 47 \times 2$

21. $^-11(^-26 \times 4)$ 22. $^-15 \times ^-30$ [11-5]

23. $(80 \times ^-3) - (67 \times ^-3)$ 24. $4(^-8 + ^-15)$

25. $207 \div ^-3 \div ^-23$ 26. $^-155 \div ^-5$ [11-6]

27. $(^-198 \div 11) \div ^-2$ 28. $^-104 \div ^-8 \div 13$

Solve.

29. $x + 8 = 3$ 30. $y - ^-8 = ^-21$ 31. $\frac{1}{^-6}n = 8$ [11-7]

In each exercise, graph the ordered pairs on the same coordinate plane.

32. $(0, ^-3), (5, 2), (^-4, 3)$ 33. $(^-1, 3), (5, 0), (^-2, ^-4)$ [11-8]

Graph the given equation. Use values of x from $^-2$ through 2.

34. $y = 4x$ 35. $y = x - 4$

Cumulative Review (Chapters 1–11)

Exercises

Simplify.

1. $3.714 + 0.039 + {}^{-}1.71$

2. $6.83 - {}^{-}2.47 + 4.61$

3. $9.2 - {}^{-}3.75 - {}^{-}4.034$

4. $3.62 \times 4.1 \times 5$

5. $10.2 \times {}^{-}0.3 \times 1.6$

6. $20.05 \div {}^{-}0.05 \times 0.14$

7. $0.937 \times 4.8 \div 0.12$

8. $\frac{11}{3} + \frac{7}{8} - \frac{11}{12}$

9. $\frac{21}{25} - \frac{7}{10} + \frac{5}{4}$

10. $\frac{9}{11} \times \frac{8}{3} \times \frac{33}{10}$

11. $\frac{15}{7} \times \frac{8}{25} \div \frac{10}{49}$

12. $\frac{12}{5} \div \frac{9}{25} \times \frac{7}{20}$

13. $2\frac{3}{8} + 7\frac{5}{6} - 4\frac{19}{24}$

14. $6\frac{2}{3} \times 5\frac{5}{8} \div 3\frac{1}{3}$

15. $4\frac{1}{2} \div 2\frac{1}{4} \times 1\frac{1}{4}$

Find the perimeter or circumference and the area. Use $\pi \approx 3.14$.

16. square
    side: 2.4 cm

17. equilateral triangle
    side: 8.4 m
    height: 7.3 m

18. circle
    radius: 5 m

19. rectangle
    length: 2.5 km
    width: 0.75 km

20. parallelogram
    length: 11.4 cm
    width: 7.1 cm
    height: 5.3 cm

21. trapezoid
    sum of bases: 18 mm
    each side: 10 mm
    height: 8 mm

Find the square root.

22. $\sqrt{64}$

23. $\sqrt{196}$

24. $\sqrt{256}$

25. $\sqrt{441}$

Find the GCF of each pair of numbers.

26. 32, 56

27. 40, 64

28. 45, 63

Find the LCM of each pair of numbers.

29. 9, 24

30. 12, 28

31. 16, 36

Solve.

32. $6x - {}^{-}49 = 181$

33. $9x + 81 = 567$

34. $\frac{1}{3}a + 41 = 132$

35. $\frac{1}{7}c - {}^{-}84 = 92$

36. $\frac{3}{8}y - 16 = 58$

37. $\frac{5}{6}d + 61 = 204$

38. $2.4x + 3.28 = 11.728$

39. $0.35y - 1.97 = 1.3795$

40. $1.04z + {}^{-}0.037 = 7.3886$

41. $4.3a + 1.2864 = 40.5024$

Problems

PROBLEM SOLVING REMINDERS

Here are some reminders that may help you solve some of the problems on this page.
- Determine whether a formula applies.
- Think of a simpler, related problem to help you plan.
- Determine whether an equation can be used.
- Consider whether drawing a sketch will help.

1. Cero went to the fruit stand. He bought $4\frac{1}{2}$ lb of apples at $.78 per pound, a bag of oranges for $2.29, $2\frac{1}{3}$ lb of bananas at $.39 per pound, and a $10\frac{2}{3}$ lb melon at $.27 per pound. If Cero paid for his fruit with a $10 bill, what was his change?

2. A scale drawing of a house has the scale 2 cm : 1.5 m. If the house has a length of 16 cm on the drawing, what is its actual length?

3. A cylindrical tank has a height of 20 m and a base radius of 45 m. Find the volume. Use $\pi \approx 3.14$ and round to three digits.

4. Louis Chang bought a new car for $10,395. Ed Goldman bought a used car. If the new car cost 3 times as much as the used one, how much did Ed pay?

5. A flower garden is in the shape of a triangle with area 27 m² and height of 6 m. Find the base of the triangle.

6. When the stock market opened, Exer Corporation stock was priced at $34\frac{1}{8}$. By noon the stock had risen $2\frac{1}{4}$ points. At 3 o'clock it had fallen $1\frac{7}{8}$ points from the noon price. When the market closed the stock had fallen another $1\frac{3}{4}$ points from the 3 o'clock price. What was the price of the stock at noon? at 3 o'clock? at closing?

7. A store is having a sale on winter coats. If a certain coat has a regular price of $149.50 and is being sold at a discount of 15%, what is the sale price?

8. Sara has $12 less than twice as much money as Bart. If Sara has $19, how much money does Bart have?

9. A circle has a diameter of $7\frac{7}{11}$ in. Find the circumference. Use $\pi \approx \frac{22}{7}$.

10. Luella Sanders receives a 6% commission on her real estate sales. Last month she sold two houses. If one house sold for $98,000 and the other for $127,000, how much did Luella receive last month?

12 Statistics and Probability

APPLYING MATHEMATICS
RESEARCH

The quest for discovery involves research to evaluate new ideas. Researchers test their ideas using the scientific method. Using statistical procedures, they organize, illustrate, and analyze their findings. Research may include investigations to determine the properties of distant stars, or to test the effectiveness of a new drug. It has helped produce artificial hearts and provide new methods of curing and preventing birth defects. Research takes place in all fields from engineering and medicine to industry. The future of our planet rests on research involving our environment. In this chapter you will learn to collect, compare, and analyze data using the methods of statistics.

CAREER CONNECTION

BIOMEDICAL ENGINEER

Biomedical engineers combine science and technology to diagnose, treat, and prevent human diseases. Their work includes physical and biological research. Some biomedical engineers design machines that are used in the diagnosis and treatment of illnesses. Some engineers design artificial limbs and devices for the physically handicapped. Biomedical engineering requires a degree in engineering as well as courses related to particular medical specialties.

Photo: Flasks and beakers are essential to the research scientist's work of gathering and analyzing data.

12-1 Picturing Numerical Data

Many scientific, social, and economic studies produce numerical facts. Such numerical information is called **data.** At the right are some data about the number of automobiles sold in the United States.

These data can be pictured by using a **bar graph** (below left) or a **broken-line graph** (below right). On the bar graph the height of each bar is drawn to the scale marked at the left and so is proportional to the data it represents. All bars have the same width. The broken-line graph can be made by joining the midpoints of the tops of the bars.

We can see from either graph that the most rapid 10-year increase in auto sales occurred between 1940 and 1950.

Car Sales	
Year	Number Sold (nearest 100,000)
1920	2,200,000
1930	3,400,000
1940	4,500,000
1950	8,000,000
1960	7,900,000
1970	8,200,000
1980	8,000,000

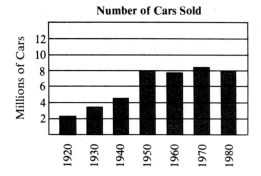

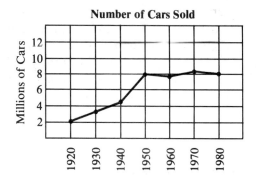

To draw a graph we must choose a **data unit** to mark off one of the axes. If the data are small numbers, the data unit can be a small number, such as 1 or 5. If the data are large numbers, a larger data unit should be chosen so that the graph will be a reasonable size. For example, the data unit in the graphs above is 2,000,000 automobiles.

EXAMPLE The following table gives the average monthly temperatures in Minneapolis, Minnesota. Construct a bar graph to illustrate the data.

Month	J	F	M	A	M	J	J	A	S	O	N	D
°C	⁻11.1	⁻8.3	⁻2.2	7.2	13.9	19.4	22.2	21.1	15.6	10.0	0	⁻7.2

Solution Label the horizontal axis with symbols for the months. Label the vertical axis using a data unit of 5°. Then draw bars of equal widths and proper lengths. Draw the bars downward for negative data. Finally, give the graph a title.

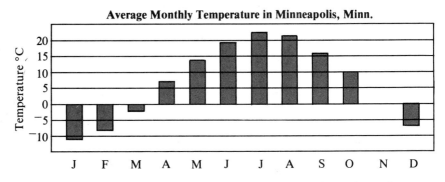

Average Monthly Temperature in Minneapolis, Minn.

Sometimes it is more convenient to arrange the bars in a graph horizontally. In the graph at the right, the data unit for the horizontal axis is 10,000 km² and the vertical axis is labeled with the names of the lakes.

We can estimate data from graphs. For example, we see from the graph that the area of Lake Erie is approximately 25,000 km².

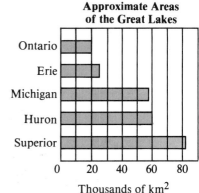

Approximate Areas of the Great Lakes

Class Exercises

Exercises 1–5 refer to the bar graph below.

1. What data unit is used on the vertical axis?

2. Which mountain has the lowest elevation? What is its elevation?

3. Which mountain has the highest elevation? What is its elevation?

4. Which two mountains have nearly the same elevation?

5. Find the ratio of the elevation of Mount Vinson to the elevation of Mount McKinley.

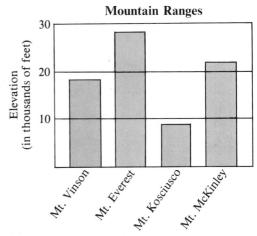

Mountain Ranges

Exercises 6–10 refer to the broken-line graph at the right.

6. What data unit is used on the vertical axis?

7. What was the approximate population in 1900? In 1950?

8. In approximately what year did the population pass 100 million? 150 million? 200 million?

9. In which 20-year period did the population increase the most?

10. Find the approximate total increase in population during the twentieth century.

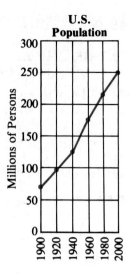

Written Exercises

The bar graph below shows the seven nations having populations over 100 million. Use the graph for Exercises 1–6.

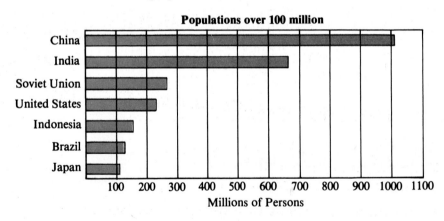

A 1. What data unit is used on the horizontal axis?

2. Estimate the total population of the three largest nations.

3. Estimate the total population of the three smallest nations.

4. Estimate the total population of the seven nations.

5. To the nearest percent, what percent of the world's 4.5 billion people live in China?

6. To the nearest percent, what percent of the world's 4.5 billion people live in the seven nations shown on the graph?

In Exercises 7–9, make a bar graph to illustrate the given data.

7. The six longest highway tunnels are: Saint Gotthard, 16.2 km; Arlberg, 14 km; Frejus, 12.8 km; Mont Blanc, 11.7 km; Enasson, 8.5 km; and San Bernadino, 6.6 km.

8. The areas of the world's five largest islands in thousands of square kilometers are: Greenland, 2175; New Guinea, 792; Borneo, 725; Madagascar, 587; and Baffin, 507.

9. The table below gives the length of each continent's longest river.

Continent	River	Length (km)
Africa	Nile	6632
Asia	Yangtze	6342
Australia	Murray-Darling	3693
Europe	Volga	3510
North America	Mississippi-Missouri	5936
South America	Amazon	6400

10. Make a broken-line graph to illustrate the given data.

Number of U.S. High School Graduates (in thousands)

1920	1930	1940	1950	1960	1970	1980
311	667	1221	1200	1864	2896	3078

B 11. Make a bar graph to illustrate the data. Net profits of the XYZ Company in thousands of dollars were: 30 in 1981; −20 (loss) in 1982; −5 (loss) in 1983; 45 in 1984; and 60 in 1985.

12. Make a broken-line graph to illustrate the average monthly temperatures in Minneapolis. (Use the table in the Example in this lesson.)

Review Exercises

Perform the indicated operation.

1. $\frac{47}{60} \times 360$
2. $\frac{74}{83} \times 249$
3. $\frac{118}{37} \times 111$
4. $\frac{85}{156} \times 312$

5. 25% of 540
6. 47% of 360
7. 73% of 180
8. 81% of 360

12-2 Pictographs and Circle Graphs

Nontechnical magazines often present data using pictures. These **pictographs** take the form of bar graphs with the bars replaced by rows or columns of symbols. Each symbol represents an assigned amount of data. This amount must be clearly indicated on the pictograph. For example, the pictograph below illustrates the data on automobile sales given in the previous lesson.

Number of Cars Sold

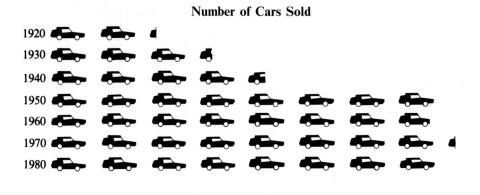

= 1,000,000 cars

EXAMPLE 1   The approximate numbers of different book titles published in the United States in selected years are: 11,000 in 1950; 15,000 in 1960; 36,000 in 1970; and 42,000 in 1980. Illustrate the data with a pictograph.

Solution   Stacks of books are appropriate symbols. We let one thick book represent 5000 titles and one thin book represent 1000 titles.

Books Published in the U.S.

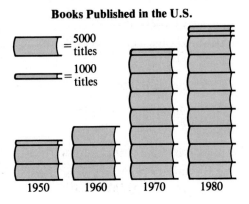

The **circle graph** at the right shows how the world's water is distributed. Circle graphs are often more effective than other graphs in picturing how a total amount is divided into parts.

The following example illustrates how to make a circle graph.

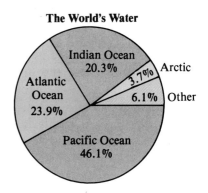

The World's Water

EXAMPLE 2 The seventh-grade class voted to decide where to have their year-end picnic. The results were as follows: Mountain Park, 62 votes; State Beach, 96 votes; City Zoo, 82 votes. Make a circle graph to illustrate this distribution.

Solution The whole circle represents the total number of votes. We plan to divide the circle into wedges to represent the distribution of the votes. Since the sum of all the adjacent angles around a point is 360°, the sum of the angle measures of all the wedges is 360°.

First find the total of all votes cast.

$$62 + 96 + 82 = 240$$

Then find the fraction of the vote cast for each place and the corresponding angle measure.

For Mountain Park:

$\frac{62}{240} \times 360° = 93°$

For State Beach:

$\frac{96}{240} \times 360° = 144°$

For City Zoo:

$\frac{82}{240} \times 360° = 123°$

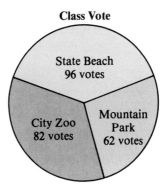

Class Vote

Now use a compass to draw a circle and a protractor to draw three radii forming the angles found above. Finally, label the wedges and give the graph a title.

Class Exercises

1. Draw a circle and divide it into 4 equal parts.

2. Draw a circle and divide it into 6 equal parts.

3. Draw a circle and divide it into 9 equal parts.

4. Draw a circle and divide it into 12 equal parts.

The circle graph at the right pictures the distribution of students playing the various instruments in the school orchestra.

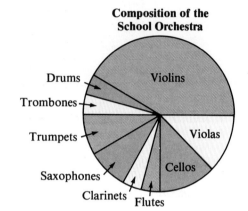

Composition of the School Orchestra

5. Which instrument is played by the greatest number of students in the orchestra?

6. How does the number of students playing stringed instruments (violins, violas, and cellos) compare with the number of students playing all the other instruments?

7. Which four instruments are played by the fewest students?

8. How does the number of saxophone players compare with the number of trumpet players?

Written Exercises

Complete the following tables and construct a circle graph for each.

A 1. The Junior Athletic Association decided to raise money by selling greeting cards. Orders were obtained for the following kinds of cards.

Kind of Card	Number of Boxes	Fraction of the Whole	Number of Degrees in the Angle
birthday	60	?	?
get well	72	?	?
friendship	48	?	?
thank you	60	?	?
Total	?	?	?

2. The winter issue of the school magazine contained the following kinds of material.

Kind of Material	Number of Pages	Fraction of the Whole	Number of Degrees in the Angle
Fiction	32	?	?
Essays	8	?	?
Sports	16	?	?
Advertisements	8	?	?
Total	?	?	?

Illustrate, using a circle graph.

3. The surface of Earth is 30% land and 70% water.

4. Earth's atmosphere is 78% nitrogen, 21% oxygen, and 1% other gases.

Illustrate, using a pictograph. The parentheses contain a suggestion as to what symbol to use.

5. The XYZ Car Rental Company rented 520 cars in July, 350 cars in August, 350 cars in September, 400 cars in October, and 110 cars in November. (cars)

6. The Meadowbrook School ordered 200 cartons of milk the first week, 220 the second week, 240 the third week, and 180 the fourth week. (milk cartons)

7. The number of fish caught in Clear Lake: 4500 in 1970; 3500 in 1975; 4200 in 1980; 4800 in 1985. (fish)

8. The cost of higher education in the United States in billions of dollars: 1965 – $13; 1970 – $23; 1975 – $39; 1980 – $55. (dollars)

Illustrate, using (a) a circle graph and (b) a pictograph. The parentheses contain a suggestion as to what symbol to use in the pictograph.

B 9. In the United States about 167 million people live in cities and about 59 million live in rural areas. (people)

10. A fund-raising event made $420 from the sale of antiques, $280 from crafts items, and $240 from food. (dollars)

Illustrate, using (a) a circle graph and (b) a pictograph. The parentheses contain a suggestion as to what symbol to use in the pictograph.

11. The average seasonal rainfall in Honolulu is 26 cm in winter, 7 cm in spring, 5 cm in summer, and 21 cm in autumn. (raindrops)

12. Of each dollar the United States government takes in, 47¢ comes from individual income taxes, 27¢ from Social Security, 12¢ from corporation taxes, and 14¢ from other sources. (piles of coins)

13. A family spends $440.75 of the monthly budget on food, $530.00 on rent, $617.00 total on clothes, medicine, and other items, and $175.25 on transportation. (dollars)

14. A total of 387 people were polled on Proposition Q, 46% favored it, 33% opposed it, and 21% had no opinion. (people)

15. The library received a $1300 grant. The librarian plans to spend 10% of the grant to extend magazine subscriptions, 35% to buy new books, 15% to repair damaged books, 30% to buy new furniture, and 10% to locate missing books. (books)

C 16. Which pictograph correctly shows that the production of a certain oil field doubled between 1975 and 1985? Explain your answer.

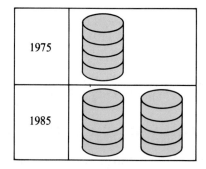

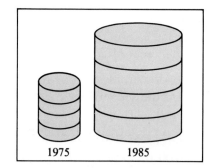

Review Exercises

Arrange in order from least to greatest.

1. 4, 2.6, 7, 0.84, 3

2. 4, ⁻8, ⁻3, 1, 10, ⁻5

3. 7, $3\frac{1}{2}$, ⁻5, $4\frac{1}{4}$, ⁻6

4. $\frac{7}{8}$, $\frac{5}{6}$, $\frac{11}{9}$, $\frac{7}{12}$, $\frac{12}{7}$

5. ⁻6, ⁻10, ⁻2, ⁻12, ⁻9

6. $3\frac{7}{8}$, $2\frac{9}{10}$, $2\frac{8}{9}$, $3\frac{11}{16}$

7. 1.09, 1.1, 0.9, 0.09

8. $\frac{17}{4}$, $\frac{11}{2}$, $\frac{15}{8}$, $\frac{9}{4}$, $\frac{7}{5}$

12-3 Mean, Median, and Range

The daytime high temperatures in °C for five days in May were

$$23°, 14°, 18°, 28°, \text{ and } 25°.$$

Here are two ways to give a numerical description of these temperatures.

(1) The **mean** of the temperatures is their sum divided by the number of temperatures.

$$\frac{23° + 14° + 18° + 28° + 25°}{5} = \frac{108°}{5} = 21.6°$$

(2) The **median** of the temperatures is the middle temperature when they are arranged in order of size.

$$14°, 18°, 23°, 25°, 28° \qquad \text{Median} = 23°$$

For an even number of data items the median is midway between the two middle numbers.

The **range** of a set of data is the difference between the greatest and least numbers in the set. For example, the range of the above temperatures is $28° - 14°$, or $14°$.

EXAMPLE   Find the mean, median, and range of each set of numbers.

a. 11, 19, 7, 45, 22, 38   **b.** 0, 1, 3, ⁻4, 4, ⁻6, 7

Solution   **a.** Mean $= \dfrac{11 + 19 + 7 + 45 + 22 + 38}{6} = \dfrac{142}{6} \approx 23.7$

Arrange the numbers in order of size: 7, 11, 19, 22, 38, 45

Median $= \dfrac{19 + 22}{2} = 20.5$ Range $= 45 - 7 = 38$

b. Mean $= \dfrac{0 + 1 + 3 + {}^{-}4 + 4 + {}^{-}6 + 7}{7} = \dfrac{5}{7} \approx 0.7$

Arrange the numbers in order of size: ⁻6, ⁻4, 0, 1, 3, 4, 7

Median $= 1$ Range $= 7 - {}^{-}6 = 13$

In everyday conversation the word *average* is usually used for mean.

Analyzing data as we have been doing is part of the branch of mathematics called **statistics.**

Class Exercises

Find the mean, median, and range of each set of data.

1. 1, 2, 3, 4, 5
2. 5, 3, 1
3. 10, 10, 6, 2
4. 3, 4, 5, 6, 8, 10
5. ⁻4, ⁻2, 0, 2, 4
6. 3, 2, 1, 0, ⁻1, ⁻2, ⁻3
7. ⁻3, ⁻1, 0, 4, 5
8. 6, 5, 5, 0, ⁻1
9. ⁻15, ⁻11, ⁻7, ⁻7, ⁻7, 0, 2, 5, 9, 15, 18, 22
10. ⁻37, ⁻28, ⁻15, ⁻15, ⁻6, 1, 13, 26, 34
11. 11, 17, 31, 43, 58, 61, 58, 89, 94, 58, 94, 107, 215

Written Exercises

Find the mean, median, and range of each set of data.

A

1. 30, 18, 21, 28, 23
2. 42, 58, 55, 61, 39
3. 7, 16, 20, 13, 26, 14
4. 85, 70, 93, 101, 116, 111
5. 47, 61, 53, 69, 45, 58
6. 17, 11, 9, 13, 7, 21, 8, 18
7. 3.6, 2.7, 2.9, 3.4, 3.4
8. 8.1, 9.2, 6.8, 7.3, 7.9, 6.9

B

9. ⁻3, 2, ⁻2, ⁻5, 3
10. 8, ⁻8, ⁻12, 16, ⁻8, 7
11. 1.3, ⁻0.8, ⁻0.1, 0.2, 0.9
12. 4.1, ⁻3.2, ⁻0.8, ⁻1.5, 2.7, ⁻0.1

13. Low Temperatures in February (°C)

⁻13°	⁻8°	⁻10°	⁻4°	1°	0°	⁻2°
⁻5°	⁻7°	⁻12°	⁻8°	⁻7°	⁻5°	0°
⁻2°	⁻3°	⁻5°	1°	2°	3°	1°
2°	4°	2°	4°	4°	5°	6°

14. Elevations Along the Salton Sea Railway (meters)

6.82	2.55	1.60	⁻0.21	⁻1.35
⁻2.68	⁻1.95	⁻2.06	⁻0.88	⁻0.02
0.41	1.15	3.15	6.51	5.86

15. Insert another number in the list 15, 23, 11, 17 in such a way that the median is not changed.

16. Replace one of the numbers in the list 15, 23, 11, 17 so that the median becomes 17.

Find the value of x such that the mean of the given list is the specified number.

17. 6, 9, 13, x; mean $= 11$

18. 8, 14, 16, 12, x; mean $= 15$

19. Janet's scores on her first four mathematics tests were 98, 78, 84, and 96. What score must she make on the fifth test to have the mean of the five tests equal 90?

20. The heights of the starting guards and forwards on the basketball team are 178 cm, 185 cm, 165 cm, and 188 cm. How tall is the center if the mean height of the starting five is 182 cm?

C **21.** If each number in a list is increased by 5, how is the median affected?

22. If each number in a list is increased by 5, how is the mean affected?

Review Exercises

Perform the indicated operations. Round to the nearest tenth if necessary.

1. $(4 \times 2 + 7 \times 5 + 6 \times 8) \div 15$

2. $(9 \times 4 + 6 \times 7 + 11 \times 5) \div 16$

3. $(14 \times 6 + 3 \times 0 + 16 \times 4) \div 10$

4. $(12 \times 1 + 8 \times 11 + 5 \times 6) \div 18$

5. $(18 \times 3 + 20 \times 5 + 7 \times 6) \div 14$

6. $(7 \times 15 + 4 \times 9 + 7 \times 2) \div 26$

7. $(11 \times 3 \times 2 + 8 \times 3 + 9) \div 33$

8. $(12 \times 2 \times 8 + 9 \times 3 \times 4) \div 15$

███ **NONROUTINE PROBLEM SOLVING:** *Decision Making*

Cellini and Valdez were each appointed to a new job. Cellini is paid a starting salary of $16,500 a year with a $1000 raise at the end of each year. Valdez is paid a starting salary of $8000 for the first 6 months with a raise of $500 at the end of every 6 months. How much does each make at the end of the first year? The third year? Who has the better pay plan?

12-4 Frequency Distributions

Forty students took a quiz and received the following scores.

8 7 10 6 8 7 9 7 8 5
9 7 8 8 7 9 3 8 8 6
7 5 6 8 10 10 7 10 8 9
7 7 9 7 8 7 9 10 10 7

In order to analyze these data, we can arrange them in a
frequency table as shown at the right. The number of times
a score occurs is its **frequency**. Since a score of 9 was received by 6 students, we can say that the frequency of 9 is
6. The pairing of the scores with their frequencies is called
a **frequency distribution**.

Score	Frequency
3	1
4	0
5	2
6	3
7	12
8	10
9	6
10	6

EXAMPLE   Find the range, mean, and median for the data above.

Solution   Since the lowest score is 3 and the highest is 10, the range is $10 - 3$,
or 7.

To find the *mean* of the data,
first multiply each possible score by
its frequency. Enter the product in
a third column as shown. The sum
of the numbers in this column
equals the sum of the 40 scores.
Therefore:

$$\text{mean} = \frac{309}{40} = 7.725$$

Score x	Frequency f	$x \times f$
3	1	3
4	0	0
5	2	10
6	3	18
7	12	84
8	10	80
9	6	54
10	6	60
Total	40	309

To find the median, first rearrange the data in order from least to
greatest. Since there are 40 scores, the median is the average of the
twentieth and twenty-first scores, both of which are 8.

$$\text{median} = \frac{8 + 8}{2} = 8$$

COMMUNICATION IN MATHEMATICS: *Reading Tables*

As you use a table, reread the headings to remind yourself what each number represents. For example, the frequency table above shows that the *score*
of 8 had a *frequency* of 10; that is, there are 10 scores of 8, not 8 scores of
10.

The **mode** of a set of data is the item that occurs with the greatest frequency. In the Example on the preceding page, the mode is 7 since it has the greatest frequency, 12. Sometimes there is more than one mode. The mode usually is used with nonnumerical data, such as to determine the popularity of car colors.

Class Exercises

Find the range, the mean, the median, and the mode(s) of each student's test score, x.

1. Evelyn

x	f
70	1
80	4
90	3
100	2

2. Bruce

x	f
75	2
85	3
90	1
100	4

3. Shana

x	f
70	4
85	3
95	2
100	1

4. Elroy

x	f
75	1
80	2
95	3
100	4

Written Exercises

In Exercises 1–6, find the range, the mean, the median, and the mode(s) of the data in each frequency table.

A **1.**

x	f
5	2
6	4
7	8
8	5
9	1

2.

x	f
0	3
1	2
2	7
3	8
4	5

3.

x	f
25	1
20	0
15	3
10	5
5	6

4.

x	f
18	1
15	0
12	3
9	6
6	7
3	1
0	2

5.

x	f
14	2
15	5
16	11
17	11
18	8
19	0
20	3

6.

x	f
28	2
27	4
26	11
25	11
24	4
23	2
22	1

In Exercises 7–12, make a frequency table for the given data, and then find the range, the mean, the median, and the mode(s) of the data. Round the mean to the nearest tenth if necessary.

B 7. The number of runs scored by Jan's team in recent softball games:
5, 1, 4, 4, 8, 6, 4, 1, 5, 0, 1, 5, 3, 8, 4, 5, 3, 4

8. Jim's 200 m dash practice times: 28 s, 29 s, 27 s, 27 s, 28 s, 29 s, 28 s, 26 s, 27 s, 26 s, 28 s, 27 s, 27 s, 25 s, 26 s

9.
April in Pleasantville
Average Temperatures (°C)

	16	15	14	16	17
17	18	18	18	19	19	18
17	18	17	18	19	20	20
19	19	18	17	18	19	20
20	20	19	20

10.
Class Test Scores

16	14	20	15	15	17
15	17	17	16	14	18
17	15	14	14	20	15
14	16	15	18	17	16
15	16	18	14	18	17

11.
Samples of Steel Rods (diameters in millimeters)

101	102	100	97	101	103	100	100	101	100	99	100
99	100	101	103	102	100	101	99	100	100	101	

12.
Ages of Members of the Moose Hill Hiking Club

15	14	15	13	16	14	18	16	15	14	14	15	18	15
13	13	14	15	14	16	16	17	14	15	13	12	14	16
14	16	15	13	16	14	15	17	12	13	16	15		

Exercises 13 and 14 refer to a class of 24 boys and 16 girls. (*Hint:* If you know the number of scores and their mean, you can find the sum of the scores.)

C 13. On test A, the mean of the boys' scores was 70 and the mean of the girls' scores was 75. What was the class mean?

14. On test B, the class mean was 75 and the mean of the girls' scores was 72. What was the mean of the boys' scores?

Review Exercises

Explain the meaning of each term.

1. mean 2. median 3. mode 4. range

5. odd number 6. even number 7. prime number 8. multiple of 7

The following computer program will find the average, or mean, of several numbers. The program finds the sum of the numbers and then divides this sum by the number of numbers. For example, if you input 2, 4, 7, 8, and 11, the computer would find their sum, 32, and divide it by 5, the number of items, resulting in an answer of 6.4.

```
10   PRINT "TO FIND THE AVERAGE,"
20   PRINT "INPUT THE NUMBERS ONE AT A TIME."
30   PRINT "TYPE -1 AT END OF LIST."
40   PRINT
50   LET N = 0
60   LET S = 0
70   INPUT A
80   IF A = - 1 THEN 120
90   LET N = N + 1
100  LET S = S + A
110  GOTO 70
120  PRINT
130  PRINT "N = ";N
140  PRINT "SUM = ";S
150  PRINT "AVERAGE = ";S/N
160  END
```

Use the program to find the average of the following. Be sure to type −1 at the end of each list.

1. 12, 19, 23, 8, 17, 31

2. 57, 3, 86, 79, 101, 9

3. 542, 863, 921, 254, 378, 511

4. 1649, 15,241, 8463, 11,684

5. 887, 3105, 6324, 7048, 2103, 1298, 5541, 7201, 4961, 1114, 2260, 1954, 7322, 5665, 5321, 3742, 4457, 8916, 9923, 4309, 2385, 3342, 4187

6.

21,542	11,372	63,982	14,320
78,864	24,953	21,419	17,160
47,922	72,315	18,560	21,000
91,254	94,456	41,215	35,743
20,964	34,290	38,730	44,287

7.

502,784	339,065	764,290	274,415
114,902	765,329	314,675	441,823
345,245	465,367	468,901	687,390
113,823	589,001	892,030	389,210
992,084	314,675	440,871	572,903

12-5 Stem-and-Leaf Plots

Like a frequency distribution, a **stem-and-leaf plot** is a method of displaying data. Consider the following centimeter heights of plants in a laboratory experiment:

25   16   32   28   25   11   29   17   43   24   37   33   30

In order to create a stem-and-leaf plot, you first draw a vertical line and list the tens' digits from least to greatest to the left of the line. These are the "stems."

1	
2	
3	
4	

Next, list the units' digit for each item of data to the right of its corresponding stem. These are the "leaves."

1	6, 1, 7
2	5, 8, 5, 9, 4
3	2, 7, 3, 0
4	3

Finally, rewrite your diagram with the leaves listed from least to greatest, reading from left to right. This is the finished stem-and-leaf plot.

1	1, 6, 7
2	4, 5, 5, 8, 9
3	0, 2, 3, 7
4	3

EXAMPLE   Construct a stem-and-leaf plot for the following test scores:

75   83   72   56   92   74   87   88   91   76   74   80

Solution

5	6
6	
7	2, 4, 4, 5, 6
8	0, 3, 7, 8
9	1, 2

Note that the stem 6 is included for completeness, even though no scores require that stem.

Class Exercises

1. List the data items from which the stem-and-leaf plot shown at the right was constructed.

0	4
1	2, 3, 3, 7
2	2, 5, 6
3	4, 7
4	5, 9, 9

Use the following data for Exercises 2 and 3:

54   65   76   83   47   62   76   89   77   88   71   80

2. List the stems for this set of data.

3. List the leaves for the stems 7 and 8.

4. What are the advantages of a stem-and-leaf plot over a frequency distribution? What are the disadvantages?

Written Exercises

Construct a stem-and-leaf plot for each set of data.

A   **1.** 22, 14, 14, 25, 27, 31, 35, 29, 18

      2. 54, 40, 41, 32, 55, 57, 58, 58, 36, 43

      3. 62, 65, 43, 44, 44, 44, 50, 53, 72, 67

      4. 81, 85, 70, 76, 92, 65, 97, 85, 87, 53, 66

      5. 7, 23, 27, 24, 9, 5, 13, 16, 5, 30, 2, 12, 10

      6. 45, 37, 28, 22, 45, 56, 25, 28, 37, 40, 42, 48

      7. 92, 90, 58, 87, 56, 77, 91, 53, 53, 91, 95, 84

      8. 11, 19, 5, 33, 9, 7, 5, 35, 16, 44, 5, 46, 41

B   **9.** Numbers of customers at a car wash on different days:
46, 42, 45, 36, 57, 72, 54, 32, 30, 44, 73, 31, 45, 53

    10. Numbers of seeds out of samples of 50 that germinated:
42, 35, 31, 30, 9, 28, 27, 37, 35, 30, 41, 22, 25, 8, 33

    11. Point totals for a basketball team in successive games:
87, 94, 82, 78, 95, 91, 87, 83, 101, 83, 82, 77, 80, 102, 75

    12. Daily patient counts at a health clinic:
47, 39, 32, 32, 58, 63, 55, 67, 52, 44, 37, 50, 40, 71, 50

C   **13.** Consider the following standardized test scores:
570, 650, 780, 460, 550, 530, 580, 610, 720, 640, 490, 520, 480

How would you alter the rule for constructing a stem-and-leaf plot so that these data could be best displayed? Construct a stem-and-leaf plot according to your rule.

12-6 Box-and-Whisker Plots

A **box-and-whisker plot** is a method of displaying data that gives a quick picture of the distribution of the data items. Consider the data below, which are scores on a job aptitude test whose maximum score is 100.

56 48 66 72 37 62 49 37 29 83 74 55 46 48 52 57 44

To make a box-and-whisker plot, first put the data items in increasing order, reading from left to right.

29 37 37 44 46 48 48 49 52 55 56 57 62 66 72 74 83

Next, find the three numbers that split the data into four equal-sized parts. The second of these numbers will be the median. In this example, the median is 52. The other two numbers, called the **first quartile** and the **third quartile,** are, respectively, the medians of the lower and upper halves of the data, not including the median.

lower half   upper half

29 37 37 44 46 48 48 49 52 55 56 57 62 66 72 74 83

first quartile: median: third quartile:

$$\frac{44 + 46}{2} = 45 \qquad 52 \qquad \frac{62 + 66}{2} = 64$$

Draw a number line that includes all the *possible* data values. Underneath the line, mark with dots the boundaries of the range, the median, and the two quartiles.

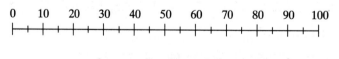

Finally, using the dots as a guide, draw a "box" around the middle half of the range, a vertical line through the median, and "whiskers" out to the two ends of the range.

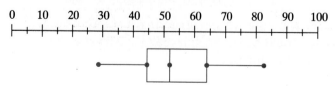

Class Exercises

Exercises 1–4 refer to the box-and-whisker plot below.

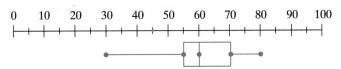

1. What is the range of the data? What is the median of the data?

2. What are the first and third quartiles?

3. Name the interval into which the middle half of the data falls.

4. Name the interval that contains the quarter of the data in which the data items are *most concentrated.*

Written Exercises

Construct a box-and-whisker plot for each set of data.

A 1. 18, 32, 35, 37, 45, 50, 53, 55, 60, 75, 80

2. 36, 38, 40, 45, 46, 55, 57, 60, 70, 77, 82

3. 6.6, 5.4, 8.3, 9.2, 9.0, 7.4, 8.2, 5.8, 6.3, 6.5

4. 114, 128, 105, 122, 130, 136, 118, 110, 129, 140

For each pair of sets of data construct two box-and-whisker plots using a common number line.

B 5. Monthly rainfall (in inches):

Antrim: 2.5, 2.0, 4.9, 3.4, 2.1, 1.6, 1.3, 0.7, 1.4, 3.6, 3.5, 3.5

Brewster: 3.2, 4.1, 5.5, 7.2, 3.6, 2.1, 1.5, 1.4, 2.5, 3.8, 5.0, 4.4

6. Scores on a math test (out of 100):

Class 1: 92, 86, 74, 56, 82, 85, 78, 94, 95, 98, 80, 72, 63, 77

Class 2: 82, 84, 83, 48, 56, 64, 72, 90, 88, 86, 80, 79, 68, 92

Construct a set of data that would give rise to each box-and-whisker plot.

C 7.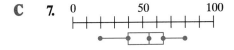

8.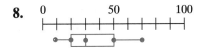

12-7 Histograms and Frequency Polygons

When a bar graph is used to picture a frequency distribution, it is called a **histogram.** No spaces are left between the bars. The histogram for the quiz-score data of the table is shown at the left below.

The broken-line graph shown at the right below is the **frequency polygon** for the same distribution. The broken-line graph of the frequencies is connected to the horizontal axis at each end to form a polygon.

We can find the range, the mode, the mean, and the median from a histogram and from a frequency polygon.

Score x	Frequency f	$x \times f$
3	1	3
4	0	0
5	2	10
6	3	18
7	12	84
8	10	80
9	6	54
10	6	60
Total	40	309

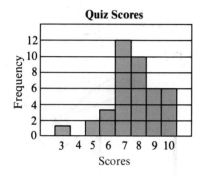

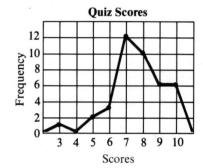

EXAMPLE Find the range, the mode, the mean, and the median for the data represented in the graphs above.

Solution The range is the difference between the least number representing data on the horizontal axis and the greatest number.

The range is 10 − 3, or 7.

The tallest bar or highest point represents the mode.

The mode is 7.

To find the mean, we first multiply each data item by its frequency.

$3 \times 1 = 3$ $4 \times 0 = 0$ $5 \times 2 = 10$ $6 \times 3 = 18$
$7 \times 12 = 84$ $8 \times 10 = 80$ $9 \times 6 = 54$ $10 \times 6 = 60$

We then add the products.

$3 + 0 + 10 + 18 + 84 + 80 + 54 + 60 = 309$

We then add the frequencies.

$$1 + 0 + 2 + 3 + 12 + 10 + 6 + 6 = 40$$

We then divide the sum of the products by the sum of the frequencies.

$$309 \div 40 = 7.725$$

The mean is 7.725.

Since there are 40 data items, the median is the average of the middle two items, both of which are 8. Thus, their average is 8.

The median is 8.

Class Exercises

Refer to the histogram at the right.

1. What is the mode of the scores?

2. What is the range of the scores?

3. How many students received scores of 90? 60? 50? 40?

4. How many students took the test?

5. What is the median score?

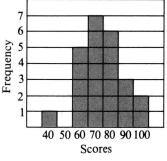

6. What is the mean of the scores? Round to the nearest tenth.

Written Exercises

Exercises 1–10 refer to the frequency polygon below.

A 1. What is the range of the data?   2. What is the mode of the data?

How many students did the following numbers of pushups?

3. 25   4. 30   5. 35   6. 40

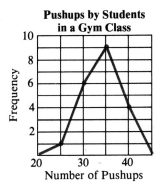

7. How many students are in the class?

8. What is the median of the data?

9. What is the mean of the data?

10. Draw a histogram for the data.

Draw a histogram and a frequency polygon for the data in the following exercises of Lesson 12-4.

B **11.** Exercise 7 **12.** Exercise 8 **13.** Exercise 9

14. Exercise 10 **15.** Exercise 11 **16.** Exercise 12

C **17.** Arrange the data listed below into the following intervals.

10–15, 15–20, 20–25, 25–30, 30–35, 35–40, 40–45

Then draw a histogram for the seven intervals.

23, 43, 27, 41, 12, 13, 19, 32, 43, 22, 36, 28, 44, 29, 31, 24, 34, 44, 37, 23, 17, 14, 23, 32, 36, 33, 43, 28, 39, 19

Self-Test A

The number of people employed in farming in the United States was: 11,100,000 in 1900; 10,400,000 in 1920; 9,500,000 in 1940; 5,400,000 in 1960; and 3,400,000 in 1980.

1. Draw a broken-line graph.   [12-1]

2. Draw a pictograph. Use people as symbols.   [12-2]

3. Find the mean, median, and range of 13, 6, 20, 20, 9, 15, 11, 10.   [12-3]

4. Make a frequency table for 12, 18, 15, 12, 9, 15, 15, 16, 9, 12, 18, 12.   [12-4]

5. Make a stem-and-leaf plot for 83, 75, 91, 63, 66, 77, 83, 89, 78, 82.   [12-5]

6. Make a box-and-whisker plot for 25, 28, 52, 55, 65, 82, 88, 90.   [12-6]

Exercises 7–10 refer to the histogram.

7. How many runners had a time of 16 s?   [12-7]

8. How many runners were there in all?

9. Draw a frequency polygon for the data.

10. What are the range, the mode, the mean, and the median of the data?

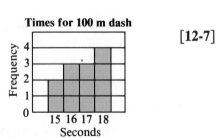

Self-Test answers and Extra Practice are at the back of the book.

12-8 Probability of an Event

Two of five unmarked envelopes contain $100 bills. The other three are empty. Suppose that you could pick one envelope and keep it. How likely is it that you will choose one with a bill in it?

When you pick one of the envelopes, the result is called an **outcome.** Since there are 5 envelopes, there are 5 possible outcomes, all of which are **equally likely,** and 2 of which are **favorable.** We say that the **probability** of drawing an envelope with a bill in it is $\frac{2}{5}$.

If we let A stand for the **event** of drawing an envelope with a bill in it, we can write $P(A) = \frac{2}{5}$ to mean that the **probability of event** A is $\frac{2}{5}$. In general, we have the following formula.

> ### *Formula*
>
> For equally likely outcomes, the probability of event A is
>
> $$P(A) = \frac{\text{number of outcomes favoring event } A}{\text{total number of possible outcomes}}.$$

When you select something by chance only, such as picking a sealed envelope, you say that you are selecting **at random** or **randomly.**

EXAMPLE 1   A jar contains 2 red marbles, 4 white marbles, and 4 blue marbles. One marble is drawn at random. Find the probability of each of these events.

A: The marble is blue.	*B:* The marble is red.
C: The marble is red or white.	*D:* The marble is green.
E: The marble is not green.	

Solution   Since there are 10 marbles, there are 10 possible outcomes.

Since 4 marbles are blue, $P(A) = \frac{4}{10} = \frac{2}{5}$.

Since 2 marbles are red, $P(B) = \frac{2}{10} = \frac{1}{5}$.

Since 6 marbles are either red or white, $P(C) = \frac{6}{10} = \frac{3}{5}$.

Since no marbles are green, $P(D) = \frac{0}{10} = 0$.

Since all the marbles are not green, $P(E) = \frac{10}{10} = 1$.

Events D and E in Example 1 illustrate the following.

> The probability of an *impossible* event is 0.
>
> The probability of a *certain* event is 1.

EXAMPLE 2 A student is chosen at random from the class of 24 whose scores are shown in the histogram. What is the probability that the student's score was **a.** 80? **b.** at least 80?

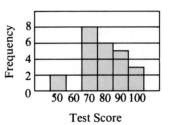

Solution There are 24 possible outcomes.

a. The histogram shows us that 6 students had scores of 80.

Therefore, $P(\text{score} = 80) = \frac{6}{24} = \frac{1}{4}$.

b. For a student to have a score of at least 80, the student must have a score of 80, 90, or 100. There are 6 scores of 80, 5 scores of 90, and 3 scores of 100.

Therefore, $P(\text{score} \geq 80) = \frac{6 + 5 + 3}{24} = \frac{14}{24} = \frac{7}{12}$.

PROBLEM SOLVING REMINDER

When you solve a problem, make use of the full range of your knowledge of mathematics and problem solving strategies. For Example 2, ask yourself what facts are needed and read only the necessary information from the histogram. You translate the phrase *a score of at least 80* into the inequality $s \geq 80$ and solve it. In the last step, you use the probability formula.

Class Exercises

Exercises 1–4 refer to the jar of marbles in Example 1. Find the probability that a randomly drawn marble is the following.

1. white   **2.** not white   **3.** not red   **4.** yellow

Exercises 5–10 refer to the histogram in Example 2. Find the probability that a randomly chosen student's score was the following.

5. 50   **6.** 100   **7.** 60   **8.** less than 80

9. equal to the mode of the distribution

10. equal to the median of the distribution

Written Exercises

Twenty-four cards are numbered 1, 2, 3, . . . , 24. The cards are put into a box and mixed. A card is drawn at random. Find the probability that the number on the card is as given.

A   **1.** 3   **2.** 12   **3.** 1, 2, or 3   **4.** 5, 10, 15, or 20

     5. even   **6.** odd   **7.** prime   **8.** not prime

     9. a multiple of 3   **10.** divisible by 4

When the pointer on the dial at the right below is spun, it will stop at random on a number, but not on any line. Find the probability that the pointer stops on a wedge of the type described.

11. red   **12.** odd-number

13. even-number   **14.** blue or white

15. number greater than 5

16. number less than 6

17. both even-number and red

18. even-number or red (or both)

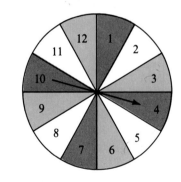

Exercises 19–26 refer to the histogram at the right. It shows the frequency distribution of test scores of a class of 36 students. Find the probability that a randomly chosen student's score was as given.

B   **19.** 80   **20.** 40

     21. 50   **22.** 90 or 100

     23. less than 80   **24.** greater than 70

     25. equal to the median score   **26.** less than 60

Review Exercises

Perform the indicated operations. Simplify.

1. $\dfrac{14}{330} \times \dfrac{3}{70}$ **2.** $\dfrac{55}{204} \times \dfrac{36}{121}$ **3.** $\dfrac{9}{25} \div \dfrac{27}{125}$

4. $\dfrac{120}{7} \div \dfrac{64}{77}$ **5.** $\left(\dfrac{1}{4} + 2\dfrac{1}{8}\right) \div \dfrac{2}{9}$ **6.** $\left(1 - \dfrac{8}{9}\right) \div \dfrac{4}{27}$

7. $\dfrac{7}{4} \div \left(1 - \dfrac{35}{40}\right)$ **8.** $\dfrac{4}{3} \div \left(1 - \dfrac{7}{9}\right)$ **9.** $\dfrac{8}{15} \div \left(12 - 7\dfrac{4}{5}\right)$

■■■■ COMPUTER INVESTIGATION: *Probability*

If we toss a coin, there are two possible outcomes—a head or a tail. If these two outcomes are equally likely, then the probability of each is $\frac{1}{2}$. Does this mean that if we toss a coin 10 times, we will get 5 heads and 5 tails? (Not necessarily.)

The following program will simulate tossing a coin. The program is based on a list of "random numbers" that are decimals between 0 and 1. (Usage of the RND function varies. Check this program with the manual for the computer that you are using, and make any necessary changes.)

```
10   PRINT "HOW MANY TOSSES";
20   INPUT N
30   LET H = 0
40   FOR I = 1 to N
50   LET A = RND (1)
60   IF A < .5 THEN 90
70   PRINT TAB( 6);"TAIL"
80   GOTO 110
90   LET H = H + 1
100   PRINT "HEAD"
110   NEXT I
120   PRINT
130   PRINT "H = ";H; TAB( 10);"T = ";N - H;
140   PRINT  TAB( 20);"H/N = ";H/N
150   END
```

1. Run the program 10 times for N = 25.
   a. For how many runs was $0.45 < H/N < 0.55$?
   b. What percent was this?

2. Delete lines 70 and 100 and repeat Exercise 1 for N = 250.

12-9 Probability and Odds

Suppose you are playing a game with a spinner. In order for you to win the game, the pointer must stop on a red wedge. Since there are two red wedges and four white wedges, you have

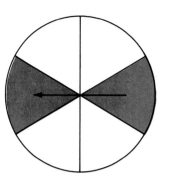

$$P(\text{win}) = \frac{2}{6} = \frac{1}{3}$$

and

$$P(\text{not win}) = \frac{4}{6} = \frac{2}{3}.$$

This example illustrates the following general fact.

> If the probability that an event occurs is p, then the probability that the event does not occur is $1 - p$.

In the example above there are 2 ways of winning and 4 ways of not winning. We therefore say:

> The odds in favor of winning are 2 to 4, or 1 to 2.
> The odds against winning are 4 to 2, or 2 to 1.

We can calculate the odds of an event if we can count the number of outcomes that are favorable and unfavorable.

> Odds of an event $A = \dfrac{\text{number of outcomes favoring } A}{\text{number of outcomes not favoring } A}$

EXAMPLE 1 A cube whose faces are numbered 1 through 6 is thrown. Find the odds in favor of the top face showing (a) 4, (b) a number less than 5, and (c) a prime number.

Solution

a. One face of the cube has a 4 and five faces do not. There is 1 favorable outcome and there are 5 unfavorable outcomes. Thus, the odds in favor of the top face showing a 4 are $\frac{1}{5}$ (read "1 to 5").

b. Four faces of the cube have a number less than 5 and two faces do not. There are 4 favorable outcomes and 2 unfavorable outcomes. Thus, the odds in favor of the top face showing a number less than 5 are $\frac{4}{2}$, or $\frac{2}{1}$ (read "2 to 1").

(Solution continued on page 432.)

c. The prime numbers on the cube are 2, 3, and 5. There are 3 faces with a prime number and 3 faces without a prime number. Thus, the odds in favor of the top face showing a prime number are $\frac{3}{3}$, or $\frac{1}{1}$ (read "1 to 1").

If the odds in favor of an event are 1 to 1, we say that the **odds are even** that the event will occur. Thus, in Example 1, the odds are even that a prime number will be thrown.

COMMUNICATION IN MATHEMATICS: *Mathematical Terms in Context*

You learned the meanings of *odd number* and *even number* in an earlier chapter. In the statement "the odds are even" the words *odds* and *even* take on a different meaning. The context of a statement provides clues that can help you figure out how the words are being used.

We can also calculate the odds of an event if we know the probability of the event.

Formula

If the probability that an event occurs is p ($p \neq 0, p \neq 1$), then:

$$\text{Odds in favor of the event} = \frac{p}{1-p}$$

$$\text{Odds against the event} = \frac{1-p}{p}$$

EXAMPLE 2 The probability that an item on an assembly line will be defective is $\frac{4}{135}$. Find (a) the odds in favor of the item being defective and (b) the odds against the item being defective.

Solution

a. Use the formula $\frac{p}{1-p}$ where $p = \frac{4}{135}$.

$$\frac{p}{1-p} = \frac{\frac{4}{135}}{1 - \frac{4}{135}} = \frac{\frac{4}{135}}{\frac{131}{135}} = \frac{4}{135} \times \frac{135}{131} = \frac{4}{131}$$

The odds in favor of a defective item are $\frac{4}{131}$, or 4 to 131.

b. Use the formula $\frac{1-p}{p}$ where $p = \frac{4}{135}$.

$$\frac{1-p}{p} = \frac{1 - \frac{4}{135}}{\frac{4}{135}} = \frac{\frac{131}{135}}{\frac{4}{135}} = \frac{131}{135} \times \frac{135}{4} = \frac{131}{4}$$

The odds against a defective item are $\frac{131}{4}$, or 131 to 4.

Class Exercises

For each event below, state (a) the odds in favor and (b) the odds against.

 1. A tossed coin shows a head.

 2. A cube numbered 1 through 6 is thrown and shows a 3.

 3. A cube numbered 1 through 6 is thrown and shows a 1 or a 6.

A deck of 10 cards is marked A1, A2, A3, A4, A5, B1, B2, B3, B4, and B5. For each event, state (a) the odds in favor and (b) the odds against.

 4. The card has an A.

 5. The card has a 4.

 6. The card has an odd number.

Written Exercises

Exercises 1–9 refer to the spinner shown at the right. If the pointer stops on the type of wedge described, find (a) the probability of the event occurring, (b) the probability of the event not occurring, (c) the odds in favor of the event, and (d) the odds against the event.

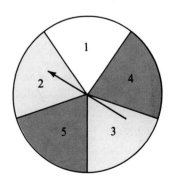

A **1.** red   **2.** white

 3. odd number   **4.** even number

 5. number less than 5

 6. number greater than 2

 7. blue or white

 8. a prime number

 9. red or blue

Exercises 10–15 refer to a jar that contains 2 red marbles, 1 white marble, and 3 blue marbles. One marble is drawn at random. Find the odds in favor of the marble being the given color.

10. red   **11.** white   **12.** blue

13. white or blue   **14.** blue or red   **15.** red or white

In Exercises 16–37, a card is drawn from a 24-card deck. Twelve of the cards are red, twelve of the cards are blue. The red cards are marked A1, A2, A3, A4, B1, B2, B3, B4, C1, C2, C3, and C4. The blue cards are marked D1, D2, D3, E1, E2, E3, F1, F2, F3, G1, G2, and G3. Find the odds in favor of drawing a card of the type described.

16. a D   **17.** a 2   **18.** a 4   **19.** a B

20. a C   **21.** an E   **22.** a 1   **23.** a G

24. a blue card   **25.** a red 3

26. a blue 3   **27.** an even number

28. an odd number blue   **29.** an even number red

30. an odd number   **31.** a prime number

B   **32.** not a G   **33.** not an A

    34. not a 1   **35.** not a 4

    36. not a blue 2   **37.** not a red 1

C   **38.** If the odds of drawing a green marble from a jar are $\frac{3}{20}$, find (a) the probability of drawing a green marble and (b) the probability of not drawing a green marble.

    39. If the odds of a blue car finishing first in a race are $\frac{7}{112}$, find (a) the probability that a blue car finishes first and (b) the probability that a blue car does not finish first.

Review Exercises

Perform the indicated operations. Simplify.

1. $\frac{5}{6} + \frac{7}{12} - \frac{11}{24}$ **2.** $\frac{7}{8} + \frac{15}{16} - \frac{7}{24}$ **3.** $\frac{11}{20} + \frac{9}{10} - \frac{8}{15}$ **4.** $\frac{5}{9} + \frac{25}{27} - \frac{71}{81}$

5. $\frac{17}{18} - \frac{2}{3} + \frac{5}{12}$ **6.** $\frac{37}{40} - \frac{41}{60} + \frac{11}{12}$ **7.** $\frac{11}{14} - \frac{17}{28} + \frac{9}{49}$ **8.** $\frac{7}{9} - \frac{5}{12} + \frac{13}{18}$

12-10 Combined Probabilities

The pointer shown at the right stops at random, but not on any line. Consider the following events.

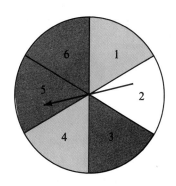

The pointer stops on a blue wedge.
The pointer stops on a red wedge.
The pointer stops on an even number.
The pointer stops on an odd number.

The event that the pointer stops on an odd number and the event that the pointer stops on an even number cannot both occur at the same time since a number is either odd or even, but not both. Such events are called **mutually exclusive.** Events such as stopping on an odd number and stopping on a blue wedge are not mutually exclusive, since the pointer can stop on the blue wedge with the odd number 1.

Let us consider the mutually exclusive events of stopping on red and stopping on blue. Since 5 of the 6 wedges are colored red or blue,

$$P(\text{red or blue}) = \frac{5}{6}.$$

Notice that $P(\text{red}) = \frac{3}{6}$ and $P(\text{blue}) = \frac{2}{6}$ and that $\frac{3}{6} + \frac{2}{6} = \frac{5}{6}$.

Formula

If A and B are mutually exclusive events, then

$$P(A \text{ or } B) = P(A) + P(B).$$

EXAMPLE 1 Use the spinner above to find $P(\text{odd or white})$.

Solution $P(\text{odd}) = \frac{3}{6}$ and $P(\text{white}) = \frac{1}{6}$

$$P(\text{odd or white}) = P(\text{odd}) + P(\text{white})$$
$$= \frac{3}{6} + \frac{1}{6} = \frac{4}{6} = \frac{2}{3}$$

Now let us consider the events of stopping on an odd number and stopping on a blue wedge. These are not mutually exclusive events since the wedge numbered 1 is also blue. Since there are 4 wedges that are either blue or odd or both, we have

$$P(\text{blue or odd}) = \frac{4}{6} = \frac{2}{3}.$$

However,

$$P(\text{blue}) + P(\text{odd}) = \tfrac{2}{6} + \tfrac{3}{6} = \tfrac{5}{6},$$

so $\qquad\qquad\qquad P(\text{blue or odd}) \neq P(\text{blue}) + P(\text{odd}).$

The formula for two events that are not mutually exclusive is given by the following.

> **Formula**
>
> For any two events A and B,
>
> $$P(A \text{ or } B) = P(A) + P(B) - P(A \text{ and } B).$$

EXAMPLE 2 Using the spinner on the preceding page, find $P(\text{blue or odd})$.

Solution $\qquad P(\text{blue}) = \tfrac{2}{6}, P(\text{odd}) = \tfrac{3}{6},$ and $P(\text{blue and odd}) = \tfrac{1}{6}$

$$P(\text{blue or odd}) = \tfrac{2}{6} + \tfrac{3}{6} - \tfrac{1}{6} = \tfrac{5}{6} - \tfrac{1}{6} = \tfrac{4}{6} = \tfrac{2}{3}$$

Class Exercises

Use the spinner at the right to find the following probabilities.

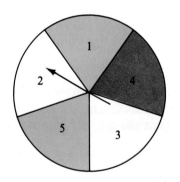

1. $P(\text{blue or even})$ 2. $P(\text{red or odd})$

3. $P(\text{white or odd})$ 4. $P(\text{red or white})$

5. $P(\text{white or even})$ 6. $P(\text{blue or odd})$

7. $P(\text{blue or white})$ 8. $P(\text{red or even})$

Written Exercises

Use the spinner at the top of the next page to find the following probabilities.

A 1. $P(\text{blue or white})$ 2. $P(\text{red or blue})$

    3. $P(\text{white or red})$ 4. $P(\text{even or red})$

    5. $P(\text{odd or blue})$ 6. $P(\text{even or white})$

7. P(prime or red)   **8.** P(prime or white)

9. P(multiples of 3 or white)

10. P(multiples of 3 or red)

11. P(multiples of 4 or blue)

12. P(multiples of 5 or red)

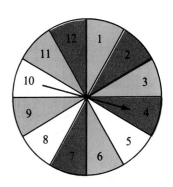

A set of 24 cards is numbered 1, 2, 3, . . . , 24 and placed in a box. A card is drawn at random. Find the indicated probabilities.

B **13.** P(even or prime)   **14.** P(odd or prime)

15. P(even or multiple of 3)   **16.** P(odd or multiple of 3)

17. P(multiple of 5 or multiple of 6)   **18.** P(perfect square or multiple of 7)

19. P(perfect square or multiple of 2)   **20.** P(multiple of 3 or multiple of 4)

The faces of each of two cubes are numbered 1, 2, 3, 4, 5, 6. Find the following probabilities when the cubes are thrown. (*Hint:* List all the possible results before you begin.)

C **21.** P(the sum of the numbers on the top face is 3)

22. P(the sum of the numbers on the top face is 7)

Self-Test B

Fifty cards are numbered 1, 2, 3, . . . , 50, put into a box, and mixed. A card is drawn at random.
Find the probability that the number on the card is as given.

   1. 19   **2.** 3, 6, 9, or 12   **3.** prime   **4.** even   [12-8]

Find the odds in favor of and the odds against the card having the number as given.

   5. odd   **6.** prime   **7.** multiple of 5   **8.** multiple of 3   [12-9]

Find the following probabilities.

   9. P(multiple of 12 or multiple of 13)   **10.** P(multiple of 5 or even)   [12-10]

11. P(odd or prime)   **12.** P(even or prime)

Self-Test answers and Extra Practice are at the back of the book.

Statistical Sampling

Suppose you wish to know the mean height of all buildings taller than three stories in your state. It would be impractical for you to measure all the buildings one by one. But you could get a *sample*. In statistics, **sampling** is the process of selecting a part from the whole. For example, you could get the height of all buildings within a 5 mi radius. Then calculate the mean of this sample to estimate the true mean of all the buildings in the state.

In order that the sample be representative of all the buildings in the state, it is important to select a sample that is **random.** For example, if you chose to use the height of buildings in the financial district of a large city, then the data would not be a random sample. The results would be biased on the too-tall side. On the other hand, if you chose to use a rural area, then the results would be biased on the too-low side.

To avoid biased results you need to select sample data with care. The information must reflect a range wide enough to match the precision and confidence you need in the results.

In the example above, the data will be more random if you select information from many different areas. You might get data from small towns as well as from medium- and large-size cities.

Deciding where to collect data, what appropriate sample size to use, and how to interpret the results are some of the concerns *statisticians* must consider. They have developed methods in which relatively small samples can be used to give precise results. For example, one widely used nationwide television program rating is based on approximately 1000 households.

Some other situations in which sampling results play a major role in decision-making are:

> opinion polls
> population shifts
> industrial quality control
> service assurance
> economic projections
> medical research
> life-style trends

Explain why the sampling method will give biased results. Suggest a more random method to collect the data.

1. To determine the nation's favorite spectator sport, an investigator polled fans at a tennis match.

2. To predict the results of a school election, a reporter for the school newspaper interviewed the campaign managers of all the candidates.

3. To help maintain production standards, a quality-control engineer tests 10 vacuum cleaners every Monday. Assume that 2000 vacuum cleaners are produced during a seven-day workweek.

4. Before marketing a new record album, the producers field-tested the album in one city.

5. To determine the lunch menu for next month, the school dietician surveyed 10 seniors out of 530 students.

Research Activity: Statistical Sampling

Computers are vital in statistical sampling. Find out how they are used by statisticians to help (a) design surveys, (b) compile information, and (c) interpret data. Ask your school librarian to recommend some references to help you answer the questions.

Career Connection

Epidemiologists, economists, and advertisers all use data sampling in their work. Find out some more about these professions. For example, what type of background do they require, and how do they use sampling data?

Chapter Review

Complete.
Refer to the bar graph for Exercises 1–3.

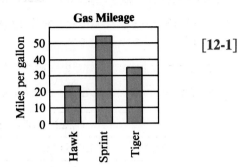

Gas Mileage

1. The car with the best gas mileage is the __?__   [12-1]

2. The Tiger gets approximately __?__ miles per gallon.

3. If we join the midpoints of the tops of the bars in the bar graph, we obtain a __?__ graph.

4. To show on a circle graph that 25% of a team is in the seventh grade, use a wedge of a circle that has an angle measure of __?__ degrees.   [12-2]

Use the data 65, 67, 67, 69, 70, 73 for Exercises 5–10.

5. The range is __?__ .   6. The median is __?__ .   [12-3]

7. The mean is __?__ .   8. The mode is __?__ .   [12-4]

9. The frequency of 67 is __?__ .

10. A stem-and-leaf plot of the data has __?__ leaves for stem 6.   [12-5]

11. Data are __?__ concentrated in the smallest interval of a box-and-whisker plot.   [12-6]

State whether Exercises 12–18 are true or false.
Refer to the frequency table for Exercises 12 and 13.

12. If you drew a histogram for the data, the tallest bar would represent 62¢.   [12-7]

13. The range of the data is 4.

Cost of a Quart of Milk			
Price	59¢	60¢	61¢	62¢
Frequency	4	5	2	1

Twenty cards are numbered 1, 2, 3, . . . , 20. The first 10 cards are red. The cards numbered 11 through 20 are blue.

14. The probability that a randomly selected card will be prime is $\frac{2}{5}$.   [12-8]

15. The odds in favor of choosing a blue card are 1 to 2.   [12-9]

16. The odds against choosing a multiple of 3 are 7 to 3.

17. $P(\text{blue or prime}) = \frac{7}{10}$ 18. $P(\text{prime or multiple of 5}) = \frac{3}{5}$.   [12-10]

Chapter Test

Refer to the bar graph for Exercises 1 and 2.

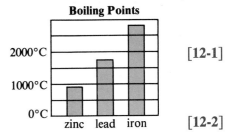

Boiling Points

1. Give the approximate boiling points of the three elements. [12-1]

2. Draw a broken-line graph for the data.

3. Draw a pictograph for the data below. [12-2]

Number of Shares of Stock Sold			
1980	1,546,000	**1981**	2,341,000
1982	3,995,000	**1983**	4,784,000

4. Draw a circle graph for the given data: 25% of the baseball team are seniors, 35% are juniors, 20% are sophomores, 20% are freshmen.

5. Find the mean, the median, and the range of 28, 14, 19, 24, 30. [12-3]

Refer to the frequency table for Exercises 6–10.

Number of Minutes	Frequency
155	2
158	3
159	1
162	1
163	1
166	2
167	3
168	5

6. Give the mean, the median, the range, and the mode of the data. [12-4]

7. Make a stem-and-leaf plot for the data using stems 15 and 16. [12-5]

8. Make a box-and-whisker plot of the data. [12-6]

9. Draw a histogram for the data. [12-7]

10. Draw a frequency polygon for the data.

Refer to the spinner below for Exercises 11–13.

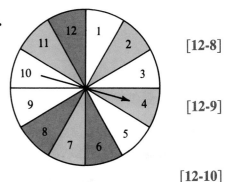

11. Find the probability that the spinner stops on the given wedge. [12-8]
    a. 7   **b.** 2, 9, or 11   **c.** white

12. Find the odds in favor of and the odds against the spinner stopping on the wedge. [12-9]
    a. odd   **b.** blue   **c.** prime number

13. Find the following probabilities. [12-10]

    a. *P*(red or odd) **b.** *P*(white or prime) **c.** *P*(blue or multiple of 4)

Cumulative Review (Chapters 1–12)

Exercises

Perform the indicated operations. Simplify.

1. $8.41 + 6.92 - 11.05$

2. 6.1×4.5

3. $19.7722 \div 4.06$

4. $(4.2 + 2.85)1.8$

5. $17.5908 \div 3.21 + 6.09$

6. $7.876 \div 1.1 \times 0.25$

7. $3\frac{7}{8} + \frac{11}{12} - 2\frac{5}{6}$

8. $\frac{7}{30} \times \frac{2}{11} \times \frac{6}{35}$

9. $4\frac{7}{12} \div \frac{11}{3} \times 2\frac{2}{15}$

10. $8\frac{2}{3} \times 1\frac{5}{13} + \frac{17}{9}$

11. $\left(9\frac{8}{15} - 6\frac{5}{6}\right) \div 3\frac{3}{5}$

12. $6\frac{1}{6} \div \left(8\frac{11}{12} - 4\frac{3}{8}\right)$

13. $^-11 + 15 - {}^-9$

14. $^-13 \times {}^-107$

15. $^-486 \div 9$

Find the surface area and volume. Use $\pi \approx 3.14$ and round to three digits.

16. cube
side: 5.3 cm

17. cylinder
base radius: 2.1 m   height: 8.5 m

Draw a broken-line graph for the given data.

18.

Number of New Subscribers						
Month	Jan.	Feb.	Mar.	Apr.	May	June
New Subscribers	58	32	47	43	50	65

Find the prime factorization of each number.

19. 110

20. 216

21. 180

22. 1024

23. 1062

Solve.

24. $7x = 266$

25. $x + 81 = 219$

26. $4n - 16 = 88$

27. $3n + 51 = 27$

28. $\frac{2}{3}c + 3\frac{5}{8} = 9\frac{11}{24}$

29. $\frac{3}{8}c - \frac{39}{10} = \frac{18}{5}$

30. $2.54y - 8 = 8.7132$

31. $0.31y + 4.4 = 6.8769$

32. 20% of 220 is what number?

33. 180 is what percent of 15?

34. 17 is 5% of what number?

35. 21 is what percent of 60?

36. 93 is 75% of what number?

37. 125% of 104 is what number?

Problems

Solve.

1. The temperature on a day in January reached a high of 3°C. If the low temperature for the day was ⁻14°C, how much higher was the high temperature than the low temperature?

2. Yvonne and Bill bought 80 wood planks. If each plank cost $4.50 and the sales tax was 6%, how much did Yvonne and Bill pay for the planks?

3. A cylindrical tank is 18 m high and 4 m wide. Find the volume. Use $\pi \approx 3.14$ and round to three digits.

4. A stack of bricks is $4\frac{1}{2}$ ft high. If each brick has a height of $2\frac{1}{4}$ in., how many rows of bricks are there?

5. The tallest tree in Hamsho's yard is 75 ft high. This is 13 ft more than twice the height of the tallest tree in Lynn's yard. Find the height of the tallest tree in Lynn's yard.

6. A square field has an area of 225 m². How much fencing is needed to enclose the field?

7. The Dead Sea is 1312 ft below sea level. Death Valley is 282 ft below sea level. How much higher is Death Valley than the Dead Sea?

8. Sue Ling bought a $6000 bond that pays 9% interest compounded quarterly. To the nearest cent, how much interest does she receive in all at the end of one year?

9. The value of Ed Jenkins' house has increased $8000 more than 3 times what he paid for it 15 years ago. If the house is worth $119,000 now, what did Ed pay for it originally?

10. The exterior of 8 boxes is to be treated with preservative. Each box is 3 m long, 2 m wide, and 1.5 m high. A can of preservative covers 9 m². How many cans are needed to treat all the boxes?

Skill Review

Addition

615
+174
789

236
4
108
+ 57
405

Add.

1. 52
+ 37

2. 30
+ 31

3. 84
+ 15

4. 48
+ 26

5. 15
+ 18

6. 39
+ 57

7. 347
+ 268

8. 756
+ 179

9. 330
124
+ 89

10. 709
25
+ 48

11. 2007
730
+ 104

12. 951
6485
8
+1027

13. 257 + 631   **14.** 463 + 451   **15.** 469 + 164

16. 104 + 325   **17.** 196 + 462   **18.** 478 + 313

19. 23 + 41 + 34   **20.** 26 + 15 + 39   **21.** 107 + 24 + 8

22. 5326 + 703 + 9427 + 8   **23.** 1027 + 349 + 8 + 12

24. 4420 + 914 + 7 + 82   **25.** 15 + 3029 + 174 + 6

26. 115 + 20 + 9 + 7603   **27.** 70 + 1328 + 94 + 5

Subtraction

756
−435
321

630
−249
381

Subtract.

1. 64
− 51

2. 98
− 37

3. 56
− 30

4. 84
− 26

5. 61
− 18

6. 93
− 29

7. 475
− 168

8. 627
− 499

9. 712
− 168

10. 2106
− 935

11. 4846
− 728

12. 5673
− 3986

13. 6002
−4789

14. 7030
−3904

15. 36,412
−12,548

16. 63,021
−47,569

17. 57 − 32   **18.** 86 − 45   **19.** 49 − 26   **20.** 98 − 34

21. 55 − 37   **22.** 42 − 29   **23.** 431 − 215   **24.** 760 − 429

25. 1314 − 197   **26.** 6240 − 3078   **27.** 7017 − 3468

28. 4320 − 2006   **29.** 23,025 − 18,769   **30.** 55,317 − 40,769

Skill Review

Multiplication

```
   476
 ×315
 2 380
 4 76
142 8
149,940
```

Multiply.

1. 13   × 2

2. 21   × 4

3. 53   × 3

4. 47   × 3

5. 16   × 5

6. 90   × 4

7. 84   × 12

8. 63   × 23

9. 429   × 15

10. 287   × 32

11. 602   × 234

12. 713   × 423

13. 20×30

14. 60×50

15. 600×80

16. 400×200

17. 700×4000

18. 5000×50

19. 52×4

20. 74×2

21. 55×66

22. 37×85

23. 18×345

24. 583×27

25. 408×70

26. 412×304

27. 805×758

Division

```
      15
13)195
      13
      65
      65
       0
```

```
      21 R4
23)487
      46
      27
      23
       4
```

Divide. Be sure to state the remainder if necessary.

1. $5\overline{)85}$

2. $8\overline{)96}$

3. $23\overline{)713}$

4. $71\overline{)1633}$

5. $8\overline{)86}$

6. $6\overline{)50}$

7. $49\overline{)172}$

8. $32\overline{)424}$

9. $315 \div 9$

10. $513 \div 7$

11. $536 \div 8$

12. $405 \div 5$

13. $341 \div 6$

14. $111 \div 4$

15. $6403 \div 3$

16. $3882 \div 9$

17. $2232 \div 8$

18. $832 \div 50$

19. $984 \div 70$

20. $720 \div 60$

21. $765 \div 45$

22. $507 \div 24$

23. $169 \div 32$

24. $2166 \div 28$

25. $1275 \div 51$

26. $7407 \div 26$

27. $3762 \div 19$

28. $8205 \div 41$

29. $1066 \div 27$

30. $17,063 \div 33$

31. $24,474 \div 60$

32. $19,412 \div 15$

33. $29,919 \div 56$

34. $79,992 \div 72$

35. $15,960 \div 38$

36. $87,048 \div 403$

37. $21,364 \div 628$

38. $13,113 \div 279$

Extra Practice: Chapter 1

Evaluate each expression when the variable has the values listed.

1. $5h$; 0, 2, 4, 10   **2.** $7a$; 2, 6, 9, 10

3. $4c$; 0, 3, 7, 9   **4.** $16 - s$; 3, 5, 8, 13

5. $37 + t$; 5, 12, 23, 30   **6.** $w \div 3$; 9, 21, 39, 45

7. $59 - r$; 12, 17, 19, 22   **8.** $89 + f$; 15, 18, 24, 32

Evaluate each expression if $m = 4$ and $k = 6$.

9. $m + k$ **10.** $2mk$ **11.** $m + 5 + k$

12. $k - m$ **13.** $k + 12 + m$ **14.** $15 - m - k$

Simplify, using the properties.

15. $38 + 23 + 17$ **16.** $14 \times 10 \times 6$ **17.** $114 + 34 + 16$

18. $15 \times 17 \times 1$ **19.** $19 \times 0 \times 21$ **20.** $87 + 42 + 0$

21. $23 \times 14 \times 10$ **22.** $87 + 25 + 63$ **23.** $32 \times 0 \times 17$

24. $20 \times 8 \times 50$ **25.** $98 + 112 + 73$ **26.** $13 \times 27 \times 1$

Write the related inverse facts for each of the following.

27. $41 - 21 = 20$ **28.** $58 + 19 = 77$ **29.** $17 + 47 = 64$

30. $87 - 23 = 64$ **31.** $56 \div 7 = 8$ **32.** $17 \times 5 = 85$

33. $91 + 51 = 142$ **34.** $144 \div 16 = 9$ **35.** $9 \times 12 = 108$

36. $111 - 48 = 63$ **37.** $13 \times 11 = 143$ **38.** $210 \div 14 = 15$

Simplify, using inverse operations.

39. $0 \div 23$ **40.** $52 \div 1$ **41.** $76 - 76 + c$

42. $31 - 0$ **43.** $16 \times 21 \div 21$ **44.** $92 \div 1$

Simplify, using the distributive property.

45. $5(18 + 12)$ **46.** $21(10 - 7)$ **47.** $(33 + 7)9$

48. $(27 - 17)13$ **49.** $14(25 + 5)$ **50.** $27(13 + 16)$

51. $4(19 - 4)$ **52.** $(3 \times 7) + (3 \times 8)$ **53.** $(6 \times 12) + (6 \times 18)$

54. $(5 \times 28) - (5 \times 8)$ **55.** $(23 \times 4) - (13 \times 4)$ **56.** $(32 \times 8) + (8 \times 8)$

Simplify.

57. $15 \times 6 + 17$

58. $46 + 18 \div 6$

59. $(15 - 7)22$

60. $(27 \div 9)30$

61. $34 + 23 - (12 \times 2)$

62. $(87 + 13) \div (15 - 11)$

63. $218 - (21 \div 3)$

64. $(31 - 12)(11 + 9)$

65. $(18 + 36) \div 6$

66. $(28 \div 4) - (39 \div 13)$

67. $123 + 10 \times 8$

68. $(6 \times 11) + (81 \div 9)$

For each problem, answer the following questions.
a. What number, or numbers, does the problem ask for?
b. Are enough facts given? If not, what else is needed?
c. Are unneeded facts given? If so, what are they?
d. What operation or operations would you use to find the answer?

69. Peter swims 1 hour every day. Last week he missed 2 days. How far did Peter swim last week?

70. Holly bought 4 concert tickets for $52. How much was each ticket?

71. A truck can carry 2 tons of gravel. If a driveway is to be covered with 1 inch of gravel, how many loads of gravel are needed?

72. Scott spent 4 hours doing chores, 2 hours playing basketball, 3 hours doing homework, and 2 hours watching television. How much time did he spend doing these activities?

73. On the first day of a two-day trip, Tom traveled 15 km. The entire distance is 33 km. How far does Tom have to travel the second day?

Solve, using the five-step plan.

74. Wendy played in 18 softball games. In the first 6 games she got 11 hits. In the second 6 games she got 8 hits. How many hits did Wendy get in the third 6 games if she had 31 hits all season?

75. Ingrid has a bird feeder that holds 2 kg of bird seed. Last week she filled the empty bird feeder 3 times. How much bird seed did she put into the bird feeder last week?

76. Herb commutes 28 km by train and 2 km by bus to get to work. How far is Herb's commute to work each week if he works 5 days?

77. Jeanne climbed from the base camp which is 1563 m above sea level to a shelter 3681 m above sea level. How far did she climb?

78. The football team has 60 players. When the season starts in 15 days the team can only have 49 players. How many players must be cut before the season starts?

Extra Practice: Chapter 2

Write a variable expression for each word phrase.

1. Seven less than a number p

2. A number t divided by 4

3. Eleven times a number f

4. The total of a number m and twenty-one

5. Six more than five times a number g

6. A number z minus eight

7. The sum of three and a number b, times seven

8. Nineteen plus a number r

9. A number d minus twenty-two, divided by four

10. The product of fifteen minus a number c, and nine

Write an equation for each word sentence. Use n as the variable.

11. A number divided by three is seven.

12. The sum of nine and a number is thirty-two.

13. Fifty-two is eighteen plus a number.

14. Seventy-two is the product of a number and eight.

15. The difference between thirty-five and a number is sixteen.

16. A number is ten more than sixty-six.

17. Two more than a number minus forty-eight is seventy.

18. Nine times a number is three plus forty-two.

19. Six is eighteen more than a number times twelve.

20. The product of a number and seven is forty minus five.

Replace __?__ with < or >.

21. 15 _?_ 23

22. 57 _?_ 49

23. 35 _?_ 18

24. 7 + 11 _?_ 31

25. 17 _?_ 12 + 4

26. 29 − 15 _?_ 17

27. 29 + 42 _?_ 72 − 16

28. 8 + 20 _?_ 6 + 8

Write an inequality for each word sentence.

29. Seventeen is greater than twelve.

30. A number plus twelve is less than twenty-two.

31. Twice a number is greater than sixty-nine.

32. Seven is smaller than two times five.

33. Eighty minus twenty-six is greater than two times twenty-one.

34. Thirty-three is less than six times a number.

Solve, using inverse operations.

35. $x - 13 = 27$	**36.** $9 + n = 53$	**37.** $22 + x < 72$
38. $p - 121 > 72$	**39.** $63 = n - 81$	**40.** $82 > m + 37$
41. $93 = c + 41$	**42.** $t - 31 > 93$	**43.** $132 = 73 + w$
44. $h - 151 = 89$	**45.** $66 < n + 44$	**46.** $m - 73 < 121$
47. $27n = 81$	**48.** $36 \div z = 6$	**49.** $28 > 4n$
50. $51 = 3b$	**51.** $60 > 10p$	**52.** $24 = w \div 4$
53. $32 < 4t$	**54.** $48 > 6n$	**55.** $11n = 121$
56. $14 < 154 \div x$	**57.** $36 = n \div 6$	**58.** $6 < 28 - k$

Write an equation for each word sentence. Then solve.

59. Sixteen less than a number is thirty-eight.

60. A number divided by seven is twenty-one.

61. Eight times a number is ninety-six.

62. Fourteen more than twice a number is forty.

63. Sixty-two is eight less than five times a number.

64. Fifty-six is twenty less than a number plus six.

Solve.

65. John owes Tom $18. John earns $5 an hour and already has $3. How long must John work to earn enough to pay Tom back?

66. Rosa sells newspapers at the bus stop. If each paper costs $.25, how many must Rosa sell to take in $10?

Extra Practice: Chapter 3

Evaluate.

1. 3^4 2. 13^2 3. 25^3 4. 34^2

5. 17^3 6. 7^5 7. 30^3 8. 9^4

Multiply.

9. $9^2 \times 3^4$ 10. $10^3 \times 2^4$ 11. $7^3 \times 13^2$ 12. $15^3 \times 4^5$

13. $6^3 \times 100^2$ 14. $4^3 \times 1^5$ 15. $2^5 \times 11^3$ 16. $3^3 \times 2^6$

Write in words.

17. 7029   18. 53,100   19. 141,278   20. 1,310,529

Write the number.

21. seven thousand eighty-four   22. two hundred fifty thousand

23. three million, sixteen thousand, six hundred eleven

24. seven hundred four million, fifty-eight thousand, two hundred nine

Write the number in expanded notation with exponents.

25. 972   26. 169   27. 5613   28. 1942

29. 37,603   30. 17,452   31. 102,511   32. 741,295

a. Write in words. b. Write in expanded notation.

33. 0.005   34. 0.09   35. 0.0062   36. 0.357

37. 0.42   38. 0.0157   39. 0.407   40. 0.091

Write as a decimal.

41. eleven thousandths   42. eighty-nine hundredths

43. seven and nine tenths   44. six hundred nineteen ten-thousandths

45. $\frac{7}{10}$ 46. $\frac{41}{10^3}$ 47. $\frac{9}{10^2}$ 48. $\frac{17}{10,000}$

Write the numbers in order from least to greatest.

49. 8.34, 8.43, 8.4   50. 5.005, 5.050, 5.006

51. 4.90, 4.09, 4.49   52. 3.3000, 30.300, 3.0030

Add or subtract.

53. 42.07 − 38.78

54. 0.81 + 16.99

55. 5.82 + 6.05

56. 86.58 + 94.07

57. 8.75 − 3.04

58. 56.24 − 33.06

59. 61.4 + 3.65

60. 9.518 + 4.34

61. 76.5 − 2.97

62. 843.52 + 12.9

63. 42.9 − 25.24

64. 14.7 + 251.92

Multiply each number by (a) 100, (b) 1000, and (c) 10,000.

65. 0.27

66. 0.2008

67. 90.95

68. 4.8

69. 0.0084

70. 0.02027

71. 13.451

72. 6.3141

Divide each number by (a) 100, (b) 1000, and (c) 10,000.

73. 59.1

74. 6.2

75. 99.09

76. 0.075

77. 25,126

78. 124.7

79. 0.007

80. 217,351

Write in scientific notation.

81. 65,814

82. 6339

83. 70,121

84. 185,562

85. 390,012

86. 12,350,921

87. 5,768,147

88. 7,232,858

Multiply.

89. 4.16 × 3.2

90. 14.7 × 28.3

91. 106.8 × 3.6

92. 10.21 × 4250

93. 0.38 × 84.1

94. 347 × 0.211

95. 0.62 × 0.082

96. 0.0012 × 0.312

Divide and check. If necessary, round to the nearest tenth.

97. 17.86 ÷ 4.7

98. 1.82 ÷ 0.28

99. 2.89 ÷ 0.34

100. 9.314 ÷ 0.35

101. 57 ÷ 0.3

102. 48.5 ÷ 0.6

103. 555.9 ÷ 1.7

104. 4.523 ÷ 0.24

Solve, using the five-step plan. Estimate to check the solution.

105. Jean bought 10 lb of ground beef. What was the price per pound if Jean paid $19.60?

106. Ken bought six shirts on sale for $9.99 each. The shirts usually cost $15.99 each. How much money did Ken save?

107. Katy drove 315 mi in 6.4 h. To the nearest tenth, how many miles per hour did she average?

108. A customer paid $19.00 for 13.6 gal of gasoline. To the nearest cent, what was the price per gallon?

Extra Practice: Chapter 4

Draw a sketch to illustrate each of the following.

1. Three points on a line

2. Two intersecting lines

3. Three noncollinear points

4. Two intersecting planes

5. Two rays with a common endpoint, A

6. Two segments with a common endpoint, B

Complete.

7. 10 km = __?__ m

8. 0.27 km = __?__ m

9. 9 m = __?__ cm

10. 0.5 km = __?__ m

11. 77 m = __?__ cm

12. 175 mm = __?__ m

13. 1500 m = __?__ km

14. 81 cm = __?__ mm

15. 0.1575 km = __?__ m

16. 900 mm = __?__ m = __?__ cm

17. 2 m = __?__ cm = __?__ mm

18. If the sum of the measures of two angles is 180°, the angles are __?__ .

19. A small square is often used to indicate a(n) __?__ angle.

20. Perpendicular lines form __?__ ° angles.

21. The __?__ is the common endpoint of two rays that form an angle.

22. If $m \angle A = 40°$, the complement of $\angle A$ measures __?__ °.

23. A(n) __?__ angle has a measure between 90° and 180°.

24. A triangle with at least two sides congruent is called a(n) __?__ triangle.

25. Triangles can be classified by their __?__ or their __?__ .

26. The sum of the measures of the angles of a triangle is __?__ °.

27. A(n) __?__ triangle has two perpendicular sides.

28. A scalene triangle has __?__ equal sides.

29. A right angle measures __?__ °.

30. The sum of the lengths of any two sides of a triangle is __?__ than the length of the third side.

31. A triangle with three congruent sides is called a(n) __?__ triangle.

32. A(n) __?__ triangle has one angle that is greater than 90°.

33. A triangle with all its angles less than 90° is called a(n) __?__ triangle.

True or false?

34. A regular polygon has all the sides equal.

35. A quadrilateral has four congruent sides.

36. All the angles of a rectangle have a measure of 90°.

37. A trapezoid always has one pair of congruent sides.

38. The opposite sides of a parallelogram are congruent.

39. A hexagon has six sides.

40. Only two sides of a rhombus are congruent.

41. A square with a perimeter of 24 cm has 4 sides that measure 6 cm.

42. A regular decagon, 5 cm on a side, has a perimeter of 50 cm.

Solve. Use $\pi \approx 3.14$ and round answers to three digits.

43. The radius of a circle is 30 cm. Find the diameter.

44. The radius of a circle is 56 mm. Find the circumference.

45. The diameter of a circle is 3 m. Find the circumference.

46. The diameter of a circle is 16 mm. Find the circumference.

47. The circumference of a circle is 20 m. Find the diameter.

48. The circumference of a circle is 100 m. Find the radius.

49. The radius of a circle is 9 cm. Find the circumference.

50. The circumference of a circle is 25.8 m. Find the radius.

51. The diameter of a circle is 50 cm. Find the circumference.

Complete the statements about the pair of congruent figures.

52. $\overline{KL} \cong$ __?__   53. $\overline{NK} \cong$ __?__

54. $\overline{LM} \cong$ __?__   55. $\overline{SP} \cong$ __?__

56. $\angle N \cong$ __?__   57. $\angle S \cong$ __?__

58. $\angle L \cong$ __?__   59. $\angle Q \cong$ __?__

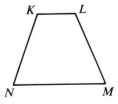
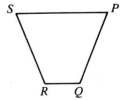

Use a compass and a straightedge to make each construction.

60. Draw a segment AB. Construct the perpendicular bisector.

61. Draw an acute angle ABC. Construct $\overrightarrow{BX}$ so that it bisects $\angle ABC$.

62. Construct an angle congruent to $\angle ABC$ of Exercise 61.

Extra Practice: Chapter 5

List all the factors of each number.

1. 6	**2.** 7	**3.** 10	**4.** 13	**5.** 15	**6.** 18
7. 19	**8.** 25	**9.** 27	**10.** 31	**11.** 35	**12.** 39
13. 41	**14.** 42	**15.** 52	**16.** 56	**17.** 59	**18.** 64
19. 72	**20.** 75	**21.** 81	**22.** 89	**23.** 96	**24.** 97

Which of the numbers 2, 3, 4, 5, 9, and 10 are factors of the given number?

25. 155	**26.** 168	**27.** 189	**28.** 210	**29.** 272	**30.** 305
31. 421	**32.** 512	**33.** 637	**34.** 888	**35.** 953	**36.** 962
37. 1080	**38.** 1100	**39.** 1260	**40.** 1362	**41.** 1423	**42.** 1485
43. 1534	**44.** 1560	**45.** 1651	**46.** 1710	**47.** 1743	**48.** 1803

Evaluate each expression.

49. 3^2 **50.** 6^2 **51.** 8^2 **52.** 10^2 **53.** 11^2 **54.** 13^2 **55.** 14^2 **56.** 16^2

Evaluate the square root of each number.

57. 25 **58.** 4 **59.** 225 **60.** 49 **61.** 64 **62.** 169 **63.** 196 **64.** 121

Determine whether each number is prime or composite. If the number is composite, give the prime factorization.

65. 10 **66.** 21 **67.** 34 **68.** 54 **69.** 41 **70.** 30 **71.** 18 **72.** 25

Find the GCF of each pair of numbers.

73. 54, 64	**74.** 27, 81	**75.** 4, 6	**76.** 34, 51
77. 42, 56	**78.** 12, 28	**79.** 40, 64	**80.** 45, 80
81. 36, 54	**82.** 20, 30	**83.** 35, 56	**84.** 16, 80
85. 15, 75	**86.** 13, 52	**87.** 33, 77	**88.** 9, 15

Find the LCM of each pair of numbers.

89. 9, 24	**90.** 15, 20	**91.** 2, 5	**92.** 8, 36
93. 12, 42	**94.** 18, 27	**95.** 8, 12	**96.** 3, 4
97. 14, 42	**98.** 9, 48	**99.** 3, 7	**100.** 3, 9
101. 8, 10	**102.** 16, 36	**103.** 19, 76	**104.** 21, 84

Extra Practice: Chapter 6

Complete.

1. $\frac{1}{5} + \frac{1}{5} + \frac{1}{5} = \underline{\ ?\ } \times \frac{1}{5}$

2. $6 \times \frac{1}{6} = \underline{\ ?\ }$

3. $\frac{1}{7} + \frac{1}{7} = \frac{1}{7} \times \underline{\ ?\ }$

4. $5 \times \frac{1}{8} = \underline{\ ?\ } \div 8$

5. $5 \times \frac{1}{9} = \underline{\ ?\ }$

6. $3 \div 4 = 3 \times \underline{\ ?\ }$

In a class of 24 students, 14 bring their lunch from home. The rest buy their lunch at school.

7. What fractional part of the students bring their lunch from home?

8. What fractional part buy their lunch at school?

Find the value of n.

9. $\frac{4}{9} = \frac{n}{36}$

10. $\frac{n}{7} = \frac{72}{126}$

11. $\frac{n}{144} = \frac{5}{12}$

12. $\frac{11}{33} = \frac{n}{3}$

13. $\frac{25}{40} = \frac{n}{8}$

Write in lowest terms.

14. $\frac{40}{88}$

15. $\frac{16}{18}$

16. $\frac{27}{81}$

17. $\frac{64}{96}$

18. $\frac{34}{51}$

19. $\frac{56}{104}$

Change to a mixed number or a whole number in simple form.

20. $\frac{17}{7}$

21. $\frac{39}{26}$

22. $\frac{36}{9}$

23. $\frac{14}{4}$

24. $\frac{121}{11}$

25. $\frac{10}{6}$

Change to an improper fraction.

26. $3\frac{5}{8}$

27. $12\frac{3}{4}$

28. $9\frac{6}{7}$

29. $21\frac{1}{3}$

30. $1\frac{2}{11}$

31. $17\frac{5}{9}$

Replace each $\underline{\ ?\ }$ with $<$, $>$, or $=$ to make a true sentence.

32. $\frac{5}{8} \underline{\ ?\ } \frac{10}{16}$

33. $\frac{5}{16} \underline{\ ?\ } \frac{9}{32}$

34. $\frac{10}{3} \underline{\ ?\ } \frac{11}{4}$

35. $\frac{6}{11} \underline{\ ?\ } \frac{5}{8}$

Express each fraction as a terminating decimal or a repeating decimal.

36. $\frac{14}{21}$

37. $\frac{13}{16}$

38. $\frac{5}{44}$

39. $\frac{5}{11}$

40. $\frac{15}{6}$

Express each decimal as a fraction in lowest terms or as a mixed number in simple form.

41. 0.054

42. 0.506

43. 1.75

44. 0.1015

45. 1.66

Extra Practice: *Chapter 7*

Add or subtract. Simplify.

1. $\frac{3}{8} + \frac{5}{8}$ 2. $\frac{2}{5} + \frac{4}{5}$ 3. $\frac{9}{11} - \frac{6}{11}$ 4. $\frac{7}{12} + \frac{3}{12}$ 5. $\frac{15}{21} - \frac{8}{21}$

6. $\frac{13}{32} - \frac{3}{32}$ 7. $\frac{1}{4} + \frac{3}{8}$ 8. $\frac{7}{11} - \frac{3}{22}$ 9. $\frac{5}{7} + \frac{1}{3}$ 10. $\frac{1}{5} + \frac{5}{7}$

11. $\frac{5}{16} - \frac{1}{4}$ 12. $\frac{2}{3} + \frac{1}{4}$ 13. $5\frac{5}{8} + 2\frac{3}{8}$ 14. $4\frac{5}{16} + 1\frac{7}{16}$ 15. $11\frac{13}{32} - 3\frac{2}{32}$

16. $21\frac{2}{5} + 9\frac{4}{5}$ 17. $7\frac{7}{11} - 2\frac{9}{11}$ 18. $8\frac{3}{13} - 4\frac{8}{13}$ 19. $4\frac{3}{5} + \frac{1}{4}$

20. $12\frac{3}{4} - 3\frac{2}{3}$ 21. $9\frac{3}{16} - 5\frac{1}{8}$ 22. $6\frac{7}{8} - 1\frac{1}{3}$ 23. $15\frac{2}{11} + 4\frac{1}{4}$

Multiply. Simplify.

24. $\frac{12}{15} \times \frac{2}{3}$ 25. $\frac{5}{7} \times \frac{1}{4}$ 26. $\frac{4}{5} \times 2$

27. $\frac{7}{8} \times \frac{3}{11}$ 28. $\frac{9}{17} \times \frac{11}{32}$ 29. $\frac{12}{13} \times \frac{9}{16}$

30. $\frac{21}{25} \times \frac{17}{21}$ 31. $\frac{56}{63} \times \frac{31}{35}$ 32. $\frac{81}{99} \times \frac{11}{27}$

33. $\frac{19}{20} \times \frac{5}{8} \times \frac{16}{17}$ 34. $\frac{13}{16} \times \frac{4}{35} \times \frac{7}{26}$ 35. $\frac{16}{17} \times \frac{21}{24} \times \frac{34}{48}$

Divide. Simplify.

36. $\frac{9}{16} \div \frac{2}{5}$ 37. $\frac{5}{7} \div \frac{9}{14}$ 38. $\frac{11}{12} \div \frac{3}{4}$

39. $\frac{6}{11} \div \frac{12}{13}$ 40. $\frac{2}{9} \div \frac{6}{45}$ 41. $\frac{8}{15} \div \frac{32}{18}$

42. $\frac{7}{27} \div \frac{21}{30}$ 43. $\frac{13}{36} \div \frac{39}{40}$ 44. $\frac{9}{14} \div \frac{18}{35}$

45. $\frac{9}{10} \div \frac{13}{16}$ 46. $\frac{15}{22} \div \frac{10}{13}$ 47. $\frac{6}{7} \div \frac{9}{28}$

Multiply or divide. Simplify.

48. $3\frac{3}{7} \times 11\frac{2}{5}$ 49. $6\frac{2}{5} \div 2\frac{3}{11}$ 50. $12\frac{13}{16} \div 4\frac{2}{3}$

51. $7\frac{6}{13} \div 1\frac{25}{39}$ 52. $15\frac{6}{7} \times 3\frac{5}{16}$ 53. $8\frac{3}{25} \times 10\frac{1}{2}$

54. $13\frac{11}{13} \div 9\frac{4}{9}$ 55. $16\frac{4}{5} \div 11\frac{1}{10}$ 56. $5\frac{3}{8} \div 2\frac{5}{11}$

57. $18\frac{2}{7} \times 6\frac{9}{12}$ 58. $3\frac{10}{13} \div 12\frac{1}{2}$ 59. $4\frac{26}{39} \times 2\frac{5}{17}$

Express each ratio as a fraction in lowest terms.

60. $\dfrac{10 \text{ min}}{1 \text{ h}}$

61. $\dfrac{6 \text{ cm}}{2 \text{ m}}$

62. $\dfrac{250 \text{ mL}}{2 \text{ L}}$

63. $\dfrac{6 \text{ kg}}{600 \text{ g}}$

64. $\dfrac{7 \text{ days}}{4 \text{ weeks}}$

65. $\dfrac{3 \text{ h}}{45 \text{ min}}$

66. $\dfrac{15 \text{ mm}}{5 \text{ cm}}$

67. $\dfrac{60 \text{ cm}}{150 \text{ mm}}$

Solve. Express each ratio in lowest terms.

68. A student walked 25 km in 4 h. What was the average speed in kilometers per hour?

69. A special typewriter has 46 keys. Of these 46 keys, 26 are used for letters of the alphabet. What is the ratio of the number of keys not used for letters to the total number of keys?

Solve.

70. $\dfrac{19}{20} = \dfrac{n}{10}$

71. $\dfrac{8}{48} = \dfrac{n}{4}$

72. $\dfrac{4}{13} = \dfrac{12}{n}$

73. $\dfrac{n}{27} = \dfrac{12}{81}$

74. $\dfrac{40}{n} = \dfrac{5}{9}$

75. $\dfrac{n}{64} = \dfrac{12}{8}$

76. $\dfrac{100}{40} = \dfrac{20}{n}$

77. $\dfrac{7}{3} = \dfrac{n}{18}$

78. Joe bought 4 shock absorbers for the price of 3 at a clearance sale. He paid a total of $39. How much would the 4 shock absorbers cost at their regular price?

79. Billie runs 4 km in 25 min. How long will it take to run 10,000 m?

80. A supermarket sells 12 oranges for $1.30. How much would 18 oranges cost at the same rate?

A map has a scale of 1 cm:8 km. What actual distance does each map length represent?

81. 8 cm

82. 5.5 cm

83. 3 cm

84. 7.9 cm

85. 3.75 cm

86. 10.2 cm

87. 6.25 cm

88. 15.25 cm

Solve.

89. The length of a drawing is 3 cm. If the scale is 1 cm:20 m, what is the actual length of the object?

90. The scale on a map is 1 cm:5 km. If the distance from Avon to Birmingham is actually 95 km, how far apart are the two cities on the map?

91. In a scale drawing the length of a truck is 4 cm. If the scale is 1 cm:3 m, what is the actual length of the truck?

Extra Practice: Chapter 8

Find the value of each variable expression for the replacement set {1, 2, 3, 5, 9}.

1. $7 + n$ **2.** $3n + 3$ **3.** $23 - 2n$ **4.** $\dfrac{6n}{2}$

5. $\dfrac{1}{2}n + 2$ **6.** $\dfrac{2}{3} + \dfrac{n}{3}$ **7.** $7 - \dfrac{n}{4}$ **8.** $\dfrac{10n}{2} - 5$

Solve each equation using the given replacement set. If the equation has no solution in the replacement set, so state.

9. $y + 2 = 10$; {4, 7, 8} **10.** $8 + a = 19$; {10, 11, 12}

11. $15 - 2n = 1$; {3, 5, 7} **12.** $4 + 6x = 22$; {2, 3, 4}

13. $(4 + 2)y + 10 = 70$; {9, 10, 19} **14.** $2k - 3 = 33$; {12, 15, 18}

15. $\dfrac{m}{3} + 15 = 42$; {18, 24, 27} **16.** $56 - \dfrac{2n}{3} = 28$; {24, 36, 42}

17. $\dfrac{1}{5}(2 + 3n) = 4$; {1, 3, 6} **18.** $6\left(\dfrac{1}{3}x - 2\right) = 30$; {9, 15, 21}

Use transformations to solve each equation. Write down all the steps.

19. $r + 30 = 80$ **20.** $31 + d = 47$ **21.** $\dfrac{1}{4}b = \dfrac{3}{4}$

22. $x - 21 = 19$ **23.** $79 - a = 17$ **24.** $14 + 12 = 17 + a$

25. $1.23 = 1.50 - a$ **26.** $\dfrac{7}{8} + a = 4$ **27.** $a - \dfrac{2}{5} = 12$

28. $0.5 + 1.7 = 5 - a$ **29.** $13t = 52$ **30.** $84 = 14k$

31. $\dfrac{n}{6} = 12$ **32.** $15 = \dfrac{x}{3}$ **33.** $\dfrac{t}{7} = 5(3 + 4)$

34. $3(27) = 9v$ **35.** $(10)(5) = \dfrac{w}{4}$ **36.** $\dfrac{1}{7} = \dfrac{3}{7}k$

37. $0.25a = 1.0$ **38.** $\dfrac{5}{9} = \dfrac{12}{5}k$ **39.** $6.25n = 1.25$

40. $\dfrac{3}{8}c = \dfrac{9}{16}$ **41.** $1.414x = 21.21$ **42.** $\dfrac{p}{6} - 12 = 3$

43. $3.6x - 2.5 = 15.5$ **44.** $17 = 5y - 3$ **45.** $\dfrac{8}{3} = \dfrac{2}{5}v - \dfrac{1}{3}$

46. $\dfrac{m}{3} = \dfrac{1}{3}(6 + 12)$ **47.** $2x - 3 = 15 - $ **48.** $12.75 = 6.75 + 2.4w$

49. $4 + \dfrac{2}{3}m = 22$ **50.** $\dfrac{w}{7} + 5 = 5$ **51.** $\dfrac{7}{8} + \dfrac{1}{2}c = \dfrac{21}{4}$

Write an equation for each word sentence.

52. The product of six and a number n is fifty-four.

53. Twelve less than two times a number n is seventy.

54. The sum of a number n and nineteen is sixty-one.

55. Eighty-one divided by a number n is the same as the product of nine and the same number.

56. Seven times the sum of ten and a number n is eighty-four.

Choose a variable and write an equation for each problem.

57. An astronaut enters a space capsule 1 h 40 min before launch time. How long has she been in the capsule 2 h 32 min after the launch?

58. The Torrance baseball team scored 10 runs in the first 3 innings. Gardena scored 2 in the first and 5 in the fourth. If Torrance does not score again, how many more runs does Gardena need to win?

Write an equation for each problem. Solve the equation using the five-step method. Check your answer.

59. Mercury melts at 38.87° below 0°C and boils at 356.9°C. What is the difference between these temperatures?

60. Yolanda rode the bus from a point 53 blocks south of Carroll Avenue to a point 41 blocks north of Carroll Avenue. How many blocks did she travel?

61. John sailed for 7 hours on Swan Lake. If he sailed for two more hours than he fished, how long did he fish?

62. The width of a rectangle is 7 cm less than the length. If the perimeter is 410 cm, what are the dimensions of the rectangle?

63. Together a house and lot cost $90,000. The house costs seven times as much as the lot. How much did the lot cost? How much did the house cost?

64. In an election 1584 people voted. The winner received 122 votes more than the loser. How many votes did each candidate receive?

65. It takes Len 55 min to ride to and from work. The ride home takes 7 min less than the ride to work. How long does it take each way?

66. Tickets to hockey games cost $9 for adults and $8 for children. If the Jones family spent $60 on tickets and brought 3 children, how many adult's tickets did they buy?

Extra Practice: Chapter 9

Express as a fraction in lowest terms or as a mixed number in simple form.

1. 5%   **2.** 10%   **3.** 72%   **4.** 163%   **5.** 215%

Express as a percent.

6. $\frac{3}{4}$ **7.** $\frac{1}{10}$ **8.** 7   **9.** $\frac{7}{16}$ **10.** $\frac{43}{20}$

Express each percent as a decimal.

11. 15%   **12.** 71%   **13.** 5%   **14.** 15.2%   **15.** 98%

16. 2.4%   **17.** 7.5%   **18.** 625%   **19.** 0.42%   **20.** 200%

Express each decimal as a percent.

21. 0.45   **22.** 0.23   **23.** 1.33   **24.** 0.05   **25.** 12.5

26. 0.0025   **27.** 10.2   **28.** 0.53   **29.** 0.008   **30.** 0.125

Express each fraction as a decimal, then as a percent.

31. $\frac{2}{5}$ **32.** $\frac{1}{4}$ **33.** $8\frac{3}{4}$ **34.** $\frac{13}{16}$ **35.** $5\frac{1}{5}$

Answer each question by writing an equation and solving it. Round to the nearest tenth of a percent if necessary.

36. 12% of 50 is what number?   **37.** 110% of 99 is what number?

38. What percent of 81 is 27?   **39.** 85% of what number is 425?

40. 15% of $30 is how much?   **41.** What percent of 256 is 32?

42. 5% of 1000 is what number?   **43.** 140% of what number is 35?

44. What percent of 825 is 25?   **45.** 30% of what number is 23.7?

Find the percent increase or decrease from the first number to the second. Round to the nearest tenth of a percent if necessary.

46. 45 to 66   **47.** 140 to 84   **48.** 15 to 75   **49.** 360 to 234

Find the new number produced when the given number is increased or decreased by the given percent.

50. 64; 25% increase   **51.** 80; 65% decrease   **52.** 121; 20% decrease

53. 324; 50% decrease   **54.** 78; 150% increase   **55.** 480; 35% increase

Solve.

56. Mervyn's is having a sale on batteries. The regular price of $2.40 is decreased by 20%. What is the sale price?

57. The number of fruit bars in a box is increased from 60 to 72. What is the percent of increase?

58. Helen received an 8% raise in her salary. She made $350 per week before the raise. How much does she make after the raise?

59. A bicycle that usually sells for $120 is on sale for $96. What is the percent of discount?

60. Great Hikes purchases backpacks from the manufacturer at $10 each. Then the backpacks are sold at the store for $25 each. What is the percent of markup?

61. A set of tools that usually sells for $38 is on sale at a 40% discount. What is the sale price?

62. A wheelbarrow sells for $36. Next month the price will be marked up 6%. How much will the wheelbarrow cost next month?

63. The Thort Company made a profit of $32,175 on sales of $371,250. To the nearest tenth, what percent of the sales was profit?

64. Dora's commission last month was $621. Her total sales were $8280. What is her rate of commission?

65. Foster Realty Co. charges a 6% commission for the sale of property. If a homeowner wishes to clear $130,000 after paying the commission, for how much must the home be sold?

66. Ivan works for salary plus commission. He earns $500 per month plus 4% commission on all sales. What sales level is needed for Ivan to earn $675 in a given month?

67. Phil borrowed $5000 for one year. The interest on the loan came to $689.44. To the nearest tenth, what was the interest rate?

Round to the nearest cent.

68. Consider a principal of $750 earning an interest rate of 5.5%. If compounded semiannually for one year, what is the total interest earned on $750?

69. A $600 deposit is left in an account for 9 months. If the account earns an 8% interest compounded quarterly, what is the total interest earned at the end of the 9 months?

Extra Practice: Chapter 10

Find the area and perimeter of a rectangle with the given dimensions.

1. 100 m by 50 m   **2.** 27 mm by 13 mm   **3.** 125 cm by 61 cm

4. If a rectangle has a width of 57 km and an area of 3648 km², what is (a) the length and (b) the perimeter?

5. If a rectangle has an area of 324 m² and a length of 27 m, what is (a) the width and (b) the perimeter?

Find the area of a parallelogram with the given dimensions.

6. $b = 12$ cm, $h = 11$ cm   **7.** $b = 105$ m, $h = 28$ m   **8.** $b = 17$ km, $h = 7$ km

9. If a parallelogram has a height of 13 cm and an area of 201.5 cm², what is the base?

10. If a parallelogram has an area of 27 m² and a base of 6 m, what is the height?

Find the area of each polygon.

11. Triangle: base 23 cm, height 7 cm

12. Triangle: base 35 m, height 41 m

13. Trapezoid: bases 11.5 m and 6.5 m, height 15 m

14. Trapezoid: bases 110 km and 55 km, height 67 km

15. If a triangle has a height of 113 cm and an area of 4576.5 cm², what is the base?

16. If a triangle has an area of 963 m² and a base of 18 m, what is the height?

17. If a trapezoid has an area of 531 mm² and bases of 32.1 mm and 21 mm, what is the height?

Solve. Use $\pi \approx 3.14$ and round to three digits.

18. A circle has a radius of 42 cm. What is the area?

19. A circle has a diameter of 22 m. What is the area?

20. A circle has an area of $12\frac{4}{7}$ ft². What is the diameter?

21. A circle has a radius of 56 m. What is the area?

Copy each figure and show on your drawing any lines or points of symmetry.

22. 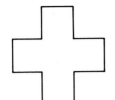 **23.** 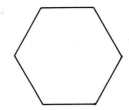 **24.**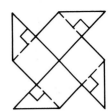

Make a sketch of each polyhedron.

25. A tetrahedron

26. An octagonal prism

Solve. Use the formula $F + V = E + 2$.

27. 10 faces, 16 vertices. How many edges?

28. 24 vertices, 36 edges. How many faces?

29. 13 faces, 24 edges. How many vertices?

30. 9 faces, 8 vertices. How many edges?

Solve. Use $\pi \approx 3.14$ and round to 3 digits if necessary.

31. What is the volume of an elevator that is 2.2 m high, 2 m long, and 1.5 m wide?

32. What is the volume of a fish tank that is 56 cm high, 113 cm long, and 45 cm wide?

33. A building, shaped like a triangular prism, has a volume of 10,000 m³ and a roof area of 400 m². How tall is the building?

34. A circular pool has a diameter of 7 m and is 1.5 m deep. What is the volume of the pool in cubic meters?

Use the table on page 351 to solve Exercises 35–38.

35. A steel ingot is 30 cm high, 7 cm long, and 5 cm wide. What is its mass?

36. A piece of cork, shaped like a cylinder, is 20 cm in diameter and 89 cm long. What is its mass?

37. A sheet of aluminum is 120 cm wide, 240 cm long, and 5 cm thick. What is its mass?

38. A bottle that measures 10 cm high and has a diameter of 5 cm is filled with mercury. What is the mass of the mercury?

Extra Practice: Chapter 11

Graph the given integer and its opposite on the same number line.

1. 4 **2.** 10 **3.** ⁻6 **4.** ⁻11 **5.** 12 **6.** ⁻9

True or false?

7. The absolute value of a number is its distance from zero on a number line.

8. Opposite numbers have the same absolute value.

9. The farther to the left you go on a number line the smaller the numbers.

Use an arrow diagram to represent the integer described.

10. 8, starting at 0 **11.** ⁻7, starting at 0 **12.** 9, starting at 0

13. ⁻2, starting at 0 **14.** 3, starting at 5 **15.** ⁻7, starting at 5

16. 8, starting at ⁻3 **17.** ⁻2, starting at ⁻3 **18.** 9, starting at ⁻5

List the integers that can replace x to make a true statement.

19. ⁻1 < x < 3 **20.** 2 < x < 8 **21.** ⁻5 < x < ⁻1

22. 4 < x < 7 **23.** ⁻4 < x < 0 **24.** ⁻6 > x > ⁻8

Draw an arrow diagram to represent each sum.

25. ⁻5 + ⁻2 **26.** ⁻4 + ⁻3 **27.** 6 + ⁻2 **28.** 8 + ⁻6

29. ⁻2 + ⁻3 **30.** ⁻4 + 7 **31.** ⁻2 + 4 **32.** ⁻7 + 12

Find each sum.

33. ⁻16 + 8 **34.** ⁻6 + 18 **35.** 6 + ⁻81 **36.** ⁻60 + ⁻80

37. ⁻5 + 70 **38.** 9 + ⁻30 **39.** ⁻20 + ⁻20 **40.** 40 + ⁻40

41. (17 + ⁻6) + 23 **42.** (⁻11 + 4) + ⁻63 **43.** 10 + (⁻2 + 31)

44. (15 + ⁻32) + ⁻13 **45.** 112 + (⁻71 + ⁻23) **46.** (⁻51 + 41) + ⁻37

Find each difference.

47. 16 − 27 **48.** 12 − 71 **49.** 14 − ⁻23 **50.** 25 − ⁻31

51. 12 − 12 **52.** 21 − ⁻21 **53.** 0 − ⁻12 **54.** ⁻15 − ⁻73

55. ⁻10 − ⁻53 **56.** ⁻71 − 43 **57.** 86 − 100 **58.** ⁻83 − 43

Multiply.

59. $5 \times {}^-10$ **60.** $12 \times {}^-4$ **61.** $9 \times {}^-13$ **62.** $6 \times {}^-78$

63. ${}^-12 \times 3$ **64.** $11 \times {}^-5$ **65.** ${}^-20 \times 19$ **66.** $15 \times {}^-11$

67. $12 \times 0 \times {}^-1$ **68.** $3 \times {}^-11 \times 5$ **69.** $17 \times 10 \times {}^-3$

70. ${}^-10(3 \times {}^-9)$ **71.** ${}^-7(20 \times {}^-4)$ **72.** $({}^-9 \times {}^-7)5$ **73.** $({}^-3 \times {}^-8)6$

Simplify.

74. $3(6 + {}^-7)$ **75.** $(6 - {}^-7)3$ **76.** $9(2 - 2)$ **77.** $({}^-5 + 2)7$

78. $({}^-2 - {}^-3)10$ **79.** $({}^-5 + {}^-12)11$ **80.** ${}^-11(7 + 3)$ **81.** ${}^-5(12 - 9)$

82. ${}^-3({}^-24 \div 8)$ **83.** $(49 \div {}^-7)10$ **84.** ${}^-81 \div (3 \times {}^-3)$

85. $({}^-12 \div {}^-3)({}^-15 \div 5)$ **86.** $({}^-9 \times 12) \div (3 \times {}^-6)$ **87.** ${}^-72 \div ({}^-4 \times {}^-3 \times {}^-1)$

Solve.

88. ${}^-15n = 45$ **89.** ${}^-7 + y = {}^-7$ **90.** $\frac{{}^-60}{w} = {}^-20$ **91.** $m + {}^-17 = 12$

92. $\frac{256}{q} = {}^-16$ **93.** ${}^-3n = {}^-51$ **94.** $c - 5 = {}^-5$ **95.** ${}^-12r = 180$

96. $f - 23 = {}^-7$ **97.** $\frac{p}{16} = {}^-9$ **98.** $15 - h = 27$ **99.** $27n = {}^-135$

100. $15 + t = 5$ **101.** ${}^-7 + b = 35$ **102.** $\frac{125}{n} = {}^-5$ **103.** ${}^-7 - w = 5$

In each exercise, graph the ordered pairs on the same coordinate plane.

104. $(4, {}^-2), (2, {}^-3), (5, {}^-3), ({}^-2, {}^-7)$ **105.** $({}^-7, {}^-2), ({}^-5, 5), (4, 3), (6, {}^-9)$

106. $(5, 0), ({}^-5, 1), ({}^-7, 6), (3, 5)$ **107.** $(0, 7), (7, 0), (0, {}^-7), ({}^-7, 0)$

108. $({}^-3, {}^-5), ({}^-3, 7), (7, {}^-5), (7, 7)$ **109.** $(3, {}^-3), (3, {}^-7), ({}^-2, 3), (4, {}^-1)$

In each exercise, graph the ordered pairs, join them in the order given, and identify the figure.

110. $(4, 8), (8, 8), (11, 8), (15, 3), (8, 3), (4, 8)$

111. $({}^-2, 2), ({}^-1, 8), (4, 8), (8, 3), (4, {}^-2), ({}^-2, 2)$

112. $({}^-2, {}^-7), ({}^-6, {}^-7), ({}^-6, {}^-2), ({}^-6, 2), ({}^-2, 2), ({}^-2, {}^-7)$

Graph the equation for values of x from ${}^-2$ to 2.

113. $y = {}^-x + 1$ **114.** $y = x + 2$ **115.** $y = {}^-3x$

116. $y = 2x + 2$ **117.** $y = 4 - x$ **118.** $y = x - 1$

Extra Practice: Chapter 12

Illustrate.

1. Make a broken-line graph to illustrate the given data.

Class Typing Speed

Words per minute	20	19	18	17	16	15	14
Number of students	1	5	1	12	6	4	1

2. Make a bar graph to illustrate the given data.

Height in Inches of Students in a Gym Class

Height	62	63	64	65	66	67	68	69	70	71	72
Frequency	1	0	2	3	2	4	3	1	2	0	2

3. During the baseball season, Tom hit 16 home runs, Fred hit 12, Jamie hit 10, Dale hit 6, and Corey hit 6. Illustrate the data using both a pictograph and a circle graph.

4. Jean used the elevator 5 times on Monday, 8 times on Tuesday, 4 times on Wednesday, 8 times on Thursday, and 2 times on Friday. Illustrate the given data using both a pictograph and a circle graph.

Find the mean, the median, and the range of each set of data.

5. 2, 4, 5, 8, 8, 10, 12

6. 6, 7, 7, 9, 11, 12, 12, 16

7. 1, 2, 3, 3, 3, 4, 4, 7, 8, 9

8. 310, 220, 300, 300, 240, 220, 300

9. 210, 250, 190, 180, 155

10. 1.4, 1.7, 2.7, 1.9, 2.1, 2.2

Make a frequency table for the given data. Then find the mean, the median, the range, and the mode.

11. 8, 9, 10, 11, 9, 12, 12, 16, 12, 14, 11, 10, 10, 11, 10

12. 9, 7, 9, 12, 10, 11, 5, 8, 8, 7, 12, 7, 11, 10

Make the suggested plot of the given data.

13. Stem-and-leaf; 7, 21, 32, 25, 4, 46, 38, 39, 27.

14. Box-and-whisker; 45, 19, 23, 38, 56, 15, 65, 28, 20, 35, 45.

Make a table, and arrange the data listed below into the following intervals: 4.5–34.5, 34.5–64.5, 64.5–94.5. Then use the table to make a histogram and a frequency polygon.

15. 64 91 86 23 67

16 42 63 25 46

44 88 48 67 86

68 25 46 86 67

52 25 67 32 86

16. 61 84 88 8 17

23 27 46 10 23

65 42 65 46 65

23 35 46 27 46

5 42 27 46 84

A jar contains two red, one orange, three green, and four blue marbles. Find the probability that a randomly drawn marble is the following.

17. blue
18. orange
19. green
20. purple

21. blue or red
22. orange or green

23. red, orange, or green
24. blue, red, orange, or green

A dial has 2 white, 3 red, 1 green, and 4 blue sections. When the pointer is spun, it will stop at random on a section. Find the odds in favor of the section being the given color.

25. white
26. red
27. green
28. yellow

29. white or blue
30. red or green

The words Monday, Wednesday, and Friday are written on blue cards and placed in a box. The box already contains 4 white cards, each with one of the remaining days of the week written on it. A card is randomly drawn from the box. Find the given probability.

31. P(the card is blue or the day begins with the letter S)

32. P(the day begins with the letter T or S)

33. P(the day begins with the letter M or T)

34. P(the card is blue or the day begins with the letter W)

35. P(the card is white or the day begins with the letter S)

36. P(the card is blue or the card has a weekday on it)

37. P(the card is white or the day begins with the letter T)

38. P(the card is white or the day begins with the letter F)

39. P(the card is blue or the card is white)

Table of Square Roots of Integers from 1 to 100

Number	Positive Square Root	Number	Positive Square Root	Number	Positive Square Root	Number	Positive Square Root
N	$\sqrt{N}$	N	$\sqrt{N}$	N	$\sqrt{N}$	N	$\sqrt{N}$
1	1	26	5.099	51	7.141	76	8.718
2	1.414	27	5.196	52	7.211	77	8.775
3	1.732	28	5.292	53	7.280	78	8.832
4	2	29	5.385	54	7.348	79	8.888
5	2.236	30	5.477	55	7.416	80	8.944
6	2.449	31	5.568	56	7.483	81	9
7	2.646	32	5.657	57	7.550	82	9.055
8	2.828	33	5.745	58	7.616	83	9.110
9	3	34	5.831	59	7.681	84	9.165
10	3.162	35	5.916	60	7.746	85	9.220
11	3.317	36	6	61	7.810	86	9.274
12	3.464	37	6.083	62	7.874	87	9.327
13	3.606	38	6.164	63	7.937	88	9.381
14	3.742	39	6.245	64	8	89	9.434
15	3.873	40	6.325	65	8.062	90	9.487
16	4	41	6.403	66	8.124	91	9.539
17	4.123	42	6.481	67	8.185	92	9.592
18	4.243	43	6.557	68	8.246	93	9.644
19	4.359	44	6.633	69	8.307	94	9.695
20	4.472	45	6.708	70	8.367	95	9.747
21	4.583	46	6.782	71	8.426	96	9.798
22	4.690	47	6.856	72	8.485	97	9.849
23	4.796	48	6.928	73	8.544	98	9.899
24	4.899	49	7	74	8.602	99	9.950
25	5	50	7.071	75	8.660	100	10

Exact square roots are shown in red. For the others, rational approximations are given correct to three decimal places.

Summary of Formulas

Circumference

$C = \pi d$

$C = 2\pi r$

Area

Rectangle: $A = lw$

Triangle: $A = \frac{1}{2}bh$

Parallelogram: $A = bh$

Trapezoid: $A = \frac{1}{2}(b_1 + b_2)h$

Circle: $A = \pi r^2$

Volume

Prism: $V = Bh$

Cylinder: $V = \pi r^2 h$

Lateral Area

Cylinder: lateral area $= 2\pi rh$

Surface Area

Cylinder: total surface area $= 2\pi rh + 2\pi r^2$

Distance

distance $=$ rate $\times$ time

Percentage

percent of change $= \dfrac{\text{amount of change}}{\text{original amount}}$

amount of commission $=$ percent of commission $\times$ total sales

percent of profit $= \dfrac{\text{profit}}{\text{total income}}$

Interest

Interest $=$ Principal $\times$ rate $\times$ time

APPENDIX A: Estimation

Sometimes an exact answer to a problem is not needed. We *estimate* when we need to find only an approximation of the answer or to test the reasonableness of the calculated answer. **Estimation** is a quick and easy way to find a number that is close to the actual answer without doing long and involved calculations. For example, suppose that we want to buy two books, which cost $3.97 each. To figure out how much money we need, we estimate the total cost. Determining the exact answer would take time and, in this case, an exact answer is not needed. We *round* $3.97 to $4 and then multiply $4 by 2 to get $8. Thus we would need about $8 to buy the books.

Estimation strategies that are frequently used include *rounding, clustering, front-end estimation,* and choosing *compatible numbers.* The example above illustrates the use of **rounding** in estimation. Refer to pages 73–74 for a detailed explanation of rounding. When rounding more than one number in order to estimate an answer, round each number to its highest place value. This allows for fast computation.

EXAMPLE 1 During the summer, an average of 1895 people visit Central Valley Zoo each day. About how many people go to the zoo during a summer month?

Solution Round 1895 to 2000, and round 1 month to 30 days.

$$2000 \times 30 = 60,000$$

About 60,000 people visit the zoo each summer month.

Choosing **compatible numbers** makes solving multiplication and division problems simpler. Select numbers that are easy to multiply or divide and that are close to the actual numbers.

EXAMPLE 2 A total of $1927.25 was collected from ticket sales for the school play. Tickets cost $3.25 each. About how many tickets were sold?

Solution Find an estimate for $1927.25 ÷ $3.25. First approximate the divisor. $3.25 is close to $3. Then choose a number close to $1927.25 that is a multiple of 3. Pick $1800.

$$3.25 \overline{)1927.25} \longrightarrow \overset{600}{3\overline{)1800}}$$

About 600 tickets were sold.

The **clustering** method of estimation is appropriate to use when finding a sum in which the addends are all close to the same number.

EXAMPLE 3   There are 493 ninth-grade students, 521 tenth-grade students, 514 eleventh-grade students, and 486 twelfth-grade students enrolled in a school. About how many students attend the school?

Solution   Since 493, 521, 514, and 486 all cluster around 500, each grade contains about 500 students. Thus the total number of students at the school is about 4×500, or 2000.

Front-end estimation helps us to add or subtract numbers quickly. Determine the highest place value shown for the given numbers. Add or subtract all the digits in that place value. Then adjust the answer by calculating with the digits in the next highest place value.

EXAMPLE 4   Which is the shorter route from Brownsville to Port Town, the northern route or the southern route?

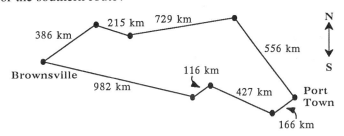

Solution
Northern route:		Southern route:	
	386		982
	215		116
	729		427
	+ 556		+ 166

Add the hundreds' digits.
$3 + 2 + 7 + 5 = 17$ hundreds $9 + 1 + 4 + 1 = 15$ hundreds

Add the tens' digits.
$8 + 1 + 2 + 5 = 16$ tens $8 + 1 + 2 + 6 = 17$ tens
$1700 + 160 = 1860$ $1500 + 170 = 1670$

Since 1670 km $<$ 1860 km, the southern route is shorter.

Exercises

Select the best estimate.

A   **1.** $37 + 41 + 39 + 44$
   a. 16   **b.** 160   **c.** 1600   **d.** 16,000

2. $28,431 - 17,987$
   a. 100   **b.** 1000   **c.** 10,000   **d.** 100,000

Select the best estimate.

3. 268 ÷ 88

   a. 0.3   **b.** 3.0   **c.** 30   **d.** 300

4. 4792 × 81

   a. 400   **b.** 4000   **c.** 40,000   **d.** 400,000

B   **5.** 1876 × 3.7

   a. 8.0   **b.** 80   **c.** 800   **d.** 8000

6. 7111 ÷ 79

   a. 0.9   **b.** 90   **c.** 900   **d.** 9000

7. 673.8 + 112.0 + 2.6

   a. 8   **b.** 80   **c.** 800   **d.** 8000

8. 771.8 × 5.0

   a. 40   **b.** 400   **c.** 4000   **d.** 40,000

C   **9.** 481.62 + 243.9 + 48.73

   a. 80   **b.** 800   **c.** 8000   **d.** 80,000

10. 598.1 ÷ 19.8

   a. 0.3   **b.** 3   **c.** 30   **d.** 3000

Problems

Estimate each answer.

A   **1.** Brian's Bookstore sold 630 books in April, 575 books in May, 644 books in June, and 606 books in July. About how many books were sold during the four months?

   2. About how much will the cost be for 2 flashlights at $4.88 each and 3 packages of batteries at $1.09 each?

B   **3.** Ellen multiplied 1.75 × 4.3. Where should she put the decimal point if the digits in her answer are 7525?

   4. A recipe calls for $2\frac{1}{4}$ cups of white flour and $1\frac{2}{3}$ cups of whole wheat flour. About how much flour is needed to make the recipe?

C   **5.** Pens imprinted with the school's emblem cost $1.19 each. Can Mr. Godeke buy a pen for each of his 77 students with $100?

   6. At Yontville High School 34% of the students walk to school each day. If 879 students attend the high school, about how many students walk to school?

Glossary

Absolute value (p. 366) The distance from 0 to the graph of a number on the number line.

Acute angle (p. 114) An angle between 0° and 90°.

Acute triangle (p. 119) A triangle with three acute angles.

Angle (p. 113) A figure formed by two rays starting from the same endpoint.

Annual rate of interest (p. 303) Percent of the principal figured on a yearly basis.

Area (p. 320) Amount of surface measured in square units.

Axes (p. 389) Two perpendicular number lines intersecting at *O,* the origin.

Bar graph (p. 404) A graph in which the length of each bar is proportional to the number it represents.

Base of the decimal system (p. 63) Ten. The value of each place in a number is a power of 10. *See* Expanded notation.

Base of a geometric figure (pp. 320, 325, 326, 339) A selected side or face.

Base of a power (p. 60) One of the equal factors in a product.

Bisect (p. 138) Divide into two equal parts.

Box-and-whisker plot (p. 422) A data display that uses a box to indicate the middle 50% of the data and whiskers to indicate the lower and upper 25% of the data.

Broken-line graph (p. 404) A graph made by joining successive plotted points.

Chord (p. 128) A segment joining two points on a circle.

Circle (p. 128) A plane figure all of whose points are at a given distance from a given point.

Circle graph (p. 409) A graph that uses the area of a circle to show the sum of data, and divides the area into parts proportional to the separate data.

Circumference (p. 128) The perimeter of a circle.

Collinear points (p. 104) Points that lie on the same line.

Common denominator (p. 191) A common multiple used as the denominator of two or more fractions that are equivalent to the original given fractions.

Common factor (p. 163) A number that is a factor of two or more numbers.

Common multiple (p. 166) A number that is a multiple of two or more numbers.

Compass (p. 128) A tool used to draw a circle.

Complementary angles (p. 114) Two angles the sum of whose measures is 90°.

Composite number (p. 160) A whole number greater than 1 that is not prime.

Congruent figures (pp. 109, 113, 132) Figures that have the same size and shape.

Consecutive whole numbers (p. 33) Whole numbers that increase by 1, such as the numbers 3, 4, 5, and 6.

Coordinates (p. 389) The ordered pair of numbers associated with a point on a graph.

Coordinate plane (p. 389) A plane marked with two perpendicular number lines, called axes, used to graph ordered pairs of numbers.

Corresponding angles (p. 132) The angles at matching vertices of congruent figures.

Counting numbers (p. 5) The set of numbers 1, 2, 3, 4, ...

Cross-multiplying (p. 231) A method for solving and checking proportions.

Cube (p. 339) A rectangular prism having square faces.

Cylinder (p. 347) A space figure having two congruent circular bases and one curved surface joining the bases.

Data (p. 404) Numerical information.

Decimal system (p. 63) The place-value numeration system that uses 10 as a base.

Degree (p. 113) Unit of angle measure.

Diagonal (p. 123) A segment joining two nonconsecutive vertices of a polygon.

Diameter (p. 128) A chord passing through the center of a circle.

Dimensions (p. 320) Length, width, and height of a space figure.

Edge of a polyhedron (p. 339) A segment which is the intersection of two sides, or faces, of a polyhedron.

Endpoint (p. 104) The points on each end of a line segment or ray.

Equation (p. 3) A mathematical sentence using the equals sign between two expressions naming the same number.

Equilateral triangle (p. 119) A triangle with all three sides congruent.

Equivalent equations (p. 251) Equations that have the same solution.

Equivalent fractions (p. 182) Fractions that name the same number.

Estimation (p. 78) The process of approximating an answer.

Evaluate (p. 3) Replace a variable in an expression by a number, and carry out the indicated operation.

Even number (p. 151) Any multiple of 2.

Expanded notation (p. 63) A method of representing a number as the sum of products of each digit and powers of 10.

Exponent (p. 60) The number that shows how many times the base is used as a factor. *See* Base of a power.

Factor (pp. 60, 150) Any of two or more numbers multiplied to form a product.

Fraction (p. 178) An indicated quotient, for example $\frac{2}{5}$. The denominator, 5 in the example, tells the number of equal parts into which the whole has been divided. The numerator, 2, tells how many of these parts are being considered.

Frequency (p. 416) The number of times that an item appears in a set of data.

Frequency distribution (p. 416) The pairing of the items from a set of data with their frequencies.

Frequency polygon (p. 424) A broken-line graph of a frequency distribution.

Frequency table (p. 416) Data arranged in a table to show how often each item appears in a set of data.

Function (p. 393) A set of ordered pairs in which no two ordered pairs have the same first number.

Geometric construction (p. 138) Geometric figure(s) drawn using only a compass and straightedge.

Graph of a number (pp. 39, 367) The point on a number line that is paired with the number.

Graph of an ordered pair (p. 389) The point in a plane that represents the ordered pair of numbers.

Graphs *See* Bar graph, Broken-line graph, Circle graph, Histogram, Pictograph.

Greatest common factor (GCF) (p. 163) The greatest whole number that is a factor of two or more given whole numbers.

Grouping symbols (p. 16) Symbols such as parenthesis, ( ), and brackets, [ ], used to enclose an expression.

Height (pp. 320, 325, 326, 347) The perpendicular distance between the bases. In a triangle, the perpendicular distance from the opposite vertex to the base line.

Histogram (p. 424) A bar graph that shows a frequency distribution.

Identity (p. 249) An equation satisfied by all values of the replacement set.

Improper fraction (p. 186) A fraction whose numerator is greater than or equal to its denominator.

Inequality (p. 39) A statement formed by placing an inequality symbol between two expressions.

Inscribed polygon (p. 129) A polygon that has all of its vertices on the circle.

Integers (p. 366) The whole numbers and their opposites: . . . ⁻2, ⁻1, 0, 1, 2, ...

Interest (p. 303) The amount of money paid for the use of money.

Inverse operations (p. 9) Mathematical operations that *undo* each other. Such as addition and subtraction, or multiplication and division.

Isosceles triangle (p. 119) A triangle with at least two sides congruent.

Lateral surface (p. 354) The surface of a space figure other than its bases.

Least common denominator (LCD) (p. 211) The least common multiple of two or more denominators.

Least common multiple (LCM) (p. 166) The least number that is a multiple of two or more nonzero given numbers.

Line (p. 104) A straight line extending in both directions without end.

Lowest terms (p. 183) A fraction is in lowest terms when the GCF of its numerator and denominator is 1.

Mass (p. 351) The measure of the amount of material an object contains.

Mean (p. 413) The value found by dividing the sum of several numbers by the number of items. Also called *average*.

Median (p. 413) The number that falls in the middle when data are listed from least to greatest. If the number of data is even, the median is the mean of the two middle items.

Midpoint (p. 109) The point of a segment that divides it into two congruent segments.

Mixed number (p. 186) A number that is expressed as the sum of a whole number and a fraction less than 1.

Mode (p. 417) The number from a set of data that occurs with the greatest frequency.

Multiple (p. 150) A product of a given number and any whole number.

Mutually exclusive events (p. 435) Events that cannot both occur at the same time.

Noncollinear points (p. 104) Points not on the same line.

Number line (p. 39) A line on which consecutive integers are assigned to equally spaced points on the line in increasing order from left to right.

Numerical expression (p. 2) An expression that names a certain number such as $4 + 6$.

Obtuse angle (p. 114) An angle whose measure is between 90° and 180°.

Obtuse triangle (p. 119) A triangle with an obtuse angle.

Odd number (p. 151) A whole number that is not a multiple of 2.

Odds of an event (p. 431) The ratio of the number of outcomes favoring an event to the number of outcomes not favoring the event.

Opposites (p. 366) A number and its negative, such as 7 and ⁻7.

Ordered pair (p. 389) A pair of numbers whose order is given.

Origin (p. 389) The point of intersection of the axes on a coordinate plane.

Outcome (p. 427) Result of a probability experiment.

Parallel lines (p. 105) Lines in the same plane that do not intersect.

Parallel planes (p. 105) Planes that do not intersect.

Parallelogram (p. 123) A quadrilateral with both pairs of opposite sides parallel.

Percent (p. 282) The ratio of a number to 100, shown by the symbol %.

Percent of change (p. 292) The result when the amount of change is divided by the original price.

Perfect square (p. 157) *See* Square number.

Perimeter of a figure (p. 124) The distance around the figure.

Perpendicular bisector (p. 138) The line that is perpendicular to a segment at its midpoint.

Perpendicular lines (p. 113) Two lines that intersect to form 90° angles.

Pi (π) (p. 128) The ratio of the circumference of a circle to its diameter.

Pictograph (p. 408) A form of bar graph with the bars replaced by rows or columns of symbols.

Plane (p. 105) A flat surface that extends without limit in all directions.

Point (p. 104) The simplest figure in geometry, pictured by a dot.

Polygon (p. 123) A closed figure formed by joining segments (sides of the polygon) at their endpoints (vertices of the polygon).

Polyhedron (p. 339) A figure formed by polygonal parts of planes that enclose a region of space.

Power of a number (p. 60) A product in which all the factors, except 1, are the same. For example, $2^4 = 2 \times 2 \times 2 \times 2 = 16$, so 16 is the fourth power of 2.

Prime factorization (p. 161) An expression showing a positive integer as the product of prime factors.

Prime number (p. 160) A whole number greater than 1 that has exactly two whole-number factors, 1 and itself.

Principal (p. 303) The amount of money on which interest is paid.

Prism (p. 339) A polyhedron with two congruent polygonal regions (called bases) that are parallel.

Probability (p. 427) The ratio of the number of outcomes favoring an event to the total number of possible outcomes.

Proper fraction (p. 186) A fraction whose numerator is less than its denominator.

Proportion (p. 231) An equation which states that two ratios are equal.

Protractor (p. 113) An instrument used to measure an angle.

Pyramid (p. 337) A polyhedron with a base that is a polygonal region and having three or more triangular faces.

Quadrilateral (p. 123) A polygon with four sides.

Quartile (p. 422) A value that divides a data set into four equal parts.

Radical sign (p. 157) The symbol, $\sqrt{}$, used to denote the square root of a number.

Radius (p. 128) A segment from the center of a circle to a point on the circle. *See* Circle.

Random selection (p. 427) Choice by chance only.

Range (p. 413) The difference between the greatest number and the least number in a set of data.

Rate (p. 227) A quotient of measures in different kinds of units, for example, 35 km/h.

Ratio (p. 226) A quotient of two numbers or two measures in the same units.

Ray (p. 104) A part of a line with one endpoint.

Reciprocals (p. 219) Two numbers whose product is 1.

Rectangle (p. 124) A parallelogram with four right angles.

Regular polygon (p. 123) A polygon with all its sides congruent and all its angles congruent.

Regular polyhedron (p. 340) A polyhedron with all its faces bounded by congruent, regular polygons.

Relatively prime (p. 164) Two or more whole numbers having 1 as their greatest common factor.

Replacement set (p. 248) The given set of numbers that a variable may represent.

Rhombus (p. 124) A parallelogram with all its sides congruent.

Right angle (p. 114) A 90° angle.

Right prism (p. 354) A prism in which all faces that are not bases are rectangles.

Right triangle (p. 119) A triangle with a right angle.

Rigid motions (p. 133) Motions such as translations, rotations, and reflections that move a figure to a new position without changing the shape or size.

Rounding (p. 73) A method of approximating a number.

Scalene triangle (p. 119) A triangle having no congruent sides.

Scientific notation (p. 83) A way of writing a number in which the number is expressed as a product of a number greater than or equal to 1, but less than 10, and a power of 10, for example 9.3×10^7.

Segment (p. 104) A part of a line.

Semicircle (p. 129) Half of a circle.

Sides (pp. 113, 118, 123) The rays forming an angle; the segments forming a polygon.

Simple form (p. 186) A mixed number is in simple form if its fractional part is expressed in lowest terms.

Simplify (p. 2) Replace a numerical expression by the simplest name of its value.

Skew lines (p. 106) Two nonparallel lines that do not intersect.

Solid (p. 343) An enclosed region of space bounded by planes.

Solution (pp. 43, 248) Any value of the variable that makes an equation or inequality a true sentence.

Square (p. 124) A rectangle with congruent sides and congruent angles.

Square number (p. 157) A whole number that is the product of two equal factors.

Square root of a number (p. 157) One of the two equal factors of a number.

Statistics (p. 413) The study of data, including gathering, organizing, and analyzing it.

Stem-and-leaf plot (p. 420) A data display that lists the last digits ("leaves") of the data values to the right of the earlier digits ("stems").

Supplementary angles (p. 114) Two angles the sum of whose measure is 180°.

Surface area (p. 354) The sum of the areas of a solid.

Terms of a proportion (p. 231) The numbers in a proportion.

Transformation (p. 251) Rewriting an equation into an equivalent equation.

Trapezoid (p. 123) A quadrilateral with only one pair of parallel sides.

Triangle (p. 118) A polygon with three sides.

Variable (p. 2) A symbol used to represent one or more numbers.

Variable expression (p. 20) An expression that involves a variable.

Vertex of an angle (pp. 113, 118, 123, 339) The common endpoint of two rays.

Vertex of a polygon or polyhedron (pp. 118, 123, 339) The point at which the sides of a polygon or the edges of a polyhedron intersect.

Volume (p. 343) The measure of the space occupied by a solid.

Whole numbers (p. 5) The counting numbers and 0: 0, 1, 2, 3, 4, ...

x-axis (p. 389) The horizontal number line on a coordinate plane.

y-axis (p. 389) The vertical number line on a coordinate plane.

Index

congruent, 119, 124
corresponding, 132, 133
of a polygon, 123, 124
of a triangle, 118, 119
Sieve of Eratosthenes, 160
Simple form, 186
Simple interest, 303, 304
Simplified expression, 2
Skill Review, 444–445
Solution, 43, 248
of equations, 43, 46, 47, 248
of inequalities, 43, 46
Solving word problems, 18, 21, 49
    See also Problem Solving, Problem Solving Reminder
Solid, 343
Square, 124
Square
centimeter, 320, 321
kilometer, 321
meter and millimeter, 321
unit, 322
Square numbers, 157, 169
Square of a number, 60
Square root, 157, 342
table of, from 1 to 100, 468
Statement, computer, 52, 53
Statistics, 413, 438, 439
sampling, 434
Stem-and-leaf plot, 420
Stevin, Simon, 66
Subtraction, 9, 32
basic facts, 43
of decimals, 77
of fractions, 210, 211
of integers, E21, 375
inverse of, 9, 252
of mixed numbers, 214
related facts, 9, 10, 43
transformation by, 251, 360, 375

Sum, 5, 32, 36
estimated, 78
of series, 240, 241
Surface area, 354, 355
Symbols, *xv*
in BASIC, 52, 53
grouping, 16
for inequalities, 39
Symmetry, 335

Terminating decimal, 195, 199
Terms of proportion, 231
Tetrahedron, 339, 340
Theorem
Fundamental, 161
Pythagorean, 358, 359
Transformations, 251, 255
with integers, 386
Translation, 133
Trapezoid, 123
area of, 326
Triangles, 118, 119, 123
acute, 119
area of, 325
equilateral, 119
isosceles, 119
naming, 119
obtuse, 119
right, 119, 358, 359
scalene, 119

Unit area, 320, 322
Unit volume, 343
Unique, 219

Value, 2, 3
absolute, 366, 370, 371
input in computer programs, 53
place, 63

Variable, 2, 33, 43, 248, 249
in computer programs, 53
expressions, 2, 3, 32, 33, 36, 248
in proportions, 231, 232
in word problems, 46–50, 234, 264, 267, 270
Venn diagram, 391
Vertex, 113, 118, 123
Vertices, 339
corresponding, 132
nonconsecutive, 123
Volume, 343
of cylinder, 347
of prism, 343, 351
unit, 343

Whole numbers, 5, 6, 33, 63
consecutive, 33, 39
in the decimal system, 63
with decimal fractions, 67
factors, 150
preceding, 33
rounding, 73
    See also Numbers, Properties
Width, 320
Word phrases, 32, 33, 49

x-axis, 389

y-axis, 389

Zero, 6, 7, 10, 11
basic facts, 6, 7, 10
in decimals, 67
in powers of ten, 60, 61
properties of, 6, 7, 10, 11
in rounded numbers, 73

Answers to Selected Exercises

1 Operations with Whole Numbers

Page 4 WRITTEN EXERCISES **1.** 511
3. 85 **5.** 918 **7.** 72 **9.** 4, 8, 12, 16 **11.** 28,
30, 34, 36 **13.** 21, 7, 2 **15.** 120 **17.** 79
19. 37 **21.** 28 **23.** 67 **25.** 98 **27.** 720
29. 12 **31.** 46 **33.** 25,920 **35.** 96 **37.** 10
39. 532 **41.** 2560

PAGE 4 REVIEW EXERCISES **1.** 5345
3. 10,121 **5.** 760 **7.** 9072

PAGE 4 NONROUTINE PROBLEM
SOLVING 27 days

PAGE 8 WRITTEN EXERCISES **1.** 79
3. 69 **5.** 910 **7.** 69 **9.** 102 **11.** 351 **13.** 92
15. 143 **17.** 0 **19.** 190 **21.** 1400 **23.** 300
25. 12,000 **27.** 870 **29.** 18,000 **31.** 10,800

PAGE 8 REVIEW EXERCISES **1.** 4217
3. 5 **5.** 682 **7.** 7

PAGES 11-12 WRITTEN EXERCISES
1. $58 - 26 = 32$; $58 - 32 = 26$; $26 + 32 = 58$
3. $62 + 41 = 103$; $41 + 62 = 103$; $103 - 62 =$
41 **5.** $273 \div 13 = 21$; $273 \div 21 = 13$; 13×21
$= 273$ **7.** $68 + 149 = 217$; $149 + 68 = 217$;
$217 - 68 = 149$ **9.** $56 + 249 = 305$; $249 + 56$
$= 305$; $305 - 56 = 249$ **11.** $649 - 288 = 361$;
$649 - 361 = 288$; $288 + 361 = 649$ **13.** 38
15. 0 **17.** 24 **19.** 48 **21.** 32 **23.** y **25.** 16
27. b **29.** 36 **31.** 29 **33.** z **35.** c **37.** t
39. 41 **41.** x **43.** y **45.** y

PAGE 12 REVIEW EXERCISES **1.** 3122
3. 1102 **5.** 490 **7.** 8961

PAGE 12 CALCULATOR INVESTIGATION
8192 people

PAGES 14–15 WRITTEN EXERCISES
1. 60 **3.** 80 **5.** 240 **7.** 180 **9.** 800 **11.** 490
13. 301 **15.** 328 **17.** 804 **19.** 506 **21.** 420
23. 720 **25.** 950 **27.** 3434 **29.** 1368 **31.** 630
33. 3330 **35.** 5130 **37. a.** true **b.** true; the
quotients are not whole numbers. **c.** false
d. Div. is not distributive with respect to add.

PAGE 15 SELF-TEST A **1.** 168 **2.** 72
3. 33 **4.** 154 **5.** 4 **6.** 648 **7.** 12 **8.** 18
9. 50 **10.** 107 **11.** 172 **12.** 0 **13.** 17,000
14. 8400 **15.** 32 **16.** b **17.** 62 **18.** e **19.** d
20. f **21.** 540 **22.** 612 **23.** 1968 **24.** 5712

25. 8580 **26.** 20,090

PAGE 17 WRITTEN EXERCISES **1.** 25
3. 4 **5.** 19 **7.** 28 **9.** 12 **11.** 20 **13.** 68
15. 33 **17.** 182 **19.** 20 **21.** 11 **23.** 12
25. 44 **27.** 87 **29.** 37 **31.** 172 **33.** 176
35. 78 **37.** 9 **39.** 78

PAGE 17 REVIEW EXERCISES **1.** 418
3. 44,918 **5.** 1110 **7.** 74,154

PAGE 20 WRITTEN EXERCISES **1. a.** the
number of model planes **b.** no; the number of
model planes that Sam bought **c.** no
d. addition **3. a.** the cost of 5 bats **b.** yes
c. no **d.** multiplication **5. a.** the difference in
mile per gallon **b.** yes **c.** yes; the model
years **d.** subtraction **7. a.** the amount spent
on tennis equipment **b.** yes **c.** yes; the
amount spent for a bicycle tire tube and a
bicycle pump **d.** addition **9. a.** the number
of bags left after the party **b.** yes **c.** no
d. addition and subtraction

PAGE 20 REVIEW EXERCISES **1.** 13,170
3. 20,536 **5.** 84 **7.** 39,894

PAGES 22–23 PROBLEMS **1.** $65
3. 2316 m **5.** $57 **7.** $32 **9.** $1086

PAGE 23 SELF-TEST B **1.** 350 **2.** 1
3. 104 **4. a.** the number of tokens Marcie can
buy **b.** yes **c.** multiplication and division
5. a. the number of rocks in the collection
after vacation **b.** no; the number of rocks in
the collection before vacation **c.** addition
6. 50 home runs

PAGE 26 CHAPTER REVIEW **1.** 91 **3.** 8
5. D **7.** A **9.** H **11.** C **13.** a **15.** c **17.** c
19. a **21.** a **23.** b

PAGES 28–29 CUMULATIVE REVIEW
EXERCISES **1.** 975 **3.** 207 **5.** 1102 **7.** 30
9. 438 **11.** 12,996 **13.** 7178 **15.** 7 **17.** 80
19. 5 **21.** 12 **23.** 24 **25.** 16 **27.** 9 **29.** 6
31. 63 **33.** 1 **35.** 945 **37.** 3400 **39.** 0
41. 1900 **43.** 18 **45.** 0 **47.** 100 **49.** 3100
51. $5c$ **53.** 72 **55.** 2368 **57.** 7800 **59.** 7
PROBLEMS **1.** $81 **3.** $22 **5.** 12 driveways
7. $26 **9.** $857

2 Using Variables

PAGES 34–35 WRITTEN EXERCISES
1. $10 + b$ **3.** $7 + m$ **5.** $3x$ **7.** $11u$
9. $5 + m$ **11.** $k - 78$ **13.** $6a - 5$
15. $z \div 14$ **17.** $m + 2$ **19.** $5n$ **21.** $100w$
23. $w + 1$ **25.** $24d$ **27.** $10y$ **29.** $3k$
31. $t \div 12$ **33.** $t + x$ **35.** $m + 2$ **37.** $d - gx$

PAGE 35 REVIEW EXERCISES 1. 595
3. 252 **5.** 30 **7.** 52

PAGES 37–38 WRITTEN EXERCISES
1. $4n = 8$ **3.** $9 \div n = 1$ **5.** $n - 14 = 41$
7. $n \div 9 = 333$ **9.** $28 - n = 2n$ **11.** $4n = 2n - 6$ **13.** $n - 10 = 43$ **15.** $x + 8 = 23$ **17.** $5n = 2755$ **19.** $10k = 127{,}000$ **21.** $n + (n + 1) + (n + 2) + (n + 3) = 106$ **23.** $a + b + c = 2a$
25. $r + t = 2r - t$ **27.** $6s + 2 = s - 10$
29. $ta + pb = 100k$

PAGE 38 REVIEW EXERCISES 1. 390
3. 148 **5.** 371 **7.** 131 **9.** 182

PAGES 40–41 WRITTEN EXERCISES
1. $>$ **3.** $<$ **5.** $<$ **7.** $<, <$ **9.** $>, >$
11. $>$ **13.** $>$ **15.** $>, >$ **17.** $6 > 0$
19. $22 < 33$ **21.** $52 > 25 > 5$
25. **27.** $27 < 3m$
29. $a < b$ **31.** $m > 25y$ **33.** $10 > r + 1 > 4$
35. $m > 4x > n$ **37.** $0 < x < 10 < y < 14$
39. $m - 1 < m < m + 1 < m + 2 < m + 3$

PAGE 42 SELF-TEST A 1. $h - 9$ **2.** $7a$
3. $x + 15$ **4.** $6 + 2z$ **5.** $y \div 5 = 31$
6. $17 + t = 60$ **7.** $14a = 98$ **8.** $<$ **9.** $<$
10. $<, <$ **11.** $30 < 48$ **12.** $11 < 17 < 22$
13. $15 > 6$ **14.** $2 < y < 13$

PAGE 45 WRITTEN EXERCISES 1. 6
3. 14 **5.** 8 **7.** 0 **9.** 10 **11.** All the numbers less than 7. **13.** All the numbers greater than 11. **15.** All the numbers greater than 13.
17. All the numbers greater than 0. **19.** 84
21. 86 **23.** 47 **25.** All the numbers greater than 45. **27.** All the numbers less than 72.
29. All the numbers greater than 14. **31.** 100
33. 134 **35.** 1000 **37.** 2000 **39.** 1452
41. 3087 **43.** 1632 **45.** 851 **47.** 2874
49. 4811 **51.** 7622 **53.** 0

PAGE 45 REVIEW EXERCISES 1. 68
3. 144 **5.** 36 **7.** 21 **9.** 1

PAGE 48 WRITTEN EXERCISES 1. 7 **3.** 9
5. 27 **7.** All the numbers greater than 1.
9. All the numbers less than 9. **11.** All the numbers greater than 30. **13.** 19 **15.** 13
17. 102 **19.** All the numbers greater than 14.
21. All the numbers less than 14. **23.** All the numbers less than 117. **25.** 100 **27.** 1
29. 9999 **31.** 3 **33.** 7 **35.** 12 **37.** 21 **39.** 19
41. 18 **43.** 0; 1

PAGE 48 REVIEW EXERCISES 1. $x + 13$
3. $20n$ **5.** $18d + 54$

PAGES 50–51 PROBLEMS 1. $12n = 252$; 21
3. $n - 45 = 100$; 145 **5.** $6n + 2 = 86$; 14
7. $5n - 1 = 114$; 23 **9.** $7n + 23 = 107$; 12
11. $13n = 221$; 17 games
13. $770 + 5n = 1575$; 161 nickels
15. $35 \times 13 + 20n = 2055$; 80 stamps

PAGE 51 SELF-TEST B 1. 13 **2.** All the numbers less than 8. **3.** 25 **4.** All the numbers greater than 44. **5.** 8 **6.** All the numbers less than 48. **7.** 50 **8.** All the numbers greater than 13. **9.** 7 **10.** 35
11. 84 **12.** 169 nickels

PAGE 54 CHAPTER REVIEW 1. false
3. true **5.** true **7.** false **9.** c **11.** a **13.** a
15. c

PAGES 56–57 CUMULATIVE REVIEW
EXERCISES 1. 1344 **3.** 4663 **5.** 1278
7. 828 **9.** 17,430 **11.** 51 **13.** 2112 **15.** 5821
17. 1505 **19.** 3082 **21.** 24,612 **23.** 54
25. 767 **27.** 2142 **29.** 550 **31.** 80 **33.** 146
35. 150 **37.** 232 **39.** 0 **41.** 9 **43.** 52
45. All the numbers greater than 90. **47.** 112
49. All the numbers less than 70. **51.** 6
PROBLEMS 1. 165 books **3.** $2.55 **5.** $3.75
7. 18 students **9.** 9600 lines

3 The Decimal System

PAGES 61–62 WRITTEN EXERCISES 1. 5^6
3. 8^9 **5.** 1,000,000 **7.** 10,000
9. 1,000,000,000 **11.** 10,000,000 **13.** 16
15. 256 **17.** 400 **19.** 3375 **21.** 6400 **23.** 256
25. 1296 **27.** 4096 **29.** 400 **31.** 1,680,700
33. 0 **35.** 961 **37.** 256 **39.** 6912 **41.** 72,000
43. 0 **45.** 27 **47.** 218 **49.** 25 **51.** 225

PAGE 62 REVIEW EXERCISES 1. 5000
3. 300 **5.** 3047 **7.** 236 **9.** 80,502

PAGES 64-65 WRITTEN EXERCISES
1. one thousand, nine hundred sixty-two
3. fifty-seven thousand, four hundred nineteen
5. one million, thirty-seven thousand, nine hundred eight 7. one billion, four hundred sixteen million, nine hundred eighty thousand, sixteen 9. 3004 11. 113,000
13. 3,014,000,702 15. $3(10^2) + 2(10) + 9(1)$
17. $1(10^4) + 0(10^3) + 4(10^2) + 7(10) + 2(1)$
19. $3(10^2) + 6(10) + 9(1)$
21. $7(10^2) + 2(10) + 3(1)$
23. $9(10^4) + 6(10^3) + 2(10^2) + 0(10) + 9(1)$
25. $8(10^5) + 0(10^4) + 4(10^3) + 7(10^2) + 2(10) + 5(1)$ 27. $5(10^3) + 9(10^2) + 0(10) + 2(1)$
29. $9(10^5) + 0(10^4) + 5(10^3) + 7(10^2) + 2(10) + 0(1)$ 31. $1(10^5) + 0(10^4) + 7(10^3) + 0(10^2) + 4(10) + 7(1)$ 33. $1(10^8) + 0(10^7) + 4(10^6) + 3(10^5) + 1(10^4) + 7(10^3) + 5(10^2) + 1(10) + 0(1)$ 35. $1(10^{10}) + 4(10^9) + 0(10^8) + 4(10^7) + 9(10^6) + 5(10^5) + 9(10^4) + 6(10^3) + 1(10^2) + 1(10) + 1(1)$ 37. $1(10^{10}) + 9(10^9) + 4(10^8) + 1(10^7) + 0(10^6) + 0(10^5) + 0(10^4) + 2(10^3) + 5(10^2) + 0(10) + 0(1)$ 39. $7(10^7) + 1(10^6) + 2(10^5) + 1(10^4) + 4(10^3) + 5(10^2) + 1(10) + 1(1)$ 41. $1(10^7) + 8(10^6) + 4(10^5) + 1(10^4) + 2(10^3) + 9(10^2) + 3(10) + 1(1)$ 43. $10t + 7$
45. $3(10) + u$ 47. $10t + 5t$ 49. $10t + 4t$
51. $100h + 10t + 0$ 53. $100(2t) + 10t + u$

PAGE 65 REVIEW EXERCISES

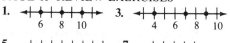

PAGES 68-69 WRITTEN EXERCISES
1. a. four hundredths b. $0(1) + 0(0.1) + 4(0.01)$ 3. a. seven thousandths
b. $0(1) + 0(0.1) + 0(0.01) + 7(0.001)$
5. a. twelve hundredths b. $0(1) + 1(0.1) + 2(0.01)$ 7. a. seventy-eight ten-thousandths
b. $0(1) + 0(0.1) + 0(0.01) + 7(0.001) + 8(0.0001)$ 9. a. one and three tenths
b. $1(1) + 3(0.1)$ 11. a. seventeen and eight thousandths b. $1(10) + 7(1) + 0(0.1) + 0(0.01) + 8(0.001)$ 13. 0.5 15. 0.017 17. 6.9
19. 0.000161 21. 9.000076 23. 0.01
25. 0.0001 27. 0.1 29. 0.01 31. 0.3
33. 0.007 35. 0.6 37. 0.04 39. 68.0099
41. 40.0431 43. 462.00071

45.
0.68

0.0 0.2 0.4 0.6 0.8 1.0

PAGE 69 REVIEW EXERCISES 1. 234; 324; 423 3. 154; 451; 15,400 5. 6; 60; 600
7. 219; 912; 920 9. 138; 803; 80,300

PAGE 69 CALCULATOR INVESTIGATION
1. 35,108 m

PAGE 72 WRITTEN EXERCISES 1. $>$
3. $>$ 5. $<$ 7. $=$ 9. $>$ 11. a 13. c
15. 3.12; 3.19; 3.21 17. 6; 6.08; 6.80
19. 532.78; 532.882; 532.9 21. 1.821; 1.823
23. 15.0001; 15.0002 25. 0.1211; 0.1212

PAGE 72 REVIEW EXERCISES 1. 700
3. 10,000,000 5. 0.8 7. 0.4 9. 1

PAGE 75 WRITTEN EXERCISES
1. 613,572,950 3. 613,570,000 5. 613,572,900
7. 610,000,000 9. 196,037,910
11. 196,040,000 13. 196,037,900
15. 200,000,000 17. 216.1 19. 220 21. 216
23. 216.098 25. 509.7 27. 510 29. 510
31. 509.690 33. a. 645 b. 654 35. a. 7500
b. 8499 37. a. 2,534,650 b. 2,534,749
39. a. 7,560,250,000 b. 7,560,349,999
41. a. $5975 b. $5984.99 43. a. $8515
b. $8524.99

PAGE 76 SELF-TEST A 1. 225 2. 256
3. 900,000 4. 200 5. $6(10^2) + 1(10) + 7(1)$
6. $5(10^3) + 0(10^2) + 3(10) + 8(1)$
7. $1(10^4) + 2(10^3) + 4(10^2) + 0(10) + 2(1)$
8. $2(10^5) + 5(10^4) + 6(10^3) + 0(10^2) + 3(10) + 0(1)$ 9. $0(0.1) + 6(0.01)$ 10. $1(1) + 3(0.1)$
11. $2(1) + 0(0.1) + 0(0.01) + 7(0.001)$
12. $0(0.1) + 1(0.01) + 4(0.001) + 2(0.0001)$
13. 0.09 14. 0.05 15. 0.00003 16. 0.0002
17. 1.23; 1.30; 1.32 18. 9; 9.08; 9.8 19. 400
20. 372 21. 372.1 22. 372.069

PAGE 76 CALCULATOR INVESTIGATION
1. 58 3. 56 5. 41 7. 285 9. 335

PAGES 79-81 WRITTEN EXERCISES
1. 10.98 3. 3.99 5. 4.35 7. 6.35 9. 290.239
11. 166.438 13. 10.9609 15. 4.1925
17. 2212.48506 19. 163.87554
21. 3.472 23. 1.1422 25. 3.698 27. 6.4398
29. 14.65 31. 10.063 33. 24.179 35. 0.0485
37. 36.35 39. 6.867 41. 58.937 43. 45.196
45. 23.62 47. 0.321

PAGES 80–81 PROBLEMS **1.** 5 min 27 s
3. 79.3 g **5.** $166.55 **7.** $1.70

PAGE 81 REVIEW EXERCISES **1.** 39,000
3. 9,000 **5.** 42 **7.** 7

PAGES 84–85 WRITTEN EXERCISES
1. a. 52,000 **b.** 520,000 **c.** 52,000,000
3. a. 5700 **b.** 57,000 **c.** 5,700,000
5. a. 12,700 **b.** 127,000 **c.** 12,700,000
7. a. 5069 **b.** 50,690 **c.** 5,069,000
9. a. 89.01 **b.** 890.1 **c.** 89,010 **11. a.** 16,475
b. 164,750 **c.** 16,475,000 **13. a.** 240 **b.** 2.4
c. 0.24 **15. a.** 0.757 **b.** 0.00757 **c.** 0.000757
17. a. 0.048 **b.** 0.00048 **c.** 0.000048
19. a. 0.028 **b.** 0.00028 **c.** 0.000028
21. a. 1600 **b.** 16 **c.** 1.6 **23. a.** 5140
b. 51.4 **c.** 5.14 **25.** 5.58×10^5 **27.** 3.8×10^3
29. 8.1507×10^7 **31.** 5.27×10^{11}
33. 3.269×10^9 **35.** 1.27376×10^{11}
37. 1.5936×10^9 **39.** 2.9715×10^7
41. 1.01×10^5 **43.** $\$4.02 \times 10^7$

PAGE 85 REVIEW EXERCISES **1.** 1666
3. 16,632 **5.** 30,576 **7.** 266.526

PAGES 87–88 WRITTEN EXERCISES
1. 13.6 **3.** 189.6 **5.** 13.344 **7.** 0.9652
9. 221.136 **11.** 0.1188 **13.** 9600
15. 0.0000468 **17.** 90,075 **19.** 0.0000756
21. 198.1 **23.** 7.23 **25.** 0

PAGE 88 PROBLEMS **1.** 1.25 in.
3. 23,105.026 ft **5.** $258.83

PAGE 88 REVIEW EXERCISES **1.** 9 **3.** 48
5. 57 **7.** 85

PAGES 91–92 WRITTEN EXERCISES
1. 75.5 **3.** 2.7 **5.** 15.6 **7.** 423.3 **9.** 0.04
11. 1015 **13.** 27.57 **15.** 61.88 **17.** 0.48
19. 21.43 **21.** 0.08 **23.** 2188.89 **25.** 314.29
27. 16.67 **29.** 603.4 **31.** 3.8

PAGE 92 PROBLEMS **1.** $7.14 **3.** $9.80
5. a. $0.84 **b.** $0.61

PAGE 92 REVIEW EXERCISES **1.** 6706
3. 14,782 **5.** 28 **7.** 16

PAGES 94–95 PROBLEMS **1.** $55.85
3. 388.9 km/h **5.** under $1; $.45 **7.** 9 gal;
9.6 gal **9.** $9.50, $9.01

PAGE 95 SELF-TEST B **1.** 14.59 **2.** 88.902

3. 10.3 **4.** 5.64×10^6 **5.** 1.749×10^{10}
6. a. 4,578,300; 457.83 **b.** 45,783,000; 45.783
7. a. 263.5; 0.02635 **b.** 2635; 0.002635
8. a. 51.66; 0.005166 **b.** 516.6; 0.0005166
9. 0.573 **10.** 3.64 **11.** 700 **12.** 0.16
13. 3 rose bushes

PAGE 97 EXERCISES **1.** $291.62 **3.** $95.14
5. $798.33

PAGE 98 CHAPTER REVIEW **1.** G **3.** A
5. B **7.** H **9.** E **11.** false **13.** 17.985
15. 10.13 **17.** 730,000 **19.** 10^5 **21.** 693
23. 0.175 **25.** 7 **27.** c

PAGES 100–101 CUMULATIVE REVIEW
EXERCISES **1.** 16 **3.** 100 **5.** 60 **7.** 8
9. 5 **11.** 31 **13.** 10 **15.** 112 **17.** 16 **19.** 32
21. 5.36 **23.** 105.7 **25.** 1150 **27.** 28.8
29. 24.5 **31.** 203 **33.** All the numbers greater
than 18. **35.** 110 **37.** 42 **39.** All the numbers
less than 648. **41.** $x - 17$ **43.** $n + 14 = 68$
45. $17 - n = 11$
PROBLEMS **1.** 192 calculators **3.** 40 lb
5. $18 **7.** 4 packages **9.** economy; $9

4 Geometric Figures

PAGES 107–108 WRITTEN EXERCISES
1. $\overleftrightarrow{YX}$ **3.** $\overrightarrow{PQ}$ **5.** $\overleftrightarrow{XY}$; $\overline{XZ}$, $\overline{XY}$, $\overline{YX}$ **7.** S, P,
O or T, Q, O **9.** $\overrightarrow{PQ}$, $\overline{PS}$, $\overline{PO}$ **11.** $\overline{ST}$, $\overline{PQ}$
13. $\overrightarrow{QT}$ and $\overrightarrow{PS}$ **15.** Answers may vary; for
example, $\overrightarrow{OS}$ and $\overrightarrow{OT}$ **17.** $\overrightarrow{OS}$ or $\overrightarrow{PS}$ **19.** $\overrightarrow{OS}$,
$\overrightarrow{OP}$, $\overrightarrow{OQ}$, $\overrightarrow{OT}$ **21.** Answers may vary; for
example $\overrightarrow{AB}$ and $\overrightarrow{AX}$; A. **23.** Answers may
vary; for example $\overleftrightarrow{AB}$ and $\overleftrightarrow{XY}$; plane ABX.
25. true **27.** false **29.** false **31.** true

PAGE 108 REVIEW EXERCISES **1.** 2.9
3. 4.6 **5.** 3.0 **7.** 9.3

PAGES 111–112 WRITTEN EXERCISES
1. a. 8 cm **b.** 80 mm **3. a.** 9 cm **b.** 92 mm
5. a. 8 cm **b.** 82 mm **7.** $\overline{AE}$ and $\overline{PT}$; $\overline{VZ}$ and
$\overline{GJ}$ **9.** 450 cm, 4500 mm **11.** 2.5 m, 2500 mm
13. 60 m, 6000 cm **15.** 2 km **17.** 0.625 km
19. 4500 m **21.** 3.74 m by 5.20 m **23.** 4.675 m
by 7.050 m **25.** 27 mm **27.** 65 cm
29. 2.1875 **31.** 35

PAGE 112 REVIEW EXERCISES **1.** 90
3. 40 **5.** 140 **7.** 105 **9.** 65

PAGES 115–117 WRITTEN EXERCISES
1.   3.

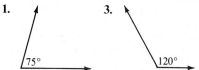

5. 50°, acute 7. 140°, obtuse 9. 47°, 137°
11. 45° 13. 19°, 161° 19. $\overleftrightarrow{AB}$ and $\overleftrightarrow{BC}$, $\overleftrightarrow{AB}$
and $\overrightarrow{AD}$ 21. Any 2 of ∠BEC and ∠CED;
∠AEB and ∠AED; ∠AEB and ∠BEC;
∠AED and ∠DEC
23.   25.   90° 27. true

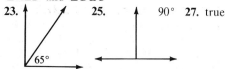

PAGE 117 SELF-TEST A 1.
2.   3.
4. Answers may vary; for example, $\overleftrightarrow{AB}$ and
$\overleftrightarrow{XY}$. 5. Answers may vary; for example, plane
ABY and plane CDW. 6. Answers may vary;
for example, $\overrightarrow{AX}$ and $\overrightarrow{AB}$. 7. Answers may
vary; for example, plane ABY and plane BCZ.
8. 4 9. 0.87 10. 0.785 11. 10.9 12. MB, $\overline{MB}$
13. 90° 14. congruent 15. is perpendicular to
16. acute 17. 48° 18. 73°

PAGES 121–122 WRITTEN EXERCISES
1. 80° 3. 90° 5. isosceles 7. equilateral
9. isosceles, obtuse 11. scalene, acute
13. △AED, △DEC, △ABC 15. △BDC
17. a.   b.   19. 60° 21. 15°

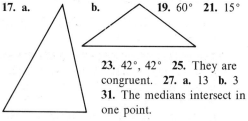

23. 42°, 42° 25. They are
congruent. 27. a. 13 b. 3
31. The medians intersect in
one point.

PAGE 122 REVIEW EXERCISES 1. 15.08
3. 15.52 5. 20.33 7. 21.873 9. 24.768

PAGES 125–127 WRITTEN EXERCISES
1. pentagon 3. hexagon 5. triangle
7. square 9. 14.1 11. 312 cm 13. 72.6 mm
15. 1356 m 17. 108° 19. 2.56 m 21. 12 m
23. 3 25.   27. 22

29. a. 360° b. 1440° c. 360° d. 1080° 31. 5

PAGE 127 REVIEW EXERCISES 1. 22.4
3. 49 5. 10.9 7. 44.8

PAGES 130–131 WRITTEN EXERCISES
1. 25.1 cm 3. 2830 mm 5. 134 m 7. 90.1 m
9. 143 km 11. 199 m 13. 1.59 mm
15. 3.74 km 17. 2.79 cm 19. 40,074 km
21. 47.1 km 23. 94.2 m 25. 35.7 27. 41.4
29. 22.7 31. $S = \frac{1}{2}\pi d$ 33. Draw a circle and
label three points, A, B, C on the circle. Let
Point D be any point not on the circle.
Quadrilateral $ABCD$ cannot be inscribed in a
circle. 35. ∠APB is a right angle. An angle
inscribed in a semicircle is a right angle.

PAGE 131 REVIEW EXERCISES 1. 18
3. 27 5. 8 7. 14

PAGES 135–137 WRITTEN EXERCISES
1. c 3. b 5. a. △GFE b. ∠G c. $\overline{CA}$
7. a. quad. $YZWX$ b. ∠D c. $\overline{XW}$
9. reflection or rotation 11. rotation, two
reflections, or a translation and a reflection
13. true 15. false 17. true 19. a, c
21. a. ∠N b. ∠Y c. $\overline{NS}$ d. $\overline{RL}$
23. a. $\overline{FG}$ b. $\overline{EH}$ c. ∠EFG d. $\overline{CD}$
25. a. △ABF ≅ △EDF, △BCF ≅ △DCF
b. quad. $ABCF$ ≅ quad. $EDCF$ c. pentagon
$ABCDF$ ≅ pentagon $EDCBF$ 27. Yes; if three
sides of one triangle are congruent to three
sides of another triangle, the triangles are
congruent. 29. Yes; if in one triangle two
angles and the side between them are
congruent to two angles of another triangle and
the side between them, the triangles are
congruent.

PAGE 137 REVIEW EXERCISES 1. 7
3. 11 5. 72 7. 4

PAGE 137 CALCULATOR INVESTIGATION
1. 3.1604938 3. 3.14$\overline{16}$ 5. 3.1416
The closest approximation is $\frac{355}{113}$.

PAGES 140–141 WRITTEN EXERCISES
1.   5.

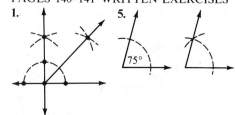

7. 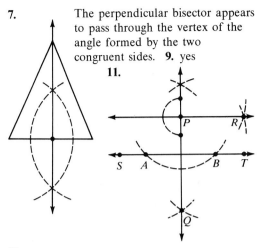 The perpendicular bisector appears to pass through the vertex of the angle formed by the two congruent sides. **9.** yes

11.

13. yes

PAGE 141 SELF–TEST B **1.** equilateral
2. 180 **3.** 3 **4.** octagon **5.** parallelogram
6. 33 cm **7.** 100 cm **8.** true **9.** false
10. a. $\overline{FG}$ **b.** J **c.** IJF
11. 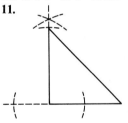 **12.**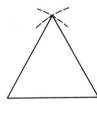

PAGE 143 ENRICHMENT **1.** 57,960,000 km
3. 149,730,000 km **5.** 12 **7.** 3.2186×10^{10} or
32186000000
9.
```
10   PRINT "DISTANCE TRAVELED";
15   FOR I = 1 TO 5
20   PRINT "HOW MANY HOURS";
30   INPUT T
40   LET R = 760
50   PRINT R * T; "MILES."
55   NEXT I
60   END
```

PAGE 144 CHAPTER REVIEW **1.** collinear
points **3.** midpoint **5.** false **7.** true
9. false **11.** d **13.** c
15.  $\triangle ABC$ is
equilateral, thus
$\angle CAB = 60°$.
$\triangle ABC \cong \triangle DAC$,
thus $\angle DAC = 60°$,
$\angle DAB = 120°$.

PAGES 146–147 CUMULATIVE REVIEW
EXERCISES **1.** 869 **3.** 352 **5.** 9072
7. 1239 **9.** 1786 **11.** 2557 **13.** 246 **15.** 268
17. 11.94 **19.** 2.12 **21.** 4.07 **23.** 3.96
25. 3.42 **27.** 5547 **29.** 17,556 **31.** 24,345.85
33. 311 **35.** 136 **37.** 119 **39.** 7 **41.** 36
43. 75 **45.** 55 **47.** 55 **49.** 9
PROBLEMS **1.** $31.11 **3.** $124 **5.** 52 m
7. 127 boxes **9.** 22 m

5 Number Theory
PAGES 151–152 WRITTEN EXERCISES
1. 1, 2, 3, 6, 7, 14, 21, 42 **3.** 1, 2, 4, 8, 16,
32 **5.** 1, 2, 4, 7, 8, 14, 28, 56 **7.** 1, 2, 3, 4, 6,
7, 12, 14, 21, 28, 42, 84 **9.** 1, 41, **11.** 0, 12,
24, 36, 48 **13.** 0, 17, 34, 51, 68 **15.** 0, 10, 20,
30, 40 **17.** 0, 24, 48, 72, 96 **19.** 0, 36, 72, 108,
144 **21.** 9 **23.** no **25.** yes; 8 **27.** yes; 283
29. yes; 273 **31.** 0, 6, 12, 18, 24, . . . ; yes
33. no **35.** even **37.** even **39.** 40,320
41. 17 **43.** 1, 4, 9, 16; answers may vary, one
such number is 25 **45.** no; $a + b$ is not a
multiple of c

PAGE 152 REVIEW EXERCISES **1.** 63
3. 89 **5.** 99.46 **7.** 183.53

PAGES 155–156 WRITTEN EXERCISES
1. 2, 3, 4 **3.** 3, 5 **5.** 3, 9 **7.** 2, 3, 4, 5, 10
9. none **11.** 2, 4 **13.** 2, 3, 4, 9 **15.** 2, 3, 5,
10 **17.** yes; yes; yes **19.** yes; yes; yes **21.** yes;
yes; yes **23.** 0 **25.** 8 **27.** 5 **29.** no **31.** yes
33. 8 pages **35.** $28 = 1 + 2 + 4 + 7 + 14$

PAGE 156 REVIEW EXERCISES **1.** 289
3. 529 **5.** 27 **7.** 41

PAGES 157–158 WRITTEN EXERCISES
1. 64 **3.** 169 **5.** 441 **7.** 130 **9.** 11 **11.** 20
13. 40 **15.** 5 **17. a.** 15 **b.** 15 **c.** yes
19. a. 13 **b.** 17 **c.** no **21.** 18 **23.** 25
25. 17; 19 **27. a.** 1; 3; 6; 10; 15; 21; 28; 36;
45; 55 **b.** Each sum is a perfect square.
c.

29. The result is 25, another odd perfect square.

$3 + 6 = 9$, a perfect square.

PAGE 159 SELF–TEST A **1.** 1, 2, 3, 4, 5, 6,
10, 12, 15, 20, 30, 60 **2.** 1, 2, 3, 4, 6, 7, 12, 14,
21, 28, 42, 84 **3.** 1, 2, 4, 5, 10, 20, 25, 50, 100
4. 1, 23 **5.** 13, 26, 39, 52, 65 **6.** 19, 38, 57, 76,

95 **7.** 24, 48, 72, 96, 120 **8.** 31, 62, 93, 124, 155 **9.** 2, 3, 4, 9 **10.** 2, 3, 5, 9, 10 **11.** 2, 4 **12.** 3, 9 **13.** 3, 5, 9 **14.** 2, 3, 4, 5, 9, 10 **15.** 3 **16.** none **17.** 196 **18.** 20 **19.** 16 **20.** 289 **21.** 19 **22.** 625 **23.** 1296 **24.** 50

PAGE 162 WRITTEN EXERCISES
1. composite **3.** composite **5.** composite **7.** prime **9.** composite **11.** composite **13.** $2^2 \cdot 3$ **15.** $2^3 \cdot 3$ **17.** $3 \cdot 13$ **19.** $2 \cdot 3 \cdot 11$ **21.** $2 \cdot 3^3$ **23.** $2^2 \cdot 3 \cdot 7$ **25.** $2^2 \cdot 7^2$ **27.** $2^2 \cdot 7 \cdot 11$ **29.** $2 \cdot 3 \cdot 19$ **31.** All other even numbers have 2 as a factor. **33.** Prime numbers greater than 2 are odd numbers. The sum of two odd numbers is an even number. **35.** 1, 3, 7, 9 **37.** 1001; the number represented by the last 3 digits

PAGE 162 REVIEW EXERCISES **1.** 343 **3.** 64 **5.** 6561 **7.** 100,000 **9.** 12,500

PAGES 164–165 WRITTEN EXERCISES
1. 8 **3.** 12 **5.** 1 **7.** 14 **9.** 15 **11.** 28 **13.** 40 **15.** 28 **17.** 350 **19.** 4 **21.** 10 **23.** false **25.** false **27. a.** 18; 30; 6 **b.** 20; 50; 10 **c.** The third number is the GCF of the first two numbers. **29.** answers may vary; 6 and 9, or 18 and 30 **31.** GCF(8, 15) = 1. Because 8 and 15 are relatively prime, if 15 is a factor of $8 \times n$, 15 must be a factor of n.

PAGE 165 REVIEW EXERCISES **1.** 1, 2, 4, 5, 8, 10, 20, 40 **3.** 1, 2, 3, 4, 6, 8, 12, 16, 24, 48 **5.** 1, 2, 4, 8, 11, 22, 44, 88 **7.** 1, 2, 5, 10, 11, 22, 55, 110 **9.** 1, 2, 3, 6, 17, 34, 51, 102

PAGES 167–168 WRITTEN EXERCISES
1. 60 **3.** 225 **5.** 72 **7.** 540 **9.** 390 **11.** 540 **13.** 150 **15.** 240 **17.** the second number **19. a.** 30; 75; 150 **b.** 36; 90; 180 **c.** 150 = LCM(30, 75); 180 = LCM(36, 90) **21.** every 720th bar **23.** 5 rows of 12 cm bricks; 3 rows of 20 cm bricks **25.** 120 and 4; 24 and 20; 40 and 12; 8 and 60

PAGE 169 SELF-TEST B **1.** composite; $2^2 \cdot 3^3$ **2.** prime **3.** composite $3 \cdot 29$ **4.** prime **5.** 30 **6.** 14 **7.** 1; relatively prime **8.** 15 **9.** 140 **10.** 189 **11.** 195 **12.** 450

PAGE 169 COMPUTER INVESTIGATION
1–10 The results of running the program for Exercises 1–10 are similar to Exercises 11–20, except that each pair of factors is given twice.

11. 1×216; 2×108; 3×72; 4×54; 6×36; 8×27; 9×24; 12×18 **13.** 1×576; 2×288; 3×192; 4×144; 6×96; 8×72; 9×64; 12×48; 16×36; 18×32; 24×24; $\sqrt{576} = 24$ **15.** 1×168; 2×84; 3×56; 4×42; 6×28; 7×24; 8×21; 12×14 **17.** 1×625; 5×125; 25×25; $\sqrt{625} = 25$ **19.** 1×1840; 2×920; 4×460; 5×368; 8×230; 10×184; 16×115; 20×92; 23×80; 40×46

PAGE 171 ENRICHMENT
1.
3. MCMLXXXVII **5.** 323 **7.** 37,806 **9.** 286

PAGE 172 CHAPTER REVIEW **1.** 4, 6, 8, 12, 24 **3.** odd **5.** 1, 2, 4, 5, 8, 10, 20, 40 **7.** c **9.** b **11.** c **13.** true **15.** false **17.** false **19.** true

PAGES 174–175 CUMULATIVE REVIEW EXERCISES **1.** 8424 **3.** 3538 **5.** 10,810 **7.** 148 **9.** 2508 **11.** 0.1091 **13.** 0.5369 **15.** 7.738 **17.** 59,088 **19.** 856 **21.** 672 **23.** 0.47592 **25.** 9.16 **27.** 25.7 **29.** 5.0303 **31.** 577 **33.** 953 **35.** 317 **37.** 1126 **39.** 14 **41.** 180° **43.** complementary angles **45.** GCF PROBLEMS **1.** 40 min **3.** 38.285 m **5.** 268 **7.** 37.92 cm **9.** 6.85 cm

6 Fractions: Definitions and Relationships

PAGES 180–181 WRITTEN EXERCISES
1. $\frac{3}{10}$ **3.** $\frac{5}{8}$ **5.** $\frac{2}{4}$ **7.** $\frac{5}{8}$ **9.** 1 **11.** 3 **13.** $\frac{10}{13}$ **15.** 3; 4 **17.** 6 **19.** 4 **21.** $\frac{20}{27}$ **23.** 3 **25.** 17; 14 **27. a.** $\frac{9}{20}$ **b.** $\frac{11}{20}$ **29. a.** $\frac{17}{32}$ **b.** $\frac{15}{32}$ **31.** $\frac{10}{45}$ **33.** $\frac{2}{45}$ **35. a.** $\frac{13}{60}$ **b.** $\frac{47}{60}$

PAGE 181 COMPUTER INVESTIGATION
1. 300 **3.** 126 **5.** 1020 **7.** 2640

PAGE 181 COMPUTER BYTE **1.** 300 **3.** 126 **5.** 1020 **7.** 2640

PAGES 184–185 WRITTEN EXERCISES
1. 5 **3.** 20 **5.** 28 **7.** 49 **9.** 242 **11.** 70 **13.** $\frac{4}{7}$ **15.** $\frac{4}{7}$ **17.** $\frac{2}{5}$ **19.** 9 **21.** 8 **23.** $\frac{15}{20}$, $\frac{8}{20}$ **25.** $\frac{15}{18}$, $\frac{4}{18}$ **27.** $\frac{21}{24}$, $\frac{20}{24}$ **29.** $\frac{10}{44}$, $\frac{33}{44}$ **31.** $\frac{27}{36}$, $\frac{30}{36}$, $\frac{14}{36}$ **33.** $\frac{96}{120}$, $\frac{45}{120}$, $\frac{20}{120}$ **35.** $\frac{5}{8}$ **37. a.** The products are equal. **b.** If $\frac{a}{b} = \frac{c}{d}$, then $ad = bc$. **39.** 4

41. 10 **43.** 15 **45.** 20

PAGE 185 REVIEW EXERCISES **1.** 37
3. 27 **5.** 96 **7.** 11 **9.** 420

PAGE 188 WRITTEN EXERCISES **1.** $3\frac{3}{4}$
3. $6\frac{2}{9}$ **5.** 10 **7.** $6\frac{1}{3}$ **9.** 9 **11.** $11\frac{2}{3}$ **13.** $\frac{20}{3}$
15. $\frac{59}{8}$ **17.** $\frac{77}{6}$ **19.** $\frac{131}{9}$ **21.** $\frac{413}{4}$ **23.** $\frac{907}{12}$
25. $261\frac{2}{3}$ **27.** $322\frac{12}{13}$ **29.** $271\frac{2}{5}$ **31.** $255\frac{10}{29}$
33. 3 **35.** 13

PAGES 188–190 PROBLEMS **1.** $2\frac{1}{2}$
sandwiches **3.** $3\frac{3}{4}$ lb **5.** $6\frac{1}{3}$ ft **7.** $11\frac{3}{4}$ min
9. $5\frac{2}{5}$ in. **11.** 7 min **13.** 12 pieces; $8\frac{1}{3}$ in.²

PAGE 190 SELF-TEST A **1.** $\frac{4}{7}$ **2.** 7 **3.** 9;
17 **4.** 8 **5.** 5 **6.** 100 **7.** 81 **8.** $\frac{9}{10}$ **9.** $\frac{7}{15}$
10. $\frac{2}{3}$ **11.** $1\frac{8}{9}$ **12.** $3\frac{1}{6}$ **13.** $8\frac{1}{18}$ **14.** $\frac{22}{9}$
15. $\frac{119}{8}$ **16.** $\frac{469}{11}$

PAGES 192–193 WRITTEN EXERCISES
1. $\frac{3}{8}$ **3.** $\frac{5}{6}$ **5.** $\frac{8}{25}$ **7.** $\frac{17}{24}$ **9.** $\frac{14}{33}$ **11.** $\frac{7}{36}$ **13.** $\frac{33}{60}$
15. $\frac{5}{42}$ **17.** $\frac{7}{14}$, or $\frac{1}{2}$ **19.** $\frac{41}{72}$ **21.** $\frac{15}{32}$ **23.** $\frac{4}{9}$
25. $\frac{17}{21}$ **27.** < **29.** > **31. a.** $\frac{ad}{bd}, \frac{bc}{bd}$ **b.** $\frac{a}{b}$

PAGES 193–194 PROBLEMS **1.** Joan
3. 60-watt bulbs **5.** 9 shots **7.** 27 first serves

PAGE 194 REVIEW EXERCISES **1.** 4.68
3. 20.33 **5.** 20.17 **7.** 41.57

PAGE 194 CALCULATOR INVESTIGATION
1. $\frac{5}{8} < \frac{9}{14}$ **3.** $\frac{17}{25} > \frac{10}{17}$ **5.** $\frac{53}{62} < \frac{71}{81}$

PAGES 197–198 WRITTEN EXERCISES
1. 0.625 **3.** 0.76 **5.** 0.6875 **7.** $0.8\overline{3}$ **9.** $0.\overline{72}$
11. $1.0\overline{6}$ **13.** 1.125 **15.** $2.08\overline{3}$ **17.** 1.84
19. $0.2\overline{7}$ **21.** $1.\overline{63}$ **23.** $0.\overline{405}$ **25.** $0.\overline{4}$, 0.45,
$0.\overline{45}$, $0.4\overline{5}$ **27.** 0.562, $\frac{9}{16}$, $0.\overline{562}$, $0.5\overline{6}$ **29.** $\frac{62}{99}$,
$0.6\overline{26}$, $\frac{2}{3}$, 0.67 **31.** $0.\overline{418}$ **33.** 6.25 **35.** 2.2
37. $0.3141\overline{6}$ **39.** The value of the largest
exponent gives the number of digits in the
decimal expansion. **41. a.** 5^3 **b.** 3 **43. a.** 2^5
b. 5 **45. a.** 5^4 **b.** 4

PAGE 198 REVIEW EXERCISES **1.** 549.3
3. 6983.2 **5.** 100.8 **7.** 8349.62 **9.** 192,000.8

PAGE 198 CALCULATOR INVESTIGATION
3. 1110 **5.** 111,110 **7.** 11,111,110
9. 1,111,111,110 **11.** 222,222 **13.** 444,444
15. 666,666 **17.** 888,888 **19.** 1,111,110

PAGE 200 WRITTEN EXERCISES **1.** $\frac{8}{25}$

3. $\frac{3}{8}$ **5.** $5\frac{13}{50}$ **7.** $9\frac{3}{40}$ **9.** $\frac{69}{400}$ **11.** $\frac{7}{9}$ **13.** $\frac{16}{111}$
15. $\frac{1}{37}$ **17.** $\frac{31}{74}$ **19.** $\frac{25}{41}$ **21.** $\frac{2}{5}$; 0.4 **23. a.** $0.8\overline{3}$
b. $\frac{1}{2} + \frac{1}{3} \times \frac{5}{6}$ **c.** $\frac{5}{6} = \frac{5}{6}$ **25. a.** $0.5\overline{6}$
b. $\frac{1}{6} + \frac{2}{5} = \frac{17}{30}$ **c.** $\frac{17}{30} = \frac{17}{30}$ **27. a.** $0.63\overline{8}$
b. $\frac{5}{12} + \frac{2}{9} = \frac{23}{36}$ **c.** $\frac{23}{36} = \frac{23}{36}$ **29. a.** $1.\overline{18}$
b. $\frac{17}{33} + \frac{2}{3} = 1\frac{2}{11}$ **c.** $1\frac{2}{11} = 1\frac{2}{11}$
31. a. $0.\overline{606879}$ **b.** $\frac{4}{11} + \frac{9}{37} = \frac{247}{407}$ **c.** $\frac{247}{407}$

PAGE 201 SELF-TEST B **1.** $\frac{3}{8}$ **2.** $\frac{4}{7}$ **3.** $\frac{83}{290}$
4. $\frac{5}{8}$ **5.** $\frac{91}{110}$ **6.** $\frac{11}{14}$ **7.** 0.225 **8.** 0.555
9. 0.6875 **10.** $0.\overline{78}$ **11.** $\frac{21}{25}$ **12.** $\frac{271}{500}$ **13.** $\frac{317}{999}$
14. $\frac{283}{990}$

PAGE 201 CALCULATOR INVESTIGATION
1. a. $0.0\overline{45}$; $0.14\overline{5}$ **b.** yes **c.** 0.1

PAGE 204 CHAPTER REVIEW **1.** 1 **3.** $\frac{7}{9}$
5. 8 **7.** $3\frac{1}{3}$ **9.** false **11.** false **13.** false
15. c **17.** b

PAGES 206–207 CUMULATIVE REVIEW
EXERCISES **1.** 29,535 **3.** 9.5949 **5.** 2.4406
7. 16,796 **9.** 17.223 **11.** 6.5197 **13.** 12,512
15. 40.8988 **17.** 41.2419 **19.** 275 **21.** 8.12
23. 5.11 **25.** 80 **27.** 467 **29.** 642 **31.** false
33. false **35.** 42 **37.** 105 **39.** 15 **41.** 14
PROBLEMS **1.** 28.69 km **3.** 47.6 cm **5.** 373
7. $65.63 **9.** 7 trips; 2 tons

7 Operations with Fractions

PAGE 212 WRITTEN EXERCISES **1.** $1\frac{6}{13}$
3. 3 **5.** $\frac{4}{11}$ **7.** $\frac{35}{41}$ **9.** $1\frac{5}{12}$ **11.** $\frac{17}{36}$ **13.** $1\frac{1}{6}$
15. $1\frac{21}{50}$ **17.** $1\frac{5}{33}$ **19.** $1\frac{33}{40}$ **21.** $2\frac{1}{10}$ **23.** $\frac{9}{20}$
25. $\frac{2}{7}$ **27.** $\frac{1}{2}$ **29.** $\frac{333}{1000}$ **31.** $\frac{787}{1000}$ **33.** d **35.** $\frac{1}{3}$
37. $\frac{7}{18}$ **39.** $\frac{5}{6}$

PAGE 213 PROBLEMS **1.** $\frac{15}{16}$ in. **3.** $\frac{8}{15}$
5. $\frac{37}{60}$ h **7.** $\frac{1}{4}$ **9.** No; after she makes the first
three shelves, there is only $\frac{2}{3}$ ft left; $\frac{2}{3} < \frac{3}{4}$.

PAGE 213 REVIEW EXERCISES **1.** $4\frac{5}{8}$
3. $5\frac{3}{5}$ **5.** $10\frac{2}{7}$

PAGE 215 WRITTEN EXERCISES **1.** $12\frac{1}{3}$
3. $6\frac{5}{7}$ **5.** $14\frac{1}{3}$ **7.** $7\frac{1}{2}$ **9.** $5\frac{7}{8}$ **11.** $3\frac{7}{18}$ **13.** $4\frac{11}{15}$
15. $16\frac{3}{20}$ **17.** $18\frac{9}{16}$ **19.** $3\frac{11}{20}$ **21.** $13\frac{1}{12}$
23. $11\frac{7}{16}$ **25.** $12\frac{2}{3}$ **27.** $1\frac{3}{4}$ **29.** $8\frac{5}{12}$ **31.** $8\frac{5}{6}$
33. $2\frac{5}{6}$ **35.** $11\frac{12}{35}$

PAGE 216 PROBLEMS **1.** $5\frac{7}{8}$ lb **3.** $66\frac{3}{4}$ ft
5. $\frac{19}{24}$ ft **7.** $10\frac{1}{4}$ in. **9.** $3\frac{1}{6}$ mi

PAGE 216 REVIEW EXERCISES **1.** 6 **3.** 5
5. 8 **7.** 15

PAGE 218 WRITTEN EXERCISES **1.** $5\frac{1}{3}$
3. 18 **5.** $\frac{5}{12}$ **7.** $\frac{2}{25}$ **9.** $\frac{2}{3}$ **11.** $\frac{15}{32}$ **13.** $1\frac{7}{11}$
15. $\frac{8}{45}$ **17.** $\frac{1}{9}$ **19.** $\frac{12}{35}$ **21.** 1 **23.** 6 **25.** $\frac{2}{3}$
27. $3\frac{3}{5}$ **29. a.** $\frac{3}{8}$ **b.** $1\frac{9}{280}$ **31. a.** $\frac{17}{18}$ **b.** $1\frac{10}{21}$

PAGE 218 REVIEW EXERCISES **1.** 11
3. 24 **5.** 60 **7.** 81

PAGES 220–221 WRITTEN EXERCISES
1. $\frac{2}{21}$ **3.** 21 **5.** $\frac{5}{24}$ **7.** $\frac{1}{6}$ **9.** $\frac{2}{15}$ **11.** $4\frac{1}{2}$ **13.** $\frac{5}{12}$
15. $1\frac{1}{3}$ **17.** $\frac{2}{5}$ **19.** $1\frac{3}{4}$ **21.** $\frac{13}{14}$ **23.** $\frac{15}{28}$ **25.** $4\frac{1}{2}$
27. $\frac{11}{12}$ **29.** 14

PAGE 221 REVIEW EXERCISES **1.** $\frac{32}{9}$
3. $\frac{31}{7}$ **5.** $\frac{131}{17}$ **7.** $\frac{151}{16}$ **9.** $\frac{408}{31}$

PAGE 221 CALCULATOR INVESTIGATION
1. $0.\overline{09}$, $0.\overline{18}$, $0.\overline{27}$, $0.\overline{36}$, $0.\overline{45}$, $0.\overline{54}$, $0.\overline{63}$, $0.\overline{72}$,
$0.\overline{90}$; the repeating block for the first fraction
multiplied by the numerator of a following fraction
gives the repeating block for that decimal.
3. $0.\overline{027}$, $0.\overline{054}$, $0.\overline{081}$, $0.\overline{108}$, $0.\overline{135}$, $0.\overline{162}$,
$0.\overline{189}$, $0.\overline{216}$, $0.\overline{243}$, $0.\overline{270}$; the repeating block
for the first fraction multiplied by the numerator
of a following fraction gives the repeating block
for that fraction **5.** $0.\overline{037}$, $0.\overline{074}$, $0.\overline{1}$, $0.\overline{148}$,
$0.\overline{185}$, $0.\overline{2}$, $0.\overline{259}$, $0.\overline{296}$, $0.\overline{3}$, $0.\overline{370}$; the repeating
block for the first fraction multiplied by the
numerator of a following fraction gives the
repeating block for that fraction

PAGES 223–224 WRITTEN EXERCISES
1. 2 **3.** 15 **5.** $7\frac{1}{2}$ **7.** $13\frac{1}{5}$ **9.** $\frac{5}{8}$ **11.** $\frac{1}{6}$
13. $2\frac{1}{10}$ **15.** $5\frac{5}{6}$ **17.** 20 **19.** 39 **21.** $\frac{14}{27}$
23. $1\frac{1}{9}$ **25.** $1\frac{1}{4}$ **27.** $1\frac{1}{2}$ **29.** $24\frac{39}{64}$ **31.** $26\frac{2}{3}$
33. $1\frac{4}{15}$

PAGES 224–225 PROBLEMS **1.** 8 shares
3. $52\frac{1}{2}°$ **5.** 33,250 oz, or $2078\frac{1}{8}$ lb **7.** $2\frac{1}{4}$ qt
9. 240 rolls **11.** 50 lb

PAGE 225 SELF-TEST A **1.** $\frac{13}{17}$ **2.** $\frac{19}{32}$
3. $\frac{11}{27}$ **4.** $8\frac{1}{2}$ **5.** $2\frac{5}{16}$ **6.** $6\frac{11}{12}$ **7.** 25 **8.** $\frac{7}{32}$
9. $\frac{3}{25}$ **10.** $\frac{1}{5}$ **11.** $\frac{9}{20}$ **12.** $1\frac{1}{5}$ **13.** $4\frac{13}{18}$ **14.** $4\frac{4}{5}$
15. $11\frac{3}{7}$

PAGES 228–229 WRITTEN EXERCISES
1. a. $\frac{5}{7}$ **b.** $\frac{5}{12}$ **c.** $\frac{12}{7}$ **3. a.** $\frac{9}{4}$ **b.** $\frac{9}{13}$ **c.** $\frac{13}{4}$
5. $\frac{3}{8}$ **7.** $\frac{2}{7}$ **9.** $\frac{15}{4}$ **11.** 2.5 km/L **13.** $15\frac{1}{2}$ mi/gal
15. $2\frac{1}{2}$ ft/s **17.** 10.4 mi/h **19. a.** $\frac{5}{21}$ **b.** $\frac{21}{26}$
c. $\frac{26}{5}$ **21. a.** $\frac{1}{3}$ **b.** $\frac{2}{1}$ **c.** $\frac{3}{2}$ **23.** $\frac{3}{5}$ **25.** $\frac{14}{9}$

PAGES 229–230 **1.** \$1.68/kg **3.** $\frac{80}{3}$
5. $62\frac{1}{2}$ lb/ft³ **7. a.** $\frac{3}{2}$ **b.** $\frac{3}{2}$ **9.** $\frac{11}{9}$ **11.** $\frac{13}{18}$
13. $\frac{27}{95}$

PAGE 230 **1.** 9 **3.** 9 **5.** 5 **7.** 12

PAGES 232–233 WRITTEN EXERCISES
1. 4 **3.** 56 **5.** 35 **7.** 60 **9.** 72 **11.** 45
13. $7\frac{1}{2}$ **15.** $8\frac{1}{2}$ **17.** 10 **19.** 12 **21.** 20
23. 15 **25.** $\frac{1}{3}$ **27.** $\frac{4}{1}$ **29.** Answers will vary; for
example, $\frac{1+2}{5+1} = \frac{1}{2}$, however, $\frac{1}{5} \neq \frac{1}{2}$ and $\frac{2}{1} \neq \frac{1}{2}$.

PAGE 233 REVIEW EXERCISES **1.** $13\frac{1}{3}$
3. $22\frac{7}{9}$ **5.** $8\frac{11}{18}$ **7.** $43\frac{1}{2}$ **9.** $60\frac{3}{10}$

PAGE 233 CALCULATOR INVESTIGATION
1. 0.4375 **3.** 9.84 **5.** $9.05\overline{6}$

PAGES 235–236 PROBLEMS **1. a.** 880 km
b. 14 h **3. a.** \$3.75 **b.** 28 oranges
5. a. $5.\overline{3}$ cm³ **b.** 337.5 cm³ **7.** \$1.20
9. 6 min **11.** 12 wins **13.** 76,800 km

PAGE 236 REVIEW EXERCISES **1.** $\frac{200 \text{ cm}}{15 \text{ cm}}$

3. $\frac{30 \text{ ft}}{5 \text{ ft}}$ **5.** $\frac{2000 \text{ m}}{450 \text{ m}}$ **7.** $\frac{36 \text{ in.}}{20 \text{ in.}}$

PAGE 236 CALCULATOR INVESTIGATION
1. 1.4925373 **3.** 3.9385584 **5.** 0.208982

PAGES 238–239 WRITTEN EXERCISES
1. 1104 in. **3.** 576 in. **5.** 960 in. **7. a.** 2 cm
b. 800 km **9. a.** 10.5 cm **b.** 4200 km
11. a. 3 cm **b.** 1200 km **13.** 400 km
15. 1,384,300 km **17.** 109 times

PAGE 239 SELF-TEST B **1.** $\frac{3}{2}$ **2.** $\frac{17}{9}$ **3.** $\frac{2}{11}$
4. 2 **5.** 4 **6.** 135 **7.** \$.67 **8.** \$110 **9.** 1 in.
10. 1 : 16

PAGES 240–241 ENRICHMENT **1.** 1.75,
1.875, 1.9375 **3.** 1.49382716, 1.49931413,
1.49992379, 1.49999153; the sums are
approaching $1\frac{1}{2}$ **5.** $1.8\overline{3}$, $2.8\overline{3}$, 2.59285714,
2.82896826, 3.59773966, 4.49920534, 5.18737752;
the sums are increasing without approaching a
specific value. **7.** 3.04, 3.13, 3.14; 3.14 or π

PAGE 242 CHAPTER REVIEW **1.** b **3.** c
5. a **7.** b **9.** true **11.** false **13.** true

**PAGES 244–245 CUMULATIVE REVIEW
EXERCISES** **1.** 34,892 **3.** 4.485 **5.** 16.033
7. 281 **9.** 0.38316 **11.** 6.58 **13.** $n > 14$
15. $27 < 41$ **17.** 164 **19.** 22 **21.** 67 **23.** 72
25. quadrilateral **27.** is perpendicular to
29. 28 **31.** 60 **33.** 2 **35.** 2 **37.** $8\frac{2}{5}$ **39.** $5\frac{6}{11}$
41. $8\frac{21}{52}$ **43.** $\frac{39}{5}$ **45.** $\frac{247}{14}$ **47.** $\frac{43}{50}$ **49.** $\frac{8}{11}$ **51.** $\frac{14}{15}$

PROBLEMS **1.** 1840 works **3.** 38 in.
5. 315 **7.** 7.265 cm **9.** 1356 tickets

8 Solving Equations

PAGES 249–250 WRITTEN EXERCISES
1. 31 **3.** 7 **5.** 27 **7.** 4 **9.** 3 **11.** 3, 6, 9, 10
13. 11 **15.** 15 **17.** 15 **19.** 8 **21.** 6 **23.** no
solution **25.** yes **27.** no **29.** yes **31.** no
33. identity **35.** 0

PAGE 250 REVIEW EXERCISES **1.** 5 **3.** 4
5. 9 **7.** y; 17 **9.** 8; a

PAGES 253–254 WRITTEN EXERCISES
1. 12 **3.** 25 **5.** 15 **7.** 23 **9.** 17 **11.** 7
13. 12 **15.** 6 **17.** 8 **19.** $1\frac{2}{5}$ **21.** $3\frac{2}{3}$ **23.** 1.1
25. 0.253 **27.** 1.196 **29.** $9\frac{3}{4}$ **31.** $2\frac{7}{12}$
33. 0.358 **35.** $3\frac{4}{5}$ **37.** 1.73

PAGE 254 REVIEW EXERCISES **1.** 5 **3.** 3
5. 9 **7.** $\frac{1}{15}$ **9.** x

PAGE 254 NONROUTINE PROBLEM
SOLVING 40°F

PAGE 256 WRITTEN EXERCISES **1.** 15
3. 18 **5.** 6 **7.** 54 **9.** 84 **11.** 28 **13.** 5
15. 10 **17.** 91 **19.** 11 **21.** $7\frac{1}{2}$ **23.** 221
25. 252 **27.** $\frac{5}{6}$ **29.** $9\frac{2}{3}$ **31.** 364 **33.** 247
35. $\frac{2}{19}$ **37.** $10\frac{1}{2}$

PAGE 256 REVIEW EXERCISES **1.** $\frac{3}{14}$
3. $\frac{2}{15}$ **5.** $3\frac{1}{19}$

PAGE 259 WRITTEN EXERCISES **1.** 88
3. 20 **5.** 1.5 **7.** 24 **9.** 60 **11.** 19.5 **13.** 18
15. 20 **17.** 30 **19.** 49.5 **21.** $13\frac{1}{2}$ **23.** $10\frac{1}{2}$
25. 6.5 **27.** 0.8 **29.** $\frac{1}{9}$ **31.** $\frac{5}{6}$ **33.** 7.595
35. 0.02148 **37.** 5.7 **39.** 15.6 **41.** 3.3

PAGE 259 REVIEW EXERCISES **1.** 30
3. 55 **5.** 103 **7.** 17 **9.** 19

PAGE 259 CALCULATOR INVESTIGATION
1. 0.3 **3.** 2.7203791 **5.** 3.3807

PAGES 262–263 WRITTEN EXERCISES
1. 11 **3.** 7 **5.** 11 **7.** 10 **9.** 3 **11.** 80
13. 30 **15.** 55 **17.** 24 **19.** $4\frac{1}{3}$ **21.** 22.5
23. 7.5 **25.** $3\frac{1}{3}$ **27.** $1\frac{7}{9}$ **29.** $1\frac{17}{21}$ **31.** $4\frac{3}{7}$
33. $7\frac{7}{39}$ **35.** $\frac{25}{66}$ **37.** $\frac{5}{11}$ **39.** $\frac{2}{15}$ **41.** 7 **43.** 4
45. 6 **47.** 27

PAGE 263 SELF-TEST A **1.** 3 **2.** 4 **3.** 0, 1,
2, 3, 4, 5 **4.** no solution **5.** 9 **6.** 56 **7.** 13
8. 68 **9.** 150 **10.** $2\frac{7}{13}$ **11.** 8 **12.** 1.74
13. $27\frac{1}{2}$ **14.** 120

PAGES 265–266 WRITTEN EXERCISES
Answers for Exercises 1–4 will vary. **1.** An
isosceles triangle has a base of 7 in. If the
triangle has a perimeter of 37 in., what is the
length of each of the two congruent sides of
the triangle? **3.** The perimeter of a square is
56 cm. What is the length of each side? **5.** b
7. a **9.** e **11.** $n - 6 = 17$ **13.** $5n = 80$
15. $n + 2n = 24$ **17.** $3n - \frac{1}{2}n = 2(n + 1)$
19. $\frac{1}{2}n + \frac{1}{3}n = n - 4$ **21. a.** $500 + w$
b. $3(500 + w) = 1545$

PAGE 266 REVIEW EXERCISES **1.** $n - 4$
3. $n \div 7$ **5.** $40 - n$ **7.** $2n$

PAGES 268–269 PROBLEMS **1.** $9n = 1170$
3. $6n = 90$ **5.** $144 - n = 116$
7. $29 + 43 + n = 100$ **9.** $26 + 26 + n = 65$
11. $\frac{3}{10}n = 240$ **13.** $48 + 2(16 - n) = 74$

PAGE 269 REVIEW EXERCISES
1. $n - 8 = 43$ **3.** $14 + n = 70$
5. $n - 17 = 34$

PAGE 269 NONROUTINE PROBLEM
SOLVING 20 seconds

PAGES 272–273 PROBLEMS **1.** 30 cm
3. 2.5 **5.** 15 cm **7.** 14 m² **9.** $750 **11.** 5 cm
13. 24 gallons

PAGE 273 SELF-TEST B **1.** d **2.** c **3.** a
4. Let n = number of gallons; $21n = 189$
5. Let n = original amount; $n - 450 = 1845$
6. 31 yd **7.** 412 new balls

PAGE 274 ENRICHMENT **1.** 3 **3.** 3
5. 2; 7

PAGE 276 CHAPTER REVIEW **1.** true
3. false **5.** divide **7.** a **9.** c **11.** c **13.** d

PAGES 278–279 CUMULATIVE REVIEW
EXERCISES **1.** 14,409 **3.** 7.3254 **5.** $7\frac{1}{24}$
7. $2\frac{49}{72}$ **9.** $3\frac{1}{36}$ **11.** 657 **13.** 26.752 **15.** 3.524
17. $\frac{21}{34}$ **19.** $1\frac{3}{11}$ **21.** $1\frac{1}{4}$ **23.** $93 - n$ **25.** true
27. false **29.** 13 **31.** 94 **33.** 139 **35.** 216
37. 237 **39.** 16 **41.** 12 **43.** 189 **45.** 504
47. $\frac{21}{50}$ **49.** $1\frac{308}{333}$
PROBLEMS **1.** $6\frac{3}{8}$ cups **3.** 7.16 cm **5.** 24
shares **7.** $2\frac{2}{3}$ in. **9.** $\frac{29}{43}$ of the puzzle

9 Percents

PAGE 284 WRITTEN EXERCISES **1.** $\frac{3}{4}$
3. $\frac{9}{20}$ **5.** $\frac{3}{25}$ **7.** $1\frac{1}{4}$ **9.** $\frac{43}{800}$ **11.** $\frac{43}{400}$ **13.** 80%
15. 30% **17.** 48% **19.** 62% **21.** 220%

23. 102% **25.** 87.5% **27.** 0.5% **29.** 0.75%
31. 302.5% **33.** $\frac{1}{6}$ **35.** $\frac{5}{12}$

PAGE 285 PROBLEMS 1. 38% **3.** 60%
5. 5% **7.** 62.5% **9.** 10%; 70%; 80%

PAGE 285 REVIEW EXERCISES 1. 0.45
3. 0.275 **5.** 0.04 **7.** $0.\overline{72}$ **9.** $0.5\overline{73}$

PAGE 288 WRITTEN EXERCISES 1. 0.93
3. 1.14 **5.** 2.60 **7.** 0.495 **9.** 0.006
11. 0.0005 **13.** 59% **15.** 9% **17.** 260%
19. 1283% **21.** 0.7% **23.** 8.67% **25.** 0.375,
37.5% **27.** 0.006, 0.6% **29.** 1.625, 162.5%
31. 0.5875, 58.8% **33.** $0.708\overline{3}$, 70.8%
35. $0.\overline{285714}$, 28.6% **37.** $16\frac{2}{3}$% **39.** $88\frac{8}{9}$%
41. $83\frac{1}{3}$%

PAGE 288 REVIEW EXERCISES 1. 2.95
3. 15.438 **5.** 23.8576

PAGES 290–291 WRITTEN EXERCISES
1. 40% **3.** 270 **5.** 1300 **7.** 5.4 **9.** 83.3%
11. 104.5 **13.** 87 **15.** 0.896 **17.** 114.3%
19. 224 **21.** 54 **23.** 252

PAGE 291 PROBLEMS 1. $12.50 **3.** 77.5%
5. 22,715 million barrels

PAGE 291 REVIEW EXERCISES 1. 3.7792
3. 7.434 **5.** 7.095

PAGES 293–294 WRITTEN EXERCISES
1. 15% **3.** 40% **5.** 82.5% **7.** 46.9% **9.** 0.8%
11. 27.5% **13.** 132 **15.** 57.2 **17.** 205.8
19. 124.5 **21.** 60 **23.** 336 **25.** 338.8 **27.** 64
29. 120

PAGES 294–295 PROBLEMS 1. 1134
employees **3.** 25% **5.** 7511 books **7.** 16.7%

PAGE 295 SELF–TEST A 1. $\frac{27}{100}$ **2.** $\frac{83}{100}$
3. $1\frac{16}{25}$ **4.** $2\frac{9}{10}$ **5.** 5% **6.** 37.5% **7.** 400%
8. 325% **9.** 0.45 **10.** 0.78 **11.** 3.48
12. 0.008 **13.** 64% **14.** 81% **15.** 785%
16. 6.8% **17.** 25% **18.** 205% **19.** 11
20. 120 **21.** 6% decrease **22.** 10% increase
23. 30% increase **24.** 64% decrease

PAGES 298–299 PROBLEMS 1. $67.15
3. 14% **5.** $26.46 **7.** $30 **9.** 25% **11.** $12.50
13. 72% **15.** The final prices are the same.

PAGE 299 REVIEW EXERCISES 1. radius
3. diameter

PAGES 301–302 PROBLEMS 1. $129
3. $978 **5.** $10,900 **7.** $64,893.62
9. $58,510.64 **11.** 12.5% **13.** $19,500

PAGE 302 REVIEW EXERCISES 1. 10
3. 6 **5.** 128 **7.** 0.4

PAGES 305–306 WRITTEN EXERCISES
1. $384, $1664 **3.** $745.20, $3505.20 **5.** $1692,
$7332 **7.** $5550.60, $11,930.60 **9.** 14%
11. 8.5% **13.** 16% **15.** 6 months **17.** $4450
19. $6720 **21.** $1850 **23.** $102.12

PAGES 306–307 PROBLEMS 1. $577.50
3. $96.25 **5.** 7.5% **7.** 8 years

PAGE 307 REVIEW EXERCISES 1. 0.375
3. 0.05 **5.** 1.496 **7.** $0.8\overline{3}$ **9.** $2.3958\overline{3}$

PAGE 307 CALCULATOR INVESTIGATION
1. 16 **3.** 48% **5.** $86.\overline{6}$%

PAGES 309–310 WRITTEN EXERCISES
1. $7056 **3.** $1560.60 **5.** $3149.28
7. $2137.84 **9.** $3975.35 **11.** $9724.05
13. $7.71 **15.** $1240

PAGE 310 PROBLEMS 1. $1852.20 **3.** 12%
simple interest **5.** 13.2% per year

PAGE 311 SELF–TEST B 1. 15%
2. $11.20 **3.** $5700 **4.** 18% **5.** $157.50
6. $247.30

PAGE 311 COMPUTER INVESTIGATION
1. $235.61 **3.** $235.88 **5. a.** $16,819.01
b. $15,995.05 **c.** $14,763.99

PAGE 313 ENRICHMENT 1. 20% **3.** 15%
5. 37.5% **7.** 87.5% **9.** 24 **11.** 336 **13.** 10
students **15.** 1.4 kg **17.** 37.5%

PAGE 314 CHAPTER REVIEW 1. E **3.** H
5. K **7.** L **9.** B **11.** 18 **13.** 700% **15.** 25%
17. 95 **19.** c **21.** c

**PAGES 316–317 CUMULATIVE REVIEW
EXERCISES 1.** 70 **3.** 1287 **5.** 31 **7.** 1.35
9. 1.95 **11.** 132.665 **13.** 196 **15.** 265
17. $4\frac{1}{40}$ **19.** $6\frac{14}{27}$ **21.** $\frac{44}{189}$ **23.** 1230.88
25. 239.96 **27.** 4308.08 **29.** 1% **31.** 75%
33. 1237.5% **35.** 50.2 mm **37.** 18 m
39. 90 mm **41.** 48 **43.** 128 **45.** 24.4 **47.** 35
PROBLEMS 1. 1 min 45.73 s **3.** about 2
hours **5.** $\frac{2}{3}$ yd **7.** 18 m **9.** 58.125 L **11.** 4 m

10 Areas and Volumes

PAGES 322–323 WRITTEN EXERCISES
1. 1050 cm²; 130 cm **3.** 2665 km²; 212 km
5. 4416 mm²; 280 mm **7.** 2490.67 km²;
205.6 km **9.** perimeter: 40; area: 93.75
11. length: 80; perimeter: 250 **13.** width: 0.4;
area: 3.44 **15.** 74 **17.** 0.5 **19.** 4 **21.** 37
square units **23.** 30 square units **25.** 72
square units

PAGE 324 PROBLEMS 1. 24 m²
3. a. 720 ft² **b.** $1080 **5.** 15 m **7.** 2025 m²

PAGE 324 REVIEW EXERCISES 1. 28
3. 1.04 **5.** 40 **7.** 0.078

PAGES 328–329 WRITTEN EXERCISES
1. 67.34 m² **3.** 2127.5 cm² **5.** 290 mm²
7. 1830 km² **9.** 44.4 cm² **11.** 24 cm **13.** 4 m
15. 8 mm **17.** 15 **19.** The base and the height
are the same for each triangle.
21. a. 450 cm² **b.** 450 cm² **23.** 9 : 1; 3 : 1

PAGE 329 REVIEW EXERCISES 1. 75
3. 6.76 **5.** 292 **7.** 1.33 **9.** 4868

PAGES 332–333 WRITTEN EXERCISES
1. 78.5 km² **3.** 2.54 square units **5.** 616 cm²
7. $9\frac{5}{8}$ square units **9.** 100π m² **11.** 4π square
units **13.** 5 cm **15.** 14 km **17.** 8π
19. 75π m² **21.** $\frac{45\pi}{4}$ mm² **23.** 9π square

units **25.** $A = \pi \left(\dfrac{d}{2}\right)^2$

PAGES 333–334 PROBLEMS 1. $1099
3. 314 m² **5.** 462 cm² **7.** 16-inch quiche
9. $\dfrac{\pi}{4}$

PAGE 334 REVIEW EXERCISES 1. 16
3. 9 **5.** 18 **7.** 15

PAGES 337–338 WRITTEN EXERCISES
1. **3.**

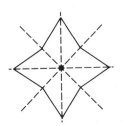 

5.

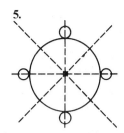

7. 84 m²
9. 50π square units
11. 135 square units
13. 16 square units
15. $(200 + 50\pi)$ cm²

PAGE 338 SELF-TEST A 1. 273 cm²
2. 84 m² **3.** 72 cm² **4.** 36 m² **5.** 707 mm²
6. 616 cm² **7.** **8.** 28 square units

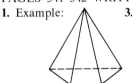

PAGES 341–342 WRITTEN EXERCISES
1. Example: **3.** Example:

5. $7 + 7 - 12 = 2$ **7.** $7 + 10 - 15 = 2$ **9.** 6,
4, 8, 8 **11.** 12, 6, 14, 14 **13.** 30, 12, 32, 32
15. 12 **17.** 12 **19.** 16

PAGE 342 REVIEW EXERCISES 1. 17.6
3. 880 **5.** 4.5

PAGE 342 CALCULATOR INVESTIGATION
1. 37 **3.** 62 **5.** 72 **7.** 118 **9.** 102.8

PAGES 344–345 WRITTEN EXERCISES
1. 24 cm³ **3.** 180 mm³ **5.** 72 cm³
7. 1.331 cm³ **9.** 9 m³ **11.** 8 : 1 **13.** 9 cm²
15. 160 m³

PAGE 346 PROBLEMS 1. 72,000 cm³
3. 720 mm³ **5.** 8 cm deep **7.** 69,888 cm³

PAGE 346 REVIEW EXERCISES 1. 4
3. 0.5 **5.** 12 **7.** 28

PAGES 348–349 WRITTEN EXERCISES
1. 314 cubic units **3.** 12,600 cubic units
5. 60π cubic units **7.** 3 cm **9.** 4 m² **11.** 4
13. 2 **15.** The volume is doubled. **17.** The
volume is multiplied by 8.

PAGE 350 PROBLEMS 1. 2260 m³
3. 2.40 L **5.** short jar **7.** 1.62 cm **9.** 30.6%

PAGE 350 REVIEW EXERCISES 1. 18.24

3. 15.408 **5.** 1800 **6.** 0.00125

PAGE 352 WRITTEN EXERCISES **1.** 870
3. 0.95 **5.** 0.02 **7.** 60 g **9.** 5000 g
11. 19,300 kg **13.** 135 g **15.** 37.1 g **17.** cork,
oak

PAGE 353 PROBLEMS **1.** 154.4 kg
3. 1,413,000 t **5.** 162,000 t **7.** 70 g

PAGE 353 REVIEW EXERCISES **1.** 8
3. 150 **5.** 12 **7.** 5

PAGES 356–357 WRITTEN EXERCISES
1. 150 cm² **3.** 104 m² **5. a.** 72 m² **b.** 84 m²
c. 36 m³ **7. a.** 75.4 cm² **b.** 132 cm²
c. 113 cm³ **9. a.** 500 square units **b.** 788
square units **c.** 1440 cubic units **11.** 121
square units **13.** 922 square units

PAGE 357 SELF–TEST B
1. Example: **2.** Example:

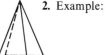

3. 160 cm³ **4.** 42 m³ **5.** 75.4 mm³
6. 62.8 cm³ **7.** 6630 g **8.** 69 g **9.** 96 m²
10. 87.9 cm²

PAGE 359 ENRICHMENT **1.** 10 **3.** 12
5. 8 **7.** 26 **9.** 16 **11.** 30 m **13.** 15 ft

PAGE 360 CHAPTER REVIEW **1.** b **3.** c
5. d **7.** prism, pyramid **9.** false **11.** false
13. false

PAGES 362–363 CUMULATIVE REVIEW
EXERCISES **1.** 126 **3.** 29 **5.** 4.24 **7.** 8.14
9. 3.2 **11.** $\frac{2}{25}$ **13.** 5 **15.** $1\frac{7}{8}$ **17.** 54 **19.** 2.16
21. 39.48 **23.** 38.5 ft² **25.** 456 m² **27.** 135
29. 34 **31.** 6.7 **33.** 6.56 **35.** $13\frac{23}{100}$ **37.** 0.8
39. 75% **41.** 85
PROBLEMS **1.** 134.7 m **3.** 5 h 15 min
5. 144 lb **7.** $1.94 **9.** 22.5 m

11 Integers and Graphs
PAGES 368–369 WRITTEN EXERCISES

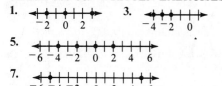

PAGE 369 REVIEW EXERCISES **1.** 102
3. 217 **5.** 300 **7.** 215 **9.** 699

PAGE 369 COMPUTER INVESTIGATION
1. a. 14 **b.** 14 **3. a.** 39 **b.** 39
5. $(a + b) \times c = (a \times b) + c$

PAGE 373 WRITTEN EXERCISES

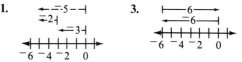
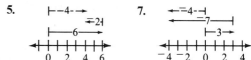

9. ⁻3 **11.** 5 **13.** ⁻25 **15.** 19 **17. a.** ⁻5
b. ⁻5 **19. a.** ⁻4 **b.** ⁻4 **21.** 1 **23.** 8 **25.** ⁻1
27. true **29.** 7 **31.** 6 **33.** 8

PAGE 374 PROBLEMS **1.** 918 ft **3.** 8°C
5. $109 **7.** 46°S

PAGE 374 REVIEW EXERCISES **1.** 17
3. 0 **5.** 24 **7.** ⁻78

PAGE 376 WRITTEN EXERCISES **1.** ⁻4
3. 5 **5.** 15 **7.** ⁻25 **9.** 18 **11.** ⁻39 **13.** 52
15. ⁻50 **17.** 444 **19. a.** 5 **b.** 45 **21. a.** 20
b. 12 **23.** true **25.** true **27.** false **29.** true

PAGE 376–377 PROBLEMS **1.** 17°C
3. 14,776 ft **5.** 20,484 m **7.** 124°; 13,764 km

PAGE 377 REVIEW EXERCISES **1.** 462
3. 0 **5.** 58,344 **7.** 58,362

PAGE 379 WRITTEN EXERCISES **1.** ⁻64
3. ⁻90 **5.** ⁻660 **7.** ⁻320 **9.** ⁻8487

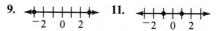

11. −16,023 **13.** −76,893 **15.** −47,772
17. −65,016 **19. a.** −60 **b.** −60 **21. a.** −270
b. −270 **23. a.** −72 **b.** −72 **25. a.** 0 **b.** 0
27. distributive property **29.** −30 **31.** −111
33. −24

PAGE 379 REVIEW EXERCISES **1.** 33
3. 80 **5.** 125 **7.** 41 **9.** 81

PAGES 381–382 WRITTEN EXERCISES
1. 243 **3.** −486 **5.** 2222 **7.** 625 **9.** 3000
11. 1040 **13.** 120 **15.** −7560 **17.** −640 **19.** 0
21. 64 **23.** 60 **25.** 10 **27.** 46 **29.** 0
31. −12 **33.** true **35.** false **37.** false

PAGE 382 REVIEW EXERCISES **1.** 109
3. 64 **5.** 361 **7.** 473 **9.** 1336

PAGE 384 WRITTEN EXERCISES **1.** −14
3. −4 **5.** 11 **7.** −15 **9.** −28 **11.** −22 **13.** 3
15. −3 **17.** −5 **19.** −13 **21.** 9 **23. a.** 2 **b.** 18
25. −32 **27.** −6 **29.** *n* **31.** −1 **33.** 1 **35.** *n*

PAGE 385 SELF–TEST A **1.** −6; 5 **2.** 3; 3
3. 7; 7 **4.** 0; 0 **5.** −4; 4 **6.** < **7.** > **8.** >
9. −4 **10.** −13 **11.** 3 **12.** −23 **13.** −26
14. −76 **15.** 2 **16.** −71 **17.** −105 **18.** −1232
19. −216 **20.** 342 **21.** 152 **22.** −54 **23.** 2
24. 2

PAGE 385 CALCULATOR INVESTIGATION
1. −9 **3.** 16 **5.** −1470

PAGES 387–388 WRITTEN EXERCISES
1. 25 **3.** −25 **5.** −5 **7.** 1 **9.** −13 **11.** −13
13. 0 **15.** −17 **17.** −50 **19.** −150 **21.** −99
23. 210 **25.** −4 **27.** −3 **29.** 14 **31.** −4
33. 14 **35.** 3 **37.** 2 **39.** 30 **41.** 28 **43.** −2
45. −27 **47.** 0 **49.** 7 **51.** 6 **53.** −12

PAGE 388 REVIEW EXERCISES **1.** Lines
that intersect to form right angles. **3.** A
parallelogram with 4 right angles. **5.** A
quadrilateral with one pair of parallel sides.
7. A polygon with 6 sides. **9.** A triangle with
one obtuse angle.

PAGES 390–391 WRITTEN EXERCISES
1.   **3.**

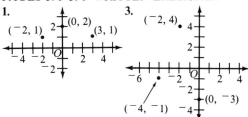

5.   **7.**

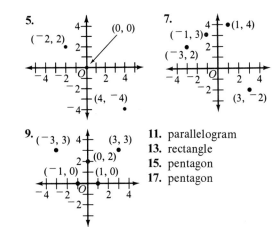

9.   **11.** parallelogram
13. rectangle
15. pentagon
17. pentagon

PAGE 391 REVIEW EXERCISES **1.** 17
3. 18 **5.** 45 **7.** 1 **9.** 19

PAGES 393–394 WRITTEN EXERCISES
1. −4, (−3, −4); −3, (−2, −3); −2, (−1, −2); −1,
(0, −1); 0, (1, 0); 1, (2, 1); 2, (3, 2)
3.   **5.**

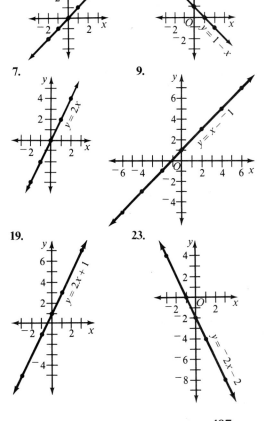

7.   **9.**

19.   **23.**

39.

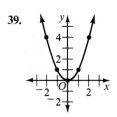

PAGE 395 SELF-TEST B **1.** 39 **2.** ⁻25
3. ⁻52 **4.** ⁻21 **5.** 7 **6.** 12

7.

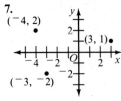

8.

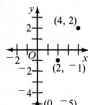

9.

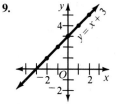

PAGE 397 ENRICHMENT
1.

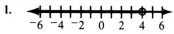

3.

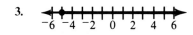

5. **7.**

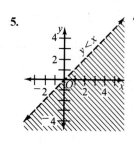
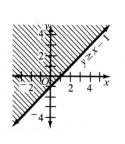

9. **11.**

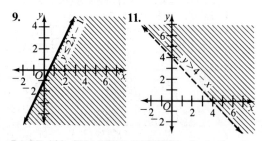

PAGE 398 CHAPTER REVIEW **1.** 4 **3.** <

5. G **7.** K **9.** A **11.** M **13.** J **15.** c **17.** a
19. c

PAGE 400 CUMULATIVE REVIEW
EXERCISES **1.** 2.043 **3.** 16.984 **5.** ⁻4.896
7. 37.48 **9.** $1\frac{39}{100}$ **11.** $3\frac{9}{25}$ **13.** $5\frac{5}{12}$ **15.** $2\frac{1}{2}$
17. 25.2 m; 30.66 m² **19.** 6.5 km; 1.875 km²
21. 38 mm; 72 mm² **23.** 14 **25.** 21 **27.** 8
29. 72 **31.** 144 **33.** 54 **35.** 56 **37.** $171\frac{3}{5}$
39. 9.57 **41.** 9.12
PROBLEMS **1.** $.41 **3.** 127,000 m³ **5.** 9 m
7. $127.08 **9.** 24 in.

12 Statistics and Probability

PAGES 406–407 WRITTEN EXERCISES
1. 100 million persons **3.** approx. 400 million
5. about 22% **7.**

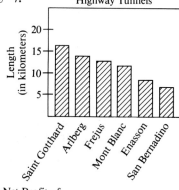

11.

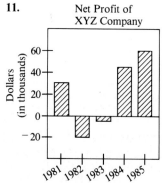

PAGE 407 REVIEW EXERCISES **1.** 282
3. 354 **5.** 135 **7.** 131.4

PAGES 410–412 WRITTEN EXERCISES
1.

$\frac{1}{4}$	90°
$\frac{3}{10}$	108°
$\frac{1}{5}$	72°
$\frac{1}{4}$	90°
240 1	360°

3. Surface of Earth

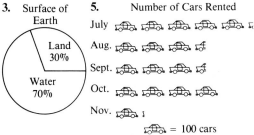

5. Number of Cars Rented

July 🚗🚗🚗🚗🚗 🚗

Aug. 🚗🚗🚗🚗

Sept. 🚗🚗🚗🚗

Oct. 🚗🚗🚗🚗

Nov. 🚗

🚗 = 100 cars

7.

x	f	
8	2	range = 8
6	1	mean = 3.9
5	4	median = 4
4	5	mode = 4
3	2	
1	3	
0	1	

9.

x	f	
14	1	range = 6
15	1	mean = 18.1
16	2	median = 18
17	5	mode = 18
18	8	
19	7	
20	6	**13.** 72

9. People Living in U.S.

People Living in United States

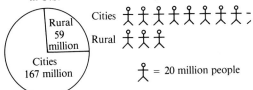

Cities 🚶🚶🚶🚶🚶🚶🚶🚶

Rural 🚶🚶🚶

🚶 = 20 million people

PAGE 418 **REVIEW EXERCISES   1.** the average of a set of scores   **3.** the score that occurs most often   **5.** an integer not evenly divisible by 2   **7.** a number greater than 1 whose only factors are 1 and itself

PAGE 419 **COMPUTER INVESTIGATION**
1. 18.$\overline{3}$ **3.** 578.1$\overline{6}$ **5.** 4494.1304   **7.** 489,439.2

15. Distribution of Library Grant

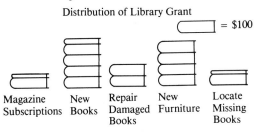

Distribution of Library Grant

📚 = $100

Magazine Subscriptions   New Books   Repair Damaged Books   New Furniture   Locate Missing Books

PAGE 421 **WRITTEN EXERCISES**

3.
4	3, 4, 4, 4
5	0, 3
6	2, 5, 7
7	2

11.
7	5, 7, 8
8	0, 2, 2, 3, 3, 7, 7
9	1, 4, 5
10	1, 2

13. Since the data are all multiples of ten, disregard the last digit and use the hundreds' digits as stems and the tens' digits as leaves.

4	6, 8, 9
5	2, 3, 5, 7, 8
6	1, 4, 5
7	2, 8

PAGE 423 **WRITTEN EXERCISES**

1. 10   20   30   40   50   60   70   80

5. 0   1   2   3   4   5   6   7   8

A:

B:

7. Example: 20, 40, 50, 55, 62, 65, 80

PAGE 412 REVIEW EXERCISES   **1.** 0.84, 2.6, 3, 4, 7   **3.** ⁻6, ⁻5, 3½, 4¼, 7   **5.** ⁻12, ⁻10, ⁻9, ⁻6, ⁻2   **7.** 0.09, 0.9, 1.09, 1.1

PAGES 414–415 WRITTEN EXERCISES
1. 24, 23, 12   **3.** 16, 15, 19   **5.** 55.5, 55.5, 24
7. 3.2, 3.4, 0.9   **9.** ⁻1, ⁻2, 8   **11.** 0.3, 0.2, 2.1
13. ⁻2°, ⁻1°, 19°   **15.** 16   **17.** 16   **19.** 94
21. It is increased by 5.

PAGE 415 REVIEW EXERCISES   **1.** 6.1
3. 14.8   **5.** 14   **7.** 3

PAGES 417–418 WRITTEN EXERCISES
1. 4, 6.95, 7, 7   **3.** 20, 10, 10, 5   **5.** 6, 16.75, 17, 16 and 17

PAGES 425–426 **WRITTEN EXERCISES**
1. 15   **3.** 1   **5.** 9   **7.** 20   **9.** 34
11.

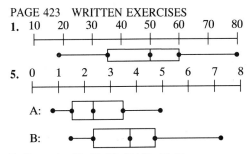

Runs Scored

17.
x	f
10–15	3
15–20	3
20–25	5
25–30	4
30–35	5
35–40	4
40–45	6

Answers **499**

PAGE 426   SELF-TEST A

1.

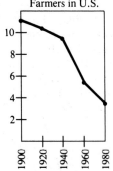
Farmers in U.S.

2.   Farmers in United States

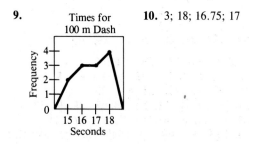

$\dagger$ = 1,000,000 people

3. 13, 12, 14   **5.** 6 | 3, 6

4.
x	f
9	2
12	4
15	3
16	1
18	2

    7 | 5, 7, 8
    8 | 2, 3, 9
    9 | 1

6. 0   50   100

7. 3   **8.** 12

9.   Times for 100 m Dash

10. 3; 18; 16.75; 17

PAGE 429   WRITTEN EXERCISES   1. $\frac{1}{24}$
3. $\frac{1}{8}$ **5.** $\frac{1}{2}$ **7.** $\frac{3}{8}$ **9.** $\frac{1}{3}$ **11.** $\frac{1}{3}$ **13.** $\frac{1}{2}$ **15.** $\frac{7}{12}$
17. $\frac{1}{6}$ **19.** $\frac{1}{4}$ **21.** 0   **23.** $\frac{7}{12}$ **25.** $\frac{5}{18}$

PAGE 430   REVIEW EXERCISES   1. $\frac{1}{550}$
3. $1\frac{2}{3}$ **5.** $10\frac{11}{16}$ **7.** 14   **9.** $\frac{8}{63}$

PAGE 430   COMPUTER INVESTIGATION
1. Answers may vary; 1

PAGES 433–434   WRITTEN EXERCISES
1. $\frac{2}{5}; \frac{3}{5}; \frac{2}{3}; \frac{3}{2}$ **3.** $\frac{3}{5}; \frac{3}{5}; \frac{3}{2}; \frac{2}{3}$ **5.** $\frac{4}{5}; \frac{1}{5}; \frac{4}{1}; \frac{1}{4}$
7. $\frac{3}{5}; \frac{3}{5}; \frac{3}{2}; \frac{2}{3}$ **9.** $\frac{4}{5}; \frac{1}{5}; \frac{4}{1}; \frac{1}{4}$ **11.** $\frac{1}{5}$ **13.** $\frac{2}{1}$ **15.** $\frac{1}{1}$
17. $\frac{7}{17}$ **19.** $\frac{1}{5}$ **21.** $\frac{1}{7}$ **23.** $\frac{1}{7}$ **25.** $\frac{1}{7}$ **27.** $\frac{5}{7}$
29. $\frac{1}{3}$ **31.** $\frac{7}{5}$ **33.** $\frac{5}{1}$ **35.** $\frac{7}{1}$ **37.** $\frac{7}{1}$ **39.** $\frac{1}{17}; \frac{16}{17}$

PAGE 434   REVIEW EXERCISES   1. $\frac{23}{24}$
3. $\frac{11}{12}$ **5.** $\frac{25}{36}$ **7.** $\frac{71}{196}$

PAGES 436–437   WRITTEN EXERCISES
1. $\frac{2}{3}$ **3.** $\frac{7}{12}$ **5.** $\frac{7}{12}$ **7.** $\frac{7}{12}$ **9.** $\frac{7}{12}$ **11.** $\frac{2}{3}$ **13.** $\frac{5}{6}$
15. $\frac{2}{3}$ **17.** $\frac{1}{3}$ **19.** $\frac{7}{12}$ **21.** $\frac{1}{18}$

PAGE 437   SELF-TEST B   1. $\frac{1}{50}$ **2.** $\frac{2}{25}$ **3.** $\frac{3}{10}$
4. $\frac{1}{2}$ **5.** $\frac{1}{1}; \frac{1}{1}$ **6.** $\frac{3}{7}; \frac{7}{3}$ **7.** $\frac{1}{4}; \frac{4}{1}$ **8.** $\frac{8}{17}; \frac{17}{8}$ **9.** $\frac{7}{50}$
10. $\frac{3}{5}$ **11.** $\frac{13}{25}$ **12.** $\frac{39}{50}$

PAGE 440   CHAPTER REVIEW   1. Sprint
3. broken-line   **5.** 8   **7.** 68.5   **9.** 2   **11.** most
13. false   **15.** false   **17.** true

PAGES 442–443   CUMULATIVE REVIEW
EXERCISES   1. 4.28   **3.** 4.87   **5.** 11.57
7. $1\frac{23}{24}$ **9.** $2\frac{2}{3}$ **11.** $\frac{3}{4}$ **13.** 13   **15.** $^-54$
17. 140 m², 118 m³   **19.** $2 \times 5 \times 11$
21. $2^2 \times 3^2 \times 5$ **23.** $2 \times 3^2 \times 59$
25. 138   **27.** -8 **29.** 20   **31.** 7.99
33. 1200%   **35.** 35   **37.** 130

PROBLEMS   1. 17°C   **3.** 226 m³   **5.** 31 ft
7. 1030 ft   **9.** $37,000

Extra Practice

PAGES 446–448   CHAPTER 1   1. 0, 10, 20, 50
3. 0, 12, 28, 36   **5.** 42, 49, 60, 67
7. 47, 42, 40, 37   **9.** 10   **11.** 15   **13.** 22
15. 78   **17.** 164   **19.** 0   **21.** 3220   **23.** 0
25. 283   **27.** $20 + 21 = 41, 21 + 20 = 41$
29. $64 - 47 = 17, 64 - 17 = 47$
31. $7 \times 8 = 56, 8 \times 7 = 56$
33. $142 - 51 = 91, 142 - 91 = 51$
35. $108 \div 9 = 12, 108 \div 12 = 9$
37. $143 \div 13 = 11, 143 \div 11 = 13$ **39.** 0
41. c **43.** 16   **45.** 150   **47.** 360   **49.** 420
51. 60   **53.** 180   **55.** 40   **57.** 107   **59.** 176
61. 33   **63.** 211   **65.** 9   **67.** 203
69. a. distance Peter swam   **b.** no; need the
rate at which Peter swims   **c.** no   **d.** multiply
by the number of hours   **71. a.** number of
loads of gravel   **b.** no; need length and width
of driveway and volume of gravel   **c.** 2 tons
d. division   **73. a.** distance remaining to
travel   **b.** yes   **c.** no   **d.** subtraction
75. 6 kg   **77.** 2118 m

PAGES 448–449   CHAPTER 2   **1.** $p - 7$
3. $11f$ **5.** $6 + 5g$ **7.** $(3 + b)7$
9. $(d - 22) \div 4$ **11.** $n \div 3 = 7$
13. $52 = 18 + n$ **15.** $35 - n = 16$
17. $2 + n - 48 = 70$ **19.** $6 = 12n + 18$
21. $<$ **23.** $>$ **25.** $>$ **27.** $>$ **29.** $17 > 12$
31. $2n > 69$ **33.** $80 - 26 > 2 \times 21$ **35.** 40
37. All the numbers less than 50.   **39.** 144
41. 52   **43.** 59   **45.** All the numbers greater
than 22.   **47.** 3   **49.** All the numbers less than
$6\frac{3}{4}$.   **51.** All the numbers less than $6\frac{2}{5}$.   **53.** All
the numbers greater than $7\frac{3}{4}$.   **55.** 11   **57.** 216
59. $n - 16 = 38$; 54   **61.** $8n = 96$, 12
63. $62 = 5n - 8$; 14   **65.** 3 h

PAGES 450–451   CHAPTER 3   **1.** 81
3. 15,625   **5.** 4913   **7.** 27,000   **9.** 6561
11. 57,967   **13.** 2,160,000   **15.** 42,592
17. seven thousand twenty-nine   **19.** one
hundred forty-one thousand, two hundred
seventy-eight   **21.** 7084   **23.** 3,016,611
25. $9(10^2) + 7(10) + 2(1)$
27. $5(10^3) + 6(10^2) + 1(10) + 3(1)$
29. $3(10^4) + 7(10^3) + 6(10^2) + 0(10) + 3(1)$
31. $1(10^5) + 0(10^4) + 2(10^3) + 5(10^2) +$
$1(10) + 1(1)$ **33. a.** five thousandths
b. $0(1) + 0(0.1) + 0(0.01) + 5(0.001)$
35. a. sixty-two ten thousandths   **b.** $0(1) +$
$0(0.1) + 0(0.01) + 6(0.001) + 2(0.0001)$
37. a. forty-two hundredths   **b.** $0(1) + 4(0.1) +$
$2(0.01)$ **39. a.** four hundred seven thousandths
b. $0(1) + 4(0.1) + 0(0.01) + 7(0.001)$
41. 0.011   **43.** 7.9   **45.** 0.7   **47.** 0.09
49. 8.34, 8.4, 8.43   **51.** 4.09, 4.49, 4.90
53. 3.29   **55.** 11.87   **57.** 5.71   **59.** 65.05
61. 73.53   **63.** 17.66   **65. a.** 27   **b.** 270
c. 2700   **67. a.** 9095   **b.** 90,950   **c.** 909,500
69. a. 0.84   **b.** 8.4   **c.** 84   **71. a.** 1345.1
b. 13,451   **c.** 134,510   **73. a.** 0.591   **b.** 0.0591
c. 0.00591   **75. a.** 0.9909   **b.** 0.09909
c. 0.009909   **77. a.** 251.26   **b.** 25.126
c. 2.5126   **79. a.** 0.00007   **b.** 0.000007
c. 0.0000007   **81.** 6.5814×10^4
83. 7.0121×10^4 **85.** 3.90012×10^5
87. 5.768147×10^6 **89.** 13.312   **91.** 384.48
93. 31.958   **95.** 0.05084   **97.** 3.8   **99.** 8.5
101. 190.0   **103.** 327.0   **105.** \$1.96
107. 49.2 mi/h

PAGES 452–453   CHAPTER 4
1.   **5.**
7. 10,000 A

9. 900   **11.** 7700   **13.** 1.5   **15.** 157.5   **17.** 200,
2000   **19.** right   **21.** vertex   **23.** obtuse
25. sides, angles   **27.** right   **29.** 90
31. equilateral   **33.** acute   **35.** false   **37.** false
39. true   **41.** true   **43.** 60 cm   **45.** 9.42 m
47. 6.37 m   **49.** 56.5 cm   **51.** 157 cm   **53.** $\overline{PQ}$
55. $\overline{MN}$ **57.** $\angle M$ **59.** $\angle K$ **61.**

PAGE 454   CHAPTER 5   **1.** 1, 2, 3, 6   **3.** 1, 2,
5, 10   **5.** 1, 3, 5, 15   **7.** 1, 19   **9.** 1, 3, 9, 27
11. 1, 5, 7, 35   **13.** 1, 41   **15.** 1, 2, 4, 13, 26,
52   **17.** 1, 59   **19.** 1, 2, 3, 4, 6, 8, 9, 12, 18, 24,
36, 72   **21.** 1, 3, 9, 27, 81   **23.** 1, 2, 3, 4, 6, 8,
12, 16, 24, 32, 48, 96   **25.** 5   **27.** 3, 9   **29.** 2, 4
31. none   **33.** none   **35.** none   **37.** all
39. all   **41.** none   **43.** 2   **45.** none   **47.** 3
49. 9   **51.** 64   **53.** 121   **55.** 196   **57.** 5
59. 15   **61.** 8   **63.** 14   **65.** composite, 5×2
67. composite, 2×17 **69.** prime
71. composite, $3^2 \times 2$ **73.** 2   **75.** 2   **77.** 14
79. 8   **81.** 18   **83.** 7   **85.** 15   **87.** 11   **89.** 72
91. 10   **93.** 84   **95.** 24   **97.** 42   **99.** 21
101. 40   **103.** 76

PAGE 455   CHAPTER 6   **1.** 3   **3.** 2   **5.** $\frac{5}{9}$
7. $\frac{7}{12}$ **9.** 16   **11.** 60   **13.** 5   **15.** $\frac{8}{9}$ **17.** $\frac{2}{3}$
19. $\frac{7}{13}$ **21.** $1\frac{1}{2}$ **23.** $3\frac{1}{2}$ **25.** $1\frac{1}{3}$ **27.** $\frac{51}{4}$ **29.** $\frac{64}{3}$
31. $\frac{158}{9}$ **33.** $>$ **35.** $<$ **37.** 0.8125
39. $0.\overline{45}$ **41.** $\frac{27}{500}$ **43.** $1\frac{3}{4}$ **45.** $1\frac{33}{50}$

PAGES 456–457   CHAPTER 7   **1.** 1   **3.** $\frac{3}{11}$
5. $\frac{1}{3}$ **7.** $\frac{5}{8}$ **9.** $1\frac{1}{21}$ **11.** $\frac{1}{16}$ **13.** 8   **15.** $8\frac{11}{32}$
17. $4\frac{9}{11}$ **19.** $4\frac{17}{20}$ **21.** $4\frac{1}{6}$ **23.** $19\frac{19}{44}$ **25.** $\frac{5}{28}$
27. $\frac{21}{88}$ **29.** $\frac{27}{52}$ **31.** $\frac{248}{315}$ **33.** $\frac{19}{34}$ **35.** $\frac{7}{12}$ **37.** $1\frac{1}{9}$
39. $\frac{13}{22}$ **41.** $\frac{3}{10}$ **43.** $\frac{10}{27}$ **45.** $1\frac{7}{65}$ **47.** $2\frac{2}{3}$
49. $2\frac{102}{125}$ **51.** $4\frac{35}{64}$ **53.** $85\frac{13}{50}$ **55.** $1\frac{19}{37}$ **57.** $123\frac{3}{7}$
59. $10\frac{12}{17}$ **61.** $\frac{3}{100}$ **63.** $\frac{10}{1}$ **65.** $\frac{4}{1}$ **67.** $\frac{4}{1}$ **69.** $\frac{10}{23}$
71. $\frac{2}{3}$ **73.** 4   **75.** 96   **77.** 42   **79.** 1 h and
$2\frac{1}{2}$ min   **81.** 64 km   **83.** 24 km   **85.** 30 km
87. 50 km   **89.** 60 m   **91.** 12 m

PAGES 458–459   CHAPTER 8   **1.** 8, 9, 10, 12,
16   **3.** 21, 19, 17, 13, 5   **5.** $2\frac{1}{2}$, 3, $3\frac{1}{2}$, $4\frac{1}{2}$, $6\frac{1}{2}$
7. $6\frac{3}{4}$, $6\frac{1}{2}$, $6\frac{1}{4}$, $5\frac{3}{4}$, $4\frac{3}{4}$ **8**   **11.** 7
13. 10   **15.** no solution   **17.** 6   **19.** 50   **21.** 3
23. 62   **25.** 0.27   **27.** $12\frac{2}{5}$ **29.** 4   **31.** 72

33. 245 35. 200 37. 4 39. 0.2 41. 15
43. 5 45. $7\frac{1}{2}$ 47. 6 49. 27 51. $8\frac{3}{4}$
53. $2n - 12 = 70$ 55. $\frac{81}{n} = 9n$
57. $t = 1$ h 40 min + 2 h 32 min
59. 395.77° 61. 5 h 63. $78,750
65. to work, 24 min; from work, 31 min

PAGES 460–461 CHAPTER 9 1. $\frac{1}{20}$ 3. $\frac{18}{25}$
5. $2\frac{3}{20}$ 7. 10% 9. 43.75% 11. 0.15
13. 0.05 15. 0.98 17. 0.075 19. 0.0042
21. 45% 23. 133% 25. 1250%
27. 1020% 29. 0.8% 31. 0.4, 40%
33. 8.75; 875% 35. 5.2; 520% 37. 108.9
39. 500 41. $n\% \times 256 = 32$; 12.5% 43. 25
45. $30\% \times n = 23.7$; 79.0 47. 40% 49. 35%

PAGES 462–463 CHAPTER 10 1. 5000 m²,
300 m 3. 7625 cm², 372 cm 5. a. 12 m
b. 78 m 7. 2940 m² 9. 15.5 cm 11. 80.5 cm²
13. 135.0 m² 15. 81 cm 17. 20 mm
19. 380 m² 21. 9850 m² 23.
25.

27. 24 29. 13 31. 6.6 m³
33. 25 m 35. 8190.0 g 37. 388,800 g, or
388.8 kg

PAGES 464–465 CHAPTER 11
1.
3.   7. true
                                        9. true

11.

15.   19. 0, 1, 2
                             21. ⁻4, ⁻3, ⁻2
                             23. ⁻3, ⁻2, ⁻1

25.

33. ⁻8 35. ⁻75 37. 65 39. ⁻40 41. 34
43. 39 45. 18 47. ⁻11 49. 37 51. 0
53. 12 55. 43 57. ⁻14 59. ⁻50 61. ⁻117
63. ⁻36 65. ⁻380 67. 0 69. ⁻510 71. 560
73. 144 75. 39 77. ⁻21 79. ⁻187 81. ⁻15
83. ⁻70 85. ⁻12 87. 6 89. 0 91. 29 93. 17
95. ⁻15 97. ⁻144 99. ⁻5 101. 42 103. ⁻12
111.   113.

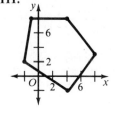

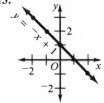

PAGES 466–467 CHAPTER 12
1.

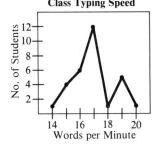

3.

5. 7, 8, 10 7. 4.4, 3.5, 8 9. 197, 190, 95
11. 11, 11, 8, 10 13. 0 | 4, 7
                       1
                       2 | 1, 5, 7
                       3 | 2, 8, 9
                       4 | 6

17. $\frac{2}{5}$ 19. $\frac{3}{10}$ 21. $\frac{3}{5}$ 23. $\frac{3}{5}$ 25. $\frac{1}{4}$ 27. $\frac{1}{9}$ 29. $\frac{3}{2}$
31. $\frac{5}{7}$ 33. $\frac{3}{7}$ 35. $\frac{4}{7}$ 37. $\frac{4}{7}$ 39. 1